KU-020-176

REGIONS OF THE BRITISH ISLES

EDITED BY W. G. EAST M.A.

# THE BRISTOL REGION

& Research
dents

.SSUE

*Titles already published in this series*

### THE EAST MIDLANDS AND THE PEAK
G. Dury, MA, PHD, FGS

### SOUTHWEST ENGLAND
A. H. Shorter, MA, PHD; W. L. D. Ravenhill, MA, PHD; K. J. Gregory, BSC, PHD

REGIONS OF THE BRITISH ISLES

EDITED BY W. G. EAST M.A.

# The Bristol Region

FRANK WALKER

*Senior Lecturer in Geography*
*University of Bristol*

NELSON

THOMAS NELSON AND SONS LTD
36 Park Street London WIY 4DE
PO Box 18123 Nairobi Kenya

Thomas Nelson (Australia) Ltd
597 Little Collins Street Melbourne 3000

Thomas Nelson and Sons (Canada) Ltd
81 Curlew Drive Don Mills Ontario

Thomas Nelson (Nigeria) Ltd
PO Box 336 Apapa Lagos

Thomas Nelson and Sons (South Africa) (Proprietary) Ltd
51 Commissioner Street Johannesburg


First published in Great Britain 1972

© Frank Walker 1972

All rights reserved. No part of this publication may
be reproduced, stored in a retrieval system, or transmitted,
in any form or by any means, electronic, mechanical,
photocopying, recording or otherwise, without the prior
permission of the publishers.

ISBN 017 133005 6

Printed in Great Britain by Willmer Brothers Limited, Birkenhead

# CONTENTS

Introduction    1

1   The Structural Basis    3

2   The Evolution of the Landscape    52

3   The Soils    64

4   The Vegetation and Climate    91

5   The Prehistoric Occupation    105

6   The Roman Occupation    125

7   The Growth of Settlements and Communications until the Eleventh Century    137

8   The Changing Economy from the Eleventh to the Eighteenth Centuries    160

9   The Bristol Region in 1800    195

10   Nineteenth-century Changes    229

11   The Bristol Region Today    279

Selected References    364

Index    381

# Introduction

To identify an area that comprises the whole of Somerset and Gloucestershire and much of west and northwest Wiltshire as 'The Bristol
Region' is to ensure that homogeneity can hardly be regarded as a
regional characteristic.

Indeed, in the realm of physical geography variety is the keynote
of almost every aspect of its structure, relief, climate and soils, and to a
considerable degree this is the outcome of the region's essentially
marginal position. On the one hand, it straddles the western limits of
the Mesozoic English scarplands extending from the upper Thames
basin well into the fringes of Palaeozoic upland Britain in northwest
Gloucestershire and in west Somerset. On the other hand, it stretches
over a hundred miles from the south Midlands to the margins of the
southwest peninsula.

In the field of human geography variety is equally characteristic of
the Bristol region but in this respect there have been periods when some
degree of regional identity might be discerned. In its early history such
periods tended to be short-lived but, on the other hand, a common
interest in the wool textile industry, for a time focused on Bristol itself,
survived longer and left lasting impressions on patterns of settlement and
industry throughout the region. Similarly the predominance of animal
husbandry and, since the seventeenth century, specialization in dairying
have been fairly permanent features of the region's agricultural
economy. However, such traits have never been universally distributed
throughout the region, nor have they been wholly absent from neighbouring areas, so that additional circumstances must underlie any real
distinctiveness which may characterize the Bristol region today.

Recent studies have shown that it largely coincides with an area
where population is growing at a more rapid rate than in southwestern
England generally, whilst it has also been recognized as an area of
considerable economic growth where there has been a marked concentration of West Country manufacturing industry, in particular. Such
growth could be interpreted as a westward spread of prosperity from

1

southeastern Britain and from the Thames–Merseyside economic axis, but it is also possible to regard Bristol itself as the essential focal point of a thriving region. Continued industrial activity and recent expansion of the city's commercial and administrative functions are tending to make it more obviously a regional 'capital', and there are grounds for expecting this tendency to continue. If, following publication of the report of the Severnside Study, further economic growth were to be encouraged on Severnside and if, as has been suggested, very considerable increases in population are to be envisaged in the Bristol district, it would perhaps become even more appropriate in the future that the 'Bristol region' should be named after its 'capital' city and economic focus.

### ACKNOWLEDGEMENTS

The map on the front endpaper and the maps on pages 4, 58, 118, and 127 are reproduced from the Ordnance Survey maps with the sanction of the Controller of H.M. Stationery Office. The maps on pages 93 and 102 are based upon the Ordnance Survey maps with additional information provided by the Department of the Environment.

# CHAPTER I

# *The Structural Basis*

THE marginal nature of the Bristol region is clearly shown by its distribution of rock outcrops and by the structures with which this pattern of outcrops is associated. A measure of the resulting variety of geological phenomena lies in the fact that formations from the Cambrian to the Chalk outcrop within twenty miles of Bristol, and that structures in the region have been attributed to almost all the earth movements which have affected Britain since pre-Silurian times.

The Bristol region straddles the western margin of the scarplands of England, which follows the well-defined line of the Cotswold scarp as far south as Bath, crosses the uplands between Bath and eastern Mendip and then traverses the succession of low scarps of southeastern Somerset past Bruton, Castle Cary and Yeovil to Crewkerne. To the east of this margin there is a continuous cover of Mesozoic rocks which in the Bristol region are predominantly of Jurassic age. Though structures in the underlying Palaeozoic rocks are reflected in the lithology of the Mesozoic cover and influenced the development of the surface, it is nevertheless the outcrops of the Mesozoic rocks which dominate the geology of the area.

To the west of the scarplands the geology of the Bristol region is more varied, and it is necessary to make an initial division between areas to the north and south at a line almost parallel with Mendip from Frome through Shepton Mallet, Wells and Axbridge to Brean Down near Weston-super-Mare. With the exception of a very small inlier of Carboniferous Limestone at Cannington Park near Bridgwater, the Palaeozoic rocks to the south of Mendip are entirely covered by younger materials until they reappear in the hill areas of the Quantocks and Exmoor. Here in the south central part of the region it is local variations in the nature of the Trias and the Lias and the Quaternary deposits of alluvium and peat overlying the Mesozoic rocks in the great basins of the Somerset levels that give diversity to a generally low-lying area. On the other hand in Mendip, and in a large triangular area to the north bounded by lines from Brean Down to Ross-on-Wye on the west and

3

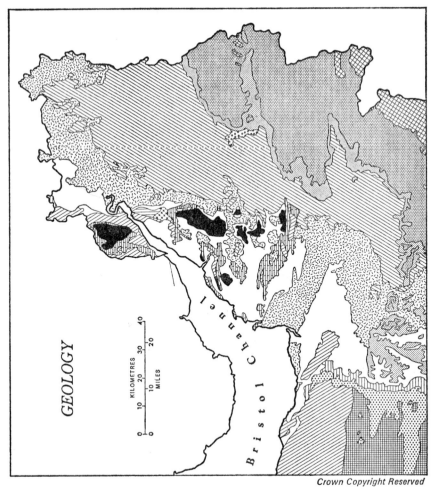

GEOLOGY

KILOMETRES
0    10   20   30   40
0    10        20
MILES

Bristol Channel

Crown Copyright Reserved

 Ologocene and Eocene

Chalk

Upper greensand and gault

Lower greensand and Speeton series

Oolitic

Liassic and Rhaetic

Keuper marl and sandstone

Bunter sandstone

Red sandstone, etc.

Coal measures

Millstone grit and culm measures

Carboniferous limestone, etc. and calciferous sandstone

Lower old red sandstone and Downtonian

Silurian

Cambrian

from Frome to Ross-on-Wye on the east, Palaeozoic rocks appear at the surface or are thinly covered by later strata. Here the pattern of outcrops and of marked relief features is complex, and has been determined by both the structural and the depositional history of the area as well as by later denudation, so that it contrasts sharply with the unbroken stretches of Mesozoic sediments to the northeast, east and south.

Structurally too, the Bristol region is a transitional one since in broad terms it embraces a part of Stille's boundary between Palaeozoic and Mesozoic Europe. The fact that the NE–SW Caledonoid and the N–S Malvernoid structures are crossed here almost at right angles by the predominantly E–W trending Armoricanoid folds is responsible for many of the structural complexities of the region and of the Bristol and Somerset coalfields in particular. It appears to have led, for example, to the remarkable intensity of movement where two of the N–S and E–W axes intersect in the Vobster area at the southern end of the Radstock coal basin.

The main N–S structures of the Malvern Hills lie outside the Bristol region, but the Malvernoid trend can be traced southwards along the eastern edge of the Forest of Dean coalfield. In the southern part of the May Hill inlier this trend recurs in elongated N–S domes with strata dipping westward towards the Forest of Dean, though at May Hill itself an anticline with a NNW–SSE trend may represent an intersection of the Malvernian trend with the NW–SE Charnian trend of the Woolhope inlier in Herefordshire. Across the Severn the Malvernoid trend is traceable southwards round Berkeley; thereafter anticlines diverge round the synclinal area of the Tortworth inlier, and it has been suggested that they continue as two separate axes, the western one forming the Lower Severn axis on a NE–SW Caledonoid trend and the eastern one the Bath axis following a slightly sinuous N–S Malvernoid direction. The Lower Severn axis may be traced through the Thornbury anticline to Avonmouth and on to Weston-super-Mare, whilst the Bath axis passes close to Wotton-under-Edge, immediately east of Chipping Sodbury and thence in an almost straight line through Bath to the neighbourhood of Yeovil. There is therefore a very close parallelism between this axis and the remarkably straight scarp of Cotswold from Wotton-under-Edge to Bath and the Inferior Oolite scarp from Mendip to Milborne Port in southeast Somerset. In the northern part of the area, enclosed by the diverging Lower Severn and Bath axes, lie the Bristol and Somerset coalfields, though their structure is further complicated by the crossing of other folds and faults following both N–S and E–W strikes.

In the west of England the 'Armorican Front' is most easily seen following the anticlinal area of Mendip in a broadly E–W direction, which is rendered apparently sinuous by the position of the four periclines lying progressively northwards in echelon from Beacon Hill to Blackdown. South of Mendip, Armorican structures do not have an immediately apparent effect upon the geology of the lowland areas of Somerset, but if the axis of the intense Armorican movement in Exmoor and the Quantocks is to be traced eastwards to link with an anticlinal axis in the Vale of Wardour, then Armorican structures may well underlie folds in the Mesozoic rocks of Somerset, which significantly pitch westwards away from the presumed southward continuation of the N–S Bath axis into the Yeovil district. North of the Mendip axis, folds along an E–W Armoricanoid trend cross the Bristol and Somerset coalfields and in some cases are continued westwards into the Cardiff area. Thus the important Kingswood anticline in the Bristol coalfield follows a broadly E–W trend and the Broadfield Down pericline is similarly aligned, whilst E–W faults divide and mark the limits of the basins in the Somerset part of the coalfield. Where the Armorican folds intersected pre-existing axes, the impact of earth movements on areas already stiffened produced intense local movement; the interaction of two sets of structure lines may also account for the anomalous alignment of structures to the west of the Bristol coalfield in the Westbury-on-Trym–Portishead–Clevedon area and to the east of it in the Wick district of the Kingswood anticline.

The only Cambrian outcrop in the Bristol region occurs in the Tortworth inlier, which stretches nine miles southwards from Tites Point on the Gloucestershire bank of the Severn. The Cambrian rocks consist of great thicknesses of grey shales, the Lower Tremadoc Breadstone Shales in the north and the Upper Tremadoc Micklewood Beds further south, though thick siliceous bands in the latter may suggest a shallowing of the sea in which they were deposited. The fact that the Ordovician and some part of the Lower Silurian rocks are absent from the Bristol region may indicate that by this time the area formed part of a land mass extending northwards into the Midlands. Thus, though the precise age and relationships of the oldest rocks in the southeastern part of the May Hill inlier are doubtful, they are regarded as Silurian, and the rest of the inlier consists mainly of Upper Llandovery Sandstones with narrow N–S outcrops of Woolhope Limestone, Wenlock Shales and Limestones and Ludlow Sandstones dipping conformably below the Old Red Sandstone surrounding the Forest of Dean. In the Tortworth inlier, too, it is the Silurian rocks which succeed the Cambrian; the Upper Llandovery and Wenlock series rest unconformably on the Tremadoc Shales in the south, whilst in a narrow two-mile belt running south from Tites Point the Ludlow Beds are faulted against the Cambrian. It has been suggested that the nature of the unconformity in this district may arise in part from erosion following movement on the Lower Severn axis along which the Cambrian inlier is aligned. Other outcrops of Silurian material exist at Sharpness and Wickwar, quite near the Tortworth inlier, but the only other area where the Silurian is seen in the Bristol region is in the Beacon Hill pericline of eastern Mendip to the northeast of Shepton Mallet. Rocks of Wenlock and possibly Llandovery age are exposed in a narrow belt in the core of an anticline through the erosion of the Old Red Sandstone which lies unconformably on the Wenlock Mudstones. An unusual feature of the Mendip Silurian inlier is that it contains igneous material including no less than 400 feet of andesite, tuffs and an ash-andesite conglomerate, and it may be noted that the Llandovery series in the Tortworth inlier also includes two extrusive lavas with a thickness of 100 feet. It has been suggested that such Silurian volcanicity is to be related to the proximity of important Armorican structures crossing the region from Mendip northwards, since the rare examples of Silurian lavas in western Europe all lie along the line of Armorican folding from central Europe to southwestern Ireland.

In the early part of the upper Palaeozoic period the extreme south of the Bristol region is distinguished sharply from the rest. Here in the Quantocks–Exmoor area Devonian rocks were deposited under true marine conditions whose northern limit is presumably hidden under the later deposits of central Somerset, since the Devonian disappears before Mendip is reached. In the anticlinal cores of each of the periclines it is the Old Red Sandstone which lies between the Silurian and the Carboniferous Limestone. From here to the northern limit of the region in the Forest of Dean, deposition took place under what are usually regarded as deltaic, estuarine or inland sea conditions, the materials involved being derived from the denudation of a somewhat arid land area to the north.

The last of the Siluro-Devonian earth movements seems to have resulted in much of the area being raised to form land in Middle Old Red times, so that the Lower and Upper Old Red are here separated by a major unconformity which, particularly near the Lower Severn and Bath axes, may include the results of considerable erosion of the Lower Old Red, with the Upper Old Red overstepping onto the Silurian. However, though there is such overstepping to the west of the Wye, there is much less evidence of the unconformity in the Old Red Sandstone which forms a belt two miles wide along the eastern side of the Forest of Dean. Here the quartz conglomerate at the base of the Upper Old Red sometimes forms a capping on the Lower Old Red Brownstone ridges and these are distinctive relief features from the Herefordshire border near Micheldean to Blackeney Hill and Viney Hill in the south. Across the Severn the Lower Old Red Sandstone occupies a belt of country about a mile wide to the west of the Tortworth inlier, from

Sharpness to Lower Stone, and two smaller areas to the east and west of Thornbury, while the Upper Old Red forms a narrow belt to the east of the Bristol coal basin, from Wickwar and Charfield northwards to Tortworth, where it turns round the north and northwestern sides of the basin to Milbury Heath before curving westwards to Thornbury and Kyneton. The results of the Middle Old Red unconformity are to be seen in the overstep of the quartz conglomerate on to Wenlock strata from Tortworth to Milbury Heath, but to the west of that point it overlies the Thornbury Beds of the Lower Old Red. West of Bristol the Lower Old Red Sandstone is represented by the Black Nore Sandstone, which appears to be comparable with the Brownstones of the Forest of Dean and occurs in the core of the Westbury-on-Trym anticline, in a narrow belt crossing the Avon from Stoke Bishop to Lower Failand and Portbury and on the coast between Portishead and Clevedon. Between these towns much of the high ground at Black Hill, Weston Down and Portishead Down is composed of the Portishead Beds apparently resting conformably on the Black Nore Sandstone and possibly corresponding in part with the quartz conglomerate and Tintern Beds of the Upper Old Red. The Portishead Beds also overlie the Black Nore Sandstone in the core of the Westbury anticline, and outcrop along a curving line from Clapton-in-Gordano through Lower Failand and across the Avon immediately downstream from the gorge. In the core of the Blackdown pericline in Mendip, the Portishead Beds extend from Hale Combe to a point north of Charterhouse, while between Priddy and Chewton Mendip they form much of North Hill and Eaker Hill. Portishead Beds also occupy the whole of the core area of the Pen Hill pericline to the north of Wells and part of the Beacon Hill pericline between Maesbury Station and Whatley near Frome. In the last district the exposure of a Silurian anticlinal core shows the Upper Old Red resting unconformably on Wenlock strata and it has been suggested that this part of eastern Mendip overlies a southern prolongation of the Bath axis on which movement and later erosion may have occurred in Middle Old Red Sandstone times.

The presence of marine Devonian rocks in west Somerset appears to link this district more closely with the southwest peninsula than with the rest of the Bristol region, though structurally the anticlinal features of the Quantocks and the west Somerset coast are aligned with axes which may link them with south Somerset and south central England. In broad terms the western extension of Somerset lies in an area where the Devonian rocks emerge on the north side of the central synclinal area of Devon from below the Culm Measures of the Carboniferous. In the anticlinal structures of this area the rocks have been subjected to intense folding, faulting and compression, but though complex in detail the area to the west of the Quantocks shows a clearly discernible succession from the Lower Devonian on the coast to the Upper Devonian in the southwest of the county round Wiveliscombe, and represents an eastward continuation of the succession exposed along the Devon coast to the north of Barnstaple Bay. The Lower Devonian includes the Foreland Grits, the Lynton Beds and the lower portions of the Hangman Grits. Grits, sandstones and slates alternate in the succession but the grits, which commonly form bold hill areas, are the most characteristic element. Immediately behind the Somerset coast the Foreland Grits enter the region from a point to the east of Lynmouth through Oare to Porlock; further east they form the isolated North Hill at Minehead and the spur-like feature of Grabbist Hill at Dunster. South of the relatively narrow belt of slates and calcareous materials of the Lynton Beds, the Hangman Grits cross into Somerset on the northern slopes of Exmoor and are to be seen in the upstanding areas of Lucott Hill and Dunkery Beacon and in Croydon Hill to the north of the Brendon Hills. The upper parts of the Hangman Grits are of Middle Devonian age, as are most of the succeeding Ilfracombe Beds, which form the high parts of Exmoor Forest in the extreme west of Somerset round Simonsbath and continue eastwards through Exford and the Brendon Hills to form a broad belt of upland country overlooking the Permian and Triassic lowland to the west of the Quantocks. The Morte Slates overlie the Ilfracombe Beds and occupy a parallel belt of country entering Somerset in the southern part of Exmoor and continuing eastwards to form the edge of the older rocks between Wiveliscombe and Tolland. The Upper Devonian Pickwell Down Grits and Pilton Beds only reach Somerset in the southwest round Wiveliscombe, whilst the Culm slates and limestones, which occupy a very restricted area in the Ashbrittle district near the county boundary, are the only representatives of the Carboniferous rocks of the southwest peninsula. In the northern half of the Quantocks, NW–SE trending anticlinal structures in the Hangman Grits of the Lower and Middle Devonian pitch southwards, whilst their western margin is complicated by extensive faulting. South of a line from Bagborough to Over Stowey, the Middle Devonian Ilfracombe Beds replace the Hangman Grits in the hill area, but their relationship is made iregular by faulting, which also determines the limits of a number of limestone outcrops within the Ilfracombe Beds at Lower Asholt, Merridge and Holwell Cave.

Apart from the very small outcrop of Culm Measures in southwest Somerset, the Carboniferous rocks are represented in the Bristol region by a succession commencing with the Carboniferous Limestone series, which normally rests conformably on the Upper Old Red Sandstone. There is a very small inlier of Carboniferous Limestone in Cannington Park near Bridgwater, but the two main areas of Carboniferous rocks are in the northern half of the region. One consists of the greater part of the Forest of Dean area from the Wye to a line from Micheldean to Lydney, where the Carboniferous rocks are exposed at the surface, and the other forms a triangular area whose apices are at Tortworth, Brean Down and the eastern end of Mendip, but in this area the Carboniferous rocks are largely overlain by Triassic and Jurassic deposits.

The predominantly marine character of the Carboniferous Limestone deposition followed encroachment by the sea from the south onto the relatively uniform Old Red Sandstone landscape, but the lithology of the Carboniferous Limestone series shows the effect of gradual shallowing of the water northwards, across the region. Thus through much of the period deeper water in the southeastern Mendip area led to the deposition of dark-coloured massive crinoidal limestones, whereas round the Avon massive dolomites developed in a somewhat shallower sea. In even shallower water and lagoon-like conditions, oolites and china-stones (calcite mudstones) replaced the dolomites from time to time, and approaching the northern shore, from the Bristol coalfield to the Forest of Dean, the limestones pass laterally into grits and sandstones, particularly in the upper parts of the series. Apart from this overall lithological change from south to north, sedimentation was also affected by earth movements which occurred during the deposition of the Carboniferous Limestone. These led to successive shallowing or deepening of the sea, thereby affecting the nature of sedimentation over the whole region, whilst local lithological variations also occur especially over the axes along which such movements are presumed to have taken place.

Rocks of the Carboniferous Limestone series outcrop in a belt about half a mile wide round the eastern edge of the Forest of Dean, running northwards from Drybrook to Micheldean Station before turning south past Cinderford and Upper Soudley to disappear below an overstep of the Coal Measures near Danby Lodge. They reappear in the Lydney syncline and continue round the southwestern edge of the coal basin, with an extension along the Tidenham Chase syncline reaching the Wye between Chepstow and Tintern. East of the Severn the Carboniferous Limestone forms a rim round the northern part of the Bristol coalfield, commencing on the west in the narrow ridge from Over through Almondsbury and Ridgway to Alveston, where the outcrop widens out around the nose of the southward-plunging Thornbury anticline to reach Olveston. The exposure continues northeastwards from Alveston to beyond Cromhall, where it turns sharply southwards and continues in a remarkably straight line on the eastern side of the basin past Charfield and Wickwar to Chipping Sodbury, beyond which point the location of the edge of the basin may be deduced from the existence of

Carboniferous Limestone inliers at Codrington and Wick to the east of Bristol. To the west of Bristol, on the Gloucestershire side of the Avon, Carboniferous Limestone rings the northeastern end of the Westbury anticline, forming the ridge from Shirehampton along Kings Weston Hill to Westbury-on-Trym and recurving through the high ground of Durdham Down to the Avon gorge. On the Somerset side of the river a broad extent of Carboniferous Limestone on the southwestern flank of the Westbury anticline produces the high ground at Failand and Tickenham, with a narrower ridge extending to Clevedon where it meets the coastal ridge between Clevedon and Portishead. Five miles southwest of Bristol a nearly circular area of Carboniferous Limestone forms the periclinal upland of Broadfield Down. The greatest extent of Carboniferous Limestone in the Bristol region, however, occurs in the massive ridge of Mendip where it forms four broad but discontinuous belts surrounding the Old Red Sandstone cores of the periclines.

For reasons which have already been discussed, each of the groups comprising the Carboniferous Limestone series shows a good deal of lithological variation within the region. Thus at the base in the Lower Limestone Shales the thickness of the passage beds of sandstones and sandy limestones ranges from 30 feet in the north to 200 feet near Bristol, and whereas the main deposit in the Forest of Dean is made up of almost equal thicknesses of limestones and shales, in Mendip there are only a few lenses of limestone in 500 feet of shale. In the latter area the Lower Limestone Shales ring the eastern end of the Old Red Sandstone core of the Blackdown pericline from Burrington to Witcombe, forming a zone of generally lower relief between Blackdown itself and the Mountain Limestone, but in the other periclines it is less important. In the Westbury anticline the Lower Limestone Shales form a narrow belt on the inner edge of the limestones, coinciding with the slopes below Abbot's Leigh and on the sides of the Trym valley in Sneyd Park, Stoke Bishop, Westbury-on-Trym and below Kings Weston Hill. Round the northern end of the Bristol coalfield the Lower Limestone Shales form only a discontinuous narrow belt from Elberton to Wickwar, and around the Forest of Dean the outcrop is extensive only to the west of the Tidenham Chase syncline near Tintern and between the coal basin and the Wye.

The Black Rock group is the basal member of the Carboniferous or Mountain Limestone which forms most of the high ground in Mendip, Broadfield Down, the downs and ridges to the west of Bristol, and the rims of the coalfields further north. The result of diminishing water depth during the deposition of this group is that an increasing thickness of the upper parts is dolomitized as one proceeds northwards. In the deeper water area of Mendip, therefore, the main deposit is Black Rock

Limestone, of which only the highest horizon is dolomitized. In Broad-field Down and near Bristol nearly 90 feet is dolomitized, whilst round the north of the Bristol coalfield the Black Rock Dolomite replaces virtually all the Black Rock Limestone. In the Forest of Dean the corres-ponding material is the Lower Dolomite, which occupies the whole of the Black Rock group and covers considerable areas on the west side of the basin.

At the base of the succeeding Clifton Down group, oolitic limestones replace crinoidal ones in the Crease Limestones of the Forest of Dean and in the Gully Oolite and the lower part of the Burrington Oolite else-where in the region. These oolites in turn are succeeded by mudstones and chinastones as far south as Broadfield Down, but not in Mendip. It has been suggested that earth movements associated with the mid-Avonian break led to a shallowing of the sea over the Lower Severn axis at this time, and from Bristol northwards there is a break in sedimen-tation between the Gully Oolite and the Clifton Down Mudstone. How-ever, at Bristol thin bands of Goblin Combe Oolite exist within the upper part of the mudstones and these oolites thicken southwards to occupy 125 feet on Broadfield Down and finally, as the upper part of the Burring-ton Oolite, replace the mudstones entirely in Mendip, implying that less shallow water conditions continued in western Mendip. To the east of the Pen Hill pericline crinoidal Vallis Limestone, resting on the Black Rock Limestone, replaces the Burrington Oolite and suggests that even deeper water existed throughout the period in this district. The possibility of mid-Avonian movement on the Lower Severn axis is also indicated by the presence of volcanic rocks in the Clifton Down Mudstones in areas near to the line of the axis on Broadfield Down and at Tickenham, Cadbury Camp and Uphill. The Clifton Down Limestone which forms the upper two-thirds of the group shows no abrupt lithological change in the Bristol area from the mudstones, but in the upper parts important changes occur. Southwards from the line of the Avon an increasing thick-ness is silicified until 150 feet are affected in Mendip. On the other hand, northwards from Bristol arenaceous deposits occupy an increasing part of the succession, probably associated with materials transported by the rivers of St George's Land to the north and northwest, which may have been rejuvenated as a result of mid-Avonian elevation. The first of these is the Lower Cromhall Sandstone, which forms a thin band at the base of the limestone and first appears northwards round the rim of the Bristol coalfield, outcropping in a narrow belt from Elberton and Olveston through Tytherington to Cromhall and then turning south past Wickwar to Yate Rocks. West of the Severn the Lower Drybrook Sandstone corresponds with the Lower Cromhall Sandstone and is succeeded by the Drybrook Limestone which is to be correlated with the Clifton Down Limestone. Apparently, therefore, the conditions of arenaceous sedimentation were replaced even in much of the northern half of the region by a return to the deposition of limestones in the upper parts of the Clifton Down group. However, within the Forest of Dean the Lower Drybrook Sandstone thickens rapidly northwards at the expense of the limestone; to the north of Cinderford the latter disappears and the Lower and Upper Sandstones merge to form the main mass of the Drybrook Sandstone.

The alternation of sedimentation conditions is continued in the lower part of the Hotwells group, since at the base conditions of arenaceous deposition spread southwards again and led to the formation of the Middle Cromhall Sandstone which outcrops in the Bristol district to the west of Brentry and to the east of Wick. Further north the Middle Cromhall Sandstone appears between Yate and Chipping Sodbury, to the north of Yate Rocks and round Cromhall, while in the Forest of Dean it merges into the Drybrook Sandstone north of Cinderford and may correspond with the base of the Upper Drybrook Sandstone further south. Southwards from Bristol to Providence Hill and Long Ashton, and in narrow belts round Broadfield Down and the Mendip periclines, the Hotwells Limestone is the basal member of this group, but renewed elevation in the north seems to have resulted in the appearance, even here, of sandy materials in the upper parts of the group forming the Upper Cromhall Sandstone. In this case the sands spread as far as Broadfield Down, where they appear as small patches about a mile south of Winford, but they thicken rapidly northwards to over 300 feet at Bristol. From here the Middle Cromhall Sandstone at the base and the Upper Cromhall Sandstone at the top of the group thicken at the expense of the Hotwells Limestone between them, until they replace it entirely when the northern end of the coalfield is reached at Cromhall. Further north still in the Forest of Dean the whole of the group is occupied by the upper parts of the Drybrook Sandstones.

The intra-Carboniferous earth movements which have been suggested as the cause of sedimentation changes in the Carboniferous Limestone series culminated in the Forest of Dean area in folding on the N–S Malvernoid trend, which also characterizes the anticline at May Hill in the southern part of the inlier. Rocks up to and including the Upper Drybrook Sandstone were involved in the folding, which produced generally synclinal structures in the Forest of Dean. Within this basin, however, the Clanna anticline in the south and the Hope Mansell anticline in the north separate the western synclines near Coleford and in Tidenham Chase from the eastern ones at Lydney and Wigpool. In consequence of these earth movements and the denudation which followed, especially towards the May Hill anticline, rocks of the Millstone Grit series are entirely absent from the Forest of Dean and the Coal Measures rest unconformably on rocks ranging from the Upper Drybrook Sandstone on the west to the Brownstones of the Lower Old Red Sandstone on the east. Moreover, as one moves eastwards across the basin, Coal Measure deposition commences progressively later, until in the extreme east it starts only a little way below the base of the Pennant Sandstone. It has been suggested that to the east of the Severn the synclinal structure of the Bristol and Somerset coalfields between the Lower Severn and Bath axes may have been initiated at the same time as the folding of the Lower Carboniferous rocks of the Forest of Dean, but for this there is very little direct evidence. Movement on the Lower Severn axis may possibly be deduced from the fact that the Millstone Grit series does not exist in Mendip to the west of a line from Churchill to Cheddar nor in the Clevedon–Portishead area, whilst in the western coal basins at Nailsea, Clapton and Avonmouth there are apparently unconformities involving the Millstone Grit, the base of the Coal Measures and the base of the Pennant. On the other hand, within the main synclinal area these unconformities are apparently of less importance, and indeed the Quartzitic Sandstone group which has been placed in the Millstone Grit series has its greatest development in the Bristol coalfield area, where it appears on Brandon Hill and near the Royal Fort in Bristol and on the eastern side of the basin from Cromhall to Chipping Sodbury, as well as in a narrow belt along the southern edge of the Radstock basin of the Somerset coalfield from Ashwick to Mells.

The Ashton Vale Marine Bed is regarded as the base of the Lower Coal Measures series in the Bristol district and as it has been identified in the Somerset as well as the Bristol basins there is a basis for the assumption that everywhere to the east of the Severn the lowest beds of the Coal Measures have comparable ages. In the Bristol coalfield four marine incursions have been recognized but none is known in the Forest of Dean and this has been taken to suggest that all the Coal Measures in the latter area are of more recent date than the uppermost of the marine beds to the east of the Severn. At all events precise correlation of the Coal Measures to the east and west of the river is impossible and it seems likely that the differences of sedimentation history between the northern and southern parts of the region during Lower Carboniferous times were maintained during the deposition of the Coal Measures. The present structure of the coal basins was determined mainly by the Armorican earth movements of Permo-Carboniferous times, but if earlier intra-Carboniferous movement on the Lower Severn and possibly the Bath axes can be inferred, then the gradual emergence of the whole region created swamp conditions in a low-lying syncline between the two diverging axes, and it was in this triangular area to the north of the Mendip axis that the Lower Coal series was deposited. It includes coal seams some of which have been worked in the extreme south of the Somerset coalfield at the Newbury, Vobster, New Rock and Moorewood pits, whilst the important Ashton and Kingswood Great seams have been extensively worked on the Kingswood anticline to the east of Bristol. In the northern part of the Bristol coalfield, however, the Lower Coal series thins out and seams have only been worked on a small scale near Yate.

It has been suggested that continued uplift and the resultant rejuvenation and rapid denudation of land areas to the north and northwest caused a vast spread of sandy materials which form the major part of the succeeding Pennant series throughout the Bristol region. Sandstones which in places exceed 2,500 feet in thickness make up the greater part of the Pennant but there are important exceptions. In the north of the Forest of Dean, Coal Measures sedimentation commences with red measures, possibly indicative of arid conditions, but from Coleford southwards the Pennant is underlain by the Trenchard group, which is itself mainly composed of sandstones almost identical with those of the Pennant. Locally, however, swamp conditions suitable for the formation of coal developed during this period of dominantly arenaceous deposition and the Trenchard group includes two coal seams, whilst near the base of the Pennant itself the 4' 6" Coleford High Delf seam has been the main source of coal in the Forest of Dean, more than 90 per cent of the coalfield's total production coming from this one seam. Coal seams do exist in the Pennant of the Bristol coalfield but they are quite unimportant in the north and it is only in the Warmley–Oldland district in the extreme southeast that the Millgrit, Rag Ruff and Parrot seams near the base of the Pennant have been widely worked. In Somerset, too, there are some coal seams in the lower half of the Pennant which have been worked in the southern parts of the Radstock basin.

In the Upper Coal series there is again a considerable contrast between the north and south of the region. In Somerset the lowest element is the Farrington group containing seams which were worked throughout the field. Above this the Barren Red group contains no workable coal and includes red measures apparently indicative of arid conditions. The succeeding Radstock group again contains coal seams recently worked in the Pensford area and formerly of some importance in the Radstock basin, and finally the top of the series is formed by the Publow group in which there is no workable coal. In the Bristol coalfield, on the other hand, Upper Coal seams are confined to the base of the series which corrresponds to the Farrington group and includes the High Vein, Parkfield, Hollybush and Great seams from which the main production came in the area to the north of the Kingswood anticline. Above this the Radstock and Publow groups do not occur and appear to have been replaced by the great thickness of red measures and sandstones which occupy the central part of the basin from Iron Acton to Pucklechurch. Similarly in the Forest of Dean the supra-Pennant group consists of a lower productive division with eight seams suitable for working and an upper division composed almost entirely of great thicknesses of sandstone which form the scarps and plateaus in the wooded part of the Forest to the west and southwest of Cinderford.

Regarded as a whole, the Carboniferous and Permo-Carboniferous earth movements in the Bristol region were brought about by movement from the east, producing N–S or Malvernoid trends, and movement from the south and southeast, producing the main Armorican E–W trends. Though both movements probably continued throughout the period, the Malvernoid trends of the Forest of Dean and the May Hill area are clearly associated with early intra-Carboniferous movements; Moore and Trueman (1939) suggested that such movements also affected the area to the north of Mendip, where there is evidence of activity over the Lower Severn axis during the deposition of the Carboniferous Limestone and over the Bath axis before the deposition of the Upper Coal Measures. Such movement may well have initiated the generally synclinal structure of the Bristol and Somerset coalfields and have stiffened the pre-existing Lower Severn and Bath axes so that they resisted the later main Armorican pressure from the south. The structures resulting from the Armorican folding were therefore conditioned to some extent by the disposition of the N–S structures, and a general picture is given in the analogy suggested by Welch and Crookall (1948) of waves breaking against two promontories representing the Lower Severn and Bath axes. The analogy is attractive because the consequential modifications of the E–W Armorican 'waves' are remarkably similar to the results of refraction in marine waves. Thus to the south of Mendip, before the 'promontories' are reached, the structures follow a little modified Armorican trend, if it may be assumed that the anticlinal structures of north Devon, west Somerset and the Quantocks are continued below the Trias and Lias of south Somerset to link up with an anticlinal axis in the Vale of Wardour. The Mendip axis, however, has a distinctly sinuous form. Beacon Hill, the most easterly pericline, lies due south of the stiffened eastern side of the coal basin and at the point of impact of the Armorican 'wave' on the Bath axis 'promontory'. Here resistance would have been at a maximum and the pericline forms the most southerly part of Mendip, whilst violent contortions of the strata mark its northern limb and the adjacent parts of the Radstock basin. To the east and west of Beacon Hill, however, the Armorican structures of the Mendip axis were apparently carried further north. On the east the evidence is slight but suggests a continuation of the axis in a curving line northeastwards through Frome to link up with anticlinal structures in the Vale of Pewsey. On the west the structures are exposed and the northward progression in echelon of the Pen Hill, North Hill and Blackdown periclines is well known. Here, it is suggested, there was little resistance from Malvernoid structures and the Armorican pericline at Blackdown was carried forward several miles, the displacement occurring to the west of a line through the very heavily disturbed area of Pen Hill. It has also been suggested that lateral displacement along such a line may exist further north along the west side of the coalfield, thereby explaining marked structural dissimilarities between the eastern and western sides of the basin.

Continuing the marine analogy, the Armorican 'waves' diminish in amplitude northwards from Mendip between the Bath and Lower Severn axes. The next fold belt is along a line from Broadfield Down to Bath, where the generally anticlinal structures are largely masked by later deposits. However, in Broadfield Down itself, where the Carboniferous Limestone is exposed, dips are low and the E–W trend is by no means universal, especially at its eastern end where a N–S direction is approached. Immediately north of the Bristol Avon the Kingswood anticline forms the most northerly major E–W structure. Over most of its length erosion has exposed the Lower Coal Measures, which show intense folding and thrust faulting, though the underlying Carboniferous Limestone is thought to be less affected and the complexity of the structures in the Coal Measures may have arisen from the incompetence of the strata involved. Throughout the central portion of the anticline trends are dominantly E–W, but at its eastern end near Wick N–S structures may suggest the early stiffening of the adjacent eastern flank of the coal basin, while at its western end in Bedminster N–S structures again cut across the general trend and may mark the limit of the main basin. To the west and northwest of this basin between Bristol and the Severn it is the 'promontory' of the Lower Severn axis which may have affected the trend of the structures. If one were to press the marine analogy still further, the fold waves might be said to swing round or be rotated, as in wave refraction, to line up with the NE–SW trend of the Lower Severn axis at this point. Thus the Westbury-on-Trym anticline on the Gloucestershire side of the Avon has a NE–SW orientation which continues in its southern limb across the river through Failand to Clevedon. The structures of the northern limb of the anticline are very complex and the same is true of the Clevedon–Portishead ridge, which locally appears to have a synclinal character and may represent the westward continuation of part of the northern limb combined with part of the southern limb of another anticline which formerly lay to the northwest, but all the trends appear to be related to that of the Lower Severn axis. Connections between the Westbury-on-Trym anticline and the southward-plunging Thornbury anticline are as yet unknown but the latter also shows folding along the line of the Lower Severn axis, though here the trend becomes NNE–SSW. Still further north the structures which flank the Tortworth inlier are thought to have a N–S alignment parallel with the eastern border of the Gloucestershire coal basin. North of Thornbury, therefore, Armorican trends virtually disappear and are largely replaced by N–S Malvernoid features. Thus in the Forest of Dean the folding which affected the Coal Measures has a predominantly N–S trend comparable with that of the intra-Carboniferous folding in the Old Red Sandstone and in the Carboniferous Limestone of this area. In the extreme north there are instances to the west of Micheldean where the folds of the two earth movements are in coincidence, but in the south, especially to the northwest of Lydney, there is no such coincidence, and the centre of a gently dipping Coal Measures syncline lies in marked discordance over the steeply dipping eastern limb of the older Lydney syncline.

Faulting associated with Permo-Carboniferous earth movements in the Bristol region also occurs on mainly E–W and N–S lines, though again with important divergences, especially in the west and northwest of the region. Predominantly E–W faults mark the area from the northern outskirts of Bristol to Mendip. In Mendip itself E–W thrust faults are associated with each of the periclines, whilst the coal basins between Mendip and the Bath–Broadfield Down anticline are crossed by a large number of E–W faults which appear to have arisen from the relief of stress by thrust faulting as the shales and sandstones of the Coal Measures were compressed between the folds to the north and south. In particular two fault belts of major importance divide the Somerset coalfield into three portions. Near to Kilmersdon the Southern Overthrust separates the area of highly contorted measures between Nettlebridge and Mells, where the coals of the Lower Coal series were extensively worked, from the Radstock basin to the north where it was the Upper Coal series which was exploited. Within the Radstock basin further E–W faults, notably the Temple Cloud and Paulton faults, separate the Radstock, Camerton, Paulton and Clutton coal districts. The second major fault belt separates the Radstock–Clutton area from the Pensford part of the coalfield to the north, in which seams of the Upper Coal series were worked. This is the Farmborough Compression Belt between Farmborough and Marksbury, in which a number of thrusts of major amplitude are thought to exist. In Broadfield Down the Wrington, Cleeve, North Hill, Lulsgate, Brockley and Hartcliffe faults all curve slightly to the north of a true E–W alignment, but in the limestones between Failand and Clevedon the Avon, Tickenham, Naish House and

Clevedon faults have a general E–W orientation. In the Kingswood anticline considerable thrusting appears to have occurred, especially on the southern flanks of the main exposure of the Lower Coal series, where E–W faults follow the general trend of the anticline. Further north, however, as in the case of the folding, the E–W orientation becomes a much less marked feature in the fault lines, the only important examples being the Stoke Gifford and Kidney Hill faults which approximately bisect the Coalpit Heath basin of the Gloucestershire coalfield. Though a major E–W fault crosses the May Hill inlier, in the main basin of the Forest of Dean the Moorgreen and Crumpmeadows faults tend more to the WNW and are in any case relatively minor ones. N–S faults, on the other hand, are rather more important in the northern parts of the region. In the Forest of Dean the general N–S alignment of the fold structures is followed by the Cannop Fault Belt and its southward continuation in the Pillowell and Whitecroft faults, which mark a line of division between the main basin and the Worcester syncline to the west. In the Tortworth inlier, too, the western edge of the Cambrian and Silurian rocks is marked by a long N–S fault from Tites Point to Stone, whilst the closely linked Iron Acton, Ram Hill and Shortwood faults extend N–S from Tortworth to the Kingswood anticline, crossing the E–W Kidney Hill fault at right angles near the centre of the Coalpit Heath basin. The Kingswood anticline, especially at its western end, is also crossed by N–S faults, some of which, including the East Flower Hill fault, continue these lines southwards towards the Somerset coalfield. Here the numerous E–W faults are crossed by several N–S ones, which include the Clutton, Hunstrete and Marksbury faults in the north, the Clandown fault in the Radstock basin, and the Luckington fault in the extreme south. Finally in Mendip N–S faults cross the central and eastern periclines and it has been suggested that those of the greatly disturbed Pen Hill area may show lateral movement associated with the forward movement of the Blackdown pericline and possibly with wrenching along the concealed western side of the Gloucestershire coalfield to the north.

In addition to the main coal basins three smaller ones occur within the folded and faulted Armorican structures to the west and northwest of Bristol, where the trends swing to a NE–SW direction aligned with the Lower Severn axis. The Avonmouth basin, concealed beneath the Trias and alluvium, is a syncline to the NNW of the prow of the Westbury-on-Trym anticline. Within the basin the Pennant, which outcrops at Kings Weston, is thought to rest unconformably on the Quartzitic Sandstone and Clifton Down Limestone. A small area of the Upper Coal series occupies the centre of the basin between the railway lines to the Severn Tunnel and to Hallen Marsh Junction, and includes the Avonmouth 1 and 2 coal seams. The small Nailsea field is also a synclinal one to the northwest of the Broadfield Down pericline, though in this case with the Lower Coal series, which was formerly worked, partially overlain by Pennant. There is some doubt whether the Lower Coal series in this area rests conformably on the Quartzitic Sandstone or on the upper parts of the Carboniferous Limestone; its complex relationship with the overlying Pennant is determined in the northern part of the basin by ENE–WSW faulting. The structural relationships of the Pennant in the Clapton basin are also obscure. It is thought that the northern as well as the southern edge may be faulted but in any case its suggested relationship with the underlying Old Red Sandstone and Lower Limestone Shales implies a major unconformity possibly related to Carboniferous movement on the Lower Severn axis.

The Armorican folding and uplift of west Somerset and of the Bristol and Mendip areas was succeeded by a period of rapid erosion during which most of the Coal Measures were removed from the higher areas. Presumably the debris of this erosion was deposited in basins in central Somerset and to the east and west of the Malvern–Bath axis. However, in the Bristol region later rocks entirely conceal any material of Permian age and the Bunter at the base of the Trias, except in a very small area behind the west Somerset coast. From this small exposure and from borings north of Bridgwater there is proof that the Bunter Pebble Beds, unlike those further south, contain pebbles of grit and Carboniferous Limestone which may indicate that the limestone cores of the Armorican folds had been exposed by this time.

There is a good deal of evidence to suggest that, following the Armorican uplift, arid conditions prevailed during most of the Permian and Triassic periods. The almost complete absence of fossil flora and fauna apart from land reptiles gives the impression of desert conditions, which is confirmed by some geomorphological and lithological evidence. Thus where erosion has removed the greater part of the Triassic material from the flanks of the Carboniferous Limestone hill areas to the south and southwest of Bristol, the resultant relief of cliff-like features is structure controlled and would be appropriate to the desert erosion of limestone anticlines once the Coal Measures had been stripped away. Typical examples of such relief are to be seen in the impressive northern face of the Blackdown pericline in Mendip, in parts of the western and southern flanks of the Broadfield Down pericline, and in the ridges between Bristol and Clevedon. Moreover, the brilliant red of the sandstones which in places overlie the Coal Measures and the presence of truly rounded sand grains in sandy beds within the Keuper Marls also suggest arid conditions.

Under such conditions some part of the eroded materials tended to accumulate as vast screes of angular rock debris around the foot of the mountainous country of the Bristol region. That this material is named Dolomitic Conglomerate is rather unfortunate, since it is more usually a breccia, its fragments ranging from massive boulders below the steep flanks of the folds to tiny particles in the fine-grained breccias stretching below the Keuper Marl several miles away from the upland edges. The most extensive deposits of Dolomitic Conglomerate surround Mendip, whilst more restricted spreads occur within the core areas of the periclines, especially at the western end of Blackdown to the north of Shipham. Broadfield Down similarly is fringed by Dolomitic Conglomerate which extends up the floors of the Combes on its western side. On the landward and seaward sides of the Clevedon–Portishead ridge there are narrow belts of the Conglomerate, and rather wider belts lie on both flanks of the Clevedon–Failand ridge. North of the Avon the wide valley of the Trym in the core of the Westbury anticline is floored with Dolomitic Conglomerate, which also flanks the northern limb in Henbury and Lawrence Weston. Further north along the western edge of the coal basin the material crops out in a small area below the limestone ridge at Lower Almondsbury and reappears just north of Thornbury to the west of the Palaeozoic rocks forming the northern rim of the coalfield round Cromhall. Across the Severn two fairly large areas of Dolomitic Conglomerate lie on the southern slopes of the Carboniferous Limestone extending southeastwards from St Briavels, one to the west of Chepstow and the other to the north of Undy.

Though the formation of the Dolomitic Conglomerate may well have proceeded through Bunter and into Keuper times on the flanks of the Armorican mountains, the more normal sequence of Lower Keuper Sandstone followed the Bunter in the basins of central Somerset and Gloucestershire. Both Bunter and Lower Keuper Sandstone occur in an irregular belt in the extreme southeast of the region round Langard Budville in Somerset, whilst the Keuper Sandstone reappears in the far northwest where the Trias is faulted against the older rocks between the May Hill inlier and the Malverns to the north of Huntly. Elsewhere in the Bristol region, however, these rocks are masked by the Marls and later deposits, and their presence has been demonstrated only in borings near Bridgwater and Gloucester. Apart from the diachronous Dolomitic Conglomerate fringing the Palaeozoic uplands, the Triassic rocks which occur commonly at the surface in the Bristol region are the Keuper Marls. Throughout the basins of central Somerset they lie below more recent deposits, but to the southwest of Bridgwater the Marls occupy virtually all the lower ground surrounding the Palaeozoic rocks of the Quantocks. Northwards they disappear below the recent materials of the moors of the Parrett basin but reappear on the higher edges and in 'islands' within the levels. Two such 'islands' form the higher ground from Othery through Middlezoy to Weston Zoyland and at Chedzoy, whilst the Marls occupy much of the higher ground around High Ham and the slopes along the southwestern flank of the Polden Hills from Charlton Mackrell and Dundon to Bawdrip in the west. To the north of the Polden Hills the Trias is again hidden by the moors of the Brue and Axe basins, but here too it reappears at the surface in the 'islands', notably that of Wedmore where it outcrops below the Rhaetic and Lias on the northeastern slopes and includes the site of the village of Wedmore. Along the foot of the southern face of Mendip the Keuper Marls occupy a belt of gently rising ground above the levels, some two to three miles wide in the southeast between Pilton and Henton but narrowing to less than half a mile at Axbridge and Bleadon Hill. The Marls extend up the valley of the Lox Yeo to the east of Bleadon Hill and then continue along the northern side of Mendip. Here, as on the southern flank, the Keuper Marls stop short of the limestone hill mass and are replaced by the encircling Dolomitic Conglomerate as explained above, whilst in places both are masked by Head deposits and gravels below the steeper slopes. Between Mendip on the south and the hills of Broadfield Down and Dundry on the north, the broad valleys of the Chew and the upper Yeo are largely floored with Keuper Marl, though to the west of Congresbury the Trias is hidden below the more recent deposits of the moors of the Yeo basin. To the east near the Somerset coalfield the Marls are overlain by patches of Rhaetic and Liassic material which become continuous east of an irregular line from Midsomer Norton to Compton Dando. In some districts to the north and west of the Chew valley and the Blagdon reservoirs, a local development of Butcombe Sandstone replaces the Marls and this combines with cappings of Rhaetic and Lias to produce considerable diversity of landscape in this central part of the vale.

The Carboniferous Limestone of Broadfield Down and the Jurassic outlier of Dundry Hill together make a complete break in the Triassic exposures, and from here northwards to the Severn at Tites Point there is an irregular pattern of outcrops governed in part by the strike of the exposed Carboniferous rocks and in part by the distribution of remnants of the overlying Rhaetic and Lias. The eastern limit of exposures of Keuper Marl is marked by the main continuous outcrop of Rhaetic and Lias which runs southward from Tites Point through Berkeley Road, between Charfield and Kingswood, immediately east of Wickwar through Chipping Sodbury, Siston and Wick to Upton Cheyney. Immediately west of this line a belt of Keuper Marl at most a mile but commonly only a few hundred yards wide lies between the low Rhaetic scarp and the Palaeozoic rocks of the Tortworth inlier and the Bristol and Gloucestershire coal basin. From the Severn the Triassic belt is continuous as far south as Wickwar, where it is broken by an over-step of the Rhaetic and Lias onto the Carboniferous Limestone around the coalfield. Within the coal basin patches of Keuper Marl extend from the neighbourhood of Cromhall southwards towards Yate and from here there is again a continuous belt of Marl between the Rhaetic and the Coal Measures as far south as Upton Cheyney. On the south side of the Bristol coalfield the Keuper Marls outcrop below the Lias and Rhaetic at the foot of the Dundry outlier, forming a curving belt about a quarter of a mile wide to the south of the Avon from Keynsham through Arnos Vale and Totterdown to the Malago valley and the lower slopes of Bed-minster Down. Westwards from Bedminster the Marls floor the Long Ashton gap between the Failand ridge on the north and Dundry and Broadfield Down on the south, though they give way to Dolomitic Conglomerate at the foot of the limestone uplands and elsewhere they are masked by Head deposits. Westwards again the outcrop of the Trias bifurcates around the Nailsea coal basin and finally disappears below the recent deposits of the Yeo basin.

Immediately to the west of the Bristol and Gloucestershire coal basin a sandstone like that of Butcombe in Somerset again locally replaces the usual slightly calcareous silts and muds of the so-called Red Marls of the Keuper. This sandstone occupies a narrow belt of country from Frampton Cotterell and Winterbourne through Hambrook to the north-eastern outskirts of Bristol, where it widens out into a triangular area between Eastville in the north, Bedminster in the southwest and Brisling-ton in the southeast. The sandstones therefore underlie the greater part of central, east and southeast Bristol and form the rounded hillocks surrounding and rising through the alluvium of the Avon and Frome valleys which played a vitally important part in the early history of the city. Further west again the Marls resume their usual character and in Bristol cover the Clifton and Redland districts below the level of the Carboniferous Limestone downs. Northeastwards from Bristol the Marls run parallel with the sandstones as a narrow belt east of Stoke Gifford to Latteridge and Itchington near to the northern end of the coal basin. The large remnant of Rhaetic and Lias which extends from north Bristol to Alveston covers the Keuper Marls and further masks the structural relationships in this area between the Westbury-on-Trym anticline and the Thornbury anticline to the north. To the west of the higher ground formed by the anticlines and the Almondsbury Carboniferous Limestone ridge, however, the Keuper Marl reappears and occupies about half a mile of sloping ground down to the 50-foot contour, below which it disappears under the alluvium of the Severn lowlands. Round the Thornbury anticline the exposures of Marl widen out westwards at Olveston and Littleton and reappear again in the higher ground behind

Aust Cliff and in the English Stones and other reefs in the Severn. North of Oldbury the outcrop of the Marl again narrows along the west side of the Tortworth inlier and finally disappears below the alluvium south of Berkeley, apart from a small area near the mouth of the Berkeley Pill.

Across the Severn the western limit of the Trias is sharply defined along a frequently faulted boundary with the Palaeozoic rocks of the Forest of Dean. In the south the line starts half a mile east of Blakeney, where the Marls are faulted against the Old Red Sandstone, and runs northwards along the May Hill inlier through Huntley, where the Keuper Sandstones appear, and Newnham towards the southern end of the Malverns. The only area where the Triassic rocks extend further west is in a narrow belt of Marls along the Severn from Alvington to the mouth of the Wye and in alternating patches of Marls and Dolomitic Conglomerate beyond that point. To the east the Keuper Marls floor the Vale of Severn almost to the right bank of the river upstream to the limit of the Bristol region at Tewkesbury, the western edge of the Rhaetic and Lias lying only a little way to the west of the river from Awre, opposite Tites Point, to within four miles of Tewkesbury.

In the area southwest of Bridgwater and in exposures in the cliffs of west Somerset, the top hundred feet of the Marls are green or grey in colour, which may imply the onset of less arid conditions. The Tea Green and the Grey Marls retain a considerable thickness as far north as the 'island' at Wedmore, but to the north of Mendip the Grey Marls are absent and the Tea Green Marls themselves are reduced to about 15 feet in thickness. During the deposition of the Red Marls under arid conditions the concentration and drying out of saline lakes gave rise to the presence of deposits of evaporites including rock salt, gypsum and celestine (strontium sulphate). Just north of Bridgwater there is evidence of a Lower Gypsum Bed at about 1,000 feet and of salt deposits at about 750 feet below the top of the Red Marls, whilst there is also an Upper Gypsum Bed in the red and green variegated Marls above the true Red Marls. North of Mendip the lower parts of the Red Marls and consequently the Lower Gypsum and the saliferous beds are absent, but the Upper Gypsum Bed is present at about 50 feet below the top of the Red Marls and is exposed in the cliff section at Aust. Though quantities of strontium have been found in evaporites to the south of Mendip, by far the most important deposits of celestine occur about 30 feet below the top of the Red Marls in the narrow belts of Trias to the east and west of the Bristol and Gloucestershire coal basin, especially at Tytherington in the northwest and from Bitton to Yate in the east, the working of the deposits being of considerable importance in the area immediately south of Yate.

Throughout the Bristol region the Rhaetic Transgression was preceded by erosion of the Keuper surface and this, combined with earlier Triassic erosion, apparently resulted in a remarkably flat land surface onto which the Rhaetic sea spread so that the Rhaetic deposits, despite their thinness (seldom as much as 50 feet), covered virtually the whole region between the land areas of South Wales and Exmoor, except where remnants of Armorican uplands still emerged as islands from the shallow sea. These islands, termed the Mendip Archipelago by Richardson, certainly included Mendip itself, the Quantocks and the Cowbridge area in South Wales and probably also the limestone uplands of Broadfield Down, Clevedon, Portishead, Failand and the Westbury-on-Trym anticline, as well as the higher parts of the Kingswood anticline. The areas to the north and south of the Mendip axis, however, again had somewhat different physical histories in this period. In south and central Somerset the erosion which preceded the deposition of the Lower Westbury Beds of the Rhaetic appears to have been relatively slight and below the Ceratodus Bone Bed shales usually overlie the Green and Grey Keuper Marls. North of Mendip, on the other hand, erosion appears to have been more prolonged and severe so that commonly the Bone Bed is the lowest of the Rhaetic deposits, whilst in places this too is missing and the Rhaetic consists only of the upper part of the Westbury Beds and the overlying few feet of Cotham Beds. Moreover, to the north of Mendip the erosion was such that in places the Rhaetic rests on the exposed Palaeozoic rocks of the coal basin and its margins as well as on the Keuper.

Tertiary and Quaternary uplift and erosion, which followed the later Mesozoic deposition, has led to the re-excavation of the Palaeozoic hill areas and the stripping of the Rhaetic deposits from much of the Bristol region, so that their present extent is continuous only to the east of an irregular curving line from Tewkesbury to the southern limit of the region in the Black Down Hills, broken for a short distance, however, at the Mendip 'island'. To the west only narrow tongues and residual patches of Rhaetic and Lias remain. From the Black Down Hills south of Pitminster a low ridge through Stoke St Mary to Langport and Somerton marks the edge of the continuous Rhaetic outcrop in south Somerset. From this point it follows an irregular course with westward extensions below the Lias of the Polden Hills and the Pennard and Glastonbury outliers before it reaches the southern edge of Mendip, where there are isolated patches on the south side of the central periclines. North of the Mendip break there are again patches of Rhaetic round Chewton Mendip but the continuous outcrop is confined to the eastern half of the Somerset coal basins, the line of its western edge being deeply notched by the valleys of the Cam brook and Wellow brook draining northeastwards to the Avon. At Keynsham there is again a major westward extension of the Rhaetic below the Dundry outlier but the main area, though broken by faulting round the eastern end of the Kingswood anticline, continues northwards in a great curve over the Gloucestershire coal basin through Siston and Pucklechurch to Chipping Sodbury, where it resumes a remarkably straight S–N course to the Severn at Tites Point. Between Chipping Sodbury and Charfield there are some of the best examples of the Rhaetic resting unconformably on the Carboniferous Limestone round the eastern edge of the coal basin. Across the Severn opposite Tites Point there are small areas of Rhaetic and Lias round Awre and on the slightly higher ground between Westbury-on-Severn and Walmore, the latter including the famous Garden Cliff exposures of the Rhaetic. The western edge of the outcrop again crosses to the west of the Severn near Minsterworth and continues northwards through Lassington and Hartpury before swinging back to the east bank four miles south of Tewkesbury.

There is some parallelism between the regional strike and the distribution and shape of the remnants of Rhaetic and Lias to the west of the main outcrop. To the south of the Bristol Avon the two main extensions are therefore aligned approximately E–W. In the more southerly of these, the Polden Hills continue the Rhaetic and Lias from the Somerton district slightly north of west, past Street and Cossington to Puriton, and detached areas continue further west at Pawlett, along the Somerset coast belt from Otterhampton to Quantoxhead, and round Watchet. In the north, too, the Dundry outlier from Keynsham to Barrow Gurney has an E–W orientation, which appears to be continued further west in isolated patches of Rhaetic and Lias on Broadfield Down. Between Dundry and Mendip no clear alignment can be discerned in the small patches of Rhaetic and Lias round Butcombe and the larger extents near Farrington Gurney which form scarp features between Farrington Gurney and Litton and round Hinton Blewett, but the location of both is clearly related to the very numerous E–W faults which cross the area. On the other hand, between Mendip and the Poldens the outlying hills of the Pennards, Glastonbury, Meare, Wedmore and Brent Knoll follow lines parallel to the major features to the north and south and have been preserved in a slightly sinuous E–W synclinal belt possibly of Armorican origin but certainly active in post-Liassic times. The structural relationships of the Polden Hills are not clear but they lie north of and parallel to a proposed eastward continuation of the north Devon Armorican axis through Langport and Sparkford towards the Vale of Wardour, where post-Jurassic activity was important. The structural position of the Dundry outlier is even more problematical. It has been suggested by Arkell that it may overlie a synclinal area comparable with that to the south of Mendip, but in such a case the syncline would be very close indeed to the suggested anticlinal axis from Bath to the pericline at Broadfield Down onto which patches of Rhaetic and Lias extend westwards from Dundry.

To the north of the Bristol Avon there are three main outlying areas of Rhaetic and Lias aligned with the NE–SW strike of the area near the Lower Severn axis. By far the largest extends from the northern outskirts of Bristol to Alveston and contains unusually large extents of exposed Rhaetic northwest of Filton. In the south round the prow of the Westbury-on-Trym anticline from Westbury itself to Brentry, the Rhaetic again rests unconformably on the Carboniferous Limestone, whilst in the north for five miles between Alveston and Almondsbury it again rests on the limestones which appear to form the discontinuous western edge of the coal basin. The other outlying areas of Rhaetic on a similar alignment are materially smaller, one between Falfield and Rockhampton, parallel with the southern end of the Tortworth inlier, and the other running NE–SW from Whitcliff Park to Hill, to the southwest of Berkeley. Finally a number of even smaller patches surround the western end of the complex plunging anticlinal structures at Thornbury and include the capping of Rhaetic and Lias at the famous Aust Cliff section.

At the beginning of the Liassic period a phase of shallower water conditions saw the deposition of the White Lias south of the Bristol Avon and southeast of the Lower Severn axis. This was followed by an extension and deepening of the sea to cover most of the Bristol region during the deposition of the Blue Lias Limestones and the Lower Lias Clay, though Mendip and possibly the Quantocks remained as islands even at this stage and, as in the Rhaetic, there were important contrasts to the north and south of the Mendip axis. Thus in the lowest portions of the Blue Lias the area south of Mendip has limestones and clays indicative of deep water deposition, whereas to the north in the angle between the Mendip and Bath axes as far as Dursley there are shelly limestones and marls characteristic of shallower water. Beyond the Bath axis northward from Dursley throughout the Vales of Gloucester and Evesham, however, deep water deposits reappear. Progressive deepening of the seas resulted in the upper parts of the Blue Lias consisting of clays and deep water limestones throughout the region except for a belt between Mendip and the Bristol Avon where shallow water shelly limestones were deposited over what has been termed the Radstock shelf. The existence of this shelf has been attributed to intra-Liassic earth movements along fold lines which have been traced between Mendip and Farmborough and which are on the same general E–W orientation as the main Armorican structures of the district. Mendip itself appears to have remained as an island or islands and around eastern and central Mendip and Broadfield Down a littoral form of Lower Lias exists. Away from the Mendip axis to both north and south limestones in the Blue Lias thicken, though very gradually to the north. Over the Radstock shelf limestones continued to be deposited through much of the Lower Lias period so that thicknesses up to 50 feet exist, but in the deeper basins of Gloucestershire and of Somerset to the south of Mendip the upper part of the Lower Lias consists almost entirely of clays and shales. The total thickness of the Lower Lias also increases away from Mendip and the presumed tectonic shelf to the north of it. In Gloucestershire the maximum thicknesses of over 900 feet lie beyond the Bath axis in the Vales of Gloucester and Evesham, whilst in Somerset over 400 feet of Lower Lias has been proved in the central basin of the Brue.

Owing to the thinness and uniformity of the Rhaetic outcrop, the western edge of the main Lower Lias outcrop follows that of the Rhaetic very closely indeed from Tewkesbury in the north to Langport and the Black Down Hills in the south, whilst in the detached areas to the west the distributions are very similar in west Somerset, the Polden Hills, the Somerset 'islands', Dundry and the area to the northwest of Bristol. In Gloucestershire, therefore, the main area of Lower Lias consists of clays at the surface forming a flat or very gently undulating plain from one to three miles wide from the north of Bristol as far as Dursley, where it widens out into the Vales of Gloucester and Evesham. Limestones are seldom seen and the only material worked has been the upper part of the clays, which has been used for brick and tile making at Stonehouse and near Cheltenham. The basin of Somerset to the south of Mendip is also largely floored by Lower Lias Clay though more recent deposits cover much of it. However, the basal limestone of the Blue Lias and the White Lias Limestone are exposed in the eastern part of the county and in the Polden Hills, and have been quarried for lime and building stone. Between these two main basins the area of north Somerset and south Gloucestershire has much less clay, and near Mendip and over the Radstock shelf considerable thicknesses of limestone exist throughout the Lower Lias succession. Around Radstock itself the White Lias Limestone has been quarried for lime and building stone whilst the Downside stone, quarried in eastern Mendip, belongs to the local littoral aspect of the Lower Lias.

The eastern limit of the Lower Lias exposures is normally marked by the higher ground of the Middle Lias. The basins in which the Lower Lias Clays were deposited appear to have become sufficiently shallow to be partially filled with silts and sands, so that throughout the region the lower parts of the Middle Lias consist of marly silts or sands. Apart from a very small area on the Dundry outlier, however, the Middle Lias thins out and disappears over the Mendip axis and much of the adjacent part of north Somerset, so that the broad geographical pattern of sedimentation is comparable with that of Lower Lias times, especially as there are again significant lithological contrasts on either side of the Mendip–north Somerset zone of division. From the extreme south of Somerset, where there is a thickness of over 150 feet, the Middle Lias thins progressively northwards towards the Mendip axis. Throughout this area marls and silts form the lowest parts but they are commonly succeeded by yellow sands, which in the south occur widely from Chard to Ilminster and Yeovil and further north appear in the outlier at the Pennards, from which they derive the name Pennard Sands. Similarly on the Gloucestershire side the Middle Lias thins from a maximum of about 250 feet near Cheltenham to 150 feet at Stroud, 100 feet at Wotton-under-Edge, and finally disappears immediately north of Bath. Here, however, no major deposits of sands occur, the whole being composed of silts comparable with those at the base in Somerset. There is palaeontological evidence that in the upper part of the Middle Lias a change in sedimentation conditions spread gradually southward from Gloucestershire into Somerset, leading to the formation of a ferruginous limestone known as the Marlstone Rock. North of Bath this material forms the top 10–20 feet of the Middle Lias and, because it is much harder than the silts below and the Upper Lias Sands and Clay above, it forms a ledge-like platform which is a highly characteristic feature at the foot of the Cotswold scarp from Bath northwards. In Somerset the Marlstone Rock is commonly thinner, especially in the south of the county where the Middle Lias outcrop swings southwest and west from Corton Denham through Yeovil and Martock. Here the Marlstone may be as little as one foot thick and was mapped along with the limestones at the base of the Upper Lias as a junction bed.

Apart from small areas at Claphanger Common and Hornsbury north of Chard, the main outcrop of the Middle Lias enters the region from the Axe valley near Winsham and then curves northward through Herne Hill to Ilminster, forming the higher ground to the east of the Isle valley. From Ilminster it occupies a wider belt of country running eastward past Martock and Yeovil before curving northwards to Corton Denham. In general terms the Middle Lias forms the rising ground on the south side of the Yeo valley but within it the three divisions appear as distinct relief features. At the base the silts and marls occur in the gently rising ground above the 50-foot contour which provides the sites of a long line of settlements from Ilminster through Stocklinch, Barrington, Kingsbury Episcopi and Martock and the villages of Ash Tintinhull, Chilthorne Domer and Trent. On the other hand, the harder ferruginous sandy limestone of the Junction Bed at the top of the Middle Lias stands out in definite hill areas. In the faulted area in the west round Ilminster these take the form of isolated ridges from Kingstone to Herne Hill, from Seavington St Michael to Puckington, and at Beacon Hill north of Ilminster. Eastwards from Cripple Hill at Bower Hinton, however, the Junction Bed occurs in the slopes of the continuous Upper Lias scarp through Stoke-sub-Hamdon and round the northern outskirts of Yeovil, whence it curves northwards at Nether Compton through Sandford Orcas to form the Corton ridge to the west of Corton Denham. Between the silts and the Junction Bed the Pennard Sands usually form the lower slopes of the hills, but the whole of the hills at Burrow and New Cross southwest of Kingsbury Episcopi are composed of the sands, as are the steeper slopes of Marshes Hill northwest of Yeovil. North of Corton Denham the thinning outcrop of the Middle Lias narrows and it is no longer possible to distinguish separate relief features within it. It forms the sloping ground below the Upper Lias scarp round Cadbury Castle, through North Cadbury and to the west of Castle Cary and Ansford, before curving eastwards along the south side of the Brue valley and then northwards through Lamyat and Milton Clevedon to Batcombe, where the outcrop ceases. To the west, outliers of the Middle Lias form the greater part of Pennard Hill, all the hill area at Glastonbury surrounding the Upper Lias tor itself, and Brent Knoll where the characteristic outline of the hill is due to the ledge formed by the Marlstone Rock.

Beyond the Mendip–north Somerset break the Middle Lias is first seen in a detached area at Upton Cheyney to the west of the Jurassic rocks of Lansdown Hill near Bath, and then the continuous outcrop runs northwards at the foot of the remarkably straight Cotswold scarp from Freezing Hill to Hillsley. Here the exposure is extremely narrow but the platform of the harder Marlstone Rock is well defined and on it are situated the villages of Old Sodbury, Little Sodbury, Horton, Hawkesbury and Hillsley. Between Hillsley and Stonehouse the line of the scarp is broken by westward-facing valleys. The Middle Lias forms a platform across the mouths of the smaller valleys in the south, on which are situated Alderley, Wotton-under-Edge and North Nibley, but in the larger and deeper valleys of the Cam and the Frome the Middle Lias forms part of the floor and the lower slopes, and provides the valley-side sites of Cam, Dursley, much of Stroud and the upper parts of Stonehouse. From Stonehouse the Middle Lias continues round Harefield Beacon to Witcombe and round Leckhampton Hill to curve eastwards and northwards round the east of Cheltenham to reach Cleeve Cloud, Nottingham Hill and Winchcombe. From here a great northern extension takes the Middle Lias as far as Chipping Camden, where it turns southwards along the western side of the Vale of Moreton. In this area to the north of Stonehouse the Middle Lias usually forms the lowest parts of the steep Cotswold scarp without any pronounced Marlstone platform, and the sites of settlements like Witcombe, Winchcombe and Broadway are on the Lower rather than the Middle Lias. Exceptionally there is a distinct platform in the Middle Lias southeast of Gloucester at Upton St Leonards and in the extreme north round Chipping Camden and the Ebrington Hill outlier, whilst in Burrell Hill above Broadway and Dorn Hill above Aston Magna it forms spur-like features. The lower slopes of the outliers of Robin's Wood Hill, Churchdown, Dumbleton and Oxenton are of Middle Lias, as are the unfaulted northern slopes of the larger Bredon outlier.

During the deposition of the Upper Lias the area between Mendip and Bath again forms a transitional belt. Maximum deposition appears to have moved southwards across the country so that the lower or Whitbian part of the Upper Lias is dominant in the north, whereas in Somerset and Dorset the upper or Yeovilian part is the more important. Though the change is progressive there is a marked contrast to the north and south of Bath, the Cotteswold Sands of the Upper Lias in Cotswold being of Whitbian age, whereas the Midford Sands between Bath and Mendip and the Yeovil Sands further south are of Yeovilian age. In addition to this north–south change it has been suggested that the Upper Lias sedimentation of the Bristol region was affected by intra-Liassic earth movements. These may well have occurred along any of the pre-existing axes but their apparent effect is greatest in consequence of presumed movement on N–S Malvernoid lines especially over the Bath axis and over anticlinal structures in the Vale of Moreton. Under these circumstances sedimentation would have proceeded over two N–S axes, with a synclinal area between them extending southwards from the neighbourhood of Cleeve Hill. It might be expected that sandy deposits, whether of Whitbian or Yeovilian date, would be laid down over the axes whilst clays would be deposited in the synclinal area, and in general the changes of facies in the Upper Lias conform to such a pattern. There are breaks in the Upper Lias exposures over the Mendip axis partly because of the removal of the Lias by the Bajocian (Inferior Oolite) denudation and partly because of later erosion. With the exception of the Mendip area, however, the western edge of the Upper Lias runs parallel with, and a little to the east of, the line of the Bath axis from Dursley to Yeovil and throughout the whole of this section the Upper Lias is predominantly sandy. In the extreme south where the exposures swing westwards through Yeovil and Crewkerne they actually cross the axis and here the Yeovil Sands are about 200 feet thick with only 5–10 feet of clay at the base. There are still between 150 and 200 feet of sand in the main scarp to the east of the break over the Mendip axis and in the outliers at Glastonbury Tor and Brent Knoll, though the clays may be nearly 50 feet thick at the base. Around the Avon tributaries south of Bath the

31

Upper Lias outcrop again approaches the axis and lies over it as far north as Little Sodbury. In this area there are again great thicknesses of sand, about 100 feet of Midford Sands south of Bath and 185 feet of Cotteswold Sands at Little Sodbury, here resting directly on the Middle Lias Marlstone. From Little Sodbury to Stinchcombe the scarp still lies very close to the line of the Bath axis and at Stinchcombe the Cotteswold Sands are 230 feet thick, though a thin Upper Lias Clay underlies them. From Stinchcombe to Chipping Camden, however, the scarp and the Upper Lias outcrop swing in an irregular northeasterly direction across the structures and traverse the synclinal area between the Bath and Vale of Moreton axes. Along this belt the thin Upper Lias Clay of Stinchcombe gradually replaces the Sands from below, so that near Cheltenham the Sands have virtually disappeared and in Cleeve Hill and the Bredon outlier 270 feet of clay form the whole of the Upper Lias. Further to the northeast, on the other hand, as the outcrop approaches the Vale of Moreton axis near Chipping Camden, the clays thin to about 80 feet and borings have shown the presence of sandy deposits above them.

Over most of the region the Upper Lias occurs as a narrow outcrop in the steeper parts of the Jurassic scarp, but in the south where the Jurassic rocks turn westward beyond the Yeo valley the Upper Lias occupies a much wider belt of very rolling country south of the Cripple Hill–Hamdon–North Yeovil scarp, usually at heights between 200 and 300 feet. The belt has its widest extent of some five miles to the west of the Parrett between Martock and Crewkerne, whilst between the Parrett and the Yeo it is about two miles wide. Virtually the whole of the Upper Lias here is composed of Yeovil Sands on which are situated the town of Yeovil in the east and Crewkerne in the south, with a large number of sizeable villages especially in the area to the north of Crewkerne. In this area Yeovil Sands contain locally a considerable thickness of ferruginous shelly limestone known as Ham Hill Stone, which is a warm-coloured building stone suitable for elaborate working and sculpture, Sherborne Abbey and Montacute House being well-known examples of its local use. Topographically the Ham Hill Stone forms three considerable hill masses rising above the general level of the sands near the centre of this southern part of the Jurassic belt, Hamdon Hill above Stoke-sub-Hamdon, Chiselborough Hill nearby and West Chinnock Hill to the northeast of Crewkerne. East of the Yeo the Upper Lias outcrop narrows and curves northward through Over Compton, forming the high ground on the Dorset border between Yeovil and Sherborne, and at Sandford Orcas it assumes a course almost due north to Corton Denham. Here it is reduced to its more usual width of a few hundred yards but nevertheless it occupies the greater part of the steepest slopes of the main Jurassic scarp in Holway Hill and Corton

Hill and continues to do so northwards round Pen Hill and to the east of Compton Pauncefoot and Yarlington. The town of Castle Cary occupies a site on the Upper Lias scarp which then recurves eastwards along the valley of the Brue to Shepton Montague and the west side of Bruton, before resuming its northward course in the steep slopes of Creech Hill above Lamyat and of the Alham valley above Batcombe. The Upper Lias then forms most of the higher slopes round Westcombe and continues northwards in the scarp until it ends in Ingsdons Hill east of Shepton Mallet. North of Mendip the Midford Sands of the Upper Lias appear in the valley sides of the Avon below Freshford and of the Cam brook and Wellow brook tributaries, continuing through Priston and English-combe to Bath where the sands occur in steep slopes at Beechen Cliff and in the southeastern suburbs.

North of Bath the Upper Lias occurs in the slopes of Lansdown Hill and on the sides of the Swainswick, St Catherine and Box valleys to the northeast of the city, but on the main scarp it has a continuous exposure northwards from Dyrham Park. Above Old Sodbury, Little Sodbury, Horton, Hawkesbury, Hillsley, Alderley and Wotton-under-Edge, the Cotteswold Sands form the greater part of the scarp face, though round Wotton thin Upper Lias Clays appear at the base. From Wotton to Stinchcombe and Dursley the Clays remain quite thin and the scarp still consists of the Sands though with a capping of increasing thicknesses of Inferior Oolite. Between Dursley and Stonehouse, however, in the valleys of the Cam and the Frome, the Upper Lias Clays have some importance. They form the lower slopes of the Cam valley sides below Uley, whilst in the valleys above Stroud and Woodchester the Cotteswold Sands form the steep sides whilst the clays occupy much of the actual valley floor, a fact of great significance in terms of the dense settlement and consider-able industrial importance of the area. As the scarp continues north-wards past Upton St Leonards and Great Witcombe to Leckhampton Hill, the thickening of the Clays at the expense of the Sands becomes rapid, so that at Leckhampton there is only a thin remnant of the Sands and the scarp is composed of nearly equal thicknesses of Inferior Oolite and Upper Lias Clay resting on a slightly thinner Middle Lias outcrop. The northward extension of Cotswold in Cleeve Hill is in effect an Inferior Oolite outlier, since the Upper Lias which surrounds it on the scarp side also floors the valley of the Coln above Andoversford to the south of it. At its northern end in Nottingham Camp and in the outliers in the vale, the Cotteswold Sands finally disappear and the clay forms the whole of the Upper Lias. The Clays continue to make up the greater part of the scarp as it runs northeastwards above Broadway, Weston and Chipping Camden, where it turns southwards through Bourton-on-the-Hill and above Upper Slaughter, but it will be recalled that there is

33

evidence of a return of sandy facies in the higher parts of the Upper Lias as the Vale of Moreton axis is approached round Chipping Camden, and sandy forms as well as clays have been mapped where the dry valleys and the Windrush valley in this part of Cotswold are cut down to the Upper Lias. The exposure of the Upper Lias Clay below the Sands and the Inferior Oolite Limestones in the valleys of north Cotswold appears to have been of considerable importance as a factor influencing settlement sites. Apart from those on the thin Fuller's Earth Clay, the vast majority of Cotswold villages to the north of a line from Painswick to Northleach are on the Upper Lias Clays or near their junction with the Sands.

In general terms the deposition of the Inferior Oolite of the Bristol region took place in comparatively shallow seas off the coral reef shore of a land area in Wales, so that the rocks concerned are commonly composed of neritic materials and themselves frequently include corals. The progress of sedimentation during this period was interrupted or modified by considerable earth movements within the region, the greatest of which, at the end of the Middle Inferior Oolite sedimentation, was sufficiently important to make necessary separate consideration of the periods before and after it. Moreover, before this period of earth movements, in Lower and Middle Inferior Oolite times, the contrast between the northern and southern parts of the region which had existed during the deposition of the Lias persisted. Since the Lower and Middle Inferior Oolite of the Dundry outlier resembles that of Somerset and Dorset and contrasts sharply with that of Cotswold, it would appear that the line of division is not along the Mendip axis but further north. Perhaps the area over the Radstock shelf in which intra-Liassic earth movements took place should still be regarded as a boundary zone between the northern and southern areas.

To the north, Lower and Middle Inferior Oolite sedimentation took place in the same synclinal zone of Cotswold between the Bath and Vale of Moreton axes in which the Middle and Upper Lias had been deposited. Here the Lower Inferior Oolite (Aalenian) consists in the main of oolitic limestones and freestones, separated in the area to the north of Stroud by thin beds of Pea Grit and oolitic marls, so that the sequence in the northern part of the basin is:

Upper Freestone
Oolitic Marl
Lower Freestone
Pea Grit
Lower Limestone

The Lower Limestone and more particularly the Lower Freestone are good building stones and both have been extensively quarried in the past, the former round Stroud and the latter round Cheltenham and Chipping Camden.

After the deposition of the Upper Freestone the long-continued sedimentation of the Cotswold basin was interrupted by earth movements which led to the erosion of an emerging land surface, except locally round Cleeve Hill where a minor synclinal area still received deposits of sands, clays and later limestones. The final phase of the Aalenian was reached when the whole basin was submerged in the Middle Bajocian transgression in which the Lower Trigonia Grit was laid down. This is the basal element of the rocks, generally termed the Ragstones, which make up the Middle Inferior Oolite succession of Cotswold and which were apparently deposited in a redeveloping basin between the Bath and Vale of Moreton axes with its deepest area in the neighbourhood of Cleeve Hill where they are thickest. In Cotswold the Bajocian succession is incomplete and therefore the precise dating of later events is impossible, but at some time after the deposition of the Ragstones earth movements were renewed on a greater scale, resulting in the folding of the main basin into the two synclines of Painswick in the west and Cleeve Hill in the east, separated by the Birdlip anticline. The whole area was then elevated and subjected to such erosion that virtual planation took place, which removed much of the Middle Inferior Oolite especially over the Birdlip anticline so that the Upper Trigonia Grit (Upper Inferior Oolite) which was laid down during the ensuing Vesulian or Upper Bajocian transgression rests on rocks ranging from the Lower Freestone west of Cirencester, and even the Upper Lias over the Vale of Moreton axis, to the upper parts of the Ragstones which were preserved in the syncline of Cleeve Hill. In the latter district the Lower and Middle Inferior Oolite has a thickness of about 300 feet but this thins rapidly from Painswick and tapers out near Chipping Sodbury over the Bath axis, so that in the area around Bath the Upper Inferior Oolite rests on the Upper Lias as it does over the Vale of Moreton axis. The Lower and Middle Inferior Oolite is of little importance in the southern half of the region. It is completely missing from the Jurassic scarp itself as far south as Bruton, where it is preserved in a small syncline southwest of the town at Cole, and beyond here it recurs only as very thin beds in restricted areas near Yeovil and Crewkerne. Such deposits of Lower and Middle Inferior Oolite as may have occurred in the south had therefore been largely removed before the deposition of the Upper Inferior Oolite, but the palaeontological evidence of the remnants suggests that the rocks in Somerset and Dorset were laid down in a separate basin from the corresponding ones of Cotswold. Moreover, nearly 20 feet of Lower and Middle Inferior Oolite are preserved to the north of Mendip in a syncline on Dundry Hill and here the fossils are of the Somerset and Dorset type, so that a connection must be postulated round Mendip between the Dundry area and a Somerset and Dorset basin to the south, there being apparently no fossil evidence of a link between Dundry and the adjacent Cotswold basin to the north.

The results of the uplift and erosion which marked the end of Lower and Middle Inferior Oolite times were so extensive that the transgression leading to Upper Inferior Oolite or Vesulian deposition affected virtually the whole north-south extent of the Bristol region, and though the axes probably still influenced sedimentation conditions and there are considerable regional variations in the rocks of this period, yet on the whole contrasts from north to south became of diminished importance. Thus the Upper Trigonia Grit, which is the lowest member in the Upper Inferior Oolite of Cotswold, extends from the far north of the region to central Somerset, though around the edges of Mendip it is replaced by a conglomerate presumably indicating the existence of littoral conditions round a Mendip island over which the equivalent of the Upper Trigonia Grit is missing. Above the Upper Trigonia Grit there is considerable lithological variation from Cotswold southwards into Somerset, but all the rocks involved are limestones despite the misnomer of 'grits' applied to many of them; from a palaeontological point of view each of the zones except the lowest is represented throughout. From north Cotswold to about Stroud the whole of the Upper Inferior Oolite above the Upper Trigonia Grit is composed of Clypeus Grit which, like the other so-called grits of this area, is really a highly granular limestone. South of Stroud this is replaced by massive limestones overlain by oolite and rubbly limestones; these continue southwards and, unlike the lower members of the Inferior Oolite, cross the Mendip axis where they rest unconformably on the Carboniferous Limestone. Beyond Mendip the massive limestones continue east of Shepton Mallet and into the district of Doulting, where they were quarried as the Doulting stone used in many buildings south of Mendip, of which Wells Cathedral is the best-known example. Locally at the base of the Doulting stone there is a thin coral bed and even more locally on Dundry Hill below the coral bed there is another massive limestone known as Dundry Freestone, which was used in a number of Bristol churches including that of St Mary, Redcliffe. In the north–south section of the Jurassic scarp from Bruton to the neighbourhood of Milborne Port, the Upper Inferior Oolite is comparatively thin, but where the outcrop swings southwest-wards and widens between Sherborne and Yeovil it thickens to include two 20-foot limestones separated by rubbly limestone, the lower beds including the Sherborne building stone. Where the Inferior Oolite is crossed by the Yeo to the south of Yeovil, however, the thickness is again reduced to about 6 feet apparently over the southern part of the

Bath axis, whilst westwards towards Crewkerne the Upper Inferior Oolite is commonly to be measured in inches.

In the extreme south of the Bristol region, therefore, the very thin Inferior Oolite does not form important relief features. It appears in small irregular patches among the complex pattern of faults round Crewkerne and to the northwest. From Bradford Abbas southeast of Yeovil the outcrop is continuous along the gentle dipslopes above the river Yeo through Sherborne to Milborne Port and Charleton Horethorne. To the west of Milborne Port, however, the Inferior Oolite extends as far as the main scarp, where it forms a capping on Holway Hill and Corton Hill, as it does from here northwards along the scarp as far as Mendip. Thus it occurs on the top of Pen Hill, where it also forms the outlier at Cadbury Castle, and continues in Lodge Hill to the southeast of Castle Cary and through Bruton to Creech Hill and Batcombe, where it swings westward in Small Down and Maes Down to reach the southern edge of Mendip near Doulting. Beyond this point only the upper parts of the Inferior Oolite cross the Mendip axis. From the scarp at Doulting to Nunney they therefore rest alternately on the Lower Lias and on the Carboniferous Limestone or Old Red Sandstone of eastern Mendip, forming the relatively low-lying and gently rolling country followed by the Shepton Mallet–Frome road. At Frome a narrow outcrop of Inferior Oolite continues round the eastern end of the Carboniferous Limestone to Mells, with an outlier between the two at Tedbury Camp. From Mells the Inferior Oolite rests successively on Dolomitic Conglomerate, Coal Measures and the Lower Lias as far as Dunkerton and Wellow, its western edge forming minor scarp features east of Radstock and Paulton and at Tunley Hill near Timsbury. From here it forms a narrow outcrop in the higher valley slopes of the Avon and its tributaries the Cam and Wellow brooks, besides continuing in the scarp through Englishcombe to Bath. In this area the Inferior Oolite also forms two detached upland areas, one between Dunkerton and Radstock on Clan Down and the other as an outlier in the ridge immediately east of Marksbury, whilst further west on the Dundry ridge Inferior Oolite forms the highest ground from Maes Knoll to Dundry itself.

It will be recalled that north of Bath Inferior Oolite sedimentation was far more important than in the southern half of the region and it plays a correspondingly greater part in the formation of the Jurassic scarp northwards from the slopes of Lansdown Hill and the outlier on Hanging Hill. It forms the crest of the scarp at about 600 feet from Freezing Hill and Tog Hill in an almost straight line above Old Sodbury, Little Sodbury, Horton, Hawkesbury and Hillsley, though it occupies a belt of country which is normally only a few hundred yards and never more than half a mile wide. This narrow exposure of the Inferior Oolite continues northwards from Hillsley round the upper slopes of the Kilcott and Ozleworth valleys and Tyley Bottom and Waterley Bottom, above the upper valley of the Cam and around the valleys converging on Stroud. Here, however, the overlying Great Oolite does not approach close to the much eroded and indented scarp, so that great spurs capped by Inferior Oolite mark the western edge of Cotswold. These form the high ground from Coombe Hill and Wotton Hill above Wotton-under-Edge to Niblcy Knoll, the long ridge to Stinchcombe Hill, the West Hill ridge north of Uley, and Selsey Common and Rodborough Common to the south of Stroud. Further north the Great Oolite outcrop lies well to the east of the scarp so that the spurs which surround the Painswick valley are of Inferior Oolite. The Maiden Hill, Haresfield Beacon and Scottsquar ridge to the west and the Wickridge–Longridge Hill to the east unite in the Cranham area, where they are met by the tongue of the Inferior Oolite which extends up the Frome valley from Stroud through Miserden to Cranham. To the north of a line from Cranham to Northleach and Sherborne the outcrop of the Great Oolite is even more remote from the scarp and the great northward sweep of Cotswold, where heights of over 1,000 feet are reached towards Cleeve Hill and Chipping Camden, is therefore largely of Inferior Oolite, as are the outliers of Bredon, Ebrington, Oxenton and Langley Hill. Apart from small isolated patches the Great Oolite here overlies the Inferior Oolite in only three districts, on either side of the Birdlip anticline in Overtown and Coopers Hill and along Ermine Street to the south of Birdlip, in the high ground from Northleach and Aston Blank to Rael Hill above Winchcombe which is followed by the Salt Way, and in an area round Summer Hill and Chalk Hill to the north of Naunton which continues northwards in the exposures of Chipping Norton Limestone past Condicote to Burton Downs.

The transgression which initiated the deposition of the Great Oolite series appears to have involved a shallow sea over a remarkably uniform surface throughout the Bristol region, because the clays at the base of the Fuller's Earth are continuous throughout the area, even over the axes, and appear to be of identical age from south Somerset as far north as the Birdlip anticline and possibly as far as the present northern limit of the Great Oolite. However, the contrasts between the northern and southern halves of the region redeveloped subsequently and it is therefore convenient to consider separately two areas with very different Great Oolite stratigraphies, the line of division being near Hinton Charterhouse between Bath and eastern Mendip.

In Somerset to the south of Hinton Charterhouse the Great Oolite below the Forest Marble consists mainly of clays called Fuller's Earth Clay from the very sporadic occurrence of fuller's earths within them.

They have a considerable thickness, ranging between 100–150 feet in the north and over 400 feet between Frome and Sherborne. As far south and west as Bradford Abbas near Yeovil they are divisible into Upper and Lower Fuller's Earth, with about 30 feet of rubbly limestone known as Fuller's Earth Rock between them. Where the Great Oolite swings westwards over the presumed continuation of the Bath axis south of Yeovil, however, the whole of the Fuller's Earth thins rapidly, the Fuller's Earth Rock disappears, and between Yeovil and Crewkerne the only break in the clays is a thin bed of marly limestone known as the Wattonensis Bed which occurs further north within the Upper Fuller's Earth Clay. Between the headwaters of the Parrett and the Yeo and to the south of a line from West Chinnock to Bradford Abbas the Fuller's Earth Clays occupy a nearly rectangular area of some twenty square miles. Except where the overlying Forest Marble forms pronounced hills and ridges, the clays themselves extend at heights between 100 and 150 feet into the upper valleys of the Parrett and the Yeo and around the Chinnock brook and Broad river tributaries of the Parrett. The generally low-lying character of the Fuller's Earth belt continues as it curves northwards along the Yeo valley to the southeast of Sherborne and by Purse Caundle to Milborne Port and Charleton Horethorne. From here through Maperton to Bratton Seymour the headwaters of the Cam lie on the Fuller's Earth, as do those of the Brue tributaries to the east of Shepton Montague. The outcrop continues round Bruton and along the Combe brook almost to Batcombe, to the north of which it is broken by faulting parallel to the nearby Mendip axis. Between Yeovil and Mendip, however, the Fuller's Earth Rock between the Upper and Lower Clays is of considerable importance, since its western edge commonly forms ridges or scarp-like features within the valleys. Thus in the south the road from Thornford to Sherborne follows the slight ridge of the Fuller's Earth Rock which continues as Dancing Hill south of Sherborne and reappears as the scarps of Hanover Hill and East Hill near Milborne Port. Cattle Hill, west of Bratton Seymour, Cliff Hill, near Shepton Montague, and Lusty Hill, south of Bruton, are also formed by the Fuller's Earth Rock, which then continues as a marked shelf above the Alham valley and below the Forest Marble scarp round Batcombe. From West Cranmore the Fuller's Earth runs ENE parallel with eastern Mendip in the upper part of the Nunney brook valley and then along a right-bank tributary round the west of Frome to form lowlands at the confluence of the Mells river and the Frome to the north of the town. In this area on the southern flanks of eastern Mendip, the Fuller's Earth Rock forms three more extensive upland areas, one at about 600 feet to the south of West Cranmore and the others at 350 feet to the north-east at Nunney and around Whatley. Finally from Mells to Hinton

Charterhouse the Fuller's Earth occupies the lower ground followed by the Frome–Radstock railway past Newbury Hill, turns northeastwards round the foot of Terry Hill and then forms a platform at about 350 feet between the Forest Marble scarp and the valley of the Wellow brook which is excavated into the Lias. Beyond the main Forest Marble outcrop to the north of Buckland Denham and northwest of Norton St Philip, areas of Fuller's Earth Clay have also been exposed in the tributary valleys of the Mells river, the Frome and the Wellow brook.

The main change in the Great Oolite series as one passes into the second area to the north of Hinton Charterhouse is the diminished importance of the thinning Fuller's Earth and its gradual replacement laterally by the Great Oolite Limestones. The precise nature of the change is uncertain because correlations between the northern and southern areas have to be based on restricted palaeontological evidence. However, in north Cotswold the Great Oolite Limestones rest on the Stonesfield Slate Beds, which are Passage Beds at the top of the Lower Fuller's Earth Clay, whereas at Bath the limestones rest on Upper Fuller's Earth Clay with Fuller's Earth Rock and the Lower Clay below, suggesting that changed sedimentation conditions migrated southwards. This appears to be confirmed by evidence further south round Radstock, where it is the uppermost beds of the Great Oolite Limestones which replace only the top of the Upper Fuller's Earth Clay.

From Hinton Charterhouse to Bath the Fuller's Earth still consists of a Lower Clay about 30 feet thick, 10 feet of Fuller's Earth Rock and an Upper Clay more than 70 feet thick, but beyond Bath it thins rapidly, the Great Oolite Limestones replacing the Upper Clay and finally the Fuller's Earth Rock in the neighbourhood of Old Sodbury. From here northwards the Fuller's Earth is only represented therefore by the very thin Lower Clay below Passage Beds of about 30 feet of sandy oolites, which in north Cotswold become the flaggy Stonesfield Slate Beds with their characteristic sandy shale partings. Between Hinton Charterhouse and Bath the Fuller's Earth occurs high on the valley sides of the Avon below Bradford-on-Avon, of the Frome below Farleigh Hungerford and along the Cam and Wellow brooks, though near the eroded scarp to the west the Fuller's Earth Rock forms high ground where it caps the ends of spurs at Peasdowne between Cam brook and Wellow brook and at Dunkorn Hill near Priston. Round Bath the Fuller's Earth occurs in the valleys to the east and northeast of the city and in the slopes of Lansdown Hill and Charmy Down. To the north it is exposed rather more extensively, flooring the valleys of the Fuddle, Dancombe and Broadmead brooks on the top of Cotswold round Marshfield, and then continues in the scarp from Pennsylvania to Hawkesbury. It forms a belt of country a few hundred yards wide sloping gently back from the crest of the Inferior Oolite scarp and bounded on the east by an almost indistinguishable rise which marks the outcrop of the Great Oolite Limestones. In Clay Hill at Hawkesbury the Fuller's Earth itself exceptionally occupies a hill feature near the top of the scarp, which is the site of the Hawkesbury Upton monument. From Hawkesbury to Stroud the Fuller's Earth appears high on the sides of the valleys cut into the scarp but its only extensive outcrop is in the relatively flat ground round the village of Nympsfield. North of Stroud where the Great Oolite moves away from the scarp the very thin Fuller's Earth Clay at the base continues as an exceedingly narrow belt round the edge of the Great Oolite Limestones to Cranham and then along a much indented line to Northleach and Sherborne, with similar belts round the prolongation of the Great Oolite towards Birdlip and Hawling and around Notgrove. It is in this area that the Stonesfield Slate Beds at the top of the Fuller's Earth Clay occur fairly extensively at the surface beyond the limit of the outcrop of the Freestones. They cover the high ground north of Bisley and around Miserden, extending towards Overtown near Cranham, and occupy much of the upland round Summer Hill and Chalk Hill to the north of Naunton, as well as a smaller area at the southern end of West Down on Cleeve Hill. Northwards from Aston Blank as one approaches the Vale of Moreton, the Chipping Norton Limestone underlies the thin Fuller's Earth Clay which it finally replaces to the east and north of Chalk Hill, the limestone occurring widely at the surface in north Cotswold in the Swell area and in the hills westwards from Bourton Downs.

The working of Fuller's Earth, originally for the woollen industry and more recently for the chemical industry, has been confined to a bed in the Upper Fuller's Earth Clay immediately south of Bath. Formerly it was obtained above Combe Hay on the Cam brook and downstream near Midford, but later workings are situated around the western end of Odd Down. Throughout the region, however, the Fuller's Earth Clays underlying the limestones of the Forest Marble in the south and of the Great Oolite in the north have also a considerable indirect importance in providing the sites of a great many settlements. In the south these include a line of villages from Purse Caundle, Stowell, Charleton Horethorne and Bratton Seymour to the towns of Bruton, Wanstrow, Frome and the settlements on the Avon from Bradford-on-Avon to Bath. In south Cotswold there are comparatively few settlements on the upper parts of the dipslope but Marshfield and Tormarton are good examples of villages near the junction of the Great Oolite Limestones with the Fuller's Earth Clay. North of Stroud, however, where the clays form a narrow belt round the edge of the Great Oolite outcrops of central and north Cotswold, the vast majority of the more numerous villages, apart from those sited on the Upper Lias Clays of the deeper valleys, are situated on the Fuller's Earth Clay. In the past the Stones-field Slate Beds have had very considerable economic importance as a source of the so called 'slates' or roofing tiles so characteristic of Cots-wold architecture. They were formerly worked at many points along the edge of the Great Oolite outcrop to the north and northwest of Ciren-cester, including Througham, Miserden, Rendcombe and Chedworth, but with diminishing demand later working was confined to the good ex-posures of the 'slate' beds in north Cotswold.

Between the Fuller's Earth and the Bradford Clay, or its equivalent, the lithology of the Great Oolite series shows considerable lateral varia-tion. South of Old Sodbury it has merely been divided into Upper and Lower Great Oolite Limestones, the latter including the more famous building Freestones. To the north of Sodbury, however, the lowest beds resting on Stonesfield Slate Beds are the Taynton and Minchinhampton Freestones overlain by White Limestone, the two being separated in the north by 30 feet of the Hampen Marly Beds. Moreover, from Tetbury northeastwards to Cirencester the White Limestone is overlain by the Kemble Beds of oolite, which to the ENE at Cirencester were originally mapped as the very similar Forest Marble.

First appearing at the top of Hinton Hill, west of Hinton Charter-house, the outcrop of the Great Oolite Limestones crosses the Frome at Farleigh Hungerford and the Avon at Bradford-on-Avon and follows the crest of the valley of the Avon on its right bank to Monkton Farleigh, before turning northwestwards above the steep-sided valley of the By brook to continue on top of Kingsdown and along Box Hill to Common Hill above Slaughterford. This continuous outcrop along the crest of the scarp is seldom a mile and often only a few hundred yards wide, the Limestones being everywhere overlain a little way to the east by the Bradford Beds and the Forest Marble. To the west of the main outcrop, however, the Great Oolite Limestones cap larger areas of upland in Bath Hill between the Cam and Wellow brooks and in the Odd Down–Combe Down districts immediately south of Bath. To the north of the city there is a similar situation where outlying hills at Lansdown, Charmy Down and around Colerne are also capped by the Limestones. To the north of the Bristol–Marshfield–Chippenham road the Great Oolite Limestones occupy a more continuous and extensive area on the Cots-wold dipslope. From Cold Ashton to Hawkesbury Upton their western edge is never more than half a mile from the scarp, though it seldom forms a pronounced relief feature. As far north as Tormarton the out-crop is about four miles wide but from there to Hawkesbury Upton its width is greatly varied by the much indented edge of the overlying Forest Marble. Further north the Great Oolite Limestones cap the three great spurs extending westward from the high ground round Kingscote towards Wotton-under-Edge and Nympsfield, as well as the Commons to the west of Minchinhampton and the whole of the upland to the north and west of the Stroud Frome round Bisley. From the upper Frome the Limestones then swing away almost due east in a belt about four miles wide, whose northern edge follows a line from Miserden through North-leach to Burford. Beyond this the Great Oolite Limestones only extend northwards along the three belts of higher ground towards Birdlip, Winch-combe and the area north of Naunton, whilst southwards the limestones are overlain by the Forest Marble along a line running ENE-wards from the neighbourhood of Cirencester to the Oxfordshire border. The free-stones of the Great Oolite include the very famous Bath stone, which has been quarried in the hills surrounding the city, especially at Combe Down, and has been used since Roman times. More recently, however, Bath stone working has been concentrated in the Box–Corsham district between Bath and Chippenham, where it is mined from below the Forest Marble. Apart from the Bath area, Great Oolite freestones were formerly worked at Minchinhampton on a large scale and in smaller quantities in individual quarries elsewhere. Although the Forest Marble forms the uppermost beds of the Great Oolite series all the way from south Somerset to Cirencester and the Oxfordshire border, there are important contrasts from south to north both in its relationship with the underlying rocks and in its own character and thickness. To the south of Hinton Charterhouse the Forest Marble overlies the Upper Fuller's Earth Clay, though in the extreme south the thin marly Boueti Bed between the two contains some of the fossils characteristic of the Bradford Clays which lie between the Great Oolite Limestones and the Forest Marble to the east of Bath, and this correspondence is thought to demonstrate a uniform date for the Forest Marble throughout. In Somerset the Forest Marble has a thickness of about 130 feet to the south of Frome and maintains fully 90–100 feet over the Mendip axis before thinning slightly towards the Avon. Though it consists in the main of clays with local sands, there is an important middle division of limestones which usually produce upstanding relief features, so that the Forest Marble forms the most easterly and often the most pronounced of the Jurassic scarps in Somerset. From Hinton Charter-house to the Oxfordshire border the Forest Marble overlies the Great Oolite Limestones, separated from them by the thin clays of the Bradford Beds in the south with which the Acton Turville Beds at the top of the limestones further north are contemporary. Clays and limestones make up the greater part of the Forest Marble in the northern half of the region, though at Hinton Charterhouse itself the upper part consists of the Hinton Sands and these do recur locally throughout the area. In the north round Cirencester flaggy limestones become the most characteristic feature of the Forest Marble and near Poulton these were worked in the past for Poulton 'slates'. There is, too, a great contrast in thickness, the beds thinning rapidly northwards from Hinton Charterhouse so that over most of Gloucestershire the normal thickness is about 15 feet, which is again reduced beyond Cirencester to less than 10 feet. In consequence the Forest Marble to the north of Bath does not form the bold relief features associated with it in the southeastern parts of Somerset.

The Forest Marble enters the region to the southwest of Yeovil, where it forms a radiating pattern centred on East Coker with the ridges of Coker Hill, Windmill Hill and Abbot's Hill and the circular Birts Hill rising above the undulating country of the Fuller's Earth Clays. The main Forest Marble scarp, however, starts at Knighton Hill and Lillington Hill southeast of Yeovil, and continues south of Sherborne to Goat Hill where faulting carries the outcrop southeastward to Holt Hill. It then curves northwards to Toomer Hill east of Milborne Port, Windmill Hill overlooking Charleton Horethorne and Bratton Hill reaching heights of over 600 feet. It occupies the high ground to the east of Bruton and the ridge of Seat Hill near Upton Noble, before being displaced westward by faulting at Wanstrow to reach over 650 feet near West Cranmore. From here the Forest Marble outcrop runs ENE–wards, forming steep slopes from Cheese Hill at Marston Bigot to Frome, where it creates the platforms of Innox Hill and Gibbet Hill on which much of the town is built. The finger-like extension of Forest Marble northeastward from Frome almost to North Bradley is directed towards the Vale of Pewsey, and the alignment of the Forest Marble, Cornbrash and Oxford Clay outcrops in this area is one of the pieces of evidence used to suggest a structural link between the axes of Mendip and Pewsey. Northwards from Mells the Forest Marble outcrop widens rapidly so that it occupies virtually all the high ground in the triangular area between the Frome on the east and the Wellow brook on the northwest, the third side of the triangle being formed by its scarp-like edge in Barrow Hill, Mells Down and Terry Hill between Frome and Radstock. The Forest Marble, now overlying the Great Oolite Limestones, continues to the east of the Frome at Farleigh Hungerford, round the east and north of Bradford-on-Avon by Monkton Farleigh to Corsham and then northwards as a narrow belt to Yatton Keynell. Here, however, the beds are thinning rapidly so that the outcrop, some way back from the steeper slopes capped by the Great Oolite Limestones, has little topographical significance. From Yatton Keynell northwards the width of the Forest Marble outcrop again increases rapidly to six miles at Acton Turville, so that in a sweeping curve through Tetbury to Cirencester it occupies the greater part of the Cotswold dipslope. Here, too, there are few relief features of any amplitude but locally where rivers have cut down through the underlying limestones the Forest Marble forms a capping on the higher valley slopes. Thus to the north of Castle Combe the Forest Marble appears on top of Gatcombe Hill overlooking the By brook valley and at Tetbury it lies on top of the pronounced spur on the south side of the town which was the site of the Castle.

Numerous large estates occupy an appreciable proportion of the Forest Marble area of Cotswold. Of these Badminton Park is the best known but the estates round Westonbirt are also very large, as are Cirencester Park and Williamstrip Park at Colne St Aldwin in the north. Grittleton House and Pinkney House in the south and Eastcourt House near Tetbury all have extensive grounds. The presence of these estates combined with the maintenance of many coverts and plantations, for which the clays and local sands of the Forest Marble are well suited, gives to this belt of Cotswold a well-wooded parkland landscape which contrasts sharply with the open arable landscape on the Great Oolite Limestones and the Inferior Oolite towards the scarp between Bath and Wotton-under-Edge.

Throughout the region the Forest Marble is overlain by the limestones and marls of the Cornbrash, but again there is considerable lateral change in its lithology and in the relative importance of its upper and lower divisions. In a central area from Frome to Malmesbury the lower division consists of massive limestones which locally round Malmesbury may reach a thickness of 50 feet and have been quarried at Corston just south of the town. The upper division in this area is much thinner and is normally marly. Southwards from Frome, however, the upper and lower divisions are of comparable thickness and in general throughout Somerset they produce together about 10–20 feet of limestones, sandy limestones and marls. Similarly from Malmesbury to Cirencester and on to Fairford and Oxfordshire the upper division again becomes more important, though here both divisions consist of flaggy limestones and thin marly bands with a total thickness of 10–20 feet.

Apart from the Corston Beds the Cornbrash has not yielded rocks of economic importance, but in spite of its narrowness across parts of the region its outcrop has considerable significance in terms of settlement. This appears to have arisen partly because the Cornbrash contains water-bearing limestones which normally overlie the clays of the Forest Marble. Moreover, soils developed on the Cornbrash were well suited to cereal production at a time when the Oxford Clay vales to the east were materially less favourable from the point of view of both agriculture and settlement.

There are patches of Cornbrash on the hills round East Coker and Yetminster to the south of Yeovil and in the faulted area round Long Burton and North Wootton south of Sherborne, and there is a more continuous belt followed by the road from Bishop's Caundle to Stourton Caundle and Stalbridge Weston. The main outcrop enters the region at heights between 250 and 350 feet on the western valley slopes of the Stour and its tributary the Cale and is marked by an almost continuous string of settlements from Stalbridge through Henstridge, Yenston, Temple Combe, Abbas Combe, Horsington, North and South Cheriton and Holton to Wincanton. To the north of Wincanton there is no comparable concentration of settlements on the Cornbrash, though the villages of South Brewham, Upton Noble and Witham Friary follow its junction with the Oxford Clay round the headwaters of the Cale, the Brue and the Frome. Beyond Witham Friary faulting displaces the outcrop westward to Cranmore. From here it continues as a narrow belt into the eastern suburbs of Frome and then extends northeastward towards North Bradley, including a fairly extensive upland area northeast of Beckington. Apart from outlying patches round Woolverton and a long inlier to the east between Trowbridge and Semington, the Cornbrash has a very narrow exposure in the slopes above the right bank of the Frome from Beckington to Farleigh Hungerford and then curves round the east of Bradford-on-Avon to Broughton Gifford, South Wraxall and Lacock. Here the widening of the outcrop to cover as much as four miles of the lower Cotswold dipslopes above the clays of the Avon valley means that there is no linear pattern of settlements comparable with that of south Somerset. Nevertheless, both Chippenham and Malmesbury are on the Cornbrash, and at or near its irregular junction with the Forest Marble there are smaller settlements at Corsham, Biddlestone, Yatton Keynell, Kingston St Michael, Sevington, Leigh Delamere, Stanton St Quintin, Hullavington, Norton and Easton Grey. Just north of Malmesbury the Cornbrash outcrop again becomes narrow, turns northeastwards almost to Cirencester and then continues ENE-ward to Fairford and the Oxfordshire border at Broughton Poggs. Here the villages and hamlets of Brokensborough, Charlton, Crudwell, Oaksey, Poole Keynes, Kemble, Ewen, Siddington, Preston, Ampney St Peter and Poulton and the town of Fairford form a continuous line close to its junction with the Forest Marble.

Throughout its whole extent the Cornbrash is overlain by a thickness of about 500 feet of Oxford Clay, which, with Kellaways Beds at the base, floors the vales extending eastward and southward to the limits of the Bristol region from the Oxfordshire and Berkshire borders near Lechlade to the boundary of Dorset near Stalbridge. Everywhere the vales tend to have a gently undulating surface with many small streams as well as major rivers, so that there is a considerable measure of uniformity throughout.

Blackmoor Vale enters the extreme south of the region in the valley of the Stour between Stalbridge and Marnhull and follows its tributary the Cale almost to Wincanton. To the east the valley is bounded by the Corallian scarp and at Stoke Trister a narrow spur of Corallian extends two miles southwestwards, nearly meeting the high ground of the Forest Marble and Cornbrash round Wincanton, thereby virtually closing off the vale at its northern end. No specific name has been given to the section of the clay vale northwards through the gap at Frome to Dilton Marsh near Westbury, but in common with most of the clay area it was formerly heavily wooded and formed the greater part of the Forest of Selwood (though Penselwood village lies to the east on the Greensand), which was of great significance as a zone of division in the early history of southwestern England. In the south this part of the vale is occupied by the headwaters and tributaries of the Cale and the Brue, in the centre by the Frome and its right-bank tributaries, and in the north by the upper course of the Biss tributary of the Avon. Here its eastern boundary is formed by the Gault and the scarp of the Greensand and Chalk overstepping between the Vale of Wardour and the Vale of Pewsey. To the southeast of Frome a Greensand outlier stands 250 feet above the general level of the vale at Roddenbury Hill near Longleat Park, whilst to the east of Frome the spur of Greensand in Lodge Hill at Chapmanslade constricts the width of the clay outcrop to barely a mile.

Between Dilton Marsh and Calne the clay outcrop widens to about five miles round Melksham in the vale of west Wiltshire. At Trowbridge, however, the southern part of the vale is divided by the slight ridge of the Cornbrash inlier extending northeastwards from the town to Hilperton and Semington, whilst to the north of Melksham the vale is again reduced to a mile in width near Lacock by the westward extension of the Corallian and the overstepping Lower Greensand in Bowden Hill and Nash Hill. The Avon drainage system occupies virtually the whole of this section of the clay vale, the main stream draining it southward from Chippenham to Melksham and Staverton, with the Marden and the Semington brooks as left-bank tributaries and the Biss tributary flowing northwards from Dilton Marsh and Westbury through Trowbridge to join the Avon downstream from Staverton.

To the north of Chippenham and Calne the Oxford Clay vale again widens and turns eastwards, its western and northern boundary being marked by the narrow outcrop of Cornbrash between Malmesbury and the Oxfordshire border. On the southeast and south the clay stretches as far as the line of ridges and low hills of the Corallian, which runs from Calne and Lyneham through Purton and round the north side of Swindon to Highworth and the Berkshire border near Coleshill. Much of this part of the vale long remained wooded and as late as the seventeenth century the Forest of Braydon remained extensive in the west near Malmesbury, where there is still a considerable number of woods, plantations and wooded commons. This district coincides approximately with the water parting between the drainage systems of the Avon and the Thames, the former occupying the north–south section of the vale from Malmesbury to Chippenham and Melksham and the latter the wide extension eastwards into the White Horse Vale.

The relatively uniform conditions of sedimentation which led to the deposition of the Oxford Clay were replaced by fluctuations of sea conditions with at least three periods of shallow water permitting coral growth, the whole sequence being demonstrable to the south of the Bristol region in the Corallian Beds of the Dorset coast. From there the Corallian extends inland as a discontinuous narrow outcrop along the eastern and southern margins of the Oxford Clay and for considerable distances its minor scarps and low hills may be regarded as marking the eastern boundary of the Bristol region. It was mapped on the basis of a simple lithological division into a Lower and Upper Calcareous Grit with coralline oolite or Coral Rag between them.

The Corallian enters the region in the southeast where it outcrops in a narrow belt from Sturminster Newton to Stour Provost and crosses the end of the Vale of Wardour to Bourton and Zeals. Here the Lower Calcareous Grit along the west of the outcrop forms a definite scarp feature from Stour Hill near Kington Magna through Slave Hill at Buckthorne Weston and Tinkers Hill north of Cucklington to the long spur at Stoke Trister. To the east of the scarp lies the undulating high ground of the Coral Rag, so that Corallian as a whole forms a belt of hilly country with the Oxford Clay vale to the west and the Kimmeridge Clay of the Vale of Wardour to the east. At Zeals and Bourton the Corallian is faulted against the Upper Cretaceous rocks which form the northern edge of the Vale of Wardour and which overstep westwards concealing the Corallian, except for a small area in Longleat Park, as far as Dilton Marsh near Westbury.

From its reappearance at Dilton Marsh the Corallian outcrop runs across the end of the Vale of Pewsey towards Calne, though it does not form such a marked or continuous relief feature here as it does across the Vale of Wardour to the south. It runs as a minor ridge at about 200 feet to the west of Westbury Station from Dilton Marsh to Heywood, is then hidden for half a mile beneath the Kimmeridge and is then continued in the hilly country at about 250 feet through West Ashton, Steeple Ashton and Great Hinton to Seend Cleeve, where it again disappears below the Kimmeridge and Greensand of Seend Hill. From Chittoe northwards towards Calne the Corallian once more forms an upland area with a pronounced scarp on the west which reaches a height of over 500 feet, though the highest parts round Bewley Common and Spye Park are formed by a capping of the Lower Greensand.

Beyond Calne the Corallian no longer marks the boundary of the Bristol region because to the southeast and south of it a widening exposure of the Kimmeridge extends the generally low-lying clay vale up to the Cretaceous scarp. Nevertheless out into the vale the Corallian still forms relief features of some importance. Immediately north of Calne there are two ridges, an outlying one of Lower Calcareous Grit at about 400 feet from Bremhill through Wick Hill and Charlcott Hill to Spirthill, and that of the Rag and Upper Calcareous Grit to the east of Cowage brook from Calne to Hilmarton. Round Lyneham the Corallian occupies a wider area of upland at about 400 feet, surrounded by a very pronounced scarp above the Oxford Clay, but beyond Tockenham the outcrop narrows abruptly and disappears two miles southeast of Wootton Bassett leaving a gap in the Corallian scarp which was used by the Wiltshire and Berkshire canal and in which the London–Bristol and London–South Wales railway lines diverge. To the north of Wootton Bassett the Corallian of the hilly country round Purton reaches a height of 450 feet and has a westward-facing scarp at Kingsbury Camp and Paven Hill. On its eastern side the outcrop is again broken at the valley of the river Ray draining northwards to the Thames and this gap was used by the railway to Cricklade and Cirencester. Beyond the Ray the outcrop turns northeastwards in the hills round Blunsden, Red Down and Highworth with a northward-facing scarp at Blunsden Hill and Castle Hill and then continues into Berkshire at Coleshill and Badbury Hill.

The Kimmeridge Clay which succeeds the Corallian occurs in the Vales of Wardour and Pewsey, but here it only reaches the margins of the Bristol region where it interrupts the Corallian scarp for short distances near Westbury and at Seend, so that its only extensive development within the region is to the north of Calne as it widens and turns northeastwards past Swindon and into the Vale of White Horse and Berkshire. At a height of a little over 300 feet it forms a flat or very slightly undulating plain comparable with that of the Oxford Clay to the north of the Corallian, with a similar abundance of streams draining westwards to the Bristol Avon and eastwards to the Thames.

The only appearance of the Upper Jurassic Portland and Purbeck Beds in the Bristol region is in a small outlier in the old town district of Swindon which stands more than 100 feet above the general level of the Kimmeridge Clay vale. Here a small syncline involving the whole of the Kimmeridge Clay has preserved the Portland Beds above it and a small patch of the Purbeck Beds. Besides providing the hill site on which the original Swindon developed, the existence of the Portland Beds, in

**49**

particular, has been of some importance in affording a local source of building stone.

It will be seen therefore that the eastern and southeastern boundary of the Bristol region commonly coincides with the outcrop of the Corallian and that elsewhere it is the appearance of the Cretaceous rocks which marks its limits. In south Somerset the Upper Greensand of the Black Down Hills and Staple Hill lies astride the county boundary, whilst in a southeastward curve the Chalk and Greensand of Coombe Beacon, Stony Down and Storridge Hill continue the upland area past Chard to the extreme southern tip of the county. East of Chard the county boundary and the limit of the Bristol region straddle the Cretaceous scarp running eastwards from Sprays Hill to Warren Hill, round the south of Crewkerne at Shore Hill, Knowle Hill and Masterton Down, and then turn eastwards to Chelborough Hill and Bubb Down Hill. From this point the Cretaceous rocks of the Dorset Downs, curving northward towards the Vale of Wardour, lie beyond the Corallian outcrop which marks the limit of the region between Sturminster Newton and Zeals.

Between the faulted northern edge of the Vale of Wardour and Dilton Marsh, the Cretaceous rocks overstep westwards onto the Oxford Clay, a narrow and discontinuous outcrop of Gault Clay being overlain by the Upper Greensand in a pronounced scarp which continues northwards the line of the Corallian hills. It starts near Ballands Castle and continues by Aarons Hill and Kingsettle Hill through King's Wood Warren and Witham Park to Gare Hill. It then forms the amphitheatre of hills round Longleat Park and continues through Lane End and Corsley to Chapmanslade, before turning northeastwards along the southern edge of the Vale of Pewsey. Here the Cretaceous again passes beyond the limits of the Bristol region and is replaced on the boundary by the Corallian between Dilton Marsh and Seend.

The small outcrops of Lower Greensand between Seend, Calne and Compton Bassett, resting successively on Kimmeridge Clay, Corallian and Oxford Clay, do mark hill areas overlooking the Oxford Clay vale, especially in Spye Park. Nevertheless, from the northern edge of the Vale of Pewsey at Roundway the limit of the Bristol region is best defined by the main Cretaceous scarp, which is formed by the Lower Chalk with a relatively narrow outcrop of the Upper Greensand below it. From Roundway the scarp projects northwestwards to Beacon Hill near Heddington, recurves round Cherhill and Compton Bassett, and then forms a broad sweeping curve overlooking the Kimmeridge Clay plain through Clyffe Pypard, Broad Town and Wroughton to the Berkshire border.

The details of the pattern of outcrops and their associated relief features which have been described in this chapter are, of course, largely the outcome of recent geomorphological processes. Some of its broader outlines, on the other hand, had already been determined by the region's pre-Cretaceous physical history and the emergence of others will be described in the next chapter when the exhumation of pre-Jurassic landscapes and structures and the establishment of a modern relief and drainage pattern, following earth movements, transgression and denudation in the Tertiary and Quarternary periods, are considered.

# CHAPTER 2

# The Evolution of the Landscape

THE absence of Tertiary rocks and the fact that denudation has removed from most districts the Cretaceous and much of the Jurassic cover have made difficult the reconstruction of the Bristol region's Tertiary physical history, and of necessity it has to be largely based on the possibility of correlating restricted local data with structural hypotheses and denudation chronologies formulated under more favourable conditions for areas further east. However, the general course of events is reasonably clear and the main differences of interpretation have concerned the emphasis to be placed on Tertiary and pre-Tertiary developments in explaining the evolution of the surface features.

Lithological evidence of Jurassic earth movements over the ancient axes of the Bristol region has already been considered and it has also been suggested (Arkell 1933) that a branch of the Jurassic trough lay over the present line of the Bristol Channel which sagged as sedimentation occurred, taking Triassic and Liassic materials to depths below present sea level. Thus a major structural feature which was of vital importance in the later Tertiary physical history of the surrounding area appears to date at least to Jurassic and possibly (North 1955) to Old Red Sandstone times, though its later geomorphological importance may have been principally the outcome of its accentuation by the Miocene earth movements.

There can be little doubt that both Jurassic and Cretaceous rocks covered virtually the whole of the Bristol region and probably reached Wales, though opinions have varied as to the extent of the Mesozoic cover beyond the Severn and the Bristol Channel. From Cretaceous to mid-Tertiary times intermittent uplift combined with gentle eastward tilting, at whatever date it may have been initiated, produced a land surface from which subaerial erosion stripped away many of the younger rocks, the general drainage pattern resulting in their debris being transported eastward out of the region. This relatively minor Cretaceous and early Tertiary uplift and tilting culminated in late Oligocene and Miocene times in the more important earth movements which were the local consequences of the Alpine orogeny. This was certainly the most important phase of the region's later physical history, since some movement appears to have taken place at this time on almost all of its structural components irrespective of the time at which they first came into being.

In the southern half of the region movements took place with E–W trends largely following the lines of the Armorican structures. In mid-Tertiary times, however, it has been suggested that anticlinal structures, like those of the Miocene folding in northern France, were arranged discontinuously in echelon, so that folds in the Cretaceous rocks and in the Lias to the west are not necessarily present at the line of the Jurassic scarp. Thus the generally anticlinal structures of north Devon continue into west Somerset and run parallel with the coast past Porlock, Watchet and Minehead to the axis of the Quantocks. From the neighbourhood of Taunton this southern fold belt is continued in the marked anticlinal structures of the Lias round Somerton and Langport, and though there is little evidence of folding in the Jurassic rocks an anticline reappears in the Vale of Wardour and is continued eastwards into south central Britain. To the south of the anticlines the great westward extension of Cretaceous rocks to the Black Down Hills may have been preserved in synclines corresponding with structures in the Hampshire basin, whilst to the north another synclinal belt has been described as the master structure of the Bristol Channel area. Whatever may have been the earlier history of the channel itself, it appears to have been further down-folded in Miocene times along with the Glastonbury syncline to the south of Mendip and its structural continuation below the uplands of Great Ridge between the Vale of Wardour and the Vale of Warminster. Below the latter the Cretaceous and Jurassic rocks are folded in a Miocene anticline which does not appear to have affected the Lias further west and therefore barely reaches the margin of the Bristol region. In the case of Mendip the NW–SE arrangement of the Armorican periclines, possibly occasioned by resistance from the stiffened Bath axis in the east, persisted in the uplift of Miocene times, and this departure from the general E–W trend has been said to have its mirror image in the suggested northeastward swing of anticlinal structures to link up with those of the Vale of Pewsey and so with folding in the Kingsclere monocline and the Hog's Back. Between Mendip and the Kingswood anticline it seems likely that the Miocene synclinal structures of the London basin are continued westwards, but there remains some doubt as to whether they follow the general line of the Bristol Avon or curve somewhat southwards round or through the Dundry outlier.

To the north of the Kingswood anticline, it will be recalled, Armorican trend lines largely disappear and mid-Tertiary earth movements were therefore influenced by the alignment of the older axes. It has been suggested that movement on Pennine trends extended into the Bristol region over the Vale of Moreton axis and that activity also occurred along the N–S Malvern-Bath axis with which the Birdlip anticline was associated. In consequence, at least some part of the Jurassic and Liassic rocks of central and north Gloucestershire were affected by a series of anticlines and synclines, which fan outwards through the Cotswold scarp to the north of Stroud. The Painswick syncline is the most southerly one, running from the direction of Bisley past Painswick itself to reach the scarp round the south of Painswick Hill. Near Miserden the upper course of the Stroud Frome follows closely the line of the Birdlip anticline, which then swings northwestward to leave the scarp in the large embayment at Great Witcombe and pass into the vale to the north of Gloucester. The third structure is the Cleeve Hill syncline which approaches the scarp from Andoversford and underlies the high ground forming the northward extension of Cotswold in Cleeve Common, Cleeve Hill, Nottingham Hill and the Oxenton outlier. Immediately east of Cleeve Hill the upper valley of the Isbourne cuts deeply into the Cotswold scarp over the Winchcombe anticline, whilst in the extreme east of the region the last of the anticlinal axes underlies the Vale of Moreton. There is evidence that these structures have had some influence on the pattern of river development in north Cotswold and the contrasts between the massive projection of Cleeve Hill and the embayments of Great Witcombe and Winchcombe on either side of it illustrate their effect on the rate of erosion and recession of the Cotswold scarp.

In general Miocene uplift appears to have preserved conditions in which post-Cretaceous subaerial erosion was continued, with rivers still draining southeastwards over the continuous Mesozoic cover towards the Thames in the north and, it has been suggested, towards the Solent or the Dorset coast further south. The limits of the basins clearly cannot be precisely defined but if the apparent alignment of the northeastward-flowing Wellow brook, Cam brook and other left-bank tributaries of the Avon with valleys on the dipslope of Cotswold implies that they formerly drained to the Thames, then the division must presumably be placed near the Mendip axis. This period of subaerial denudation was sufficiently long to initiate the exhumation of the Palaeozoic landscapes of the Bristol region, since the rivers must already have cut down to the summits of the old hill masses if erosion surfaces on the Mendip plateau between 800 and 900 feet o.d. can be regarded as western parts of the peneplain established in southern England in this period (Wooldridge and Linton 1955). Moreover, it has been suggested that the Miocene period saw the evolution of an early form of the river Severn draining into the now deepened Bristol Channel, foreshadowing even greater changes following the establishment of a western drainage system.

Even though the Pliocene/Pleistocene seas over southeastern England may not have reached the Bristol region through a so-called Pliocene channel and despite the absence of marine deposits in the area, it is thought likely that transgression did occur from the sea inlet over the Bristol Channel to the west. One basis for this assumption is the recognition of erosion surfaces at 600 to 700 feet O.D. to the northeast of Mendip, which are thought to correspond with similar surfaces cut into the Chalk in southeast England and attributed to Pliocene/Pleistocene marine erosion (Wooldridge 1960). Particularly in south Gloucestershire and round the basin of the Bristol Avon a very large number of erosion surfaces at lower levels have been recognized. Whilst it is possible that some of the higher ones may be products of the general subaerial denudations of the area, they may equally be of marine origin and those below 300 feet O.D. are fairly generally thought to represent stages in the gradual retreat of the western sea. One of the clearest examples of the higher surfaces between 550 and 600 feet O.D. is seen in the summit level of Broadfield Down which cuts across the Carboniferous Limestone and the Lias, but similar surfaces exist on some of the lower plateau areas of eastern Mendip and possibly on the Quantocks. Surfaces between 400 and 450 feet O.D. are best developed from the southern side of the Dundry outlier round the margins of Broadfield Down and on the northern and southern flanks of eastern Mendip. By far the most widespread surfaces, however, are those with heights between 200 and 300 feet O.D. and it is these which are most characteristic of the basins of the Bristol Avon and its tributary the Frome in south Gloucestershire. On the lower Avon overlooking the Clifton gorge they form the flat surface of the Carboniferous Limestone downs stretching away northward across Carboniferous and Liassic rocks towards Filton and Patchway, whilst on the Somerset side of the river they cross the high ground between Leigh Woods and Pill. To the east of Bristol surfaces between 200 and 300 feet O.D. occupy large parts of the Whitchurch–Queen Charlton district to the south of the river and form most of the Staple Hill–Kingswood–Hanham area to the north, where they cut across Coal Measures sandstones and clays. Further upstream they again cut across Carboniferous and Liassic rocks in the Bitton, Bridgeyate and Wick areas and reappear above Bath particularly in the neighbourhood of Bradford-on-Avon. Away from the line of the Avon, 200–250-foot O.D. levels continue round the south side of Bristol through Knowle and Bishopsworth to the western end of the Dundry ridge at Barrow Gurney. Northward they surround the eastern side of the valleys of the Frome and its tributaries in a belt running from Westerleigh between Iron Acton and Yate past Rangeworthy to Wickwar, and then turn southwards over Liassic, Triassic and Carboniferous rocks on the west side of the Ladden brook tributary to meet the corresponding lower Avon surface at Patchway. The upper course of the Frome is thought to have been graded to a sea level between 200 and 300 feet O.D., but below a nick point at Cogmill between Iron Acton and Frampton Cotterell it enters a gorge section through Winterbourne to Frenchay and northeast Bristol. Deeply incised immature valleys below the 200–300-foot O.D. level are also characteristic of the right-bank tributaries joining the Avon in its gorge section between Keynsham and Bristol and of the Malago brook which cuts through the erosion surfaces to the south of the city.

If the 200–300-foot O.D. surfaces are assumed to be of marine origin and of late Tertiary date, it might follow (Trueman 1938) that the Avon, first entering the sea from the higher ground at Bath, would later flow northwestwards across the emerging land surface. The Dundry ridge, higher ground at Flax Bourton and the Carboniferous Limestone of the Failand–Clevedon ridge must have risen above the level of such a surface and prevented the Avon from turning westwards, so that it may have followed approximately its present course to a point somewhere between Avonmouth and Portishead where it joined the Severn, which by then drained into the Miocene (or earlier) Bristol Channel. On such an assumption the lower Avon from the outset flowed in the present general direction and was superimposed onto the Carboniferous Limestone of its Clifton gorge section from a late Tertiary erosion surface between 200 and 300 feet O.D. rather than from a massive mantle of Mesozoic rocks on which its ancestral river flowed southeastwards from Wales prior to its capture by the developing Severn. In any event the later evolution of the Avon drainage system was presumably greatly retarded by the gradual downcutting of the Clifton gorge and it has been suggested (Trueman 1938) that the preservation of so many remnants of the supposed 200–300-foot O.D. marine erosion surface in and around its basin is the product of this delay in the process of subaerial denudation. To the north of the Bristol coal basin and to the south and west of Mendip the development of the other river systems of the region was not impeded by resistant exhumed Palaeozoic rocks so that there are only a few uncertain traces of the 200–300-foot O.D. surfaces on the face of the scarps and ridges which surround the basins of Somerset and the Gloucestershire vale to the north of Wickwar. In these lower areas evidence of erosion surfaces at 100 feet O.D.. and 50 feet O.D. is more common, and conversely these are absent over the more resistant Palaeozoic rocks which were nowhere planed below the 200–300-foot O.D. level.

The development of the Severn and the initiation of drainage westwards introduced a new phase of subaerial denudation in which the main features of the physiography of the Bristol region emerged. In

Somerset the excavation of the great central and western basins by the Parrett, the Brue, the Axe and the Yeo and their tributaries may have involved the capture of the headwaters of the Dorset rivers as the upper Mesozoic cover was stripped away, whilst the streams on the dipslope of north Cotswold may have been similarly beheaded by the development of the Severn and the Warwickshire Avon. In central Gloucestershire to the north of the Bristol coal basin the Little Avon and the Cam cut deep notches into the Mesozoic rocks and the Stroud Frome cut its valley back through the line of the present scarp to capture the southward-flowing section of its course above Sapperton from a Cotswold dip stream. After the removal of the Cretaceous and Upper Jurassic rocks the rivers were therefore pushing the scarp of the Middle Jurassic Limestones further and further eastwards, leaving to the west an evolving pattern of exhumed Palaeozoic structures modified by Triassic erosion and overlain to varying extents by uneroded Triassic and Liassic rocks. A more complete Jurassic and Cretaceous succession, apparently preserved in a synclinal belt, curves westwards to the Black Down Hills round the southern edge of the Bristol region, but in central and north Somerset erosion etched the Jurassic outcrops into lines of hills and narrow scarps which have already been described. To the north of Wotton-under-Edge the Great Oolite was cut back far from the scarp, which was itself deeply notched by strong streams in valleys cut down to the Upper Lias Clays. In the centre of the region, overlooking the basin of the Bristol Avon among the exhumed Palaeozoic rocks, the Jurassic scarp is less broken and the Great Oolite still occupies high parts of the Cotswold plateau. However, though the Bristol Avon excavated its lower course slowly, its headwaters ultimately occupied much of the Oxford Clay vale and in its middle course through the intervening Jurassic uplands between Bradford-on-Avon and Saltford it is thought to have captured streams formerly flowing northeastwards to the Thames. Thus, though many details of the present landscape have been created in more recent times, it seems likely that before the onset of glacial or periglacial conditions in Pleistocene times a gentler shallower form of the present relief features and the main drainage systems of the Bristol region had been established.

In the first Great Welsh glacial period, ice not only occupied the vale between Malvern and Gloucester but also just overrode the then low scarp of north Cotswold along the Vale of Moreton and possibly elsewhere (Wills 1938, 1950; Beckinsale and Smith 1953). Though ice again advanced into the Vale of Severn in the second and third Great Welsh glacials, it never again directly affected other parts of the Bristol region. Here the consequences of the Pleistocene glaciations were therefore mainly indirect and arose either from the prevalence of special

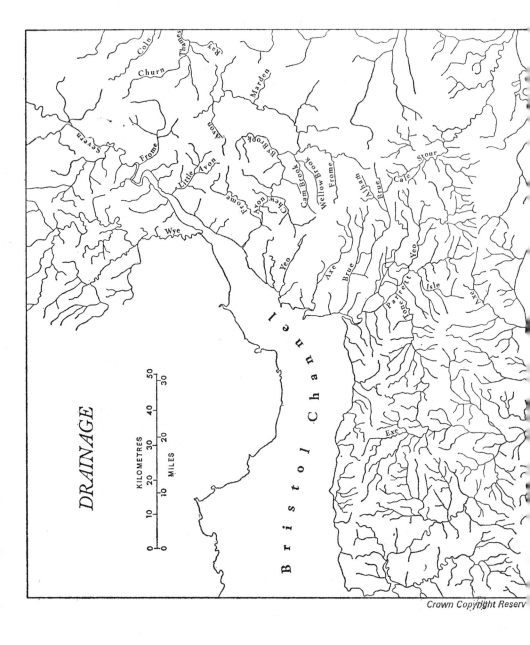

DRAINAGE

KILOMETRES

0  10  20  30  40  50

MILES

0  10  20  30

Bristol Channel

Crown Copyright Reserv

forms of weathering and erosion under periglacial conditions or from the fluctuations of sea level which characterized the late and post-glacial periods.

Good examples of the effects of periglacial conditions are found on and around the upland areas in the form of Head deposits. In general terms these are products of solifluxion, occurring when alternate freezing and thawing combined with the presence of ice or melt water to allow mass downslope movement of shattered local materials over a presumably frozen subsoil. Normally they consist of unsorted gravels, but loamy or clayey Head deposits exist and in many cases an original gravel constitution has been altered by the subsequent addition of colluvium and by water sorting. However, these superficial materials are essentially the product of local conditions and must be considered separately in individual districts. Very extensive deposits of this kind have been recognized in the Cotswold sub-edge zone, particularly in the north from the neighbourhood of Mickleton, north of Chipping Camden, to Whitminster near the entrance to the Stroud valley, on whose flanks they also occur, and similar materials surround the Bredon outlier. They consist of unsorted subangular fragments of local Oolite and Middle Lias Marlstone in what have been described as taele fans (Tomlinson 1941), from the foot of which, however, stratified and current-bedded materials stretch out into the vale as fan deltas probably created by summer meltwater. There is a tendency for the fans to be well developed below embayments in the Cotswold scarp and it is significant that the best-known group of deposits at Barnwood, where they stretch out onto the Main terrace of the Severn near Gloucester, lies opposite the large embayment at Great Witcombe over the Birdlip anticline, whilst there is another considerable spread of gravels and wash material opposite the similar Winchcombe embayment further north. Attempts have been made to correlate the Barnwood and Stroud valley deposits with stages of terrace formation and erosion recognized in the Severn and Warwickshire Avon valleys, but something of a diachronous character must be inherent in the processes involved in the complete establishment of such spreads of gravel and wash material and precise correlation with any one phase of river development may be impracticable.

Round Mendip there is even closer relationship between the location of the main Head deposits and the outlets of the coombes and gorges of the upland area. Since small pockets of conglomerate of Triassic age have been found in the coombes it seems reasonable to assume that these features were initiated during the period of Triassic erosion, and since Mendip must have been early stripped of its Mesozoic cover the re-excavation of these early valley forms may well date to Tertiary and early Pleistocene times. It has therefore been suggested (Findlay 1965) that

59

c

when the snowfield meltwaters swept frost-shattered debris from Mendip, it was carried down pre-existing channels to form the fans and spreads of Head which now surround their outlets at the margins of the plain, evidence of frost heaving in the resulting deposits indicating that this happened when periglacial conditions still prevailed. Rain and valley wash added colluvium to the Head deposits and in some areas water sorting and redeposition comparable with that in the Cotswold sub-edge deposits took place. However, the gorges and coombes themselves were not subjected later to any great degree of normal water erosion nor have the Head deposits been swept clear of their entrances because the post-glacial drainage of Mendip appears to have followed the present cave system, from which the water emerges in springs at the foot of the hills commonly well away from the main deposits. To the north of the hills gravelly Head, apparently derived from the Lias and Trias of Harptree Hill, stretches to the margins of the new Chew Valley lake, but the greatest spread emerged from the coombes of northwestern Mendip between Burrington and Churchill and round the western end of Blackdown past Sandford, where the gravels are mainly derived from the sandstones in the core of the pericline. On the south, where the gravels are largely composed of limestone, there is a large composite fan, on the eastern end of which the whole of the village of Cheddar is built round the mouth of the gorge. The fans from five small coombes to the west have merged with that from the Cheddar gorge to floor the whole of the amphitheatre ringed by the steep Mendip slopes between Cheddar and Axbridge and extending outwards to the Axbridge reservoir. Smaller fans surround the mouths of the coombes further east round Draycott and there are spreads in which redeposition is often marked where the Ebor gorge emerges near the headwaters of the Axe at Wookey Hole and in the valleys and coombes to the northeast and east of Wells. Some of the periglacial debris on the summit areas of Mendip away from the coombe heads was not swept down to the fans but formed in situ a narrow ring round the eastern end of the Blackdown pericline, smaller patches round North Hill and Stock Hill to the east of Priddy and a rather larger area on Beacon Hill to the north of Shepton Mallet, much of the evidence for which is now confined to the character of the derived soils.

The gravelly Head round the Quantocks is mainly made up of locally derived sandstones. In the northwest there appear to be relatively compact fans and patches opposite the smaller coombes, but around the mouths of the longer coombes to the south and along the eastern side of the hills there are larger spreads extending over the surrounding Lias Clays and Keuper Marls.

Head deposits were by no means confined to the margins of the larger hill masses, however. They cover considerable areas round the mouths of Goblin Coombe and Brockley Coombe on the western side of Broadfield Down, and below the slopes of the Failand ridge to the west of Bristol they stretch through Bower Ashton and Long Ashton towards Flax Bourton. There are also large patches of Head towards the eastern end of the Gordano valley from Pill to Portbury and smaller ones below the Almondsbury ridge at Compton Greenfield, near Stoke Gifford and to the east of the Kingswood anticline, whilst it has been suggested (Findlay 1965) that a former great extent of gravelly Head may be deduced from the existence of many small gravel patches on minor ridges in the area and from the frequent occurrence of stones in the upper parts of soils apparently derived from the Keuper Marls.

Periglacial conditions are also thought to have prevailed during the formation of Pleistocene breccias which have been described at Barnwood and in Somerset on the landward slopes of the Portishead–Clevedon ridge, on the southward facing slopes of Hope Hill, Worlebury Hill and Brean Down near Weston-super-Mare and at Bleadon (Palmer 1934), and which may also occur on the Polden Hills and near Wedmore. Archaeological evidence suggests a late Pleistocene date for the formation of the breccias, which may have developed under conditions of cold and excessive ground moisture during temporary glacial readvances. However, in all cases there is an upper and lower breccia each with a sandy matrix and the two are separated by a sandy zone. There is evidence that the sands involved are wind-blown and they do not appear to be of local origin, so that the suggestion has been made that they were derived from the erosion of Tertiary deposits in the southwest peninsula under cold and arid conditions associated with the late glacial readvances. The probable late date of the breccias would mean that their formation followed that of much of the gravelly Head and this has led to the further suggestion (Findlay 1965) that their subsequent downslope movement and modification by solifluxion and later rain wash converted them into the loamy Head which partially overlies the gravelly Head on the lower slopes of western Mendip round Churchill and was evidently in that position before frost heaving ceased.

The prevalence of periglacial conditions over the uplands of the Bristol region may also be responsible for some of the morphological features of the north Cotswold valleys. In the case of the Windrush and its tributaries, in particular, it has been suggested (Beckinsale and Smith 1953) that the 'valley in valley' forms may have been created by temporarily increased surface flow over frozen subsoils, though in some cases the misfit may have been accentuated by the volume of meltwater flowing down the dipslope valleys after ice locally overrode the Cotswold scarp. On the other hand, though the Coln is likely to have had a similarly enlarged volume in glacial times, its later shrinkage has been attributed (Dury 1953) to decreased rainfall from late Pleistocene times.

There is now little evidence of the direct impact of periglacial conditions on the low-lying areas of the Bristol region but the related late Pleistocene and post-Glacial fluctuations of sea level had profoundly important indirect consequences, particularly in the Somerset levels. During one of the earlier interglacials the sea level is thought to have reached about 20–25 feet O.D., producing shallow water conditions in which the shelly marine sands of the Burtle Beds were deposited. In the basin of the Parrett these deposits partly cover the extensive low ridges rising above the levels between Middlezoy and Weston Zoyland, round Chedzoy and near the margins of the basin. They have been important as dry winter land for stock summered in the levels and they afford sites for the villages in the central parts of the basin. To the north of the Poldens the sands only occur in small 'batches' in the basins of the Brue, the Axe, the Yeo and the Kenn, but even these have considerable agricultural value and provide village sites. South of High-bridge the villages of Huntspill and Stretcholt occupy two such low ridges, near the centre of the Brue levels many of the settlements round Catcott Burtle and Edington Burtle are on the sands, and the village of Kenn covers most of a similar 'batch' in the extreme north of the lowland. These remnants of marine deposition in earlier glacial times are exceptional because by late glacial times the sea level may have been as much as 100 feet below that of the present day and erosion by the rejuvenated rivers produced a considerable degree of denudation in the lowland areas. The Severn itself occupied a now buried channel at a depth of −75 feet O.D. near the line of the Severn tunnel, −50 feet O.D. at Sharpness and −19 feet O.D. at Gloucester, so that down-cutting and the further development of the Bristol Avon as well as the Somerset and Gloucestershire tributaries must have been greatly accelerated.

A renewed rise of the sea at about 6000 B.C. led to the inundation of the Somerset levels and parts of the Severn valley and to the deposition of silty clay which mantled the lowlands up to the present-day sea level. There followed a period of nearly 6,000 years during which the sea level remained relatively stable or fell very slightly, and conditions developed in which reed swamps and fen peat covered much of the alluvium in the Somerset levels. In some areas by about 3500 B.C., however, the growth of raised moss became possible and this subsequently acquired a woodland cover. This phase covered much of the prehistoric period and some archaeological evidence for dating the physical changes in the levels is discussed in a later chapter. Towards the end of the Bronze Age and during the Iron Age in the last millenium B.C., increased precipitation led to flooding in many parts of the levels so that locally fen conditions replaced the raised bogs, but at about 250 A.D. a further marine transgression led to the deposition of the so-called Romano-British estuarine clay over a coastal belt some five miles wide, though extending inland as much as ten miles in places. The settlement and reclamation of much of this clay belt had been initiated before the end of the Roman occupation so that later peat growth was confined to the inland river basins where fairly regular landwater flooding also led to the deposition of riverine clays in post-Roman times, whereas on the coast between Weston-super-Mare and Burnham dune formation followed the deposition of the Romano-British clay.

The later physical history and the drainage and reclamation of the Somerset levels has been largely governed by this pattern. In the inland parts of the basins, despite intermittent drainage work over centuries, flooding and the deposition of riverine clays continued until modern times and it was only in the nineteenth century that some areas of fen peat were effectively drained. This process and attempts to minimize or shorten the duration of flooding by river water have been complicated by the very large tidal range in the Severn estuary and by the fact that the coastal zone of the Romano-British clay belt is at a slightly higher level than the inland basins, especially where the latter have been affected by peat shrinkage. In consequence modern drainage schemes have necessitated not only the excavation of the new Huntspill river through the slightly elevated coastal clay belt but also the provision of pumps at the edge of the clays to raise the water from the inland drains into the natural or artificial river outfalls across the coastal rise.

The end of periglacial conditions and the comparatively stable sea level since 6000 B.C. has allowed a fairly uninterrupted normal pattern of subaerial erosion by which the denudation of the Mesozoic cover of the Bristol region and the exhumation of the Palaeozoic landscapes has been continued. Meanwhile the general spread of alluvial materials along the valleys and into the lowlands, the deposition of colluvium below the hill slopes and the more local accumulation of wind-borne deposits added even further variety to the pattern of parent materials from which the soils of the region have been derived.

# CHAPTER 3

# *The Soils*

ALTHOUGH climatic and biological factors are of vital importance in considering the formation of soils, it is nevertheless the nature of their parent materials and the configuration of the land surface which determines the broad pattern of soil conditions in the Bristol region. It is therefore convenient to describe the soils initially in terms of the geological outcrops, superficial deposits, and major morphological units. In some localities within such a broad outline a multiplicity of soil series indicates the variety and complexity of the factors involved in soil genesis, but elsewhere less varied conditions are reflected in the widespread occurrence of one or two highly characteristic soil series.

The lowlands which form the eastern margin of the region from southeast Somerset to north Wiltshire and the Gloucestershire boundary illustrate such relative uniformity since broadly similar soils have developed over the greater part of the Oxford and Kimmeridge Clays which floor the vales. They usually consist of heavy dark-coloured clays commonly showing the mottling of imperfect or poor drainage. The Denchworth series is particularly characteristic of the Oxford Clay and has been described in agricultural terms as a cold heavy clay. The alternative local name of Forest Clay is indicative of its former extensive cover of oak forest and though it supported arable agriculture in the Middle Ages it has for centuries been mainly used for grass farming. Soils on the Kimmeridge Clay to the east of the Corallian outcrop sometimes contain appreciable amounts of sand and have been described as 'warmer' than those on the Oxford Clay, but nevertheless they have shared the almost universal problem of imperfect drainage on the clay lands of the vales. In sharp contrast with this broad uniformity of soil conditions in the surrounding lowlands, the Corallian ridges and upland areas which divide the vales provide such a variety of parent materials, slopes, drainage and biological history that complexity is the keynote of their soils. However, in general terms, two main types of soil reflect the lithological divisions of the Corallian rocks. On both the Upper and Lower Calcareous Grits they are largely stone-free brown soils with as much as 80 per cent of sand, whereas on the Coral Rag the characteristic dark brown loams commonly contain a large number of limestone fragments. All the variants of both types of soil, however, tend to be relatively light, easily worked and well drained; they were probably free of the true damp oak forests of the vale and in most districts have remained in arable use. More varied soil conditions are also characteristic of the margins of the vales, where the clays are replaced by other rocks or are overlain by superficial deposits. Thus towards the Chalk scarp, north of the Vale of Pewsey, sandy soils of the Goldhill and Bromham series occur on the discontinuous narrow outcrop of the Lower Greensand, which separates the Kimmeridge and Gault Clays, but widens out round Bromham to overstep the Corallian. In this area and in particular where the Greensand overlies the Coral Rag, the soils drain freely and with a sand content approaching 90 per cent produce conditions well suited to market gardening. On the western side of the vales, approaching the Cornbrash and Oolites of Cotswold and of the Somerset scarplands, the clays are sometimes overlain by superficial deposits of calcareous oolitic gravels on which loamy soils have developed. The Badsey series occurs where such gravels reach to within 30 inches of the surface and facilitate the drainage of quite light loamy soils, whilst the heavier soils of the Honeybourne series are found where the gravels thin out or are at greater depths. Under intensive cultivation both series can provide good agricultural soils and locally they have led to more variety of husbandry than characterizes the clays of the rest of the vales.

Some broad similarities also exist among soils developed on the Jurassic Limestones of Cotswold and the Somerset scarplands, though in the latter area the narrow outcrops, the limited extent of the Great Oolite Limestones and the greater importance of the Fuller's Earth, in particular, produce a far greater variety of soils. Over most of the high ground of Cotswold where the Jurassic Limestones form the main parent material and in those parts of Somerset where similar conditions prevail, the most characteristic soils are those of the Sherborne series. They are well drained, red-brown to brown calcareous soils which range from medium or heavy silt loams to silty clay loams and generally have structures sufficiently stable to withstand prolonged cultivation. Under grass the A horizon is an almost stoneless dark brown loam and the B horizon a dark or strong brown loam with a great many subangular limestone fragments. Since the greater part of the land in question has long been in arable use, however, and since the A horizon seldom exceeds 6 inches in depth, ploughing has brought the limestone fragments to the surface and given the fields their characteristic stony appearance. The soils are shallow and average figures of 12–14 inches have been suggested, but on Cotswold and in particular on the high plateau areas of the Inferior

Oolite in the north, the thickness ranges from as little as 3 inches to about 9 inches. Moreover, on steep and convex slopes, again characteristic of the northern areas and the scarp face, there are highly porous loose stony soils with a single horizon. In prehistoric times vegetation appears to have consisted of mixed scrub and dry forest with beech as the predominant species; this survived on parts of the scarp but gave way to grassland over most of the plateau and dipslope. On the plateau areas near the scarp to the north of Stroud, greater elevation and exposure combine with extreme shallowness and porous conditions to produce very poor Sherborne soils which readily suffer drought and may undergo wind erosion. Here there are, therefore, appreciable areas of poor pasture and common land which contrast sharply with the general practice of continuous arable cultivation that has been followed on the deeper loams of the less exposed parts of the plateau and dipslope at least since the eighteenth century. There is a tendency for the soils to be deeper and somewhat heavier further down the dipslope and particularly where the outcrop of the Cornbrash is reached. Moreover, it is thought that the Sherborne series may be replaced by the fairly widespread Marnhull series, in which dull grey-brown heavy loams or clay loams are underlain by yellowish marly clay, where impervious strata or the configuration of the land lead to imperfect drainage. However, the most important exceptions to the general soil character of the Jurassic uplands occur where there are outcrops of the clays of the Fuller's Earth and Forest Marble or of the Upper Lias in the valleys north of Stroud, giving rise to the moderately well-drained deep calcareous soils of the Chickerell and Trip series. In Cotswold there are only narrow outcrops of the Fuller's Earth Clays, and superficial deposits modify the soils on the Upper Lias Clay of the northern valleys, but on the Forest Marble, particularly round Badminton, there are considerable areas of clay soils on which extensive plantations and parkland alternate with arable land. In Somerset soils of this type occur on the more continuous outcrops of the Fuller's Earth Clays and the Forest Marble in the scarp belt to the south of Bath and are quite extensive in the lowlands to the southwest of Yeovil.

In Gloucestershire the Cotteswold Sands of the Upper Lias and the Marlstone of the Middle Lias occur only in the scarp face of Cotswold and in the sides of valleys cut into it, so that their outcrop is a very narrow one. On the sands the steep slopes of the scarp and the valley sides not only affect soil development, drainage and movement but also limit cultivation, so that they often have a woodland or scrub cover or provide indifferent pasture land. On the ledge of the Marlstone, however, slopes are greatly reduced and parent materials include colluvium from the sands above as well as the Marlstone itself; these together produce a narrow belt of deep well-drained yellow-brown sandy soils which locally spread out onto the Lower Lias Clay at the margin of the vale. On steep slopes, especially on the face of the Marlstone ledge, orchards are commonly established, but elsewhere these very valuable sandy soils have been used continuously for arable cultivation since Saxon times. In south Somerset the Yeovil Sands of the Upper Lias occupy a much wider belt of rolling country west of Yeovil, extending towards Crewkerne and Ilminster past South Petherton, after which their characteristic soil series is named. They consist of deep sandy loams and sands which are very easily worked and, having been long in high cultivation, are of great agricultural value. Similar deep sandy soils continue into the steep slopes of the Liassic scarp belt south of Castle Cary, but here they have been included in the Antrim series which is mapped on all the sandy materials of the Middle and Upper Lias further north, where the soils are materially heavier with a loam or silt loam texture at the surface and silty clay loam in the subsoil. At the base of the sands in this district the limestones of the Junction Bed at the top of the Middle Lias form cappings on Pennard Hill and ledge-like features elsewhere, on which soils of the Pennard series have developed. They are usually friable silty clay loams which are easy to work and fairly well drained so that a good deal of arable agriculture is possible on them. Most of the Middle Lias, however, and in places parts of the Upper and Lower Lias consist of micaceous siltstones and silty mudstones in Somerset, on which the most characteristic soils are the greyish brown loams of the Martock and Long Load series. The former does show some gleying and species indicative of imperfect drainage occur in permanent pastures, but arable agriculture is increasing and high quality cider apple orchards are important round West Pennard and North Cadbury. Drainage is actually poor in the Long Load series, which tends to develop in hollows at the foot of steep mudstone slopes and round the 'islands' of the levels, the largest extents being below the scarp between Sparkford and Castle Cary and to the south of Pennard Hill. Here the maintenance of permanent pasture depends on a combination of pipe and ditch drainage, but flooding does still occur.

To the west of the Jurassic scarps very varied extents of younger rocks, surrounding and sometimes capping exhumed Palaeozoic landscapes, combine with an irregular distribution of superficial deposits to produce great diversity of parent materials. This, in an area of varied relief, ensures that there is no general uniformity of soil conditions comparable with that in the Oxford and Kimmeridge Clay vales to the east. There is none, for example, in the vales of Gloucestershire to the north of the coal basin where the Lower Lias Clay extends from the Cotswold scarp foot zone to the western bank of the Severn, since in this area much of it is overlain by a variety of superficial deposits. Further south the Lower Lias Clay is confined to a comparatively narrow belt

**67**

between the coal basin and Cotswold, and occurs only in patches and narrow outcrops from the line of the Kingswood anticline to Mendip. From Shepton Mallet, however, it again covers extensive areas on the tableland to the south of Mendip, round the east and southeast of the levels, in the 'islands' and ridges within the alluvial lowlands and on the coast to the west of the Parrett. By far the most common soils on the Lower Lias Clay are those of the Evesham series. Imperfect drainage means that they are gleyed calcareous soils with 9 or 10 inches of dark greyish brown clay in the A horizon and up to 25 inches of olive brown to pale olive mottled clays below. Until early historic times they had a cover of damp oak forest but in general only hedge timber of oak and elm now exists. Clearance was followed by arable cultivation employing rudimentary drainage methods and traces of this phase of land use remain in the ridge and furrow which is easily seen on the Lias Clay lands of Gloucestershire but has not been widely recognized in Somerset. Some mixed arable farming is still practised in the coast belt to the west of the Parrett but elsewhere the Evesham soil areas have been largely given over to grass farming, formerly almost all on permanent pasture but in recent years with some rotation grasses and barley. Ensuring adequate drainage has been a common problem on the Lower Lias Clays but in Somerset an additional difficulty has been caused locally by high concentrations of molybdenum in the soil and herbage which are thought to cause the scouring in cattle experienced on these so-called 'teart' pastures. Where the drainage is poor or very poor in hollows and in some flat and low-lying districts in the Vale of Gloucester and on the margins of the Somerset levels, in such areas as the upper basin of the Brue round Baltonsborough, round Pennard Hill and in parts of Wedmore, surface water gley soils occur in the Charlton Bank series. At the surface and to varying depths these soils are non-calcareous and have an acid reaction. They usually support pastures of moderate quality with weeds indicative of wet conditions and some liability to the growth of rush and sedge patches.

Some variation of soil conditions occurs where the lithology of the Lower Lias parent material changes or where the underlying Rhaetic and Upper Triassic rocks approach the surface. In the case of soils in the Ashton series, which occupy very small areas in Somerset, particularly on the western slopes of the Isle of Wedmore near the village of Ashton, the difference appears to have little effect on vegetation or land use despite the fact that non-plastic shales significantly alter the soil structure below the B horizon. On the other hand, where limestones are involved in the soil genesis more significant changes occur. It will be recalled that around the Mendip axis a littoral facies of shallow water Lower Lias Limestones was deposited and on these rocks the Ston Easton soil series is sometimes developed. The most continuous extent of such soils is therefore on the ledge of Lower Lias round Shepton Mallet which extends along the southern side of Mendip to West Harrington, while on the low plateau to the north of the hills patches occur east of Chewton Mendip. The series consists of Brown Earths with free drainage from which all calcium carbonate has been leached, possibly because of the elevation and high rainfall of the areas involved. The A and B horizons consist of clay loams which may be silty and sometimes humose near the surface. There are few steep slopes and the soils are generally well suited to arable cultivation, though in recent times they have commonly been left under long grass leys. Away from the Mendip axis there is a change to the more usual facies of the Lower Lias Limestones which include shale bands and combine with broadly similar Rhaetic Limestones and Shales as parent materials for soils of the Somerton series. These occur from about two miles south of Shepton Mallet round the eastern and southern margins of the levels past Somerton itself and extend northwestwards along the gentle dipslope of the Polden Hills. To the north of Mendip there is a similar change and Somerton soils recur from the neighbourhood of Farrington Gurney. The Somerton series is one of brown calcareous soils with free drainage which normally have an alkaline reaction and at least 50 per cent of the clay throughout the profiles. They too were used for arable agriculture after the clearance of woodland and some cereal growing occurs on them today, but large areas have also been used for permanent pastures in recent times or have been left in grass leys. Over much of the plateau area to the north of eastern Mendip and in small areas south of Shepton Mallet, an intergrade has been suggested between the Ston Easton and Somerton series with mainly non-calcareous soils, which have a somewhat lower percentage of clay than the true Somerton soils and are rather better adapted to arable cultivation. Apart from differences of facies in the Lower Lias Limestones and differences of elevation and rainfall, it has been shown that the graduation between the Somerton and Ston Easton soils may be partly due to the presence of wind-borne silts and superficial material derived from non-calcareous rocks in the latter series in the Mendip area. Where the Rhaetic consists of clays and occurs above the Triassic Tea Green Marls in steep slopes marking the western edge of the main Liassic outcrop and the edges of the Liassic 'islands' and ridges in the Somerset levels, the Hurcot soil series has developed. It consists of imperfectly drained calcareous clays which on level ground are used for permanent pasture, but the more characteristic steep slopes have considerable areas of rough grazing, thorn scrub and small woods. Indeed the steep slopes combine with water from springs at the base of the Lower Lias Limestone to produce slumping and intermingling. This leads to great complexity, with Evesham and Charlton Bank soils

69

from the Lower Lias Clay being mixed with the Hurcot soils and then spread out over the Keuper Marl as the Ham complex in the High Ham–Othery–Somerton district on the southern side of the Polden Hills. On the other hand, where sands overlie the Rhaetic Clays in very small areas in the southern half of the Isle of Wedmore, loam soils of the Wedmore series and sandy loams of the Sand Hall series occur. Both are gleyed Brown Earths because underlying clay on the characteristically level sites leads to imperfect drainage, though both could be made agriculturally more valuable by artificial drainage.

In central and south Somerset the Triassic and Permian rocks are largely overlain by the alluvium and organic materials of the levels and by gravelly Head and other superficial deposits which spread into the vales round Blackdown, the Quantocks and the Brendon Hills. In north Somerset and Gloucestershire, on the other hand, they appear at the surface in an intricate pattern surrounding and partially overlying the coal basins and the Carboniferous Limestone ridges and downs from Mendip northwards. This pattern contributes much to the diversity of soil conditions in the western part of the Bristol region, especially as there is considerable lithological variety in the Triassic rocks themselves. Nevertheless the Keuper Marl is more widely represented than the other rocks involved and soils of the Worcester series are so commonly developed on this parent material that they may be regarded as generally characteristic of the Triassic lowlands. They are classified as gleyed Brown Earths because there is some evidence of impeded drainage, presumably caused by unweathered marl. Normally they are deep and fertile dull red calcareous loams or clay loams which, after the clearance of woodland, were used for arable agriculture until the establishment of dairying in the West Country vales in the seventeenth and eighteenth centuries. They were then turned over to permanent grass and improved by cutting ditches and by laying stone or pipe drains to prevent poaching; in recent times they have undergone further drainage improvement with a return to a certain amount of arable and grass ley farming. Some variations do occur including a shallow and less fertile phase where hard dry marl approaches the surface, whilst soils with a greyish colour but otherwise almost identical characteristics occur where the Grey Marls overlie the Red Marls. The shallow phase is fairly common to the south of the Polden Hills in central Somerset, and on steep slopes like those round Dundon a good deal of erosion has taken place as a result of run-off caused by poor internal drainage. Where even greater changes occur in the character of the Keuper Marl, however, with the presence of sandstones, sands or siltstones, soils of the Greinton series become more characteristic. Sandy materials in the Marls appear to be particularly common in the area between Mendip and the Bristol Avon. Greinton soils are typically developed over fairly wide areas on the flat or nearly flat surfaces formed by hard bands of sandstones and siltstones near the top of the Red and Grey Marls in the hilly area to the west of the new Chew Valley lake, as well as to the south of the Polden Hills near Othery and near Greinton itself. Very similar soils, though derived from different sandy materials, occur on lower ground to the east of the Chew Valley lake and near Churchill, and others are likely to be identified further north where broadly similar lithological conditions occur locally in the Trias. They are non-calcareous loams or silty loams in the upper horizons, with clay loams like those of the Worcester series below. They have similarly imperfect drainage but where this is improved artificially they provide good arable land, much of which has, however, been used for grass leys in recent times. On concave slopes below the adjoining higher land of other formations and in depressions within the normally undulating landscape of the Keuper Marls, relatively small pockets of the poorly drained Spetchley series occur. These are surface water gley soils with a dull dark greyish brown and slightly mottled silty clay at the surface and heavily mottled clays below. Locally, woodland with alder and poplar occurs on the Spetchley soils but over most of their limited extent permanent grassland is the general land use. Unless artificial drainage is maintained, however, these soils are liable to be excessively wet and the value of the pasture is diminished by patches of rushes.

Although the Keuper Marls cover by far the greater part of the Triassic outcrop in the lowlands of Gloucestershire and Somerset, sandstones do occur to the east of the Forest of Dean, from the Newent district northwards, in south Somerset, and in the Bristol district, with very much smaller patches between the Bristol Avon and Mendip. In these areas the Worcester, Greinton and Spetchley series are replaced by less fine-textured soils, of which the North Newton series is perhaps the most characteristic. It takes the name of a village on the Keuper Sandstone outcrop to the southeast of the Quantocks, where the parent material consists either of soft red calcareous sandstone interbedded with Keuper Marl or of very sandy marls. Here the soils are freely drained reddish brown sandy loams in the A horizon and sandy clay loams in the B horizon, with a preponderance of fine sands and some silt throughout. This, combined with weak structures near the surface, may make the soils unstable under arable cultivation, but the depth of the sandy soil and favourable climatic and site factors have encouraged a considerable degree of specialization in intensive vegetable production. Similar soils occur over the smaller outcrops of sandstone to the east of the Quantocks but elsewhere round the western margins of the Vale of Taunton Dene and below the Brendon Hills the Triassic sandstones are commonly overlain by superficial deposits, and other soil series have a wider distribution. North Newton soils have also been mapped in the Paulton–West Harptree–Chew Stoke districts between eastern Mendip and the Bristol Avon, but here the less favourable climate and factors of elevation and configuration tend to curtail their use for either horticulture or arable agriculture. In the same area, where Keuper Marls are locally replaced by the fine-grained Butcombe Sandstone, usually overlying the margins of the Coal Measures outcrops, soils of the Chelwood series occur. These are well-drained fine sandy loams and loamy fine sands which work easily and are well suited to arable agriculture, but their commonest use is for grass leys and again elevation and exposure restrict horticulture to a few more favoured sites. Similar Triassic sandstones also follow the western margins of the Coal Measures outcrops in the Kingswood anticline and the south Gloucestershire coal basin. At their southern end they are largely hidden below the urban area of Bristol but beyond the northeastern outskirts they give rise to a narrow belt of sandy loam soils extending to a point just beyond Frampton Cottrell. On the adjacent western edge of the Coal Measures Sandstones a similar tongue of red loam soils extends from Bristol to Iron Acton, and together these easily worked and generally well-drained soils form the core of a district which has long specialized in market gardening and intensive vegetable production. Where the sandstones become less fine grained, soils resemble more closely those of the Bridgnorth series of the Midlands. This occurs chiefly in the northern parts of the Bristol region where a range of warm, freely draining sandy soils on the Keuper Sandstones and Bunter to the north of Newent, together with some of the sandy medium loams and coarse sandy loams of the Bromyard and Ross series on the adjacent Old Red Sandstone, account for the importance of sugar beet production in the large arable component of the northwest Gloucestershire mixed farming district.

As in the Oxford and Kimmeridge Clay vales to the east, superficial deposits, mainly derived from nearby higher ground, also overlie the Trias and Lias of the western vales and commonly form parent materials for the lowland soils. Here, however, such deposits are not confined to the outer margins of the lowlands and similar materials occur on the plains and in valleys surrounding and intersecting the Palaeozoic uplands which break the continuity of the vales between Mendip and south Gloucestershire. In the extreme north of Gloucestershire round Tewkesbury and in the Vale of Moreton, the presence of glacial deposits results in great diversity of soil conditions, governed partly by the patchy distribution of boulder clay, glacial sands and gravels and river terrace deposits and partly by variations of site, configuration and drainage in such a landscape. Here important market gardening and fruit growing activities are profoundly influenced by quite small relief features and in particular by variations in the thickness of sands and gravels whose water tables are based on the uneven surface of the underlying Boulder Clay or Lower Lias Clay. The drainage class and surface texture of soils in such localities can be exceedingly variable over very short distances but on such parent materials the generally coarse sandy soils of the Pershore series are broadly typical. To the south of these small areas of glacial deposition as far as the neighbourhood of Slimbridge, the Lower Lias Clay of the Vale of Gloucester has a variable and discontinuous cover of superficial deposits, mainly calcareous gravels derived from the Cotswold Oolites. Under these circumstances the thickness of the gravels and the depths at which they occur below the surface clays and loams greatly influence soil drainage in particular and this underlies the distinction between two of the most widespread soil series in this area. The Badsey series, which occurs where there are appreciable thicknesses of gravel within 30 inches of the surface, tends to have reasonably free drainage and a surface texture which can be a clay but is more normally a loam or even a light loam. The deeper Badsey soil areas are therefore ones which, after woodland clearance, contained some of the most valuable agricultural land in Gloucestershire. The Honeybourne series, on the other hand, develops where the gravels only occur at greater depth, are thinning out or are virtually absent. Here drainage conditions may be less satisfactory and surface soils are commonly heavier. Nevertheless, loams and even light loams do occur in the Honeybourne series and it too can provide valuable land when good artificial drainage and cultivation are maintained. In the immediate vicinity of Cheltenham and to the north of the town, below the slopes of Nottingham Hill, very localized deposits of Cheltenham Sand give rise to soils of the Cheltenham series. These are freely draining deep calcareous coarse sandy soils which are particularly well suited to the highly specialized market gardening, intensive vegetable production and glasshouse industry of the Cheltenham district.

In northern and central Somerset the extent of Badsey soils is smaller since the series only occurs as patches on terraces below the scarps, particularly in the Castle Cary–Sparkford area, where arable and grass ley farming is the normal land use. In the same area less well-drained soils of the Podimore series are much more extensive and correspond in a general way with the Honeybourne soils of Gloucestershire. Their parent material is re-sorted clay, derived from the Oolites and the Lias with beds of calcareous gravel and sandy materials, but these are usually thin and tend to become waterlogged. Here arable agriculture has again become common but, as on the Honeybourne soils, it needs good artificial drainage and the heavy soils call for careful management. Nearby somewhat less extensive superficial deposits of Head and old alluvium from the Middle and Upper Lias occur in the valleys emerging from the scarp belt, especially to the east of Sparkford and to the north of Castle Cary. These form parent materials for the deep stoneless loams of the Isle Abbotts series, which are generally in high cultivation or support good quality pastures.

At the southern end of the Bristol region the pattern of superficial deposits is somewhat more complex because a wide variety of materials derived from the Black Down Hills, the Brendon Hills and the Quantocks is involved. On the narrow belt of Cretaceous rocks along the southern border of Somerset round the Black Down Hills, soil series normally characteristic of Chalk and the Greensands occupy comparatively small areas, partly because the configuration of the land produces great local variability of slope, aspect and drainage, and partly because there are extensive deposits of Clay-with-Flints on the plateau area and hill tops. In such areas medium to heavy loams are usual but quite light loams do occur. However, the influence of Cretaceous materials on soil genesis extends far beyond the outcrop area because flinty gravels and coarse sands derived particularly from the Upper Greensand extend down the valleys of the Isle and the Firehead and well out into the southern and southeastern parts of the Vale of Taunton Dene. In the river valleys to the northwest of Ilminster these superficial deposits give rise to the Isle Brewers and Hambridge soil series. In both cases the surface consists of heavy flinty loam below which the flinty gravel occurs. Where there are appreciable thicknesses of gravel near the surface the relatively freely draining Isle Brewers series is developed, but where the gravels are thinner and at greater depth drainage may be impeded and mottling occur in the heavier soils of the Hambridge series. In the adjacent parts of the Vale of Taunton Dene superficial deposits of Cretaceous sands and gravels provide much of the parent material for the soils of the Taunton series, which usually consist of sandy loams overlying sandstone gravels. Elsewhere in the Vales of Wellington and Taunton Dene, in the lowlands to the east of the Quantocks and along the fault corridor and the coastal lowlands, superficial deposits from the Brendon Hills and the Quantocks become important. The great lithological range of the Permian rocks, which include sandstones, conglomerates, marls and clays, ensures that there is a wide variety of soils where they outcrop below the slopes of the Brendon Hills along the western edge of the vales and the fault corridor, especially as the pattern of parent materials is further complicated by the presence of Devonian gravels from the hills. Similar gravels from the Quantocks spread along the eastern side of the fault corridor and the slopes from the Quantocks towards the Parrett and occur extensively in the northern and central parts of the Vale of Taunton Dene, but here they consistently rest on Keuper Marls or on the Lower

74

Lias Clay near the coast, so that there are fairly extensive tracts of land where soils of the characteristic Huntworth series are developed. There is normally a considerable thickness of gravel so that material from the underlying Trias or Lias is not greatly involved in the soil profile. They are free-draining non-calcareous soils and at the surface consist of sandy loams with few stones, but below about 8 inches an Eb horizon becomes very stony; from 18 inches the clay loam of the Bt horizon is similarly stony and below about 24 inches much of the C horizon is made up of sandstone fragments. The Huntworth soils provide some very good agricultural land on which mixed farming has normally been practised, though locally specialist vegetable production and market gardening has been of some importance. Variations of drainage characteristics do occur with changes in the thickness and depth of the gravels, and imperfect drainage is more common over the Lower Lias Clay where in some localities in south Somerset and near Glastonbury the Huntworth series is replaced by the Polsham series. At the surface these have loams or sandy clay loams above an Eb(g) horizon of very stony sandy loam and B horizons which change downwards from sandy clay loam to sandy clay merging into the calcareous clay of the C horizon. These less freely drained soils are more commonly used for pasture than the better soils of the Huntworth series in the Vale of Taunton Dene.

Taken together the areas of superficial deposits in the north between Slimbridge and Gloucester and those in and around the Vale of Taunton Dene provide the largest extents of good quality agricultural land in the Bristol region. In the former district it is possible to distinguish between the zone of South Petherton soils below the Cotswold scarp and zones of lighter Badsey and Honeybourne soils alternating with the clay soils of the Evesham series in the vale. In the Vale of Taunton Dene, on the other hand, the distribution of soils in the Evesham, Worcester, Huntworth, Hambridge and Isle Brewers series has been described as a random one and the agricultural quality of the land, though generally high, shows correspondingly localized variations.

Superficial deposits in the central parts of the Bristol region occur mainly on the flanks of the Carboniferous Limestone uplands and in the valleys between them. Where the thickness of the gravelly Head deposits opposite the coombes and gorges of Mendip and round the Carboniferous Limestone hills further north is sufficient to permit free drainage, soils of the Langford series occur. They have normally dark brown, almost stone-free loamy surface soils over an Eb horizon of stony loam and very variable subsoils in which the gravels are mixed with sands and silts from the overlying drift and with the underlying marls. Since Langford soils usually occur in sheltered positions on gentle slopes below the hills and since they are freely drained and medium-textured, many of the important strawberry-growing and market-gardening concerns are located on them, but otherwise, despite their suitability for arable cultivation, they are mainly used for pasture. Where the gravelly Head thins out, usually round the margins of the fans and in depressions away from the hills, the marls approach sufficiently near to the surface to cause the impeded drainage characteristic of the Brinsea series. Mottling and greyer colours are indicative of the imperfect drainage of the loamy Brinsea soils, whose exact texture varies with the nature of the Head deposits. North of Mendip, round Langford, where the gravels are of sandstone, the soils are sandy loams, but over the chert gravels further east the loams are silty and the same is true over the Carboniferous Limestone gravels to the south of Mendip. The mode of origin of the Brinsea soils means that they normally occur on flat land or in hollows where the problems of their impeded drainage are difficult to overcome despite the use of both pipe and ditch systems, and they are mostly used for permanent pastures. Superficial deposits are also involved in the development of the Tickenham series on gentle slopes round the western end of Mendip, below the western slopes of Broadfield Down, in the Gordano valley and at the foot of the Bristol–Clevedon ridge. In some areas thin deposits of gravel do underly them, but elsewhere the soils pass directly downwards into the Keuper Marl so that the main superficial parent materials appear to have been Pleistocene silts and fine sands, which may share the aeolian origin suggested for silts in the Mendip soils (see below). The deep reddish brown loamy soils of the Tickenham series occupy topographical situations comparable with those in which the Langford soils are used for strawberry growing and market gardening on the south side of Mendip, and similar developments have taken place especially in the neighbourhood of Banwell, Winscombe and Clevedon. Arable agriculture is fairly important on Tickenham soils in the upper basin of the Lox Yeo between Bleadon Hill and Wavering Down, but elsewhere most are in pasture with orchards on the lower hill slopes west of Burrington.

Above the gentle slopes where the Langford and Tickenham series occur, the Palaeozoic uplands have a number of characteristic soil series developed over the Carboniferous Limestones. They exist on all the larger outcrops of these limestones but they are most extensive on Mendip where their distinctiveness is accentuated by unique conditions of elevation and exposure. In western and southern Mendip and on the other limestone areas of north Somerset, notably Broadfield Down on which Lulsgate is situated, the most important of these is the Lulsgate series which occurs on the limestones themselves, on old limestone screes and on adjacent massive forms of the Dolomitic Conglomerate. Their largest extent, therefore, forms an almost continuous belt of country on the southern limestone rim of Mendip, from the neighbourhood of Wookey Hole in the east to Bleadon Hill and the isolated limestones of Brean Down in the west, with a shorter and narrower belt on the northern limestone limb of the upland from Bleadon Hill to Burrington Coombe. Though solution residues from the Carboniferous Limestone clearly enter into the genesis of the Lulsgate soils, it has been suggested (Findlay 1965) that loessial silts were also of considerable importance and help explain the presence of silty loams or silty clay loams throughout the A and B horizons of deeper soils and the A/B horizon of shallower ones. On steep slopes and near the small isolated rock outcrops, soils may be less than 3 inches deep and consist of little more than dark brown fine earth surrounding a mat of roots, but elsewhere they are normally between 6 inches and 14 inches in depth. The traditional land use of the Lulsgate areas has been as winter pasture for animals from the lowland farms using cultivated or semi-natural grass. Where the soil is shallow, pastures tend to 'burn' rather readily in dry summers and there may be a good deal of bracken and some gorse and thorn scrub especially near abrupt upper slopes and around limestone outcrops. Most of the remaining Mendip woodland occurs on Lulsgate soils on the steep lower slopes, particularly along the northern face of Mendip from Burrington to Bleadon Hill and in the Cheddar–Axbridge area in the south, whilst there are extensive woodlands on similar soils on Worlebury Hill to the north of Weston-super-Mare, at the western end of Broadfield Down, and on the ridges between Bristol and Clevedon. On the less wooded southern face of Mendip the lower slopes of the Lulsgate soils adjoin the Langford soils round Cheddar and in places share the production of strawberries and vegetables, whilst similar activities and anemone growing at the foot of the hills between Cheddar and Wells take place on soils of both the Lulsgate and the Wrington (see below) series.

Where the Dolomitic Conglomerate is less massive the rubbly subsoils characteristic of the Wrington soil series tend to develop. These conditions occur near the limestones of the Bristol district and in a curve round the western and southern sides of Broadfield Down where Wrington itself is situated. In Mendip Wrington soils occupy the northern slopes between Burrington and East Harptree, occur patchily along the southern side of the hills and on the plateau, and cover the lower ground round Shipham, sloping westwards from the core of Blackdown. The soils are clay loams but, because they have strongly developed structures and because they become stony below 6 inches and very stony in the B horizon below about 10 inches, they are porous and very well drained. Their use in strawberry and vegetable growing near Cheddar has already been mentioned and similar use is made of them round the margins of Broadfield Down and locally round the limestone ridges near Bristol.

In most parts of Mendip, however, they are usually maintained under grass because their very good drainage characteristics make them suitable for winter grazing. Some improvement by reseeding has taken place in more favoured localities but, in general, site characteristics tend to minimize their agricultural value. Woodland, orchards with grass for winter grazing and rough grazing with bracken and scrub alternate on Wrington soils on the northeastern face of Mendip where slopes are too steep or rock outcrops too numerous for other use, and the same pattern is repeated on less favoured sites round the southern and western margins of the hills, whilst in the area to the north of Shipham, where natural conditions might not have been too unfavourable, innumerable shallow calamine and lead workings, particularly round Rowberrow, hamper land improvement.

Over much of central and eastern Mendip by far the most widespread soils are the dark brown silty loams of the Nordrach series. One of the most interesting characteristics of all these soils is a high silt content and this contributes to their uniformity over a wide range of other parent materials including Triassic, Rhaetic and Liassic rocks as well as many lithological divisions of the Carboniferous Limestone. It has therefore been suggested that a cover of loessial silty drift played an important part in the development of the Nordrach soils, combining with residues from underlying rocks to produce soils which regularly have a thickness of 36 inches. The 17–21 inches of the loamy A and Eb horizons have been shown to contain as much as 60 per cent of silt and not more than 25 per cent of clay, the latter increasing to about 40 per cent in the Bt horizon, but there is evidence that the thickness of loessial and other materials varied considerably and there may be little uniformity in the texture profiles of these soils. Over most of the Carboniferous Limestone rocks the silty loams are virtually stoneless, but a stony phase has been mapped to the south of East Harptree and round Emborough, where chert fragments derived from underlying Mesozoic rocks or from silicified bands in the Carboniferous Limestone are involved in the soils. Though the Nordrach soils may formerly have had a cover of oak-ash woodland, there are now remarkably few trees on the plateau and almost all the land is kept in long grass leys. In the central parts of Mendip, round the flanks of eastern Blackdown, in a belt on the plateau stretching from the head of Cheddar gorge past Priddy and in small patches elsewhere, a Mendip complex has been mapped as an intergrade between the shallow (6–14 inches) Lulsgate soils of western and southern Mendip, which have poorly developed texture profiles, and the deeper (normally over 30 inches) Nordrach soils to the east and northeast, where there is a marked increase in clay content with depth. In general soils of the Mendip complex have a depth of 14–24 inches and are used for grass farming but in many areas between Priddy, Charterhouse and Cheddar, where rock outcrops surround pockets of deeper soil, land use and vegetation are correspondingly patchy. To the northeast of Wells on the flanks of Pen Hill and round the south of Beacon Hill near Shepton Mallet, soils occur in which the superficial layers closely resemble those of the Nordrach series but the lower horizons consist of thick clays, possibly of Liassic age, which lead to impeded drainage. The upper layers of these soils of the Bodden series may contain more stones and sand, derived from the sandstones in the nearby cores of the periclines, than do the Nordrach soils, but silts are still the most important component and despite less satisfactory drainage they are also used for grass leys or for permanent pastures in the stonier areas.

Two other soil series occur very locally on Mendip. Within the main area of Nordrach soils there are a number of small patches of land where podzolization characteristic of the Priddy series has taken place. Three such patches occur on high ground north of Priddy at Townsend, round the Priddy Circles and at the top of Smitham Hill, and there are others at Nordrach and at Whitnell Corner. An important feature of the Priddy soils is the presence of an iron pan at a depth of about 7 inches, above which there is a 4–5 inch A horizon of very humose silty loam and a 2–3-inch Ea horizon of dark grey silty loam. Below the iron pan there is a silt loam Eb horizon above a frangipan at the junction with the Bt horizon of silty clay. It has been suggested (Findlay 1965) that raw humus collected above the iron pan when heath vegetation may have covered much larger areas in the post-Roman period. In these areas the vegetation in modern times included some *Calluna* as well as bracken and gorse, until very recent improvements were carried out by ploughing and reseeding. The other soils with a limited extent are those of the Tynings series which occurs only on the narrow outcrops of the Carboniferous Limestone Shales round the Old Red Sandstone core areas. There is therefore a very narrow discontinuous belt of such soils round Blackdown from Winscombe to Nordrach and Dolebury, similar belts to the east and west of Pen Hill and a slightly wider area between North Hill and Priddy. In addition to the Carboniferous Limestone Shales the parent materials include superficial deposits of loessial silt with Head and colluvium from the adjacent sandstone areas. The soils, therefore, consist of stony silt loams and silty clay loams above a bedrock of impermeable shales which causes impeded drainage in the subsoil, but on the generally steep slopes the effects of this are usually minimized by good site drainage. Round Pen Hill the very steep slopes on the Tynings soils are wooded in Biddle Coombe and on the valley sides at Rookham, and round Blackdown they provide pasture which is liable to invasion by bracken and thistles, but the area on the west side of North Hill has much gentler slopes and is continuously cultivated.

Though rock exposures and the thinness of many soils in the Lulsgate series reduce the agricultural value of considerable areas especially in the west and south, the same is very seldom true of the more extensive areas covered by soils of the Nordrach series and the Mendip complex, and limitations on Mendip agriculture must be imposed at least as much by the configuration of the land and by climatic conditions arising from elevation and exposure as by any deficiencies of the soils.

On the Carboniferous rocks of the Bristol region away from the limestone hills a great variety of soils occur over the Coal Measures and by no means all of them have been identified as belonging to named series. In the Forest of Dean and in the Bristol and south Gloucestershire area where Coal Measures outcrop over fairly large continuous areas, there are extensive developments of their characteristic soils, but in the Somerset coalfield where a patchwork of more recent rocks overlies the Coal Measures the occurrence of soil types is exceedingly irregular. The Nibley series is developed on hard coarse-grained sandstones and grits and in the Bristol region these occur most commonly in the Pennant series, since there are only limited exposures of the Quartzitic Sandstones of the Millstone Grit series. There are, however, some coarse-grained sandstones elsewhere in the Coal Measures succession, and in Somerset at Temple Cloud, on Highbury Hill near Clutton, and round Stanton Wick, patches of soil in the Nibley series occur over sandstones in both the Upper and Lower Coal series. Moreover, at least some of the sandstones in the Upper Coal series in the northern part of the Somerset coalfield and in the Brislington district, and others occurring in the centre of the South Gloucestershire coal basin in the Red Measures, are sufficiently coarse-grained to form broadly comparable soils. However, the only extensive areas of Nibley soils in this area occur where the Pennant flanks the Kingswood anticline and curves round the western, northern and northeastern sides of the coal basin from north Bristol through Frampton Cottrell and Rangeworthy to Nibley itself. In the Forest of Dean the Pennant series is again important and Nibley soils occur commonly wherever its coarse-grained sandstones outcrop. The soils normally have an A horizon of reddish grey sandy clay loam to a depth of about 6 inches and a B/C horizon of reddish brown sandy loam to about 24 inches. They have a coarse texture and sandstone fragments throughout the profile make them stony but they have the advantage of draining freely. In lowland areas like south Gloucestershire where there are few really steep slopes the Nibley soils are reasonably suitable for grass ley and some other forms of arable agriculture since they have satisfactory drainage and are easily ploughed and drilled; but where they are thin and on steep slopes or at high elevations they are regarded as poor agricultural soils. All three limitations are characteristic of the Forest of Dean where Nibley soils often remained under oak woodland until this was largely replaced with conifers, whilst the configuration of the land in the southern coalfield area of Somerset involves steep slopes where patches of woodland alternate with pasture on the Nibley soils. Where softer and finer-grained Coal Measures sandstones occur, deep and less coarse-textured reddish brown loams may develop which still have free drainage and are therefore of considerable agricultural value. Soils of this type occur over Upper Coal series sandstones in the Pensford–Compton Dando area of north Somerset, and between northeast Bristol and Iron Acton similar red loamy soils on the Coal Measures cover part of the area which has long specialized in potato production and general market gardening.

The shales which occur quite frequently near the junction of the Pennant with the Upper Coal series but also exist elsewhere, particularly near its base, give rise to poorly drained clay loam soils of which the Coalpit Heath series is typical in this region. Soils of this kind are not common in the Forest of Dean but they are important in south Gloucestershire where long narrow outcrops of shale alternate with Pennant Sandstones in a zone about a mile wide surrounding the rocks of the Upper Coal series in the centre of the basin. The poor drainage of the Coalpit Heath soils results in pronounced mottling throughout the upper 15 inches, which consist of stoneless clay loams. Below these there are reddish yellow and brownish yellow plastic and tenacious clays in the B and B/C horizons, passing downwards at about 44 inches through dark grey shaly clay to the shales themselves. Most of these soils in the neighbourhood of Coalpit Heath itself, Frampton Cottrell, Iron Acton and Nibley occur on almost flat land in the shallow valley of the Frome and its tributaries, where winter flooding has created problems in the past. With adequate artificial drainage they can support good grassland but invasion by rushes and excessive growth by moisture-loving species have to be guarded against. In the central and southern parts of the Somerset coalfield, on the other hand, where a complex of soils of this kind has been mapped to the north of Chelwood and Stanton Wick, round Clutton and High Littleton and in the Nettlebridge valley, relief features are pronounced and woodland occurs much more commonly. Here poorly drained soils truly characteristic of the Coalpit Heath series are confined to depressions and concave slopes where the woodland includes alder and willow, and pastures are comparable with those in south Gloucestershire. Where site drainage is more favourable a better, but still imperfectly, drained variant occurs which supports mixed deciduous woodland on the steeper slopes and rather better pastures elsewhere.

Soils derived from rocks of pre-Carboniferous age cover large areas only in the extreme northwest and southwest of the Bristol region, though they do occur in small areas over the cores of the Mendip periclines and very locally round the lower Bristol Avon. In the northwest great variations of site factors combine with lithological differences to produce a considerable range of soil types on the outcrops of the Old Red Sandstone round the margins of the Forest of Dean. Thus round the Brownstone ridges of the Old Red Sandstone running southwards from Micheldean, soils of the Ross series occur. These are generally characteristic of areas where sandstone phases of the Old Red appear and consist of well-drained reddish brown coarse sandy loams. In level or gently sloping country they can provide quite good, easily worked, arable land though under either crops or grass they may suffer from drought. However, much of the sandstone outcrop in this area occurs in ridges, sometimes with a capping of Quartz Conglomerate, where slopes are steep, exposures of the bedrock fairly common and a considerable area is wooded or under permanent pasture. To the west and south of the Forest the Old Red Sandstone includes both sandstones and marls, but the marl phase becomes dominant to the north of the May Hill inlier round Dymock and here soils of the Bromyard series are more typical. They are usually quite well-drained fine sandy medium loams but their agricultural value varies considerably with the depth of soil above unweathered marl. However, in the extreme northwest of Gloucestershire many of the Bromyard soils are deep and the area includes a fair proportion of arable land which shares with the neighbouring Triassic area some specialization in sugar beet production. Between the two Old Red areas the May Hill inlier consists largely of hard Silurian sandstones and has thin soils on many of the steep wooded slopes and under poor pastures, so that deeper and more valuable soils are confined to small pockets of colluvial material near the base of the hills. Across the Severn Silurian rocks and the Old Red Sandstone reappear in the Tortworth inlier. The Old Red on its western side round Berkeley is continued southwards to the Thornbury district and throughout gives rise to Bromyard soils whose agricultural value depends partly on their depth and partly on site drainage. The Silurian outcrop occurs in the low-lying area to the east, crossed by the Little Avon and its tributaries between Tortworth and Tites Point. Here the rocks themselves are mainly softer shales and limestones on which silty and fine sandy medium or heavy loams have developed. Since site drainage in such an area is usually poor and many of the rocks are impermeable, soil drainage is imperfect and land use is usually indistinguishable from that characteristic of most clay areas in the low-lying parts of the vale.

In the southwest of the Bristol region the Devonian rocks form upland areas where soil genesis is profoundly influenced not only by elevations which exceed 1,000 feet over wide areas but also by the high annual rainfall, with values in excess of 60 inches in parts of Exmoor. Podzolization is consequently widespread and since hard grits and slates are common parent materials many soils are thin. In general these are therefore areas of poor soils so that much of Exmoor and the northern Quantocks is occupied by heath and moor or by woodland. In detail, however, lithological differences within the Devonian rocks and more particularly site factors of slope, aspect and exposure produce a great diversity of soil conditions, amongst which a general distinction may be drawn between the areas of Lower and Upper Devonian rocks. The Lower and Middle Devonian includes a somewhat greater proportion of the hard grits and slates which form the very high ground running eastwards from the summits of Exmoor Forest to Dunkery Hill. Since the effects of low temperatures, high rainfall and exposure are at their greatest in this area of hard rocks, the thin soils are likely to be heavily podzolized and of poor quality, so that arable land and even woodland is largely confined to sheltered valley sites particularly on the seaward side above the Porlock valley, round Catcombe and in the rather lower North Hill–Dunster area. Similar rocks also form the higher northern part of the Quantocks and it is significant that woodland and plantations alternating with heath characterize the hills to the north of the outcrop of the Hangman Grits. The Upper Devonian rocks occupy the somewhat lower ground extending south and southeastwards from the summits of Exmoor and Dunkery to the Simonsbath–Exford–Withypool area and along the Croyden, Brandon and Haddon Hills to the south Quantocks. Even here many uplands exceed 1,000 feet in elevation and it seems likely that the smaller proportion of hard rocks in the parent material accounts at least as much as reduced elevation and rainfall for more favourable conditions. On valley sides in the west and on the slopes of the eastern hills there are Acid Brown Earths and a related valley-side soil complex which cover more than 40 per cent of the land in the Exmoor Forest district and together form the moderately well-drained brown loams of the so-called Exmoor dry land. On the other hand, on spur tops and the summit areas thin iron pans developed and peat growth occurred so that peats, peaty gley podzols, podzols and humic gley soils occupy virtually all the remaining areas. When reclamation was started following the sale of Forest lands in 1815, the application of lime was the only treatment thought necessary for the dry lands, but the provision of open-ditch drainage for the peats was essential and elsewhere improvement was achieved by stripping the vegetation and superficial litter layers, followed by deep ploughing of alternate furrow widths to break the iron pan. Arable agriculture was attempted and is still practised in some more favourable localities in the west but most of the improved land is now in permanent grass. Ploughland is more widespread in the east and on the lower southeastern slopes of the Quantocks where deep well-drained brown loams have developed over most of the Upper Devonian rocks except the shales, which produce shallow and less well-drained grey-brown medium loams.

The pre-Carboniferous rocks of Mendip consist of Old Red Sandstone cores in each of the periclines, with a very small Silurian inlier in that of Beacon Hill, so that, with the exception of a lower area round Shipham, they outcrop at heights above 750 feet O.D. On the sandstones themselves the most extensive soils are those of the Maesbury series covering much of Blackdown, Pen Hill and Beacon Hill, with smaller patches to the east and south of Eaker and Stock Hill. They generally occur on sloping ground since the flatter summit areas usually have soils of the Ashen series. In addition to sandstone residues the Maesbury soils are thought to include fine wind-borne silts comparable with those present in the other Mendip soils of the Nordrach and Langford series. The surface layers therefore consist of dark reddish brown loams involving both sands and silts below a thin acid mull A horizon. From 4 inches downwards the loams are very stony through the A/B, B and B/C horizons, extending to depths of about 26 inches, so that conditions of texture, stoniness and slope ensure that they have free drainage. A good deal of gorse and bracken formerly existed amongst semi-natural grassland on the Maesbury soil areas, particularly on Blackdown, but in recent times some changes in land use have been brought about by clearance of gorse and bracken, by the use of fertilizers and some reseeding of the pastures, and by afforestation on Stock Hill and Beacon Hill.

The Ashen series has been mapped on the Old Red over fairly extensive summit areas of Blackdown, the southern parts of North Hill and Stock Hill and in smaller patches on Beacon Hill. These districts are mainly at heights above 900 feet O.D. with an annual rainfall approaching 50 inches and all had a heathland vegetation, mainly of *Calluna,* before wartime ploughing and reseeding initiated improvements which have left heath in only a small area near Priddy and on Blackdown. Elsewhere most of the land is now in pasture but the leaching characteristic of podzols has removed many minerals and in particular cobalt deficiency may be serious. There is evidence that the existence of heath was essential to the genesis of the podzolized Ashen soils which under this kind of vegetation have a black peaty A horizon of some 3–6 inches over a very stony grey or greyish brown loam in the Ea horizon down to about 10 inches. Below this humus accumulation may occur in a Bh horizon succeeded by a thin Bfe horizon, though there is seldom any large extent of continuous iron pan. The subsoils often consist of freely draining stony reddish brown loams over the Old Red Sandstone but on many level or only slightly convex summit areas the parent materials also include silty clay overlying the sandstone and this may lead to impeded subsoil drainage. Drainage can also be impeded locally in the superficial layers when small patches of iron pan and other concretions make the Bfe horizon less permeable, so that the surface may be spongy and wet.

It will be recalled that not all periglacial gravelly Head was swept by meltwater down the coombes and gorges of Mendip; some remained where it had accumulated by solifluxion processes at the foot of the sandstone slopes and in hollows over much of the outcrop of the surrounding Lower Limestone Shale. In these areas, round the margins of all the pericline cores, the Ellick series occurs where the sandy gravels are thick and allow free drainage in the soils for which they are the principal parent material. Ellick soils are essentially very stony sand loams which are acid and deficient in bases and usually have a cover of rather poor semi-natural grassland. This is commonly invaded by bilberry and gorse as well as bracken, which itself actually forms an almost continuous cover on parts of Blackdown above Burrington Coombe that are not regularly grazed, and in such localities bracken litter and a thin humose horizon overlie the loams. The Thrupe series occurs where a thinner cover of gravelly Head overlies shales and clays, and especially where the latter cause water passing vertically or laterally through the Old Red Sandstone to form springs or seepages through the subsoil. Thrupe soils therefore tend to occur in hollows or on flat sites below the Old Red Sandstone outcrops particularly round Beacon Hill and to the northeast of Pen Hill, though there are also belts of these soils round Priddy Hill, Eaker Hill and the eastern end of Blackdown. They are poorly drained and generally infertile soils which are used for permanent pastures, under which they consist of grey brown loams or silt loams passing downwards through silty clay loams to dense, sticky and commonly wet subsoils. In some cases semi-natural vegetation, mainly of *Molinia,* has survived on Thrupe soils under bog conditions with an organic surface layer and humose loams overlying very wet stony loams.

The soils over the very small area of Silurian igneous rocks on the southeastern flanks of Beacon Hill are mapped as the Moons Hill complex, since they involve Moons Hill and Knapp series in close association. The former consist of dark brown loams, humose at the surface and becoming progressively stonier until the deeply weathered pyroxene andesite is reached. This weathered rock subsoil permits free drainage of the Moons Hill soils, in sharp contrast with those in the Knapp series which overlie small pockets of very firm almost impermeable clay derived from Silurian mudstones and argillaceous tuffs. The soils of both series are used in this locality for grass farming, the contrast in their drainage regimes being evident from the distribution of rushes and moss in shallow depressions which are the characteristic sites of the Knapp soils.

The most important of the remaining soils of the Bristol region are those of the alluvial lowlands. These include the fine silt and silty clay soils near the Severn, which, when drained, can provide some of the finest pasture land in Gloucestershire, and the more complex assemblage of soils in the central basins and levels of Somerset.

In the latter area by no means all the soils have parent materials of recent alluvium, two locally important series, for example, occurring on the marine sands of the Burtle Beds. Over these deposits in the Parrett basin well-drained fine sandy loams of the Chedzoy series overlie an alternation of calcareous sands and sandstones, whilst elsewhere, especially in the northern levels, the Catcott series and Catcott complex consist of sandy loams above subsoils which do not include appreciable thicknesses of sandstone and may have a loam or even a sandy clay loam texture. Favourable site factors on elevations above the levels and free drainage, at least of the Chedzoy series, mean that arable agriculture can be practised, whilst under grass these areas are invaluable as winter grazing for animals summered on the alluvial lowlands.

Of the recent alluvial deposits in central Somerset and the Severn lowlands the greatest continuous extent is that of the Romano-British estuarine calcareous silty clay, which runs parallel with the river and the estuary and, in the Somerset basins, forms most of the coastal belt at a uniform height of about 20 feet o.d. Similar uniformity exists in the soils: nearly identical profiles are found wherever the occurrence of the Wentlloog series marks the extent of largely unmodified estuarine clay. In the A and B horizons the grey-brown and the grey silty clays are non-calcareous and consistenly contain more silt than clay whilst as little as one per cent of sand may be present, but at about 18 to 20 inches in the Cga horizon the clay content reaches a maximum as the base of the carbonate-free horizons is reached. Though these are groundwater gley soils in low-lying sites, open drainage by rhynes and field grypes, now supplemented by the new cuts and modern drainage techniques which have drastically reduced winter flooding, normally keeps the water table below a depth of 2 feet. Before the nineteenth century arable farming was practised on at least some areas of Wentlloog soils and in one or two localities they are still ploughed for grass leys, but in most places they have indifferent permanent pasture which is regarded solely as summer grazing and which is liable to develop rushy patches. Near the landward margins of the estuarine clay, where large quantities of run-off water are received from the higher land of Mendip or the 'islands', the imperfectly drained Wentlloog series is sometimes replaced by the poorly drained Allerton series, particularly in the Axe levels between Axbridge and

86

Panborough, on the western side of the Isle of Wedmore and immediately east of Brent Knoll. Below about 14 inches the Allerton soils, like the Wentlloog, consist of silty clays derived from the estuarine parent materials of this texture, but the upper horizons of the Allerton have a much higher clay content, sometimes over 70 per cent, and it has been suggested that clays from the Lower Lias areas surrounding the levels may be involved. Former liability to winter flooding is indicated by the humose nature of the superficial clay layers, but the Allerton areas are no longer inundated regularly though standing water does appear occasionally and the rushy nature and low quality of most of the pastures demonstrate the poor drainage regime of the soils. In the same area of the Axe levels it is thought that silts and fine sands laid down on top of the estuarine clays in creek systems may account for a very high proportion of silt in the upper horizons which distinguishes the small patches of the Latcham series to the east of Wedmore from the surrounding Wentlloog, Allerton and Compton soils.

Fine-textured alluvial and colluvial materials derived from the clays and calcareous shales of the Lower Lias form the parent material for the clay soils of the Butleigh series. Their mode of origin, mainly by downwash from the slightly higher ground of the Lias, means that these soils occur as very narrow rings surrounding the Liassic 'islands' at Wedmore, Mark and Brent Knoll, in the valleys and on the lower slopes on the north side of the Polden Hills, in similar sites in the Somerton-Langport district, and on the coastal Liassic area beyond the Parrett from Stockland Bristol westwards. The drainage of the Butleigh soils is imperfect and within the levels they receive a good deal of water from the higher ground of the 'islands', so that they can become waterlogged along with the estuarine clay on which they rest. Waterlogging at depth may also occur in Butleigh soils at higher levels in the Lias valleys, but this is less common and arable agriculture is practised on some of these soils in the Poldens and the coastal area, in contrast with their general use for permanent grass in the levels. Liassic alluvium is also the main parent material of soils in the Fladbury series and, like those of the Allerton and Butleigh series, they have at least 60 per cent of clay in the upper layers. They occur most widely in the eastern and southeastern parts of the basins, particularly round the upper Brue on Kennard Moor and Butt Moor and along the courses of the river Cary and the river Parrett where they cross the Lias upstream from Somerton and Langport respectively, but smaller extents occur in many other low-lying localities adjoining the higher ground of the Lias. Humose clay at the surface suggests the prevalence of waterlogging in these poorly or very poorly draining soils where site drainage must also be generally unfavourable; even today it is common to encounter waterlogging at a depth of

18 inches and winter inundation is not unknown. Inevitably most land on Fladbury soils is used as summer grazing but the pastures are usually poor and the prevalence of rushes and sedges greatly reduces their value for hay. Adjacent to the Fladbury soils, particularly in the upper basin of the Brue, patches of soil of the Lydford series occur. A higher proportion of silt in these soils is derived from the Middle and Upper Lias and, correspondingly, the clay percentage is usually below 50, but even so drainage is poor and the pastures are little better than those on the Fladbury soils.

In valleys on the Keuper Marls and below its slopes down to the edges of the levels, there are accumulations of alluvial and colluvial material, mainly derived from the Marls, on which the Compton soil series has developed. Locality within the basins determines whether the Keuper material overlies estuarine clay or peat but in either case Compton soils usually occur only where the thickness of alluvium is greater than 3 feet. Stream courses on the Keuper Marls, like those of the Chew, the Cam brook and the Sheppey, have characteristic elongated strips of Compton soils, whilst similar patterns are created by strips along the river levées of the levels, particularly in the Axe basin. Away from the rivers somewhat wider patches of soils of this type spread outwards from the edge of the Keuper Marl outcrop, particularly onto the margins of the levels immediately south of Mendip, and there are narrow bands of the Compton series on the southern side of the Poldens especially below the steeper slopes of the Trias round Compton Dundon and High Ham. The clay becomes calcareous below about 4 inches and its proportion increases downwards through the profile with ranges variously estimated as from 40 to 60 or from 60 to 90 per cent, the remainder being virtually all silt so that percolation is slow and soil drainage is imperfect. On the levées somewhat coarser textures and better site drainage reduce the risk of waterlogging, which is most common in flatter areas of the levels where the permanent water table is higher. Almost all the Compton soils are used for permanent pastures, the quality of which is partly governed by the efficiency of artificial drainage. The Max series occurs on similar and often adjacent sites, particularly in the floors of lowland valleys opposite the Mendip gorges and coombes, but its parent materials are different. These consist of clay alluvium and gravels carried down from the hills as well as the Keuper Marls on which they are deposited, and the proportions in which each is involved vary greatly. The colour of the clay soils therefore ranges from reddish brown to grey and the amounts of gravel and sand in the subsoil are equally variable. Nevertheless the soils are invariably poorly or very poorly drained so that in some parts of the stream courses and in small wet depressions elsewhere unimproved marsh still exists, whilst the growth of rushes is a considerable problem in maintaining the permanent grass-land which covers almost all the remaining areas of Max soils.

Round the margins of the peat moors and along river courses across them, standing floodwater formerly laid down over the peat super-ficial deposits in which the clay content was normally at least 60 per cent. Where these clays have a thickness of about 18 inches but do not reach the 30 inches or more of the Compton or Fladbury series, they form parent materials for soils of the Midelney series. In the Axe basin such soils occupy quite small areas on the margins of the Wedmore, Stoke, Westbury and Knowle Moors but further south they occur not only in narrow belts round the edge of the peat in the basins of the Brue and the Parrett but also over wider tracts round the western side of Glastonbury and on the moors of the Parrett basin downstream from Langport. When the clays of the surface layers are mainly derived from the Keuper Marl they tend to be pink or reddish but elsewhere Liassic or mixed materials lead to predominantly grey colouring. From about 12 to 19 inches in depth the clays may be replaced by peaty loams but elsewhere there is a rapid transition from clay to peat at about 18 inches. Despite recent great improvements in the drainage of the levels brief flooding does still take place occasionally over the Midelney soils and in winter the water table is commonly within a few inches of the surface. These are therefore areas of permanent pasture but they can also yield early and heavy crops of good quality hay provided they are kept clear of rushes and sedges.

The moors thus encircled by strips of Midelney soils are themselves almost entirely occupied by organo-mineral and organic soils. Of these the Sedgemoor series covers large parts of the inland basins of the Parrett and the Brue including King's Sedge Moor, Queen's Sedge Moor, West Sedge Moor and Catcott Heath, where 5–10 feet of pre-Roman fen peat normally rest on post-Glacial clays whose surface is little above present sea level. Since the top of the peat was therefore commonly below 10 feet O.D. and the river outfalls lay across the somewhat higher coastal Romano-British clay lands, these areas suffered regular and prolonged inundations prior to the increase of pumping and the excavation of the Huntspill river and the new North Drain in recent decades. Above the peat there are therefore flood deposits of clay and silt which produce surface layers on the Sedgemoor soils with textures ranging from peaty loams to peaty clays. These layers of soil with a higher mineral content are usually less than 12 inches thick and the Midelney series is mapped where greater thicknesses of predominantly clay soils overlie the peat. Traditionally the Sedgemoor areas were summer pastures and hay land for farms situated on nearby higher ground and the practice continues, but recent drainage improvements make it poss-ible to leave the stock longer on the low ground and may improve the quality of the heavy grass crops if rushes and sedges can be eliminated.

In the Axe basin above Cheddar Moor and on Godney Moor, peat and organo-mineral materials overlie the Romano-British estuarine clay and give rise to soils of the Godney series. In the central part of Godney Moor and in small areas on Draycott and Knowle Moors a deep phase of these soils has between 3 and 5 feet of peat above the clay, the top 9 inches of which are usually completely humified. Since these are slightly higher areas flooding does not now take place and the permanent pastures can be used throughout the year. The shallower Godney soils, in which peaty materials seldom exceed 12 inches in depth, show considerable variations in the proportions and thickness of organic matter. They too are used for pasture, but lower elevations commonly lead to waterlogging, winter flooding and the prevalence of species characteristic of wet sites.

Where raised mosses developed in the central areas of the Brue basin, notably on the heaths of the Westhay, Shapwick and Ashcott area and on Westhay Moor to the north of the river, there are acid peat soils of the Westhay series. There are considerable variations of colour and of the plant remains found in the great thicknesses of fibrous peat which make up the profile below about 8 inches of black well-humified peat of the surface. Moreover, considerable local variations arise from the effects of long-continued peat cutting, and soils of the Westhay series have therefore been mapped in a Turbary Moor complex. Scattered pastures of the characteristically tiny farms have a hummocky surface on these soils and are often almost isolated by present-day peat cuttings and trackways, and the scrub and pools of former ones. They seldom develop a real sward, suffer alternately from excessive moisture and drought, and are sometimes little better than rough grazing.

Despite such a variety of configuration and soil, particularly to the west of the Jurassic scarps, most of the land of the Bristol region was placed in the medium quality category of the classification used by the University of Bristol Reconstruction Research Group, and substantial areas in south Somerset and the vales of north Gloucestershire were described as land of good quality. Appreciable extents of poor quality land were recognized only in the Forest of Dean and the uplands of southwest Somerset, whilst the low quality of very small patches of land elsewhere was commonly due to the occurrence of steep slopes, rock outcrops or very localized flooding and waterlogging rather than the character of the soils themselves. The greater part of the land of the region has therefore long been in continuous agricultural use, so that cultivated forms of vegetation are virtually universal and there are few remnants of early semi-natural forms of woodland or grassland.

# CHAPTER 4

# The Vegetation and Climate

## Vegetation

IT is probable that deciduous woodland became established over the greater part of the Bristol region after the disappearance of periglacial conditions, though the complex post-glacial physical history of the alluvial lowlands, particularly in the central basins of Somerset, resulted locally in the prevalence of other forms of vegetation. In the lowlands elsewhere, however, woodland, with oak as the dominant species, was almost universal, and fairly continuous damp oak forest covered the clay vales. It has been suggested that on limestone uplands ash was generally the dominant species but this does not seem to have been completely characteristic of the Bristol region since beech appears to have been more common on Cotswold, whilst ash, oak and other species occurred in very varied proportions on the Carboniferous Limestones.

It is unlikely that any of the individual small woodlands of the present day represents a true relic of this early semi-natural vegetation, but a study of a considerable number of woodlands (Hope-Simpson and Willis 1955) did suggest what appear to be ecologically significant regional variations of tree species on limestones in the central part of the Bristol region. Thus the former importance of beech on the Cotswold oolites is suggested by its present-day dominance in the woodlands of the Stroud district and in one woodland between Stroud and Bath, and this seems to be confirmed by the importance of beech in the wooded valley of the By brook round Castle Combe, Ford and Slaughterford and that of the Avon between Bradford-on-Avon and Bathford. On the oolites to the south of Bath, however, beech becomes relatively unimportant and it is virtually absent from the Carboniferous Limestones except in very small patches on the ridges between Bristol and Clevedon. The proportion of ash in woodlands on the oolites within ten miles or so of Bath varies greatly from about 20 to 80 per cent of the total, but the average is probably about 50 per cent, whereas it is only at the western end of Broadfield Down that the proportion of ash appreciably exceeds 25 per cent on the Carboniferous Limestones, and on the ridges to the north-west of Bristol it amounts to little more than 10 per cent of the woodland. Oak, on the other hand, was the most important individual species in most of the woodlands studied on the Carboniferous Limestones and in one woodland to the north of Bath, whilst on the oolites between Bath and Frome about a quarter of the woodland was of oak. Of the other species which may have been involved in semi-natural vegetation on the limestones, wych elm forms between a quarter and a half of the woodland round the lower Bristol Avon and on the oolites near Bath, whilst at the western end of Mendip more than a quarter of the woodlands are of lime. Apart from plantations and parks, the woodland of the oolites is virtually restricted to steep slopes, so that it is impossible to differentiate between woodland sites except in terms of the contrast between the beechwoods of the scarp and the deep valleys round Stroud and on the lower dipslope and the mixed woods of oak, ash and wych elm further south. On the other hand, on Mendip, ash is most characteristic of the steep slopes whereas on the plateau, apart from modern coniferous plantations, oak is the most important tree species.

One of the largest and most compact areas of deciduous woodland which remains in the Bristol region is that included in about 30,000 acres of hilly Coal Measures country in the Forest of Dean which came under the control of the Forestery Commission in 1919. However, by that time the semi-natural damp oak forest of the area had already been subjected to at least two thousand years of intermittent exploitation, conservation and spasmodic afforestation so that the mixed oak wood-land with beech, chestnut and sycamore can hardly be regarded as a simple remnant of the original forest, and in modern times the deciduous area has been surrounded and in places penetrated or replaced by conifers, mainly firs and larch. In the far southwest of the Bristol region there are compact areas of woodland on the Devonian uplands, particularly on the seaward slopes to the north of Exmoor, on the Croyden, Haddon and Brendon Hills, and on the northern and eastern sides of the Quantocks. Here again the semi-natural woodland may well have been mainly of oak and ash but there was subsequently a far greater extension of beech, which often dominates copses and hedgerows in the area, and in any case replacement and new plantations of conifers have left no continuous extents of largely deciduous woodland comparable with those in the Forest of Dean.

In the vales little forest survived the spread of cultivation in the Dark Ages and the early medieval period, though early enclosure of much of the land into a patchwork of small fields led to the planting of a maze of hedgerows with sufficient trees to give to the landscape the well-wooded appearance which still exists in many areas. Most of the hedge-

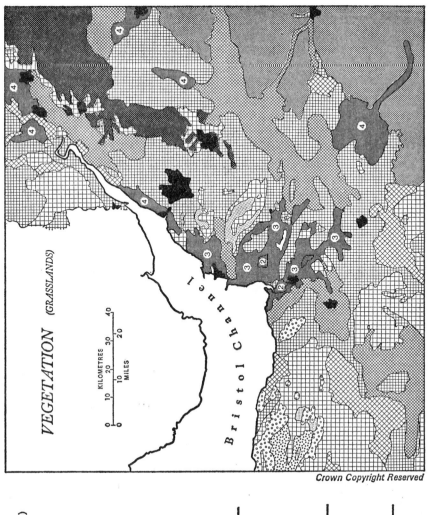

VEGETATION *(GRASSLANDS)*

Crown Copyright Reserved

row trees are oak, ash or English elm, but sycamore and horsechestnut are also common, beech is plentiful in the south and pollard trees are characteristic of parts of the alluvial lowlands, especially in Somerset. However, few stretches of actual woodland now exist which might be remnants of the semi-natural damp oak forest with hazel, though such an association did cover a considerable area on the Lower Lias Clay to the east and southeast of Wickwar until the present century, when felling left much of it as scrub and hazel coppice. Round Braydon on the Oxford Clay to the northwest of Swindon there are also small areas of oak woodland with an undergrowth of hazel and hornbeam, which are probably relics of the ancient Forest of Braden, and to the southeast of Trowbridge the once extensive woodland of oak and elm may have been seminatural in origin. One of the largest stretches of present-day wooded country covers much of the Greensand plateau from Penselwood northwards to Longleat, along the eastern margins of the vales of Wiltshire and Somerset where the Forest of Selwood still stretched far out into the lowlands in the Middle Ages. Local remnants of a fairly dense cover of oak still exist but much of the Greensand country has long been enclosed as parkland estates, and in the central districts of Witham Park and King's Wood the deciduous woodlands have been almost entirely replaced by conifers during the last hundred years. On the ridges and slopes of the Corallian outcrops there is more woodland than in most parts of the vale but it is almost entirely preserved in parks and estates and has consequently been very considerably modified.

Continuous cultivation for many centuries means that over the greater part of the Bristol region modern grassland is the product of a long history of some sort of husbandry and semi-natural forms are rare, particularly on the pasture land of the vales. Surveys earlier in the present century, before the position was further modified by reseeding with new strains and by the very recent increase in cereal cultivation, revealed a tendency for swards to contain a rather high proportion of *Agrostis,* but there were significant variations within the region and ordinary *Agrostis* pastures, as such, were common only in the agriculturally less favoured areas. Thus they were characteristic of grassland areas within the Forest of Dean and among the uplands of southwestern Somerset and they were fairly widespread on the Lower Lias Clay below the Cotswold scarp, particularly on the extensive common lands. Throughout the rest of the vales of Gloucestershire, Somerset and west Wiltshire there was considerable variation in the proportions of ordinary *Agrostis* and of *Agrostis*-with-Ryegrass (up to 15 per cent Ryegrass), the former being concentrated mainly round the margins of the Forest of Dean and the Devonian uplands and in some localities in north Somerset and South Gloucestershire, whilst *Agrostis*-with-Ryegrass was rather more important on the better soils of the vales of north Gloucestershire, south and southeast Somerset and some better-drained areas of the vale of west and north Wiltshire. *Agrostis*-with-Ryegrass was only dominant in good pastures near the Severn in Gloucestershire and in Somerset extending some way inland into the levels from the coast belt between Clevedon and Pawlett, where there were also limited areas of true Ryegrass pasture.

Somewhat different associations occurred on the limestone uplands of the Bristol region, though prolonged intensive cultivation of most of the Cotswold plateau has left few traces of semi-natural grassland. In the limited uncultivated areas, however, evidence of calcicolous vegetation is to be expected since soils on almost all grassland sites, irrespective of slope, aspect or drainage, tend to involve free carbonate. Semi-natural grassland therefore contained the fine-leaved fescues— sheep's fescue (*Festuca ovina*) and red fescue (*Festuca rubra*)—as well as common bent (*Agrostis tenuis*), the fescues becoming dominant on very shallow soils over the limestones. However, under early semi-natural conditions the dominant calcicoles were probably tor grass (*Brachypodium pinnatum*) and brome (*Zerna erecta*) and tor grass has appeared in Cotswold grasslands in the past. Because of the almost universal presence of free carbonate in the soils but possibly also because of the extent of continuous cultivation in this part of Cotswold, there is no evidence that an oolite heath involving more or less calcifuge species ever existed. On Mendip, on the other hand, conditions favouring calcicolous vegetation are limited to quite small areas of thin and possibly immature soils on drier, usually south-facing, slopes and here the dominant form was sheep's fescue (*Festuca ovina*) along with red fescue (*Festuca rubra*). Over much of the Mendip upland, however, where soils in the Nordrach and Lulsgate series and in the Mendip complex are non-calcareous, at least near the surface, and in the case of the Nordrach series are very much deeper, there was an approach towards a calcifuge association so that common bent (*Agrostis tenuis*) and heath grass (*Seiglingia decumbens*) accompanied the fescues and in the past considerable areas of the higher Mendip plateau had a limestone heath vegetation which also involved ling (*Calluna vulgaris*), heather (*Erica cinerea*) and tormentil (*Potentilla erecta*). On north-facing slopes and especially on the acid brown earths on the sandstone slopes of Blackdown, on Maesbury and Ellick soils, bracken (*Pteridium aquilinum*) was dominant along with patches of gorse (*Ulex gallii*), bilberry (*Vaccinium myrtillus*), wavy hair grass (*Deschampsia flexuosa*) and the fescues, but only limited areas of this heath now remain following reclamation and reseeding in recent times. On the summits of the Old Red Sandstone hills, mainly on soils of the Ashen series, small areas of true heath or heather moor still exist, generally dominated by ling but with heather, bilberry and gorse in well-drained areas and with purple moor grass (*Molinia caerulea*), cotton grass (*Eriophorum angustifolium*), rushes and mosses on wetter sites which are even more common on adjacent areas of Thrupe soils.

Heath and moor of ling and heather also formerly occupied large areas in the Devonian uplands of western Somerset and the northern Quantocks. In the Exmoor area prolonged grazing and the reclamation work of the nineteenth century meant that grasses to a considerable extent replaced the heather, but ling still covers some of the higher areas in the west round Simonsbath and on Dunkery Hill and, where drainage is impeded on summit areas, some *Molinia* and cotton grass occur, while bracken was common on steep slopes or where reclaimed areas were neglected and understocked in the 1930s. However, in recent decades reclamation has been resumed and the Exmoor Society estimated that some 8,000 acres of moorland were put into agricultural use in the area of the Exmoor National Park between 1958 and 1966. Similar conditions existed in those parts of the northern Quantocks which did not have a cover of semi-natural woodland, but the extent of heath has been greatly reduced by new plantations and by the replacement and extension of old woodlands.

The distinctive physical history of the Somerset levels and their coastlands means that they have had in the past specialized forms of vegetation, but it is only near the coast and in the raised bog districts that this is reflected in the modern vegetation. Elsewhere the grassland of the levels appears to have been established by reclamation direct from fen-like conditions, of which there is now little evidence except that derived from the former fen vegetation of the Glastonbury area and the assemblage of fen plants with rushes and sallow carr found in the Gordano valley. In the raised bogs peat growth ceased in Romano-British times and was followed by the growth of woodland, mainly of birch, alder, sallow (*Salix atrocinera*), oak and pine. Prolonged peat cutting, however, has left little of this other than birch scrub, and the highly disturbed surface produces a mixed environment of acid peats but base-rich surface water, which results in a variety of both bog and fen plants, mainly ling and purple moor grass but also cross-leaved heath (*Erica tetralix*), the cotton grasses (*Eriophorum angustifolium* and *E. vaginatum*) and bog moss (*Sphagnum spp.*), with bracken and willow herb often colonising the open areas of recent peat cuttings. In the coastal area along much of this part of the Severn, sea or rice grass (*Spartina Townsendii*) is coming to dominate the halophytic plants of the lower secondary marsh and spreads far out onto the mud flats. On the primary marsh, usually a few feet higher, there is a usable turf of common salt marsh grass (*Puccinellia maritima*) and red fescue (*Festuca rubra*), which grades into the grassland of the pastures further inland. In the area of dunes there is a marked change both of morphology and vegetation from north to south. Near Brean Down in the north the dunes are narrow and really consist of a single line of sandhills covered with marram (*Ammophilia arenaria*) but in the Berrow–Burnham district there is pronounced zoning. The outer dunes at the head of the beach have a covering of sea crouch (*Agropyron junceiforme*) which is succeeded inland by some marram and then by a dune pasture of red fescue and sand sedge (*Carex arenaria*). During the present century, however, this zoned pattern has been complicated by the presence of sea buckthorn (*Hippophae rhamnoides*) which has spread from plantations to cover and dominate the whole dune system in some localities.

## Climate

The position and extent of the Bristol region, stretching along the margins of the English plain from the Devon border to the west Midlands, suggests that its climate might be transitional between that of the southwest peninsula and those characteristic of southeast England and the rest of the Midlands. In general marine influences, carried far inland by the presence of the Bristol Channel and the Severn estuary, maintain moist conditions over the region and keep its winters warmer and its summers a little cooler than areas further east, but these effects are less marked than in the southwest peninsula and they are more liable to interruption. For example, winds predominantly from the southwest and west ensure long periods in which the Bristol region shares the very mild moist winter weather of Devon and Cornwall, but at any time from October onwards and very frequently in spring the establishment of high pressure conditions to the north may create gradients for northeasterly and easterly winds, which can bring to the area very cold and often dry air more characteristic of inland areas in southeast England. The effects of such temporary but important changes of wind direction, temperature and humidity, however, depend largely on the aspect, elevation and exposure of particular localities, and this augments the continuous influence of relief on temperature and, more particularly, on precipitation within the region. Thus, though a general climatic transition across the region from southwest to northeast unquestionably exists, it is of far smaller significance than more local climatic contrasts between the exposed uplands of Cotswold, Mendip and southwestern Somerset and sheltered areas in the surrounding vales.

*Wind.* Study of records from Long Ashton, near Bristol, has shown that, as might be anticipated, the most common wind directions are from the southwest and west. However, such winds occurred over only about 40 per cent of the time observed and even in the months of June and July, when they are most frequent, they are normally experienced for very little more than half of the period. During August and September there is an increased occurrence of winds from the east and northeast which is maintained throughout the winter as a result of the fairly regular establishment of high pressure to the north of the region. Such conditions are even more common in the spring so that in March and May the frequency of winds from the northeast and east actually exceeds that of westerly and southwesterly winds. Thus it is only in early summer that there is little chance of the occurrence of winds from an easterly or northeasterly quarter, the importance of which lies in the fact that they interrupt what might otherwise be a regular pattern of mild or warm maritime conditions over almost all of the region. Thus the usual low relative humidity of the easterly and northeasterly winds of spring makes this the driest season of the year, whilst in the autumn and winter these winds regularly bring in cold or very cold and often dry air. When westerly or southwesterly winds prevail conditions may be fairly uniform over the whole region, except for the higher precipitation and greater liability to mist and hill fog on the uplands and the slight regional decline in precipitation towards the northeast especially in the northern vales of Gloucestershire. Marked climatic contrasts within the region are therefore much more the product of exposure to or shelter from easterly and northeasterly winds, particularly in winter and early spring. Thus Cotswold's reputation for bleakness and the 'lateness' of its agriculture is largely the outcome of the exposure of the dipslope and plateau to winds from those directions, and similar effects are felt on the high and exposed plateau surfaces of Mendip. On the other hand, the influence of easterly and northeasterly winds becomes far less marked in the extreme south of the region so that, despite greater elevation, heavier precipitation and exposure to strong winds from the southwest, conditions in the uplands of southwest Somerset in winter and spring are commonly much less bleak than on Mendip or Cotswold. Similarly some localities have the double advantage of a southerly aspect and shelter from the easterly, northeasterly and, less frequent, northerly winds and consequently enjoy a climate which is particularly favourable in late winter and spring. The best-known example is that of the strawberry-growing district of the Cheddar Vale below the curving southern face of Mendip which, in the immediate vicinity of Cheddar itself, also affords shelter from westerly and northwesterly winds, but similar effects occur in the Vale of Wrington to the southwest of Broadfield Down, round Wraxall below the Failand ridge and on the Somerset coast in Porlock Vale and in parts of Weston-super-Mare and Clevedon.

*Temperature*. The absence of a good network of stations with comparable long-term records makes it impossible to study variations of temperature over the region with any degree of precision, and only approximate values can be quoted because considerable differences are revealed when it is possible to compare mean figures based on recent records with those based on longer series for the same station. Nevertheless it is clear that the mean monthly temperature for January in the neighbourhood of Bristol is about 4·7°C: this may be reasonably indicative of winter conditions over much of the region since the corresponding value for Cheltenham is about 4·4°C, for Bath 4·3° C and for Weston-super-Mare about 5°C. The slightly higher figure for Weston-super-Mare can be related to its coastal position and the shelter effect already referred to. The lower temperatures of Bath and Cheltenham may be due to local siting considerations as well as their position further inland; a mean monthly figure for January of about 3·1°C at Cirencester reflects exposure to easterly and northeasterly winds and elevation (443 feet O.D.) as much as its inland location. On the other hand, January mean daily ranges of 6·2°C and 6·5°C at Bristol and Cirencester are broadly comparable, whereas on the coast at Weston-super-Mare the mean daily range is as low as 4·9°C. However, a fairly common alternation of winter weather types associated with southwesterly and northeasterly winds suggests that winter mean monthly temperature values have only limited significance and this is indicated by the fact that in the Bristol area the January mean monthly temperature itself has ranged from −0·7°C to 8·7°C and the extreme recorded temperature range at both Bristol and Cirencester over the months of January and February is from −14·5°C to 15°C. However, large upward departures from the seasonal mean temperatures either in winter or summer are quite infrequent and by far the most common departures are the downward ones in winter and early spring associated with the establishment of easterly and northeasterly winds. Over much of the region the earliest air frost is usually in late October, though ground frost may occur at any time between late August and mid-May. Near Bristol the latest air frost is usually at the end of April but on Cotswold and Mendip air frost is common in May. The morphology of Mendip is such that frost hollows are fairly small but over considerable areas in the Cotswold valleys cold air with frost, mist and fog may accumulate under calm or near calm conditions at any time between September and late May. In the vales snow normally falls on about 10 days each year between December and March, with the largest number of falls in February and January, but reports of snow lying are made on an average of only about 5 days a year.

On the uplands, however, snow usually falls on 15–25 days a year and snow lying is reported on more than 15 days on the higher parts of Cotswold, Mendip and the moors of southwest Somerset. Following spells of cold weather, snowfalls in south Somerset and on Mendip are often associated with the passage of depressions or fronts actually crossing the area from the southwest or west, but under similar temperature conditions, when the depressions move along the English Channel and moist easterly winds to the north of them rise up the dipslope of Cotswold, snowstorms may occur which produce exceptionally heavy falls as the higher plateau areas are reached. Exposure to the east and northeast therefore gives to large areas of Cotswold prolonged winter liability to cold winds, frost and heavy snowfall, which is shared by only the high areas of the Mendip plateau and the summits of the moorlands in the southwest. It is this bleakness and lower temperatures caused by greater elevation which create the most important contrasts within the Bristol region in the winter half of the year since they can reduce the growing season from about 43 weeks near the Somerset coast to barely 34 weeks on the uplands.

Temperature conditions are somewhat more uniform in summer than in winter since the mean monthly figure for July is about 16·5°C at Weston-super-Mare, 16·4°C near Bristol and 17° C further inland at Bath and at Cheltenham, the only other significant variations being attributable to the effects of greater elevation on Cotswold and Mendip and in southwest Somerset. Mean daily ranges of 9°C and 7·3°C near Bristol and Cirencester are a little higher than the corresponding winter figures of 6·2°C and 6·5°C respectively, but on the coast at Weston-super-Mare the July mean daily range of 5·7°C (winter 4·9°C) is still very low. The absence of important departures from the mean temperatures in summer is shown by the fact that the recorded range of the July monthly mean itself at Bristol is only 5°C (14·3°C–19·3°C) compared with the corresponding January range of 9·4°C. Maximum recorded temperatures of 34°C or 35°C seem to have occurred in most parts of the Bristol region but on only very rare occasions, whereas the lowest recorded July temperatures show a little more variation between districts, 6·1°C being fairly typical of lowland areas and 3·4°C of the uplands.

*Sunshine.* In all parts of the region June is the sunniest month but in Gloucestershire relatively dry conditions in spring mean that by May the duration of sunshine has almost reached that of June. December is in all cases the month with least sunshine. Examination of sunshine figures for the period 1921–50 at Long Ashton has shown (G. E. Clothier 1950) that the June mean value of 7·07 hours per day represents only 43 per cent of the theoretical maximum whilst the December figure of 1·52 hours per day represents only 19 per cent and the annual mean of 4·19 hours per day only 34 per cent of the maximum possible. That such low values are reasonably typical is demonstrated by the fact that the range of recorded annual means of daily sunshine is only between 4·1 and 4·4 hours over the whole region, thus illustrating the prevalent cloudiness arising from the general dominance of maritime influences.

*Precipitation.* A much larger number of stations have recorded rainfall over fairly long periods and it is therefore possible to consider a rather more complete picture of precipitation over the region. Such a picture immediately reveals the very close connection which exists between rainfall totals and the configuration of the land, since there is a striking resemblance between maps showing rainfall and those showing relief. This resemblance is most marked in areas of pronounced relief so that there is a fairly precise coincidence between the uplands and the areas of maximum rainfall, but though precipitation totals are invariably smaller in the lowlands their variations may be quite significantly influenced by circumstances other than relief. In general annual rainfall totals between 30 inches and 35 inches are characteristic of the western vales of the Bristol region but in Somerset the central parts of the levels have somewhat lower figures, like that of 28·4 inches at Ashcott. The rainfall of 30 inches at Taunton and 30·8 inches at Bridgwater is typical of the rest of the basins, however, and round their margins amounts increase slightly on the higher ground to totals of 32·9 inches at Castle Cary and 34·7 inches at Crewkerne, for example, and on the highest parts of the Jurassic and Cretaceous uplands on the eastern and southern borders of the county rainfall locally exceeds 37·5 inches. Somewhat higher ground and less regular relief in north Somerset results in rather greater variation of rainfall, with figures of 35·1 inches at Yatton, 35·8 inches at Long Ashton, 36·2 inches at West Town and 37·6 inches at Chew Magna, but with only 32·4 inches on the coast at Weston-super-Mare, 33·6 inches in the sheltered Gordano valley at Walton and 30·9 inches in the Avon valley near Bath. In the Severn lowlands from the Bristol Avon northwards annual rainfall is again approximately 30 inches but it diminishes northeastwards to below 27·5 inches near Gloucester and 25 inches round Tewkesbury. This northern part of the Gloucestershire vales no doubt feels some effect of shelter from the west and southwest by the high ground of Wales, the Malverns and the Forest of Dean, so that in low-lying areas to the south and east of Tewkesbury rainfall is actually below 25 inches. To the east of the Jurassic uplands the Oxford Clay vale has a rainfall of about 30 inches at the foot of the dipslopes but this decreases steadily eastwards so that in the extreme east of the region at Lechlade it is 26·2 inches, though slight increases occur on the higher ground of the Corallian and as the

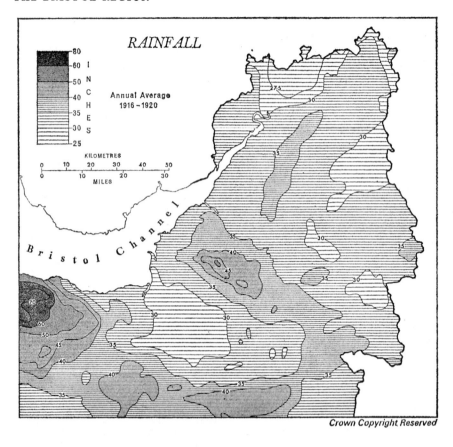

Crown Copyright Reserved

Chalk is approached beyond Swindon where the rainfall is 29 inches.

The highest rainfall figures on the uplands of the Bristol region occur at elevations above 1,200 feet on Exmoor and Dunkery Hill, where considerable areas have more than 60 inches. Here the influence of relief and exposure is clearly seen when the rainfall of 70·7 inches at West Dunkery (elevation 1,580 feet) is contrasted with that of 35 inches eight miles away in the sheltered lowland at Dunster. Similarly on the Quantocks, despite elevations of well over 1,000 feet, rainfall figures between 35 inches and 40 inches indicate the effect of shelter afforded by even higher land to the west. The greater part of the high Mendip plateau has a rainfall of over 42·5 inches, the summit areas from Blackdown to Pen Hill and on Beacon Hill have over 45 inches, and a small area between Smitham Hill and the Castle of Comfort has over 50 inches. On the other hand, in north Gloucestershire the less exposed position of the high ground of May Hill and the eastern parts of the Forest of Dean means that it has rainfalls between 32·5 and 37·5 inches and it is only in the west near the Wye that the figure exceeds 40 inches. Partly because of the alignment of the scarp and partly because elevations above 800 feet O.D. are far inland to the northeast of Stroud, most of the Cotswold plateau has a rainfall of only about 32·5 inches and there is only a small area near the steep N–S portion of the scarp to the north of Bath where it exceeds 35 inches.

Everywhere in the Bristol region rainfall is well distributed throughout the year. Near Bristol about 30 per cent of the total falls in the months of autumn from September to November, 26 per cent in winter from December to February, 20 per cent in spring from March to May and 24 per cent in summer. These proportions are fairly typical of the region as a whole but in the northeast where marine influences are a little less marked summer becomes the wettest season and the autumn a little less wet, so that at Tewkesbury 26 per cent of the total falls in autumn, 24 per cent in winter, 21 per cent in spring and 29 per cent in summer. Spring is invariably the driest season but in different localities the driest month may be any from February to June.

Calculations of potential transpiration published by the Ministry of Agriculture, Fisheries and Food show that at average heights for each county the average potential transpiration for the months from April to September would be 17·65 inches in Somerset and 17·55 inches in Gloucestershire. The relationship between these figures and the corresponding rainfall amounts indicates the development of a soil moisture deficit for which average maximum potential values of 2·8 inches in Somerset and 3·0 inches in Gloucestershire have been calculated. These figures are appreciably higher than those of counties on the west coast (Devon 1·5 inches, Cornwall 1·7 inches, Pembrokeshire 1·7 inches,

Glamorgan 0·5 inches, Lancashire 1·5 inches) but they are much lower than those of most eastern and southeastern counties (Kent 6·6 inches, Lincolnshire 5·6 inches). In the lowlands the accumulated deficit tends to reach a value of 2 inches in June and this is maintained until September, but in many upland areas there may be a very small deficit in the months of June and July only. From an agricultural point of view, in most years these deficits are only likely to be of significance on very thin well-drained soils in parts of Mendip and Cotswold where 'burning' does occur, or in one or two localities on some well-drained coarse-textured soils in the lowlands. For the months from October to March the average potential transpiration falls to 2·85 inches in Somerset and 2·75 inches in Gloucestershire so that the soil moisture deficit disappears in October and there is a winter excess of rainfall, the average amounts being 16 inches in Somerset and 12 inches in Gloucestershire. These figures, too, may be contrasted with 25 inches in Devon and Cornwall, 24 inches in Lancashire and 39 inches in Glamorgan or with figures between 4 inches and 9 inches in the eastern counties. In the Bristol region the excess is clearly appreciable so that fair amounts of water percolate through and cause some leaching of the soils.

There is a characteristically high degree of short-term variability in the rainfall of the Bristol region. Where a station normally has between 2·5 and 3·0 inches of rain in every month of the year, months with almost double these values are by no means rare and months with less than 1 inch occur fairly frequently. Moreover, there is a wide range of annual totals since the Bristol district, for example, has had as much as 49 inches and as little as 25 inches in a year, compared with a mean value of 35 inches, but such occurrences are very much rarer and it is distinctly uncommon for annual variations to exceed 20 per cent. Exceptionally heavy rain has been recorded from time to time but this is much more characteristic of Somerset and the Bristol district than of Gloucestershire and north Wiltshire. Totals of between 6 and 9 inches of rain in a day are usually associated with a succession of violent summer storms affecting extremely small areas, but the disastrous floods of the summer of 1968 occurred when several inches of rain fell over large parts of Somerset and the basin of the Bristol Avon in a single night.

Fairly extensive, though seldom really dense, fog does occur between October and March, but it is only at all common in November, December and January, December being the month with most calms and most fogs. However, local valley mist and fogs occur much more frequently, particularly in some of the deeper Cotswold valleys, whilst on all the uplands, but especially on the moors of southwest Somerset, hill fog and mist can occur at any time of the year during the passage of depressions and fronts across the region.

# CHAPTER 5

# *The Prehistoric Occupation*

ALTHOUGH the Bristol region lies outside that area of south central Britain which was the most important part of the country during the prehistoric period, nevertheless recent discoveries have all tended to show that it shared to a considerable extent with the rest of southern Britain a fairly complete history of the development of early human cultures; and this participation can be demonstrated continuously from lower Palaeolithic times right up to the Roman conquest.

Constant chance finds of Palaeoliths still continue to show how incomplete is our knowledge of the full distribution of the earliest human cultures, but the large number of finds in three widely separated localities demonstrate that in all probability groups of lower Palaeolithic men existed throughout the Bristol region during the Pleistocene period. The largest group of lower Palaeolithic implements has been found in the gravels of the Bristol Avon, over 500 of them in the Bristol collection being regarded as comparable with any collection from Britain or northern France. Most of the implements belong to the middle Acheulean period of the Mindel-Riss interglacial and they include advanced examples which show the use of the levallois technique. The richest locality is on the gravel terrace below the Clifton gorge at Shirehampton and across the river round Ham Green, but considerable numbers of Palaeoliths have also been found on the terraces between Bristol and Bath as well as further afield throughout the southwestern part of the Severn basin and along its tributaries. The second group of lower Palaeolithic finds occurs in the extreme south of the Bristol region where the well-known south coast cultures in the valleys of the Otter and the Axe have been traced northwards into the Taunton area of Somerset and more recently to gravel deposits on the coast of west Somerset. Here too the finds are predominantly of middle Acheulean hand-axes. Similarly in the northern part of the region Acheulean objects have also been found at the remarkable prehistoric site of Barnwood, two miles east of Gloucester, in the Cotswold sub-edge deposits of solifluxion material probably of Riss glacial age. At this site the middle Palaeolithic is also represented by implements of Mousterian form, whilst Barnwood has been described as the most important open site of the upper Palaeolithic in England, the numerous Aurignacian artifacts including some of the gravette stage.

It is, however, in the gorges, rock shelters and caves of the Mendip area that the upper Palaeolithic cultures are most elaborately represented in the Bristol region. In the Pleistocene period infilling with solifluxion material suggests conditions in the caves which would have rendered them unsuitable as habitations for lower Palaeolithic man, so that occupation usually commences with upper Palaeolithic cultures, most of which have been regarded as belonginng to the post-glacial period, though some recent work may indicate a late glacial rather than a post-glacial date. Aurignacian blades have been found in the caves at Cheddar, at Wookey Hole near Wells, and at Aveline's Hole and Uphill, whilst strong British Solutrean influences are evident in the hyena den at Wookey, and in Soldier's Hole and Gough's cave at Cheddar. In the later stages of the upper Palaeolithic, corresponding with the French Magdalenean, artifacts of a Creswellian type have been found in considerable numbers in all the occupied Mendip caves, in Chelms Combe, in the Ebbor gorge and in a cliff site at Brean Down near Weston-super-Mare. For the final stages of the upper Palaeolithic cultures the name Cheddarian has been proposed and a dating in the Younger Dryas of the Würm glaciation suggested. It is uncertain whether the *bâton de commandement* from Cheddar and 'harpoons' of a Magdalenean VI type indicate the presence of true Magdalenean cultures.

Some Mesolithic traits have been observed in the final stages of the upper Palaeolithic, and in the Mendip caves, notably Aveline's Hole, as well as at King Arthur's cave at Ross, there is evidence to suggest that the local Mesolithic cultures were in fact epi-Palaeolithic developments from this stage. Such locally derived cultures probably explain scattered finds of Mesolithic implements in the Mendip–Bristol–Bath area, over much of Cotswold and sporadically over Somerset to the south of Mendip. A second epi-Palaeolithic element in the Mesolithic of the Bristol region is identical with and probably derived from the Sauveterrian of France. It includes many of the Mesolithic finds in Gloucestershire and is also represented in the characteristic assemblage of geometrical microliths at the Birdcombe Mesolithic site near Wraxall in Somerset. Evidence of a third Mesolithic component in the form of heavy tranchet implements found at Shapwick and Middlezoy to the south of Mendip has been taken to suggest a possible link by way of the Kennet valley with the Maglemose culture of eastern England, the North Sea basin and the Baltic, whilst finds of large numbers of microliths along the Avon and By brook in the lowland area of west Wiltshire also suggest the possible importance of valley routes in this period.

Though it is now appreciated that Mesolithic influences continued throughout the Neolithic period, their cultural consequences became apparent only in its later stages with the emergence of the secondary cultures produced by contact with the intrusive Neolithic forms which must therefore be described first. For one of these, the Windmill Hill culture, two different continental origins and approach routes have been proposed, one involving movement into Britain from the north coast of France from Brittany eastwards with points of entry along the south coast from Devon eastwards, and the alternative suggesting that the roots of both the Windmill Hill culture and the continental Michelsberg might lie further to the east along with those of the funnel-beaker groups of the Baltic. In either case the outcome was a major concentration of the culture on the chalk uplands to the south of the Thames. Except at Cadbury Camp, pottery evidence does not suggest that the outlying Windmill Hill area in Devon (Hembury) had any important influence on developments in Somerset or Gloucestershire and therefore the main question to be resolved is the extent to which this culture extended westwards beyond the chalk scarp into the Bristol region. The distribution of the causeway camp enclosures affords no evidence of such a westward extension of the Windmill Hill culture despite their concentration on the area of chalk immediately above the scarp, the only possible exception being at Cadbury Camp in the scarp belt of east Somerset, where finds of western Neolithic pottery have led to the suggestion that a Neolithic causeway camp might underlie the Iron Age structures.

On the other hand, the distribution of the long mounds or earthen non-chambered long barrows does indicate that one aspect of the burial practice of the Windmill Hill culture spread westwards, because they are found in the eastern part of Mendip, in the area between Mendip and the Bristol Avon, and on Cotswold immediately to the north of that river. It is perhaps significant that finds of western Neolithic pottery of the Windmill Hill type in the Bristol region are also largely confined to Cotswold and Mendip and the intervening area round the Bristol Avon, and are rare in the vale in Gloucestershire (except on the gravels at Barnwood) and in most of Somerset to the south of Mendip. By the Neolithic period it is likely that the chalk areas of Wiltshire had a relatively light woodland cover well suited to the wheat and pastoral economy of the Windmill Hill culture, and very similar conditions may have existed on Mendip, which has been described as a connecting link between Wessex and the West Country. Between the chalk scarp and Mendip the heavily wooded clay vale narrowed near Frome to form the gap across which the culture may well have reached Mendip, since

Windmill Hill pottery has been found at Sun Hole and Chelms Combe, whereas at Windmill Hill itself pottery of a characteristic Frome type has been discovered. Cotswold with its relatively thicker woodland of beech may have been less attractive to the inhabitants of the chalk country and the area has been described as a kind of halfway-house between lowland and highland Britain where Mesolithic cultures may have lingered on. Even so, the evidence of pottery and the non-chambered long barrows does indicate some limited extension of the Windmill Hill culture to Cotswold, probably across a second narrowing of the clay vale round Lacock and Corsham between the Chalk and Greensand of Swindon, Devizes and Sandy Lane and Cotswold round Chippenham and Bath.

By contrast, the northern part of the Bristol region formed the essential British home of the intrusive early Neolithic Severn–Cotswold culture. Apart from a group near the Medway and a small number in south Dorset, Devon and Cornwall, the chambered long barrows associated with this culture are all distributed around the lower Severn. Within this main area such barrows exist along the South Wales coast and round the Black Mountain, but by far the heaviest concentration is on Cotswold where there are 75 and in north Somerset where there are 15. The continental point of departure for this Neolithic group was probably in western France to the south of Brittany, and the general distribution along the lower Severn might imply an approach by way of the Severn estuary itself. In detail, however, the distribution within the Bristol region with its heavy concentration on Cotswold and in the area between eastern Mendip and the Bristol Avon, especially round Frome, might suggest an alternative approach from the south coast by way of the Wessex chalk, particularly in view of the total absence of such barrows from the western parts of Mendip, from the Carboniferous Limestone hills overlooking the estuary near Clevedon, Portishead and Failand, and from the whole of Gloucestershire to the west of the Cotswold scarp. At all events some contact between the Bristol region and the Wessex chalk country must be inferred from the presence of oolitic material in the stonework of Wiltshire barrows and the presumed use of Wiltshire flint by the Neolithic folk of Cotswold.

The practice of using these megalithic gallery graves seems to have continued for a long period because carbon 14 dates have established their existence by 3000 B.C., but finds associated with them include not only early Neolithic Windmill Hill pottery but also secondary Neolithic and Beaker materials of a much later date. Indeed the idea of assimilation and culture continuity gains considerable support from the evidence on Cotswold, where there is not only some overlap of the distribution of the chambered and non-chambered long barrows, but also a tendency for long barrows and the later round barrows to occupy closely adjacent sites and for considerable admixture of ceramic types to occur. The chambered long barrows commonly occur in pairs and occupy distinctive sites above spring heads or valley heads where it might be inferred that Neolithic trackways approached the streams across Cotswold, though in contrast some individual barrows occupy commanding sites immediately above the scarp itself.

The emergence of the secondary Neolithic cultures in Britain is seen as a consequence of interactions between surviving Mesolithic traits and the intrusive primary Neolithics. The Peterborough culture is thought to represent such a development mainly near river routes in eastern England as a result of Neolithic cultures arriving across the North Sea, and to have spread westwards by way of the Thames valley to Cotswold. Here the physical conditions of the beech woods favoured the redevelopment of a Mesolithic hunting economy which seems to have characterized the secondary Neolithic cultures. The possibility of assimilation of Neolithic traits by a surviving local Mesolithic population has already been mentioned, so that it is not surprising that both the Peterborough and Rinyo-Clacton secondary Neolithic cultures had important concentrations in the Cotswold area.

However, on Cotswold the stage of the secondary Neolithic cultures merely represents part of a continuing settlement story, whereas in Somerset it has additional interest because there is conclusive evidence of such cultures occupying lowland sites not only in the Chew valley and round Mendip but also at Williton and in the Somerset levels round Shapwick Heath. As a result of stratigraphical and pollen studies, more recently combined with carbon 14 dating, Godwin and others have built up a detailed account of the sequence of events in the Somerset levels after 3500 B.C. when a fresh-water fen replaced the saltmarsh. At the end of the Mesolithic period at 3000 B.C. the VIIa–VIIb boundary, marking the change from Atlantic to sub-Boreal conditions, has been identified and shown to be followed at 2800 B.C. by the growth of fen wood, on top of which wooden trackways of Neolithic age were constructed to allow movement over the difficult terrain in times of flood. Four of these have been dated by radiocarbon methods at approximately 2850, 2800, 2500 and 2235 B.C., in confirmation of the pollen evidence. Here in the Somerset levels the VIIa–VIIb boundary is marked by the normal decline in elm pollen, possibly indicating woodland clearance in the surrounding area, and in the ensuing VIIb period pollen of the characteristic agriculture indicating plants is present. At the same time there is a very high hazel count and since hazel poles were used in the Neolithic trackways the possibility exists of deliberate coppicing on the higher ground surrounding the levels or on the Poldens or the 'islands' like Wedmore within the levels. There is also the possibility that the pollen evidence of a sharp decline of Linden at 2000 B.C. indicates a more deliberate development of agriculture in the surrounding area later in the Neolithic period. Apart from secondary Neolithic pottery, finds in the area include two Neolithic bows whose carbon 14 dates are approximately 2665 and 2690 B.C. and a Craig Llwyd polished stone axe of a kind commonly associated with secondary Neolithic cultures. This last, indicating northwestern contacts, may possibly imply a link with Cotswold along which a route of entry has been suggested for the Craig Llwyd axes found in Wessex.

The appearance towards the end of the Neolithic period of B and A type beakers, especially on sites round Mendip and on Cotswold, presumably arose from an approach of beaker folk along two converging routes which led to an overlap of the two forms in much of the Bristol region. B type beakers arrived on the western part of the south coast and may have spread northwards into Somerset, though the close similarities between the beakers found at Brean Down and those of Wessex have been taken to infer a route by way of the Wiltshire chalk and the Frome gap almost identical with that followed by the Windmill Hill culture earlier. B beakers have been found between Mendip and the Bristol Avon but further north only a few have been discovered on Cotswold and exceptionally in the vale of Gloucestershire at the beaker burial site at Barnwood.

On the other hand, the arrival on the east coast of the A type beakers from areas to the north of the Rhine was followed by their westward spread along the chalk ridgeways to Wessex and along the Thames to Cotswold. In the latter area A type beakers are consequently more numerous than the B type from the south, though the total numbers are small and there is nothing to indicate any considerable settlement of beaker folk in the Cotswold region. However, the beakers of South Wales are very similar to the A type beaker of Woodchester (Glos.) and penetration of Cotswold may have led to this extension of beaker movement across the Severn, whilst the large number of stray finds of arrowheads could indicate that the wooded Cotswold acted as a hunting ground for beaker people within an essentially Neolithic province.

A beakers between the Bristol Avon and Mendip and at Corston near Bath link the Cotswold group with those on Mendip but it seems equally likely that the Mendip beakers of this type may again have arrived by way of the Frome gap from the Wiltshire chalk. In the barrows near Tynings Farm on Mendip there was some evidence of B beakers being replaced by the A type, and the excavation of what is probably a single causeway henge monument at Gorsey Bigbury indicates that it was built, possibly during the secondary Neolithic period, by B beaker folk and subsequently occupied for a short period by A beaker folk. A still more extensive overlap of the distribution of the two forms is illustrated by the discovery of both beaker types near the coast far to the southwest at Stogursey, whilst a further movement of A beakers to South Wales by sea from Somerset might be inferred from the similarities between the beakers of west Somerset and Brean Down and those found in South Wales.

The development of the Bronze Age in Britain has been thought to represent the outcome of a continuing process whereby Neolithic influences on the pre-existing Mesolithic population led to the emergence of the secondary Neolithic cultures and these in turn received the stimulus of the beaker and subsequent true Bronze Age immigrant cultures. In consequence it may well have been that the areas heavily settled by the primary Neolithic cultures on the uplands of southern Britain tended to remain significant chiefly as burial places, whereas the lowland areas, certainly used by the Peterborough secondary culture, may have tended to become economically more important. Such a set of circumstances would certainly help to explain anomalous aspects of the Bronze Age distributions of the Bristol region, where the round barrow burials are very heavily concentrated on the uplands whilst the finds of individual artifacts show no such concentration and most of the hoards have been discovered on low ground. Taken together, the two distributions suggest a considerable population but, apart from Mendip caves, no true living sites are known and this anomaly, too, may well be explained by the assumption that in the lowlands they have been obliterated by later land use.

To the north of the Bristol Avon about 350 round barrows are known within the region and, apart from a small group in the Forest of Dean and another on the Carboniferous Limestone hills round Bristol, virtually all of them are on Cotswold. In Somerset, however, there are over 750 round barrows—a number which seems to indicate during the Bronze Age a fairly rapid rise in the importance of the area not fully shared by Gloucestershire. More than 700 of the Somerset barrows are on the uplands, no less than 320 of them on Mendip with its great groupings on Beacon Hill and Blackdown and round Priddy, Charterhouse and Tynings Farm. Barrows along the great arc of scarp country in east Somerset link those of Mendip with the other great concentration on the Quantocks, the Brendon Hills, Exmoor and all the hill country behind the west Somerset coast.

Towards the end of the early Bronze Age there grew up on the chalk country to the east of the Bristol region the elaborate Wessex culture which was responsible for much of the distinction of the Bronze Age in Britain. One of the characteristic features of this culture was the construction of the more specialized forms of round barrow such as the bell and later the disc and saucer barrows. The presence of these types in the Bristol region must imply some continued contact with developments on the chalk downlands. Among the Cotswold barrows there are only one or two such examples, possibly because contact was with the less advanced areas of Wessex to the north of the Vale of Pewsey. A link across the Frome gap between Mendip and the richer Wessex culture of Salisbury plain is also shown by the presence of a small number of bell barrows and one disc barrow on Mendip, but equally strong evidence of the connection is afforded by finds of Wessex type biconical urns in the barrows round Tynings Farm and at Brean Down and of pigmy cups at Camerton, Priddy, East Harptree and Blackdown.

Large numbers of finds of Bronze Age artifacts, not associated with barrows, have been made throughout the region both on the uplands and in low-lying areas, and it is possible to discern a pattern which throws some light on the settlement of the period. Individual finds have been very numerous round the edges of the levels and lowland parts of Somerset, notably at the foot of the hills in the south and southeast of the county and near the ridges and hills which rise as 'islands' within the levels, particularly along the Poldens and at Wedmore and Glastonbury. This, combined with the fact that almost all the Somerset hoards have been found in low-lying areas at such places as Glastonbury, Eddington-on-Polden, Stogursey, Taunton, Compton Martin and West Buckland, leads to the conclusion that in the Bronze Age lowland Somerset must have been quite heavily settled. Such a view appears to be confirmed by the evidence of Bronze Age activity within the levels themselves. In the raised bog which grew above the Neolithic trackways round Shapwick Heath, six Bronze Age wooden trackways have also been found. Pollen analysis and carbon 14 determinations indicate dates between 900 and 500 B.C. for these tracks, which antedate a period of flooding by land-water at about the latter date, presumably the consequence of the onset of the wetter conditions of the sub-Atlantic period. The tracks link the higher ground of the Poldens with the Lias 'islands' to the north towards Wedmore and were probably rendered increasingly necessary by the approach of the innundation at the very end of the late Bronze Age. The date of the trackways is confirmed by the late Bronze Age axe techniques with which their timbers were dressed and by their probable stratigraphical relationship with middle Bronze Age spears and amber beads found in the locality. The pollen analyses of late Bronze Age deposits in the levels show a considerable increase for plants indicative of active cereal cultivation within the lowland areas of Somerset; with this evidence the numbers of sickles found in the Bronze Age hoards accords well.

On Mendip Bronze Age finds, as distinct from the barrows, are more heavily concentrated on the western end of the hills, but in north Somerset the distribution seems closely related to the line of the Bristol Avon. In its lower course and round Bristol two hoards and individual objects have been found in close association with the river valleys, whilst upstream all the hills surrounding Bath have yielded numbers of finds.

In Gloucestershire, as in Somerset, the distribution of Bronze Age objects shows less contrast between uplands and lowlands than was the case in the preceding period when there was little or no evidence of occupation of the vale but, even so, there is nothing to suggest here quite such a rapid growth of agriculture or of population as seems to have occurred in Somerset.

The gold-plated sun disc found at Lansdown near Bath and the gold torque from Yeovil are perhaps the best-known Bronze Age objects from the Bristol region, but others have greater geographical interest in that they throw light on the space relations of the region. For example, the presence in Somerset of three double looped palstaves implies contacts with Spain, whilst an analysis of the very characteristic sickles and other contents of the hoards shows similar contacts with the middle Bronze Age of northern Europe, and numerous finds, especially of flat axes, afford ample evidence of links with Ireland. It is therefore clear that, at least from the Bristol Avon southwards, the region had some share in the widespread culture contacts which are thought to lie at the root of the elaborate Bronze Age developments in Wessex. Closer at hand to the west there is equally clear evidence of connections with South Wales. Indeed there now seems to be some consensus of opinion that the connecting route between Stonehenge and the source of the Prescelly blue stones in Pembrokeshire lay through the Bristol region, though it remains in doubt whether the route followed the Bristol Avon or a Mendip trackway.

In the succeeding Iron Age the historical geography of the Bristol region continues to show the effects of its distinctive position in relation to the rest of southern Britain and this is well illustrated by reference to the provinces and regions into which Hawkes[1] has proposed to divide the country for a study of this period. The Bristol region lies at the junction of his southern, western and southwestern provinces. It comprises the western end of the 6th (Upper Thames) and the 12th, 13th and 14th (North, Mid-and South Wessex) regions of the southern

[1] Hawkes, C. F. C., 'The A.B.C. of the British Iron Age', in *Antiquity* Vol. 33, 1959 pp. 170–82.

province, much of the 18th and 19th (Exmoor/Quantock and Mid-Somerset) regions of the southwestern province, and the whole of the 20th (East Somerset) and part of the 21st (Wye/Cotswold) regions of the western province. From this it might be deduced, in anticipation of what follows, that an interesting admixture of cultures would result from the convergence of movements made through the three provinces from southern Britain, from the southwest peninsula and possibly from the west by way of the Severn estuary.

In the first period of the Iron Age between 550 and 350 B.C. the Iron First A culture (Hallstatt I and II, La Tène I a, b) occupied the greater part of the southern province and consequently approached the Bristol region along its eastern side, one of its type stations being close at hand at All Cannings Cross in the Vale of Pewsey. The First A culture of Cotswold and Mendip is thus regarded by Hawkes as a westward extension from his southern province, presumably once again by way of the Lacock/Corsham and Frome gap routes and unconnected with the Western First A of north Wales and the Southwestern First A of Devon and Cornwall.

In Cotswold finds of Iron Age A pottery are fairly numerous and on Cleeve Hill near Cheltenham, at Salmonsbury near Bourton-on-the-Water and near the hill-fort at Leckhampton these may indicate actual settlement sites. A number of small hill-forts round the upper Thames may well represent an early occupation of the dipslope of Cotswold and an initial Iron Age A stage of the hill-fort itself at Leckhampton and of the camp on the Oxenton outlier implies that the westward spread reached the scarp. In the extreme south overlooking the valley of the Avon the hill-fort of Little Solsbury near Bath was constructed by Iron First A folk, and occupation of the course of the river downstream seems probable in view of the existence of a late Iron Age A hill-fort on Kings Weston Down about two miles from Avonmouth.

The Iron First A culture appears to have spread into Somerset earlier and more extensively than into Gloucestershire and there is even a possibility that in the uplands in the east the culture which is represented in the first stages of the hill-fort of Cadbury Castle may have antedated the first occupation of the type site at All Cannings Cross in Wiltshire. The greatest density of Iron Age A sites, however, is the district immediately west of the Frome gap in eastern Mendip and round the Chew and Avon valleys. Here finds of pottery have been sufficiently numerous to permit of a classification into early forms found at Pagan's Hill, Burledge Camp, Chew Park Farm and Stanton Wick in the Chew valley, at Freshford on the Avon and in several of the Mendip caves, a middle group found at Little Solsbury, and a late type again found in the Chew valley and at Camerton near Radstock. Further north Iron Age A pottery was found at Maes Knoll on the Dundry outlier, whilst at Brean Down at the western limit of the uplands a local variant of the All Cannings Cross A has been identified.

In the Bristol region the later part of the second period of the Iron Age between 350 and 150 B.C. is characterized by the development of the Second B cultures in their southern, western and southwestern forms. These represent the outcome of the stimulus of Iron First B on the pre-existing First A cultures and therefore involve no obviously new intrusive elements here. Occupation sites at Gloucester, Hucclecote and Eastington and the hill-forts at Salmonbury, Meon Hill and Bury Hill at Winterbourne are demonstrably associated with these evolving Iron B cultures, but there are grounds for supposing that virtually the whole of Gloucestershire and Somerset gradually developed an Iron Second B culture. By this time there is evidence of a spread of the Iron Age beyond the Severn into the Forest of Dean and as far afield as Lydney, whilst to the south of Mendip it seems likely that a Southwestern Second B preceded the emergence of the Southwestern Third B of the lake villages, though throughout the region Iron Age A cultures probably lingered and no clear-cut division between them is possible. Linear ornamented pottery is a characteristic feature of the Second B in both the southern and western provinces and its slow evolution and spread is shown by a possible ancestral form in Iron Age A contexts at Little Solsbury and by its long survival at the hill-fort on Bredon.

Whatever may have been the degree of cultural uniformity achieved by the end of the second period of the Iron Age, however, this was soon disrupted in the third period by the appearance of the Third B cultures of the west and southwest. Of these the Western Third B is thought to be completely intrusive and to be the product of a sea-borne approach by way of the Bristol Channel to the lower Severn and the Wye. Associated with this culture is stamped pottery often including the so-called duck pattern which probably indicates its origin in the northwestern parts of the Iberian peninsula. In Gloucestershire the distribution of finds shows a spread up the Severn tributaries as far as the Cotswold scarp, in the central portion of which there is a minor concentration of the culture, whilst further north one of the few known occupation sites is on the Bredon outlier. Movement up the Wye and the Severn led to a second concentration outside our area in Herefordshire and Worcestershire, from which it may be inferred, however, that Gloucestershire to the west of the Severn was also occupied, possibly as a result of a search for iron in the Forest of Dean. This Western Third B culture was probably short-lived on Cotswold because it is thought to have been replaced within about sixty years by the Belgic Western Third C culture, but it probably survived longer to the west of the Severn and in any case its main interest lies in the evidence it affords of the importance of the western seaway and the Severn in late prehistoric times.

The Southwestern Third B culture, best known from the excavations of the lake villages at Glastonbury and Meare, had a greater inherent importance. No continental counterpart is known to exist and it is thought to have evolved in southwest Britain from the pre-existing Second B cultures as a result of trading contacts with Brittany which led to the introduction of most of the culture traits of the continental La Tène III. The extent of the area influenced by this 'Glastonbury' culture is best indicated by finds of the very distinctive moulded and incised curvilinear decorated pottery, which is found commonly in the lowland areas of Somerset at the lake villages themselves and at Brent Knoll, Cannington Park, Combwich and Somerton. Finds of Glastonbury pottery in the Ham Hill and Cadbury Castle hill-forts show at least some contact with the scarp lands of east Somerset, and numerous examples from Burrington, Cheddar, Dolebury, Wookey, Worlebury and Mells prove an occupation of the Mendip area which was formerly regarded as the northern limit of the culture. Later evidence, however, showed that the influence of the Southwestern Third B culture may have spread further afield. To the north the pottery has been found in the hill-fort across the Bristol Avon at Blaise Castle, and at Little Solsbury near Bath the defences of the Iron Age A hill-fort were destroyed at about 150 B.C. and the site occupied by Southwestern Third B folk. Further north, Glastonbury ware has also been found at Bury Hill, Winterbourne, whilst at Barnwood some connection with this culture has been suggested. In particular, occupation of the Little Solsbury hill-fort brought the 'Glastonbury' folk onto the southern part of the Jurassic routeway, which in the Iron Age and possibly earlier marked a line of movement from central Somerset and Mendip by way of Bath and the upper part of the Cotswold dipslope past Old Sodbury, Rodmarton and west of Cirencester to Birdlip, Andoversford, Stow and Banbury and on to the English Midlands. The extent to which this Southwestern Iron Age B culture affected developments in the Midlands is by no means certain but the presence of Glastonbury type iron currency bars and fine metal work along the Jurassic belt proves at least that some influence extended along this route throughout the northern part of the Bristol region and probably beyond.

A good deal is known about the economy of this culture from the excavations at Glastonbury and Meare and from pollen studies in the levels. In the Shapwick area the flooding towards the end of the Bronze Age at about 500 B.C. was followed by further growth of pale unhumified peat in the raised bog under materially wetter conditions, which culminated in a further inundation in the last years B.C. Finds of a brooch at Shapwick, an Iron Age scabbard and a boat illustrate the Iron Age occupation of the area between the two flood periods, during which the growth of wet peat explains the necessity for the boats and for the nearby villages at Meare and Glastonbury to be constructed in the form of crannogs floated on horizontally laid timbers. From the peat growing immediately before the second flooding, the pollen evidence points to a maximum development of prehistoric agriculture in the area, both of arable and pasture, whilst Meare and Glastonbury were occupied. The actual finds of grain and grain casts in the excavation of these sites confirms the growth of wheat, two forms of barley and some oats, in addition to beans which seem to have been a Somerset speciality. The wider extent of such arable activity is demonstrated by the finds of wheat, barley and beans at Worlebury hill-fort near Weston-super-Mare and of wheat at Little Solsbury. Evidence of field systems are not so readily apparent as on the chalk country of Wessex, but traces of such enclosures on Bathampton Down near to Little Solsbury and at West Littleton on Cotswold may belong to this period, as may a number on Mendip and on the limestones round the lower Bristol Avon at Wraxall, Failand and Ashton Court. The fact that nearly 90 per cent of the animal bones found at Glastonbury were of sheep is regarded by Clark and others as proving the existence of what was virtually a sheep-rearing economy, probably on Mendip and the Poldens, though the sheep concerned could also have been kept in the levels themselves. Based on wool from this source a textile industry apparently grew up in the lake villages and it is significant that quite elaborate textile equipment, including distinctive combs, is a characteristic feature of the culture. The considerable use of fishing has a double interest since the making of lead line-sinkers has been taken to show that the Iron Age folk had started to work the Mendip lead. Iron for their often beautiful metal work probably came from the neighbourhood of Westbury in Wiltshire or from the Forest of Dean, whilst the material for the bronzes must have come from much farther afield.

So many of the Iron Age hill-forts of the Bristol region either are unexcavated or were excavated before modern classifications of Iron Age cultures were available that it is impossible to describe them fully in terms of such a classification. In their geographical distribution they fall into three main groups associated with Cotswold, Mendip and the uplands of central and southern Somerset, easily the largest being that of Cotswold.

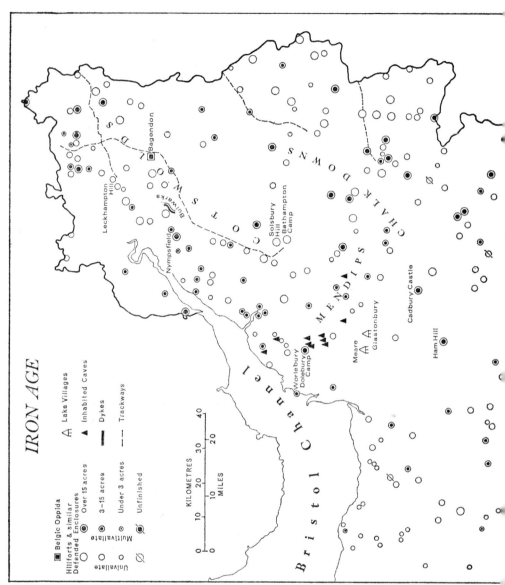

IRON AGE

Belgic Oppida ■

Hillforts & similar
Defended Enclosures
Over 15 acres ◉
3-15 acres ◉
Under 3 acres ◉
Unfinished ⌀

Multivallate
Univallate

Lake Villages ⌂
Inhabited Caves ▲
Dykes ▮
Trackways - - -

KILOMETRES 0 10 20 30 40
MILES 0 10 20

Bagendon

Leckhampton Hill
Bulwarks
Nympsfield

COTSWOLDS

CHALK DOWNS

Solsbury Hill
Bathampton Camp

MENDIPS

Worlebury
Dolebury Camp
Meare
Glastonbury
Cadbury Castle
Ham Hill

Bristol Channel

Crown Copyright Rese

From Meon Hill in the north to Solsbury Hill and Bathampton Camp overlooking the Bristol Avon, no less than 31[1] hill-forts are strung out along the 50 miles of the crest of the Cotswold scarp. All of these either use the scarp face as part of their defences or are on eminences near it, but in addition the Cotswold group includes others away from the line of the scarp. On the dipslope and concentrated round the head-waters of the Thames and its tributaries there are 16[2] such camps, many of them of comparatively small size. Of the total of nearly 50 hill-forts actually on Cotswold in Gloucestershire, only 14 are multivallate and the majority are small. From this and from their location an early date might be anticipated for many of them, possibly as early as the first period of the Iron Age when the approach to Cotswold was up the dipslope, though this has been demonstrated by excavation only in a limited number of cases. It is also possible that future excavation will show that the replacement of an Iron Age A culture by that of Iron Age B, as at Little Solsbury, Oxenton and Leckhampton, occurred widely in other parts of Cotswold. Possibly connected with an extension of the Iron Age occupation of Cotswold, but equally likely to have been connected with the Severn and Wye approach of the Western Second B culture, a number of hill-forts lie to the west of the scarp. These include the camps on the outliers in the north at Bredon and Oxenton and across the Severn in the Forest of Dean at Westbury, Lydney and Symonds Yat. Further south on the higher ground which crosses the vale towards Aust round the northern and northwestern end of the Bristol coalfield, a group of 7 camps, Burn Hill, Knole Park, Bloody Acre, Camp Hill, The Castle and Abbey Camp at Thornbury, almost reaches the Severn at the Toots near Oldbury.

From Worlebury at the seaward end of the limestones the Mendip group extends along the northern flank of the hills through Banwell, Dinghurst, Dolebury, Burrington, Blackers Hill, Wadbury and Tedbury, with only Maesbury Castle on the central area and Westbury Camp on the southern flank, a distribution which implies defence against possible attacks from the valleys to the north, for which the Dinghurst and Dolebury Camps, commanding the gap at Churchill, and the small camp at Burrington above the approach to the Combe, would be specially valuable. In the hilly country between eastern Mendip and the southern

---

[1] Meon Hill, Willersley Hill, Toddington Camp, Beckbury Camp, Upper Coscombe, Langley Hill, Diston Hill, The Knolls, Nottingham Hill, Cleeve Cloud, Battledown Camp, Leckhampton Hill, Crickley Hill, Norbury Camp, Birdlip Camp, High Rotheridge, Kimsbury, Haresfield Beacon, Randwick Wood, Nympsfield, Uley Bury, Brackenbury Ditches, Hawkesbury Knoll, Horton Camp, Old Sodbury Camp, Dyrrham Camp, Bury Camp, Royal Camp, Little Down Camp, Solsbury Hill, Bathampton Camp.

[2] The Brum, Idbury Camp, Ilbury, Norbury Camp, The Roundabout, Windrush Camp, Dean Camp, Ranbury Ring, Juniper Hill, Pinbury, Green Ditches, Trewsbury, Bury Hill, Salmonsbury, Chastleton, Eubury.

end of Cotswold at Bath, Stantonbury Camp, Tunley Camp, the fort on Burledge Hill and Maes Knoll, a little to the west on Dundry Hill appear to link the two main groups.

A smaller group lies to the north of Mendip on the Carboniferous Limestone hills extending from Broadfield Down to the Failand ridge and the downs to the west of Bristol. Here there seems some possibility that the hill-forts were sited mainly to control movement up the valleys from the Severn. The camp on Cadbury Hill at Congresbury overlooks the river Yeo, whilst Cleeve Toot and two small forts near Brockley could control routes up Goblin Combe and Brockley Combe onto Broadfield Down. To the north the Wains Hill Camp at Clevedon lies above the mouth of the Land Yeo and Cadbury Camp on Tickenham Hill above its middle course. On the Bristol Avon the 3 camps of Stokeleigh, Burgh Walls and Clifton have fine sites above the gorge section at a possible crossing point, whilst its right bank tributary the Hen is similarly straddled by the 3 camps of Kings Weston Down, Blaise Castle and Combe Hill.

To the south of Mendip the Small Down Camp appears as a link with the third main group of hill-forts on the great semicircle of hills surrounding the Somerset lowlands on the east and south. This group is continued southwards by Creech Hill Camp to the famous Cadbury Castle and then by Milborne Wick Camp, turning westwards to Ham Hill and Castle Neroche, with Ruborough Camp and Downsborough Camp on the Quantocks completing the series. It has been suggested that in the extreme south and west of Somerset the typology of some of the multivallate hill-forts links them with those of the southwest peninsula where the ramparts are normally widely spaced. On the other hand, the multivallate forts of Ham Hill, Cadbury Castle and north Somerset have close-set ramparts like those of the hill-forts of the Wessex chalk country. It is usual to regard the latter type as having evolved by the multiplication of original univallate defences to meet an increasing need for security. The southwestern type often seems to have originated in its multivallate form and two possible explanations for this have been proposed. The first regards this type, with its wide spaces within the outer earthworks, as an insular development to meet the needs of the southwestern areas with their predominantly pastoral economy. Alternatively they may have been introduced from the continent and a possible source has been suggested in the northwestern part of the Iberian peninsula where generally similar forts occur. In this case it is of some interest to notice that the same region may be the home of the intrusive Western Second B culture with its duck-stamped pottery, and it may be significant that at an outlying example of this kind of fort in the north at Bredon the duck pottery has also been discovered.

In Devon and Cornwall southwestern and western forms of the Third B cultures (with duck-stamped pottery and curvilinear Glastonbury ware) lasted throughout the first century B.C. and right up to the Roman conquest. It seems possible that this situation may have applied too in the southwestern parts of the Bristol region beyond the Parrett and conceivably even as far north as Mendip. However, culture boundaries were not necessarily coincident with political ones and there is no certainty that the territory of the Iron Age B Dumnonii of the southwest peninsula extended north to Mendip as would be implied by the identification of a site at the mouth of the Somerset Axe as the Uxella which, according to Ptolemy, lay in their lands.

In any case, over a major part of the Bristol region the history of the later Iron Age was dominated by the spread of Belgic Iron Age C cultures into areas which later became the territories of the Dobunni, the Durotriges and the peoples between them for whom the Romans kept the name Belgae. In the case of the Durotriges this territory was mainly outside the Bristol region since it was very nearly coincident with the county of Dorset, but the evidence of coins and pottery at the hill-forts of Cadbury Castle and Ham Hill could indicate Durotrigan influence spreading northwestwards to the edge of the hill country of southeast Somerset. Coins and pottery of the Durotriges also occur sporadically on Mendip so that a boundary between them and the Dobunni of Cotswold might well have run across north Somerset into Wiltshire. Evidence from the hill-forts of northern France and the coin hoard of Le Catillon in Jersey, combined with that of Maiden Castle, which acted virtually as the capital of the Durotriges, is now regarded as showing a replacement of Iron Age A cultures at Maiden Castle by those of Iron Age B between 150 and 100 B.C. This in turn was replaced by a Belgic Iron Age C culture, presumably from Sussex and Hampshire at least as early as 50 B.C. However, before the latter date Glastonbury ware is found at Maiden Castle, pointing to some degree of contact at least with areas outside the Durotrigan sphere and showing that no hard and fast lines of demarcation should be imagined between cultural and embryonic political regions at this time.

The growth of the most important tribal group in the Bristol region, the Dobunni, involves the general history of the Belgic peoples in Britain. From south coast landings the groups of Atrebates who came under the rule of Commius eventually occupied a belt of territory from Sussex to the middle Thames and it was the westward spread of associated groups which brought Belgic Third C cultures to the chalk country of Wiltshire. Other groups of Belgic people, not under Atrebatic rule and therefore not having Atrebatic coins, were also moving westwards through Wiltshire at the same time and they may have been the origin of the later Belgae of north Somerset and Wiltshire. From Wiltshire the Belgic groups apparently moved across the clay vale by way of Lacock and Corsham into the south Cotswold area between Stroud and the Bristol Avon, where coins first appear which are attributable to the Belgic Dobunni, a people with a culture presumably the product of Belgic influence on the pre-existing Western Second B of the Cotswold dipslope.

From this base the power of the Belgic Dobunni certainly spread over the rest of the Cotswold dipslope in Gloucestershire, where they established the oppidum at Bagendon near Cirencester. At the same time they continued their westward movement to displace the Western Third B folk from the scarp and the outliers as far afield as Bredon, where a massacre round the hill-fort may have been a consequence of this advance. Possibly before A.D. 25, therefore, all of Gloucestershire to the east of the Severn was under the control of the Dobunni and the oppidum at Bagendon was becoming an important tribal capital.

To the south the Dobunni extended their power across the Bristol Avon into the area between Bath and eastern Mendip, where the sites at Freshford, Camerton and Kingsdown Camp near Mells have all yielded Dobunnic coins and pottery very similar to that at Bagendon. It seems likely that the spread of Iron Age Third C cultures into northeast Somerset may be entirely attributable to this movement southwards of the Dobunni from Cotswold, though the possibility of a spread of the Belgae to this area by way of the Frome gap from Wiltshire must not be overlooked. From whatever source they arrived the Iron Age C folk then seem to have moved westwards along Mendip to reach the Severn near Weston-super-Mare, where a massacre at Worlebury is usually regarded as dating to their conquest of the hill-fort.

In the meantime the Catuvellauni, from the first Belgic landings in southeastern Britain, had spread northwestwards across the Thames, whilst the Dobunni, moving eastwards had obtained control over neighbouring Belgic groups in Oxfordshire so that eventually a common boundary was established between them along the line of the Cherwell. To the north and northwest the Dobunni appear to have extended their territories into the Forest of Dean and the nearby areas of Herefordshire and Worcestershire, presumably after forcibly taking control of the forts beyond the Cotswold scarp. Between A.D. 10 and 40, therefore, the Dobunni came to hold lands extending from Herefordshire on the north and from Oxfordshire to the Severn and southwestwards to Mendip. They were therefore powerful neighbours of the Catuvellauni under Cunobelin, but the two tribal groups appear to have existed on relatively good terms, to judge from the evidence found at Bagendon of massive imports of pottery from the Catuvellaunian territories.

At Bagendon there is evidence, too, of Iron Age agricultural achieve-

ments on Cotswold which can be compared with that which the Glastonbury and Meare excavations revealed in Somerset. Typical Belgic grain
jars indicate arable activity, and cattle and pigs were kept, but in
particular the very large number of sheep bones implies a considerable
rearing industry and it has been pointed out that the maturity of many of
the animals might indicate that year-round grazing was possible. The
wealth and importance of the Dobunni, however, must have depended
to a large extent also on their access to metals. Sources of iron from the
Forest of Dean and lead from Mendip may well have been under their
own control, whilst they were admirably placed for the trade in Welsh
copper, Cornish tin and Irish gold. In consequence metal work of the
highest order was carried out in Bagendon itself in the production of
elaborate brooches, in such sophisticated techniques as plating and in the
work of the Bagendon mint.

After A.D. 40 the evidence of two distinct coinages, that of Boduoc on
Cotswold and that of Corio in parts of south Gloucestershire and north
and northeast Somerset, may have arisen from a political division
within the extensive lands of the Dobunni. Uneasy tribal alignments on
the eve of the Roman conquest might lie behind such a split, but in any
case the possibility is of considerable interest in the light of later terri-
torial arrangements when the Romans attached the southern area not to
the Dobunni but to the confederation of the Belgae based on their capital
at Winchester.

This last arrangement, however, lay in the future, and immediately
before the conquest a political map of the Bristol region would still
have shown the area as far south as Mendip in the hands of the Dobunni,
whilst the southern and southeastern parts of the region lay in the sphere
of the Dumnonii and the Durotriges. However, it is obvious that the
boundaries are ill-defined and the distribution of culture traits seldom
coincides with tribal areas. Indeed the overlap of currency bars, coins
and the pottery of Glastonbury and Bagendon is so frequent and extensive
that some kind of loose confederation between the three tribes has been
suggested. This would help to explain, for example, the apparently
important Dobunnic trade through Durotrigan territory to the port at
Hengistbury Head and the distribution of currency bars with its marked
concentrations both in the north from Cotswold to the Malvern Hills and
in the south Somerset–Dorset area.

Through much of the prehistoric period, therefore, it is the position
of the Bristol region which is the predominant influence on its culture
associations. Lying round the western margins of the chalk country and
the upper Thames basin, its upland areas to some extent shared with
more important centres to the east such cultures as the Neolithic of
Windmill Hill, the Wessex culture of the Bronze Age and the Southern

123

E

First A of the Iron Age. Alternatively the Bristol region can be regarded as a wide coastal belt along the English side of the Severn estuary and certainly from Mendip northwards it shared fully such cultures of the Bristol Channel and the Severn basin as that associated with the Severn–Cotswold long barrows or with the duck-stamped pottery of the Iron Age. And finally from the south the Bristol region received influences from the Dorset coast and the southwest peninsula which may have been important on the eve of the Bronze Age but which reached a culmination when the Southwestern Third B culture spread northwards during the Iron Age, leading to the development in Somerset of the very important Glastonbury culture.

The convergence of these three streams of culture influences was responsible for the considerable complexity of the prehistoric period in the Bristol region. Different orientation with respect to them was also responsible for the significant contrasts which developed within the region to the north and south of the Mendip–Bristol Avon area, notably during the Bronze Age and on the eve of the Roman conquest.

# CHAPTER 6

# *The Roman Occupation*

THE rapidity with which the Roman conquest brought lowland Britain under control is well demonstrated by the fact that much of the Bristol region on its western fringe, was occupied quite soon after the landings of A.D. 43. In the north the Kingsholm site at Gloucester is thought to have been established in 49, in the centre the Romans had certainly taken over the working of the Mendip lead mines by the same date, whilst in the south there is good evidence of occupation of the site of Ilchester (Lindinis) in the middle of the first century.

There is both literary and archaeological evidence of the nature of the Roman advance into the south of the region where, according to Suetonius, the second Augusta legion under Vespasian conquered two important tribal groups, presumably the Belgae and the Durotriges, in their drive towards the southwest. The archaeological evidence from the hill-forts at Maiden Castle and Hod Hill bears out the story of forcible conquest, and if the defeat of the Durotriges and Belgae was complete it would imply early Roman control of at least the eastern margins of the Bristol region as far north as Bath, thereby giving access to Mendip and allowing the early start of Roman lead mining.

Less certainty attaches to the literary evidence of the more northerly Roman advance into Cotswold and the Vale of Severn, since it hinges on a long-disputed interpretation of the account of early moves by Ostorius Scapula against the Silures. However, archaeological evidence from the Kingsholm site in the northern part of Gloucester now shows with reasonable certainty that this was the base established in 49 for the second legion's advance across the Severn against the Silures. Before this could be undertaken Cotswold must presumably have been brought under effective control, one aspect of which may well have been the replacement of the oppidum of the Dobunni at Bagendon by the creation nearby of Cirencester (Corinium), for which a date between 43 and 47 has been suggested. The actual advance into Cotswold may therefore have taken place as part of the initial Roman reduction of southern Britain, and it has even been suggested that earthworks like The Bulwark near the scarp at Minchinhampton could mark the line of a temporary boundary of the Silures under Caratacus, maintained by a ford across the Severn at the Arlingham bend until a Roman campaign from the Berkshire ridgeway, possibly marked by small unexcavated earthworks on the dipslope, and the outflanking move to the Kingsholm site led to their final withdrawal across the river.

It is therefore reasonably certain that by the middle of the first century the military phase of the occupation of the Bristol region was virtually over and the rapid return to peaceful conditions explains the almost complete absence of Roman military structures found in the area, apart from the temporary legionary fort at Kingsholm, Gloucester. The importance of this site, however, and of the Severn crossing after the second legion was moved forward to reach Caerleon by 75, explains the early construction of the Ermine Way from Silchester (Calleva) to Cirencester (Corinium) and on to the north side of Gloucester (Glevum). At Cirencester the Ermine Way crosses the line of the Fosseway, but the detailed lay-out of the Roman roads converging on the town has been taken as affording evidence that the Silchester–Gloucester road ante-dated the construction of the Fosseway. This has great relevance to one of the most difficult problems associated with the pattern of Roman roads in Britain. The fact that the Fosseway from Exeter or Lyme Bay through Ilchester, Bath, Cirencester and Leicester to Lincoln is so remarkably straight, but is apparently unrelated to any of the major lines of advance or supply of the Roman armies, led Collingwood to suggest that it was constructed, possibly as one operation, to act as a supply road along the line of a temporary boundary marking the limit of Roman penetration at a probable date of about 47. Since this line approximates in a very general way to the limit of lowland Britain, it is geographically an attractive hypothesis, but there is no example elsewhere of the construction of frontier roads at such an early date. At this time natural features were more commonly used and recent supporters of this inter-pretation of the Fosseway have suggested that the real limit of the Roman advance may have been the Severn and the Trent, with the Fosseway acting as part of a system of defence in depth. To help prove such a theory it would be useful to discover evidence of fortifications in the zone in advance of the Fosseway and between it and the Severn, but the results of excavations have been inconclusive and sections cut into the southern part of the Fosseway itself, with the possible exception of one near Camerton, have failed to prove definitely its early date. On the other hand, if the interpretation of the road pattern at Cirencester is correct, before the Fosseway was built the threat of the Silures to the Cotswold area had been largely controlled by the establishment of the legionary fortress at Kingsholm and the building of the Ermine Way, so that the

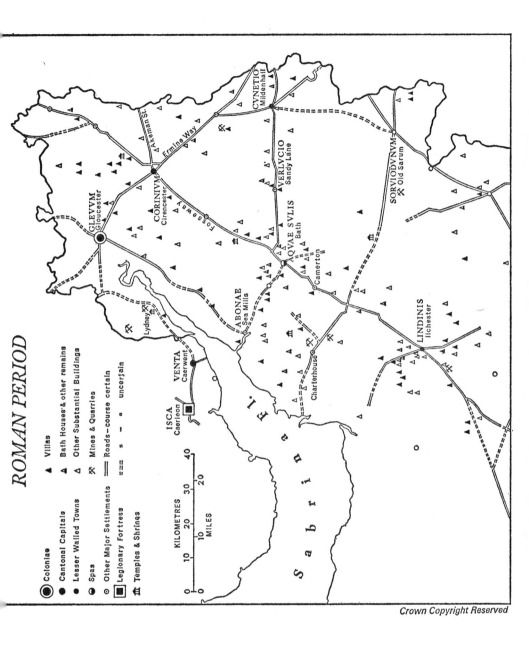

# ROMAN PERIOD

**Legend:**

- ◉ Coloniae
- ● Cantonal Capitals
- ● Lesser Walled Towns
- ◐ Spas
- ◎ Other Major Settlements
- ▣ Legionary Fortress
- ⚹ Temples & Shrines
- ▲ Villas
- ◮ Bath Houses & other remains
- △ Other Substantial Buildings
- ✕ Mines & Quarries
- ═══ Roads—course certain
- ═ ═ ═ uncertain

KILOMETRES 0 10 20 30 40
MILES 0 10 20

**Labels on map:**

- CVNETIO Mildenhall
- GLEVVM Gloucester
- CORINIVM Cirencester
- VERLVCIO Sandy Lane
- AQVAE SVLIS Bath
- SORVIODVNVM Old Sarum
- Camerton
- ABONAE Sea Mills
- LINDINIS Ilchester
- Charterhouse
- Lydney
- VENTA Caerwent
- ISCA Caerleon
- Akeman St.
- Ermine Way
- Fosse Way
- S a b r i n a  F l.

Crown Copyright Reserved

need no longer existed for a frontier road. The Cirencester evidence, however, does suggest that the second road to be built in that district was the part of the Fosseway which continues to the northeast past Leicester to Lincoln, through country in which there is little other evidence of Roman activity, and in this section it may well have acted as a transverse supply road near the Roman boundary. Again, if the sequence of events at Cirencester is correctly determined, the town was next connected by Akeman Street with St Albans (Verulamium) and Colchester (Camulodunum) and, since the name Akeman Street was also used to describe the part of the Fosseway south of Cirencester, this could be regarded as an extension southwestwards to link up with existing Roman centres at Bath, Camerton and Ilchester. On such an interpretation the remarkable overall straightness of the Fosseway would be largely accidental at least in the southern part and indeed the post-Roman use of the name Fosseway for the whole of its length incorrect.

To interpret the southern part of the Fosseway as a road link between early centres of Roman occupation also provides a basis for understanding the framework of other main roads in the region, since they too connect these centres with the road system of the rest of southern Britain. A second road leaves the strategic Silchester–Gloucester Ermine Way about twenty miles northwest of Silchester and follows a more southerly course to Mildenhall and the presumed site of Verlucio at Sandy Lane, to be crossed by the Fosseway at Bath. Like the Ermine Way the southern branch also continued beyond the line of the Fosseway through Bitton and the urban area of Bristol to Sea Mills on the Avon, two miles upstream from Avonmouth. The Roman site at Sea Mills is now recognized as that of Abona and is thought to have been occupied at about A.D. 50. Abona was a ferry terminal for the crossing of the Severn to supply and support troops moved forward from Gloucester towards Caerleon and it has been suggested that the Roman occupation of the nearby Blaise Castle hill site involved the provision of a signal station visible across the estuary. There seems, therefore, to have been a considerable similarity of function between the Ermine Way and the southern road to Sea Mills and it is possible that both preceded the construction of the Fosseway from Cirencester to Bath.

The third road from central southern Britain ran westwards from the focus of roads at Old Sarum, past Maiden Bradley and across the Frome gap, to intersect with the Fosseway on Beacon Hill and then continue along the Mendip summits to the lead-mining centre of Charterhouse and possibly from there along western Mendip to reach the sea at Uphill south of Weston-super-Mare. There is no real evidence of a Roman port at Uphill and indeed the continuation of this road to the west of Charterhouse is based less on actual identification than on probability, suggested by the location of the Roman site at Brean Down and of the villas at Star and near Banwell. It is difficult to escape the conclusion that the primary function of this road was to give access to the lead-mining area at Charterhouse, and early Roman control of the mines implies that this road too was in use at an early date.

In south Somerset the last connection with the road system of the rest of southern Britain was made by the road from Dorchester to Ilchester. Again a road on a very similar alignment extends beyond the line of the Fosseway northwestwards to the Poldens and probably continued along the crest of the hills to reach Puriton, where Roman buildings have been found near the Parrett.

In addition to the four roads which extended beyond the Fosseway from the east and south, there were also a number of connecting and branch roads to the west of it. Of these the longest and possibly the most important was that which connected Sea Mills and Gloucester along the Kings Weston and Almondsbury ridges and through the Vale of Berkeley. The possible military significance of such a link between two bases concerned with the advance against the Silures is obvious, but in addition civil use of the road is suggested by the situation near it of the villas at Kings Weston and near Tockington and Cromhall. On Cotswold no Roman-built roads are known to exist to the west of the Fosseway apart from the continuation of the Ermine Way from Cirencester to Gloucester, but it seems possible that pre-Roman trackways may have continued in use and Margary suggests that two of these may have functioned as Roman roads. The first followed the line of the prehistoric Jurassic way near the Cotswold scarp from Bath almost to Cirencester, with a branch descending the scarp near Nympsfield towards the Severn crossing at the Arlingham bend, and the second led northwards from Cirencester past a considerable group of villas along the line of the White Way and the Salt Way towards the scarp at Winchcombe.

In Somerset a short road descended the northern slopes of Mendip from the lead-mining area towards the groups of villas in the valleys of the Chew and Yeo, whilst to the south of Mendip it has been suggested that a road from the Polden Hills may have crossed the levels by a causeway at Street to Glastonbury and continued from there to link up with the Mendip roads. It has also been suggested that evidence of considerable settlement along the left bank of the Avon from Bath to Bristol implies that some kind of road existed, and similar arguments have been advanced for the existence of a road from Sea Mills across the Avon towards the Frome area, with a branch to the Roman site at Gatcombe near Long Ashton.

It is evident, therefore, that the Roman road system of the Bristol region had three focal points, the most important apparently at

Cirencester and the other two at Bath and Ilchester. Although strategic considerations obviously affected the construction of roads through Cirencester and Bath, the continued importance of all three centres after the phase of military occupation emphasizes their civil importance and in the case of two of them their role in the pattern of cantons. The exact boundaries of these tribal areas in the Roman period are no more clearly known than in the prehistoric period, but it is reasonably certain that the lands of the Durotriges extended into south Somerset from Dorset where the 'capital' at Dorchester was the successor to their hill-fort stronghold of Maiden Castle. In south Somerset it appears that a similar pattern emerged, with Ilchester succeeding the Ham Hill and Cadbury Castle forts as the main centre of the Durotriges in this area. Excavations at Ilchester have shown that Roman occupation of a small hut settlement near the crossing of the Yeo, where the ground rises slightly to the southeast of the levels, certainly dates to A.D. 55. By the end of the first century this small village had been cleared, to be replaced by a well laid-out Romanized settlement, which remained as an important open town until in the late fourth century walls were constructed, within which town life continued into the early fifth century. There is a good deal of evidence, especially from the distribution of villas, that this south-eastern corner of Somerset became a remarkably rich agricultural area in the Roman period, with increasing emphasis on pastoral as well as arable activity, and it has been suggested that its economic importance may well have outstripped that of the Durotrigan lands to the east, so that Ilchester (Lindinis) came to act as a second 'capital' with an importance at least equal to that of Dorchester itself.

It is possible that the canton of the Belgae was in part a deliberate Roman creation designed as a territory for a loose confederation of tribes between the Durotriges on the south and the Dobunni and Atrebates on the north, but little is known of its extent except that it included oppida corresponding to Winchester and Bath. The character of Bath in Roman times was so highly specialized that it is perhaps unlikely that the town can have functioned as a normal tribal centre but, like Ilchester, one of its roles may have been as a successor to Iron Age hill-forts on the surrounding hills of Solsbury, Bathampton and Lansdown. Roman occupation here too dates to the middle of the first century but there is little evidence that as a town it ever had major military or normal commercial importance since, as the name Aquae Sulis implies, the mineral springs and baths account for its rise, and its fame throughout its Roman history. The lay-out of the elaborate system of baths is now almost completely known but there are only small remains of the great temple of Sulis Minerva, fortunately including the famous pediment with its extraordinary sculptured boss of a gorgon's head. The double dedication to a pre-Roman deity Sul and to Minerva is matched by the odd mixture of Roman and Iron Age styles in the sculpture and both are perhaps indicative of some measure of assimilation even in such an essentially Roman town as Bath. The importance of the spa may be judged from the fact that it is known to have had visitors from many of the civil towns and legionary centres throughout Britain as well as from Gaul. It was apparently still active at the beginning of the fifth century and the fact that it was one of the towns said to have been captured after the battle of Deorham in 577 may indicate its survival for at least another century and a half.

Excavation of Corinium (Cirencester) is still proceeding but already enough is known to show that it was one of the largest towns in Roman Britain, with a well-developed rectangular street pattern, an amphitheatre and very fine town buildings. Its establishment, largely to replace the nearby Dobunnic oppidum of Bagendon, in the middle of the first century, has already been mentioned and it will be recalled that it soon became the centre of a converging road pattern which made it a well-situated 'capital' for the canton of the Dobunni, which embraced most of Gloucestershire and parts of Oxfordshire, and beyond the Severn and the Forest of Dean extended into Worcestershire and Herefordshire. By the beginning of the third century the construction of walls had begun and excavation has shown that this continued until the town must have had a very elaborate system of defences by 296, when it is thought that it may have become the capital of Britannia Prima, one of the provinces into which Britain was divided under the reforms of Diocletian. Here too there is evidence that town life survived throughout the fourth century and some form of building was going on even outside the walls as late as the early fifth century.

The only other urban centre in the Bristol region during the Roman period was at Gloucester, where excavation also continues from time to time when sites are exposed during building operations. This has shown that whilst the second legion was based at Kingsholm in the north of the city between A.D. 49 and 75, a Roman settlement also existed around a harbour on the Severn near the present docks. Iron Age settlements had previously occupied a small sandy hill overlooking this harbour and the ford, and to this higher ground the Roman occupation spread some time between 75 and 97 when, as Glevum, it was given the status of a colonia for the second legion, which had been moved forward to occupy Caerleon in 75. As a colonia for time-expired legionaries it had a guaranteed economic function of a specialized kind but in addition it probably had a vital role as a link between the wool- and grain-producing Cotswold lands of the Dobunni and the areas across the Severn, especially the Forest of Dean, from which iron, coal and building stone are known to have been brought. The use of iron slag in construction work suggests some metal smelting in the town itself, and potters were making Glevum ware here well before the founding of the colonia in 97, after which date finds of this pottery in the middle and lower valleys of the Severn and the Warwickshire Avon and over central Cotswold are thought to be indicative of the probable extent of the territorium of the colonia of Glevum. As at Cirencester the building of walls was in progress at about 200 and evidence of reconstruction in the third and early fourth centuries has been found, but it is doubtful if the town shared all the later prosperity of Cirencester or its continued activity into the fifth century.

If one considers the distribution of the Roman villas shown on a small-scale map of the Bristol region, immediate confirmation seems to be afforded of the present view that those aspects of country life in Roman Britain which the villas represent were vitally linked with the existence of towns and roads. Well over a hundred villas are known to have existed in the region and more than two-thirds of these were situated in three concentrations within about twelve miles of Ilchester, Bath or Cirencester, usually very near the roads converging on those towns. If to these are added the villas round the smaller towns at Verlucio (Sandy Lane), Abona (Sea Mills) and the Charterhouse lead-mining centre on Mendip, something like 90 per cent of the villas are accounted for and most of the remainder lie within a short distance of the roads between the towns.

The Ilchester villas form two groups, one to the north of the town at the southeastern end of the Polden Hills and on the rolling country round Somerton and Langport, and the other to the south approaching the hills of south Somerset round Yeovil. Parallel with the Fosseway and to the east of it between Ilchester and Bath, a line of six villas occupied sites along the scarp country of eastern Somerset, and near Camerton they connect with the Bath group. Here villas follow the line of the intersecting Fosseway and Silchester–Sea Mills roads but they also cluster thickly round the valleys of the Avon and its tributaries above Bath and continue downstream towards Sea Mills, spreading round the foot of the Carboniferous Limestone hills on either side of the Avon below Bristol. Immediately north of Bath there are only five villas on Cotswold close to the line of the Fosseway towards Cirencester but to the north and west of Cirencester about twenty villas occupied favoured sites near springs at valley heads within the higher parts of Cotswold, six of them near to the line of the Ermine Way from Cirencester to Gloucester and eight close to the White Way and Salt Way to the north.

In addition to these three great concentrations of villas there are two other interesting groupings. The first consists of five villas spaced out along the line of the road between Sea Mills and Gloucester the most southerly one occupying a low-lying site under Kings Weston Down just above the alluvium of the Vale of Severn, whose cultivation may have formed an essential part of the economy of a group of settlements in this area and possibly of the other villas along the road. The second group may well have been connected with the lead-mining area of Mendip, possibly to supply it with food. Near the actual lead-working sites at Charterhouse no villa is known to have existed on the hills and only one has been identified on the southern slopes, but at least nine villas surround the northern and western end of Mendip along the course of the Yeo, down the Vale of Wrington and round the hill-enclosed lowland to the west of Shipham.

Only a minority of the villas have been adequately excavated but enough evidence has been accumulated to make possible a tentative summary of the history of villa life in the region. Some degree of continuity of land use from pre-Roman times can be deduced from the fact that the Hucclecote villa in Gloucestershire occupies a site which had been used in both Bronze Age and Iron Age times and the same may be true of the villa at Littleton near Somerton, whilst the replacement of a primitive circular structure of Iron Age type by a Romanized rectangular building has been proved at the nearby Catsgore villa. First-century structures have also been found at the Star villa near Shipham and at Witcombe in Gloucestershire, but perhaps the main period of villa building was in the second century when the Chedworth, Wood-chester, Whittington and Bourton-on-the-Water villas seem to have been started. The later part of the second century certainly appears to have been a prosperous period in the Ilchester area because it is marked by the creation of the large and luxurious villas in the Yeovil area like Westland, Lufton and Low Ham, which contrast sharply with the earlier and humbler buildings at Littleton and Catsgore. Though the early third century may not have been specially prosperous, there is again evidence in the later part of the century of the elaboration of existing buildings and the construction of new villas of considerable sophistication at Lufton and Keynsham, so that villa life may well have been very active at the beginning of the fourth century.

The increasing threat from barbarian attacks and in particular the severe raiding of 367-8 has been thought to have caused the breakdown of villa life after the middle of the fourth century. In the Bristol region it is true that the coin evidence suggests the end of the active use of certain villas about this time. The Wraxall villa in Somerset may have ceased to function about the middle of the century; no coins prove the occupation of the Kings Weston villa after the year 367, of Yeovil after 370 or of Chedworth after 386, and the villa at Star seems to have survived for only a short period after fire damage about 355. However, more recent views are tending to regard the existence of villa life well into the fifth century as certain and some of the evidence from the villas of the Bristol region may bear this out. At Low Ham in Somerset, for example, occupation certainly went on long after the raids of 367, whilst in Gloucestershire the villa at Hucclecote and probably that at Whittington survived in use into the fifth century. The same is almost certainly true of the villas at Bourton-on-the-Water and Witcombe, where reconstructions were carried out at the very end of the fourth century.

The villas of the Bristol region are remarkable not only for their numbers but also because they provide examples of early primitive forms at Catsgore and Littleton, as well as some of the most elaborate villas in Britain. Close at hand the great villas of the Yeovil area include at Low Ham truly exceptional mosaics, whilst in the north the villa at Woodchester was probably among the most luxurious in the country and at Chedworth there is one of the best-preserved examples of the larger type of villa. Throughout the region ample local supplies of building stone were available and it is therefore interesting evidence of affluence that in a number of Cotswold villas such as Chedworth, Hucclecote and Witcombe the builders, despite the plentiful supply of materials at hand, were prepared to bring from the Forest of Dean Pennant flagstones and Old Red Sandstone roofing material for the greater embellishment of their work.

Apart from information obtained during the excavation of some of the villas, few details are known of land use during the Roman period, but there seems no reason to suppose that agricultural developments by the Belgic peoples in the later Iron Age did not continue. Evidence of field systems round the foot of the limestone ridges near Bristol indicates continued arable cultivation and similar fields have even been identified round Charterhouse on Mendip. Nor is there any reason to doubt that the evidence of grain production at individual villas is typical of the whole. Nevertheless, it has been suggested that a considerable shift of emphasis to pastoral farming may underlie the vastly increased importance of the lowland margins of Somerset, especially round Ilchester, and the large-scale production of wool in the later Iron Age shown at Glastonbury and Bagendon almost certainly continued, particularly on Cotswold and in north Somerset, providing much of the wealth of the Dobunni and of the owners of some of Britain's most magnificent villas.

Some measure of continuity must also have marked the development of the mineral wealth of the region during the Romano-British period. The fact that the lead mines of Mendip were being operated under direct imperial control as early as 49 is almost certain proof that the Iron Age workings were known to the Romans and deliberately sought out in the earliest stages of the occupation. It is possible that the imperial control did not last throughout the Roman period and there were times of diminished production, but lead and silver were certainly still being produced at the end of the fourth century. Operations were probably extensive in the whole of the area from Shipham to Priddy but intermittent working of the same ores right up to the beginning of the present century makes it quite impossible to reconstruct details of the lay-out of the workings or of the smelting and silver extraction plant, except to demonstrate the probable focus of the industry near Charterhouse in the upland basin leading down to Velvet Bottom and the head of Cheddar gorge. In the Forest of Dean, too, the mining of iron for the Dobunni appears to have continued with little change into the Roman period, because on the site of the later Roman temple in Lydney Park a prehistoric settlement from about 100 B.C. is succeeded by a first phase of Roman occupation between A.D. 50 and 350, during which mines were probably worked by small groups of people living in huts. Subsequently iron working extended northwards into the Forest and the Wye valley past Monmouth, and the township of Ariconium (Weston-under-Penyard) became its chief centre. There is less certainty about the sequence of events in other iron-producing areas but there is evidence that the Romans obtained iron from Treborough and Luxborough in the Brendons as well as from deposits round Westbury in Wiltshire.

Besides affording evidence of Roman iron working, the excavations at Lydney Park revealed a second phase of Roman occupation commencing at 364 with the construction of a most impressive temple to the deity Nodens. This seems to have flourished and possibly rivalled the great temple to Sulis Minerva at Bath until the year 400, and to have been in some kind of use well on into the fifth century. Possibly because of the great distance involved in pilgrimages from the main centres of population to this remote spot beyond the Severn, the Lydney temple is remarkable for the elaboration of the buildings associated with it to provide for the hospitality and 'tourist trade' of its large numbers of visitors. At almost the same date (367) another fine temple on an octagonal plan, with Bath stone facings and tufa used as a lightweight material for an apse roof, was built on Pagan's Hill north of Chew Stoke, and it too was in active use throughout the fourth century and again possibly into the early fifth century. The smaller temple on Brean Down near Weston-super-Mare appears to have had a life of only about thirty years in the second half of the fourth century. As yet no precise dating is possible for the more recently excavated temple on Cadbury Hill near Yatton, for a possible temple on the Blaise Castle site near Sea Mills or for the small wayside temple near the Fosseway at Nettleton Shrub ten miles north of Bath.

Of the distribution of other finds of the Roman period, only that of the coin hoards calls for special comment. The majority of these occur in parts of Gloucestershire and Somerset which are known on other grounds to have been heavily settled in the Roman period, but it is a little surprising that pottery coin moulds as well as numbers of hoards have been found not only round the Polden Hills but also in southern and western Somerset beyond the Parrett, in areas where no great degree of Roman civil occupation is otherwise evident. It is, of course, possible that these hoards represent one consequence of increasing turmoil and a retreat to less favoured areas as the period of secure Roman control came to an end.

However, it is no longer regarded as certain that there was anything in the nature of a complete breakdown of Roman life in Britain in the late fourth century and it is thought likely that town life in particular may well have survived throughout the century. In the Bristol region this seems to have been the case at least at Ilchester, Bath and Cirencester, whilst the long continued life of the temples at Lydney and Pagan's Hill and their possible survival into the fifth century serve to confirm the town evidence. Moreover, from the excavations at Hucclecote, Low Ham and elsewhere it seems that a Romanized way of life even in the country-side continued, in places, beyond the end of the fourth century. In the case of the Cotswold villas and the temple at Lydney, however, this may merely reflect the comparative security enjoyed in these secluded sites in a part of the country whose position meant that it did not feel the full impact of the barbarian invasion of lowland Britain until a comparatively late date.

# CHAPTER 7

# The Growth of Settlements and Communications until the Eleventh Century

THE long survival of Romanized institutions revealed by recent excavations is more understandable when it is remembered that the systematic conquest of the Bristol region by the Saxons apparently only started at about 577 when Gloucester, Cirencester and Bath were captured after the battle of Deorham, fought six miles north of Bath on the Cotswold scarp above the village of Dyrham.

A great controversy has centred round the question of the approach routes by which the West Saxons reached this critical stage in their conquest of southwestern England and the divergent views are perhaps best appreciated by considering separately the archaeological, place-name and literary evidence.

Archaeological evidence of early Saxon penetration is normally in the form of burial places which belong to the pagan period. There is a remarkable concentration of such finds in the upper Thames valley above Dorchester-on-Thames, which continues westwards between the river and Akeman Street into Gloucestershire past Cirencester and the cemetery sites at Fairford and Kemble, to reach the Cotswold scarp at Leckhampton and to approach it near Avening. The fact that this distribution is linked near Dorchester-on-Thames with a line of pagan burials along the north side of the Icknield Way is one basis of E. T. Leeds's suggestion that the West Saxon approach to the upper Thames was by the fenland rivers and the Icknield Way rather than along the Thames itself, though more recently the view has been expressed that the Thames may have been the more important route, especially as the cremation burials, which are presumably the oldest, have a definite riverside distribution and the whole pattern of burial sites might be taken to imply movement along the valley. In either case there seems little doubt on archaeological grounds that the pagan Saxons whose burials occur throughout the central and northern parts of Cotswold approached from some area or areas in eastern England by way of the upper Thames. The type of brooches sometimes associated with the burials indicates that the greater part of this westward advance had been achieved as early as 450, whilst pins with inturned spiral heads found near Stow-on-the-Wold and Bourton-on-the-Water seem to confirm the connection with eastern England. The nine sites of pagan Saxon burial in the vale of west Wiltshire and the seven sites in Somerset do not appear to be as early as those of the upper Thames and Cotswold, and there was certainly no evidence of the early practice of cremation at the very large cemetery at Camerton (Som.) or that further west at Cannington.

In the west of England the use of place-name evidence to trace early settlement is not wholly satisfactory since the earliest 'ham' endings are very rare, but the 'tun' form, besides being indicative of secondary settlement in eastern England, is also characteristic of the earliest advances into western England, so that for this region it may, along with demonstrably early 'ing' endings, represent the initial settlement, however late when compared with southeastern England. In Gloucestershire the distribution of such relatively early names tends to confirm the archaeological evidence in so far as their greatest concentration is in the east where the boundary with Oxfordshire cuts across the upper basin of the Thames and its tributaries towards the Warwickshire Avon. Moreover, just as the pagan Saxon finds suggest a penetration into central Cotswold, so too a very similar line is followed by the early place-names through Sapperton, Cherrington, Minchinhampton, Leighterton and others to Wotton-under-Edge at the scarp. A continued advance along the upper Thames and over the watershed into the upper basin of the Bristol Avon seems to be indicated by the grouping of early names in the extreme southeast of Gloucestershire and by their concentration round the upper Bristol Avon itself, round its tributaries the Biss, the By brook and the Semington brook in the vale of west Wiltshire, and in the part of northeast Somerset drained by the Frome, Wellow, Chew and Cam brook tributaries—near the last of which is the site of the Camerton pagan cemetery.

It is possible that less heavily wooded conditions in the southern part of Cotswold encouraged early Anglo-Saxon movement across the upland from the upper Bristol Avon, which is to be inferred from the names West Littleton, Tormarton, Badminton, Hinton, Doynton, Siston, Cold Ashton, Horton and Bitton, whilst the lower course of the Avon probably linked the inland settlements with a large coastal group along the Severn. Despite the apparent eastward orientation of early settlement, there is a considerable number of early names in the vale in Gloucestershire. In the south such places as Elberton, Olveston, Alveston, Tytherington, Iron Acton and Frampton may have been settled from south Cotswold, the lower Avon or the coast, whilst in the extreme north of the county the large group of 'tun' names around the Oxenton outlier may be the result of movement along the Coln or Windrush valleys from the main area of early settlement on the upper Thames above Oxford.

If the many detailed differences of interpretation are ignored, the literary evidence of early West Saxon history in England can be summed up as indicating a landing on the south coast in 495 and an extremely slow northward advance, marked by the capture of Old Sarum (Salisbury) in 552 and of Barbury Castle, on the edge of the Marlborough Downs south of Swindon, in 556. Thus the West Saxons of the Chronicles entered the Bristol region about fifteen miles south of Fairford in Gloucestershire, for whose pagan Saxon cemetery a date nearly a century earlier would be acceptable on archaeological grounds. Moreover, there is no archaeological evidence from districts south of Barbury Castle which would suggest a northward movement of Saxons at dates earlier than those given in the Chronicle. The two main sources of information are therefore wholly incompatible in terms of both the direction and the timing of the West Saxon approach and, unless it seems proper to regard the literary evidence as valueless, it is necessary to view the evolution of Wessex as stemming from a dual approach. Since the nature of much of the literature of this period is heroic, it is perfectly possible that the Chronicles describe the arrival only of the Gewissae, from whom the royal house of Wessex emerged. In their subsequent advance into the vale to the north of Barbury Castle, the Gewissae may have established political control over the pre-existing Saxon groups of the upper Thames and Bristol Avon, though possibly not over detached groups already ranging far to the west into Cotswold and the Vale of Severn. Such an explanation is not at present susceptible of proof but at least it provides a theoretical framework capable of accommodating most of the conflicting evidence.

Partly related to this unresolved question of the origin of Wessex is the difficult problem concerned with the function and date of one of England's most impressive earthworks, Wansdyke. Even the field evidence of Wansdyke is disputed, the earthwork having been described as running south of, and parallel with, the Bristol Avon from Portbury near Portishead to Maes Knoll on Dundry Hill, thence by Newton Park and Englishcombe southwest of Bath, to cross the Fosseway on Odd Down and to continue along a rather doubtful course across the vale of west Wiltshire, where it becomes easily identifiable again on the chalk scarp at Morgan's Hill and then runs eastwards through Savernake Forest almost to the Kennet near Hungerford. The one clear fact about the structure of Wansdyke is that where a ditch and bank exist together the ditch is on the northern side, which indicates that, if it were built as a line of defence as distinct from a boundary mark, it was intended to defend the area to the south of it. Since Wansdyke is now known to be a discontinuous earthwork, with breaks in areas which can be presumed to have been heavily wooded and therefore easily defended, it is now taken, partly by analogy with Offa's Dyke, to have had a definitely defensive function. Investigations near Morgan's Hill and in the vale, however, now throw doubt on the existence of a single defence work, however discontinuous, throughout the whole length of the supposed Wansdyke from Portbury to Hungerford. Indeed it has been suggested that there are two distinct earthworks, an eastern one starting at Morgan's Hill and a western one starting from a point southeast of Bath and running west as far as Maes Knoll or alternatively all the way to Portbury according to one's reading of the field evidence. If the existence of two separate structures could be accepted, then speculation about dates would be a good deal freer, since there would be no need to regard the two parts as contemporaneous.

Before the idea was suggested that Wansdyke might be two separate earthworks, it was difficult to regard the whole earthwork as a British defence in the fifth century against the Saxons of the Thames valley, since the western end would have been needless until the presumed Saxon advance into Somerset after the battle of Deorham in 577. Similarly the whole structure could not have been built by the British after 577 if the movement of the Gewissae from Old Sarum to Barbury Castle, across the line of Wansdyke, between 552 and 556 is to be accepted.

If Wansdyke is considered as two separate earthworks, then the eastern part is outside the Bristol region, but it is necessary to consider its date and function because it may have a bearing on the whole progress of the Saxon settlement of west Wiltshire and Somerset. If it is held to be free of connections with the earthworks in Somerset, it would then be possible to accept eastern Wansdyke as a fifth-century British structure long ante-dating the arrival of the Gewissae in Old Sarum, and this view is favoured by those who regard Woden's Dyke to have been named after a deity by the Saxons, who had no knowledge of its actual human construction. The diametrically opposed view that its name implies Saxon construction is used to support the alternative theory that it was built by the Gewissae between A.D. 584 and 592. Presumably after taking control of the upper Thames and Avon region and then Cotswold in 577, the Gewissae's next major battle with the British was at FethanLeag in 584. As a site for this battle has now been suggested about twelve miles north of Oxford, it is possible that the Gewissae were campaigning in lands where there was a clash of interest with Mercian settlers. The Chronicle account of the battle is obscure but it is most unlikely that it was a decisive West Saxon victory. Indeed, it could be interpreted as a virtual defeat, after which the Saxons might have constructed the defensive line of eastern Wansdyke and possibly the fortress of Woden's Burh on the line of the earthwork where the battle which temporarily decided the Wessex royal succession was fought between Ceawlin and Ceol in 592. On the latter interpretation it is of course also possible that eastern Wansdyke remained in use into the seventh century as a West Saxon defence against the Mercians, who drove them out of Cotswold and most of the area north of the Thames after the battle of Cirencester in 628. However, it remains clear, irrespective of its date, that the function of Wansdyke was to prevent movement southwestwards from the upper Thames basin and especially along the Wiltshire continuation of the Berkshire trackway along the chalk downs.

For western Wansdyke three dates have been proposed in recent times. The first of these, suggesting British construction in the fifth century, is feasible only if it is assumed that an early foray took the Saxons as far west as Bath and that the problematical battle of Mons Badonicus at about 500 really was fought in that neighbourhood. The second suggested date of western Wansdyke as a British defensive line is immediately after the battle of Deorham in 577 when the Saxons took Bath and presumably the valley of the Avon. However, archaeological evidence in northeast Somerset indicates the possibility that the area round Wansdyke was settled by Saxons before 600 and this makes a date for the earthwork after 577 perhaps less likely. Finally, this part of Wansdyke could also be regarded as part of the West Saxon defences against an advancing Mercia after the battle of Cirencester in 628. If this were the case there might be a great similarity of function between the two parts of Wansdyke, the western part being designed to block Mercian attacks using the Cotswold trackways or the Fosseway. Those who do not think that the earthwork extends west of Maes Knoll point out that for this purpose the western end would be needless, especially as in its lower course the Bristol Avon is sufficiently difficult to cross as to afford adequate protection.

The possibility of West Saxon earthwork defences against Mercia in the early seventh century underlines the importance of the division of the Bristol region between the two kingdoms from 628 until the tenth century. This can be interpreted as a result of West Saxon preoccupation with the conquest of the southwest, leaving their northern territories inadequately defended; alternatively their advance into Somerset and Devon could be regarded as a policy dictated by the loss of their lands north of the Thames and the Bristol Avon.

It is impossible to define the boundaries of the two states precisely. Thus it is not clear how far Mercian control extended down the Cotswold dipslope and into the vale of northwest Wiltshire because in the late seventh century grants of land in that area were made to the Abbey of Malmesbury by both Mercia and Wessex. A century later grants of lands as far southeast as Purton near Swindon were made by the Mercians, and the fact that the Wessex victory over the Mercians in 825 was won at Ellandun, nearby, suggests an extension of Mercian territory almost to the chalk scarp. On the south the boundary of Mercia was probably close to the present county boundary of Gloucestershire and Somerset but actual evidence is largely limited to that afforded by the history of Bath in this period. In 676 the Mercian Osric founded the Abbey there and when Offa took its lands for the Mercian crown in 781 they included areas in Somerset probably between the Bristol Avon and Mendip. As a royal town Bath was an important centre where the Mercian Gemot met in the eighth century, but after the victories of Wessex over Mercia in 825 and 829 the boundary must have undergone adjustment, because by the tenth century Bath was an important town of the Wessex shire of Somerset. Mercian overlordship in Gloucestershire was apparently achieved when the Hwiccii, who probably took part in the West Saxon conquest of the Cotswold area after the battle of Deorham, accepted the rule of the kings of Mercia early in the seventh century, possibly after the Mercian victory at Cirencester in 628. In Saxon land charters Cotswold is referred to as Mons Huuicciorum and the territories of the Hwiccian sub-kings who signed many of the charters probably included the whole of Gloucestershire as well as the adjacent parts of southeast Worcestershire, southwest Oxfordshire and northwest Wiltshire. It is indicative of West Saxon settlement and subsequent prolonged political subordination to Mercia that the traces of dialect forms in the Gloucestershire place-names show a mixture of West Saxon and Hwiccian (Mercian) influences.

On the other hand, the conquest and settlement of Somerset was purely West Saxon, though interpretations vary as to the exact timing of the stages of the advance through the county. Pagan Saxon finds and the scarcity of pre-Saxon names or church dedications in northeast Somerset indicate an early Saxon settlement of that district and lend support to the view that the battle of Bradford-on-Avon as late as 652 can scarcely have been against the British but was either a civil conflict or a fight with raiding Mercians. Moreover, the view that the Saxon conquest was held up long after the battle of Deorham in 577 by the heavy forests of Selwood in the clay vale of west Wiltshire and east Somerset is difficult to reconcile with the Saxons' demonstrable skill in using wooded areas in warfare, and therefore it seems unlikely that the battle in 658 really represented the outcome of their breaching the forest 'barrier' at Penselwood leading to an advance to the line of the river Parrett. Instead the Parrett may have been reached materially earlier and Stenton (1943) has suggested that the 658 battle may have taken them to the extreme south of the county near the Black Down Hills, which would make understandable their recorded arrival on the coast in 682. It would also explain the grant of lands near Taunton to Glastonbury Abbey in 672 and King Ine's establishment of Taunton's defences well before 722. On these grounds it is thought possible that before the accession of King Ine in 688 the whole county of Somerset was in Saxon hands and indeed that much of Devon too may have been conquered by this date.

Though Saxon progress through Somerset may therefore have been more rapid than was once thought, there is still considerable evidence that the survival of pre-Saxon influences becomes more marked as one moves southwestwards across the county, especially beyond the Parrett. Thus Celtic place-names become more important towards the southwest, dialect changes occur near the Parrett, and pre-Saxon church dedications, largely absent from northeast Somerset, are most numerous in the western and southwestern parts of the county. Moreover, contrasts in the settlement pattern and in the weight of the assessment of the northeastern and southwestern areas in the eleventh century point to long-lasting consequences of the progressive but gradual nature of the extension of West Saxon control.

Before the surveys of the eleventh century, evidence of prevailing physical conditions and of the progress of settlement and cultivation must be derived from place-names and from direct or indirect references in Saxon land charters and the documents of religious houses. One measure of the agricultural settlement of the land is the extent to which the early woodland cover of much of the Bristol region was cleared before the Norman conquest, and references to existing woodland in the charters afford some evidence of this. In Gloucestershire the charters, especially at Woodchester for example, make it clear that considerable areas of woodland occupied the central portion of the Cotswold scarp from Winchcombe in the north to Chipping Sodbury in the south, and it is interesting that this same zone of steep slopes and deeply cut valleys was still well wooded at the time of the Domesday survey, as indeed much of it remains today. However, there were two important breaks in this woodland belt which were also evident in the eleventh century. The first marked the upper valley of the Coln and its continuation along the Vale of Andoversford to Cheltenham, a route of penetration into and through Cotswold followed by a trackway of some importance. The second break ran from the area between Minchinhampton and Nailsworth towards Wotton-under-Edge and, significantly, coincided with the line where place-names and pagan Saxon finds suggest an early penetration of Cotswold from the headwaters of the Thames. Elsewhere comparatively early Saxon settlement may have brought about a good deal of clearance on Cotswold and there is some evidence of this in the very large number of names with 'leah' endings which are commonly taken to imply woodland clearance, though the form 'leah' itself may mean little more than any poor land with or without trees, possibly something like rough pasture. These names are very numerous in the southern part of Cotswold and particularly so on the scarp to the east of Wotton-under-Edge where other evidence indicates early clearance. Nevertheless, even in south Cotswold by no means all the woodland had disappeared because charters at Dyrham refer to woodlands which existed on both the scarp and the dipslope of Cotswold.

Since the initial Saxon approach appears to have been into the clay vale of the upper Thames, it is reasonable to expect that some Saxon clearance of the heavy woodland would take place and this may be inferred from references in the charters to 'the woods' of Kemble and Braydon in north Wiltshire, which imply that these are identifiably different from the rest of the area. Moreover, place-names with 'leah' endings are quite plentiful throughout the clay vale in north and west Wiltshire and east Somerset, so that some clearance and settlement was obviously proceeding in Saxon times. On the other hand, in the Domesday surveys of both Wiltshire and Somerset there is a very marked concentration of records of woodland in the clay vale, especially in the areas of the later 'forests' of Braydon, Chippenham and Melksham. Clearance of the vale was therefore very far from complete and this was probably particularly true in the south where Saxon settlement was later; a great deal of woodland is recorded in the Somerset Domesday around Selwood.

Saxon evidence of woodland to the west of the Cotswold scarp is scanty and the Domesday survey is hardly more satisfactory since it refers only to individual small areas of wood in Pucklechurch, Thornbury and to the west of Stroud and a larger area to the south of Tewkesbury. However, the lack of references to woodland in both periods and the density of settlement in the vale in the eleventh century may be sufficient evidence of quite rapid clearance of the woodland at least to the east of the Severn. To the west of the river, however, the picture is different. Only five relatively early place-names exist and these are all close to the coast, whilst the Tidenham charters can be interpreted as evidence of small numbers of relatively unimportant settlements in forest clearings. Here again the Domesday evidence is of little value since the recorded woodland lies only round the edges of the Forest of Dean—a state of affairs which is entirely understandable if the main areas of the Forest were still largely unused in the eleventh century and therefore not worthy of comment in the Domesday survey.

In Somerset to the west of the clay vale there are few specific Saxon references to woodland except the 'Quantock wood', though settlements in woodland clearings may be inferred from some names. However, it has been suggested that the very low Saxon assessment of parts of Somerset, notably around Taunton and in the Vale of Wrington, is characteristic of cleared woodland areas. That such clearance had taken place on a large scale before the eleventh century is also evident from the Domesday survey, since there are only scattered references to woodland throughout the whole belt of oolites and Lias on the eastern and southern sides of the county, apart from isolated large entries near Bruton, Ilminster and Langport. Moreover, within this belt it appears that clearance was largely complete in three districts: the area to the west and southwest of Bath where early Saxon settlement is presumed to have taken place after the battle of Deorham, the area round Ilchester where intensive settlement certainly dates from Roman times, and the Lias ridge of the Poldens. Elsewhere in the northwest, west and southwest of Somerset the only considerable areas of woodland which remained in the eleventh century were on the lower slopes of the hills, especially round the western end of Mendip and on the northern sides of Exmoor, the Brendon Hills and the Quantocks.

Taken together, then, the evidence of Domesday and of the few Saxon sources gives a picture of the continuous woodland of the Bristol region being restricted to the compact areas of the later 'forests' of Selwood, Chippenham, Melksham and Braydon in the clay vale of Somerset and Wiltshire, to the Forest of Dean and to areas where the steeper slopes and valleys of Cotswold and the hills of Somerset may in any case have made the land unattractive for Saxon agriculture. Elsewhere there is nothing to suggest that woodland was sufficiently dense or continuous in the later part of the Saxon period as to prejudice either settlement or agriculture.

On the other hand, ill-drained ground certainly prevented the full use of considerable areas. This most obviously applies to the Somerset levels where there is evidence that in some districts intensive land use in late Iron Age times was interrupted by renewed flooding before the Roman conquest. In Saxon charters relating to parishes round the levels it is common for the part of the parish in the low-lying area to be omitted entirely from the bounds of the land grants, presumably because it was not used in any way. In High Ham, for example, the northern area on King's Sedgemoor is omitted, and the same is true to the southeast of Glastonbury round the moors of the Brue. Possibly this may have been due in part to the Saxons' supposed antipathy to fen-like areas, but certainly by the time of the Domesday survey the levels were being put to some kind of use because there is evidence of drainage on the lands of Glastonbury Abbey and of settlements on the Polden Hills; the 'islands', too, where Saxon coins have been found, had detached portions in the 'moor' which must have had a value if only for peat cutting. In Gloucestershire, also, there are some parishes like Aust where the omission of areas from Saxon charters again suggests low-lying swampy ground which was not in agricultural use; in many districts near the Severn field names including 'moor' and 'marsh' are common; a causeway was mentioned at Henbury; and at Olveston there is a reference to land 'where the reeds grow'. Few references in the Domesday survey of Gloucestershire show how far the low-lying lands in this area of relatively early Saxon settlement had been brought into use by the eleventh century but the apparent total absence of meadow land on the alluvium bordering the Severn is perhaps indicative of liability to inundation; indeed some parts of the alluvium were not effectively reclaimed until the seventeenth century.

Little information exists about the organization of the agricultural settlements of the Bristol region before the conquest but it is apparent that by the eighth century there were settlements in at least some parts of Wessex with open fields under strip cultivation, because the laws of King Ine laid down specific requirements for the regulation of the system. There is, however, no method of determining how far such a practice was general throughout Somerset and Wiltshire or whether it extended to the Hwiccian lands north of the Bristol Avon. Ine's laws have also been quoted as demonstrating royal insistence upon the maintenance of land in cultivation, since they laid down that in a landholder's absence from his territory a specific fraction of his estates should be kept in agricultural use. This, taken together with the rules governing the relationships with the pre-Saxon population, has even been regarded as evidence of deliberate agricultural 'plantations', but, of course, such rules may have been applicable only to the areas of recent Saxon conquests in south and west Somerset where the co-existence of Saxon and British populations has been deduced on other grounds. Nevertheless, in the light of the situation achieved by the eleventh century, it seems reasonable to accept the evidence of Ine's laws as indicating vigorous agricultural development during the preceding three centuries.

Of the distribution of this agricultural colonization there are only hints before the survey of the eleventh century. The only districts where the absence of land grants in the charters, combined with negative place-name evidence, indicates retarded development are the Forest of Dean, the marshy areas of the Somerset levels, the higher moors in the extreme south, and the areas of residual true forest in Selwood, Braydon and possibly Chippenham and Melksham. If it is permissible to assume that the Saxon hide (as distinct from that of Domesday) bore a direct relationship to the value of land for purely arable use, then it is possible to regard the areas of high assessment as those likely to have seen the maximum agricultural development before the eleventh century. Unfortunately it is only rarely possible to calculate the weight of the assessment from the charters but where this has been done it shows some interesting regional variations. Thus places in northeast Somerset on the lower and middle Lias to the north of the Brue valley and away from the levels were assessed almost as heavily as vale lands in Berkshire and round the upper Thames, whereas some assessments in the vale in Gloucestershire appear to have been 50 per cent less, others in south Somerset near Taunton 100 per cent less and for some lands south of the Quantocks 200 per cent less. There is no lack of evidence of settlement on the higher ground of Cotswold, but the occurrence of the name 'Starveall' could be taken to show that it was not held in high esteem by the Saxons. The frequent use of the 'leah' place-name ending could mean that cleared areas were often in pastoral use, though in the north at Bishops Cleeve there may be charter evidence of arable cultivation on the plateau. At Dyrham there is reasonably good evidence that the Saxons arranged the settlement to make use of a variety of lands across the scarp from the oolites down to the clays of the vale, and in the Evenlode valley near Stow-on-the-Wold the use of both the uplands and the riverside meadow lands may show one basis of the considerable settlement of the Cotswold dipslope at the time of the Domesday survey.

Information about the development of land use being so limited for the Saxon period, it is best to look at the eventual results of this process from the standpoint of the Domesday survey. Perhaps the most remarkable feature of the eleventh-century distribution of settlements in Gloucestershire, as shown by the location of the recorded vills, is its uniformity over the whole county apart from the empty area of the Forest of Dean. It is certainly very difficult to distinguish any real contrast between the vale and Cotswold, and even in the latter there is little sign of significant local variations or of the strings of settlements aligned along the rivers which are so characteristic of the Wiltshire chalk lands, though no doubt the importance of the arable land and the meadows of the streams of the lower dipslope far outweighed that of the higher areas in the north and near the scarp. If the distribution of plough teams and recorded population is considered, however, it is possible to distinguish not only the emptiness of the Forest of Dean but also some other appreciable variations. In the case of the plough teams there is a slight increase of density on the lower dipslope of Cotswold as the Thames is approached towards Fairford and Lechlade, and in the vale there is again a slight increase towards the northeast. Similarly for recorded population the highest density to the east of the

Cotswold scarp is in a belt along the eastern side of the county from the Thames round Fairford and Lechlade across the tributary valleys past Stow-on-the-Wold and Moreton-in-Marsh towards the Warwickshire Avon. The apparent density of population in the vale was very slightly greater than that of the higher parts of Cotswold and it too increased appreciably towards the Vale of Evesham and the northeastern corner of the county. Thus, such variations as are evident from the Domesday survey suggest the continued importance from early Saxon times of the upper Thames and the northeastern parts of the county and slightly less active development of the higher parts of Cotswold and the southern part of the vale.

Apart from the early settlement of the east and northeast and the advantage of generally favourable physical conditions, it is likely that the presence of considerable areas of meadow land in the lower dipslope valleys of the Churn, Coln, Leach and Windrush, round the Severn and its tributaries between Gloucester and Tewkesbury and along the Vale of Evesham, added greatly to the agricultural wealth of these districts. There was obviously little possibility of meadow land on the higher parts of Cotswold but its scarcity in the vale below Gloucester is remarkable. Its absence from the alluvium near the Severn has already been mentioned and if, as suggested, liability to tidal flooding were the cause, this might also afford an explanation of the total absence of eleventh-century fisheries on the east bank of the Severn below Gloucester. The middle courses of the streams in this apparently less-favoured southern part of the vale afforded comparatively small patches of meadow land and they provided the sites for only a limited number of mills. In this last respect it was naturally Cotswold that contributed most to the wealth of Gloucestershire in the eleventh century, since not only were mills numerous on the streams in the relatively densely settled areas in the east but the strong streams through the scarp, especially the Stroud Frome, also provided a great concentration of mill sites which were later to provide the power for the Stroudwater woollen district.

The Wiltshire portion of the lower dipslope of Cotswold and of the vale adjoins the more heavily settled parts of southeast Gloucestershire and, apart from the absence of vills in the Forest of Braydon, there is nothing in the Domesday record for Wiltshire to suggest that the southern part of the vale of the upper Thames was not equally well colonized. Indeed the very large areas of meadow recorded south of the Thames near Cricklade point to an area of considerable wealth and this was probably equally true of the vale in west Wiltshire, where considerable areas of meadow followed the watercourses in the upper basin of the Bristol Avon. Moreover, calculations based on the recorded population at Domesday suggest, if the wooded areas of Melksham and

Chippenham are excluded, that the well-peopled area was continued southwestwards along the vale beyond Trowbridge until the remaining forest of Selwood was approached.

Considerably less uniformity in the distribution of settlement, population and wealth is revealed by the Domesday records of Somerset than of Gloucestershire and the western parts of Wiltshire but this is to be expected, partly because Saxon penetration into much of the county was delayed and partly because of the great variability of physical conditions within the county.

In the first place the extensive levels left larger gaps in the settlement pattern than existed in the neighbouring counties. Even so, the Domesday records support the slender Saxon evidence of gradual occupation of the levels, because a grouping of eleventh-century settlements near the western end of the Poldens is linked by a line of vills through Bridgwater to another quite large group to the west of the Parrett. Moreover, the 'islands' and low ridges between the levels of the Brue and Axe basins were all occupied and vills around the lower Axe near Axbridge connect them with the more continuous settlement around Mendip and to the north.

A comparative lack of settlement in the low-lying parts of the vales immediately north of Mendip in the eleventh century confirms the Saxon evidence from Wrington of slow occupation, but elsewhere there is quite a uniform pattern of settlement in north and northeast Somerset and this is continued southwards along the eastern side of the county on the higher ground of the Jurassic scarps as well as in the Oxford Clay vale to the east and in the rolling country of the Lias to the west of it. Within this belt the slightly increased concentration of vills round the tributaries of the Bristol Avon and the Brue in the northeast and round the upper courses of the Yeo and Parrett further south is attributable in part to the attraction of the middle and upper parts of the valleys, where there were considerable tracts of meadow land and the majority of the eleventh-century mills of the county. But these were also important areas from Roman times onwards and continued intensive use through the Saxon period is possibly to be expected.

There was still a good deal of evidence at the time of the Domesday survey of the very different conditions beyond the Parrett in territory which was apparently not reached by the Saxons until the second half of the seventh century. It is true that there was considerable settlement between the Parrett and the Quantocks, and round Taunton the special character of the very large manor may mask the real state of affairs, but elsewhere this was an area of tiny manors and of vills whose wealth was small, not only from the point of view of an arable economy but also in terms of stock recorded in the *Exon. Domesday,* despite the fact that the hills of the south and southwest afforded a good deal of pasture. Indeed, poverty as well as a very different history almost certainly explains the fiscal boundary at the Parrett between areas to the north with an assessment which shows at least some signs of the five-hide basis characteristic of other parts of Wessex and Gloucestershire, and the area to the southwest where no such pattern is discernible among the mass of tiny assessments.

The extra details available from the *Exon. Domesday* make it possible to get a slightly clearer picture of the agricultural economy of eleventh-century Somerset, mainly because of the references to animals other than those of the plough teams. To judge from the distribution of the plough teams themselves, arable agriculture was practised most intensively on the higher ground of northeastern, eastern and southeastern Somerset from the slight elevations of the Lias above the levels to the oolite scarps, but not quite so markedly in the Oxford Clay vale and certainly to a much less extent in the lowlands and on the hills of the southwest. This last area also had surprisingly few cows, but elsewhere the distribution is relatively uniform, the considerable numbers round the levels suggesting their use at least for summer grazing. Pigs were kept in all parts of the county but the fact that they were most numerous in the Oxford Clay vale and on the clay areas to the west of the scarps and much less so on the oolites is presumably attributable to the use of the woodland for pannage. It is, however, the Domesday record of sheep which produces the most useful additional information. This confirms the absolute poverty of the southwestern parts of the county because even sheep were only slightly more numerous here than on the levels despite the large amounts of pasture available. On the other hand, the oolitic uplands are shown as a very important pastoral area indeed with a density of sheep nearly double that of the rest of eastern and northern Somerset, including Mendip. The fact that the oolitic uplands included lands with the highest values recorded in the Somerset Domesday presumably arose therefore from agriculture based on sheep and arable, and it seems reasonable to expect that a not dissimilar form of land use prevailed in parts of Cotswold, though the less detailed nature of the Gloucestershire Domesday means that positive evidence is restricted to isolated references to sheep in that area.

## Communications and Transport

In considering means of communication and transport until the eleventh century it is difficult to assess the importance of movement along the rivers. There is certainly some indication that the upper Thames was used in very early Saxon times but the evidence at the end of the period is not conclusive since it largely arises from the grouping of Domesday vills round the streams and this could have been occasioned by other circumstances, notably the availability of mill sites and vitally important meadow land. On the other hand, it is possible to derive a great deal of information about trackways and roads from the Saxon land charters because points on them were commonly used to define the boundaries of grants.

The ancient trackways of the prehistoric period on the Chalk and Jurassic scarps were probably never wholly out of use in the Roman period and they were certainly in active use in later times. The great chalk ridgeway of Berkshire and Wiltshire very nearly coincides with the eastern limit of our area but the Jurassic ridgeway of Cotswold from Bath to Birdlip and Snowshill may almost be regarded as an axis of pre-Conquest communications in the northern half of the Bristol region. It was referred to as the Ridgeway in some Saxon charters, but in south Cotswold it was called the Salters' Path and long before the eleventh century it had obviously become one element in the complex pattern of saltways covering most of Gloucestershire. By the time of the Domesday survey it appears that saltways crossed the northern part of the county from the salt-producing area of Worcestershire towards the upper Thames. A continuation of the Worcestershire ridgeway climbed the Cotswold scarp at Snowshill, crossed the Jurassic way and continued through Stow-on-the-Wold to Burford and possibly on to the Thames. A little way to the south the saltway from Worcestershire by way of Evesham reached the crest of the scarp and the Jurassic way at Stanway and followed the dipslope to the Thames at Lechlade along two tracks, one down the Colne valley and the other just to the west of the Windrush valley. Finally the Worcester–Tewkesbury–Cheltenham saltway approached the Jurassic ridgeway at Leckhampton and from that neighbourhood a saltway again continued eastwards through Northleach to Burford and Whitney. South of Cheltenham the ridgeway was no longer crossed by saltways from Worcestershire and was itself presumably the main route by which salt was carried into south Cotswold. Here one main track branched to the east from Tormarton to cross the vale north of Chippenham and reach the chalk ridgeway west of Marlborough. To the south of Birdlip the main Cotswold ridgeway curved eastwards avoiding the deep Stroudwater valleys, but a course nearer to the scarp was followed by a saltway from Birdlip to Stroud and Wotton-under-Edge where it divided, one branch extending out into the vale at Thornbury and the other following the Middle Lias 'ledge' at the foot of the scarp through Alderley, Hillsley and Hawkesbury to Chipping Sodbury.

At the southern end of the Jurassic way it must be presumed that communications to the west followed the Bristol Avon, or possibly the line of the Roman road parallel with it, from Bath to the settlements of the Bristol neighbourhood, because it is certain that in the Saxon period use was made of a western trackway from the lower Bristol Avon which followed the general course of the Roman road along the limestone ridge at Almondsbury and northwards through the Vale of Berkeley near the line of the present Bristol–Gloucester main road.

Whatever the function of the Fosseway in Roman times, the linking of Cirencester, Bath and Ilchester along a nearly straight line meant that in Saxon times it was the southern part which remained important. To the north of Bath the road only skirted the area of Saxon settlement round the upper Thames and it is symptomatic of its isolation that Cirencester is the only settlement site on the first 45 miles of its course. South of Bath, on the other hand, the Fosseway passed through the district of early Saxon penetration round the tributaries of the Bristol Avon in northeast Somerset, continued through the heavily settled country on the Lias round the east of the levels, and in south Somerset crossed the long-settled and well-cultivated upper basins of the Yeo and Parrett, so that in the 45 miles south of Bath it passed within a mile of more than 20 settlements. Southwards into Somerset, therefore, the Fosseway seems to have taken over the role of the Cotswold ridgeway as the main north–south route of the Bristol region, intersecting with two main east–west lines of communication.

The first of these followed the trackway from the Wiltshire Downs across the Frome gap and along the Mendip crests, parts of which were incorporated in the Roman road from Old Sarum to the Mendip lead mines. The second continued the line of the Dorset ridgeway along the southern boundary of Somerset by way of Staple Hill and Brow Down to the ridgeways of the Black Down Hills and possibly those of the Brendons, Dunkery Hill and Exmoor. Elsewhere in Somerset the trackways which are referred to in Saxon documents have a dominantly east–west direction following the 'grain' of the country. They might appear from the records as somewhat unconnected lengths of road on the Quantocks and along the slightly higher ground within the levels, especially the Poldens and the Wedmore ridge, but it is probably only the lack of evidence which prevents their appearing as east–west links with the main zone of north–south movement in east Somerset.

This pattern of roads and trackways, for which there is definite field or literary evidence, clearly provided a framework of communications over the whole of the Bristol region, but it does not take into account the unrecorded and essentially local emergence of the rest of the road system. When the generally uniform distribution of vills in the eleventh century is recalled, it will be apparent that intercommunication implies at least the beginning of paths and tracks which was to become the network of minor roads of the Middle Ages. However, the uniformity of distribution shown on a small-scale map of the vills masks considerable diversity of pattern. For example, the choice of sites on the 'ledge' of the Middle Lias Marlstone at the foot of the Cotswold scarp, especially in its long straight course north of Bath, led to the existence of a string of 16 settlements in the 17 miles between Bath and Wotton-under-Edge which were almost certainly linked by a track, the northern half of which was described as a saltway. Similarly in east and southeast Somerset strings of vills marked the lower slopes of the Upper Lias scarp, particularly between Sandford Orcas and Castle Cary, and of the Forest Marble scarp from Milborne Port to Bruton. In north, west and central Somerset it is along the slightly higher margins of the valleys and the levels that strings of settlements led to the development of distinctive road patterns. Thus the line of 14 settlements in the 15 miles along the foot of the northern slopes of the Polden Hills from Puriton in the west to West Lydford near the Fosseway was probably connected by early tracks and the same may have been true of the settlements below the southern slopes from Chedzoy to Compton Dundon. Again a line of no less than 34 vills surrounded Mendip at the foot of the steeper slopes above the Chew and Yeo valleys on the north and the levels of the Axe basin on the south, and they were soon linked by the roads which skirt the hills on the north from Uphill by way of Banwell, Churchill, Blagdon and the Harptrees to Chewton Mendip, and along the south by way of Loxton, Axbridge, Cheddar and Westbury to Wells. The margins of the levels of the Yeo and Land Yeo to the north of Mendip are similarly marked by settlements along the foot of the surrounding limestone uplands, from Wrington and Congresbury following the western side of Broadfield Down through Cleeve and Brockley to Flax Bourton and then the Failand, Tickenham and Clevedon ridges to link up with sites round the edges of the Gordano valley.

Though many aspects of the Domesday geography of the Bristol region arose from the nature of its settlement by the Saxon peoples, others reflect its political, administrative and ecclesiastical history in the period between the seventh and the eleventh centuries and particularly the somewhat different circumstances which prevailed in the parts which lay in Mercia and Wessex. It will be recalled that at least in the west the boundary between the two states had long been established near the line of the Bristol Avon, and therefore Somerset and much of Wiltshire shared in the general pre-Conquest history of Wessex.

Here the characteristically small and often irregular Hundreds imply the early development of an administrative system, and the division of the extensive West Saxon territories into shires had taken place before the ninth century when Wessex had to face the full force of Danish attacks. Raids on the Somerset coast preceded the campaign of 877 when the Danes reached Gloucester before they established their base near the borders of Wessex at Chippenham, the site of their victory in 879 which led to Alfred's retreat into his refuge at Athelney in the south of the levels. Thereafter the men of the Wessex shires, initially assembled near Selwood on the borders of Somerset, Dorset and Wiltshire, fought the campaign against the Danes, the success of which led to the ultimate, if temporary, unification of Anglo-Saxon England. It also led to the extension of the Wessex administrative system to Mercian Gloucestershire and the west Midlands so that by the beginning of the eleventh century shires had been carved out here too, though the apparent artificiality of the assessment in round numbers of hides and the complex system of Hundreds in Gloucestershire in this period bore testimony to this recent innovation and to an earlier Mercian history.

The vital necessity of providing for the security of the West Country area on which Alfred's campaign was based is thought to account for the establishment round it of a series of fortified places whose maintenance is illustrated in the burghal hidage. Of the burghs in the Bristol region the four in central and west Somerset—Watchet (513 hides), Lyng, near Athelney (100 hides), Langport (600 hides) and Axbridge (400 hides)—appear to have been small and concerned with local defence, in part against coastal raids. On the other hand, in northeast Somerset and northwest Wiltshire, along a potential corridor of attack from Danish-held eastern England, Bath (possibly over 3,000 hides) Malmesbury (1,500 hides) and Cricklade (1,300 hides) were apparently of much greater strategic significance, Cricklade, near the boundary of Wessex and Mercia, in particular being in a position to command the crossing of the Thames and the approaches to Malmesbury and south Gloucestershire and to Bath and Somerset.

There has been long controversy over the pre-Conquest origins of urban institutions in England but this has centred on the much disputed garrison theory of Maitland and on doubts about the existence of real borough courts and burgess status before the late eleventh century. There can be little doubt, however, that in parts of the Bristol region, which have been described as the 'classical land' of small West Saxon boroughs, some kind of townships did grow up around the burghs of the pre-Conquest period or occupied parts of the Roman sites at Ilchester, Bath, Cricklade and Gloucester. In Somerset at Bath, Ilchester, Milborne Port, Bruton, Langport, Axbridge and Taunton, the Domesday record suggests the possible existence of a town and all of them may have had this character in the Saxon period, though there is no evidence of a burgh at Bruton. It is also possible that the eleventh-century markets at Ilminster, Milverton, Crewkerne and Frome were held in small towns of Saxon origin which may have existed also at Cheddar and Somerton. By no means all of these townships necessarily grew around ninth-century fortifications and it has been suggested that the presence of large numbers of such small boroughs in Somerset may also be due in part to their association with royal lands and the frequent visits of the king to this important base of West Saxon power. This might well be true, for example, of Cheddar, where the Anglo-Saxon royal palace has been excavated, and it has also been suggested that complex royal administration may be indicated by the legal or fiscal grouping of pairs of such boroughs, like Somerton and Langport, Cheddar and Axbridge, Frome and Bruton, and by the fact that mints had existed at six places in Somerset by the eleventh century. The survival of these small boroughs and their subsequent medieval growth was of course determined partly by the geographical advantages of their sites in later times and partly by the extent to which they participated in the prosperity of the West Country woollen industry. Though the fortunes of many of them, especially the woollen towns, fluctuated considerably and their legal status was not defined until after the 1832 Reform Act, yet the majority survive as ingredients in the mixture of former wool towns, market towns and town-like villages which is still characteristic of the eastern and southern parts of Somerset.

The Wiltshire Domesday records the existence of boroughs only at Cricklade, Malmesbury, Bradford-on-Avon and Calne in the part of the county which lies within the Bristol region, but there is good evidence that the first three had been urban settlements for a considerable period. Cricklade and Malmesbury were certainly fortified before the Conquest; both had issued coins and it is possible that as a centre for local trade from the ninth century onwards Malmesbury had an importance which merited its special treatment at the head of the survey.

The different history of Mercian Gloucestershire might well have placed it outside the Wessex sphere of early urban growth, but the fact that only two boroughs and four other sites of markets are specifically referred to in Domesday may be due in part to the incompleteness of this aspect of the survey. Gloucester, which was fortified by Aethelflaeda of Mercia in 909, was almost certainly a place of some size throughout the Saxon period and appears to have been concerned with iron working and the manufacture of nails as a result of its close contact with the Forest of Dean since Roman times at least. Winchcombe, too, was a borough in the eleventh century whose importance may have grown after the founding of its Abbey in the early ninth century, but only a reference to burgesses and the finds of coins of the period between 979 and 1016 afford evidence of Bristol's existence before the Conquest.

**155**

F

In addition markets certainly existed at Tewkesbury, Berkeley, Thornbury and Cirencester, but they bring the total of possible urban centres to a remarkably small one in a county which had over 20 boroughs and 40 markets in the fourteenth century.

An appreciation of the ecclesiastical as well as the political and administrative aspects of Anglo-Saxon history is essential to an analysis of the Domesday survey in the Bristol region because here the church lands and those held by the king (or forfeited to him between 1066 and 1086) were of vastly greater importance than those in lay hands. Moreover, the church lands were frequently held in compact blocks of territory so that their administration by the religious houses in later times profoundly affected the economic development of whole districts, especially where they were actively concerned in wool production, the woollen industry and mineral working.

In Somerset in the eleventh century there was a broad geographical division between the south, where the king, the Count of Mortain and William of Moion held most of the lands, and the north, where the majority of the holdings were ecclesiastical. Even in south Somerset, however, the great manor of Taunton belonged to the Cathedral at Winchester and included large areas to the north and south of the town, whilst to the west of it another large area was held by the church at Wells. Glastonbury Abbey lands extended in a nearly continuous belt across the levels of central Somerset from Mells to Middlezoy and Woolavington, but also included areas to the north of Mendip between Winscombe and Wrington. The latter adjoined one of the four great blocks of territory surrounding Mendip which were held by the religious house at Wells, whilst towards the lower Bristol Avon lay the Coutances lands and upstream round Bath another compact group of holdings of Bath Abbey. Thus, apart from the royal lands on Mendip between Frome and Cheddar and those between Stanton Drew, Bedminster and Keynsham, the greater part of north and central Somerset was in ecclesiastical hands and in the county as a whole nearly one-third of the assessment was on lands held by the church, whilst the king and the religious houses together held about half the total.

Similar circumstances prevailed in north and west Wiltshire where the king held wide areas in the western vale between Calne and Warminster, but further north the lands of Malmesbury Abbey occupied large parts of the lowlands between Chippenham, Swindon and Cirencester. In Gloucestershire there is again a concentration of the church lands in the north of the county, partly because of the presence of the religious houses at Gloucester, Winchcombe and Evesham and the links with the Hwiccian see of Worcester. Other ecclesiastical holdings were scattered throughout the county, however, and Domesday shows that more than a third of its assessment was on lands held by religious establishments whilst the king and the church together held some 60 per cent of the land recorded in the county.

This situation in the west of England may have arisen from the lateness of the Saxon conquest of the area and the granting of lands to the church in many districts which were occupied only after 635 when King Cynegils was converted. Moreover, the possibility exists that a legacy of British Christianity survived in the areas which were conquered only in the mid-seventh century, probably strengthened in the fifth and sixth centuries by the influence of Welsh Christianity which is shown in the dedications to St Congar at Congresbury, St Decuman at Watchet, St Dyfrig at Porlock and St Petroc at Timberscombe, and by Irish Christians like Meldun who apparently founded Malmesbury Abbey before the middle of the seventh century. As yet there is no archaeological confirmation of traditions of the earliest history of a British church at Glastonbury and its possible associations with St Patrick, but excavations at the Abbey have certainly shown that older structures were replaced during the first main church building period about 700. The earlier charters of the Abbey are of doubtful authenticity but the archaeological evidence does not conflict with the possibility that grants of land were confirmed by King Ine at the end of the seventh century, and by that time, seemingly under his patronage, Aldhelm of Malmesbury had founded religious establishments at Bradford-on-Avon, Frome and Bruton. From soon after 625 the Hwiccii of Gloucestershire came under Mercian control but here too the founding of religious houses at Bath in 676, at Gloucester (St Peter and Paul) in 681 and at Tetbury and Whittington about the same time shows that the Hwiccian sub-kings were hardly less active in support of the church in the seventh century than King Ine, and indeed there is a possibility that Malmesbury Abbey received grants of land from both kingdoms.

From the late seventh century the ecclesiastical history of Wessex is complicated by the rearrangement of the dioceses, that of Dorchester-on-Thames being replaced before 700 by Winchester, which in turn was subdivided into the dioceses of Winchester and Sherborne in 705. There is conflicting literary evidence as to the position of the boundary between them but it seems most probable that it lay in Selwood and along the vale of west Wiltshire, leaving Aldhelm's sphere of influence as a founder of churches at Bradford-on-Avon and Frome within his diocese when he became Bishop of Sherborne in 705. Two centuries later further partition of the Wessex dioceses made Somerset largely coincident with the diocese of Wells, and the adjacent parts of west Wiltshire were probably added to the diocese of Ramsbury later to be incorporated in that of Salisbury. To the north of the Bristol Avon early diocesan history is a good deal simpler, the whole of the Hwiccian lands in Gloucestershire remaining entirely within the diocese of Worcester from its creation in 680, though the Forest of Dean was long attached to the diocese of Hereford.

Throughout the eighth and ninth centuries in both Wessex and Mercia the founding of religious houses continued. To the Gloucestershire houses at Westbury-on-Trym (720), Yate (720), Cleeve (785), Berkeley (759), Beckford (775) and Cheltenham (775) were added in the following century Deerhurst (804), Winchcombe (811), Twinging (814) and Cirencester (820), and in the early tenth century the church of St Oswald at Gloucester and the religious establishments at Tewkesbury and Stanway. In Somerset two monasteries were founded by King Ine at Muchelney (725) and by King Alfred at Athelney (888), but at Bath, Wells, Frome, Bedminster, Pitminster, Ilminster and possibly Cheddar and Taunton the religious establishments tended to take on the role of minsters exercising some form of pastoral care over their neighbourhood, and the same may well have been true of the wealthy churches on the royal manors at Milborne Port, North Curry, South Petherton and Crewkerne. Some attempts were made (at Wells, for example) to establish a more ordered monastic life but with little success until the tenth-century Benedictine revival under the influence of St Dunstan of Glastonbury.

The translation of St Dunstan from Glastonbury to the see of Worcester before he became Archbishop of Canterbury is indicative of the pre-eminence of Wessex during the tenth-century unification of England and marks the diminishing importance of the political and ecclesiastical boundary at the Bristol Avon between Mercia and Wessex. At once he set about reforming his new province by bringing the religious house at Westbury-on-Trym under strict Benedictine rule. This was followed immediately by reforms at Worcester itself and at the great Abbey of Winchcombe, and it is in no small measure due to the influence of Glastonbury and in particular of St Dunstan and his successors in Worcester that the church was both influential and exceptionally well endowed throughout the Bristol region on the eve of the Conquest.

In the long period from the end of the Roman occupation to the Norman Conquest a framework of the pattern of medieval settlements and communications in the Bristol region was therefore established and almost all the land, except for parts of the higher moors, the Forest of Dean and the levels, was brought into agricultural use.

To some extent this meant that the sharp contrasts of the prehistoric period between the uplands and the vales were softened as the centre of gravity of population and economic importance moved to the zones between them, whether at the foot of the Cotswold scarp, round the margins of the upper basins of the Thames and the Bristol Avon, at the foot of the Carboniferous Limestone hills or in the great curving belt of country below the scarps round the eastern and southern sides of Somerset. Hints were not lacking, however, that the old contrasts might redevelop. There was already evidence, for example, that the higher parts of Cotswold were not well suited to the usual forms of agriculture in the Middle Ages and a suggestion of their future distinctive character can be deduced from the extra information in the Somerset Domesday which reveals the great importance of sheep on the oolites further south. Moreover, other long-standing contrasts were sharpened rather than softened by the political history of the Bristol region before the Norman Conquest. Thus, when the boundary between Wessex and Mercia was established close to the line of the Bristol Avon, this served to reinforce old differences, particularly as parts of Somerset seem to have been of considerable importance to the rulers of Wessex whereas the development of Gloucestershire before the Conquest does not appear to have been quite so rapid, especially in respect of the origins of urban life. In the tenth century this division may have had diminished importance but, even so, at the beginning of the Middle Ages the county boundary does seem to have represented a real line of cultural and economic division.

# CHAPTER 8

# The Changing Economy from the Eleventh to the Eighteenth Centuries

As late as the seventeenth century there were remnants of manorial control in the Bristol region and Royal Forests still existed, but these were exceptional relics of earlier conditions and it is the purpose of the following discussion to trace the course of agricultural and rural changes which had virtually brought to an end the feudal patterns of the Middle Ages.

### Agriculture

Even at the start of this period it would be incorrect to imagine the existence of uniform conditions throughout the region, and in particular it is by no means clear to what extent the region was characterized by the presence of the field systems which were the normal accompaniment of the manorial pattern of the Midlands. Though there is evidence that field systems were established in Saxon times in parts of the Bristol region, it came to occupy a marginal position between the southwest Midlands with their characteristic two and three-field cultivation and the southwest peninsula where there are relatively few traces of such methods. It has been suggested that a boundary between these very different regions might be identified in northern or central Somerset, but there seems little justification for the attempted recognition of a line across the region, beyond which it might be assumed the Midland field system did not spread. In detail the actual distribution of this form of land use was probably determined by the date and density of early Saxon settlement and also by local environmental conditions. Thus there are a number of—possibly isolated—examples of open fields well into southern and western Somerset, whilst on the other hand open-field cultivation was by no means universal to the north of the hypothetical boundary in Gloucestershire. Considerable areas of Cotswold, for example, do not appear to have had a field system and the practice was almost entirely absent from the Forest of Dean.

Where open-field cultivation did exist it was characterized in the Bristol region by very early modifications. Of these, the first was the change from two-field to three-field systems which may be regarded as leading to an intensification of land use. In this there was a considerable degree of local variation and it was a rare or tardy development on the upland calcareous areas of Cotswold, east Somerset and the chalk lands on the margins of the region. Here such open-field agriculture as existed tended to remain on the older pattern. A two-field system operated on alternative fallow and wheat or barley on the estates of Winchcombe Abbey during the thirteenth, fourteenth and fifteenth centuries, and two-field agriculture was practised at Hawkesbury and Badminton in the sixteenth century, though nearby at Minchinhampton there is evidence of enclosure and exchange of holdings within a three-field system. In Somerset sixteenth-century remnants of the open fields at Curry Mallet and Bruton were of the two-field type and indeed examples of the three-field form were rare in the southern part of the region, the best-known being at Martock, South Petherton, Barrington and Stoke-sub-Hamdon. On the other hand, the improvement to the three-field system was earlier and more rapid on the richer loams and clays of the vales and reached a maximum in the prosperous period between 1250 and 1350 when the results can be illustrated by the fourteenth-century evidence of three-crop cultivation at Corsham.

However, many cases of this change of field arrangements were associated in the Bristol region with very early enclosure, which resulted in great irregularity of the remaining open-field patterns, so that true three-field cultivation was not common. During the thirteenth century, for example, enclosure was taking place on lands of the Crown and of the Berkeleys throughout the vales of Gloucestershire from the Bristol Avon to Evesham, where it was said 'wee inclose, convert and keepe in severall to our selves our grounds which before laye open with the Common fields'. This may well explain the situation that existed by the sixteenth century, when in many localities in the vale, including Yate, Horton, Frocester and Frampton Cotterell, a high proportion of the meadow and pasture had been long enclosed and the remaining open arable land had a totally irregular field system. Similarly in the vale of Wiltshire the Abbot of Malmesbury was enclosing land in the thirteenth century and at Christian Malford early enclosure had taken in 40 per cent of the land, the remaining open arable being worked on an exceedingly complex field system. By the seventeenth century 75 per cent of the land in the cheese and butter country of north and west Wiltshire was said to be enclosed. In Somerset, too, a great part of the rich lowland area was enclosed at a very early date and an example of resulting

161

complex field systems is afforded by the remaining open arable land at Kingsbury.

Such early changes, enclosure and the resultant break-up or complexity of field systems in the West Country may have arisen for several reasons. By medieval standards there was sufficient good arable land interspersed with invaluable alluvial meadow lands throughout the extensive vales to encourage progressive agriculture. Moreover, particularly in Somerset, the presence of moors, levels and marshes meant that there was abundant pasture land outside the field system itself which freed it from the rigidity of pastoral regulation. Finally, and again particularly in south and west Somerset, settlements and units of land-holding were commonly very small and some slightly more flexible attitude towards field arrangements may have existed because of traces of run-rig practice shared with the southwest peninsula. Such underlying causes of change and of the early breakdown of a far from universal open-field system were augmented, however, by local peculiarities of tenure and agricultural practice. Throughout the region, and especially in Gloucestershire, there was a high proportion of copyholders and tenants-at-will, and a peculiar copyhold for three lives (renewable) which meant that if tenants did not manage to purchase the comparative security of a leasehold, at the end of three lives the lord could arrange short leases in lieu of the defunct copyhold and enclose the land when all the short leases fell in together. In agricultural practice the process of hitching—reducing the effective fallow by using part of it each year for a crop—tended to break standard patterns, as did the existence of 'every year land', cropped continuously with beans, peas and oats, throughout Gloucestershire, the adjacent parts of Wiltshire and in lowland Somerset. It is uncertain how far early tenurial and agricultural change was matched by equally early commutation of services for rents, but there is evidence of this process on the lands of Glastonbury Abbey, where the whole of the village of Grittleton had commuted by 1189, and by the fourteenth century commutation was regarded as normal on the Winchcombe lands in Gloucestershire.

Since the region was never entirely occupied by 'normal' field systems and since enclosure started so early and continued throughout the fifteenth, sixteenth and seventeenth centuries, comparatively little land remained to be enclosed by Act. In Somerset as little as 12·7 per cent of the land was enclosed in this way, in Gloucestershire 18·7 per cent, and in Wiltshire the somewhat higher figure of 26 per cent is entirely due to the late enclosure of the chalk downs, outside our area. Much of the enclosure of land in Britain at the end of the Middle Ages is said to have been for wool production, and because this was the home of the West Country woollen industry it might be tempting to regard the early enclosed state of the Bristol region as stemming from this cause. When examined in more regional detail, however, such a thesis cannot be sustained. In Gloucestershire, Cotswold was the centre of a great deal of wool production, but it was here that the greatest proportion of land in the county remained open either as sheep walk, cow down or open-field arable to the time of the Acts. Moreover, such early enclosure as did take place on Cotswold was mainly in the area to the south of Tetbury and its connection with woollen manufacture seems to have been for the more intensive provision of meat and dairy produce for the towns rather than the production of wool. Similarly in Wiltshire the wool-producing downland was late enclosed so that in the northern areas of the Bristol region it was the vales of Wiltshire and Gloucestershire which were mainly affected by enclosure before the eighteenth century. Much of the Forest of Dean was also enclosed at an early date but the special circumstances of this district can best be discussed later in connection with an account of the extraction of its minerals. Some portion of the early enclosed lands of the northern vales remained in arable use and this was apparently still characteristic of parts of the vale of Wiltshire in Defoe's time (1724–6). They were, however, by this time rapidly becoming involved in dairy production and much of the grass enclosure of the vales of Gloucestershire in the seventeenth century was for dairying. Sheep unquestionably existed in the enclosed vales, especially in winter, but this was not an important motive for enclosure, which really represented a continuation of a long-standing process for the improved use of the rich vale lands. The early enclosed state of Somerset was commented upon by writers from the mid-sixteenth century when Leland wrote of the 'elme wood wherwith most part of al Somersetshere ys yn hegge rowys enclosid'. His references to the actual agriculture of Somerset, however, mainly concern the plenty of 'henes, whete and catelle' rather than sheep. Indeed it is likely that wool production was most important on the oolites in eastern and northeastern Somerset and, as in Cotswold to the north, it was here that a fair proportion of unenclosed land remained in the sixteenth century. Early enclosure in Somerset, too, was therefore by no means solely for wool production. By the seventeenth century almost all the available agricultural land in the county was enclosed, because the greater part of the 12 per cent affected by Acts consisted of land reclaimed in the levels, the only exception being eighteenth-century Acts for areas in the Lias ridge between Alford, Keinton Mandeville, Somerton and Curry Rivel, on the Poldens, isolated areas at Weston-super-Mare, Portishead, Ditcheat, Milborne Port and Cheddar, and the nineteenth-century enclosures at Middlezoy and Weston Zoyland.

If special local economic motives for early enclosure are to be sought it seems more likely that they will be found in the need to intensify the production of food for the urban markets in Bristol and in the wool towns and villages round Stroudwater, in the upper basin of the Bristol Avon and in south and southeast Somerset. It is true that popular resistance to enclosures did occur in the Bristol region in the seventeenth century but it arose from local grievances in the Royal Forests of Braydon and Dean and in the newly reclaimed Berkeley lands near Slimbridge. It did not arise from the widespread evils which contemporary propagandists attributed to the general conversion of enclosed lands to sheep pasture.

To minimize the importance of wool production as a cause of early enclosure is not to deny the importance of sheep in the economy of the Bristol region throughout the Middle Ages and well into modern times. In the centuries following the Conquest the considerable role of sheep in the Somerset economy, which was evident from the returns of the *Exon. Domesday,* apparently continued because in 1135 there were 3,568 sheep on the demesne lands alone of Glastonbury Abbey. In Gloucestershire much of the wealth of Winchcombe Abbey was derived from the sheep of Cotswold onto which its lands extended, and it has been estimated that by the early fourteenth century the Abbey possessed at least 8,000 sheep. The Berkeley family, too, held vast flocks in the same period. Of one of them it was reported: 'In some of the manors hee had his flocks of 1,500 sheepe. In some 1,000, 900, 800, 700, 600, 500, 400 and in none under 300. At Beverstone [on Cotswold near Tetbury] in the Seventh of Edward the Third [1334] hee did sheare 5,775 sheepe which were going in those manors thereto adjoyning.' Moreover, many of the manors were in the vale parts of the Berkeley lands which had a valuable function for wintering the flocks, as might be inferred from a description of a later Berkeley, Thomas V, as 'a perfect Cotswold sheppard, living a kind of grazier's life, having his flocks of sheep summering in one place and wintering in other places, as hee observed the fields and pastures to bee sound and could bargaine best cheape'. In many areas sheep were therefore still one of the mainstays of the agricultural economy but the wool was by no means universally of the highest quality and the relatively low esteem of Somerset wool may have been due to the county's large numbers of lowland 'moor' sheep.

Much of the wool was used in the West Country woollen industry but the fourteenth and fifteenth centuries saw increasing purchases by foreign merchants. Florentine buyers regarded the Cotswold markets of Northleach, Burford, Tetbury and Cirencester as the best sources of wool from the Abbey lands. At the end of the fourteenth century and during the fifteenth, they showed a preference for wool produced on the open north Cotswold which was collected at the nearby markets, particularly in Cirencester, and shipped by direct sailings from Southampton to the Mediterranean.

Conversely the significable of arable agriculture must not be under-estimated because it clearly remained vitally important throughout the region during the whole of the period under consideration. The Winchcombe lands afford specific examples on Cotswold of the two-year rotation of fallow followed by wheat or barley, with the addition of the characteristic Gloucestershire use of 'every year land' for peas and oats. This practice seems to have been maintained throughout the thirteenth and fourteenth centuries. In 1335 at Temple Guiting in the Windrush valley, 94 per cent of the demesne land was in spring corn, whilst a century later wheat and barley normally shared over 80 per cent of the demesne every other year. In the vales, before the rise of dairying, arable cultivation was probably even more prominent and on either side of Cotswold the upper Thames basin, the vale of Wiltshire and the lower basins of the Warwickshire Avon and the Severn have been described as a granary of Britain in the later Middle Ages. By the seventeenth century the contrast between the arable cultivation of the vale and of Cotswold had become sufficiently marked to call for the comment that in the latter area 'they sow their land but every other yeere' and that the folding of sheep on the arable was practised on 'sands, stonebrash and generally for all their barren lands upon the hills, where it is allmost the only improvement'. In the vale the system of two or three crops (either wheat–beans or barley–beans–wheat), followed by fallow, had apparently become the rule, as indeed it re-mained until the end of the eighteenth century, beans being an essential element in the rotation on the heavier clay lands. It is interesting to notice that some exchange of seed was practised between the two regions in Gloucestershire, Cotswold barley seed being planted in the vale and lowland wheat seed being sent to Cotswold. Oats seem to have been grown less commonly except on 'every year land' and rye is mentioned frequently only in the Ryelands districts round the Forest of Dean. In Somerset, too, cereal production remained the essential function of arable land throughout the Middle Ages and indeed food supplies from the Somerset 'granaries' have been suggested as a factor aiding the evolution of the woollen industrial areas of northeast Somerset and west Wiltshire. In the middle of the sixteenth century Leland des-cribed much of Somerset as 'plentiful of corne' and it should be noticed that references to corn occur over most of the county except the extreme southwest between Exford and Simonsbath, where he noted 'little or no corne or habitation'. In particular Leland's comment that there was 'great plenty of beans and great plenty of whete' in the area he traversed round Stert suggests an arable economy in lowland Somerset comparable with that of the vale of Gloucestershire. This

165

pattern probably survived through the seventeenth century and into the eighteenth, when lands in Burnham, Huntspill and Mark were said to have 'borne crops of wheat year after year without any manure for twenty years together'.

However, the coming birth of dairying is foreshadowed in other comments by Leland which show the considerable importance of cattle in the sixteenth-century economy of Somerset. On the moorlands of the southwest there was 'store and breeding of young cattelle' and during the sixteenth and seventeenth centuries cattle, grazing and dairying were mentioned in practically every part of the county. By the beginning of the eighteenth century Defoe was able to say that all the low part of Somerset was engaged in grazing and feeding cattle, and that the lower western and northern parts bred and grazed black cattle. The date when dairying became fully developed in the vale of Wiltshire is somewhat uncertain, since Defoe described some arable cultivation there in the early eighteenth century. By that time, however, considerable areas in the northwest of the vale had been engaged in dairying for generations and in any case in 1792 Marshall wrote that for at least forty years the whole of the north Wiltshire vale had been a grass dairying area. As early as the fifteenth century the production of cheese in northwest Wiltshire and in the Stroudwater area of Gloucestershire was as noteworthy as that of corn and wool, and the continued enclosure of the vale of Gloucestershire in the sixteenth and seventeenth centuries was at least in part concerned with grass farming for cattle. On the Berkeley estates some draining and reclamation of low-lying meadow land was commenced and reference was made to the advantages of a 'flourishing matt of trefoil' achieved by the use of ash and soot as a dressing for the new forms of clover.

By the start of the eighteenth century, therefore, there was some justification for the use of the term dairy vales, at least in Wiltshire and Gloucestershire, but for the region as a whole there was, by the standards of 1700, a reasonably mixed agriculture based on corn, sheep and cattle, with some local additions of pigs and poultry. One other aspect of later specialization was gradually emerging, however, as the production of fruit increased throughout the region. Orchards, particularly of cider apples, were being established throughout Somerset except on Mendip, the southern moorlands and the lowest lands of the levels, whilst in Gloucestershire there were already signs of the later concentration on horticulture in the extreme north near the Vale of Evesham. The other specialization was short-lived; the growth of tobacco for a little over thirty years, between 1622 and some time after its prohibition in 1652, was started as an experiment by John

Stafford in Winchcombe and extended rapidly as far afield as Tewkesbury, Cheltenham, Northleach and Great Burrington.

## The Woollen Industry

Agriculture was by no means the only important occupation in the Bristol region before the eighteenth century, however, and in Gloucestershire there is evidence that it accounted for only about 46 per cent of the working population in the seventeenth century. This figure is based on what has been described as a seventeenth-century census of occupations, calculated from exceptionally detailed statements of employment in muster rolls drawn up for the whole of the county. Such data lack precision, especially as the category of 'labourers' is usually undefined in the rolls, but they give a good broad picture of employment in the county. They indicate that by the seventeenth century a very wide range of occupations existed, with a surprisingly high proportion of what would now be described as service industries. However, the balance of agricultural and non-agricultural employment in Gloucestershire was affected to a very considerable degree by the fact that over 15 per cent of the working population was engaged in the manufacture of textiles. This is probably a fair measure of the importance of the Gloucestershire part of the West Country woollen industry in the seventeenth century and if figures were available it is likely that they would reveal a similar state of affairs in Somerset and in the part of Wiltshire which is included in the Bristol region.

Wool working in the Bristol region certainly dates back to prehistoric times at Glastonbury and, even after the rise of the industry on a larger scale in the towns, some of the ancient widespread woollen crafts were continued on farms and in villages throughout the west of England. Thus there is early evidence of woollen manufacture in many of the villages in southern and western Somerset and at Hawkesbury and Chipping Sodbury in Gloucestershire. However, in the twelfth and thirteenth centuries it was in towns and cities like Tewkesbury, Cirencester, Gloucester, Taunton and particularly Bristol that the industry was most important. In Bristol it was said that one-fifth of the population was engaged in woollen manufacture and well into the fourteenth century 1,500 workers were apparently involved. Indeed it was in 1339 that Thomas Blanket was contemplating the establishment of what was virtually an embryonic woollen factory in the city and throughout the fourteenth and fifteenth centuries wool cloth formed a major part of Bristol's exports, though much of this in the later period was manufactured elsewhere.

The so-called 'decay' of the industry, which prompted the enact-
ments of Edward III's reign, probably affected only these established
centres of the town and city industry and may well have been caused
by a shift of woollen manufacture away from them. Such changes, which
have been described as a thirteenth-century industrial revolution,
initiated much that came to be characteristic of the West Country
industry in succeeding centuries. The moves may in part represent an
attempt to escape from borough and gild restrictions and levies, but they
were also very closely associated with the mechanization of the fulling
process essential in the manufacture of broadcloths on which the
twelfth- and thirteenth-century industry depended. Most thirteenth-
century fulling mills were located in the north of England, the Welsh
border country and the southwestern counties and represented a
regional shift from the lowlands of the southeast to the margins of
highland Britain where water power was readily available. Moreover,
the need for unobstructed stream-side sites meant that many of them
were established in the country or in smaller towns, rather than in the
large and more heavily built-up textile towns. The existence of fulling
mills on Cotswold near Malmesbury in 1174 and at Temple Guiting in
1185 means that Gloucestershire shares with Yorkshire the earliest signs
of this revolution. Such mills became relatively common during the
thirteenth century and are known to have existed on Cotswold at
Bourton-on-Windrush, Bourton-on-the-Water, Hawkesbury, Cerney
(near Cirencester), Hinton, Minchinhampton, Overbury, Stanway,
Wheatenhurst and Winchcombe. In the part of Wiltshire within the
Bristol region there were mills at Castle Combe, Chilton Foliat, Stanley
and Chippenham, and in Somerset at Cheddar, Wells, Wookey,
Dulverton, Dunster, Wiveliscombe and in the town of Taunton. As
Lord of the very large manor of which Taunton was the centre, the
Bishop of Winchester made himself responsible for building and equip-
ping a new fulling mill in the town in 1218–9. The Winchester records
show that this mill was farmed to a fuller for £3 13s 4d when it was
built. Seven years later the 'farm' was £8 13s 4d but its almost immediate decline to figures between £2 and £3 during the rest of the
century was explicitly stated to be due to competition from other fulling
mills nearby. Lords of manors sought to extend 'suit of mill' to fulling
as such mills became commonplace throughout the region and an
example of this process is recorded at Hawkesbury in 1325. Fulling
mills had become a part of the manorial pattern of the countryside
and fulling was no longer a town monopoly. Nevertheless the towns
were slow to acquiesce and in Bristol the gild of fullers passed an
ordinance in 1346 which prohibited the movement of cloth out of the

city for fulling, whilst another ordinance of 1381 forbade the finishing in Bristol of cloth which had been fulled elsewhere.

Fourteenth-century aulnage figures indicate that up to this time the growth of the woollen industry was most marked in Somerset, where about 10,000 broadcloths were produced each year, whilst Gloucestershire produced considerably less than 5,000. In Somerset production was concentrated in four main areas. The first lay in the north and northeast near the Bristol Avon and its left-bank tributaries the Chew and the Frome, and included large producers like Pensford and Frome, where 2,000 cloths a year were manufactured, and Bath with over 1,000. In addition woollen manufacture on a smaller scale was carried on in most of the stream-side villages, including Freshford, Iford, Farleigh Hungerford, Stowford, Tellisford and Rode. The second area of woollen manufacture in Somerset followed the curve of hills round the upper basin of the Brue from Wells through Shepton Mallet to Bruton, Castle Cary and Wincanton, by far the most important centres at this stage being Wells and the neighbouring Croscombe, each of which produced over 1,000 cloths per year. Beyond Castle Cary the third wool district followed the hill country circling the upper basins of the Yeo, the Parrett and the Tone to Taunton, but it also included the towns of Langport and Bridgwater on the middle and lower course of the Parrett. This southern part of Somerset did not share the general West Country preoccupation with the manufacture of fine broadcloths but specialized rather on smaller and less fine cloths called straits, of which Taunton made over 500 per year in the fourteenth century. Here and in the much less important fourth textile area of west Somerset towns like Wiveliscombe, Dulverton, Dunster and Barnstaple, the subsequent history of textile working was also distinctive. By the seventeenth century Taunton had adopted worsted techniques and was making mainly serges, whilst the area to the west which had previously made coarse kerseys and dozens was also changing to worsted manufacture. Along the southeastern margins of the county from Castle Cary and Wincanton to Crewkerne and Chard, considerable quantities of flax were grown throughout the Middle Ages and here the early woollen industry was accompanied by home spinning of flax for the production of coarse linens like dowlas and ticking. The weaving of these fabrics was later concentrated in the wool towns of Castle Cary, Bruton, Wincanton, Yeovil, Crewkerne and Chard, and along with the manufacture of rope, netting and sailcloth remained an important industry until modern times.

The fifteenth century saw a considerable development of the woollen industry in the three western counties of Somerset, Wiltshire and Gloucestershire, which together produced one-third of all the woollen cloth manufactured in Britain in 1470. Though Somerset remained the most important, being the second largest producer in the country, the industry had made very rapid strides in Gloucestershire and Wiltshire, which now occupied the fourth and fifth positions.

In Gloucestershire this was the period when woollen manufacture was localized in what became a truly industrial region in Stroudwater and the adjacent parts of the Cotswold scarp. Here in Minchinhampton and nearer the scarp at Hawkesbury, woollen manufacture had been present since the thirteenth century and many references exist to fulling, dyeing and the digging of fuller's earth, but no further great development took place during the fourteenth century. However, the water-power potential of this location near the strong streams breaching the Cotswold scarp had long been appreciated and used in other ways. Stroudwater divides Minchinhampton from Bisley and at the time of the Domesday survey each had land in the valley where there were no less than 13 grain mills. In the middle of the fifteenth century there is evidence of a vast upsurge of interest in the letting and re-letting of ancient water rights and mill rights throughout the Golden Valley of the Stroud Frome and its tributaries. Moreover, this was accompanied by vast local increases in the new assessment for lay subsidies when compared with those of the fourteenth century. At Rodborough and Bisley, for example, the increases were five-fold and thirteen-fold respectively, whereas the assessments on long-established wool centres like Cirencester were only slightly increased or actually declined, as at Winchcombe. Much of the water which provided power in the section of the Cotswold scarp between Painswick and Hawkesbury had passed through the natural filter of the great thickness of Cotteswold Sands and was both soft and said to have special properties making it particularly suitable for textile finishing and for dyeing the distinctive scarlets for which the district became famous. Initially, therefore, this Stroud-water area became a great fulling, dyeing and finishing centre to which cloths were sent from many surrounding towns and villages, but this was only a temporary phase and it was soon carrying out all the stages of broadcloth manufacture.

It is significant that the first of the Wiltshire wool towns to develop rapidly in the fifteenth century was Castle Combe. Though situated in the upper basin of the Bristol Avon, like the rest of the west Wiltshire textile centres, its exact location is on the section of the By brook tributary which is deeply trenched into the lower Cotswold dipslope and gives topographical conditions generally similar to those in Stroud-water, with ample power and water of a quality well-suited to dyeing reds. There was a fulling mill here in the fourteenth century but real development began in the first half of the fifteenth century when

Sir John Fastolf, campaigning in France, arranged for his Castle Combe tenants to manufacture the red-and-white uniforms for his troops. This apparently initiated immediate industrial growth, because as early as 1454 the vill of Nethercombe on the valley floor had become virtually an industrial township where mill and house construction was proceeding apace, where landless men were being recruited into the service of a real class of entrepreneurs and where early mechanization is indicated by the construction of the first gig mill in England. By 1457 'Red woollen cloths called Castle Combes' were well known in London, and during the rest of the century 'Castle Combes', 'Stroudwaters' and 'Bristols' became famous all over Europe as coloured woollens of the finest quality. Though London was handling a gradually increasing proportion of wool cloth exports during the fifteenth century, a great deal was still shipped from Bristol, and the trade name 'Bristols' probably applied to fabrics manufactured in various parts of the region but exported through that city.

In spite of fluctuations in the middle of the sixteenth century, the West Country industry continued to grow and it was in this period that Wiltshire woollen manufacture expanded considerably. Centred in the inland basin of the Bristol Avon at Chippenham, Calne, Bradford-on-Avon, Trowbridge and Westbury and on the Cotswold dipslope at Castle Combe, Marshfield and Malmesbury, this growth, like that in the prospering Stroudwater district of Gloucestershire, marked a further stage in the move of the woollen industry away from the chartered cities and towns. In Wiltshire the Tudor Act of 1557, aimed at checking this process, was as ineffective as elsewhere and it is significant of the importance attached to the Stroudwater area that the Act specially excepted from its provisions 'any of the villages near adjoyning to the Water of Stroud in the county of Gloucester'. In the Wiltshire industry there appears to have been a distinct tendency for production to pass into the hands of a relatively small number of capitalist clothiers, some of whom became great landowners as well as industrialists. Stompe of Malmesbury was by far the most famous of these men but in the same town the King and Hedges families were substantial capitalists and so were the Longfords of Trowbridge and the Yerburys and Hortons of Bradford-on-Avon. The figures derived from the 1608 muster rolls in Gloucestershire suggest that about 200 clothiers were directly or indirectly responsible for the employment of the 2,545 textile workers in the county, but there is little evidence of individual employers with more than a modest labour force. The Tudor Act of 1571, which would have had the effect of prohibiting clothiers from purchasing more than 20 acres of land, would presumably have had appreciable consequences only in Wiltshire had it not also proved ineffective.

The reign of Henry VIII has been described as the golden age of the white broadcloth industry, but this was the branch of the woollen industry on which much of the West Country concentrated throughout the sixteenth century, and the growing importance of the Wiltshire area is demonstrated by the fact that in 1606 some 60 per cent of all such cloths sent to London came from that county. This is a reliable indication of Wiltshire's share in the production of the cloth because in 1559 London was already handling 93 per cent of the country's cloth exports. This, of course, had brought about a catastrophic decline in the shipments of cloth from the port of Bristol and it is scarcely surprising that the West Country was the home of 'interlopers' challenging the privileges of the London-based chartered companies, who nevertheless still sought to monopolize the trade until 1688.

The pre-eminence of the white broadcloth trade, on which the prosperity of the West Country woollen industry had grown, was coming to an end in the late sixteenth and early seventeenth centuries, however. Changed fashions and the success of worsted and the New Draperies in eastern and northern England no doubt played a part in bringing this about, but to some extent it was also the outcome of changes in the supply of wool. There is some controversy as to whether the woollen industry of the Middle Ages chose between long- and short-stapled wools and there is similarly a good deal of doubt about the exact nature of early Cotswold wools. The Cotswold sheep was apparently an animal of more than average size, whose wool may have been longer than that from Wiltshire and Somerset, but it has recently been argued that the Cotswold wool was nevertheless fine and technically of short staple. This would have made it suitable for the manufacture of the fine broadcloths of the West Country industry which surrounded the Cotswold upland—an argument which is supported by the popularity of Cotswold wools with the discerning Italian buyers. With the changed arable agriculture of the Cotswold plateau in the eighteenth century the food supply of the sheep was radically altered and this, combined with the increasing popularity of the Leicester/Cotswold crossbreds, tended to produce the long coarse wools of Cotswold commented upon by Rudder in 1779. However, this was long after the woollen industry had undergone the important technical changes of the seventeenth century, for which the cause must be sought elsewhere.

The whole of the West Country industry not only used Cotswold wools but also bought supplies from the Welsh border, the Midlands and the north of England at the Cotswold markets of Cirencester, Tetbury and Castle Combe. Following the enclosure movement in the fifteenth and sixteenth centuries and the expansion of the lowland sheep flocks, wool from many of these sources tended to become longer and coarser during the sixteenth and seventeenth centuries, and as early as 1586 West Country clothiers were complaining of the increasing coarseness of wool from the Midlands. Deprived of at least some part of its supply of short fine wool, the West Country broadcloth industry perforce had to adapt itself to the changed circumstances. The response varied from district to district and produced by the later seventeenth century a regional pattern of specialization which continued through the eighteenth and nineteenth centuries and to some extent exists in the surviving modern textile industries.

In Gloucestershire and especially in the main centre round Stroudwater and the valleys of the Cam and Little Avon, the response was to seek alternative supplies of fine short wools and to continue with the production of broadcloths. During the seventeenth century wool was still bought in the Midlands and eastern England, wherever suitable fleeces were available, but supplies were also sought in Dorset and even in South Wales, and during the eighteenth and nineteenth centuries wool of the merino and its crosses was imported through London and Bristol from Spain, later from Germany and finally from Australia and South Africa. Here, in any case, there was less immediate likelihood of collapse because the district had long specialized in the manufacture of dyed cloths, especially the scarlets of Stroudwater and the later blues of Uley, and was therefore less vulnerable to the vagaries of the country's staple exports of white broadcloths. The high degree of concentration of the Gloucestershire industry in the Stroudwater area had become evident by the time of the 'census' of the 1608 muster rolls. The five Hundreds which occupy the south central part of the county and encircle the Stroud valleys included three-quarters of the county's textile workers and probably a similar fraction of the 1,500 looms which were in use in 1622. Though the limitations of the statistical source must be borne in mind, it is still a useful indication of the dominance of the woollen industry in this district that the percentage of able-bodied workers engaged in textile crafts was 45 in the Longtree Hundred, 39 in Bisley Hundred, 38 in Berkeley Hundred, 32 in Whitstone Hundred and 28 in Grimboldsash Hundred. In the villages of the area the percentage was naturally even higher. In Dursley it was 55, in Woodmancote 68 and it reached 79 in Stinchcombe and 82 in Owlpen. Spinning and weaving were carried on throughout the whole area, but fulling and tucking were almost entirely concentrated alongside the scarp streams whose power was essential for the high degree of mechanization in these processes. This power was also used to drive the gig mills which replaced hand finishing by means of king teazles. From the sixteenth century onwards attempts were made to prohibit the use of gig mills by statute, but the Gloucestershire clothiers evaded the issue partly by declaring that the dyed cloths were not damaged by such mills and partly by describing their local machines as mozing mills. These were gig mills using embedded small teazles to finish the famous scarlet cloths; they continued in use into the nineteenth century and gave the Gloucestershire industry some advantage over that in Wiltshire, where the adoption of finishing machinery was long delayed. Localization of wool working round Stroudwater was matched by the decline of the industry elsewhere in Gloucestershire and the seventeenth century saw the gradual decay of woollen manufacture in Bristol, in the Forest of Dean, in many parts of the vale and on the plateau areas of Cotswold.

An alternative approach to the problem of changing wool supplies was to use the new longer and coarser varieties by combing them and adopting worsted techniques. It is significant that at Tetbury, where the market handled all varieties of wool, combing was carried on in the early seventeenth century. Worsted yarn was then spun from the longer combed wools in Tetbury itself and at Cirencester, Marshfield, Gloucester and Tewkesbury, all of them ancient wool centres which lacked adequate power supplies for the mechanical fulling and finishing of broadcloths. Much of this yarn was sold to worsted areas outside the Bristol region, but later in the century a West Country market arose with the growth of serge production, using a worsted warp and a weft of noils or short stapled wool. After 1650 serge was manufactured in Wiltshire at Calne and Devizes but until the eighteenth century the main West Country serge district was concentrated in and around Taunton, where straits rather than broadcloths had formerly been manufactured. The tradition,[1] that the serge industry in Taunton itself provided employment for 8,500 workers in the seventeenth century may have involved some exaggeration but the industry was certainly a very important one. Besides drawing wool from the Cotswold markets it also received supplies direct from the Midlands by way of the ports of Gloucester, Bristol and Bridgwater, and during the seventeenth, century a vast export of Irish long stapled wool was sent to the Taunton area through Barnstaple and Bideford as well as Bristol and Bridgwater.

The area which had depended most completely on the white broadcloth industry comprised the inland basin of the Bristol Avon and its left-bank tributaries in west Wiltshire and the adjacent parts of Somerset towards Frome. Here the impact of declining supplies of short fine wools was accentuated by politico-economic events of the early seven-

---

[1] Quoted by Baker, J. N. L. in Darby, H. C., (1961). An historical geography of England before 1800, Cambridge, p. 411.

teenth century and particularly by the ill-fated Cockayne's experiment of 1614. This was aimed at developing the home dyeing and finishing of white broadcloths and carried with it Cockayne's monopoly of the purchase of white broadcloths and their subsequent dyeing and finishing for export. Failure to dye adequately in the piece after fulling contributed to the collapse of the scheme in 1617, but it had already severely damaged the reputation of English cloth. Moreover, after 1618 the central European market was disrupted by wars and at home the Civil War led to the West Country being cut off from its main market in London for a considerable time. In this troubled period the woollen industry of the Wiltshire–Somerset borders turned to imported supplies of fine dyed Spanish wool for the manufacture of high quality 'Spanish' or 'Medley' cloths and as early as the 1620s this new development had been concentrated in Frome, Freshford and Bradford-on-Avon, where the Methuen and Goldney families were establishing the basis of their later pre-eminence. Later, Spanish wools were dyed in the Wiltshire and Somerset towns and supplemented by local supplies and wools from Sussex and Shropshire, acquired in the markets of Gloucestershire and at Warminster and Devizes. Most of the English wool was used to make a slightly coarser type of 'medley' cloth and eventually a technique was developed for dyeing whole cloths before the fulling process. Some export of white broadcloths from this area did continue into the second half of the seventeenth century but their manufacture was being rapidly replaced by the 'Spanish' and 'Medley' cloths at this time. Moreover, the orientation of the export trade to Europe was changing. It was no longer dominated by shipments from London to Holland and central Europe but instead increasing quantities of cloth were being sent to France, Portugal, the Mediterranean countries, India and the West Indies, not only from London but also from other ports including Bristol. Indeed, though London did not lose its legally privileged position until 1689, its capacity to dominate the export of woollens was greatly reduced after the Civil War. Moreover, the 'Spanish' cloth trade enjoyed a far greater freedom from regulation than had the manufacture of white broadcloths. London merchants were always active in encouraging the enforcement of the many regulations which the government had sought to impose on broadcloth production since Tudor times and their declining influence, particularly after 1640, may partly account for the fact that half-hearted attempts to legislate for the new cloths in a similar way were ineffective. Like the new industries in Lancashire, the evolving fancy cloth industry of Wiltshire and northeast Somerset grew up with a minimum of government intervention and in 1660 entered upon a period of rapid growth and prosperity.

By the early eighteenth century, therefore, there were three very prosperous centres in the West Country woollen industry, each with its own distinct specialization—the scarlet and blue broadcloth area of Stroudwater and the Cotswold scarp with an outlier at Castle Combe, the 'Spanish' and 'Medley' cloth area of the vale of Wiltshire and the Wiltshire/Somerset border, and the serge area of Taunton. Elsewhere wool working still existed in towns and villages throughout the region and in some cases formed the basis on which further local specialization took place during the course of the eighteenth century.

## Mining

No other non-agricultural activity before the eighteenth century can be compared in scale with the West Country woollen industry, but the Bristol region has the distinction of having two examples of very early mineral working in the metal and coal mining of Mendip and north Somerset and of the Forest of Dean. In both cases reference has already been made to evidence that these activities date back to pre-historic times but little is known of workings in either area in the Dark Ages and it is only in the post-Conquest period that it again becomes possible to trace their development.

The iron mining of the Forest of Dean was apparently the earlier of the two industries to gain importance because it seems to have enjoyed a near-monopoly of production in southern Britain which lasted through to the thirteenth century. Perhaps its most distinctive feature is that much of the productive area has been Crown land throughout its recorded history, from the post-Conquest period, when it became a Royal Forest, until the present century when the interests of the Crown were vested in the Coal Commission and the Forestry Commission and parts of it became the first National Forest Park in Britain. It seems likely that mining of both coal and iron on a considerable scale developed during the twelfth and thirteenth centuries because by 1244 there were iron workings at East Bicknor, Staunton, Abenhall, Bearse and elsewhere, and coal was being won at Blakeney, Staunton and Abenhall. It was presumably during this period or even earlier that the customary rights of the Free Miners of the Forest of Dean grew up because rivalry between the privileged miners and outsiders, whether landholders, lay, ecclesiastical and royal, or later 'foreign' mine owners, forms a continuous background to the troubled economic history of the district. The Free Miners were later defined as men who had been born within the Forest or the Hundred of St Briavels and had been engaged in mining for a year and a day. They enjoyed considerable freedom to start mines or 'gales' on any land in the area; for long periods they were entitled to cut forest timber freely and in return paid a 'royalty', which was the equivalent to one man's share in the mine, to the king on royal lands, and to a lay lord or to a religious house in the case of lands at Tintern and Flaxley. They also largely controlled the Mine Law Courts which, besides resolving all mining disputes, had a semi-legislative function and which by the seventeenth and eighteenth centuries attempted a good deal of overall economic control of the industry. In 1680, for example, these courts laid down minimum prices for ore delivered to the furnaces in and around the Forest. At the end of the seventeenth century furnaces existed in no less than 11 centres, at Tintern, Redbrook, St Leonards, Whitchurch, Blakeney, Bishopswood, Elmbridge, Linton, Gunn's Mill, Flaxley and Longhope, and these supplied about 15 forges and the wire works near Tintern. In the early eighteenth century the Mine Law Courts also sought to control mineral traffic on the Wye and to ban the sale of metal to 'foreigners' outside the Forest. Before the middle of the century market areas were laid down for the two districts 'above' and 'below' the Forest which were divided by a line from Lydney along the Lyd and Blackpool brooks to Blakeney.

By this time, however, the ancient pattern of exploitation by individual Free Miners had long been disrupted by political and commercial changes during the Stuart period. From 1611 until the end of the Civil War royal grants and sales led to a succession of 'overlords' claiming rights and making enclosures within the Forest, stoutly challenged by the Free Miners. This situation was repeated after the Restoration, following a brief period under the Commonwealth when an attempt was made to prohibit the use of timber for iron making. The Reafforestation Act of 1668 restored royal control and did lead to the preservation of some timber for naval use in the eighteenth and nineteenth centuries, but constant references to 'abuses' continued after the passing of the Act and it appears to have been in this period that large-scale exploitation took place by capitalists from outside the Forest. For example, in 1672 Paul Foley bought 'the whole of the materials and King's works in the Forest of Dean' and when a commission eventually investigated the situation in the Forest in 1831 many 'foreigners' claimed to have bought or leased 'gales' from the Free Miners. Edward Protheroe alone claimed to have gained control of 30 mines in this way and to have invested £200,000 in them and a further £100,000 in his iron works. 'Foreign' influence was greater in the iron-smelting industry than in the actual extraction of the ore and as early as 1717 two-thirds of the furnaces in the Forest area were controlled by the Foley family and their partners.

Besides modifying the structure of the industry, these changes also

177

fundamently altered the orientation of the Forest of Dean's economy. From very early times Forest of Dean iron had been used in nearby towns and in Tewkesbury, Cirencester and Gloucester, particularly in the making of nails, but throughout the Middle Ages and well on into the seventeenth century by far the greater part of the metal output was sent to Bristol by way of the Severn. Bristol dominated the market for merchant iron and was the chief customer for wire (though some of this was subsequently shipped to London), and even in the early eighteenth century agreements were normally made in terms of the prevailing Bristol iron prices. However, in 1692 the Foley family formed a series of partnerships which linked them with the west Midlands and even as early as 1717 more than half of the output of the Forest furnaces was sent out of the district as pig iron, mostly to the Midlands. This set the pattern for the eighteenth and nineteenth centuries, during which furnace capacity was rapidly increased and the links of the larger producers were first with the west Midlands and subsequently with the growing industries of South Wales, so that the economic orientation of the Forest of Dean lay almost entirely outside the Bristol region. For a time, however, the connection with Bristol itself was maintained by the sale of merchant bar and wire manufactured in the Forest forges, which in the early eighteenth century still used about 46 per cent of the output of the furnaces.

Though much of the mining on Mendip took place within the area of the Royal Forest, the legal history of the industry is very different from that of the Forest of Dean. Virtually no mention exists of mining from the end of the Roman period until the late twelfth century, when Richard I apparently granted to the Bishop of Bath the right to mine throughout Somerset. A century later the Mendip Forest area was specifically involved in permission given by Henry II to the Carthusian house at Witham to mine lead near Charterhouse. In both cases there was a royal levy of 10 per cent of the value of the lead produced and this came to be a permanent feature known as 'lot' lead. However, the amounts mined before the middle of the sixteenth century must have been very small—even in 1535 the value of the Bishop's share of the lead produced was only about £3. Indeed mining played a relatively small part in the economy of Mendip when compared with its general pastoral activities and many of the cases before the courts related to a clash of interest between mining and the all-important pasture and common rights. Mining, in fact, was commonly a part-time summer activity rather awkwardly integrated with local agriculture. Episcopal interest in lead mining in the Mendip area arose from the gradual development of four manorial lordships on the lands of the Royal Forest following their effective disafforestation after the thirteenth century. The four liberties were those of the episcopal manor of Wells, the manor of Chewton, the manor of Harptree and the manor of Charterhouse which, until it passed into lay hands at the Dissolution, was held by the religious houses of either Glastonbury or Witham. An ancient code of ten mining laws, in some ways comparable with the traditional privileges of the Free Miners of the Forest of Dean, apparently existed throughout the Middle Ages, though it was recorded only in Tudor times. Here, however, the laws were administered separately in the four liberties and since there was no single Mine Law Court the lords of the manors could dominate proceedings within their own liberties. Indeed the four lords Royal tended to regard their Mendip liberties as their own manorial land and sought, through their very important lead reeves, to extract the maximum financial benefit from the mineral wealth of their holdings. The illusory nature of the supposed freedom of mining on Mendip is well demonstrated by the enforced use of particular mineries. The general mining code allowed miners to take their ore to any minery for processing but the lords of the manors tried to make them use the minery in the manor in which the ore was won and in the case of the manor of Chewton the ancient code was specifically overruled.

The importance of the area increased rapidly after 1550 and was at a maximum between 1600 and 1670. This is shown by constant references to lead pigs and lead shot in cargoes leaving Bristol during the seventeenth century and by the fact that in the year 1608–9 well over 1,000 tons of lead were shipped from the port. The initial decline in production at the end of the seventeenth century and throughout the eighteenth century was almost certainly due to the gradual exhaustion of the shallow workings, the inability of individual miners to meet the problems of deep mining, and the failure of one or two elaborate schemes aimed at solving the special local problem of flooding. In consequence a number of attempts were made to work lead in the Carboniferous Limestone hills to the north of Mendip, on Broadfield Down, near Clevedon, at Penpole Point, on the Downs near Bristol and at Almondsbury in Gloucestershire, but all were on a small scale, short-lived and unprofitable.

The declining importance of lead mining in the Bristol–Mendip area throughout the eighteenth century was offset to a considerable extent by the rising production of calamine, the carbonate ore of zinc, over the same period. Zinc production in Britain was stimulated by the manufacture of brass after the middle of the sixteenth century, largely under the monopoly of the Society of the Mineral and Battery works. During the seventeenth century most of the calamine mined in the west of England came from Broadfield Down and Worle, near Weston-super-Mare, though production on a considerable scale must have been started on western Mendip because in 1665 it was alleged that competition from foreign brass was causing hardship in Rowberrow, Shipham, Winscombe and Burrington. After the Mines Royal Act of 1689 had effectively ended the base metal monopoly, the production of calamine in north Somerset was largely destined for use in the metal works of Bristol and Birmingham, though a considerable amount was also exported. The former concentration of the Bristol non-ferrous metal industry on lead smelting culminated in the establishment of a large plant on the Somerset side of the Avon at the end of the seventeenth century. By that time, however, copper smelting, largely to meet the needs of the brass industry, had been introduced to the Bristol region. Initially the copper works at Redbrook in the Forest of Dean used a little local ore but this was soon replaced by Cornish ore which was also shipped to Bristol from St Ives as early as 1691. In 1696 a copper plant was built at Conham and later supplied the Baptist Mills works which was completed in 1703 for the Bristol Brass Wire Company, soon to become the largest brass company in Europe with 66 furnaces in use by the middle of the eighteenth century. Another works was built in 1720 across the river from Hotwells and in 1746 and 1779 Champion's works at Warmley and Emerson's works at Hanham were among the first in Europe to produce zinc (spelter). The peak of calamine production to meet the needs of this major metallurgical industry was probably in the later eighteenth century. At that time some ore was produced in East Harptree but the greater part came from the two west Mendip villages of Shipham and Rowberrow, with smaller amounts from Winscombe and Burrington. In Shipham alone there were no less than 100 mines, but these were usually no more than surface diggings which would soon have been exhausted even if technical changes in the brass industry during the nineteenth century had not drastically reduced the demand for calamine.

The rapid expansion of coal production in the Bristol and Somerset fields, like that of the Forest of Dean, follows the national pattern and belongs to the second half of the eighteenth and the nineteenth centuries. However, the Kingswood and Somerset fields appear to have been fairly actively worked throughout the Middle Ages so that by the middle of the sixteenth century, when they were producing per annum about 6,000 and 4,000 tons respectively, their combined 5 per cent share of the total United Kingdom production was the highest in their history. By the end of the seventeenth century a ten-fold increase in output had occurred and a further two-fold increase was achieved before the middle of the eighteenth century. Even so the scale of production was very small with individual pits raising a few hundred tons per annum at the most and employing a total labour force which in

Somerset, before 1700, has been estimated as less than 500, with probably a comparable number on the Kingswood field. In the latter area the pits were situated round the southern and eastern sides of Bristol from Bedminster to Brislington and then continued eastwards along the exposed portion of the Kingswood anticline between Bristol and Warmley. There were frequent references to the use of Kingswood coal in Bristol during the seventeenth century and Norden's report on the Kingswood Forest indicates that a Mr Player had acquired a near-monopoly of the trade, which was said to be worth £500 per year. In 1687 there were no less than 70 workings in the area but even so the Bristol market called for additional supplies from the Forest of Dean and on occasion shipments were made from Swansea to meet temporary shortages. In Somerset before 1700 the mines were mainly near the margins of the field; in the north in the Upper Coal series round Pensford and in the south in the Lower Coal series round Coleford. The central portion of the field round Radstock was only opened up during the eighteenth century when the introduction of efficient pumps greatly facilitated deep working.

The markets for the Kingswood coal, apart from Bristol, lay in the neighbouring south Gloucestershire towns and villages of the Avon basin to the east and south. The Somerset coal was either collected at the pithead and used locally or sent to the towns of northeast Somerset and west Wiltshire from Frome and Shepton Mallet to Bath, Trowbridge, Bradford-on-Avon and Warminster. However, the means of communication for such a purpose were poor. The left-bank tributaries of the Bristol Avon, in particular, were small and unsuitable for navigation and roads had been degenerating throughout the Middle Ages, especially in early enclosed counties like Somerset. Even as early as 1373, when Bristol petitioned to be granted county status, one of the reasons advanced was the difficulty of travel over the bad roads to Gloucester or Ilchester which acted as administrative centres for the counties of Gloucestershire and Somerset, between which the urban area of Bristol had previously been divided. Even further dilapidation of the roads had taken place by the early seventeenth century, when it was alleged that their use by coal wagons was responsible for much of the damage. Accordingly during the Commonwealth an Act of 1654 sought to halt the deterioration by restricting the number of beasts which might be used in teams hauling the coal wagons.

### Trade

Whilst the period between the eleventh and eighteenth centuries thus saw a considerable development of some of the resources of the Bristol region, the city of Bristol itself was becoming a vastly larger and more affluent place than the admittedly important wool manufacturing and exporting town of the Middle Ages. In considerable measure the change was due not only to the steady growth of its trade and commerce but also to the rise of new industries which removed its former almost complete dependence on woollen manufacture.

Through these centuries the fortunes and orientation of Bristol's overseas trade had many vicissitudes, but there was always a background of coastwise trade and trade with Ireland which continued to grow steadily throughout the period. As early as the twelfth century Bristol is thought to have achieved a pre-eminent position among the ports of the Bristol Channel and thereafter trade round the western coasts and along the Severn and its tributaries tended to converge upon the city. During the Middle Ages the Severn was used to transport much of the corn with which Bristol was supplied from points above Gloucester, wool was brought from the Welsh border and from the Wye, and timber, coal and iron were shipped from the Forest of Dean. Overland transport was used to connect the city with the other centres of the West Country woollen industry, though there is evidence of coastwise links with the Somerset and Gloucestershire rivers and the small ports of west Somerset and north Devon. To seaward the Irish and coastwise trades were intimately linked because much of the traffic between Bristol and Ireland was handled by Irish vessels or by those belonging to the smaller ports of the Bristol Channel, especially along the coast of south and west Wales where cargoes were commonly exchanged. The inward trade consisted almost entirely of hides, skins, fish, flax and linen, and in return salt, iron, leather, cloth, wine and mixed general cargoes were shipped both to Ireland and to supply the small ports at which the outward-bound ships called.

By the fifteenth century Bristol had become established as the great collecting and distributing centre of southwestern Britain, with trading connections from Chester in the north to Plymouth in the south, and from Milford Haven in the west to London in the east. From the lower Severn Worcester, Tewkesbury and Gloucester continued to send wheat, barley and malt and from further north and east wool now came from Hereford, Leominster, Coventry and Buckinghamshire. The Forest of Dean was still a major source of supply of timber, coal and iron, but all the ports along the South Wales coast as far as Tenby and Milford Haven sent wool, hides and cloth to Bristol and served as ports of call on the voyage to Ireland, while the ports of Devon and Cornwall shipped fish and tin. Lacking direct contact in her overseas trade with the Mediterranean trading cities and with the Hanseatic League, Bristol established indirect overland and coastwise connections with them through Southampton and London. Wagons loaded with madder, alum, soap, raisins, fruit and oriental or Mediterranean luxury goods regularly travelled from Southampton to Bristol during the fifteenth century and London was the main source of supply of Baltic goods and madder from Flanders. Bristol's coastwise exports consisted partly of the re-shipment of these essential textile raw materials and luxuries from the Mediterranean and northern Europe and of her own foreign imports of wood, wine, fruit and luxuries from Gascony and Iberia. In addition, however, a great deal of cloth, manufactured iron and wire, lead and leather was shipped to other home ports. The trade to Southampton and London in particular consisted largely of fine broadcloths, since it was from these ports that they could be shipped to the Hanseatic and Mediterranean markets. Irish industry had grown appreciably by the fifteenth century and exports of linen yarn and cloth to Bristol reached considerable proportions, as can be seen from the shipment of 20,000 cloths in a single year. Nevertheless the traditional exports of fish, particularly herring, and hides continued as wider contacts grew up in Ireland in addition to the long-established centre for the Bristol trade in Waterford. Ships from Cork, Kinsale, Ross and Youghal were regular visitors to Bristol and there were occasional shipments from Limerick, Galway and Sligo. It is perhaps a measure of the prosperity of Ireland at this time that high-quality cloths came to be by far the most important item in the return cargoes from Bristol, though shipments of salt for herring curing were equally vital and there was a regular trade in iron and metal goods and an increasingly varied range of general cargo and luxuries.

When Gloucester was chartered as a port in 1580, there were vehement protests on the grounds that this could cut off from Bristol much of the trade up the Severn which in the late sixteenth century was extending to include the shipment of cloth from Kidderminster and Shrewsbury and even from Manchester and Yorkshire. However, there was no decline in Bristol's Severn trade during the sixteenth and seventeenth centuries and indeed its position at the hub of a complex system of coastal and river traffic led to its description as a 'metropolis of the west' in the eighteenth century. During the previous hundred years Bristol had come to dominate a food marketing area comparable with that of London to the east. As early as 1623 cereals and malt were brought from as far apart as Tewkesbury and Chichester, and butter and bacon were sent from the south Wales ports, which later shipped young animals through Bristol to south Gloucestershire and Somerset for fattening to meet the needs of the city and the other woollen manufacturing towns. Wool supplies continued to arrive in Bristol not only from the middle and upper Severn and the Midlands but also in increasing quantities from South and West Wales, whilst coal was brought from Shropshire and the west Midlands as well as from the Forest of Dean. It was, however, the iron trade which became specially important during the eighteenth century when Bristol's domination of the market made the Severn for a time the principal highway of the iron industry.

The state of deterioration of the roads by the end of the seventeenth century is illustrated by the claim that it was possible to use wheeled vehicles between Bristol and Stroud for only four months of the year. This situation prompted some improvement of river navigation during the seventeenth century, on the Parrett, the Tone and the Bristol Avon, for example, but it was not until a century later that the canal gave Stroud a good navigable waterway. Early turnpiking represented a token improvement of a few stretches of road during the seventeenth century, but this was largely confined to the hills where the London–Gloucester, London–Bristol and London–Bath roads climbed the scarps of Cotswold and the Chalk, and overland movement within Bristol's hinterland was little affected. It might therefore have been expected that the era of canal construction in the later eighteenth century would have been of great benefit to Bristol, dependent as its inland trade had been on the waterways of western Britain. However, in the long run, the canal network of the country as a whole served the ports of London, Liverpool and of the east coast better than it served Bristol, and the construction of the canals marked the beginning of an era of improved communications by waterway, road and later railway which made much of Bristol's eighteenth-century hinterland readily accessible to other ports and was one of the factors which initiated a period of at least relative decline in the port's fortunes during the later eighteenth century and much of the nineteenth.

To seaward, however, these changes had little effect on Bristol's trade before the era of railway construction, and the true coasting business prospered throughout the seventeenth and eighteenth centuries. A cargo list from Bristol to Barnstaple in 1623 includes considerable quantities of cloth, wine, pitch, tar, sugar, lead, iron, soap and a vast catalogue of groceries and smallware which was typical of shipments to ports round the Bristol Channel and the southwest peninsula, whilst cargoes to London commonly included such items as iron, white sugar, rosin and olives. The appearance of sugar, and later tobacco, in these lists is indicative of Bristol's early participation in the transatlantic trade, the white sugar probably being refined at the city's first sugar house which had been opened in 1616. Soap, iron and lead were also products of industries which were developing in Bristol during the seventeenth century, to which brass, brassware and glass were added during the eighteenth century. The volume of shipping involved in the coasting trade varied somewhat from year to year, but the number of coastwise vessels paying anchorage dues (excluding those engaged in river traffic on the Severn and the Wye) did not decline during the eighteenth century. In the early decades it was about 400, in the middle part about 600 and as late as 1799/1800 it was 676.

The Irish trade was also thriving throughout the sixteenth, seventeenth and eighteenth centuries, with well over a hundred sailings and arrivals in Bristol each year. Fish, skins and hides still figured largely in inward cargoes but, by the end of the seventeenth century, shipments of wool, woollen fabrics, linen, flax and rugs reflected the continued growth of the Irish textile industries, and it is interesting to recall that in 1695 Bristol merchants apparently urged Members of Parliament to take all possible steps to block the growth of the Irish woollen industry, to encourage the development of the linen industry instead, and to ensure that Ireland's status be made that of a colony. Subsequently Ireland took a share in supplying the eighteenth-century food markets of Bristol with dairy produce, salt beef and pork as well as fish, whilst continuing to send wool, fabrics, skins, hides and some timber. A cargo from Bristol to Ireland in 1679 which included hops, cider, iron, tobacco, glass, haberdashery, pewter, nails, lead, lead shot, cloth of many varieties, brassware, glue and refined sugar illustrates the outward trade in Bristol manufacturers and overseas products which was characteristic of the period.

Though a consideration of the overseas part of Bristol's trade shows significant changes in orientation, there is throughout the continuous thread of an Atlantic outlook, attributable to the position of the port. Until relatively recent times Bristol's trading contacts with northern and eastern Europe, with the Low Countries and with northern France were slight and intermittent. Before the seventeenth century its foreign trade was principally with the Atlantic seaboard of Europe, with Ireland and with Iceland, and the expansion of its commercial horizons during the seventeenth and eighteenth centuries took its ships mostly to the Atlantic coast of Africa, to the West Indies and America or into the Mediterranean in a belated extension of the long-established trade route to the Iberian peninsula.

During the later Middle Ages the evolution of Bristol's foreign export trade was intimately connected with the growth of the West Country woollen industry. Although made a Staple port in the early fourteenth century the Staple soon became in effect a purely judicial one and Bristol took little part in the actual export of wool. As early as 1303 Bristol exported 43 cloths and only $5\frac{1}{2}$ sacks of wool and during the course of the fourteenth century wool exports greatly exceeded 300 sacks in only one year (1340), when an Italian merchant shipped about 2,000 sacks from the Cotswold markets through Bristol rather than Southampton. By the end of the century the occasional small shipments of wool had virtually ceased but the export of woollens had reached the vast figure of 9,782 cloths in 1398–9. This was, however, the peak of the trade and over the next ninety years cloth export figures fluctuate wildly between 7,500 and less than 1,000 per year, but the average over the period was only 3,800. The diminished importance of Bristol's cloth exports during the fifteenth century was almost entirely due to the diversion of the West Country's exports through London and the south coast ports, particularly Southampton. Thus by the beginning of the sixteenth century the cloth trade was dominated in London by the merchant venturers, who shared the vital markets in the Low Countries and central, eastern and northern Europe with the Hanse, whilst at Southampton the alien merchants alone handled greater exports of woollens than did the port of Bristol, where alien merchants never played an appreciable part in commerce.

The heyday of Bristol as the great port of the West Country woollen industry was therefore clearly the late fourteenth and early fifteenth centuries and by this time it was already established as one of the main centres for the trade with Gascony. During this period, however, the extension of trading southwards to Portugal was beginning; in the year 1390 at least five shipments carried a total of 812 cloths to that country and there are records of some small shipments to Spain. Associated with the homeward voyages from Gascony in the fourteenth century was the rise of the wine trade, particularly from Bayonne and Bordeaux, as well as the continued shipment of Languedoc woad for the woollen industry. In addition olive oil was already being imported in the few ships which traded with Spain and Portugal and it is likely that the iron which was shipped from Bayonne was of Spanish origin.

Though the fifteenth century saw the contraction of Bristol's principal export it also saw a great expansion in the port's overseas trade routes and trading contacts. Until trading ceased, following the English defeat in the French wars in 1453, Gascony remained Bristol's main market for wool cloth and for occasional cargoes of coal and fish, while exports of wine to Bristol from Bayonne and Bordeaux were at their highest level in the decade before 1453. Shipments were gradually resumed after 1463 and finally the treaty of 1475 allowed almost complete freedom of trade once more, but by that time southwestern France was only a part of Bristol's sphere of interest, which now embraced the greater part of the Iberian peninsula. Shipments of wine from both Portugal and Spain increased greatly after the fall of Bordeaux in 1453 but other commodities were now involved. Friendly relations with Portugal continued into the fifteenth century and, as well as wine, olive oil, cork, wax, honey, fruit, dyestuffs and Madeira sugar were now regularly included in cargoes received in Bristol from Lisbon and Oporto. Oil, honey, fruit, almonds, saffron, figs, raisins and dates came also from Spain, along with increasing quantities of iron, salt, soap and manufactured metal goods, but political relations were more troubled than with Portugal and the Spanish trade more liable to interruption. To both countries cloth was still by far the most important item in Bristol's exports, but occasional shipments of iron, lead and fish were sent to Portugal. During the fifteenth century, however, Bristol's contacts with the Iberian peninsula were still largely through Portugal or with Castile by way of the Atlantic coast and Andalusia, and adventures far into the Mediterranean proved ill-fated. The first attempt by the Bristol merchant Sturmy to trade in the eastern Mediterranean in 1446 ended in shipwreck and his second voyage led to a disastrous defeat by the Genoese off Malta in 1457.

In the far north, despite official bans or restrictions from time to time, Bristol ships participated much more successfully in opening up commerce with Iceland. Licences were repeatedly sought to ship out mixed cargoes and to bring back large quantities of fish, and it seems likely that Bristol became the leading port in the very important fifteenth-century Icelandic trade.

Thus, despite the rivalry of London and Southampton, the fifteenth century was a reasonably prosperous one for the port of Bristol, and its trade was extending and becoming more diversified as cloth shipments declined. It was, therefore, symptomatic of changing circumstances that the fifteenth century in Bristol saw the virtual disappearance of the exporting drapers of earlier times and their replacement by a true mercantile class which later included the great shipowning merchants typified by William Canynges.

Before the middle of the sixteenth century, however, the decline in cloth shipments had reached the point where Exeter and Dartmouth together were handling more than Bristol and the position was aggravated by European wars which disrupted commerce in the port's traditional area of interest in southwestern Europe. In the early part of Elizabeth's reign there may therefore have been some justification for the statement that the trade of the port was 'decayed' and that exemption from the provisions of the Navigation Acts was merited. The improved international position later in the reign must have led to some measure of recovery, however, because Camden described Bristol as a prosperous port, though it was not until a century later, after the Civil War, that its commerce again enjoyed a period of considerable expan-

G

sion. It is possible that increased participation in Mediterranean trade in late Tudor times may have helped start Bristol's slow recovery because in 1625 it was stated that in the trade to the Levant Bristol was 'the principall and farr above any other port' except London. A continued share in the trade of the Mediterranean is also suggested by a royal decree of 1666 granting Bristol freedom to trade with Venice and Zante. By that date, too, trade with France and the Iberian peninsula had revived so that the more prosperous times after the Restoration were largely the product of the revival of a traditional orientation of trade, no doubt aided by the fact that the privileged position of the London merchants was largely eliminated in the later years of the seventeenth century.

Though Bristol ships and seamen played a significant part in early transatlantic voyages, it is clear that no great volume of trade was conducted with America before the middle of the seventeenth century, apart from that which had grown up as a result of early contacts with Newfoundland. Ships regularly sailed to the fishing ports of Newfoundland, some of them bringing their cargoes direct to Bristol, though an increasing number followed a triangular course to unload their fish in Spain and Portugal where they picked up cargoes of wine, oil and sugar for Bristol.

A general impression of the orientation of Bristol's trade during the first thirty years of the seventeenth century can be deduced from the number of vessels which were in port working cargo to and from various countries in normal years. With countries other than those listed below contact was so irregular that average figures over a number of years are insignificant.

| | |
|---|---|
| Ireland | 156 |
| France | 83 |
| Spain and Portugal | 26 |
| Newfoundland | 13 |

In spite of the decline in the shipments of cloth, it still formed by far the most important single item in the list of exports from Bristol as late as 1608. It was, however, no longer a trade dominated, as formerly, by West Country broadcloths, and no less than 38 varieties of fabric were specified in the cargoes of that year, many of which came from other parts of England and Wales. Of the other exports more than 1,000 tons each of lead, lead shot and iron, 1,024 bags of nails and coal were the most important, but diversity was increasingly the keynote of Bristol's exports and the full list forms an almost comprehensive catalogue of seventeenth-century items of trade. Wine and olive oil continued to be the most important items in Bristol's imports in the first decade of the seventeenth century, but the figures for other traditional commodities from southwest France and Iberia in 1612—wood (114 tons), raisins (46 tons), figs (15 tons), currants (6 tons), citrus fruits (158,700 pieces) and sugar (112 tons)—were increasing, and 183 tons of iron were imported, most of it from Spain. In the same year there is evidence of the start of a vitally important trade with America in the arrival of 324 lbs of tobacco.

During the next forty years there was a moderate increase in Bristol's transatlantic trade because by 1654 the shipment of tobacco had reached the figure of 3,440 hogsheads and 4,199 rolls, sugar imports from the Caribbean included 1,336 hogsheads, 242 barrels, 533 butts and 87 casks, while 11,816 lbs of indigo came from Barbados. From the middle of the century, however, the expansion was much more rapid and by 1670 imports of tobacco reached almost 2,000 tons and those of sugar were 1,350 tons. It has been estimated that in 1654 transatlantic traffic represented only one-eighth of the port's activities, whereas in 1685 it involved nearly one-third of Bristol's overseas trade. Again the number of vessels loading and discharging cargo in the port of Bristol in a normal year in the later seventeenth century gives a picture of the direction of its trade and illustrates the vital importance of the New World trade by this time:

| Ireland | 146 |
| France | 61 |
| Spain and Portugal | 48 |
| Newfoundland | 13 |
| America and West Indies | 133 |

Apart from indigo, ginger, spices and lime juice from the West Indies and some skins and hides from Virginia, transatlantic imports were virtually confined to tobacco and sugar. Antigua, Barbados, Jamaica, Nevis and Maryland all sent cargoes of tobacco but the bulk of the imports to Bristol came from Virginia. Similarly all the West Indian settlements sent sugar but more than half the total came from Barbados with which Bristol had long-standing and close commercial relations. This helps explain the report that 'The arrival of the Barbados fleete hath much quickened the trade of this towne being of greete vallew.' From Europe imports in the later seventeenth century were still headed by wine, oil and other Mediterranean produce from the Iberian peninsula and Bordeaux, together with refined sugar from Portugal, and wool from Spain for the Spanish cloth industry in Wiltshire and Somerset. However, a great deal more traffic had developed by 1685 with other western French ports, particularly St Malo, Brest, Quimper, Oleron, Morlaix, Vannes and Rochelle, all of which shipped quantities of Breton salt to Bristol. There was also some extension of Bristol's sphere of trade further northwards in Europe. Rotterdam was the source of considerable quantities of iron, brass, copper, metal manufactures and pantiles, and Norwegian ports sent cargoes of timber, pitch and tar from time to time.

The tendency for Bristol's exports to become more diversified continued throughout the seventeenth century and is especially exemplified in the trade to Virginia, Maryland and New England. The emphasis was naturally on manufactured goods for the colonies, with iron, lead, copper and brass goods as important as textiles and leather goods, but the list is a lengthy one from which few of the items of a seventeenth-century general store's stock-in-trade were missing. This tendency was a little less marked in the export trade to European countries where there was, however, the very important addition of re-exports of sugar and tobacco. Moreover, there was some revival of cloth exports in the late seventeenth century when the London merchant venturers lost their stranglehold on the trade and the best markets shifted somewhat from central Europe to Bristol's trade areas in western and southwestern Europe.

By the end of the seventeenth century Bristol's position and traditional western outlook had therefore already involved the port in the early transatlantic trade, which grew during the eighteenth century to form the basis of the city's golden age. This has been said to start in 1698, when the slave trade ceased to be the monopoly of the London Royal Africa Company, and to end with the outbreak of the American revolutionary war in 1776. The use of these dates as milestones to measure the progress of Bristol's prosperity clearly implies that its golden age reflected an upsurge in transatlantic trade. The reality of this outburst of prosperous activity can be measured by the tonnage of shipping using the port, which rose from 15,365 in 1709 to 33,462 in 1771.

Bristol ships were already engaged in the slave traffic some twenty years before the end of the Royal Africa Company's monopoly in 1698, but after that date Bristol soon replaced London as the chief participant. The number of ships concerned grew rapidly to a peak in 1738–9 when no less than 52 sailed for Africa. No details of their loading are available for that year, but in 1748–9, when 47 vessels were taking part, the enormous total of 16,640 slaves was carried across the Atlantic. These voyages were, of course, following the well-known triangular pattern, returning from the West Indies or the American mainland to Bristol with cargoes of sugar, tobacco, cotton and spices. As far as Bristol was concerned, however, this scale of operations was only very briefly maintained, because by the third quarter of the century only 20 to 30 vessels were engaged and before 1800 the number had fallen to 3. At this time between 10 and 20 slave ships were still operating from

London and nearly 100 from Liverpool, so it seems likely that Bristol's virtual disappearance from the trade is to be related partly to the rival activity of other ports and partly to the disruption of her general commerce as a result of the revolutionary war. Despite its brevity Bristol's very active participation in the slave trade had lasting consequences on the economy of the city and port, however. It had led to the accumulation of a great deal of wealth in the hands of the city's growing class of merchants for investment in new overseas ventures, and in the new commercial and industrial life of Bristol itself. It had also established firmly the port's trade contacts with the West Indies and America which were to survive the blows of the revolutionary war and the end of slaving.

When the slave traffic was growing most rapidly between 1700 and 1730, the tonnage of Bristol shipping engaged in the West Indies trade increased from 5,175 to 8,700. There was no collapse of this trade, however, when the triangular voyages virtually ceased during the second half of the century because they were replaced by direct sailings from Bristol to load cargoes of spices, cotton, logwood and the vitally important West Indian sugar. It was sugar which dominated commerce with the West Indies throughout the century and the increase in shipments to Bristol from 12,330 hogsheads in 1770 to 19,381 hogsheads in 1801 is a measure of the continued prosperity of one aspect of the port's activities.

The volume of shipping to and from the mainland of America was smaller but remained steady at about 4,200 tons per year. By far the largest item was tobacco from Virginia and here too amounts remained remarkably constant at a little over 4 million lbs per year. However, this represented a diminishing share of the rapidly increasing total imports of tobacco into the country—one of the first clear indications of the relative decline in Bristol's importance which was to become so marked by the end of the century. South Carolina, the other plantation colony with which Bristol had a considerable trade, supplied rice, skins and naval stores. From the colonies further north shipments were less regular and cargoes varied, except in the case of the continued thriving trade with Newfoundland. Here triangular voyages were still usual, outward from Bristol to the fishing areas and homeward by way of southwest Europe to unload fish and pick up cargoes of wine, oil, fruit and Spanish wool for Bristol. Thus in the three years 1764, 1775 and 1780 a total of 64 ships sailed from Bristol to Newfoundland, whereas in the same three years only 21 arrived directly from Newfoundland, others presumably being recorded with arrivals from Spain, Portugal and southwest France.

Since vessels from Bristol did not necessarily make direct outward and homeward trips, a general picture of the orientation of the port's trade can perhaps best be given by combining the number of departures and arrivals to and from particular areas over several years and this has been done for three years between 1770 and 1790. The results suggest that each year approximately the following numbers of ships were involved:

| | |
|---|---|
| Africa | 23 |
| Newfoundland | 20 |
| North America | 80 |
| West Indies | 156 |
| Europe | 201 |
| Ireland | 222 |

At this time, therefore, 53 per cent of Bristol's overseas trade (other than that with Ireland) was with the New World, well over 40 per cent was still with Europe, and less than 5 per cent with Africa and even this was directly linked with voyages to America.

To a great extent the pattern of the port's European trade was a continuation from earlier centuries. Of the average number of 201 vessels normally plying to and from Europe, 91 were engaged in trade with southern Europe, 53 with western Europe and 57 with northern Europe. All the contacts with southern Europe and almost all those with western Europe represent the traditional Bristol trade route down the west coast of France to Bordeaux, the Iberian peninsula and the Mediterranean, and there had been little change since the seventeenth century in the goods they brought back—wine, Mediterranean produce, oil, iron and Spanish wool. Some changes had taken place, however, of which the most important was the increased proportion of Bristol's trade which was conducted with northern Europe. Vessels regularly came from Hamburg and Rotterdam with metals, metal goods, linen and Rhine wines, while Norwegian and Swedish ports had become regular sources of shipments of timber and naval stores.

The commodities involved in Bristol's export trade had changed only slightly during the eighteenth century. Cloth of many varieties still figured in most cargoes but coal, lead, metal goods, glass and bottles were often more important in shipments to Europe, and vessels bound for the West Indies and America usually carried such a wide variety of manufactured goods that it is impossible to distinguish any particularly characteristic cargoes—except for the unhappily specialized shipment of 3,279 convicts and 3,707 servants to Maryland between 1745 and 1775. However, unusual difficulties in the export trade to the American colonies arose as the shadow of the coming struggle was cast before it. In 1775 the merchant venturers of Bristol petitioned Parliament to avoid restrictions on the American trade and alleged that almost all vessels sailing outward from Bristol to America were in ballast because the colonies were enforcing the non-importation agreement.

The subsequent great dislocation of Bristol's American trade by the revolutionary war did, for a time, produce an absolute reduction of the port's prosperity, but there was no such effect in the long term and any decline in the importance of the city in the late eighteenth and early nineteenth centuries was essentially a relative one. The fact that England's second largest city and second busiest port of 1700 became its fifth city and eighth port by 1800 was largely a product of its being outpaced in growth by the industrial cities and ports of the Midlands and the north. Bristol's population, trade, commerce and industry continued to grow, but grew more slowly than those of London and the newer cities and towns elsewhere. This was probably due in the main to the very different impact of the industrial revolution in the Bristol region from that in South Wales, the Midlands and the north of England. Near Bristol no new massive staple industries appeared but instead there was a steady, though slower, modification and growth of the existing pattern of industrial activity, which eventually produced the region's present great diversity of industries. However, the industrialization of South Wales was to a limited extent at the actual expense of Bristol, since the establishment of the non-ferrous metal industry in Swansea dealt a severe blow to the Bristol works, and iron manufacture in South Wales, as well as in the west Midlands and the north, put an end to the pre-eminent position in the iron trade which Bristol had enjoyed in the earlier eighteenth century. Moreover, whilst the port of Bristol's trade grew more slowly than that of Liverpool or London, the development of ports at Swansea, Cardiff and Newport broke Bristol's near-monopoly of the trade of the Severn estuary and actually diverted some of its traffic. At the same time the construction of canals and improvements in land transport allowed London, Liverpool and the Humber ports to capture the vastly increased trade of the Midlands which might have speeded Bristol's economic growth had conditions remained as they were in the days of Defoe, who described the port's hinterland as extending from Southampton to the Trent and embracing South Wales and possibly much of North Wales.

Nevertheless the century of great prosperity which was Bristol's golden age left an immediate legacy in the form of wealth which had been accumulated in the city. Much of the merchants' capital was naturally invested in the new local industries but its very existence also acted as a powerful stimulus to an emerging commercial life in Bristol. Between 1750 and 1800 seven banks were established in the city, which also became a centre of marine and fire insurance following the opening of the first provincial fire office as early as 1718 and of a number of others after 1760. New classes of merchant-industrialists in the eighteenth century, however, were far from parochial in their interests and as the physical advantages of other areas became apparent they were not unwilling to invest 'Bristol' money elsewhere. For this there were many precedents overseas, since Bristol merchants had commonly financed commerce in Barbados, for example, whilst a Bristol iron-monger owned furnaces in Virginia, and at home a great deal of Bristol capital had been invested in mining and smelting in the Forest of Dean. Great prosperity in the early eighteenth century led to similar ventures on a larger scale, like Dr John Lane's investment in copper works near Swanswea in 1717 and the establishment of the Swansea White Rock Copper Company by a group of Bristol merchants in 1737. These were forerunners of massive investment in the iron and steel industries of South Wales and elsewhere in the later eighteenth and the nineteenth centuries, of which the provision of half the Dowlais Company's capital by four Bristol men is typical. Financially at least, Bristol derived far greater benefits from investment in the progress of the industrial revolution than is immediately evident in the city itself.

# CHAPTER 9

# *The Bristol Region in 1800*

By the end of the eighteenth century the slow processes of political social and economic change which had transformed the medieval life and landscape of the Bristol region were largely complete. The nineteenth century was to see a different and more rapid transformation and it may therefore be useful to select the years at the turn of the century for a description of the region at this stage in its evolution.

It is probably fair, from an agricultural point of view, to describe the Bristol region in 1800 as part of the Berkshire, Wiltshire, Gloucestershire and Somerset dairy region. It has already been shown that even at the beginning of the century dairying had assumed considerable importance, and this had continued to grow. When the early reports on the agriculture of the western counties were written at about 1800, dairying was therefore the principal activity in many parts of the region, and here there was no wholesale nineteenth-century conversion to grass farming for dairy purposes but rather a gradual culmination of two centuries of change. Nevertheless in 1800 neither dairying nor grass farming entirely dominated the scene and in some districts arable agriculture and corn production remained vital. The general economic circumstances which occasioned the countrywide change to grass farming had not yet arisen and consequently much of the interest in the early county agricultural reports stems from the evidence they afford of continuing local variations of economy and farming practice. Moreover, in an area as physically diverse as the Bristol region, it will be seen that these variations can be related closely to the physical divisions of the counties.

This relationship can be illustrated most clearly in the case of Gloucestershire where a simple division of the county into Cotswold, the vale and the lands beyond the Severn seemed to early writers an adequate starting point for a description of its agriculture. In such a description at the end of the eighteenth century a major issue was inevitably the extent to which the agriculture of a district had undergone the changes characteristic of the so-called agrarian revolution and a necessary key consideration was the proportion of the land which had been enclosed. In this respect there were major contrasts in Gloucestershire. Beyond the Severn circumstances were exceptional, since much of the land had been within the Royal Forest of Dean and had been enclosed by one form of encroachment or another before the seventeenth century. For the rest of the county a broad generalization might be made that on Cotswold a considerable proportion of the land remained to be enclosed by Act in the late eighteenth and nineteenth centuries, whereas much of the vale had been enclosed before the time of Enclosure Acts. Evidence of very early enclosure in the southern part of the vale between Bristol and Stroud has already been cited and this process was probably largely completed during the seventeenth century. The main purpose seems to have been for dairying and the wintering of sheep, and by 1800 as much as 75 per cent of the land was said to be in grass. However, further north, and especially towards the Vale of Evesham, a higher proportion of the land remained in open fields and it is with this arable land that the enclosure, towards the end of the 1760–90 period, of 25 to 28 per cent of the land in Gloucester, Tewkesbury and Winchcombe is concerned. On Cotswold there was a similar contrast from north to south. Much of the high plateau-like area in the north remained open until the late eighteenth century and in the period between 1760 and 1790 enclosure by Act affected 40 per cent of the land in Stow-on-the-Wold, 28 per cent in Northleach and 25 per cent in Tetbury. South of Tetbury, however, in the area known as Southwold, a great deal of enclosure had taken place before the time of Parliamentary Acts and in most districts little more than 10 per cent of the land remained to be enclosed between 1760 and 1790. It has been suggested that intensification of agriculture to meet the needs of the nearby wool-manufacturing towns may have led to this early enclosure and this may also explain the fact that very few open fields remained to be enclosed by Act where Cotswold extended from Gloucestershire into the Corsham–Bradford-on-Avon district of Wiltshire and into northeast Somerset between Bath and Frome.

Rapid elimination of many of the residual open fields of Gloucestershire between 1760 and 1800 had therefore ensured that by the latter date the contrast between Cotswold and vale was no longer reflected in their degree of enclosure. It was, however, in consequence of this eventual enclosure and the introduction of new crops on Cotswold that fresh contrasts between the two areas were emerging at the turn of the century. From medieval times the agriculture of the Cotswold upland with its thin stony soils and extensive tracts of sheep walk and cow down had been compared unfavourably with that of the Lias vale, but in contemporary accounts written in the early years of the nine-teenth century the position is reversed, at least as far as arable agriculture is concerned.

On Cotswold enclosure had made possible the evolution of a six-course rotation, without a fallow year, in which turnips and seed grasses played an essential part. The thin light soils were greatly improved by folding sheep to eat off the first-year crop of turnips and this was followed by a barley year in which seed grasses were also sown for mowing in the third year and grazing in the fourth. A single shallow ploughing prepared the ground for wheat in the fifth year and for the final year in which oats, vetches or peas were grown. Throughout almost the entire vale, on the other hand, the fallow year remained standard practice and arable farming was categorized as slovenly by comparison with the newer husbandry of Cotswold. Below Gloucester virtually no change had taken place in the ancient rotation of fallow, wheat and beans, but above Gloucester it had been extended to fallow, barley, beans and wheat. Even on the newly enclosed arable lands near the Vale of Evesham fallow still existed, but here new crops were introduced in a lengthy rotation of fallow, wheat, beans, barley, clover mown, clover grazed, potatoes, wheat and beans. There were two exceptional areas within the vale where fallow had disappeared. Round the city of Gloucester high costs apparently made it necessary to use 'every year land' where somewhat lighter soil conditions made this practicable, whilst in the extreme south of the vale towards Bristol somewhat specialized farming had developed using the red sandy loams of the Trias and the Coal Measures. Here in Iron Acton, Frampton Cotterell and Winterbourne a rotation of clover, wheat, turnips, barley, seed grasses and potatoes was associated with high husbandry, no doubt rendered particularly profitable by nearness to the Bristol market. Though incomplete the 1801 crop returns do afford some limited confirmation of this pattern of arable agriculture in the county. Wheat occupied 36 per cent of the recorded land, barley 28 per cent and oats 16 per cent, leaving only 20 per cent growing turnips, beans, peas, vetches and potatoes. Of these turnips accounted for nearly 10 per cent of the arable land described and were heavily concentrated in the Cotswold parishes, whilst beans accounted for 8 per cent and were most common in the southern half of the vale.

Despite its more elaborate husbandry, however, arable land on Cotswold still commanded a rent of only about £15 per acre in 1807, when rents in the vale and even in the Forest of Dean district were about £20 per acre. This was probably due, in part, to lower yields, particularly of wheat, which gave only about 15 bushels per acre on Cotswold, whereas 20–30 bushels could be obtained on the heavier soils of the vale if they were adequately drained and ploughed three times before sowing. Moreover, the exposed aspect of the higher parts of Cotswold meant that the harvest was at least two weeks later than in the vale, and the uplands had a long-standing reputation for bleakness.

Apart from the use of stream-side meadows on the dipslope and small remnants of open 'down', grass farming on Cotswold was entirely dependent on grass leys within the arable rotation. In the vale, on the other hand, semi-natural pastures still predominated and seed grasses were important only in the more modern rotations used in the area immediately north of Bristol and near the Vale of Evesham. The grasslands on the heavier Lower Lias Clays of much of the vale were probably of indifferent quality, but on the alluvium near the Severn and along the lower courses of its tributaries richer meadows existed. Along the estuary to within a few miles of Gloucester the meadows were liable to be rendered saline by tidal inundations and only served as summer grazing. Around Gloucester and further upstream, however, only landwater inundation occurred and here good hay crops were obtained, providing a surplus which was regularly sold to farmers in the west Midlands. On Cotswold sheep were still the mainstay of animal husbandry but were now fed almost entirely on the seed grasses and turnips of the arable rotation, since very little open sheep walk remained. Moreover, the pure Cotswold breed had diminished in importance and was being replaced first by the Cotswold/Leicester cross and later by the Cotswold/Southdown. The long and coarser wools of the new breeds still found a market in the serge industry of south Somerset but London was the principal market for mutton and lamb. Flocks of sheep seldom remained continuously in the vale because of the incidence of foot-rot and were usually present only for wintering or a brief fattening period. In the northern part of the vale there was quite a close link with Cotswold and the same breeds were therefore fattened for sale in London, but in the south, Somerset, Mendip and Wiltshire varieties of sheep were more common and supplied the markets at Bristol and Bath.

By 1800 dairying had become the essential motive of animal husbandry throughout the vale, and the permanent herds were invariably of Gloucester dairy cattle. However, beef animals, like the sheep, were regularly brought into the vale for short periods, but in this case from beyond the Severn. Welsh heifers usually grazed the lattermath after mowing and then remained for winter fattening on hay, while Herefords came both in spring for summer pasture fattening and in autumn for stall feeding during the winter. Again there was a distinction between the upper vale from which the animals were sent to the London market and the lower vale which supplied Bristol and Bath.

Similar contrasts between the vale and the Chalk downlands characterized the agriculture of Wiltshire at the end of the eighteenth century, but, since the scarp of the Chalk has been taken to represent the limit of the Bristol region, it is mainly conditions in the vale which are to be considered. In the west and northwest, however, Wiltshire extends beyond the Oxford Clay vale across the Cornbrash and onto the oolites. Thus the oolite uplands between Bradford-on-Avon and Corsham share the general characteristics of the Gloucestershire 'South-wold', whilst further north round Castle Combe and Malmesbury the county extends onto the lower Cotswold dipslope. Here, and in the adjacent parts of Gloucestershire, enclosure was a little later than on the higher parts of south Cotswold, 17 per cent of the land in Malmes-bury being enclosed between 1760 and 1790 for example, but by the early years of the nineteenth century the process was largely complete. In this area the Cornbrash normally forms a reddish calcareous loam over the oolites, though locally heavy clays exist, and agricultural prac-tice has tended to be transitional between that of the arable Cotswold and that of the grass farming vale. In the period immediately after 1800, however, this was regarded as an essentially arable area and in the better farmed districts a six-course rotation identical with that on the rest of Cotswold was practised. It was separated from the dairy lands of the vale along a line through Kemble, Malmesbury, Allington and Lacock which coincides very closely with the Oxford Clay boundary.

To the southeast of this line, and its continuation in Gloucestershire from Cirencester to Burford, the clay lands had been largely enclosed by the seventeenth century and at least two-thirds of the area was devoted to grass farming in 1800. Dairy farming represented fully three-quarters of the animal husbandry here, the remainder being accounted for by occasional wintering or fattening of sheep and beef cattle. In the south, near the wool-manufacturing area, farms tended to be small, the enclosures of long standing, and the output of all kinds of dairy produce was destined to supply the local towns, especially Bath, Bradford-on-Avon, Trowbridge and Melksham. In northwest Wiltshire and the adjacent parts of Gloucestershire, on the other hand, there were some large grass farms engaged in mixed dairying and grazing which specialized in cheese making and the fattening of beef cattle, for markets not only in the west of England but also in London. Viewed as a whole the vale of west Wiltshire was nevertheless a land of small dairy farms whose main product justified its description as the 'cheese country' since it was said to make over 5,000 tons of cheese a year at the turn of the century.

Within the vale there were some local exceptions to the general rule of enclosed dairy farming. In the central low-lying areas between Melksham and Cricklade some land was still in commons as late as 1813 and apparently little progress towards enclosure had been made in the preceding decades. This was attributed to the fact that the country was 'naturally wet and deep' and local roads therefore inadequate for enclosure schemes. In the same district, in contrast, gravel deposits near the Avon and the Thames round Melksham, Chippenham, Tytherton, Christian Malford, Dauntsey, Somerford and Cricklade were occupied by enclosed arable farms where continuous cropping was possible with a variety of cereals, whereas on the surrounding clays only wheat could be grown with occasional moderate success. Discontinuous narrow belts of similar arable farming also marked the presence of lighter soils on the Corallian and occasional outcrops of Lower Greensand from Heywood to Seend and from Sandyridge, near Melksham, through Calne, Lyneham and Purton to Highworth, but elsewhere dairy farming continued across the Kimmeridge and Gault clays virtually to the foot of the Upper Greensand–Chalk scarp. Below this feature and along the margin of the Bristol region, the soils of the Upper Greensand were ideally suited to the production of potatoes, carrots, cabbages and turnips for the markets in the local wool towns and in Frome and Bath.

Though southeast Wiltshire lies outside the Bristol region, its agriculture at the beginning of the nineteenth century cannot be ignored because from here came supplies of grain and wool which were vital to the prosperity of the urbanized areas of the Avon basin. In 1813 south Wiltshire, where enclosure had been proceeding with very great rapidity for twenty years, was described as the granary 'not only of the manufacturing towns within the county but also [of] those in the east part of Somersetshire; and it sends very considerable quantities of wheat and barley to the cities of Bath and Bristol'. Moreover, despite the disappearance of the open downland, the summer sheep flock was still estimated to be about half a million and included an increasing proportion of southdowns and some Spanish merino strains. The wool was of a quality which met many of the requirements of the Wiltshire and Somerset industries, though it was somewhat quaintly described as suitable for 'an inferior kind of superfine broadcloth'.

It is therefore possible to describe the northern part of the Bristol region in 1800 in simple terms as an area of dairy farming on the clay lowlands, in the centre of which Cotswold rose to form an island with rapidly changing arable cultivation. To the south, however, the more complex physical conditions of Somerset were reflected in a pattern of varied agricultural practice which defies any such broad generalizations.

In one respect, nevertheless, the agriculture of Somerset at the end of the eighteenth century can be broadly summarized. By that time 86 per cent of the land of the county was enclosed but only 2 per cent lay in open arable fields. The remaining 12 per cent consisted of marsh and fen, moorlands and uncleared woodland, much of which was reclaimed during the course of the nineteenth century. In 1800, however, this land was little used and a more accurate impression of agricultural practice can be deduced from the fact that nearly 98 per cent of the regularly farmed land was enclosed. Moreover Somerset, like Gloucestershire and the vale of Wiltshire, was already heavily involved in grass farming, so that meadow and pasture were said to account for 70 per cent of the enclosed land, though more accurate data available for the later part of the nineteenth century suggest that contemporary writers may have exaggerated slightly the preponderance of grass farming at the turn of the century.

A three-fold division of the county into a northern area, comprising Mendip and the country extending northwards to the Bristol Avon, a central area from the southern edge of Mendip to the line of the Quantocks, Taunton and Chard, and beyond this a southwestern area, provides a reasonable framework for an account of the agriculture of Somerset at about 1800.

In the north the Carboniferous Limestone uplands of Broadfield Down and the ridges between Failand, Clevedon and Portishead shared some of the characteristics of Mendip. Thus a considerable extent of Broadfield Down as well as nearly half the area of Mendip remained unenclosed and here the land was used almost solely as summer sheep pasture. Moreover, even the areas which had been enclosed, mainly during the preceding forty years, included tracts in western Mendip and on the Failand and Clevedon ridges where the soil was too thin for arable cultivation and continuous use for sheep pasture was leading to serious overgrazing. On the other hand, conditions in eastern Mendip, in the area round Charterhouse and on the enclosed parts of Broadfield Down permitted arable cultivation which could be combined with the folding of sheep. Turnips, potatoes, cabbage, vetches and seed grasses predominated in various rotations and cereal production was limited, though concentration on the growth of oats allowed yields of between 40 and 60 bushels per acre to be achieved. Round the lower slopes of the Limestones where the Dolomitic Conglomerate and Marls provided relatively deep soils and where steep slopes reduced the risk of frost, mixed arable and dairy farming was combined with orchards and some market gardening. Such conditions were perhaps most characteristic of the long narrow belt of well-sheltered sloping ground between the levels and the steep southern face of Mendip, but the early fame of strawberries grown at Long Ashton in a similar position below the Failand ridge is indicative of comparable developments further north.

To the north of Mendip the low-lying lands round the mouth of the Avon, in the Gordano valley and at the seaward end of the Ken and Yeo basins between Clevedon and Weston-super-Mare still included some thousands of acres which were liable to flood. Here the pastures were good only in the late summer and autumn, and grazing and the fattening of stock assumed greater importance than dairying. Inland, however, where the Yeo and Ken penetrate into the Vale of Wrington and the Long Ashton lowland between Nailsea and Bedminster, the pastures were particularly rich and dairying was all-important. Where the Long Ashton lowland approaches Bristol and extends into the Avon valley towards Bath, the presence of urban markets led to some concentration on milk production and the sale of hay, while throughout the northern parts of Somerset there was a great deal of butter production for Bristol and Bath as well as the more general making of cheese.

To the east of Broadfield Down the agriculture of north Somerset was more complex. Everywhere dairying was an important aspect of the mixed farming of the district but the arable crops and rotations varied greatly in an area where physical conditions were themselves exceedingly variable. In the valleys and especially on the Lower Lias Clays to the south of the Avon somewhat old-fashioned, if long, rotations of beans, summer fallow, wheat, oats, oats with grass or beans, wheat, winter fallow and oats with grass were still common. On the Trias immediately to the north of Mendip oats were important, the two commonest rotations being oats, fallow and wheat or alternatively three years of oats followed by one of grass. On the Upper Lias and oolites between Bath and Stratton-on-the-Fosse the usual rotation consisted of three years of wheat followed by barley, along with which the following year's clover was sown.

In area the levels form a major part of the central division of Somerset to the south of Mendip and by 1800 the rapid enclosures and drainage of the preceding twenty years had given them an enhanced agricultural importance. In Brent Marsh, to the north of the Polden Hills, nearly 20,000 acres had been enclosed between 1780 and 1800. Some 3,000 acres were still unenclosed and several thousand acres of enclosures, especially round the Brue, still lacked efficient drainage, but virtually all the land was in use. In the actual levels of the Axe, the Yeo and the Brue the maintenance of permanent pasture for cattle was almost the sole form of agricultural activity. Red Somerset and Devon draught and beef animals were still grazed here in considerable numbers to supply markets over much of southern England, but they were gradually being displaced by shorthorns for dairying and for cheese making, which were nearly twice as profitable as the older enterprises. Towards the seaward end of the levels, however, there was a sharp contrast on the slightly higher ground, followed by the present A38 road from Pawlett to Highbridge and East Brent and by the road from Bawdrip to Woolavington, East Huntspill and Mark, where almost continuous corn cropping was practised. Arable cultivation was also characteristic of the Wedmore ridge between the basin of the Brue and that of the Yeo and Axe, while on the Lias Clays at the foot of the 'islands' and ridges within the levels orchards had been established.

The enclosure and drainage of much of King's Sedgemoor under an Act of 1791 had greatly increased the amount of agricultural land in the Bridgwater levels to the south of the Polden Hills, though to the southeast in the valleys of the Parrett and the Yeo and to the south along the Tone there remained large areas of ill-drained land. As the levels were improved this area, too, concentrated almost entirely on grass farming and, as in Brent Marsh, arable agriculture was confined to the continuation of the rising ground near the coast from Bawdrip to Chedzoy and Bridgwater and to the low ridge through Weston Zoyland, Middlezoy and Othery. Here relatively light soils on the Trias and Burtle Beds allowed of a varied arable agriculture producing some wheat and very good barley, as well as turnips, carrots, potatoes, hops and madder, but this district was one of the few in Somerset where appreciable areas still lay in open fields and in places the fertility of the light soils was seriously diminished.

A considerable contrast has always been evident between the agriculture of the levels and that of the great curve of rising ground which surrounds them on their eastern and southern sides. However, no sharp boundary, comparable with that of the Cotswold scarp in Gloucestershire, exists in east Somerset, partly because of the more varied topographical expression of the Lias in Somerset and partly because the oolites here do not form continuous uplands like those of Cotswold. The whole of the rolling country of this Jurassic belt was commonly described at the end of the eighteenth century as being rich corn and cattle land and most of it was enclosed and well farmed. Within it, however, it is possible to recognize distinctive forms of agriculture in three zones moving eastwards from the edge of the levels.

Immediately above the levels the first of these occupied the undulating ground, mainly on the Lower Lias clays and limestones, which stretched from the neighbourhood of Taunton to eastern Mendip, though it was broken by the marshy valleys of the Parrett, the Yeo and the Brue. To the south of the Brue there was considerable emphasis on cereal production, though sheep were also important, orchards occupied the lower slopes of the hills and locally market gardens produced early peas, potatoes and cucumbers. Most of the land in this zone was enclosed, but at Langport, Somerton and Compton Dundon, where somewhat higher ground borders King's Sedgemoor and continues along the crest of the Polden Hills, ancient open fields remained. On many of these, old farming systems persisted and on the Poldens, for example, yields of only 12 bushels per acre were produced in the rotation of wheat, beans and fallow, whereas far better farming was practised, using seed grasses, on neighbouring enclosed land. To the north of the Brue this zone comprises the upper parts of the Vale of Glastonbury and the Brue basin and extends over the low watershed into the Frome gap and the Avon valley leading into the vale of west Wiltshire. Mixed farming was the essential characteristic of this area but many of the soils were described as cold or heavy and a high proportion of the land was kept in grass, especially on the Oxford Clay near the southern margin of the Wiltshire butter district and in the area of the former Selwood Forest, nine-tenths of which had been cleared by this time. Though flocks of sheep were regularly brought in, cattle were much more important here than in the south, and pigs were also kept in large numbers, especially where dairying was the main purpose of animal husbandry.

The second zone occupied country at a slightly greater elevation running southeastwards from Taunton to Ilminster and Chard and then recurving northeastwards through South Petherton and the Vale of Ilchester to Castle Cary, Bruton and beyond the Brue valley into the district south of Shepton Mallet. More pronounced relief in this zone led to greater variations in the proportions of meadow, pasture and arable and gave rise to some local specialization in fruit and vegetable production. It was throughout, however, an area of high cultivation of enclosed farms, and in particular the Vale of Ilchester and the district between South Petherton and Taunton were singled out for favourable comment by contemporary writers. Here deep strong loamy soils were used in long rotations of wheat, turnips, barley and clover, followed by flax or peas and a sixth year of wheat. Fallowing no longer existed in this rich area of large estates and farms where the arable fields were said to look like gardens.

The final zone occupied a discontinuous belt of higher land near the Dorset border from Wincanton to Yeovil and Crewkerne. Here mixed arable and sheep farming was practised but the most distinctive feature of the district was the importance of the flax crop, which helped supply the specialized textile industries in Dorset as well as in the old wool towns of southeast Somerset.

The Vale of Taunton Dene, where the enclosed lands of the great ecclesiastical manors were now farmed by small proprietors, was by far the most important area in the western division of Somerset in 1800. Everywhere here there are deep soils on the Red Marl, tending to be lighter on the higher ground, especially in the north towards the Quantocks, but forming heavier strong loams in the south and in the valleys. Predominantly arable agriculture was more general on the lighter and drier soils, and grazing and dairying more common in the river valleys, but some arable cultivation was present everywhere. On the heavier soils it was still usual for a fallow year to precede the rotation of wheat, beans, barley, clover, clover and wheat, though locally turnips had been introduced into a rotation of wheat, turnips, beans and flax which eliminated the fallow. On the lighter soils fallowing had completely ceased and wheat, beans, barley and winter vetch was the usual rotation. To the west of the Quantocks, along the valley of the Doniford stream, and to the east between the Quantocks and Bridgwater, conditions similar to those in Taunton Dene produced an alternation of what was described as good corn land and watered meadows.

The summits of the Quantocks, however, seem to have been used almost solely for summer pasture and, apart from the ponies, summer flocks of over 20,000 sheep represented the only significant agricultural use of Exmoor before the great reclamation work of the nineteenth century.

In 1800, therefore, the new agriculture was by no means universally adopted throughout the Bristol region. It is true that new breeds of sheep were becoming popular and the growing importance of shorthorns and Gloucester cattle was to be expected in an area which specialized increasingly in dairy farming, but slower progress had been made by modern arable methods. Long rotations involving the new emphasis on turnips and seed grasses were common on Cotswold and in the northern part of the vale in Gloucestershire but the remoteness of the rest of the region from the home of the new methods in eastern England may explain its relative backwardness. Fallowing remained common on the heavier soils, seed grasses were little used in the vales and in particular turnips were not widely grown outside Cotswold.

On the other hand, the increasing influence of urban markets on the agriculture of the region is indicative of future trends. The production of hay, milk and butter in north Somerset, the growth of potatoes and other vegetables in the Iron Acton area of south Gloucestershire, the maintenance of the traditional bean crops for the Guinea ships, the intensification of agriculture in southwest Wiltshire and the 'export' of grain and wool from the Wiltshire downs were all associated with the markets of Bristol, Bath and the great concentration of textile towns where the borders of Gloucestershire, Wiltshire and Somerset meet in the inland basin of the Avon. Moreover, the future vital importance of the London markets to West Country agriculture was foreshadowed by the supplies of cheese, beef and lamb regularly sent to the capital from northwest Wiltshire, parts of central and northeast Gloucestershire and even from central Somerset, whilst the influence of new markets in the west Midlands was already felt in the northern vales of Gloucestershire.

### Woollen Industry

Except in the city of Bristol itself, the industrial aspect of the region was still dominated in 1800 by woollen manufacture, though the fluctuating fortunes and technical changes of the seventeenth and eighteenth centuries had ended in a new degree of concentration of prosperous woollen industries in three localities—round Stroudwater, on the borders of Somerset and Wiltshire, and in the Taunton–Wellington district of south Somerset.

Of these, the Gloucestershire area appears to have been the most successful because in 1803 the prosperity of the Stroud district was said to be the envy of manufacturers not only in Somerset and Wiltshire, but also in Yorkshire. At this date the industrial area still included the basins of the Little Avon and the Cam round Wotton-under-Edge, Dursley, Uley and Cam as well as the valleys converging on Stroud, where the greatest concentration of mills now stretched from Horsley, south of Nailsworth, to Painswick, whose manufactures had assumed major importance during the eighteenth century. Continued concentration on the production of high-quality scarlet and blue broadcloths, dyed in the piece except near Wotton-under-Edge, still permitted vigorous economic growth throughout this area, so that the extension of existing mills by the addition of extra floors and by construction on new sites reached a maximum between 1800 and 1830, with a peak of activity in the former year. The home demand for fine coloured woollen cloth, and especially for military scarlets, had increased markedly during the eighteenth century, but its growth had been irregular and much of the prosperity of the Gloucestershire area during the last quarter of the century was due to the fact that about half of its output was still exported to Europe, Turkey and the territories of the East India Company as well as to the newly opened markets in Russia.

For this growing production Stroud was said to need about $2\frac{1}{2}$ million fleeces a year and even if the quality of the wools of Cotswold had not declined with new breeds and the new husbandry, its supposed flocks of about 400,000 sheep could not have met the demand. During the eighteenth century, therefore, the Gloucestershire industry came to depend increasingly on the import of merino wool from Spain, but vast quantities were also brought to the nearby wool markets of Cirencester and Tetbury from the Midlands and eastern England. Though these markets long continued to serve the needs of manufacturers throughout the western counties, much of the English wool they handled was now too coarse and long-stapled for use in the characteristic West Country superfine broadcloths. The wool-combing establishments in Cirencester and Tetbury therefore sent the greater part of their combed long wools and worsted yarn to the serge region of Taunton and Wellington and to Devizes and Calne, but the availability of such wools and yarn in Cirencester was probably also responsible for the existence, about 1800, of fine worsted manufacture in the town.

Though the rest of the prosperous Gloucestershire industry depended entirely on traditional products, it was by no means out of date technically and at the beginning of the nineteenth century there was more widespread use of machinery here than in any other part of the country. After 1750 the flying shuttle had been commonly accepted and by 1806 the spinning jenny and gig mill were in general use in the Cotswold valleys. Whilst the survival of small concerns meant that the 'average' Gloucestershire clothier still had only 30–40 looms under his control, these technical changes in the later eighteenth century had favoured operations on a larger scale and in 1800 it was the great clothiers of the Stroud district who embarked on the impressive era of mill building of the succeeding decades. Austens of Wotten-under-Edge, who employed between 200 and 300 weavers, and Lloyds of Uley, who had about 150 weavers, were probably fairly typical firms of this period, but it has been suggested that as many as 1,000 workers may have been employed directly or indirectly by some of the larger companies.

By 1800 some degree of collaboration had been established between the employers and one outcome of this is thought to have been the perpetuation of extremely low wage rates in the industry. By the same date some early steps were also being taken by the textile workers to form associations, which may have seemed more necessary in this region of large employers than elsewhere in England. There seems little doubt that a major preoccupation of both groups was with wage rates and the riots in the Stroud area in 1802 are more likely to have been provoked on this account than by resistance to the introduction of machinery which was already in general use.

The woollen industry of Wiltshire had by 1800 undergone a revolutionary change of specialization not experienced in the Stroud district

of Gloucestershire. Though there was still some production of superfine broadcloths, which even increased slightly in the early decades
of the nineteenth century, the prosperity of the area now depended
increasingly on the manufacture of true wool-dyed Spanish medleys or
fancy cloths. It will be recalled that this change had started at the
beginning of the seventeenth century and as early as 1677 it was said
that over a hundred of the principal clothiers of west Wiltshire were
making Spanish medley cloths, but the arrival of Dutch textile workers
in the district in the later part of the century may have led to concentration on finer and finer fabrics of which the later types of cassimere
were an outstanding example. There were, however, local variations of
emphasis. In the great eighteenth-century textile town of Bradford-on-
Avon, for example, there was still a considerable output of broadcloths
and heavy-milled fabrics whose processing was facilitiated by the availability of water power from the Avon. Nevertheless it was a member of
the Yerbury family of Bradford who patented in 1766 the process for
making diagonally ribbed cassimeres which, by the turn of the century,
had become one of the great specialities of the neighbouring town of
Trowbridge, where the virtual absence of water power may have been
partly responsible for an early change to narrower and lighter medleys
and fancy cloths. The very rapid industrial growth of these two towns,
and particularly of Trowbridge, has been described as an outstanding
feature of the nineteenth-century industrial revolution in Wiltshire, but
in 1800 this concentration of the industry lay in the future and woollen
manufacture remained widespread in towns and villages throughout
west Wiltshire, from Chippenham and Calne in the north to Westbury,
Warminster and Heytesbury in the south.

To some extent the scattered nature of wool working in west
Wiltshire reflects the scarcity of sites with obvious advantages like those
on the powerful streams of the Cotswold scarp, but it also suggests that
the organization of the industry was changing more slowly here than
in Gloucestershire. Even in the early years of the nineteenth century
most of the weaving for the Trowbridge firms was still carried on in
cottages and small workshops rather than in factories in the town, and
the vigorous period of mill building in Stroud in the years around 1800
was not matched until later in Trowbridge and Bradford-on-Avon. In
technical matters, too, there was some resistance to change, though this
seems to have been mainly characteristic of the weaving and finishing
sections of the industry. Attempts to introduce the flying shuttle led to
riots between 1785 and 1812 and though it had been generally adopted
in Trowbridge in 1816 it was still a source of unrest in Bradford-on-
Avon as late as 1822. Similar tardiness in adopting finishing machinery
certainly placed the Wiltshire industry at a disadvantage at the end of

the eighteenth century when compared with the Stroud area, where the gig mill, for example, had long been in general use. On the other hand, in 1800 the spinning jenny had been widely used for some years, scribbling machines were universally employed and carding engines were being introduced. The industry was therefore by no means in decay and in areas where water power had been deficient the next few years saw a start to the replacement of man and horse power by steam engines. This heralded a period of mill construction between 1814 and 1835 which was quite as impressive, especially in Trowbridge, as that of Stroudwater.

Though it had largely changed over to new types of cloth by 1800, the Wiltshire industry was still entirely concerned with the production of high-quality fine materials for which Spanish wool was then essential. Most manufacturers added some home-grown fleeces but a Trowbridge firm whose purchases of English wool never exceeded one-third of its total supply, except in time of war, was probably typical. Long-established trading links with Spain resulted in the port of Bristol handling much of the wool, especially as the cost of overland carriage from Bristol to the wool towns was less than one-third of the rate from London at the end of the eighteenth century.

During the period after 1700 there was an increasing tendency for Wiltshire cloths to be sold directly to provincial buyers, but even so in 1800 the Blackwell Hall factors in London still handled a major part of both home and export sales. The long-standing cloth export trade from Bristol to Europe and America also included a share of Wiltshire woollens, but another new orientation of the industry's outlets was represented by considerable shipments to Hamburg and Holland through Southampton and Poole.

The situation of textile manufacturing in Somerset in 1800 differed somewhat from that in Gloucestershire and Wiltshire. Except in the northeast, near the Wiltshire woollen area, there had never been the same degree of preoccupation with the manufacture of superfine broadcloths and there was consequently a greater variety of products within the county; largely because of this difference manufactures were based less on Spanish than on English wool, usually yarn-dyed, which was obtained from Dorset and Wiltshire as well as from the upland areas of Somerset itself and the great wool markets of Cirencester and Tetbury. Moreover, though individual Somerset towns like Frome, Taunton and Wellington stood out as centres of the textile industries, there was less tendency towards localization than in the neighbouring counties. The textile area, therefore, still formed a great arc round the eastern side of the county from Bath through Frome and Shepton Mallet to Wincanton, Bruton, Castle Cary, Yeovil and Crewkerne, and along the south round Ilminster, Chard, Taunton and Wellington. Within this broad distribution, however, the industries of individual districts were enjoying very varied degrees of prosperity in 1800 and local specialization was already symptomatic of the mixed character of Somerset textile manufactures in the nineteenth century.

The towns and villages on the Bristol Avon and its tributaries in the northeast of the county shared to a large extent the industrial experience of neighbouring parts of Wiltshire. High-quality traditional broadcloths were still manufactured but fine Spanish medley cloths were now of greater importance and it was mainly here that quantities of Spanish wool were used. The large town of Frome, one-third of whose working population was said to be engaged in the woollen industry in the eighteenth century, dominated the southern part of this district. It lay within ten miles of the great wool towns of west Wiltshire and in 1800, whilst sharing their emphasis on textile manufacturing, had embarked on the production of metal cards and machine parts used later in the mechanization of the whole industrial area. In the northern part of this distrct the woollen industry of Bath itself was not as important as that of Frome, but the town acted as a focal point for the area of woollen manufacture in villages along the Avon from Keynsham to Twerton, Bathampton, Limpley Stoke and Freshford and on its tributaries as far south as Norton St Philip. Here, too, Spanish medleys were made but the continued importance of superfine broadcloths is illustrated by their manufacture in three mills at Twerton.

To the south of Frome the woollen industry along the eastern borders of Somerset was less concentrated and in 1800 was still rivalled by the manufacture of linen, especially in the three adjacent towns of Castle Cary, Bruton and Wincanton and further south between Yeovil and Crewkerne. These districts represented an extension of the western parts of the linen region of Dorset and the extreme southwestern parts of Wiltshire which lie outside the Bristol region. For centuries they had used yarn spun from local flax but they now depended for at least two-thirds of their supplies on imported yarn, mostly from Hamburg. Their nearness to the margins of the Bristol region is emphasized by the fact that merchants normally insisted that the yarn should be landed at London, Southampton or Poole rather than Bristol. Traditional coarse linens such as ticking and dowlas were the fabrics most widely produced but already local specialization is indicated by the making of sailcloth, netting and canvas as well as ropes and twine in Crewkerne, Yeovil, Castle Cary and Wincanton and of lace, nets and thread in Chard, Ilminster and Yeovil.

During the late eighteenth century the textile industries of eastern and southern Somerset had been further diversified by the introduction of silk manufacture, probably from London. Silk was certainly used in Bruton and Wells in 1773 and in Taunton and Glastonbury in 1778. By the end of the century silk production on a considerable scale had been achieved in Bruton and soon followed in Taunton. The manufacture of gloves in Yeovil and later in Milborne Port and smaller centres in south-west Somerset had also been an alternative to woollens for domestic employment at least since the late sixteenth century and in 1800 it involved several hundred workers. Nevertheless the woollen industry was nowhere completely absent from this belt, and in the extreme south between Ilminster and Chard fine quality cloths were still produced in the early years of the nineteenth century.

It was, however, the worsted section of the industry which was most prosperous in south Somerset in 1800. By this time worsteds had replaced woollens in all the surviving small centres of production in the extreme southwest of the county, but large-scale activity had long been confined almost entirely to Taunton. As late as 1821 about a dozen looms were still in use in the town, but during the eighteenth century the greater part of the industry had shifted to Wellington, the smaller neighbouring centres of Milverton and Wiveliscombe and even Crewkerne. This was probably done in order to use the more adequate water power of the upper river courses for fulling, though labour troubles in the larger town of Taunton may have been a contributory factor. The principal cloth made in this district was serge, a fulled cloth using a long stapled worsted yarn as its warp and a short stapled wool as its weft, which remained in considerable demand both at home and in the East India market until well into the nineteenth century. It has already been mentioned that the wool combers at Cirencester and Tetbury supplied this southern district with long-stapled Midland wool and yarn, but in addition vast imports of Irish long wools were shipped throughout the eighteenth century by way of Bristol, Bridgwater, Barnstaple and Bideford.

Immediately to the south of Mendip, and well to the west of the main textile belt of Somerset, wool working in Wells and Glastonbury was a legacy of the even more widespread distribution of the industry in earlier times. By 1800 this district, along with the important wool town of Shepton Mallet, had also developed a valuable local speciality in the making of woollen stockings, many of them for export to Spain.

In the textile industries of the Bristol region, therefore, the period around 1800 was characterized, at least locally, by continued prosperity and by early signs of the concentration, factory building and rapid mechanization which followed during the nineteenth century. In mineral production, however, the turn of the century saw a more critical phase of activity, because the life of lead and zinc mining in the area was almost at an end whilst, on the other hand, the rapid exploitation of the coalfields was under way.

## Mining

On Mendip, by the end of the eighteenth century, the winning of lead ore was virtually over, though some mines near Dolebury and the Castle of Comfort survived until the cut in duty on imported lead in 1825 and competition from the Derbyshire mines, which produced lead of a better quality for sheeting and pipes, finally led to their closure before the middle of the nineteenth century. Moreover, output from the surface workings of Mendip calamine had passed its peak in the later eighteenth century and in 1800 they were approaching exhaustion. Here again the reduction of duty on zinc imports in 1825 speeded their abandonment, though changed technology in brass manufacture greatly diminished the importance of calamine. Once the technique of alloying metallic zinc and copper was developed, the greater suitability of sulphide blende ores for the making of spelter in factories, like those established by Champions and Emmersons in Bristol in the later eighteenth century, gradually eliminated the use of calamine which had been essential in the old copper/calamine cementation process.

In contrast with the situation on Mendip, working of iron and, more particularly, coal continued in the Forest of Dean in 1800. It is true that in the later eighteenth century very little iron had been mined and the furnaces and forges at Bishopswood, Lydbrook, New Wear, Redbrook, Park End, Blodly and Flaxley were largely supplied with Lancashire ore. In 1795 some ore production and smelting had been resumed, in the face of severe competition from South Wales and Staffordshire, but another twenty-five years were to elapse before it again reached a large scale. Coal mining, on the other hand, was prosperous at the turn of the century and in the period between 1788 and 1841 between 100 and 120 workings must have had an annual production of about 100,000 tons. It was a measure of the difficulty and cost of overland transport at this date that coal was regularly shipped to Bristol, whereas in the nearby city of Gloucester coal brought by river from Shropshire and Staffordshire was as cheap as that brought overland from the Forest and was preferred because of the high sulphur content of the local coals.

With the vast increase in production from the larger coalfields of Britain the relative importance of the Somerset and Bristol fields declined slowly during the eighteenth century and rapidly in the nineteenth, their share of the United Kingdom output falling from 3½ per cent to much less than 1 per cent. Throughout the whole of this period, however, actual production was growing in both fields. By 1800 output had probably reached 300,000 tons per annum and during the nineteenth century was again increased more than four-fold, so that local coal was able to play a not inconsiderable part in the very real, but commonly ignored, industrial revolution of the Bristol region. This fuller use of local coal was eventually made possible by vastly improved communications provided by canals and railways, but neither served the Bristol and Somerset coalfields until some time after 1800, so that the appreciable increase in coal production, especially in north Somerset, in the second half of the eighteenth century was due to other circumstances. One of these was the development of larger and deeper mines, made feasible by the introduction of steam pumps and financed by the gradual emergence of partnerships of wealthy local landowning families. Even before the canal era, however, some slight improvement in communication also played a part in stimulating coal production. Despite local resistance the Avon Navigation, following its establishment by Act at the end of the seventeenth century, had brought the river into use between Bristol and Bath by 1728, whilst on the roads the turnpike trusts had begun their work. During the seventeenth century it was only in the neighbourhood of Bath that appreciable results emerged from the work of the turnpike trusts of Gloucestershire and Somerset. The Bristol trust, which was set up in 1727, made slow progress in its twelve-mile circle round the city, partly because coal miners took violent action to emphasize their claim that coal-carrying pack animals were exempt from the tolls. Riots also greeted the extension of turnpiking further into Gloucestershire and Somerset in 1748–9, but during the second half of the century more general extension of trusts throughout Wiltshire, Somerset and Gloucestershire gradually made the transport of coal by road a practicable, though costly, method of supplying markets in the towns of the Avon basin.

Estimates of employment in the Somerset part of the coalfields show an increase from about 500 in 1700 to a figure approaching 4,000 in 1800. This resulted in considerable growth in mining villages like Pensford, Chew Magna, Marksbury, Hunstrete, Stanton Drew, Farmborough, Clutton, Timsbury, High Littleton and Farrington Gurney in the north and the opening of the central section of the field produced new growth in Paulton, Midsomer Norton, Radstock, Camerton and Dunkerton, most of it associated with short-distance migration. Though the southern section of the field had been worked for a considerable period, the mining villages of Mells, Vobster, Babington, Kilmersdon, Coleford, Stratton-on-the-Fosse and Holcombe did not, however, share these rapid developments in the late eighteenth century. Indeed production in this area had begun to decline slightly just before 1800, possibly because of competition in south Somerset from coal imported from South Wales to Bridgwater or to points along the Parrett and the Tone, which had been navigable as far as Taunton since 1699. Other markets lay in southeast Somerset, Dorset and southwest Wiltshire, but road improvements and canal construction hardly affected this area, so that difficult cart haulage remained the sole method of distribution until the middle of the nineteenth century when the belated arrival of railways in the district halted this decline in production.

By 1800 the working of the Kingswood anticline coalfield had extended well beyond the limits of the Forest of Kingswood itself, particularly in the west. Before the middle of the eighteenth century Brislington had been the only important local source of coal other than Kingswood, but in 1755 the construction of a new road to a colliery in Bedminster marked the beginning of important developments in the south Bristol section of the field. Round the eastern side of the city mining had reached the St George district and to the northeast better roads linked the city with workings in Fishponds and Stapleton. To the south of the anticline, mining near Bitton approached the Avon, giving access to markets in Bath and the textile towns, whilst to the north the workings near Mangotsfield extended onto the southern margins of the synclinal coal basin of south Gloucestershire. In the latter area the main period of development followed the early nineteenth-century construction of tramways and the related alignment of the Bristol–Gloucester railway, but already in 1800 coal was being won in the south at Pucklechurch, in the centre near Westerleigh and from Iron Acton and Yate to Cromhall at the extreme northern end of the coalfield.

## Communications

The extent to which the economic growth of the Bristol region had been influenced by the availability of transport has already been suggested in particular instances and it is therefore appropriate to review the general state of communications in the region at 1800. It will be recalled that the suggested metropolitan role of Bristol in the eighteenth century was largely related to its position at the centre of a web of coastal and river waterways, and by 1800 these had undergone some improvement and extension. In the south the Parrett and the Tone had been navigable throughout the century and the Avon had been in use between Bristol and Bath for seventy years, but it was in the north that the greatest changes had taken place. Little was done to improve the actual navigation of the Severn before the establishment of the

River authority in the nineteenth century, but its importance had been greatly enhanced by early canal building. In 1766 an Act was passed for the creation of a link from the Severn at Bewdley to the new Trent and Mersey canal, and during the following twenty-three years further canal construction in the Midlands resulted in the establishment of through waterway connections between the Severn, the Mersey, the Trent and the Thames. Moreover, by 1789 direct connection with the Thames had been provided by the Thames–Severn canal. As early as 1730 a proposal had been made to canalize the Frome from the Severn to the Stroud industrial area but this was held up for half a century by the mill owners of the valley, despite ingenious schemes for by-passing their sites. However, by 1785 a canal large enough to carry Severn trows had been cut upstream as far as Stroud and four years later the connection with the upper Thames was completed.

This development of the Severn waterways accompanied the great eighteenth-century prosperity of the port of Bristol, where the average number of coastwise arrivals and departures increased from 900 to 1,700 per year between 1750 and 1770. Many of these were Severn trows, of which 28 traded weekly to Stourport and 17 weekly to Bewdley at the end of the century when Bristol directories listed the vessels sailing regularly on each suitable tide. Worcester was the most frequently served of the other Severn ports but there were also regular services to Frampton, Gloucester, Tewkesbury, Bridgnorth and Shrews-bury, and to Tintern, Ross and Hereford on the Wye, as well as weekly market boats to and from Newport and the Usk valley. At the same time advertisements appeared for trows sailing by way of the newly-opened Thames–Severn canal to Stroud in three days, Oxford in seven days and London in fourteen days.

Thus Bristol saw its traditional inland waterway communications vastly extended by canal construction before the end of its eighteenth-century golden age, during which a great deal of capital had been accumulated by its merchants. It is therefore scarcely surprising that it was one of the main centres of the canal mania of 1792, when wild scenes accompanied the formation of canal companies in the city and would-be investors raced thirty miles to storm semi-secret company meetings in the surrounding counties. From this orgy of speculation a pattern of projects emerged which would have made Bristol the focal point of canals radiating to Gloucester, South Cerney (to join the Thames–Severn), London, Newbury, Salisbury, Southampton, Poole and Taunton. The financial crises of 1793 and the outbreak of war ensured that by 1800 most of these schemes had been abandoned, though not before large sums had been spent on abortive starts of such projects as the Salisbury–Southampton canal and the Frome coal

# CANALS

**Legend:**
- —19— Canals
- ——— Rivers (navigable)
- +++++ Tramways

KILOMETRES
0  10  20  30  40  50

MILES
0  10  20  30

**Map labels:** Cheltenham, Gloucester, Oxford, Lechlade, Thames, Abingdon, Coalpit Heath, Bristol, Swindon, Chippenham, Calne, Bath, Cheddar, Frome, Bridgwater, Glastonbury, Taunton, Tiverton, Exeter, Bristol Channel, English Channel

| | |
|---|---|
| 1 Stroud canal | 15 Bath and Bristol canal |
| 2 Berkeley and Gloucester canal | 16 Somerset Coal canal |
| 3 Hereford and Gloucester canal | 17 Kennet and Avon canal |
| 4 Combe Hill canal | 18 Kennet navigation |
| 5 Lydney canal | 19 Dorset and Somerset canal |
| 6 Bristol and Taunton canal | 20 Stour navigation |
| 7 Western canal | 21 Nettlebridge branch |
| 8 Tiverton branch | 22 Wiltshire and Berkshire canal |
| 9 Exeter canal | 23 Chippenham branch |
| 10 English and Bristol Channels ship canal | 24 Calne branch |
| 11 River Parret and River Yeo navigation | 25 North Wiltshire canal |
| 12 Tone and Parret navigation | 26 Thames-Severn canal |
| 13 Glastonbury canal | 27 Thames navigation |
| 14 Avon navigation | |

branch of the Dorset and Somerset canal. On the other hand, the activities
of French privateers off the southwest coast gave added force to arguments for the construction of canals to link the English and Bristol
Channels, but again rising costs meant that no practical steps were taken
before the start of the nineteenth century.

In 1800 the Kennet and Avon was therefore the only canal directly
connected with Bristol on which construction was proceeding and this
was a project which long ante-dated the 1792 mania. As early as 1656 a
scheme to link the Thames and the Bristol Avon had been formulated
and a lengthy campaign preceded the passing of the Kennet and Avon
Act in 1794. By 1798 the stretch from Newbury to Hungerford was
open, but the western sections within the Bristol region were only
completed at very high cost during the first decade of the nineteenth
century. Rising costs also beset the Gloucester ship canal, which was by
far the most ambitious canal scheme in England when its Act was
passed in 1793, and by 1800 it had run into the financial difficulties
which were to halt progress until government aid allowed the resumption of work in 1817. Thus monetary and international crises, as well as
the rivalry of other ports, prevented Bristol's becoming the centre of a
major canal system and in 1800 there was little to show for the investment mania which had occurred eight years previously.

During the eighteenth century Defoe commented on the fact that
Bristol traders maintained 'carriers, just as the London tradesmen do,
to all the principal counties and towns from Southampton in the south
even to the banks of the Trent in the north; and though they have no
navigable river that way, yet they drive a very great trade through all
those counties'. These overland communications were maintained by
wagons and at the end of the century Bristol directories listed between
90 and 100 wagoners engaged on regular routes from the city. Their
destinations make it clear that the great majority of road journeys
terminated within the Bristol region or in the immediately adjacent
parts of Oxfordshire, Wiltshire, Dorset and Devon, but the exceptions
give some indication of long-distance roadways which carried a fair
volume of traffic in 1800. The London road by way of Chippenham was
clearly the most important, with wagons leaving daily, some of them the
so-called flying wagons. To the northeast the traffic referred to by Defoe
followed two routes. The main road climbed the Cotswold scarp at Old
Sodbury and then turned north through Tetbury to Cirencester and
Northleach, at either of which points it connected with important east–
west roads between Gloucester, Cheltenham and Oxford. From Northleach the wagons continued through Stow-on-the-Wold to Warwick,
Coventry and Leicester. However, some of the long-distance wagons
to the north apparently went by way of Gloucester, avoiding the worst

of the vale roads by travelling through Wotton-under-Edge and Dursley. Beyond Gloucester one firm advertised wagons continuing to Northampton, Cambridge, Lincoln and Yorkshire, another served Hereford and the Welsh border, and a third offered a service to Worcester, Bromsgrove, Birmingham and Liverpool. The fourth important route out of Bristol lay to the southeast through Bath and the Wiltshire wool towns to Warminster and Salisbury, with regular connections to Southampton and Portsmouth and to the coastal and inland routes and towns of Hampshire and south Dorset. Finally to the south the difficult terrain of lowland Somerset was avoided by wagons, which crossed eastern Mendip to Shepton Mallet and Wells and then followed a variety of routes in the eastern part of the county by Bruton and Castle Cary or Wincanton, Sherborne, Yeovil and Crewkerne to reach Taunton, Wellington and north Devon by way of Ilminster, or Exeter and the southwest by Axminster.

It will be appreciated that most of these more important roadways followed high ground wherever this was possible and in 1800 it remained true that no all-weather through roads existed to the north and south of Bristol in the vales of Gloucestershire or in lowland Somerset. However, turnpike trusts had been active throughout the preceding century and some improvements had been made. All the main routes from Bristol had been turnpiked before 1750, including the Cotswold route to Cirencester and the north, the London road and the Bath, Warminster and Salisbury road, while branch roads round Cirencester, Warminster, Bath and Bridgwater and some north–south roads in eastern Somerset had also been placed under trusts by the same date. The Bristol and Warminster trusts of 1726–7 were of a type established over roads within a specified radius of the town or city and this created a precedent followed in other West Country towns but very seldom copied elsewhere. Thus the Trowbridge (1751–2), Bradford-on-Avon (1751–2), Malmesbury (1755–6) and Frome (1756–7) radiating trusts formed nuclei from which grew up between 1750 and 1775 a close network of turnpiked roads covering the whole of the wool-manufacturing area of west Wiltshire and northeast Somerset, linked on the north to Chippenham, Swindon, Cricklade, Cirencester, Stroud and Gloucester and on the south to the roads of the Yeovil and Taunton areas. Between 1775 and 1800 most of the new trusts involved relatively short stretches of road within the existing turnpike network, with longer sections in the vale of Wiltshire between Calne and Cricklade and from Swindon to Highworth and Lechlade and a number in the lowland parts of Gloucestershire and Somerset, including one across the newly reclaimed portions of King's Sedgemoor. It is true that traffic, even on the turnpiked roads, was still liable to disruption by flooding; many of the roads had stretches only seven feet wide and important improvements were largely confined to the main roads and to sections where steep gradients led out of the vales. Progress was often very slow and thirty years elapsed after the formation of the Bristol trust, for example, before the turnpike reached Shirehampton, five miles away, whilst only a pack road connected Pill with the city and wheeled vehicles were rarely seen between Bristol and Clevedon in the second half of the eighteenth century. Nevertheless a system of roads comparable with that of the present day did exist in 1800, and land drainage and new surfacing techniques were to revolutionize this system within two or three decades.

Few places were therefore inaccessible to wagon traffic and, in addition, by 1800 coaches were able to provide a reasonably regular passenger and mail service all the year round between Bristol and the more important towns and cities of southern Britain. Each week 38 coaches left for London, 7 of them capable of completing the journey in one day, 31 left for Birmingham, over 100 for Bath, 6 or 7 for Exeter, Oxford, Gloucester and Wales and 3 for Weymouth and Portsmouth.

## The City of Bristol

In 1800, therefore, the pattern of communications in the Bristol region served the needs of the city which had been an almost unrivalled western metropolis during its golden age in the early and middle eighteenth century. By the end of the century, however, the continued prosperity and growth of Bristol had been rendered less evident by the changed situation which followed the American war, by the financial crises of years of war with France and by the more rapid growth of towns and cities elsewhere in England. It seems likely that the long-term effect of these adverse circumstances was to cause reduced rates of economic growth rather than an actual decline in the city's fortunes but, even so, the period around 1800 was a critical one in Bristol's history. Rapid changes and impending vital decisions characterized every aspect of life in the city from foreign trade and local industries to port improvements, street improvements and municipal administration.

In the city's foreign commerce the immediate consequences of wars and monetary crises were still being felt in 1800 and in this case there is evidence of absolute, if temporary, decline. In the year 1799–1800 only 386 vessels trading with foreign ports paid anchorage dues in Bristol compared with 478 in 1728–9 and 411 in 1764. Moreover, this situation was typical of the closing years of the eighteenth century,

H

since in 1796 only 313 ships sailed to and from foreign countries, compared with 473 thirty years previously. The extent to which this decline may be attributed to the collapse of trade with the former American colonies is possibly indicated by the fact that sailings to and from North America in 1796 represent only 38 per cent of their number in 1764, whereas in the case of the West Indies the percentage is 78 and in the case of Europe 88. However, such generalized figures may mask quite rapid fluctuations of fortune in so troubled a period. The fact that a Jamaica convoy in 1791 included 66 Liverpool ships, 28 from London and only 7 from Bristol has been used to illustrate the collapse of Bristol's West Indian commerce and to explain why Bristol refiners were forced to obtain supplies of sugar through Liverpool during the last decade of the eighteenth century. Yet by 1801 the import of sugar into Bristol reached a record figure of 19,000 hogsheads, so that the West Indian trade must have recovered quite quickly or perhaps Bristol's Barbados ships had chosen not to join a Jamaica convoy. By this date Bristol's West Indian trade was almost entirely a direct one because participation in the slave trade triangle virtually ceased at the turn of the century. Between 1795 and 1804 only two or three ships a year sailed for the African coast and by the date of abolition in 1807 not a single Bristol vessel appears to have been engaged in slaving. Most of the small decline in sailings to and from Europe arose from difficulties of commerce with many ports of western and northern Europe during the French wars, but it by no means ceased and trade with Bristol's traditional sphere in southern Europe was only slightly affected.

Nevertheless it remains true that at the end of the eighteenth century when other ports were prospering Bristol's foreign trade was at a lower level than it had been a generation earlier. It was therefore largely for this reason that the physical and administrative deficiencies of the port itself were urgently reviewed afresh and in 1800 plans were afoot which initiated a century and a half of spasmodic port improvements and ultimately changed the riverside harbour of the Middle Ages into the complex of docks that is the modern Port of Bristol.

Throughout the eighteenth century the need to improve the city's harbour facilities should have been increasingly apparent, but little was done. Somewhat surprisingly the eventual resort to the construction of out-ports was anticipated as early as 1712 when a dock was constructed at Sea Mills. It was not for another fifty years, however, that the turnpike roads connected this isolated spot with Bristol and, though the dock was favoured by privateers and whalers for a time, it had few advantages for general cargo ships and by the last quarter of the century it was disused. In 1725 a period of active quay construction on the Avon and the Frome within the city itself was probably a necessary response to the rapid expansion of Bristol's trade but during this golden age of the port little else was done to improve the harbour. It was therefore not until 1764 that more ambitious schemes were considered. At that time the annual customs revenue at Bristol was £195,000 whereas the figure for Liverpool was only £70,000, but the extraordinarily rapid growth of the latter port was already causing some concern and leading to a greater appreciation of the disabilities imposed on Bristol by the great tidal range and tortuous navigation of the Avon. The year 1764 saw the first serious proposals to 'float' or 'dockize' some portion of the Avon and the Frome in Bristol, but indifference or alarm at the magnitude of the schemes led to their abandonment. In the following year a dock, eventually capable of accommodating thirty vessels, was constructed near Rownham Ferry at the present entrance to the city docks, but it was not fully used for the next thirty years, possibly because of its distance from the established quays in the centre of the city.

While major schemes thus made little headway in 1764, the city itself showed little or no inclination to assume direct responsibility for the administration and essential maintenance of the port. By this time the need for further extension of the quays had become urgent but in the same year the Corporation agreed that the Society of Merchant Venturers, who had been responsible for many aspects of harbour management and improvement throughout the seventeenth and eighteenth centuries, should carry out the work in return for the right to levy wharfage during the following ninety-nine years. After a lapse of twenty years, rival schemes to convert various parts of the Avon and the Frome into a floating harbour were again debated at length from 1787 until 1791, when competition from other ports had made major improvements imperative. In the meantime wars and the approaching end of the slave trade had gone far to wreck the city's commerce and the same spiralling costs and credit crises which brought the canal mania to an abrupt end made port reconstruction seem impracticable. Nothing less than the survival of the port was at stake, however, by 1800, and only four more years were to pass before the first steps were taken in the construction of the city docks at the enormous cost of over £600,000.

In the industrial sphere, too, the period around 1800 represents something of a turning point in Bristol's fortunes, but the changes were more gradual and there was no crisis comparable with that in the trade of the port. The ancient woollen industry had almost reached the end of centuries of decline, accelerated in its final stages by the American war. Some woollen stuffs and serges were still made in the city and a worsted mill was in operation across the river from Hotwells, but though a directory at the end of the century asserts that 'The woollen manufactury is not entirely taken away from Bristol', it lists few people engaged in the industry. Nor had much success attended several recent attempts to reintroduce cotton manufacture, after its virtual extinction in 1720 by Parliamentary action designed to protect the woollen industry. At the turn of the century Bristol had almost ceased to be a textile-manufacturing centre. Very much the same fate had befallen the more recently prosperous Bristol potteries. Probably started in 1682, pottery manufacture was extended in the middle of the eighteenth century to include the making of 'china' and copies of Dutch tiles, and Champions, one of the leading firms, enjoyed a great reputation and prosperity in the 1760s and 1770s. Like the rest of the industry they suffered a severe setback with the loss of American markets and the company's move to the north in 1782 helped make it clear by 1800 that Bristol was unlikely to be a serious rival of the potteries of the Midlands during the nineteenth century.

On the other hand, little decline had occurred in the non-ferrous metal industry, whose expansion during the eighteenth century had added mills in Hanham, Warmley, Keynsham and in the neighbourhood of Bath. It is true that examples have already been given of the establishment of copper smelting in South Wales during the preceding century which foreshadowed the shift of metal production away from Bristol, but no less than eighteen foundries were still active in the city in the middle of the nineteenth century. Moreover, there were already signs of the later diversification of Bristol's metal-using industries in the specialized manufacture of brass wire, clocks, watches and instruments, and the production of the high-grade iron-free brass used in compass cases, while the success of the Watts patent lead shot process meant that this branch of lead working was even more prosperous than that of sheet making, which itself survived in the city throughout the nineteenth century. Other long-established Bristol activities like soap boiling and candle making, tanning and the operations of the wine trade also shared reasonable prosperity with the newer tobacco and chocolate industries at the end of the eighteenth century.

The Bristol sugar and glass industries, however, probably achieved their greatest importance at about 1800. Despite earlier disruptions of the West Indian trade there were no less than twenty large sugar-refining houses in Bristol at that time, and it was not until twenty years later that the removal of tariffs on Indian and oriental sugars and the growth of the refining industry elsewhere began to undermine its prosperity. Distilling, partly associated with the sugar industry and the city grain market, was also a growing enterprise, so that a comparably large number of residents were listed as refiners and distillers in contemporary directories. The same source suggests that the glass industry was on a similar scale. By the end of the eighteenth century it is known to have involved, in the suburbs and outskirts of the city, fourteen glass houses, at a number of which the public were encouraged to enjoy the spectacle of window glass and bottle making—the latter a speciality associated with the local wine trade, the sale of Hotwells spa water and exports to Europe. Moreover, the industry was still growing and spread as far afield as Nailsea, where the Bristol firm of Lucas was able to operate its glass houses with coal from the tiny local field.

The glass and sugar industries had a particularly heavy fuel consumption and the availability of excellent supplies of coal was regarded as a vital factor in their success. Indeed from the point of view of fuel Bristol industries as a whole were thought to occupy a specially favourable position and Mathew, writing in his Bristol Directory of 1794, described the city as standing 'in the midst of a Coal Country'. He listed the adjacent Somerset sources in Ashton, Bedminster, Brislington and Nailsea, and continued: 'But the most copious supply is from Kingswood in which there are a great number of pits and collier's houses which last are so frequent and numerous that Kingswood has from the neighbouring hills the appearance of being one vast rural suburb of Bristol.' Apparently these supplies were adequate for most industrial needs in Bristol because coal from the Forest of Dean was said to be 'chiefly used for parlours and chambers' since it burned 'very clearly and makes cheerful fires'.

The Bristol industrial scene at the end of the eighteenth century was therefore by no means entirely composed of ancient crafts and industries either dying or destined to decay during the nineteenth century. The leather, tobacco and chocolate industries continued to grow, the non-ferrous metal industries became more specialized and survived, and in 1800 there were already some examples of new iron-using and engineering activities whose vast expansion during the following century was to make engineering and allied metal working Bristol's largest group of manufacturing industries. A long-standing connection with iron production, especially in the Forest of Dean, and the city's importance in the iron and wire trade of the seventeenth and eighteenth centuries have already been emphasized, but a new element was introduced in the late eighteenth century as factories began to concentrate on the production of machinery or on more elaborate and specialized castings. One foundry in St Phillips, for example, constructed a steam boring mill in order to machine cannon from massive castings, other concerns were engaged in the manufacture of pumps, carding engines and edge tools, whilst Bristol's subsequent specialization in small wares

223

and containers was foreshadowed by the large number of tinplate workers mentioned in directories of the 1790s.

The existence of an urban market of nearly 70,000 people, with widespread regular trade connections and two yearly fairs which still attracted custom from all parts of the British Isles, meant that a great range of secondary industries existed in the city and service industries were growing. Shoe making and watch making were by far the most commonly recorded occupations in contemporary publications, but there were also large numbers of cabinet, furniture and chair makers, tobacco pipe makers, tailors and other clothing makers. The profession of accountancy evidently had many members in the city, eight banking houses had been established during the second half of the eighteenth century and in the last thirty years they had been joined by a group of fire offices and insurance companies. Even if the closing years of the century saw the port's overseas trade declining and the great fairs slowly dying, the city nevertheless had wealth, commercial and industrial momentum and a unique importance in a predominantly rural region which carried it through into the middle of the nineteenth century, when a new system of communications and a new phase of industrial development allowed its economic growth during the last hundred years more nearly to keep pace with that of the 'industrial revolution' cities.

The year 1800, however, saw the physical growth of Bristol halted so abruptly that unfinished and derelict houses and crescents must have given to parts of Clifton and Redland the appearance of a heavily bombed city suburb. This crisis marked the end of a century of unprecedented growth because in 1700 the urban area still closely followed the outlines of the medieval city, most of whose walls and gates were still recognizable. The greater part of the estimated population of about 25,000 must therefore have been contained within the ancient city. By 1801 the recorded population of the ancient city area was 40,814, so that a 65 per cent increase in population was accommodated by building near the river on such sites as Queen Square and on the adjacent lower slopes of the hills. Outside the ancient city, however, in 1801 the four parishes of St Phillips-without (8,406), St George (4,038), Mangotsfield (2,947) and Stapleton (1,541) had an additional population of 16,932, representing the spread of the urban area up the Avon valley in St Phillips and through St George towards the Kingswood coalfield, which involved the two major industrial areas round Avon Street in St Phillips and in the Crew's Hole–Conham district. In addition the population of 3,278 in Bedminster in 1801 indicates a southwestward spread beyond the Avon. Until 1755 Bristol's growth had been in the central area or predominantly eastwards and southwards, possibly in part because of the steepness of the slopes which surrounded the ancient city on the north and northwest. The only important exception to this pattern took the form of a spread along the strip of lower land on the north bank of the Avon towards the Clifton gorge and Hotwells, where the spa, established at the end of the seventeenth century, enjoyed a reputation which rivalled that of Bath in the 1740s. However, the building of King's Square on the steep slopes below Kingsdown in 1755 was followed after 1760 by the rapid development of Kingsdown itself on the plateau-like area to the north of the city, and by this time progress was also being made with the twenty-year-old plan to construct Park Street up the steep gradients to the northwest and allow the building of the Charlotte Street and Berkeley Square district. As the Park Street development spread towards the village of Clifton in the 1780s, the declining fortunes of the spa at Hotwells were accompanied by increased interest in the provision of hotels and houses up the cliff-like slopes leading to the new spa in Clifton.

The belated spread of Bristol to the north and northwest was therefore well under way in 1790, when the city was struck by the investment boom which was to lead to the excesses of the canal mania two years later. In building the outburst occurred at once in 1790 in the form of great projects covering a belt from Royal York Crescent and Cornwallis Crescent below Clifton, through Tyndall's park and Redland to Kingsdown. Three years later most of the work was halted by the consequences of war and the same credit crises which halted the canal mania, so that in 1800 half-prepared sites and partly built walls were the only outward evidence of building plans which were not finally completed until the second decade of the nineteenth century. Such spectacles were perhaps appropriate material symbols of the crisis of Bristol's prosperity at the turn of the century and were indicative of some of its causes. Nevertheless the census which was taken at this unfortunate point in the city's history measured the growth of its population during the eighteenth century from about 25,000 in 1700 to 67,000 in 1801. Moreover, the temporary nature of any actual setbacks which Bristol suffered at this time is evident if one looks forward to 1851 when its own population had reached 137,000 and the urban area was spreading across the city boundary into south Gloucestershire.

In 1800, however, the adverse circumstances of the late eighteenth century still threatened to precipitate a disastrous collapse of Bristol's prosperity and the most energetic measures were necessary to improve the port and stimulate the city's commerce and industry. At this time, unfortunately, the conduct of municipal affairs was still the prerogative of a largely unreformed Corporation which took few steps to divest itself of privileges more appropriate to the Middle Ages. The attitude of the

Corporation thirty years later to the reform movement, and their virtual condemnation as a self-perpetuating group by the Municipal Corporations Commission in 1833, suggest that this was not a body to which Bristol could look for progressive decisions in 1800. Indeed the Corporation was the instrument by which attempts were still being made at the end of the eighteenth century to enforce such medieval ordinances as those restricting commerce within the city to its burgesses. The ill-effects of this legacy of the city's privileged chartered position in the Middle Ages were not confined to the maintenance of archaic regulations, however. In evading responsibility for port improvements the Corporation mortgaged wharfage dues for ninety-nine years as the price of help from the Merchant Venturers and at the same time increased its own levy on trade by enforcing the payment of increased port dues. Thus, at a time when the traffic was declining and port dues were a critical element in competition with Liverpool, the amount collected by the Corporation for its sole use increased from £291 in 1787 to £2,448 in 1790 and £3,851 in 1800. There can be no doubt that municipal authority did little, before the provisions of the Reform Act were enforced in 1835, to help pull Bristol from the depression which followed the American war.

Nevertheless no town in the surrounding counties compared with Bristol in size and importance in 1800 and in particular the other ports of the Severn estuary continued to play a subordinate role. Direct shipments of wool to ports like Barnstaple and Bridgwater continued and cargoes of coal were just beginning to reach Bridgwater and the Tone from South Wales, but in the main the ports of Somerset, north Devon and even South Wales still depended on the coastwise trade with Bristol. Despite the financial misfortunes which held up the construction of its ship canal, Gloucester was in a slightly more favourable position, however, because the canal links in the Midlands had greatly augmented the Severn trade. Moreover, the arrival of the first cargo of Norwegian deals in 1776 marks the beginning of Gloucester's major participation in the foreign timber trade and by 1800 this had already helped in the establishment of the two oldest firms in the city's timber-using industries.

Apart from the widespread textile trades and the production of iron in the Forest of Dean, industrial activity outside Bristol was on a small scale in 1800. In the metal industries Gloucester was again something of an exception, because long-standing connection with the Forest of Dean had led to the growth of the pin-making industry, which in 1800 employed about 1,500 people in the city and had a flourishing trade at home and with Spain and America. By this date the mechanization of the West Country woollen industry had not progressed sufficiently far to give rise to ancillary engineering on any scale and the manufacture of wire cards was almost the only example of this type of activity. Card wire was made at Frampton-on-Severn and the cards themselves at Stroud, Dursley and Wotton-under-Edge, but it was only in Frome, where 400 people were said to be employed, that the industry was on a considerable scale. The only other industry which had more than local significance in the Bristol region in 1800 was paper making which at that time was growing considerably. Until the second half of the nineteenth century paper making was not concentrated in Bristol or the larger towns but was dispersed throughout the region and carried on by small firms, the middle of whose relatively brief life was commonly at the turn of the century. Paper was made in the Forest of Dean at Flaxley, Rodmore, Woolaston and Quenington between 1743 and 1890, but one mill at Rowley which was starting production in 1800 continued into the twentieth century. In the central Gloucestershire woollen area mills in Wotton-under-Edge, Dursley, Nailsworth and Stroud made paper from 1773 to 1847, but in the north the Postlip mills at Winchcombe were started in 1749 and are still in production. In Somerset the paper mills at Cheddar, Banwell, Taunton and Watchet were working in 1800 and it is possible that the development of printing in the Frome area and at Bath in the same period was associated with paper making. In west Wiltshire one of the two paper mills at Calne was in operation from 1791 to 1876 and one of the Slaughterford mills is still working, but elsewhere the normal life span of the mills was from the 1790s until the 1840s. Most of them used the water of the By brook tributary of the Avon between Castle Combe and Bathampton so that a minor short-lived concentration of the industry took place in Slaughterford and Colerne.

Whilst it is therefore true that Bristol had no commercial or industrial rivals in the west of England in 1800, Bath had in other respects a greater prestige. Its golden age, too, was in the eighteenth century and can be traced in the building of the first pump room and assembly rooms between 1704 and 1708, of Queen's Square between 1728 and 1735, of the Parades in the 1740s, of the Circus and the Crescent between 1754 and 1775, and of the later assembly rooms between 1769 and 1771. After the deaths of Nash in 1761 and of Allen in 1764, Bath's distinction changed, but it has been said that 'Bath only reached the fullness of its brilliance by the end of the century' and certainly the beginning of its decline as an exceptionally important social centre was still a quarter of a century away in 1800. By that date the city had grown considerably, its population had reached 27,000 and the splendour of its eighteenth-century architecture was a fitting monument to Ralph Allen, whose development of the building stone of Combe Down provided much of the material and established a major nineteenth-century industry which is still of considerable importance. The opening of the Avon Navigation between Bath and Bristol in 1727 widened the potential market; Allen built roads and later tramways from the quarries to the river, Bath stone became the principal cargo downstream to Bristol and after 1810 was shipped to London on the Kennet and Avon canal.

Cheltenham, the other spa of the Bristol region, had been growing in esteem for barely half a century in 1800 and its population was a mere 3,000, but it was within a decade or so of the period of phenomenal growth which gave it a population of 44,000 by the end of the nineteenth century.

## CHAPTER 10

# Nineteenth-century Changes

ALTHOUGH the Bristol region did not experience after 1800 the truly revolutionary developments which characterized the Midlands and the north of England, it did undergo very rapid changes, particularly in the second half of the century. By this time a revolution in transport was affecting every aspect of life in this area, and widespread changes of agricultural practice and marketing as well as industrial and commercial developments were in part the direct consequence of a changed system of communications.

### Communications and Transport

*Canals.* It will be recalled that political and financial troubles at the end of the eighteenth century made Bristol's belated canal mania a short-lived one; almost all the schemes were long delayed or abandoned and in consequence the region's canal age was also a brief one in the early nineteenth century. Moreover, the grandiose plans of the 1790s were finally represented by the construction of only three systems, of which the most extensive was that which linked the Severn waterways with the Thames. One part of this system, the Thames–Severn canal, had been completed in 1789, but the difficulties of the upper Thames navigation tended to retard the growth of its traffic even before the construction of the more direct route of the Kennet and Avon. The latter formed the main element in a group of four linked canals of which the first to be completed and the most profitable was the Somerset Coal canal. This was opened soon after 1800 and remained in use until 1902. It crossed the north central portion of the Somerset coalfield by following the valley of the Cam brook from Hallatrow through Camerton and Dunkerton to Combe Hay, where it was joined by a short-lived Radstock branch, and then continued past Midford to link up with the Kennet and Avon canal near the Dundas aqueduct over the Avon. The completion of the main Kennet and Avon canal was delayed until 1810 by the construction of a flight of locks near Devizes, and in consequence the Wiltshire and Berkshire branch canal which came into operation in 1809 provided the first link between the Thames and the Avon. It left the Kennet and Avon at Semington near Trowbridge and followed the vale of northwest Wiltshire to Swindon and the Vale of White Horse to Abingdon, thus by-passing the more difficult upper sections of the Thames navigation. Four years later the short North Wiltshire canal from the Thames–Severn at Cricklade to the Wiltshire and Berkshire at Swindon was designed by the two companies to allow the former's boats also to avoid the upper Thames. By this time, however, the more direct Kennet and Avon was completed and soon took over most of the through traffic, though for a few years fast fly-boats did travel between London and Bristol by way of Abingdon. However, the original purpose and, in the outcome, the main use of the Wiltshire and Berkshire canal and its branches to Chippenham, Calne, Cricklade and Wantage was to collect agricultural produce and more particularly to supply coal throughout west and north Wiltshire and the Vale of White Horse. The greater part of the coal came from Somerset on the Coal canal and the Kennet and Avon, though supplies from the Forest of Dean, South Wales and Staffordshire were also carried to the area by way of the Thames–Severn canal. As late as 1868 the Somerset Coal canal still carried 140,000 tons of coal, though railway competition had forced freight charges down to less than one-third the rate of forty years previously. Some part of this coal was widely distributed over southern Britain as far east as Reading by the canals, but within the Bristol region the most important consequence of this traffic was the supply of cheap fuel as the woollen industry turned over to steam power after 1815. From this point of view Bradford-on-Avon and Trowbridge were particularly fortunate since the Kennet and Avon canal passed within a short distance of the mills and it is known that in the latter town, where steam plant was introduced as early as 1805, small coal was available at the mills for 12s 9d per ton—a price somewhat lower than at many mills in the West Riding of Yorkshire. The woollen industry also benefited from the cheaper transport of wool by canal, since between 1811 and 1822 the London–Trowbridge charge per hundredweight was reduced from 7s to 2s 7d and the Bristol Trowbridge charge from 2s 6d to 1s.

Apart from coal, Bath stone was the most important heavy cargo regularly carried throughout the length of the Kennet and Avon canal, but a wide range of agricultural produce, imported goods and manufactures were also carried from time to time, and the needs of perishable or other urgent shipments were met by fly-boats carrying loads of up to 15 tons, which completed the London–Bristol journey in 36 hours.

The volume of traffic on this group of canals was at a maximum in 1838–9 when the tonnage carried on the Kennet and Avon was 341,878, on the Wiltshire and Berkshire 62,899, on the Thames–Severn 60,894, and on the Somerset Coal canal approaching 120,000. The large figure for the Kennet and Avon is somewhat misleading because it included considerable quantities of material needed for the construction of the Great Western railway line between London and Bristol, competition from which led to such drastic rate cutting that the canal company's takings were halved during the following five years. A further eight years of competition and negotiation ended when the Great Western Railway Company took over the canal in 1852, partly to offset the threat of rival railway proposals made by the canal company. No such bargaining power helped the Wiltshire and Berkshire canal, whose route was closely followed by the Great Western main line from Didcot to Chippenham, and its traffic had virtually ceased twenty years before its final closure in 1914. Similar competition after the opening of the Swindon and Cheltenham railway in 1845 virtually destroyed the trade of the Thames–Severn canal and though it was successively owned and operated by the Great Western Railway Company, a canal trust and the Gloucestershire County Council, its traffic was negligible and it was often out of use for long periods before it was officially closed in 1927. All four canals therefore survived in name until the twentieth century, but only the coal traffic on the Somerset Coal canal and parts of the Kennet and Avon had any real importance in the late nineteenth century.

Of the array of canals envisaged in the 1790s linking the Bristol Channel with southern England and the south coast, only a part of the proposed Grand Western canal from the Exe estuary at Topsham to the Tone, Taunton, the Parrett and Bridgwater was completed. When the scheme was revived in 1809 work started on the Tiverton branch in order to tap the quarry trade, but it was not until 1836 that the Tiverton–Taunton section was completed, giving access to the Bridgwater–Taunton canal which had been opened nine years earlier. No construction was undertaken on the southern part of the scheme, but the canal had a brief importance mainly in carrying sea-borne coal to Taunton and Tiverton and in handling stone from the Burlescombe quarries. However, eight years after the opening of this part of the canal the Bristol–Taunton–Exeter railway line was completed and its Tiverton branch was added in 1848. Immediate ruinous rate cutting on the transport of coal to Tiverton virtually forced the company to lease the canal to the railway in 1853 and finally to sell it in 1863. Thereafter coal traffic almost ceased and only small quantities of stone were carried on the canal until its eventual closure in 1929.

It was therefore only the third of the waterway systems that survived into the twentieth century as an important means of transport. The resumption of work on the ship canal, known as the Gloucester and Berkeley canal, was followed by ten years of financial difficulties before it was opened from Sharpness docks to Gloucester in 1827, but it was an immediate success, since it handled well over 100,000 tons in its first year. By 1870 this tonnage had increased to 567,000 and by 1905 to 1,053,000. In effect it confirmed Gloucester's position as a sea-port and made it the point of transhipment from sea-going vessels to river and canal craft, though larger ocean-going ships unloaded at Sharpness. The connection with the Thames–Severn, the Wiltshire and Berkshire and the very short-lived Herefordshire and Gloucestershire canals was of value for a limited period in the middle of the nineteenth century, but its main waterway connections were by way of the Severn and the Midland canals in which the company soon developed financial interests. The opening of the Gloucester ship canal was followed by some improvement in the Severn towpaths to allow horse hauling, and consequently barges from the canals began to work down to Gloucester rather than tranship to trows at Worcester. The Gloucester company therefore resisted the proposal of the Worcester-based Severn Navigation Company in 1835 to provide 12 feet of water upstream to Worcester, by the construction of locks, which might have moved the transhipment point to Worcester. Even after the Severn Commissioners took over control of the river in 1842 the clash of interest between Gloucester and Worcester remained and it was only in 1858 that a single lock at Tewkesbury was agreed upon and not until 1868 that the twin locks at Gloucester ensured a minimum of 6 feet of water upstream to Worcester. Thereafter the navigation of the river remained satisfactory and it was competition from other forms of transport alone that led to the decline in Severn tonnage from 323,000 in 1888 to 120,000 in 1927. After that date, however, there was a considerable revival of trade on the waterway, the traffic as far as Stourport, for example, having doubled to 250,000 tons per year. A fair range of commodities is carried, originating from or being transhipped at Avonmouth, Sharpness and the South Wales ports, and includes lead, aluminium, steel, timber, grains, sugar and cocoa. Much of the increase, however, was due to shipments of petroleum either direct from the South Wales refineries or through Avonmouth, which at one time shipped as much as 500,000 tons of petroleum annually up the Severn waterway. Within the Bristol region Gloucester became a base for coastal and waterway tankers and a major distribution centre for petroleum products, whilst similar centres were supplied upstream at Worcester and Stourport. At the Sharpness terminal vessels up to 7,000 tons are unloaded to dockside store or overside to waterway craft which can carry shipments of over 700 tons as far as Gloucester. Upstream to Worcester 400-ton cargoes are possible and 150-ton cargoes can be taken to the water-head at Stourport.

The city of Gloucester, in particular, derived great benefits from the construction of its ship canal. Apart from its role in transhipment for the inland canals and its subsequent share in the oil distribution industry, Gloucester also acted as a terminal point for shipments, particularly of grain for local milling and timber used in its own industries, which grew rapidly in the nineteenth century. The canal company's early agreement to rail connections for its Gloucester basins enhanced the prosperity of the port in the later part of the century when other waterways were rapidly declining in importance.

*Railways.* In the Bristol region there is a striking parallelism between the history of the 1792 canal proposals and that of a number of railway projects brought forward as early as 1824–5 and abandoned, like the canal schemes, in the face of a financial scare. It was therefore not until the period between 1830 and 1835 that really effective consideration was given to plans for a London–Bristol railway. By 1836 proposals had been approved for the main line of the Great Western Railway Company through Swindon, Chippenham and Bath, as well as for the railways which it subsequently acquired between Bristol and Exeter. Approval had also been obtained for the Cheltenham and Great Western Union railway through Gloucester and the Stroud valley to Swindon and for the alternative route from Cheltenham to Swindon through Cirencester. By 1841, after a lease of the completed section of the Bristol and Exeter railway was acquired, the main line was open from London to Bristol and Bridgwater and reached Exeter three years later, whilst the opening of the Swindon, Stroud, Gloucester and Cheltenham line in 1845 saw the completion of the 1836 projects. Basically these represented developments of the original scheme to link Bristol and the West Country with London and were unconnected with contemporary rail construction in the Severn lowlands.

Unlike the London–Bristol line, the railways between Bristol and Birmingham were not conceived as a whole. In the north a tramway between Gloucester and Cheltenham had been approved as early as 1809 and its replacement in 1840 by the Birmingham and Gloucester railway represented an extension of the growing network of the Midlands in a southwesterly direction. At the southern end of the vale a horse tramway was constructed from Coalpit Heath to carry south Gloucestershire coal to the industrial district of St Phillips in Bristol and this formed the base from which the Bristol–Gloucester railway was started. Coalpit Heath was also linked to the Avon near Bitton by another tramway, sponsored by the Kennet and Avon canal company, leaving the Bristol tramway near the site of the Mangotsfield junction from which, thirty years later, the rail branch to Bath Green Park Station was designed. Both tramways were in use by 1835, the Act authorizing the extension of the Bristol and Gloucestershire and its conversion for locomotives was obtained in 1839 and five years later the Bristol–Gloucester railway was completed. Rail communications between Bristol and Birmingham therefore came into being in 1844, but the meeting in Gloucester of the Birmingham–Gloucester and Bristol–Gloucester railways in that year was noteworthy for a less fortunate reason. The former line, like other Midland railways, was constructed on the standard gauge whereas the latter, after a sudden change of plan, had adopted the Great Western broad gauge, and their convergence on Gloucester might be regarded as a major confrontation in the 'gauge war' of the years between 1844 and 1854.

Brunel's advocacy, and later defence, of the broad-gauge system in the 1830s partly depended on his view that the Great Western Company was opening up areas physically detached from the region of early rail construction in the Midlands and north, where the future standard gauge had been adopted. He argued that any additional isolation of its rail network imposed by a different gauge would therefore be unimportant, especially as he deprecated the interchange of rolling stock between companies even when they did share a common gauge. That he could have held such views is interesting chiefly because it illustrates the isolation of the Bristol region at that stage from the first developments of modern communications which stimulated economic growth during the industrial revolution. Brunel's misjudgement and the adoption of the broad gauge did not create the isolation but certainly delayed the time when the railways brought it to an end. It has been alleged that 'war' tactics involved the deliberate aggravation of the problems of transfer between the gauges at Gloucester, but the acquisition by the Midland Railway Company of the Birmingham–Gloucester and Bristol–Gloucester railways after their amalgamation in 1845 was a strategic move aimed at stopping and reversing the northward advance of the broad-gauge system. It was said to have been done 'under the conviction of the absolute necessity of a uniformity of gauge between the northern and manufacturing districts and the Port of Bristol', and was in fact followed by the conversion of the Gloucester–Bristol section of the line to standard gauge by 1854.

The list of railway approvals in the 'mania' year of 1844 included lines forming part of a South Wales network which had been linked to the existing systems at Gloucester by the middle of the century. Another outburst of railway proposals in 1863 eventually led to three further connections through the Bristol region to South Wales. The first was the short line from Bristol to New Passage to connect with a ferry to Portskewett and the second followed the construction of the Severn bridge, near Sharpness, which was completed in 1879 to link spurs from the Bristol–Gloucester line with a branch of the Gloucester–Chepstow line near Lydney. By this date the Act for the Severn tunnel was already seven years old, but it was not until 1885 that this final connection was completed between Bristol and the railways of the South Wales coast.

Before either the bridge or the tunnel had been completed, all the Great Western tracks as far west as Bristol had been converted either to standard or to mixed gauges. This had been brought about in stages, the first as far west as Reading to meet the needs of traffic through Didcot and Oxford to the standard gauge railways in the west Midlands in which the company had invested heavily, often to the chagrin of its Bristol shareholders who regarded this as an irresponsible dissipation of the resources of what they felt was essentially a Bristol–London railway. Conversion of the line from Didcot to Swindon next became necessary for traffic through the Gloucester and Cheltenham area to South Wales, where the tracks were all on the standard gauge by 1872. It is therefore partly true that conversion was only gradually forced upon the Great Western Company by its own acquisition of lines in the standard-gauge areas to the north and northwest of its original sphere of interest. Connection with the Bristol and Exeter line and control of the Wiltshire, Somerset and Weymouth Railway after 1850 also brought the company into competition with the standard-gauge South Western Railway, so that in the extreme south of the Bristol region round Yeovil and Chard the gauge war was fought on the Great Western's other flank. Conversion of the whole system was inevitable but it was a piecemeal process and it was not until the last quarter of the century that the area round Bristol itself had uninterrupted access to the whole of the railway system of Britain.

The considerable network of railways in the southern half of the Bristol region was brought into being as a development of intersecting lines built by three companies: the Great Western itself, the associated Bristol and Exeter, and the Somerset and Dorset. The southward penetration of the Great Western was started by the short-lived Wiltshire, Somerset and Dorset Railway Company whose line from the Great Western near Chippenham to Melksham, Trowbridge and Westbury was opened in 1848. The Wiltshire, Somerset and Weymouth Railway Company which succeeded it was taken over by the Great Western in 1850 when its line extended to Frome, with a second route under construction from Westbury as far as Warminster. In 1854 a branch from Frome to Radstock was opened, initially for coal traffic, but the completion of the two main lines as far as Yeovil and Salisbury was delayed until 1856. In the following year the original projected line was completed from Yeovil to Weymouth and in addition two important connections in west Wiltshire came into use. The first ran from Trowbridge to Bradford-on-Avon and continued down the Avon valley to join the main Great Western line near Bathampton; the second was a branch from Holt to Devizes. Five years later Devizes was also reached by the Berkshire and Hampshire Extension railway from Hungerford, most of which was later to form part of the Great Western's Taunton direct line. At the same time the East Somerset railway, from the Frome–Yeovil line to Witham, reached Wells by way of Shepton Mallet and in 1863 the opening of the Chippenham–Calne branch marked the completion of this part of the railway network of the Bristol region.

Two of the branch lines constructed by the Bristol and Exeter Railway Company connected with Great Western lines in Somerset. The first was from Durston Junction, between Bridgwater and Taunton, to Langport and Yeovil, which it reached in 1853, three years before the Great Western line from Frome was completed. The second was opened in 1869, from the main line at Yatton through the Cheddar valley, and extended in 1870 to Wells where it met the east Somerset branch of the Great Western. The Taunton–Ilminster–Chard branch of the Bristol and Exeter did not link up with the Great Western but met a branch of the South Western system in Chard. All the remaining extensions of the Bristol and Exeter railway were branches which served coastal areas of Somerset and north Devon and did not intersect with other railways. The first was the line from Yatton to Clevedon opened in 1847, the second was the West Somerset railway which reached Watchet in 1862 but was not extended to Minehead until 1874, and the third reached Barnstaple in 1873 by way of Milverton and Wiveliscombe.

The Somerset and Dorset system was created by the amalgamation of the small Central Somerset and Central Dorset Railway Companies. During the 1850s the former company built lines through the Somerset levels from Burnham-on-Sea and Highbridge to Glastonbury and Wells, with a later branch to Bridgwater, and it was originally intended to join the Great Western line near Bruton. The Dorset company's line was planned to run from Poole northwestwards along the Stour valley through Blandford and Sturminster Newton. The junction of the two lines by way of Wincanton meant that by 1862 through rail communications existed between the Bristol Channel at Burnham and the south coast at Poole, with a connection to the South Western railway at Templecombe. Though it was hoped that considerable traffic might develop between the two ports, it was a later branch line which gave real significance to the Somerset and Dorset Railway Company. This branch from Evercreech crossed eastern Mendip from Shepton Mallet to Radstock, then followed the Wellow brook valley to Midford and in 1874 reached the Midland railway's Green Park Station at Bath by the Combe Down tunnel. In the same year an extension was opened from Poole to the new resort of Bournemouth and, when the Somerset and Dorset was taken over jointly by the Midland and South Western Railway Companies in 1875, Bath–Bournemouth became effectively its main line. It provided a continuation of the Midland Railway Company's north–south alignment in this area across the Great Western's east–west system, it allowed competition with the Weymouth and Bristol–Exeter lines and, until the last few years before its closure, it formed the southern end of the London, Midland and Scottish Railway Company's —later the London Midland Region's—Pines Express route between the north of England and the south coast.

In 1873 a further element was added to the Somerset network with the completion of the Bristol and North Somerset railway from Bristol across the northern and central parts of the Somerset coalfield through Pensford and Paulton to Radstock. In 1882 a branch was opened from Paulton to Hallatrow and Camerton which was later extended to Dunkerton colliery, though it was not until the Dunkerton–Limpley Stoke extension was opened in 1910 that the whole course of the Somerset Coal canal down the Cam brook valley was replaced by a railway. Unfortunately the 1854 Frome–Radstock line and its branches in the Vobster district, on the southern margins of the coalfield, had been constructed on the broad gauge and it was only when they were converted that through rail services were possible across the whole of the coalfield from Frome to Bristol.

The final links in the railway system in Wiltshire and Somerset were not forged until the completion of the Great Western Taunton direct line in 1906. The first part of this was a continuation of the old Berkshire and Hampshire Extension from Patney to Westbury in 1900 and the final stage was reached with the opening of a line from the Frome–Yeovil route at Castle Cary to the Taunton–Yeovil branch of the former Bristol and Exeter railway near Langport. Thereafter the Great Western system in Somerset and west Wiltshire may be seen as a mesh of local lines between its two main West of England routes, with extensions southwards to Yeovil and Weymouth and westwards to the Somerset coast. Across this pattern the Somerset and Dorset railway formed an extension of the Midland system from Gloucestershire to Poole and Bournemouth.

Apart from the South Wales connections already described, railway construction in the rest of the Bristol region during the second half of the nineteenth century was mainly concerned with short local lines.

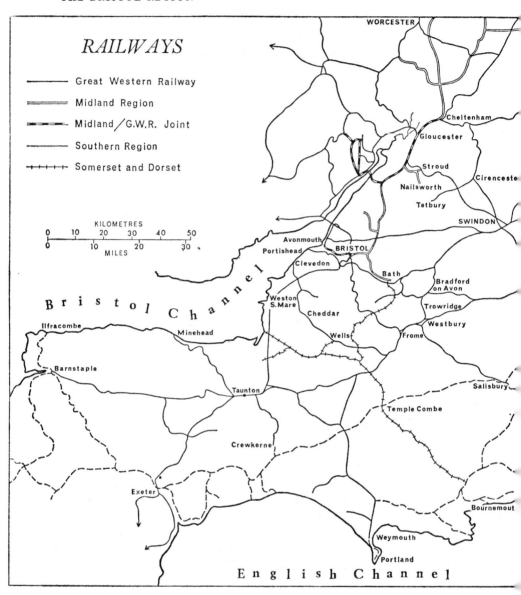

RAILWAYS

———— Great Western Railway

═════ Midland Region

━━━━ Midland/G.W.R. Joint

———— Southern Region

+++++ Somerset and Dorset

KILOMETRES

WORCESTER

Cheltenham

Gloucester

Stroud

Nailsworth

Cirenceste

Tetbury

SWINDON

Avonmouth

Portishead

BRISTOL

Clevedon

Bath

Bradford on Avon

Weston S.Mare

Cheddar

Trowridge

Ilfracombe

Minehead

Wells

Frome

Westbury

Barnstaple

Taunton

Salisbury

Temple Combe

Crewkerne

Exeter

Bournemout

Weymouth

Portland

B r i s t o l   C h a n n e l

E n g l i s h   C h a n n e l

These included the East Gloucestershire railway from Whitney to Fairford (1873), the Dauntsey–Malmesbury branch (1877), the Weston-super-Mare loop (1884), the Kemble-Tetbury branch (1889) and the line from Avonmouth to Pilning and the Severn tunnel line (1900). This last line, however, was really an extension of one of an important group of railways connected with the creation of outports at Avonmouth and Portishead. The original 1864 track of the Avonmouth Pier and Railway Company followed the Avon through the Clifton gorge to Hotwells, but no satisfactory route beyond that point was possible and it was the extension of the joint Midland and Great Western Clifton Down line through the Downs tunnel to Sea Mills and Avonmouth in 1875 which finally provided a connection with the main lines of the two companies. The Portishead Pier and Railway Company also used the Clifton gorge route but in their case connection on the left bank with the former Bristol and Exeter line below Bedminster Down was straightforward.

Like that to Taunton, the direct line to South Wales was only opened in the early years of the present century. It left the London–Bristol line at Wotton Bassett, crossed Cotswold through the Badminton tunnel and joined the Severn tunnel line at Filton Junction, north of Bristol. Though the Badminton route has been used from time to time for London–Bristol passenger trains and provides a valuable alternative freight line, its greatest importance for the Bristol region will follow the opening of Bristol's new out-of-town station.

By 1845, therefore, main railway lines had reached all the larger towns of the Bristol region and during the next five years the Somerset coalfield and most of the smaller towns of the textile area of west Wiltshire and Somerset were provided with rail services. It is true that progress was slow in completing the rail network in Somerset and Wiltshire and in constructing the Severn tunnel and its connections during the second half of the century, whilst the work of conversion to the standard gauge also delayed the emergence of a wholly satisfactory system throughout the region. On the other hand, the arrival of the Midland railway's standard gauge in Bristol in 1854 meant that the city had direct connection both with London and with the industrial Midlands and the north, albeit on different gauges for the time being. After the middle of the century there were few parts of the region, except in the far west of Somerset, where economic growth might have been retarded by the absence of rail transport.

*Roads.* The development of communications by road during the nineteenth century was less dramatic than that brought about by the advent of railways, since it mainly took the form of a very gradual improvement in the condition of the existing road network. It will be recalled that by the beginning of the century most of the main roads in the region had been turnpiked and the activities of McAdam as surveyor to the Bristol Trust between 1815 and 1825 eventually stimulated the work of road reconstruction throughout Britain. The road between Bristol and Bath in 1816 was the first in the country to have a macadamized surface and served as an example. Moreover, the local availability of excellent road metal from the Carboniferous Limestone proved a valuable asset in this work, though its general use throughout the region was itself dependent on improved transport. In the early years of the century Carboniferous Limestone, quarried in the Clifton gorge, was taken by river for road work in various parts of the Gloucestershire vale, but at that stage inland areas in Cotswold and throughout much of east and south Somerset had no easy access to good road stone and used unsatisfactory friable materials from the local Jurassic rocks. It was the canals and railways which made possible the use of road metal from Mendip and the Carboniferous Limestone hills of north Somerset and south Gloucestershire over much of the Bristol region in the later nineteenth century. In turn the improved roads and the development of motor road haulage during the present century have simplified the distribution of the Carboniferous Limestone locally and extended its use eastwards throughout the whole of southern Britain.

*Docks.* While the benefits of a revolution in inland transport were thus felt somewhat belatedly in the Bristol region, there was also a long delay before intermittent improvements and extensions, occupying the whole of the nineteenth century, equipped the Port of Bristol to handle modern sea-borne trade. It has already been explained that no major works had been undertaken before 1800 and it was not until 1804 that the long-debated plan to 'dockize' part of the Avon was embarked upon.

By the excavation of the New Cut and the construction of locks, the meandering course of the Avon through the city from Netham to the Cumberland Basin was converted into a large non-tidal lock whose level could be maintained by river water drawn through the Feeder canal. An estimated cost of £300,000 proved quite inadequate for the work involved and £600,000 had been spent when the city dock system was finally completed in 1809. The money was raised partly by subscriptions to the New Dock Company and partly from funds provided by the Merchants and by the Corporation, the latter making a charge on the citizens for this purpose. Even so the company became the legal proprietors of the dock itself and were entitled to levy the heavy dock dues necessitated by the high costs of construction. Moreover, the Corporation continued to collect Town dues, the Society of Merchant

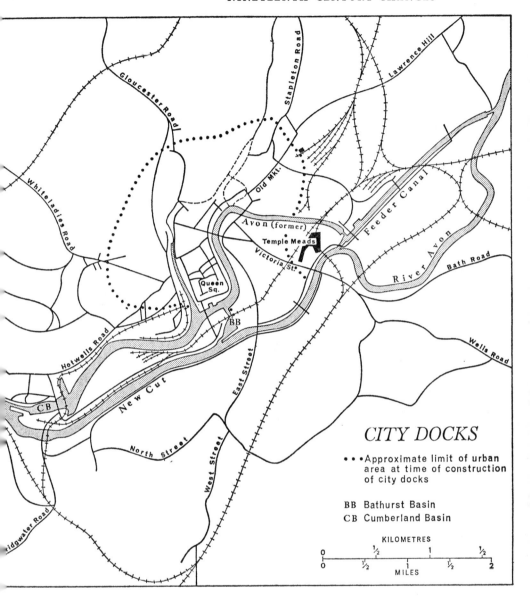

*CITY DOCKS*

• • • Approximate limit of urban
area at time of construction
of city docks

BB  Bathurst Basin
CB  Cumberland Basin

KILOMETRES

MILES

Venturers still had the right to collect wharfage, and the Mayor's due of £2 5s remained payable on all vessels entering the port, irrespective of their size. In consequence the total port charges in Bristol became excessive. Examples for specific commodities in the 1820s show that charges at Bristol could be from three to seven times as great as those at Liverpool and over a wide range of commodities in the 1830s charges remained nearly double those at Liverpool and almost three times those at Hull.

Though the costly docks in the city eliminated damage from grounding at low tide and reduced the risks of fire, they did nothing to improve the hazardous navigation of the Avon itself below the Cumberland Basin. It was ironic that Bristol led the way in 1835 in the design of the new large steamships like the *Great Western* and the *Great Britain* which finally demonstrated the inadequacy of access to the new docks. Both left Bristol for Liverpool, partly because they were forced to pay the heavy Bristol dues, despite the fact that their size made regular navigation of the Avon impracticable and they were compelled to use the open Kingroad anchorage off its mouth. Meanwhile Liverpool had established a firm hold on the ocean trade routes and in particular had captured much of the growing traffic to New York with more moderate-sized sail and steam ships. The formation of the Free Port Association represented the coordination of Bristol commercial and shipping interests to voice discontent with high charges, inadequate facilities and the loss of trade to Liverpool. Almost at once, in 1848, the Corporation was impelled to buy out the dock company.

However, municipal control of the city docks could, of itself, do little to enable Bristol to compete with the physically superior port of Liverpool and the Corporation, as the new owner, was forced to consider ways of solving the fundamental problems of the Avon navigation. Between 1840 and 1885 the river channel was deepened and straightened by a series of blasting and dredging operations and the Cumberland Basin was reconstructed, but as early as 1858 it was apparent that more ambitious developments would have to be undertaken and the Corporation had the choice of two alternative policies. The first involved a 'total dockization' scheme for the construction of a barrage across the mouth of the Avon, which would have converted the whole of the lower course of the river into an extension of the city docks. Many technical difficulties concerning sewage disposal and the effects of the barrage on coasts and anchorages in the estuary were raised by critics of the scheme, but it was still under serious consideration in the later years of the century. The alternative policy was for the construction of outports near the mouth of the river, and between 1846 and 1863 a number of schemes, some of them involving quite elaborate dock systems on the Somerset side of the river in the Portishead–Portbury area, were put forward. However, in 1863 the first practical steps were taken on the other side of the river at Avonmouth by an independent company rather than by the Corporation. The Avonmouth Pier and Railway Company was followed four years later by a pier company at Portishead which developed into a Pier and Railway Company in 1870. By this time, moreover, excavations had been in progress for two years at Avonmouth to augment the pier with an actual river-mouth dock and the same policy was adopted in 1870 by the Portishead company in which the Corporation of Bristol did have a financial interest. It will be recalled that by 1875 the railway of the Avonmouth company had been replaced by the Joint Great Western–Midland Clifton Down extension line, while the Portishead railway already gave access to the former Bristol and Exeter line. When the Avonmouth and Portishead docks were completed in 1877 and 1879, both had adequate rail connections to the main lines and formed effective but independent outports for the Port of Bristol.

At once the threat to the prosperity of the city docks was appreciated. The Corporation in 1877 sought to reduce dues charged at its own docks and might well have initiated a charge-cutting war had not Parliament intervened in response to local protests. Prevented from competing by these means, the Corporation had little alternative but to re-establish municipal control over the whole of the port system by the purchase of the river-mouth docks which it completed in 1884. By the end of the century the old 'dockization' scheme had been finally abandoned and most later development plans were concentrated on Avonmouth. Here the opening of the Royal Edward Dock in 1908 and the construction of its western and eastern arm extensions in 1928 and 1941 virtually completed the present lay-out of the dock system administered by the Port of Bristol Authority for a committee of the City Council.

### Agriculture

The most far-reaching effects of the transport revolution upon the agriculture of the west of England became apparent only in the last thirty years of the nineteenth century, at a time when the arrival of cheap grain from North America was producing other equally revolutionary changes in British agriculture. Within the Bristol region, however, both revolutions varied greatly in the date and intensity of their impact on the types of agriculture which had come to characterize the different parts of the area. Here agricultural history during the first

243

sixty years of the nineteenth century largely represents a continuation of processes which were well under way when the early accounts of the counties' agriculture were written at the end of the eighteenth century. The stage which had been reached by the late 1860s can be summarized in the form of approximate percentages of farmed land which were in arable cultivation and in permanent pasture at that time.

TABLE 1

|  | ARABLE | PERMANENT PASTURE (%) |
|---|---|---|
| Gloucestershire | 54 | 46 |
| Wiltshire | 58 | 42 |
| Somerset | 37 | 63 |

The broad similarity of the figures for Gloucestershire and Wiltshire is indicative of comparable distributions, Cotswold and the Chalk downs being predominantly engaged in arable agriculture whilst the vales of both counties had largely turned to grass farming. In Somerset the absence of any continuous and extensive tracts of calcareous upland and the pastoral activities of the central lowlands and of the far west led to an even higher proportion of permanent pasture.

It will be recalled that before 1800 there was a growing emphasis on dairying in the northern vales of the Bristol region and this trend continued throughout the nineteenth century. In the vale of west and north Wiltshire nearly 70 per cent of the land was said to be in grass as early as 1800 and by the late 1860s it is likely that a figure of over 80 per cent was characteristic of many districts. This was the 'cheese country' where manors had been early enclosed and broken up into a multiplicity of small family farms. In consequence, apart from the difficulties associated with inadequate drainage of the heavy clays, one of the chief problems of the area was the excessive growth of hedgerows. By the middle of the nineteenth century steam ploughing was being tried and hedgerows grubbed out in a number of localities but the final improvements had to await the introduction of the tile field drain. Despite these handicaps the area's production was clearly increasing rapidly during the first half of the nineteenth century. Even if the output of cheese in 1800 was grossly underestimated at 5,000 tons per year there still must have been a vast increase before 1850 when Chippenham market alone was handling 400 tons per week. By this date the old cheese longhorn cattle had largely been replaced by shorthorns and some Gloucesters, Ayrshires, Suffolks and Herefords, changes which were to prove fortunate during the second half of the century as the emphasis shifted to the sale of liquid milk and the dairy shorthorn came to enjoy a pre-eminent position until joined by Friesians and Ayrshires in the present century. Before this change took place, however, the manufacture of cheese itself underwent a rapid revolution and by 1878 Cheddar cheese, made by a largely standardized process, had virtually replaced the Wiltshire variety, whose far from uniform quality had reflected the diversity of farmhouse cheese-making methods. The change to the Cheddar variety, however, did not allow the cheese industry of Wiltshire to survive, like that of Somerset, in the face of the growing market for liquid milk; by the end of the century cheese making in Wiltshire had virtually ceased and none was made after 1914.

The completion of the branches of the Great Western railway from Swindon to Gloucester and Cheltenham and from Chippenham to Melksham, Trowbridge and Westbury meant that by 1848 most of the Wiltshire dairy vale was served by lines to London. The outbreak of cattle plague in London twenty years later accentuated the problem of supplying the city with milk and by 1871 the large-scale shipment of liquid milk from Wiltshire to the capital was under way. A short-lived, but possibly important, third factor in the change-over to the sale of liquid milk was the crisis of 1879 when massive imports of American cheese led to the price of cheese being halved. This price collapse rapidly put an end to the imports and the crisis lasted little more than a year, but it probably served to emphasize the other advantages of selling liquid milk rather than cheese, which involved delays until it matured and allowed the redemption of indebtedness to the cheese factors. At all events by 1894 all the vale farmers who could do so regularly despatched liquid milk to London and this, combined with the growth of factory milk processing in the later years of the nineteenth century, meant that by 1920 the farmhouse cheese industry was virtually extinct and only liquid milk left the farms for collecting centres for the London trade or for the local condenseries.

It is impossible to distinguish clearly between the dairy manufacturing industry and the shipment of liquid milk, since many of the large centres acted as forwarding creameries, which also made solids or condensed and evaporated the milk to compensate for fluctuations of yield and demand. The first of these was established as early as 1873 in Chippenham by the Anglo-Swiss company (later Nestlé). For the next twenty years, however, a major part of the liquid milk shipments to London was still handled by the individual farmers or small local creameries and it was not until 1896 that the amalgamation of two such creameries in Melksham and Devizes along with other smaller firms formed the basis of Wiltshire United Dairies. In 1901 this company bought a retail milk business in Paddington and started the twentieth-century expansion into a nationwide organization, with present-day milk processing plant throughout the Bristol region, which will be considered later.

The 1879 cheese crisis was almost the only adverse effect of American imports on the agriculture of the vale of Wiltshire during the nineteenth century, since most farmers actually gained by the availability of cheap imported feeding stuffs. It is true that on the clays much of the remaining arable land was now laid down to the almost universal permanent pasture, but this was in no sense disadvantageous and on the lighter soils of the Corallian ridge and round the margins of the vale where cereal growing was reduced there was usually a very profitable alternative in the production of potatoes and market-garden crops.

The availability of cheap feeding stuffs also helped in the survival of pig rearing when the end of farmhouse cheese and butter making left farmers without the residues on which the animals had been partly fed. By the last quarter of the nineteenth century Berkshires had largely replaced the Wiltshire breed in the population of some 66,000 pigs and as the demand for bacon, in particular, grew steadily, pig keeping remained a valuable supplement to dairying and still accounted for nearly 25 per cent of the income of vale farms well into the twentieth century. Nevertheless it has always been a supplementary activity and it did not increase materially with the establishment of a local bacon and pig-meat factory industry in the second half of the nineteenth century. Indeed, whereas the factory output has not declined, pigs have recently played a smaller part in the economy of Wiltshire farms, which in any case have rarely supplied more than 15 per cent of the pigs handled by the factories within the county. The slenderness of the links between the bacon factories and the dairy region within which they are located is emphasized by the early history of the industry.

Calne was a resting point on the drove route by which Irish pigs were taken from the west coast to London before the advent of railways, and it was animals from this source which were slaughtered and cured in the town by the Harris family. At one stage even the purchase of American pigs was contemplated, but as the business expanded, after the introduction of ice chilling made year-round mild curing practicable in the 1850s, the firm turned to other parts of England for supplies. This was greatly facilitated by the opening, in 1863, of the Chippenham–Calne railway, which the Harris family had supported financially, and by 1887 well over 1,000 pigs per week were being gathered from 25 counties. Before the end of the century the Calne factory was handling between 2,000 and 3,000 pigs per week, and at Trowbridge and Chippenham the Bowyer's and Wiltshire Bacon Company's factories were also in production, all of them using rail transport to collect pigs from far beyond the Bristol region and for the widespread distribution of their products.

According to one contemporary account, permanent pasture occupied only about half of the western vales of Gloucestershire in 1850, but this was probably an overall estimate which included lands near the Vale of Evesham and to the north of Bristol where arable cultivation was important. Throughout much of the central Vales of Gloucester and Berkeley, the proportion of permanent grass was certainly much higher and as early as 1840 a 500-acre farm at Frocester had 80 per cent of its land in 'old pasture'. By this time dairying was the main objective and farmers here were described as 'manufacturers' of cheese and butter. On the Frocester farm, for example, cheese was the main source of income derived from a herd of 100 head of cattle, which were usually shorthorn crosses with Gloucesters and Alderneys, though 300 sheep were also kept, usually for short periods. The Vale of Berkeley and the adjacent parts of the Vale of Gloucester probably showed the greatest similarity to the vale of Wiltshire in the predominance of dairying and the making of cheese to supply the famous cheese markets at Berkeley itself and at Yate and Thornbury. For the whole of the vale, cheese, butter, beef and mutton were listed as the main sources of income in the middle of the nineteenth century and the fattening of stock may have been a little more important than in Wiltshire. The wintering and fattening of sheep was particularly common on the meadows near the Severn but was normal practice throughout the vale, whereas there was rather more regional specialization in the fattening of beef cattle. For this the rich riverside meadows around and above Gloucester were specially famous, but in Gloucestershire to the west of the Severn young animals from the Welsh border and from the margins of the Forest of Dean were also fattened in more favoured localities.

The change to the sale of liquid milk was later and more gradual in Gloucestershire than in Wiltshire, so that cheese making continued throughout the nineteenth century and on a diminishing scale into the twentieth. The effects of rising demand in the liquid milk market of London in the 1870s and 1880s were scarcely felt to the west of Cotswold and it was only from collecting centres at Cirencester and later at Lechlade and Moreton-in-Marsh that appreciable quantities of milk were eventually taken to the capital. Instead, the existence of the Birmingham–Bristol railway meant that towards the end of the century gradually increasing amounts of liquid milk were drawn to these cities and to the growing urban areas of Gloucester and Cheltenham from all parts of the vale, whilst the dairying districts beyond the Severn met

247

some of the rapidly expanding demand in the industrial areas of South Wales.

As in Wiltshire adverse effects of the arrival of American cereals were minimized by their use in inexpensive animal feeding stuffs for both cattle and pigs. In the dairying areas the remaining arable fields had often been worked on extended versions of old rotations such as an eight-course system of fallow or vetches, barley, beans, wheat, fallow, barley, clover, wheat, and the consequent change-over to permanent pasture was probably advantageous, though some modified rotations continued locally, partly because barley grown on the clays was commonly of malting quality and therefore profitable. At the extreme northern and southern ends of the vale, however, larger areas had remained in arable cultivation and by the 1870s the success of specialized enterprises ensured that they were not entirely converted to pasture. Market gardening was of increasing importance round Bristol and along the Avon valley, round Gloucester and Cheltenham and near the northern boundary of the county on the margins of the Vale of Evesham. Between 1872 and 1895 the acreage of market gardens in the county doubled from 1,067 to 2,172 and in the same period there was a considerable increase in the growth of potatoes, especially in the triangle between Bristol, Thornbury and Chipping Sodbury and in the Gloucester and Cheltenham districts. In the last thirty years of the century the acreage of orchards in the county also grew from 11,000 to 20,000, but this activity was fairly uniformly distributed over the whole of the vale and on to the Middle Lias Marlstone 'ledge' at the foot of the Cotswold scarp and of the outliers.

In sharp contrast with the long-established dairy farming of the vales, Cotswold agriculture underwent marked changes throughout the nineteenth century. The fact that the acreage of arable land in Gloucestershire grew from 300,000 to 352,000 between 1807 and 1872 is almost entirely due to the progress of Cotswold farming. In the early part of the century the enclosure of the land on Cotswold was largely completed and by 1872 its full effects were being felt as something akin to high farming was achieved, despite the bleakness of Cotswold and its thin stony soils. Rents were still materially lower than for farms in the vale and nineteenth-century development was almost entirely based on arable cultivation of large farms with large regular stone-walled fields. Two typical examples had 83 and 85 per cent of their 1,300 acres in arable in 1840 and 1878 respectively. Grass was largely confined to riverside meadows on the lower dipslope and to patches of thin clay on the plateau itself. By the middle of the century the normal rotation had become a five-course one of roots, barley, seed grasses for hay, seed grasses grazed and wheat, the former sixth year of oats, vetches or peas now being commonly omitted. It was generally held that the maintenance of this system on the Cotswold soils was completely dependent on the manuring and treading of sheep, folded on the turnip crop and grazed on the ley after the cattle, so that a 1,300-acre arable farm with only 220 acres of pasture had 440 sheep and only 40 cattle in 1840. Much of the barley and all of the wheat were sold off the farm and it is significant that the maximum extension of arable cultivation was matched in 1872 by the maximum growth of wheat in the county, which reached a total of 97,108 acres, mostly in south Cotswold, on the Forest Marble and Cornbrash of the dipslope and on the Thames terraces.

Under these circumstances the import of cheap grain from the Prairies during the last twenty years of the century had far more serious consequences than in the surrounding vales. Since the Cotswold soils were unsuitable for the development of good permanent pasture, arable cultivation was of necessity maintained as long as possible and the problem was partly met by allowing seed grasses to occupy a greater part of the rotation. Until 1900 between 80,000 and 100,000 acres in Gloucestershire were planted with seed grasses, but thereafter leys were often left down at least semi-permanently and some real degeneration to poor grazing took place, especially on the higher northern parts of the Cotswold plateau. By this time low wool prices and declining demand for larger mutton joints meant that sheep were becoming less important, especially as the high labour cost of root cultivation had led to the growth of green crops rather than turnips. The consequent change to a mixed type of farming with some dairying and the early production of fat lambs and cattle really belongs to the twentieth century, but the old system never disappeared entirely. The stimulus to wheat production during the 1914–18 war and after the passing of the Wheat Act did help maintain some kind of arable farming on Cotswold, until national agricultural policy and a diversification of farming practice finally overcame the blows inflicted in the late 1870s and allowed its revival.

The early preponderance of pastoral activities in Somerset, the remoteness of many parts of the county from large urban markets and the relative lateness of the completion of its railway systems meant that agricultural changes in the nineteenth century were less marked than in parts of Gloucestershire and Wiltshire. Great progress was made, but the predominant types of pastoral farming remained those suited to a more remote area. Rearing and fattening of stock were more important than dairying in many districts and dairying itself long continued to be concerned with the production of cheese rather than the sale of liquid milk.

This situation is well illustrated in the west and southwest of the county where agriculture was very backward indeed at the beginning of the nineteenth century. Following the sale of Exmoor lands by the Crown in 1818, the elaborate scheme of enclosure and road and farm construction was aimed solely at the production of young stock. However, by concentrating on the cultivation of oats and grass, rather than attempting a standard rotation, the scheme was working well during the last quarter of the century and some of the stock were being fattened rather than being sold off young. Even in the more favoured and accessible lowland areas towards central Somerset the 1800 practice of fattening beef cattle continued. In the middle decades of the nineteenth century summer grazing of the best pastures round Bridgwater was used to fatten Red Devons at the rate of one animal per acre and in winter the same land was used to fatten two sheep per acre. In this district dairying was entirely concerned with cheese production and was commonly relegated to second-quality pastures of which three acres were required for each milk cow, to give a yield of 3–4 hundredweights of cheese per year.

On the other hand, far greater emphasis was placed on dairying in the northern half of the county. Between Mendip and the Bristol Avon dairying was concerned principally with the provision of local liquid milk supplies and butter for the markets of Bristol and Bath, while the Cheddar cheese belt stretched southwards from Mendip. Here the growing demands of the London market did not produce immediate effects comparable with those in west Wiltshire and shipments of liquid milk from Somerset grew only at the end of the century. Initially this affected merely the extreme northeast of the county when Wiltshire United Dairies started to draw milk from a depot in Frome, but in the early years of the present century the change was more rapid and condenseries and depots were established as far south as Templecombe and as far west as Bridgwater. Even so, the growing importance of liquid milk never produced a collapse of cheese making comparable with that in Wiltshire or even in Gloucestershire. Some farmhouse production of Cheddar cheese has continued in Somerset until the present time and was already augmented at the end of the last century by the beginnings of factory production at Frome and Yeovil.

Extreme variability was the keynote of farming practice on the small amounts of arable land in nineteenth-century Somerset. Standard four- or five-course rotations were by no means universally adopted, though they were common in the 'high farming' areas in the south of the county between Yeovil and Taunton and in the Vale of Taunton Dene, and were used by individual farmers throughout the county. Otherwise, exclusive concentration on oats and grass on Exmoor, on wheat and green crops near Bath, and an infinite variety of rotations on the levels and on the low-lying Lias are indications of the diversity. But in Somerset there were no extensive tracts of land like the Chalk downs or Cotswold where the alternative of permanent pasture was impracticable when the arrival of cheap grain from America made the growth of cereals unprofitable. In consequence the change in Somerset seems to have been remarkably rapid, since the percentage of permanent pasture on the farmed land of the county rose from 63 to 81 between the 1870s and 1900 and then rose only from 81 to 83 by the mid-1930s. The corresponding figures of the approximate percentages of permanent pasture in Gloucestershire and Wiltshire demonstrate the delayed change occasioned by the unsuitability of Cotswold and the Chalk downs for immediate conversion to permanent pasture in the last twenty years of the nineteenth century.

TABLE 2

PERCENTAGES OF FARMED LAND IN PERMANENT PASTURE

|  | 1870s | 1900 | 1930s |
|---|---|---|---|
| Gloucestershire | 46 | 60 | 75 |
| Wiltshire | 42 | 58 | 75 |

## Industry

Change and growth during the nineteenth century in aspects of the Bristol region's economy unconnected with agriculture have often been minimized, because it has been suggested that here there was no true industrial revolution comparable with that in the Midlands and north. It is probably more correct, however, to recognize a different pattern of economic change in the west of England rather than to deny its importance. In the Midlands and north the basis of the industrial revolution may perhaps be described as rapid economic growth in existing industries and the attraction of ancillary ones. In the Bristol region, on the other hand, though some long-established industries and trades did survive the nineteenth century and remain important today, it is nevertheless basically true that the end of the nineteenth century saw the virtual extinction of such fundamental elements of its earlier economy as widespread woollen manufacture and the production of metal ores. On the positive side the industrial revolution saw the replacement of these ancient activities by completely new industries, some of them widespread like food processing and engineering and others so local that they involved the adaptation of a single woollen mill.

*Mining.* In no aspect of the economy is this element of nineteenth-century replacement more apparent than in the mining industry, where

I

the rapid rise in coal output offset the final abandonment of lead and zinc working and the more gradual decline in iron-ore production. In the Forest of Dean it will be recalled that the mining of iron ore had declined considerably at the end of the eighteenth century and Lancashire ores were being used extensively in the local iron works. Strenuous efforts were made to re-establish the use of Forest ore, but heavy financial losses were incurred during the first quarter of the nineteenth century before recovery began, helped by the development of larger mines in the 1830s. Westbury Brook (1837) and Old Sling (1838), with annual outputs of 20,000 and 10,000 tons respectively, are typical of the new mines and the progress of the revival throughout the Forest is to be seen in the annual ore production figures.

TABLE 3

FOREST OF DEAN AREA—IRON ORE PRODUCTION

| 1828 | 9,800 tons |
|------|------------|
| 1839 | 72,800 ,, |
| 1871 | 170,611 ,, |
| 1905 | 7,245 ,, |

The peak production around 1870 was achieved by increased output from a limited number of mines including Oakwood, China Eugene, Perseverence, Findall, Shakemantle, St Annals and particularly Buckshraft, which alone produced 46,000 tons in 1865. During this prosperous period much of the ore was smelted locally at Sudeley, Lydbrook, Cinderford and particularly at the Park End works of the Forest of Dean Iron Company which was established in 1825 and which, by the 1860s, was using ore at the rate of 30,000 tons per year and manufacturing 15,000 tons of pig iron, some part of which was used in the tinplate works at Park End itself and at Lydney.

The stimulus for this massive increase in the output of ore came from a culmination of demand for iron as the railway network was completed and the iron-using plant of the industrial revolution came into production in the west Midlands, South Wales and, after 1855, in Bristol. The Forest of Dean was by far the most important source of supply in the Bristol region but the high level of demand encouraged a brief burst of activity elsewhere. At Seend in Wiltshire this was particularly short-lived since the workings were shut down in 1873 and only re-used briefly during the 1914–18 war to supply steel works in South Wales. At Westbury the ore discovered during railway construction in 1841 was brought into production in 1857 to supply a small local concern with four blast furnaces, which remained prosperous until the end of the century and survived long enough to enjoy a boom between 1914 and 1918 before being closed down in 1925. In Somerset local clay band ores were apparently used by the Ashton Vale works near Bristol in 1871 and, in the south, workings in the Brendon Hills were started in 1852 by the Ebbw Vale company who shipped ore to South Wales from the harbour at Watchet. Here output reached 40,000 tons per year in 1882 and continued on a diminishing scale until the early years of the present century.

Even in the Forest of Dean iron ore output had fallen to a mere 7,000 tons in 1905 but by that time coal production was reaching its peak.

TABLE 4

FOREST OF DEAN AREA—COAL PRODUCTION

| 1800 | 100,000 tons (approx.) |
|------|------------------------|
| 1856 | 460,000 ,, |
| 1898 | 1,176,712 ,, |
| 1906 | 1,310,000 ,, |

In 1841, when the limits of the 'gales' were defined under the 1838 Forest of Dean (Mines) Act, 20 such iron mines were recognized but already 104 coal 'gales' were being worked and by 1856 the number had risen to 261. However, as in the case of the iron workings, an increasing share of the coal output came from the larger collieries, and in 1856 Park End and Lightmoor were each producing 87,000 tons per year or, together, 38 per cent of the total for the field. Indeed, during the nineteenth century the two most pressing needs of this ancient mining area were for integration of the innumerable small 'gales' and provision for working the deeper seams. Though the Forest of Dean (Mines) Acts of 1838 and 1904–6 effectively confirmed the Free Miners' rights, other than that of using free Forest timber, they also provided an eventual solution of the two problems. The need for deeper working was met by making it legally possible for deep shafts to be sunk through the shallow 'gales', while the need for larger units was met by grouping the 'gales' into colliery units. The 1838 Act had established machinery to review the payment of 'royalties' every twenty-one years and the later colliery units were required to pay what were tantamount to royalties to the Free Miners. There were therefore long-established precedents for the special clauses of the Nationalization Acts of the present century, which, in the Forest of Dean, still allow Free Miners to acquire, work and sell 'gales' as their own property.

On Mendip the actual winning of lead and zinc ore was dealt what proved to be its final blow by the 1825 reduction of tariffs on imported non-ferrous metals and the last workings were closed down before

1850. By that time, however, some reworking of slag, much of it of Roman origin, had been in progress at Charterhouse for twenty years. In the second half of the nineteenth century there was a considerable revival of interest in this process, greatly stimulated by the arrival of Cornish miners and metal companies. This led to an outburst of activity at each of the 4 old mineries at Harptree for a brief period before 1875, at Chewton Mendip between 1864 and 1877, at Charterhouse on quite a large scale between 1858 and 1878, and finally at Priddy, where the St Cuthbert works was in operation from 1879 to 1897 and a rebuilt plant worked from 1900 until falling prices led to its closure in 1908.

However, these were only the final flickers of interest in the waning fortunes of Mendip metal production, and in north Somerset and south Gloucestershire it was the rapid development of the coalfields that dominated the mining industry in the nineteenth century. In Somerset only the Radstock and Paulton sections of the coalfield had been growing in prosperity in 1800 and this continued into the first quarter of the nineteenth century, greatly assisted by the opening of the Somerset Coal canal which served both districts and linked them with the industrial area of the west Wiltshire wool towns and eventually with much of southern Britain. The comparative isolation of the southern part of the field had retarded its development in the early nineteenth century, whilst in the extreme north the collieries of Brislington, Queen Charlton, Burnett and Pensford were largely out of production in 1824. However, completion of the railway from Frome to Radstock in 1854 and of the Bristol and north Somerset line in 1873 meant that no part of the coalfield lacked adequate transport facilities, and in the period between 1870 and 1879 output reached 650,000 tons per year, more than double the 1800 figure. Thereafter production continued to rise until the end of the century.

TABLE 5

SOMERSET COALFIELD—COAL OUTPUT

| 1880–1889 (average) | 850,000 tons |
|---|---|
| 1890–1899 „ | 850,000 „ |
| 1901 | 1,300,000 „ |
| 1908 | 1,130,000 „ |

In the 1860s 4 collieries in the Bedminster district of Bristol, one at Twerton near Bath, and one in the detached Nailsea basin were still working, and the northern part of the coalfield round Pensford was again active. However, the central area remained the most prosperous with 21 of the county's 34 pits in operation, 10 in the Radstock district, including Clandown and Foxcote, and 11 round Paulton, including

Timsbury, Camerton and Farrington. In the south the construction of branches from the Frome–Radstock railway caused a considerable revival and 6 collieries were working, in Nettlebridge, Newbury, New Rock, Vobster, Edford and Mells. When production reached its peak in 1901 the number of collieries had increased to 60 and employment topped the 6,000 mark, compared with just over 5,000 in the middle of the nineteenth century.

The geographical proximity of the Kingswood anticline coalfield to the eighteenth-century Bristol industrial districts of St Phillips and St George and to the metal smelters of the Avon valley encouraged its development from the turn of the century. Thirty years later the exploitation of the south Gloucestershire basin was accelerated by the construction of the coal tramways from Coalpit Heath to St Phillips and to the Avon near Bitton. In consequence the output of the combined Bristol field was nearly doubled between 1800 and the 1870s, when it reached a maximum of 524,000 tons per year. From that point production declined slowly to 483,881 tons per year in the 1880s and 395,546 tons per year in the 1890s, but it reached 411,077 tons in 1903 before exhaustion of the good seams and competition from South Wales coal led to the gradual abandonment of the field in the following forty years.

Until the nineteenth century the development of the Kingswood Forest section of this field had been characterized by a multiplicity of small shallow workings not unlike the gales of the Forest of Dean, but the expansion of production in the course of the century was achieved mainly by a limited number of large companies. The Bristol United Colliery Company and, to the north, the Oldland and the Coalpit Heath companies were relatively large organizations but by far the most important was the Kingswood and Parkfield Colliery Company. It was responsible for more than half the total output of the field in the 1890s, with a daily production approaching 1,000 tons from the Parkfield, Kingswood, Bedminster and Easton collieries as well as other pits purchased by the company in St George, in the manor of Kingswood and on the Beaufort estate at Stapleton.

*Wool.* The best-known example of a manufacturing industry which virtually disappeared during the nineteenth century is the extensive West Country woollen industry. The word 'extensive' is to be stressed because it was characteristic of this period that wool working 'drained back' into five towns where it not only survived the nineteenth century but still exists, though in greatly modified form. Moreover, in some of these centres the industry enjoyed considerable prosperity until about 1875, despite the decline that was elsewhere general throughout the century. No universal single cause can therefore have produced the

255

collapse and different circumstances have to be considered in each of the three main eighteenth-century woollen areas.

In the former white broadcloth and Spanish cloth area of west Wiltshire and northeast Somerset the making of broadcloths still continued in 1840 at Frome, Twerton and Bradford-on-Avon, where water power was available for the necessary heavy fulling. In Frome 350 looms were still in use in that year, mostly making livery cloths which were exported in considerable quantities to America in the early part of the century. The mill at Twerton, near Bath, was using a considerable variety of Spanish, Moravian and Silesian wools to make meltons and hunting pink, but in 1840 the more general broadcloth trade in Bradford-on-Avon was said to have been stagnant for twenty years. During that period 15 mills in the town had closed down, leaving only 4 in operation, with 418 employees. Here utter collapse was precipitated by a bank failure in 1841 and its consequences can be assessed from the 25 per cent decline in the town's population between 1840 and 1850.

Trowbridge, however, having virtually no water power, had long specialized in the manufacture of narrower fancy Spanish cloths and had become the principal centre of that profitable eighteenth-century trade. Moreover, after the invention in 1766 by Yerbury of Bradford-on-Avon of wool-dyed diagonally ribbed cassimeres, Trowbridge concentrated almost wholly on this fabric and produced it in finer and finer qualities at the end of the eighteenth and in the first half of the nineteenth centuries. In this highly specialized field little competition was felt from cheaper cloths and the town prospered. In the smaller towns and outlying villages, however, where broadcloths or coarser Spanish cloth were made, competition from Yorkshire was felt severely and had been commented upon since the later seventeenth century. Here a decline started as early as 1815 and of the single mills which survived at Malmesbury, Calne and Chippenham only the last was still engaged in wool working in the twentieth century. In part the drain back to Trowbridge in the nineteenth century represented a move from the cottages and small workshops of surrounding villages to the new and rebuilt mills of the town as the industry evolved a true factory stage of organization. At all events the fortunes of the woollen industry in Wiltshire from 1815 onwards are largely bound up with its history in Trowbridge.

It is a measure of the prosperity of the town that its population rose from 5,799 to 11,146 between 1801 and 1851, and that in 1838 no fewer than 19 mills in Trowbridge employed 1,278 people. The peak period of factory building was between 1814 and 1835 when several firms were competing in a scramble for river-side sites. Details are available from the records of the firm of Clarks of Trowbridge during this very prosperous period and they reveal that the company's capital increased from £500 to £59,000 between 1811 and 1824. The rapidity of the firm's expansion in this period, when London was the main market for their high-quality products, may also be judged from the fact that in 1804 they had 4 agents in the city whereas by 1819 they were using the services of 19 agents and had opened their own London office. The mills built in Trowbridge during the first half of the nineteenth century housed all the textile processes except weaving, which at this stage was still carried out in small workshops in the town or in cottages in the surrounding countryside. Between 1815 and 1835 steam power, using coal brought cheaply from Somerset by canal, was universally adopted to drive the scribbling, carding and spinning machinery which came into general use in the same period. Despite the availability of steam engines, power fulling was not common in Wiltshire until after 1840 and this, combined with the absence of gig mills in the county, put the broadcloth manufacturers at a considerable disadvantage compared with those of the Stroud district where the use of both types of machine was long established. In the Trowbridge manufacture of Spanish and fancy cloths, however, the only delay in mechanization which might have harmed the industry arose from the tardy adoption of various types of finishing machines, to which objections were made as late as 1840, but the prosperity of the town in the meantime suggests that this cannot have been a very serious handicap.

The progress of the eventual introduction of factory power weaving can be measured by the fact that in 1850 7 mills had 170 such looms in use, in 1862 16 mills had 549 looms and in 1867 all 25 mills in the district were equipped with 770 power looms. This led to a second phase of factory building after 1860 and as late as 1884 Clarks had a large new mill under construction in the town.

By this late date, however, even the Trowbridge industry was declining. For some time local mills had specialized in fancy weaves, including striped trouserings, whilst the black broadcloths for jackets to accompany the stripes were made in Bradford-on-Avon. Fashion changes at the end of the century perhaps even more than economy allowed both to be superseded by much cheaper worsted suitings. Of the 3 mills which were still in production at Bradford-on-Avon in 1880, 2 closed before the end of the century and the third in 1906. In Trowbridge 8 mills were working in 1880, 5 continued into the present century and 4 survived by constant adaptation of their products to fashion changes in the high-quality cloth trade. In Frome 3 firms have continued to manufacture buckskins as well as cords, whipcords, tweeds and high-quality coatings, but elsewhere only individual firms survived

257

until the end of the century. The mill at Chippenham was acquired by a Stroud company and did not close until 1930, at Westbury 1 of the 5 mills which were working in the early nineteenth century was kept in production by changing to worsted fabrics in 1920, and the mill at Twerton became the property of Isaac Carr and Company in the late nineteenth century and was able to prosper by concentrating on the highly specialized production of fine meltons and hunting pink.

In Gloucestershire, figures of employment in the woollen industry of the county show that it was by no means extinct at the end of the nineteenth century and that it had undergone a considerable revival after 1850. (see Table 6).

TABLE 6

GLOUCESTERSHIRE—WOOLLEN MANUFACTURE, EMPLOYMENT

| 1839 | 5,515 |
|------|-------|
| 1851 | 4,459 |
| 1861 | 7,050 |
| 1881 | 4,950 |
| 1901 | 3,321 |

Nevertheless throughout the county there was a similar story of concentration in a single town which enjoyed a period of great prosperity comparable with that of Trowbridge. The declining population of the small Gloucestershire wool towns and villages throughout the nineteenth century (see below, p. 264) is indicative of the extent to which the industry 'drained back' into Stroud, particularly after 1830. By 1839 nearly one-quarter of the county's woollen workers were employed in the town, mostly by large concerns, since at that time Stroud had only 14 mills, many of which had been rebuilt and greatly enlarged or newly built since 1800.

In the nineteenth century Stroud was unquestionably a progressive wool town and in particular it pioneered the use of new sources of supply of the fine wools essential for its products. By 1808 local manufacturers were replacing Spanish wool with supplies from Saxony, and later used Silesian and Moravian wool before turning to Australia, New Zealand and South Africa between 1830 and 1860. During the eighteenth century the use of machinery had been adopted at least as promptly as in any part of the country and after 1800 Stroud was a centre of considerable technical progress. Preparation and spinning were almost completely mechanized, the district had long led the way in the use of finishing machines and as early as 1820 attempts were being made to adapt power looms for wool weaving. In the middle of the nineteenth century, therefore, the Stroud manufacturers were well able to withstand competition from any part of the country. Elsewhere in the county, however, the almost complete collapse of the industry between 1830 and 1870 meant that by the latter date Stroud was the only prosperous wool town in Gloucestershire, in part because it was only in this district that mechanization had been wholly accepted. During the rest of the century one or two mills continued in use in the nearby centres of Nailsworth and Painswick and a little further away at Wotton-under-Edge and Dursley, in each of which a single mill survived into the early years of the present century.

Even in Stroud prosperity finally collapsed after 1875 and the reduced county employment figures for 1881 (see Table 6) are to a considerable extent attributable to the town's misfortunes during the following five years. Some part of the decline was due to tariff changes and the loss of overseas markets, but the main cause lay in changes of fashion and high costs. Not only were worsted suitings in greater demand than superfine broadcloths but their manufacture, by avoiding the difficult and prolonged finishing processes needed by the latter, was appreciably less costly. Between 1875 and 1905 no fewer than 20 mills closed down in the Stroud area, leaving only 11 working in the latter year. They continued to produce smooth, highly finished cloths like buckskins, doeskins, meltons and vicunas, for which there still remained a highly specialized market in the supply of hunting pink, military cloths in the traditional Stroudwater scarlet, billiard cloth and fabric for the new local piano industry.

In Somerset broadcloths were manufactured on a considerable scale in the nineteenth century only in the northeastern part of the county round Frome, which has already been considered with the neighbouring parts of Wiltshire. By 1840 they were being woven on only 23 looms in Chard and 9 in Ilminster, two formerly famous centres for fine woollens in south Somerset, and before the end of the century wool had been largely replaced here by other textiles. In the southern half of the county the fortunes of wool working were therefore almost entirely bound up with the manufacture of serge which, it will be recalled, had moved during the eighteenth century from its former home in Taunton to Wellington, Milverton and Wiveliscombe. In the early nineteenth century Wiveliscombe began to specialize in the production of thick blue kerseys called Penistones and the manufacture of ordinary serges was concentrated in Wellington and Milverton where, in 1837, 258 and 200 men respectively were employed. These were obviously important wool towns, though the industry was small by comparison with the making of broadcloths in Frome, which provided employment for 730 men at the same date.

From 1830 onwards the serge industry declined appreciably, partly owing to the loss of a stable export market through the former East India Company's monopoly. In the second half of the century, however, fashion changes and competition from botany worsteds also took their toll and by 1917 only 3 firms were still working in Wellington, all making serges, though 2 of them combined this with the manufacture of flannels, blankets and some woollen cloths.

Throughout the three counties the collapse of the woollen industry was therefore widespread and its causes seem to have been mainly connected with changing demand and fashion. Demand from a population which was growing rapidly during the industrial revolution was for inexpensive simply designed cloth of moderate quality and not for the superfine highly finished broadcloths, fancy cloths and serges in which the region still specialized. After 1850 this trend was accentuated by changing men's fashions and the West Riding worsted industry was given an additional advantage in exploiting the new markets by the invention of the combing machine, which made possible the manufacture of botany worsteds from many types of wool.

It has been suggested that the West Country industry declined because it was not located on a coalfield and because in the eighteenth and early nineteenth centuries it was a highly capitalized industry which therefore suffered more resistance to the introduction of machinery and the evolution of factory working than was experienced by the smaller Yorkshire concerns. It is true that the average number of employees in individual woollen concerns in the western counties was higher than that for the country as a whole in 1838.

TABLE 7

1838 AVERAGE NUMBER OF EMPLOYEES IN INDUSTRIAL
WOOLLEN MANUFACTURING CONCERNS

| | |
|---|---|
| United Kingdom | 45·8 |
| Gloucestershire | 57·4 |
| Wiltshire | 60·7 |
| Somerset | 71·1 |

Moreover, it seems clear that at about 1800 there was a certain amount of resistance to change, particularly in the finishing and later in the weaving sections of cloth manufacture in Wiltshire and in parts of Somerset. On the other hand, the Stroud district was actually long in the forefront of technological change and the prosperity of the industry here and in Trowbridge in the middle of the century suggests that any such problem had been overcome. In all the towns where the industry became concentrated during the nineteenth century, coal was available at prices which compared more than favourably with those in many localities on the Yorkshire coalfield. It seems certain that as it became concentrated in Stroud, Trowbridge, Frome and to a lesser extent near Bath and in Wellington, the West Country woollen industry could and did overcome the problems of organization and technology which faced it at the beginning of the nineteenth century. Except in the case of relatively few firms which concentrated on the manufacture of highly specialized fabrics for a steady, if limited, market, it collapsed during the later part of the century because it failed or was unable to overcome the problem of changing demand and fashion.

In a number of localities, particularly in Somerset, employment and some degree of industrial prosperity was maintained for a period after the decline of the woollen industry by turning to other textiles, of which silk was by far the most important. In the late eighteenth and nineteenth centuries the silk industry spread fairly widely before being relocalized in London and the north of England. One of the first towns to be engaged in silk manufacture on a considerable scale was Taunton, where it largely replaced the serge industry, so that by 1822 over 800 silk looms were weaving crape in the town and another 200 were in use in its immediate neighbourhood. Bruton also had a sizeable silk industry in the early nineteenth century for which yarn was being produced in nearby parts of Wiltshire in 1813. During the 1820s the industry spread to Milverton, Ilminster and as far north as Shepton Mallet, and by the middle of the century it was also established in Yeovil. In 1858, 355 men and 1,696 women were engaged in the silk industry in Somerset, whilst at about the same time there were nearly 1,000 employees in 12 mills in the Stroud valley which had turned to silk and 700 silk workers in west Wiltshire, nearly 300 of them in Malmesbury and the rest in former woollen mills at Chippenham, Calne and Devizes. In the middle of the century the industry was therefore an important one, but it declined in the second half of the century. This was partly because of the concentration of silk manufacture elsewhere, but it was also due to a falling demand for silk crape on which the West Country had concentrated. Like the woollen industry it only survived in the present century because individual firms in Taunton, Frome, Evercreech, Shepton Mallet, Malmesbury and later in Warminster, were able to adapt their production to a rapidly changing market.

The demand for ticking and dowlas, which had been the mainstay of the ancient coarse linen industry of Somerset, declined severely at the beginning of the nineteenth century, but other uses for a variety of coarse yarns in the manufacture of canvas, sailcloth, webbing and sacking continued in the southern part of the linen area at Crewkerne and in the neighbouring villages of West Hatch, Merriott, East Coker and North Perrott. Similar industries later developed further north in Martock and Castle Cary, where decay of the woollen and linen industries was also partly offset, after 1815, by the establishment of the haircloth industry. In 1858 just over 1,100 workers were employed in the manufacture of this group of coarse textiles. Even locally it never approached the woollen and linen industries in importance but some industrial activity was maintained in the small towns of east and south Somerset and survived on a significant scale into the present century at Crewkerne with 4 firms manufacturing canvas, sailcloth and webbing, at Castle Cary with 2 haircloth and 1 sailcloth factories, and on a very small scale elsewhere especially in the sack-making trade.

Though lace making was fairly widespread in the eighteenth century and was apparently of great importance in Malmesbury, it became extremely localized in the nineteenth century and by 1830 it was largely confined to Taunton, where there were 2 establishments, and to Chard. In the latter town, however, the industry was on a sufficient scale to compensate for the decline of other textile occupations, since the 5 concerns employed 1,500 hands at that time. By the end of the century lace and net were being made also in Shepton Mallet and Ilminster, but Chard remained the principal centre of the industry in the early years of the present century, manufacturing fabrics ranging from fine tulle to a grade commonly used for mosquito netting.

Elsewhere other textiles, including cotton in Tewkesbury, Bitton and Bristol, and linen in Chipping Camden and Moreton-in-Marsh, were manufactured for varying periods during the nineteenth century. The Bristol cotton industry was on a considerable scale for a time, but the only other textile industry which was still important after 1900 was that producing elasticized fabric at Kingswood and Charfield near Wotton-under-Edge, which provided employment for 700 workers in 1905.

The course of these changes in the West Country textile industries is illustrated by the trend of employment in them. In 1851 it was only in Somerset that large numbers were employed in the making of textiles other than woollens.

TABLE 8

1851 MANUFACTURE OF TEXTILES—EMPLOYMENT

| | MAKING OF WOOLLEN CLOTH | MAKING OF OTHER TEXTILES |
| --- | --- | --- |
| Somerset | 2,703 | 2,781 |
| Gloucestershire | 7,241 | 645 |
| Wiltshire | 5,671 | 681 |

By 1901 employment in the manufacture of woollen cloth had

diminished greatly in all three counties, but in Somerset and Gloucestershire this was still partly offset by continued production of other textiles.

TABLE 9

1901 MANUFACTURE OF TEXTILES—EMPLOYMENT

|  | MAKING OF WOOLLEN CLOTH | MAKING OF OTHER TEXTILES |
|---|---|---|
| Somerset | 1,611 | 2,124 |
| Gloucestershire | 3,049 | 1,702 |
| Wiltshire | 1,898 | 209 |

The Gloucestershire figure for 'other textiles' includes about 1,000 hands employed at the Great Western cotton mill and elsewhere in Bristol, and the remainder is almost entirely accounted for by employment in the elasticized fabric mills in the Kingswood–Charfield district.

In Wiltshire there was little corresponding growth in the manufacture of other fabrics and only the survival of the Trowbridge woollen mills kept a significant textile industry alive in the county at the end of the century.

*Population Distribution*

The localization and decline of the woollen industry, a changing agricultural economy, the growth of coal mining and a new pattern of communications combined to alter significantly the distribution of population in the Bristol region. In the first half of the nineteenth century these processes operated gradually but after 1850 the more rapid collapse of the woollen industry, the consequences of increasing imports of American cereals, the completion of the railway system and accelerating urbanization led to more radical changes.

In the majority of small towns and villages throughout the Bristol region, therefore, the normal trend was for a continued steady increase of population until about the middle of the century, followed by an appreciable decline. This was particularly characteristic of villages in the arable districts of Cotswold and southeastern Somerset, where falling cereal prices had their greatest effect. Thus the total population of 7 such Cotswold villages increased by 23 per cent between 1801 and 1851 and then declined by 32 per cent in the second half of the century, while in a comparable group in Somerset over the same periods the rise was 19 per cent and the subsequent fall 36 per cent. In small towns and villages which were less completely agricultural, textile industries and local commerce prospered in the early nineteenth century so that the growth of population was more marked, and in the latter part of the century their more diverse economy led to a smaller decline. In 20 of these settlements in Gloucestershire with a total population of 36,000 in 1801, there was a 36 per cent increase by 1851 and then a decrease of 18 per cent between 1851 and 1901. The corresponding increase and decrease in 7 west Wiltshire towns with a combined population of 24,000 in 1801, were 31 per cent and 19 per cent respectively. Increasing population in a considerable number of small towns in the first half of the nineteenth century was even more characteristic of Somerset than of the neighbouring counties. This was partly due to the fact that here other textile crafts supplemented and later replaced the dying woollen industry. Moreover, there was no concentration of textile industries in a single Somerset town comparable with that in Stroud and Trowbridge. The rate of increase in 20 Somerset towns with a total population of 25,000 in 1801 was therefore as high as 56 per cent between 1801 and 1851, though there was then a decrease of 21 per cent before 1901.

Exceptionally, the population of some villages and small towns decreased continuously throughout the century. In almost all cases this was a local phenomenon associated with a high degree of early specialization in wool working or mining. The most remarkable examples are provided by Alderley, North Nibley, Nympsfield, Owlpen, Uley, Miserden and Horsley, all situated in the upper parts of valleys or below the scarp of central Cotswold between Stroud and the Wotton-under-Edge district. Their combined population declined from 7,298 in 1801 to 6,515 in 1851 and 4,812 in 1901, mainly because it was from here that the woollen industry drained back into the lower valleys and Stroud, but partly because they did not share the growing prosperity of the arable plateau in the earlier part of the century. The corresponding population figures for the rather isolated Wiltshire woollen village of Castle Combe are 1801: 567; 1851: 557; 1901: 357. In Somerset, Freshford, similarly, had a declining population of 624, 622 and 533 in the same years, as had the former mining centre of Chewton Mendip (1801: 1,155; 1851: 1,139; 1901: 682). In the Hundred of Frome, which included a considerable part of the wool-working area round that town, most of the settlements had a continuously declining population, illustrated by the figures for the villages of Beckington, Berkley, Rode and the nearby Mells whose combined population fell from 4,364 in 1801 to 3,886 in 1851 and 2,521 in 1901. There was a similar situation in the south in the Hundred of Milverton and the population of the serge town itself decreased from 2,146 to 1,452 in the second half of the century. In the southeast, too, the population of almost all the villages in the Hundred of Wincanton declined steadily throughout the century.

Conversely population increased throughout the nineteenth century in the districts in which the woollen industry became concentrated. Stroud and Rodborough became virtually one urban area whose population grew from 7,070 in 1801 to 11,006 in 1851 and 14,163 in 1901, while downstream Stonehouse grew from 1,412 to 2,598 and 4,091 and the neighbouring small town of Painswick from 3,150 to 3,464 and 4,067. Before the end of the century, however, the Stroud area owed much of its continued growth to a wide range of metal-working and engineering industries as well as to the remaining textile trades, and the same was certainly true of the nearby town of Dursley where engineering was rapidly replacing the woollen industry in the last thirty years of the century. Improved communications during the nineteenth century also favoured the growth of all these larger towns in which industry survived and this almost certainly accounts for the rising population of Cirencester and the adjacent village of Stratton (combined population 1801: 4,296; 1851: 6,718; 1901: 8,929) since Cirencester's role as a market town outlived its connection with the manufacture of fabrics. Trowbridge, whose population increased very rapidly in the first half of the century and was maintained throughout the second (1801: 5,799; 1851: 11,148; 1901: 11,526) also owed some of its continued prosperity to the growth of an engineering industry, and the very large increase in the population of Chippenham after 1850 (1801: 3,366; 1851: 4,999; 1901: 12,677) was almost entirely attributable to the establishment of engineering works. Here, as at Calne (1801: 3,767; 1851: 5,117; 1901: 5,518), the opening of food-processing plants also contributed to the growth of the town; the continued existence of woollen mills was of relatively slight significance.

It will be recalled that in Somerset a considerable variety of textile working continued throughout the nineteenth century in a number of towns; moreover, several other old industries redeveloped and new ones were introduced. In consequence there is a longer list of former wool towns whose population grew throughout the period, especially as concentration of the woollen industry itself was less marked than in Gloucestershire and Wiltshire. Though the population of Frome grew appreciably before 1851 (1801: 8,748; 1851: 11,916) it had not increased further by 1901 (11,828) and Wellington (1801: 4,033; 1851: 6,415; 1901: 7,283) was the only town mainly engaged in wool working whose population grew continuously throughout the century. On the other hand, alternative textile or other trades had supplemented or replaced woollens in all of the following towns, whose population increased continuously:

265

TABLE 10

POPULATION

|  | 1801 | 1851 | 1901 |
|---|---|---|---|
| Taunton | 5,794 | 13,119 | 19,525 |
| Yeovil | 2,774 | 7,744 | 11,704 |
| Chard | 2,784 | 5,297 | 6,318 |
| Castle Cary | 1,281 | 1,860 | 1,902 |
| Crewkerne | 2,576 | 4,497 | 5,172 |
| Shepton Mallet | 5,104 | 5,116 | 5,446 |

The very considerable growth of the two larger towns of Taunton and Yeovil must be associated, in part, with early access to rail communications, with their commercial function and with the establishment of important engineering industries, but surviving textile industries and, in Yeovil, the expansion of the ancient glove-making industry also played a part.

The growth of the mining industry of the Bristol region is illustrated by the rising population of its three coal-producing areas during the nineteenth century. In the Forest of Dean by no means the whole of this rise (combined population of Lydney, Dean Forest, Newland, Flaxley and Ruarden, 1801: 7,880; 1851: 22,992; 1901: 34,831) is to be related to the increased output of coal, since iron mining did not diminish greatly until the end of the century and the iron works themselves remained active and prosperous throughout. Similarly the rapid increase in population on the Bristol coalfield outside the built-up area of Bristol itself and its immediate neighbourhood (combined population of Yate, Bitton, Frampton Cotterell, Winterbourne, Pucklechurch and Siston, 1801: 9,844; 1851: 17,102; 1901: 26,222) was affected to some extent by the growth of other industries and of the city itself, though locally coal mining was commonly the most important occupation. On the other hand, the central portion of the Somerset coalfield was an area where coal mining dominated the economy of whole districts and the growth of the combined population of Midsomer Norton, Paulton and Radstock (1801: 3,080; 1851: 7,695; 1901: 11,527) was significantly proportionate to the rising output of coal. On a much smaller scale the quarrying of building stone in Cotswold had a similar effect on the population of Box (1801: 1,165; 1851: 1,897; 1901: 2,405) and Corsham (1801: 2,402; 1851: 3,712; 1910: 4,322).

However, by far the most important population trend during the nineteenth century was that towards increasing urbanization, particularly round Bristol itself and in the seven other largest cities and towns of the Bristol region. It was characteristic of the period that in almost all cases growth reached the point where the built-up area spread beyond the administrative unit of the town or city or coalesced with that of neighbouring settlements, and the population figures listed below are approximately those of the whole of the urban area concerned, rather than of the area within the town or city boundaries.

TABLE 11

POPULATION

| THE URBAN AREA OF: | 1801 | 1851 | 1901 |
|---|---|---|---|
| Bristol | 72,000 | 166,000 | 356,000 |
| Taunton | 5,749 | 13,119 | 19,535 |
| Yeovil | 2,774 | 7,744 | 11,704 |
| Bath | 29,460 | 45,140 | 48,240 |
| Gloucester | 8,908 | 22,586 | 44,775 |
| Bridgwater | 3,878 | 11,777 | 16,666 |
| Cheltenham | 1,816 | 41,688 | 54,996 |
| Swindon | 1,198 | 4,879 | 45,000 |

Apart from the exceptionally rapid growth of Cheltenham, from 1801 to 1851 the rate of population increase in the other urban areas (from a total of about 52,000 to about 105,000) is somewhat less than that of the Bristol area (from 72,000 to 166,000). During the second half of the century it is only the very large increase in the population of Swindon which makes the total increase in all the other centres from 147,000 to 241,000 even broadly comparable with that round Bristol from 166,000 to 356,000.

Like Taunton and Yeovil, Bath still had some connection with the textile trades and a group of clothing and engineering industries, but its considerably greater size and its growth in the early part of the century reflect also a continuation of its roles as a resort and spa, a residential city and an important commercial centre. The steady and rapid growth of Gloucester throughout the century is a measure of its prosperity, both as a port and as a market centre, and of the establishment of new local industries following the completion of its canal and later rail connections. The opening of the canal to Taunton and the relatively early completion of a main-line rail connection provided the basis for similar developments, though on a smaller scale, at Bridgwater. The two remaining towns are quite exceptional, not only in the extraordinary rapidity of their growth during a fifty-year period, but also in the highly specialized courses of their development. Though some industries grew up in and around Cheltenham during the nineteenth century and it became a market centre of considerable importance, it enjoyed the most rapid rate of urban growth of any town in the Bristol region between 1801 and 1851 principally because of its emergence as a fashionable resort and spa at a time when improved communications made travel to such centres vastly easier than it had been in the previous century. The main growth of the population of Swindon, second only in rapidity to that of Cheltenham, came in the second half of the century and was entirely due to the opening of the Great Western Railway Company's main locomotive and rolling stock establishment in the town.

Elsewhere considerable population increases occurred only in the Somerset resorts after the completion of railways to the coast and with the rising popularity of seaside holidays.

TABLE 12

POPULATION—SOMERSET COASTAL RESORTS

|  | 1801 | 1851 | 1901 |
|---|---|---|---|
| Minehead | 1,168 | 1,542 | 2,782 |
| Burnham | 653 | 1,701 | 4,922 |
| Clevedon | 334 | 1,905 | 5,900 |
| Weston-super-Mare (including Kewstoke) | 487 | 4,594 | 19,448 |

In Minehead, Burnham and Clevedon the increase was fairly rapid but it did not compare with the phenomenal growth of Weston-super-Mare. To a considerable extent the obvious prosperity of Weston, Clevedon and the smaller settlements at Portishead and Easton-in-Gordano during the second half of the nineteenth century arose from their proximity to the Bristol urban area, whose population, it will be recalled, had increased almost five-fold in the course of the century.

### The Bristol Area and the growth of manufacturing industry

Clearly some of the problems which confronted the city of Bristol in 1800 had been overcome and by the end of the century the very size of its urban population ensured that it would recapture some aspects of its eighteenth-century metropolitan role, at least within its own region. This growth of Bristol arose from many changed circumstances. Physical improvements in the port and the construction of outports combined with the advent of railways to make possible a revival of its trade, whilst its banking and other financial and administrative functions increased as improved communication made it the commercial centre of a wider area. But perhaps the most characteristic aspect of economic growth in the Bristol area after 1850 was the redevelopment of a number of long-established industries and the introduction of a wide variety of new ones. Amongst this variety, however, there grew up a considerable emphasis on many aspects of metal working and engineering and it was the expansion and specialization of this side of Bristol's manufacturing activities that gave it, by the end of the century, a distinctive group of industries of considerable size for the first time since the collapse of its medieval woollen industry. Since Bristol shared this predominance of engineering industries in the nineteenth century with other towns in the surrounding counties an examination of the character and growth of the engineering industries seems an appropriate first step in a review of the new forms of manufacture which had become characteristic of the whole of the Bristol region by the beginning of the present century.

An impression of the scale and widespread nature of the growth of engineering can be gained from the vast increase in employment in this group of industries between 1851 and 1901. In Gloucestershire there were probably in 1851 about 3,600 employees engaged in some form of metal-using industry which might broadly be described as engineering. By 1901 this number had increased to 15,873 and in Bristol alone there were by then 7,850 such workers. In Wiltshire the corresponding increase was from about 1,600 to over 10,700 and of this a major part took place in the industrial area of west and north Wiltshire which lies within the Bristol region. In Somerset the increase was smaller, partly because many workers were still engaged in other crafts, particularly in the textile towns in the south of the county, but even so the numbers nearly doubled from 3,085 to 6,030.

Throughout its history West Country engineering has been characterized by a great variety of function, but during this early period of its development it is possible to distinguish five branches of the industry for which circumstances provided a climate conducive to specially rapid growth. The first arose from the mechanization of existing industries as local foundries were established to meet the needs of a new generation of millwrights working in metal rather than wood. After 1850 this group of engineering industries became increasingly specialized as machines were designed for more and more factory processes, but in the first half of the century the textile industry was still the millwrights' best customer. The establishment of foundries and small engineering works in Trowbridge in 1815 and in Bradford-on-Avon in 1816 coincides with the beginning of the real steam age in the West Country woollen industry, and within a decade or two similar concerns grew up in virtually all the wool towns from Wellington, Taunton, Martock and Bridgwater in the south to Melksham, Dursley, Nailsworth and Stroud in the north. In many of the smaller towns the industry had a brief period of growth, but by the early years of the present century it was represented only by local forges and workshops mainly concerned with the repair of machinery and later motor vehicles. However, in the larger towns and particularly in the Stroud–Nailsworth district and in Bridgwater, it was the origin of a modern general engineering industry which by the end of the century engaged in a wide range of activities unconnected with textiles. In Trowbridge the Haden company provides a somewhat specialized example of this process. Formed in 1815 as a millwright and general engineering firm, it had become involved in the problem of factory space heating as early as 1819 and grew steadily throughout the century so that it had 200 employees in Trowbridge in 1902. By this time, however, the company was also actively engaged as heating engineers in many parts of the country and was soon to grow into the present nationwide organization, which has links with other concerns including the Newman-Hender firm of valve specialists at Woodchester between Stroud and Nailsworth.

The second group of engineering activities was originally concerned with the making of quite simple agricultural machinery. During the late nineteenth century it engaged literally hundreds of small firms, and some part of the output of most of the West Country foundries and forges was used in new metal farm equipment as well as in the mill-wrights' workshops. The application of steam power to agriculture led a number of firms to turn during the 1850s to the building of farm traction engines, and Devizes, where in 1901 the firm of Brown and May employed 350 men, became the chief centre of this specialized branch of the industry. The failure of the Devizes industry in 1913 was due to competition, partly from large firms in the eastern counties and partly from the development of the internal combustion engine. In a similar way competition from the large-scale factory production of agricultural machinery in East Anglia meant that few of the agri-cultural engineers in the Bristol region survived as manufacturers, though many continued to operate repair shops and later garages in which the mass-produced machines and later tractors were serviced. As in the case of textile engineering, however, there were individual firms which had a very different history. In Melksham a small foundry, which was established in 1830 and was concerned with the production of agricultural equipment, eventually grew into the present firm of Spencers (Melksham). An early interest in grain handling and stacking machines for farms was presumably the starting point of its specializa-tion, but the company's main period of rapid growth dates from the 1880s. From then until the end of the century it concentrated to a great extent on grain handling gear for ports and by the beginning of the present century it had 500 employees and was undertaking the con-struction of plant in all the main grain ports of the country. Listers of Dursley is also a firm of agricultural engineers which grew considerably between the 1860s and 1900 and has subsequently continued to expand. The small power plants for which Listers became famous have many non-agricultural applications but at the beginning of the present century the firm was still primarily one of agricultural engineers with an interest in the new field of electrical engineering. In Yeovil the small engineering and millwrights' shops were usually connected with the textile and glove-making trades, but the large firm of Petters which was established in 1896 specialized in the manufacture of oil engines, the majority of which were still destined for agricultural use during the early decades of the present century.

Revolutions in transport during the nineteenth century were responsible for the very rapid growth of a third broad group of engineering industries, by far the most outstanding example of which followed the 1840 decision of the Great Western Railway Company to build their locomotive and rolling stock works at Swindon. The actual construction was not carried out until 1843 and variations of company policy led to considerable fluctuations of employment between 1848 and 1875, but the growth of the labour force from 4,000 to 11,500 between 1875 and 1900 is sufficient indication of the importance of the works. Indeed, until the comparatively recent introduction of other industries, Swindon was a railway town almost exclusively concerned with the building and maintenance of locomotives and rolling stock. Though not so completely a consequence of the arrival of the railway, the rapid economic growth of Chippenham in the later part of the nineteenth century was nevertheless closely connected with it. During the period of actual railway construction, the large civil and mechanical engineering firm of Brotherhood had important establishments at Chippenham as well as at Swindon, but the town's long-term association with railway engineering was in the field of signalling and brakes. Three firms engaged in various aspects of this work were founded in Chippenham in 1860, 1861 and 1894 and it was from their amalgamation in the present century that the Westinghouse Brake and Signal Company emerged as the largest single industrial concern in the district. The construction of railway wagons for other users as well as the main line companies was more widespread, but it assumed major importance in Gloucester where the Carriage and Wagon Company came to employ over 1,000 hands by the end of the century. For the frames and chassis the company operated a large foundry which, along with its own associated workshops and other similar concerns, accounted for the presence of over 2,500 engineering employees in the city in 1901. Since the wagon bodies were then mainly of wooden construction the industry also benefited from Gloucester's specialization in the import

271

of timber and from the city's long wood-working associations, while similar considerations, as well as the presence of foundries and forges, probably account for the establishment of wagon building and repairing concerns in Bristol and Bridgwater. Bristol's connection with railway engineering was by no means confined to the construction of wagons, however. Locomotives were built at the Avonside works, which remained in the St Phillips district of the city from its establishment in 1837 until the firm moved to Fishponds in 1905, while the Atlas works, which was opened in 1860, became the plant of Pecketts, who also specialized in making the smaller classes of locomotive mainly for industrial users at home and for export all over the world. The railways were, moreover, among the more important customers of the general engineering shops, foundries and forges in Bristol, and in considering the total impact of the new era of transport on the city's economy it should also be remembered that in 1901 no less than 3,351 of its workers were engaged in railway operation and maintenance. The Bristol region as a whole was little affected by the revolution in water-borne transport, since only the Bristol shipyards were involved in building sea-going steamships, but the construction of launches and craft for inland waterways at Gloucester had more than local significance and partly explains the manufacture of light marine propulsion machinery and ancillary equipment by Sissons in Gloucester itself and by Newman-Henders in Woodchester.

The fourth branch of the metallurgical industries which developed rapidly during the late nineteenth century was more miscellaneous in character. It was concerned with the production of a wide range, not only of general types of machinery such as pumps, valves, bearings, conveying gear, machine parts and tools, but also of structural materials, containers and smallware; it involved the use of non-ferrous metals as well as iron and steel in casting, forging, machining, metalling, galvaniz-ing and plating. Having long associations with the non-ferrous metal industry, Bristol was a natural centre for the development of this aspect of engineering, which therefore became largely concentrated in and around the city. Even though the main production of non-ferrous metals had moved to South Wales and elsewhere, there were still in the 1860s 18 brass foundries working in Bristol, 8 concerns making sheet lead, and the firm of Capper Pass was beginning to concentrate on the production of tin alloys and solder in the Bedminster works to which it had transferred from St Phillips in 1840—twenty years after moving there from Birmingham. Most of the firms engaged in this group of industries remained quite small, and their products were usually sold to other concerns within the engineering industry, but the Lysaght company, established in 1857, was something of an exception. It occupied the site of the former spelter works at Netham and was essentially a galvanizing concern which for a long period represented a link between Bristol and the growing metallurgical industry of South Wales since it drew its supplies of black iron sheets from Newport. These were galvanized, corrugated and packed in Bristol and their export, along with other products such as galvanized wire netting and tanks, played an important part in establishing new trading contacts for the Port of Bristol, particularly in Australia and New Zealand.

The fifth and last of this series of industries became increasingly important only in the late nineteenth century. As more and more activities moved into factories, their mechanization made new demands on the engineering concerns and led to the emergence of firms making highly specialized equipment for individual operations or for whole industries. Food processing provides one of the first examples, soon after 1850, in the manufacture of milling machinery in Gloucester to meet the needs of the large local industry which handled home and imported grains and, after 1862, oil and cake previously milled at Evesham. Similar industries soon developed in Bristol, but it was not until the last two decades of the century that the growth of the dairy and bacon factories created a demand for specialized engineering. The mechanization of the Harris bacon factories at Calne in the 1880s and 1890s led to the local manufacture of suitable machinery, and at Chippenham equipment was built for the new dairy factories, which needed not only process plant but also machines to make cans for condensed and evaporated milk from South Wales tinplate and to fill and seal them. The rubber industry in Wiltshire (see below, p. 276) dates back only to 1848 but it involved the introduction of a new technology whose requirements had to be met almost at once by the establishment of a local engineering firm in Bradford-on-Avon. As the rubber industry spread to Limpley Stoke and later Melksham, and as increasingly sophisticated machines were needed to manufacture a widening range of products, further engineering concerns grew up Bradford-on-Avon and Corsham.

It was, however, in the Bristol area that this form of engineering had its maximum development. For example, widespread hand-making of boots and shoes in small workrooms was being replaced by their manufacture in factories, most of which were located in Bristol and the contiguous parts of Gloucestershire. Similarly the output of paper and board from small mills scattered throughout the surrounding counties was being supplemented and later replaced by their large-scale production in big mills in and around the city. For both of these

273

industries equipment was made locally and in the case of the paper trade, in particular, the associated engineering industry has continued to grow more complex and specialized up to the present time as it has made machines for the manufacture and printing of prepared papers and boards, bags, envelopes, cartons and other types of container and packaging on which there has been a gradually increasing emphasis in the Bristol industry. Even the ancient Bristol tobacco trade began to make demands on the engineering industry after tobacco was first packed by machine in 1887, and by the early years of the present century the equally old cocoa, chocolate and confectionery industry was established in city factories in which increasingly elaborate processing and packing machinery was required.

Apart from engineering and food processing, one of the most widespread groups of industries which was of growing importance after 1850 was that concerned with leather working. It involved ancient crafts, because the earliest records of the Port of Bristol make reference to the import of skins and hides, but during the nineteenth century a growing population and the progress of the industrial revolution led to an increased demand which was only met when large-scale factory manufacture of boots, in particular, was established. Although leather was produced and dressed in various parts of the west of England, including north Somerset and the glove town of Yeovil, Bristol has always been by far the most important centre for tanning, and the prosperity of the industry at the end of the nineteenth century can be judged from the fact that the number of hides tanned in the city increased from 187,000 in 1872 to 250,000 in 1900. The making of boots and shoes was naturally the most important use of the leather and the following figures are indicative of changes in this branch of the industry. The decrease in Wiltshire was a consequence of the reduced importance of the small boot and shoe maker's craft and the relatively modest increase in Somerset is explained by the way in which increased employment in the Street works of C. and J. Clark from 1895 onwards was offset by declining employment elsewhere in the county. The main concentration of the growing factory industry was in the Kingswood–Hanham district straddling the Bristol–Gloucestershire county boundary, so that half (6,357) of the 11,000 operatives lived within the limits of the city itself, where there were at that time over 100 'factories'. In its early factory phase the Bristol and Gloucestershire industry concentrated increasingly on the manufacture of the heavier type of working boot, of which it was said to be capable of producing 10 million pairs annually in the early years of the present century.

TABLE 13

MAKING OF BOOTS AND SHOES—EMPLOYMENT

|  | 1851 | 1901 |
|---|---|---|
| Wiltshire | 2,138 | 841 |
| Somerset | 2,512 | 3,034 |
| Gloucestershire and Bristol | 5,482 | 11,081 |

Apart from the making of boots, shoes and belting, the other important use of leather during the nineteenth century was in the glove industry. Silk and other fabric gloves have been made in Martock, and in small quantities elsewhere, but the main industry in the Yeovil district was principally concerned with leather gloves, often of the heavier kinds. The industry had a long history before 1831 when there were 300 workers in Yeovil, 150 at Milborne Port and 45 at Stoke-sub-Hamdon, Montacute and Martock. However, the next thirty years saw employment in the industry reach a peak because in 1858 there were apparently some 9,000 people in Somerset engaged in glove making. Of these 1,156 were men and over 8,000 women, mostly engaged in the making-up process in their own homes. By 1901 this number was reduced to 3,291 (904 men, 2,387 women) partly because of changes in demand and competition from other glove-making areas, but also because of the increasing concentration of full-time working on all processes in factories in Yeovil, joined later by similar establishments in north Somerset and at Westbury and Warminster in Wiltshire. The only other related industry of importance in the nineteenth century was that using sheepskins for lined footwear and rugs which was developed in Glastonbury after 1825 by the Clark and Moreland families and has remained prosperous until the present time.

Some reference has already been made to the import of timber at Gloucester (see above, pp. 226; 233) and to the rise of wood-working industries in the city. Timber had also long figured in Bristol cargo lists, but during the nineteenth century it became increasingly important and in 1880 105,000 tons were landed, representing about 14 per cent of the port's inward foreign tonnage. By the end of the century Bristol's timber imports had increased to nearly 174,000 tons and rather more than half that amount was normally handled at Gloucester, so that the development of wood-working industries in the two cities is understandable. Much of the timber handled at Bristol was merely in transit for use in building and other industries throughout the west of England and many of the 1,600 general wood-working employees in 1901 were engaged in saw-milling and machining, though the use of timber in wagon building has already been mentioned and there were, in addition, over 2,300 furniture workers in the city at the end of the century. In

Gloucester, where 750 workers were employed in general wood working in 1901, there was a slightly greater degree of local specialization. Apart from the Carriage and Wagon Company, additional furniture firms and one manufacturing step-ladders used a great deal of timber after the 1860s, and the important local match industry was established in 1850. The wood-working industries of the Stroud–Nailsworth area differed somewhat from those of the cities in that initially they drew some part of their supplies from nearby beech woods on the Cotswold scarp. The making of walking sticks and umbrellas in old woollen mills started soon after 1800, became prosperous during the next four decades and still employed 1,700 hands in 1901, whilst the piano industry involved highly specialized metal work as well as the use of a variety of local and imported hardwoods and, later, veneers.

It will be recalled that in 1800 the paper-making industry was in the middle of a period when it was characterized by a dispersed distribution involving a considerable number of small concerns often housed in former woollen mills. Many of these were closed during the second half of the nineteenth century, but a few remained prosperous. In Bath, Frome and Midsomer Norton larger concerns concentrated increasingly on book and commercial stationery production and printing, the Postlip mills near Winchcombe continued to make blotting paper and in the Cam–Nailsworth area there was increased emphasis on specialized forms of board and stationery. Elsewhere almost every variety of paper and board was made by individual firms in Gloucester, Taunton, Creech St Michael, Yeovil, Street, Wells, Wookey, Watchet and Slaughterford. However, by far the most important development in the manufacture of paper and board was the rise of the large-scale industry in the Bristol area during the last three decades of the nineteenth century. As early as 1850 the establishment of the Golden Valley mills, in the former brass works near Bitton, marked the start of this process, but the real origins of the modern industry in the city and its immediate neighbourhood date from the opening of the Avonside mills in St Phillips in 1876 and of Mardon's mill in 1885. By this time, of course, the printing industry in Bristol was almost 200 years old and the 6,000 paper and printing workers in the city in 1901 included those of many small, but long-established, firms as well as those of the new large mills, whose growing demands for materials had led to the shipment of 1,500 tons of pulp into the Port of Bristol in the previous year.

The manufacture of rubber in west Wiltshire is the only example, on an appreciable scale, of the introduction of a totally new industry into the Bristol region during the nineteenth century. In 1848, on his return from America, a Mr Moulton established the processing of rubber in a disused woollen mill in Bradford-on-Avon, where cheap canal-borne coal was available, and within ten years had taken over two further mills. From 1860 until the growth of the motor car, aircraft and electrical industries, the firm was almost exclusively concerned with the manufacture of rubber mechanical components, such as buffer and draw-bar springs for railway rolling stock, and its prosperity can be judged from the growth of its labour force from 78 to 164 by 1900 and of the value of its output from £17,000 to £67,000 between 1857 and 1890. In 1875 a similar concern took over a former flour mill at Limpley Stoke and fourteen years later moved to a larger mill at Melksham where it employed 20 workers, also mainly engaged in the manufacture of rubber mechanicals for railway rolling stock. By the end of the century, however, it was embarking on the manufacture of cycle and motor tyres which later became the chief interest of the Avon Rubber Company and led to a period of expansion shown by the growth of its labour force to 500 as early as 1909 and to more than 3,500 in recent times.

Finally, in Bristol itself the long-established manufacture of tobacco and of cocoa and chocolate was growing rapidly and by 1900 was being progressively concentrated in large factories. In 1901 there were 3,869 tobacco workers in the city and over 2,500 engaged in the making of cocoa and chocolate.

By the end of the nineteenth century, therefore, the industrial scene in Bristol had taken on many of its modern aspects. Some traditional industries were prospering greatly, though in aggregate the engineering group of industries had already become the largest employer of labour in the city, admittedly by only a narrow margin over the paper and printing or the boot and shoe industries. Indeed, if the whole of the Bristol and south Gloucestershire boot and shoe industry in Bristol, Kingswood and Hanham is considered, this was perhaps the nearest approach to a staple industry in the Bristol area, since it was not until the growth of the aircraft industry that a single branch of engineering came to figure as one of its larger individual industries. Variety was then, as it is now, the keynote of engineering and of industry as a whole in the city and its immediate neighbourhood.

Many of the modern characteristics of the Port of Bristol were also becoming increasingly apparent as trade revived after the port improvements of the early nineteenth century and more particularly after the construction of the outports. Between 1850 and 1900 the annual net registered tonnage of vessels using the port increased from 129,254 to 847,632 and the tonnage of cargo, which was probably about 175,000 in 1850, must have passed the half million mark in the 1870s, and reached 1,368,758 in 1900. Moreover, the overriding importance of foreign imports and their character in the last twenty years of the nineteenth century gave a foretaste of the port's modern specialization. Between 48 and 54 per cent of the total import trade after 1890 consisted of grains and a further 2 or 3 per cent was accounted for by oil seeds. Timber, representing between 13 and 14 per cent of the imports, was still the next most important category, but petroleum products were already in third place and made up 4 per cent of the trade in 1900. In addition, among the smaller quantities in the foreign import lists, long-standing items like tobacco, cocoa and wine had been joined in the later part of the century by new industrial materials like non-ferrous ores, paper and paper pulp and by fruits and provisions, all of which have subsequently continued to increase in importance.

It will be recalled that whilst the economy of Bristol was thus evolving towards its present pattern, the population of the urban area had reached about 356,000 by the end of the century. Here too growth was along lines which rapidly sketched in the form of the modern city in the course of the century. The emergence of industrial east Bristol involved the parishes of St Paul, St George, St James-without, St Philip and St Jacob-without, as well as the Gloucestershire parishes of Mangotsfield and Stapleton, and in the whole of this area the population increased from about 23,000 in 1801 to 61,000 in 1851 and 177,000 by 1901. Similarly industrial and residential development to the south of the Avon is shown by the growth of the population of Bedminster and Brislington from 4,054 in 1801 to 20,684 in 1851 and 75,407 by 1901. Together Bedminster, Brislington and the east Bristol district accounted for 79 per cent of the nineteenth-century growth of population in the whole urban area. In contrast, markedly reduced populations were characteristic of all the small ancient city parishes in which a central business district was gradually emerging, while the extension of a largely residential built-up area to the north and northwest is reflected in the growth of the population of Clifton, Westbury-on-Trym and Horfield from 6,901 in 1801 to 25,583 in 1851 and 67,869 by 1901.

Away from the neighbourhood of Bristol, present-day patterns had also been largely established throughout the region by the end of the nineteenth century. Already the preponderance of grass farming had brought with it widespread marketing of liquid milk and the establishment of new food-processing industries, while in all the larger towns except Swindon a characteristic diversity of commercial and industrial activity was growing. Elsewhere specialized woollen manufacture, newer textile trades and the paper and printing industry survived in smaller towns as they do today, whilst the distinctive tendency for such towns in the Bristol region to develop highly individual single industries was already discernible in the rubber industry of Bradford-on-Avon and Melksham and the agricultural machinery industry in Dursley.

# CHAPTER 11

# *The Bristol Region Today*

DESPITE the changes of the nineteenth century, the Bristol region must still be regarded as part of rural southwestern England and in most districts it remains a good deal less industrialized and urbanized than the Midlands or much of the north of England. Nevertheless it stands somewhat apart from the rest of the southwest and in the report of the South West Economic Planning Council the Bristol region corresponds with the northern and half of the central sub-regions which are distinguished from the rest by increasing population and a greater degree of industrialization. Similarly the Bristol region, though excluding the Swindon district, was identified by Britton (1967) on the basis of increasing population, a relatively high concentration of manufacturing industry, and nodality about the city of Bristol.

The characteristic of an increasing population in recent times is illustrated by a growth of about 11 per cent between 1954 and 1964 over the region as a whole. That this was a general trend can be seen from the figures for the sub-regions used in the planning report. The Northern sub-region had a population growth of 13 per cent over the same period and within it the North Wiltshire sub-division had a growth of 25 per cent, North Gloucestershire of 13 per cent and Bristol–Severnside of 9 per cent. The exceptionally high figure for North Wiltshire is partly due to the arrival in Swindon of 17,800 people under overspill arrangements, but even if this exceptional element is excluded the growth rate remains at 18 per cent. The figure of 13 per cent for North Gloucestershire also involves inter- and intra-regional inward migration to the Gloucester–Cheltenham district, where increases of the order of 17 per cent were experienced. In the planning report's Central sub-region it is mainly the Wellington–Westbury sub-division which falls within the Bristol region and here too the growth rate was 11 per cent. Only in the Forest of Dean, in parts of Cotswold and in some areas in southern and western Somerset have appreciably slower rates been experienced within the Bristol region.

## Employment

Full employment has accompanied this increasing population; in the early 1960s unemployment rates as low as 1·2 per cent characterized the region and rates well below 1·0 per cent occurred in several districts. Activity rates, on the other hand, are not particularly high throughout the Bristol region, though around Bristol itself and in the Gloucester–Cheltenham and Swindon areas the rate for males has been broadly comparable with those in the Midlands and northern England; but even here the female rate is low, possibly because there is less established tradition of the employment of women in staple industries.

Overall, therefore, the Bristol region appears to enjoy growing prosperity and evidence of less favourable circumstances is largely confined to the Forest of Dean, which experienced an unemployment rate of over $2\frac{1}{2}$ per cent and very low activity rates in 1962. This no doubt reflected the approaching end of coal mining in the district and the decline of its older industries, but it will be seen later that even here the introduction of new industries has led to reasonably rapid economic growth in recent years, which may well lead to a level of prosperity comparable with that of the rest of the region.

The employment structure of the Bristol region at the present time is indicated in the following approximate figures:

TABLE 14

% EMPLOYMENT

| | EXTRACTIVE INDUSTRIES | MANUFACTURING INDUSTRIES | SERVICE INDUSTRIES AND CONSTRUCTION | TOTAL |
|---|---|---|---|---|
| Great Britain | 5·0 | 38·0 | 57·0 | 100 |
| Bristol region | 4·0 | 36·0 | 60·0 | 100 |

Recent trends are suggested by an employment decline of 14 per cent in the extractive industries and rises of 3 per cent and 12 per cent respectively in employment in the manufacturing and service industries during the first half of the last decade.

In the extractive group of occupations, employment in agriculture (about 3 per cent of total employment) has declined over many years at a rate broadly comparable with that of the country as a whole, whilst in mining and quarrying (about 1 per cent of total employment) the decline is associated, in particular, with what appear to be the final stages of coal production in the region. In the Forest of Dean production ceased in 1965 except from a number of extremely small workings and the recent closure of two of the three remaining collieries in the Radstock area of Somerset must inevitably reduce employment still further. In other forms of mineral working and quarrying, employment is not large but, on the other hand, production in some districts has a great deal more than local significance. The output of Carbonifcrous Limestone, for example, from Chipping Sodbury and other quarries in south Gloucestershire and from Mendip quarries, especially in the east round Frome, is of the order of 8 million tons per year, about 16 per cent of the total in England and Wales. Its principal use as road stone extends over most of southern Britain and major national companies with widespread road construction activities are established in the two neighbourhoods. Similarly a modest labour force is responsible for the excavation of vast quantities of sand and gravel in the upper Thames basin round South Cerney and Lechlade, in the Vale of Severn and by dredging in the Bristol Channel, whilst at Yate 75 per cent of the world's supply of celestine is worked and projected developments may lead to materially increased production. Elsewhere quarrying of the traditional building stones of east Somerset and Bath and of the blue and grey stones of the Forest of Dean continues, and in the latter area dolomite from a former ironstone quarry near Cinderford has recently been developed as a brick-making material. Though the Bristol region is by no means a major brick-producing part of the country, other firms in the Forest of Dean manufacture bricks from orthodox materials, and some brick and tile making of local importance exists in many districts including the Bristol–Thornbury area, Swindon, Clevedon and the Bridgwater–Highbridge area.

In greatest contrast with declining employment in the extractive industries is the rapid increase in service occupations following a trend characteristic of the country as a whole. The fact that the absolute level of employment in service industries in the Bristol region is above the national average, however, is due to a variety of local circumstances. Normal service provision in the unusually large number of small towns, which form such a characteristic feature of the settlement pattern of the region, tends to increase the labour requirements of this sector of the economy, and the presence of a considerable tourist industry on the Somerset coast and elsewhere augments the total. In addition, however, growing office employment both for national, regional and local government and for private industry and commerce plays an important part. Bristol itself is the fifth largest and most rapidly growing provincial office centre and this aspect of its economic growth has been attributed to its increasing role as a regional 'capital' and administrative centre. Bath too has a high proportion of government employees in the offices of the Ministry of Defence but, even so, at least half of the office employment in both cities is provided by private industry and commerce. Among the smaller centres, Gloucester, Taunton and Trowbridge have service sectors enlarged by the presence of county administrative offices, but office employment in Taunton has also been increased by the establishment of the central buying organization of Messrs Debenhams as part of a policy of decentralization from London, and a similar move has been made to Cheltenham by the Eagle Star Insurance Company.


## Manufacturing Industry

The percentage of regional employment in manufacturing industry remains somewhat below that of the country as a whole, but increases at about six times the national rate have been recorded in recent times. Moreover, when compared with the rest of southwestern Britain, concentration of employment in the Bristol region is most marked in this aspect of the economy. Thus about 65 per cent of all employment in the South West Economic Planning Region occurs within the Bristol region, but in manufacturing industry the percentage is as high as 75, whilst in the service and construction industries it is 60. Activity in many localities within the Bristol region will be shown to have contributed to this concentration, particularly in recent times, but nevertheless the continued vital importance of the Bristol district itself as the focus of the region is illustrated in the report of the South West Economic Planning Council. This shows that in the Bristol–Severnside sub-division, which comprises only 7 per cent of the area of the planning region, there is no less than 28 per cent of regional employment and 33 per cent of employment in manufacturing industry. Considering the Bristol region as a whole, the broader pattern of this industrial concentration is revealed by examining the areas in which the percentage of total employment provided by manufacturing industry exceeds the regional average of 36. The importance of service industries in the Bristol district to some extent masks its importance as a manufacturing centre, so that only 40 per cent of its employment is in manufacturing industry. The existence of important service functions in the growing industrial area of Gloucester–Cheltenham may also explain the fact that its employment in manufacturing (37 per cent) only slightly exceeds the regional figure. Elsewhere the towns of Swindon, Chippenham, Stroud, Yeovil and Bridgwater all have more than 40 per cent of employment in manufacturing industry and, except in Bridgwater, this proportion had increased significantly in recent years. But this is not the case in Taunton whose administrative and service functions help explain the fact that less than a quarter of its employment is in manufacturing industry. A fairly recent feature of employment patterns in the Bristol region is the increased relative importance of manufacturing in the former mining areas of the Forest of Dean and the Somerset coalfield. Whereas it must be made clear that the increase is relative, in the sense that it stems in part from the absolute decline in employment in extractive occupations, the introduction of new industries and the revival of some old ones in the Forest of Dean and in the Somerset towns and villages, particularly Frome, means that these may become economic growth centres of some significance. Thus around 50 per cent of employment in the Forest of Dean and in the Frome–Street area of Somerset is now in manufacturing industry and in the Norton–Radstock area the percentage increased from 30 to 40 in a recent ten-year period.

Within manufacturing industry diversity is an established characteristic of the Bristol region and location quotients, derived from employment figures, have values in excess of 1·0 for eight groups of the standard industrial classification, indicating that the groups Food, drink and tobacco; Engineering and electrical goods; Vehicles; Leather and leather goods; Clothing and footwear; Timber and furniture; Paper, printing and publishing; and Other manufactures are localized in the region. On the other hand, this diversity does not mean that there have been no leading elements in the industrial make-up of the region and at the time of the 1958 census of production three groups—Food, drink and tobacco; Engineering and electrical goods; and Vehicles—accounted for at least 70 per cent of its output. During the past thirty years these three industrial groups have provided much of the impetus for economic growth, though the Paper, printing and publishing and the Clothing and footwear industries, traditionally established throughout the region, have also grown appreciably and together the five groups now probably account for fully four-fifths of the Bristol region's manufacturing production.

Great internal diversity is also found within each group and this is perhaps most highly characteristic of the Engineering group. Nevertheless even here it is possible to discern fields of specialization. In mechanical engineering there is some concentration on the production of heavy mehanical handling gear, cranes and port machinery, of hydraulic mechanisms, of oil engines and agricultural machinery, of hydraulic presses and injection moulding plant, of specialized machinery for the paper, printing and packaging industry, and of components such as pistons and bearings. In electrical engineering there is rather more marked specialization in the lighter branches of the industry concerned with the production of control panels, of radio and electronic apparatus and of domestic electrical equipment. In both mechanical and electrical engineering this element of specialization is largely due to the activities of 44 concerns, each employing over 500 workers, which comprise

K

more than one-third of the largest industrial organizations in the southwest. It is equally characteristic of both branches of the engineering industry in the Bristol region that a multiplicity of very small firms maintains the traditional diversity of production.

The Vehicle group is distinguished by the highly localized nature of its various branches and by the dominant position of the aerospace industry, which is the largest individual type of manufacturing activity in the region. Six organizations in three localities make up the greater part of the region's aerospace industry: the Rolls-Royce Bristol Engines division and the British Aircraft Corporation in Bristol, the Westland and Normalair companies in Yeovil and the Dowty Group and Smiths Industries in the Gloucester–Cheltenham area. However, frequent subcontracting and the establishment of subsidiaries have been common practice in the aircraft industry and this has resulted in the creation of sizeable plant at Weston-super-Mare and many smaller associated undertakings in Bristol and Gloucestershire. On the other hand, manufacturing activity connected with rail transport has been of major importance in recent times only in Swindon and Chippenham and at one subsidiary concern near Bristol, and the motor vehicle industry is equally concentrated in Swindon and Bristol, though the manufacture of ancillary equipment is of some importance in the Gloucester–Cheltenham area and in Bath.

The Food, drink and tobacco industrial group includes a particularly wide distribution of all aspects of food processing which can best be discussed in local contexts. Nevertheless a broad classification of the group leads to the recognition of five major types of activity, each of which shows some degree of localization within the Bristol region. The processing and manufacturing treatment of milk is naturally characteristic of the dairying vales where creameries and factories are operated by the major British dairy companies. In part associated with local pig rearing in the same areas, bacon curing and the manufacture of other meat products are food industries which also have considerable regional importance, with some degree of concentration in west Wiltshire. The two remaining food industries, however, have recently been little influenced by the agricultural characteristics of the region. It is true that, in origin, milling in the Gloucester area and to some extent in Bristol depended on West Country grain, but imported supplies are now vital to both and are the mainstay of the large milling and animal feeding stuffs industry at Avonmouth. This is also true of the manufacture of cocoa, chocolate and confectionery, which shows a high degree of localization in the Bristol district, and of the tobacco industry which, apart from a single cigarette factory at Swindon, is virtually confined to Bristol itself.

Throughout the region almost equal importance attaches to the two aspects of the Paper, printing and publishing group, one concerned with the manufacture of paper and board and the other with printing, publishing and the preparation of paper products for other trades. All branches of the industry are strongly localized in the Bristol district, though this is most marked in the making of paper and board, because of the availability of imported raw materials, and in the manufacture of packaging materials, because of the needs of the tobacco and food-processing industries in particular. There is also a considerable concentration of the printing and publishing side of the industry in the Somerset centres of Paulton and Frome, but the former widespread distribution of the industrial group as a whole is still reflected in a scatter throughout the region of individual concerns making and using paper and board.

Footwear manufacture and the other clothing industries are also of comparable size but their distribution differs. There is some concentration of the general clothing industry in Bristol but its most characteristic feature is nevertheless a wide distribution in many of the smaller towns of the region. On the other hand, despite recent decentralization by individual firms and widespread sub-contracting for boot and shoe components, the footwear industry remains highly localized in the Staple Hill, Kingswood and Hanham districts to the east of Bristol and in Street.

Apart from these five dominant industrial groups, manufacturing in the Bristol region tends to have two general characteristics. It is usually carried out on a relatively small scale and in most cases it is long-established and concerned with products made traditional by the economic history of the area before the industrial revolution. It is true that there are many examples, mentioned below, of completely new small-scale industries, but the most significant exceptions to the general pattern are provided by a limited number of very large concerns which have been established in the area or have grown very greatly during the past fifty years. The Imperial Smelting Corporation and Imperial Chemical Industries are good examples of such organizations with works near Avonmouth and to these might be added the Avon Rubber Company at Melksham, British Cellophane at Bridgwater and British Nylon Spinners near Gloucester.

Industrial concentration and recent economic growth in the part of southwest England which forms the Bristol region may therefore be seen largely as the outcome of the historical evolution which has been traced in preceding chapters. During the past thirty years, however, unusually rapid changes associated with three groups of industries have introduced new elements into the economy of the region which have little direct connection with its earlier history. Thus the vast wartime expansion of aircraft production provided the base from which the aerospace industry has grown in certain localities into something like a staple industry. On the other hand, the post-war contraction of the industry in some districts and the realignment of certain of its branches have had far-reaching consequences in the redeployment of labour and the introduction of replacement industries, especially in the Gloucester–Cheltenham area. The second new element has been created by the establishment of additional large-scale chemical and petrochemical industries in the Avonmouth–Severnside area, by the increasing interest of the Imperial Smelting Corporation in chemical as well as metallurgical products, and by some growth of chemical and plastics industries elsewhere in the region, notably in Frome and Stroud. The third group of industries involved in these changes is more diverse in character but has the common characteristic of recent introduction by organizations moving into the Bristol region as a result of wartime relocation or deliberate post-war decisions. A further characteristic of the group is that it tends to involve much advanced technology in such industries as electronic and light electrical and mechanical engineering in Swindon and Stroud and in smaller centres like Cirencester, Malmesbury, Calne, Wells, Clevedon, Minehead and the towns of the Forest of Dean, and in the manufacture of instruments and of hydraulic and fluid flow equipment in Gloucester, Cheltenham and the Stroud area.

The establishment of these new industries in many small centres throughout the region combined with growth in the Gloucester, Cheltenham, Stroud, Frome and Yeovil districts might well have tended to diminish the share of the region's manufacturing industry concentrated in the Bristol–Severnside area. On the basis of employment figures Britton (1967) calculated that this share declined by at least 13 per cent during the 1950s, but it should be remembered that the new large-scale chemical, petrochemical and metal industries on Severnside have small labour requirements and if it were possible to measure the changes in terms of production rather than employment, the Bristol district's share of the total might not be found to have declined so significantly.

It might also be expected that the rapid growth of the aerospace, engineering, petrochemical and a few other industries would have tended to diminish the characteristic industrial diversity of the Bristol region and such an assumption appears to be borne out by a very slight increase (1 per cent—Britton 1967) in specialization revealed by employment figures. However, a generalized figure for the whole region hides the very real diversification which has taken place in, for example, the important industrial area of Gloucester–Cheltenham as the aircraft industry was replaced, while the use of employment data does not reveal diversity of production maintained by new large-scale capital-intensive enterprises with small labour forces. Moreover, general industrial classifications are an inadequate basis on which to measure specialization and diversification since they mask factual diversification of end-products of the kinds that have characterized areas like the Forest of Dean and Swindon, where mining and railway engineering have been replaced by a very wide variety of production, much of which, however, falls into the general categories of engineering and the manufacture of electrical goods.

The prosperity of manufacturing in the region as a whole may be deduced from the fact that it has provided new employment at a rate appreciably higher than the national one in recent times. This has been attributed not only to the success of individual industries but also to the good proportion of regional undertakings which are engaged in enterprises enjoying nationwide economic growth. In assessing the extent and distribution of this prosperity within the region, Britton (1967) carried out a multivariate analysis of sub-regions involving a number of change factors and activity rates as well as manufacturing employment levels. On this basis, while recognizing that manufacturing industry remains highly concentrated on an axis from Bristol to Stroud and Gloucester–Cheltenham, he concluded that 'a new locational pattern seems to be emerging in the region. Admittedly Gloucester–Cheltenham is polarizing manufacturing development to the north of Bristol, but the characteristics of Western-super-Mare, Frome, Yeovil and Bridgwater (and Chippenham in the east) indicate relative drifts in the location of industry through the emergence of new growth centres in the southern parts of the region'. It should be noted that the region used for this analysis excluded the Swindon district, where the absolute level of manufacturing employment and considerable change factors might now lead to the recognition of another growth centre, particularly in view of new developments in the town in the past few years. The choice of variables for the analysis and of the period covered (1952–62) also tends to minimize the effects of post-war developments in the Forest of Dean, where very real diversification may have created at least a potential growth centre if assessed in terms of a greater variety of change factors over a longer period such as 1945–65. On the other hand, the recognition of Weston-super-Mare as a growth centre for manufacturing industry is due almost entirely to the use of percentage population and employment change factors (1952–62) in the analysis, and these were influenced less by normal economic growth trends than by the effects of the 1952 Town Development Act, which provided for the movement of population and light industry to the town from London and Birmingham. Since 1958 this movement of population has been provided for by the allocation of over 400 housing units and new light industry, mostly engineering and metal working, has fully occupied the Oldmixon Crescent Town Development Estate. The announcement in March 1968 of a further project for a £4 million factory estate suggests that the recent pattern of growth may continue, but it seems likely to remain essentially part of a planned use of the resort for the relocation of population and light industries and not the spontaneous development of Weston-super-Mare as a town predominantly concerned with manufacturing industry.

However, it remains true that change and growth over recent decades in the Gloucester–Cheltenham area, in Swindon and in a number of other towns to the south and east of Bristol suggest that a prosperous manufacturing industry is, if anything, becoming more widely distributed, whilst vigorous service industries, though concentrated in Bristol, are also particularly well represented in the other large towns and in the many smaller ones which are so characteristic a feature of the Bristol region.

It follows that the existence of prosperous and growing urban and industrial activity throughout most of an area which nevertheless has a thriving agriculture and remains largely rural, precludes the systematic division of the Bristol region into urban-industrial and rural-agricultural sub-regions. In part these circumstances arise from two aspects of local economic history. The absence of a regional staple industry dating to the industrial revolution and comparable with those of the Midlands and north of England has meant that from the decline of the West Country woollen industry until very recent times industrial and commercial activity has been confined to ancient cities and towns which remained in a completely rural setting. Apart from the very special case of Swindon there are no 'industrial revolution towns' and the characteristic built environment of that era is confined to the eastern and southern parts of the Bristol urban area, to a considerable part of Gloucester and to extremely restricted parts of the other towns of the region. At the beginning of the present century only the Bristol district itself could have been regarded as a major urban-industrial area. Subsequent economic growth, combined with the redevelopment of old industrial and mining districts, however, makes possible the recognition of four or five areas whose preoccupation with a variety of non-agricultural activities may now justify their description as industrial if not urban-industrial. These are (1) the lower Avon–Severnside area, (2) the Gloucester–Cheltenham area, (3) the Stroudwater area, (4) the Swindon area and, possibly, (5) the Forest of Dean.

The presence of a considerable number of small towns, particularly in the southern and eastern parts of the region, the vast majority of which were associated with the early West Country woollen and linen industries, reflects a second aspect of the region's distinctive economic history. In consequence, though the area remains rural in appearance, its population is largely concentrated in some 35 towns—indeed, urban centres with populations in excess of 2,500 account for more than three-quarters of the total population of the region. Despite the almost complete disappearance of their early industrial basis, all the smaller towns have important non-agricultural functions which in most cases include a manufacturing industry or group of industries of appreciable size, and it is therefore only in the far west of Somerset that there are considerable areas remote from even minor industrial centres. In the smallest of these towns industry is often represented by a single plant and even in moderately sized towns the largest single manufacturing concern commonly employs a highly significant proportion of the total labour force. Thus in Table 15 it will be seen that it is only in the four largest industrial centres defined above that dependence on an individual concern falls below 10 per cent of the total labour force.

TABLE 15

% OF ALL EMPLOYEES IN LARGEST SINGLE
MANUFACTURING CONCERN

| OVER 30 | 10–30 | UNDER 10 |
|---|---|---|
| Keynsham | Tewkesbury | Bristol |
| Melksham | Chipping Sodbury | Bath |
| Dursley | Midsomer Norton | Gloucester |
| Chippenham | Trowbridge | Cheltenham |
| | Street | Stroud |
| | Bridgwater | Swindon |
| | Yeovil | |
| | Forest of Dean | |

It has been mentioned that recent changes could reflect some long-term industrial redistribution and in the future the growth of manufacturing activity may be relatively greater in some of the rural towns of the region than elsewhere. In the meantime, however, they are still quite small and some of their manufacturing functions, especially in food processing, are intimately linked with the agriculture of their locality. Moreover, their equally important function as service centres for surrounding country districts also makes it proper to discuss them along with the rural parts of the region whose principal agricultural activity is to be described next.

### The Present-Day Agriculture of the Bristol Region

A broad picture of the present-day agriculture of much of the Bristol region can be drawn from data published by the Ministry of Agriculture,

289

Fisheries and Food, for the counties of Gloucestershire and Somerset, but it has to be borne in mind that only parts of the vales of western and northern Wiltshire lie within the Bristol region and the figures for the whole of that county show features which arise from the inclusion of statistics from the chalk downland which occupies much of the remainder.

TABLE 16

| | | LAND USE IN THOUSANDS OF ACRES | | | | |
|---|---|---|---|---|---|---|
| | | Crops and grass | Arable | Rotation grass and lucerne | Permanent grass | Rough grazing |
| Gloucestershire | 1963 | 594 | 307 | 124 | 287 | 17 |
| | 1967 | 593 | 322 | 90 | 271 | 15 |
| | 1968 | 587 | 322 | 89 | 265 | 14 |
| Somerset | 1963 | 797 | 275 | 140 | 522 | 45 |
| | 1967 | 794 | 283 | 126 | 511 | 45 |
| | 1968 | 789 | 278 | 127 | 511 | 43 |
| Wiltshire | 1963 | 631 | 367 | 137 | 264 | 66 |
| | 1967 | 629 | 392 | 112 | 237 | 56 |
| | 1968 | 626 | 390 | 111 | 235 | 56 |
| England | 1963 | 21,784 | 13,000 | 4,034 | 8,780 | 2,185 |
| | 1967 | 21,669 | 13,351 | 3,153 | 8,318 | 2,118 |
| | 1968 | 21,490 | 13,379 | 3,124 | 8,111 | 2,076 |

Table 16 shows the general pattern of agricultural land use in the three counties, the preponderance of grass farming being emphasized in Table 17.

TABLE 17

TOTAL ACREAGE OF PERMANENT GRASS, SEED GRASSES AND LUCERNE AS A % OF TOTAL ACREAGE OF CROPS AND GRASS

| | | |
|---|---|---|
| Gloucestershire | 1963 | 68 |
| | 1967 | 61 |
| | 1968 | 54 |
| Somerset | 1963 | 83 |
| | 1967 | 79 |
| | 1968 | 81 |
| Wiltshire | 1963 | 63 |
| | 1967 | 55 |
| | 1968 | 55 |
| England | 1963 | 59 |
| | 1967 | 53 |
| | 1968 | 52 |

The higher percentage of grass farming in Somerset arises from the fact that the county does not include extensive areas of cropping comparable with Cotswold or the chalk downland. Since the latter lies outside the Bristol region it is reasonable to regard a figure approaching that for Somerset as generally characteristic of most parts of the region apart from Cotswold and a few much smaller areas of specialist farming. The amount of rough grazing in Gloucestershire and Somerset is small, though locally in southwest Somerset it plays an important part in the general agricultural system, whilst rough grazing in the upland areas of Wiltshire (beyond the limits of the Bristol region, but linked with it in some aspects of farming practice) accounts for the slightly higher figure for that county.

The growth of fodder crops in the Bristol region (Table 18) is also on a very limited scale and is now at a level below the national average. Apart from imported materials, therefore, locally produced barley, wheat, oats and beans (see below) are the only important feeding stuffs other than grass used in the dominant animal husbandry of the region.

TABLE 18

ACREAGE OF ALL FODDER CROPS AS A PERCENTAGE OF ACREAGE OF CROPS AND GRASS

| | | |
|---|---|---|
| Gloucestershire | 1963 | 1·7 |
| | 1967 | 1·3 |
| | 1968 | 1·5 |
| Somerset | 1963 | 3·0 |
| | 1967 | 2·0 |
| | 1968 | 2·1 |
| Wiltshire | 1963 | 2·7 |
| | 1967 | 1·9 |
| | 1968 | 2·0 |
| England | 1963 | 2·2 |
| | 1967 | 2·4 |
| | 1968 | 2·6 |

Besides being primarily concerned with animals, the agriculture of the Bristol region is further specialized towards dairy farming to an even greater extent than in southwestern Britain generally. This is illustrated in the table of farming types included in the report of the South West Economic Planning Council.

Somerset is clearly the county most typically involved in grass dairy farming, but the continuation of this type of enterprise along the vale into the Wiltshire part of the Bristol region is reflected in the high dairy

TABLE 19

% OF FULL-TIME FARMS ENGAGED IN VARIOUS
ENTERPRISES, JUNE 1964

|  | DAIRY | LIVE-STOCK | PIGS/POULTRY | CROP-PING | HORTI-CULTURE | MIXED FARMING |
|---|---|---|---|---|---|---|
| England and Wales | 39·7 | 14·8 | 6·5 | 15·9 | 9·9 | 13·2 |
| South West Planning Region | 55·0 | 12·8 | 4·9 | 3·0 | 5·9 | 18·4 |
| Gloucestershire | 48·0 | 11·1 | 6·2 | 7·4 | 11·0 | 16·3 |
| Somerset | 68·1 | 8·7 | 4·5 | 1·8 | 6·1 | 10·8 |
| Wiltshire | 66·5 | 5·9 | 7·2 | 6·8 | 3·7 | 9·9 |

figure even for the whole of that county. In this respect the contrast in Gloucestershire is most marked. The lower percentage of dairy farms is partly due, of course, to appreciable cropping activity in many parts of Cotswold and to mixed farming in the north, but it is also due to more varied agricultural practice in the vale. Thus the higher figure under 'Livestock' is a consequence of long-standing involvement in the rearing and fattening of cattle and sheep, whilst the equally large figure for horticulture represents in part market gardening round Bristol and in the Gloucester–Cheltenham district and in part the specialist production of fruit and vegetables round the Vale of Evesham.

It will be noted from the preceding tables, however, that in recent years the acreage devoted throughout the region to all types of grass and fodder crops, other than barley (see below), has shown an absolute decline, though in 1968 this decline largely ceased except in the case of Gloucestershire grass farming. Nevertheless Table 20 shows that there has been no decline in the livestock population of the region during the same period, so that considerable intensification of animal husbandry is to be inferred, possibly helped by bought-in feeds. Figures quoted for the whole of the South West Economic Planning Region show the number of livestock units per thousand acres farmed increasing from 365 to 422 between 1956 and 1964, but on 200 farms studied by the Universities of Bristol and Exeter in 1966–7 the average figure reached 580, the lowest recorded being 505 on Cotswold farms not involved in milk production and the highest 709 in parts of south Somerset.

Between 1963 and 1968 the total number of cattle and calves increased appreciably throughout the three counties and dairying re-

TABLE 20
LIVESTOCK NUMBERS

| | GLOUCESTERSHIRE | | | SOMERSET | | | WILTSHIRE | | | ENGLAND | | |
|---|---|---|---|---|---|---|---|---|---|---|---|---|
| | 1963 | 1967 | 1968 | 1963 | 1967 | 1968 | 1963 | 1967 | 1968 | 1963 | 1967 | 1968 |
| TOTAL Cattle and calves | 206,790 | 215,308 | 215,017 | 362,280 | 402,994 | 409,230 | 225,595 | 232,601 | 234,500 | 7,432,439 | 7,683,155 | 7,550,286 |
| For milk or dairy herd | 71,803 | 70,605 | 73,137 | 172,848 | 176,107 | 182,201 | 97,671 | 94,063 | 97,213 | 2,338,142 | 2,328,776 | 2,335,490 |
| Cows and heifers in milk | 62,116 | 61,314 | 63,757 | 153,199 | 157,065 | 162,747 | 86,618 | 84,041 | 87,054 | 2,019,282 | 2,024,425 | 2,041,164 |
| Cows in calf | 9,687 | 9,291 | 9,380 | 19,659 | 19,042 | 19,454 | 11,053 | 10,022 | 10,159 | 318,860 | 304,351 | 294,326 |
| Heifers in calf | 13,455 | 14,731 | 14,801 | 25,688 | 30,246 | 29,538 | 18,821 | 21,615 | 20,580 | 450,972 | 498,278 | 502,536 |
| For beef herd | 10,958 | 8,700 | 8,741 | 15,535 | 16,062 | 16,602 | 10,954 | 9,730 | 9,700 | 469,232 | 457,647 | 454,894 |
| Cows and heifers in milk | 9,220 | 7,060 | 7,068 | 12,673 | 13,164 | 13,854 | 8,885 | 8,002 | 7,570 | 394,363 | 380,618 | 397,844 |
| Cows in calf | 1,738 | 1,640 | 1,673 | 2,862 | 2,898 | 2,748 | 2,069 | 1,728 | 2,130 | 74,869 | 77,029 | 75,050 |
| Heifers in calf | 1,113 | 1,468 | 1,229 | 1,709 | 2,156 | 1,771 | 1,046 | 1,413 | 1,277 | 55,364 | 63,315 | 60,152 |
| Other cattle under 2 years | 92,967 | 103,507 | 102,176 | 121,519 | 152,483 | 155,775 | 81,818 | 92,215 | 93,470 | 3,407,561 | 3,678,750 | 3,597,195 |
| Sheep | 362,306 | 338,739 | 312,448 | 406,612 | 433,566 | 414,066 | 137,460 | 136,564 | 127,742 | 14,029,097 | 13,423,005 | 12,892,509 |
| Pigs | 108,360 | 113,193 | 116,239 | 200,082 | 195,793 | 207,713 | 105,504 | 100,916 | 100,912 | 4,985,468 | 5,387,992 | 5,588,874 |
| Total Poultry | 1,669,308 | 2,085,086 | 2,016,807 | 2,692,672 | 2,971,296 | 3,047,831 | 2,292,856 | 3,046,935 | 3,041,478 | 90,271,613 | 99,454,040 | 101,076,014 |
| Broilers | 255,079 | 370,294 | 356,465 | 551,882 | 938,733 | 1,119,618 | 536,720 | 832,778 | 1,030,275 | 20,948,252 | 29,610,035 | 32,512,457 |

293

mained the principal enterprise. Thus the categories of stock classified as forming the milk and dairy herd comprise 44 per cent of the total of cattle and calves in Somerset and 41 per cent in Wiltshire, though in Gloucestershire a more varied animal husbandry brings the figure down to 34, close to the English average of 31 per cent. Over recent years animals for the milk and dairy herd have been consistently eleven times more numerous than those for the beef herd in Somerset, between nine and ten times more numerous in Wiltshire and even in Gloucestershire this preponderance increased from seven to over eight times between 1963 and 1968.

Varying economic factors have led to much greater countrywide fluctuation in sheep and pig populations in recent years, however, and trends cannot be discerned from figures for individual years. Thus between 1963 and 1967 there was a slight overall increase in the total number of sheep in the three counties but this represented consistent increases in the numbers in Somerset throughout the period being largely offset by a sharp decline in numbers both in Gloucestershire and Wiltshire during the year 1966–7, which continued into 1968. By the latter year the number of sheep and lambs in Somerset had also declined rapidly so that over the five-year period there was an appreciable reduction for the region as a whole. Similar sharp reductions in the number of pigs in 1966 and 1967 in all three counties wiped out considerable increases which had occurred between 1963 and 1965 in Wiltshire and Somerset and greatly reduced their effect in Gloucestershire, but by 1968 numbers had again increased materially in Gloucestershire and Somerset, so that in this case over the five-year period the total number in the three counties increased by some 10,000. The most rapid change over the past five years, however, has been the increase in the poultry population, which for the three counties has been nearly 23 per cent, almost double the national average. In Somerset there has been an increase of 13 per cent, in Gloucestershire of over 20 per cent, despite a reduction in numbers in 1968, and in Wiltshire of 30 per cent. Throughout the country the recent rise of the broiler chicken industry accounts almost entirely for the growth of the poultry population, but this is less true in Gloucestershire and Wiltshire where increased broiler numbers only account for 22 and 42 per cent respectively of the increase in total poultry numbers, and broilers still only form 18 per cent of the poultry population in Gloucestershire. In Somerset, however, the broiler industry outstripped other forms of poultry keeping, since the number of broilers more than doubled to give an absolute increase greater than that of the total for all poultry, and the proportion of broilers to the total poultry population rose from 21 to 37 per cent over the five years.

A review of present-day animal husbandry in the Bristol region therefore suggests that the primary function of the dairy vales, which make up the greater part of its area, remains unchanged, that interest in sheep and pigs fluctuates with economic circumstances but remains at a fairly constant level over longer periods, and that Somerset appears to be a regional leader in the present continued swing towards broiler chicken production.

The general pattern of arable agriculture in the region and some aspects of its changing relationship with animal husbandry in recent years is shown in Table 21. The most striking feature which it illustrates is the declining area of land devoted to the production of grass, green crops and roots as animal feeding stuffs and the corresponding rise in the production of cereals, particularly barley. Thus, if the period from 1963 to 1967 is considered, the acreage in Gloucestershire devoted to wheat and barley increased by 55,170 (wheat 21,508, barley 33,662) whilst that devoted to other sources of animal feed declined by 53,292 (rotation grass, clover and lucerne 34,703, permanent grass 16,029, greens and roots 2,561). In Somerset the wheat and barley acreage increased by 31,709 (wheat 9,983, barley 21,726) and that of the feed group was reduced by 38,802 (rotation grass, clover and lucerne 13,259, permanent grass 10,771, and greens and roots 14,772) whilst in Wiltshire wheat and barley acreage increased by 54,533 (wheat 18,807 and barley 35,726) and the feed crop acreage declined by 58,216 (rotation grass, clover and lucerne 25,723, permanent grass 27,096, greens and roots 5,397). In Gloucestershire the greatest reduction was in the rotation grasses and this commonly represents their replacement on the extensive arable farms of the county by barley as a more profitable crop either for sale or for use on the farm in modern animal feeding methods. The same change also took place in Somerset, particularly in the eastern parts of the county, but a greater decline has occurred in the acreage devoted to greens and root crops for animal feeds—particularly kale. In Wiltshire adaptations of the rotation comparable with those in Gloucestershire and a reduction of the permanent grass area appear to have similar importance, but the position was profoundly affected by changes in land use in parts of the county outside the Bristol region. Overall the change was made in response to the recent profitability of cereal, and especially barley, production, partly caused by new methods of animal husbandry and a period of heavy exports of feeding barley. It represented primarily a modification of arable practice, though it has resulted in some reduction in the acreage of permanent grass throughout the region. It is therefore understandable that beans and oats were the only other feed crops of which an increased acreage was grown,

TABLE 21

CROPS—ACREAGES

| | GLOUCESTERSHIRE | | | SOMERSET | | | WILTSHIRE | | | ENGLAND | | |
|---|---|---|---|---|---|---|---|---|---|---|---|---|
| | 1963 | 1967 | 1968 | 1963 | 1967 | 1968 | 1963 | 1967 | 1968 | 1963 | 1967 | 1968 |
| Crops and grass | 594,315 | 592,866 | 586,714 | 796,745 | 794,128 | 789,456 | 631,036 | 628,797 | 625,648 | 21,784,645 | 21,669,592 | 21,489,648 |
| Arable | 307,011 | 321,594 | 321,699 | 275,301 | 283,492 | 278,409 | 367,070 | 391,926 | 390,670 | 13,004,635 | 13,351,434 | 13,378,841 |
| Permanent grass | 287,302 | 271,273 | 265,015 | 521,444 | 510,673 | 511,048 | 263,967 | 236,871 | 234,977 | 8,779,823 | 8,318,157 | 8,110,807 |
| Rough grazing | 17,195 | 14,558 | 14,388 | 45,353 | 44,524 | 43,399 | 65,338 | 55,827 | 55,571 | 2,185,003 | 2,118,046 | 2,076,582 |
| Wheat | 40,522 | 62,030 | 56,702 | 21,266 | 31,249 | 27,110 | 46,235 | 65,042 | 62,945 | 1,823,042 | 2,199,793 | 2,306,476 |
| Barley | 98,365 | 132,027 | 136,498 | 58,766 | 80,492 | 78,193 | 148,919 | 184,645 | 183,793 | 4,065,886 | 5,094,498 | 4,958,405 |
| Oats | 6,836 | 7,038 | 8,658 | 5,437 | 6,321 | 6,592 | 5,021 | 6,424 | 8,164 | 527,767 | 461,177 | 468,395 |
| Potatoes | 3,945 | 3,720 | 3,555 | 4,804 | 4,663 | 4,677 | 1,918 | 1,577 | 1,649 | 514,041 | 504,648 | 503,175 |
| Other stock feed | 10,302 | 7,741 | 8,537 | 23,810 | 9,038 | 16,542 | 17,366 | 11,969 | 12,411 | 612,342 | 522,374 | 561,566 |
| Orchards | 10,313 | 7,820 | 6,982 | 12,249 | 9,090 | 8,687 | 474 | 295 | 244 | 212,788 | 187,586 | 170,488 |
| Small fruit | 688 | 722 | 692 | 804 | 893 | 897 | 55 | 53 | 44 | 33,111 | 30,528 | 30,512 |
| Vegetables | 4,706 | 3,937 | 3,994 | 2,754 | 2,670 | 2,674 | 838 | 988 | 813 | 373,429 | 384,458 | 417,096 |
| Under glass | 74 | 123 | 132 | 81 | 136 | 110 | 43 | 60 | 104 | 4,290 | 6,320 | 6,146 |
| Bare fallow | 4,828 | 4,802 | 4,222 | 3,387 | 3,769 | 3,560 | 7,072 | 6,360 | 5,924 | 204,628 | 210,304 | 180,916 |
| Lucerne, clover and rotation grasses | 124,410 | 89,707 | 89,359 | 139,554 | 126,295 | 127,233 | 137,338 | 111,615 | 110,821 | 4,034,430 | 3,152,964 | 3,123,500 |

since both were used as break crops between what had become almost continuous production of barley and wheat in some districts.

If the figures for 1968 are considered, however, there is a little evidence that the trends of preceding years may have been halted or even reversed. In Gloucestershire the evidence is very slight indeed since the area of permanent grass and of seed grasses continued to decline whereas the arable acreage as a whole and that devoted to barley continued to increase, though more slowly than previously. Wheat acreage, on the other hand, did decline somewhat, though this was more than offset by the increased areas growing oats and field beans as break crops between the main cereal years. In Wiltshire there was in 1968 the first actual reduction in the arable acreage in recent years, but again increased production of oats somewhat offset reductions of both wheat and barley; the permanent grass and seed grass areas still declined, while field beans had an increased importance as the chief break crop. It was therefore only in Somerset, where arable acreage declined and where the slight increase in the acreage of oats did not offset the reduced area of both wheat and barley, that the trend may be said to have been reversed, especially as 1968 saw an actual increase in the acreage of both permanent grass and the seed grasses in the county. Throughout the region the need to break the near-monoculture of barley or wheat on some farms is evidenced by the fact that in the three counties between 1963 and 1968 the acreage of oats increased by 35 per cent and that of the main break crop, field beans, increased fourteen-fold.

Less widespread crops in the Bristol region which are nevertheless important in individual districts include potatoes, vegetables, orchard fruits and small fruits. Most of the potatoes grown in Glouceseshire, Somerset and the vales of Wiltshire are main crop varieties, with some concentration of production immediately to the north of Bristol round Winterbourne and Iron Acton, in parts of north Somerset and in the Gloucester–Cheltenham area. Early potatoes are by no means a characteristic crop and are normally grown only on light soils in small areas near Cheltenham, on the Corallian and near the Chalk scarp in Wiltshire and occasionally in favoured localities on the south of Mendip and in south Somerset. In similar areas both in southeast Somerset and the light-soil districts in Wiltshire, root vegetables, particularly carrots, are locally important. Elsewhere vegetable production is concentrated round the lower Bristol Avon between Bath and the Gordano valley near Portishead, to the north of Bristol round Winterbourne, round Cheltenham and in the far north of Gloucestershire, where there is a considerable degree of specialization in the growth of brussels sprouts, accounting for virtually half the acreage of vegetables in the county.

One of the more specialized and localized agricultural activities of the region is the growth of mushrooms, which has become an enterprise of major importance in the Wrington–Churchill–Yatton district of north Somerset, in the neighbourhood of Bradford-on-Avon and in the vegetable-producing area to the north of Bristol.

Orchards form an important aspect of land use in Somerset and Gloucestershire and extend into the adjacent parts of west Wiltshire, though the small figures in Table 21 show that they are not characteristic of the rest of that county. In the extreme north of Gloucestershire the orchard trees include plums, pears and some dessert and cooking apples, but throughout the rest of the region the orchards are almost exclusively composed of cider apple trees with a smaller number of pear trees for perry making. There is an important distinction to be drawn between the commercial orchards, often large and systematically laid out, which usually belong to the cider and perry manufacturing concerns, and the non-commercial orchards, which are commonly very small and irregularly disposed around farm buildings and the margins of nearby fields. A few years ago the commercial undertakings accounted for about 57 per cent of the orchards in both Somerset and Gloucestershire, but more recently there has been a slight absolute decline in the commercial acreage and since the reduction of non-commercial orchards has been even slower the percentage has declined to 54. Apart from obviously unsuitable localities like the lower areas of the Somerset levels, the Carboniferous Limestone uplands and the more exposed parts of Cotswold, almost every part of the Bristol region has a scattering of small non-commercial orchards, usually close to the farm buildings or on the lower slopes of nearby hills, particularly on the 'islands' within the levels, on the southern flanks of Mendip, below the limestone hills round the lower Bristol Avon and in south Gloucestershire, among the scarps of southeast Somerset, along the Poldens, on the Cotswold outliers and on quite minor slopes within the vale of Gloucestershire. On the other hand, there is more concentration of the commercial orchards in the vale to the north of Gloucester, round the foot of the Carboniferous Limestone hills to the north of Mendip, in a belt extending southwards from eastern Mendip and in an area surrounding Taunton and continuing southwards into Devon.

Small fruit growing in north Gloucestershire includes a considerable range of fruits and varieties and this is also true of individual small localities elsewhere, but in terms of regional output small fruit production is dominated by strawberries and blackcurrants. Strawberry growing now occupies about half of the small fruit acreage in Somerset and is very highly concentrated on the lower southern slopes of Mendip in the immediate vicinity of Cheddar, though important quantities are

TABLE 22

FARM SIZES—APPROXIMATE PERCENTAGES

| FARM SIZE IN ACRES | TOTAL | UNDER 5 | 5–15 | 15–20 | 20–30 | 30–50 | 50–100 | 100–150 | 150–300 | 300–500 | 500–700 | 700–1,000 | OVER 1,000 |
|---|---|---|---|---|---|---|---|---|---|---|---|---|---|
| (A) By numbers of farms | | | | | | | | | | | | | |
| England | 100 | 22·0 | 18·0 | 4·0 | 6·0 | 10·0 | 16·0 | 8·5 | 10·5 | 3·0 | 1·0 | 0·5 | 0·5 |
| Gloucestershire | 100 | 24·5 | 18·0 | 3·5 | 5·5 | 8·0 | 14·0 | 8·5 | 11·0 | 4·0 | 1·0 | 0·5 | 0·5 |
| Somerset | 100 | 21·0 | 15·5 | 3·5 | 6·0 | 11·0 | 19·0 | 10·0 | 10·5 | 2·5 | 0·5 | — | — |
| Wiltshire | 100 | 21·5 | 14·0 | 5·5 | 4·0 | 9·0 | 16·0 | 8·5 | 12·5 | 6·0 | 2·5 | 1·5 | 1·0 |
| (B) By acreage of crops and grass involved | | | | | | | | | | | | | |
| England | 100 | 0·7 | 1·9 | 0·8 | 1·9 | 4·9 | 14·3 | 13·2 | 27·7 | 16·7 | 7·3 | 5·0 | 5·5 |
| Gloucestershire | 100 | 0·8 | 1·9 | 0·7 | 1·7 | 3·9 | 12·5 | 13·0 | 28·5 | 17·5 | 8·7 | 5·1 | 6·0 |
| Somerset | 100 | 0·8 | 2·0 | 0·9 | 2·2 | 6·3 | 20·0 | 17·9 | 31·7 | 14·0 | 2·8 | 0·9 | 0·5 |
| Wiltshire | 100 | 0·5 | 1·0 | 0·4 | 0·9 | 3·0 | 9·4 | 8·7 | 21·8 | 18·3 | 12·1 | 10·1 | 14·0 |

grown at the foot of the limestones to the north, particularly round Clevedon, in the Avon valley near Bath and in a number of localities in south Somerset. Blackcurrants take up a further 43 per cent of the Somerset soft fruit acreage and, though there is no concentration comparable with that of strawberries at Cheddar, individual localities in east Somerset produce them on a large scale. In Gloucestershire blackcurrants occupy 60 per cent of the area devoted to small fruits, most of it in the north of the vale and in the Forest of Dean, where the greater part of the region's crop is processed in the Ribena plant of H. W. Carters at Coleford.

Underlying this broad pattern of agricultural land use in the Bristol region is the more intricate pattern of varying husbandry and practice on over 20,000 farms and holdings of all sizes. Table 22 shows the percentage distribution of these farms by size in terms both of numbers of holdings and of total acreage involved. It will be seen that all three counties follow the national pattern in having the largest proportion of their agricultural land on farms with an acreage between 150 and 300. In other respects it is Gloucestershire whose figures correspond most closely with the national ones but even in this case the variations are significant. For all sizes of holdings over 300 acres the Gloucestershire figures are equal to or above those for the country as a whole, whether numbers of holding or acreage is considered, and this is largely due to the preponderance of large farms on Cotswold. Conversely Gloucestershire has fewer farms and less land involving holdings from 5 to 150 acres, though the importance of extremely small units in the vale, especially in the neighbourhood of Bristol, Gloucester and Cheltenham, results in the Gloucestershire figures for holdings of less than 5 acres exceeding the national average. Somerset, on the other hand, shares the preponderance of small farms characteristic of the southwestern counties and each size of holding below 300 acres accounts for a larger percentage of its agricultural land than is the case in the county as a whole, whereas the Somerset figures are below average for all the six groups above 300 acres. Moreover, if the number of holdings, rather than acreage, is considered, holdings between 30 and 100 acres assume greater importance (30 per cent of all holdings) and the range from 30 to 300 acres accounts for more than half the Somerset farms. In Wiltshire the many large farms on the Chalk, outside the Bristol region, account for the fact that three-quarters of the agricultural land in the county is on farms of over 150 acres and well over half of it on farms of over 300 acres. Within the Bristol region, however, much smaller farms are characteristic of most parts of the vale and this is reflected in the number of holdings in the various size groups, those between 30 and 100 acres accounting for a quarter of all

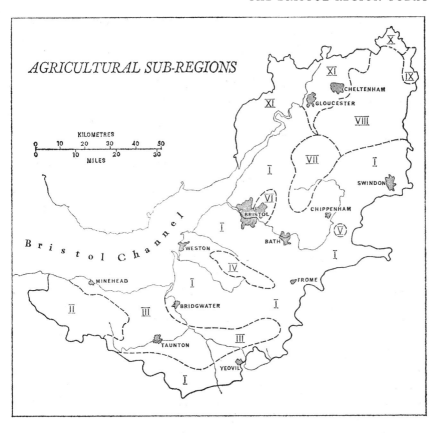

AGRICULTURAL SUB-REGIONS

Wiltshire farms. In so far as it is possible to generalize about farm sizes it is therefore true to say that the large farms of Cotswold are exceptional in the Bristol region. Elsewhere farms tend to be of smaller than average size and this tendency is most marked in Somerset.

The general characteristics of the agriculture of the Bristol region may be summarized in terms of the eleven agricultural sub-regions shown on Map 11. The predominant position of dairying in the agricultural economy of the region is emphasized by the great extent of sub-region I, which comprises almost all the lowlands of Somerset, west and north Wiltshire and south Gloucestershire. Here dairying is completely dominant and no other enterprise is of major significance; it should be emphasized that dairying is also important in most other districts with the exception of sub-region II, and parts of III and VIII. The greater part of sub-region II is formed by the Brendon Hills and part of Exmoor, where rearing and livestock farming are the mainstays of the economy. Sub-region III has been described as a mixed farming belt because this type of practice is everywhere present, but it is only specially characteristic of a small area forming the centre of the Vale of Taunton Dene and extending round the southern end of the Quantocks towards Bridgwater. Mixed farming is also fairly common at the seaward end of the belt, but varied topographical conditions are reflected in local specialization. Thus, in the lowlands, particularly to the west of Bridgwater, dairying is dominant, on and around the Quantocks live-stock farming is widespread, and in the lowlands between the Quantocks and the Brendons there is some concentration on arable cropping. On the other hand, in the eastern and southern parts of the belt round the basins of the Parrett, the Isle and the Tone, mixed farming and some horticultural activity to the north of Ilminster are definitely subordinate to the prevailing dairy farming. Mendip forms sub-region IV and here livestock farming occupies almost all the summit area, with highly localized horticulture and strawberry production at the foot of the steep southern slopes round Cheddar. Horticulture is also characteristic of sub-region V, which coincides with the light soil areas on the Corallian round Sandy Lane in Wiltshire, and sub-region VI, which is the Winterbourne–Siston–Hanham area to the north and east of Bristol.

Sub-regions VII and VIII correspond with the predominantly arable areas of Cotswold. To the south of an approximate line from Stroud to Malmesbury (sub-region VII), however, dairying is the principal farming objective, and the feeding of other cattle and sheep, the sale of cereals and true mixed farming have been of only minor importance. To the north, on the other hand, in sub-region VIII, dairying is almost entirely absent and is replaced by cereal production and arable farming with an animal husbandry involving sheep, pigs, beef cattle and more recently poultry. It is only in the extreme northeast, where sub-region IX marks the margins of the Vale of Moreton, that dairying is again of major importance and largely replaces other forms of animal husbandry, while sub-region X extends into the southern half of the Vale of Evesham and shares its specialization in horticulture and orchard crops. The area of northwest Gloucestershire which forms sub-region XI includes the northward extension of the dairy vales through the Severn lowlands and the Vale of Gloucester. Indeed dairying is the only common feature throughout this sub-region, where other aspects of agriculture are influenced by very varied physical conditions and by proximity to the urban markets of Gloucester, Cheltenham and the west Midlands. Thus between the two cities and especially in the immediate neighbourhood of Cheltenham, highly specialized market gardening, glasshouse production and pig and poultry keeping are as important as dairying. Elsewhere it is usually mixed farming which accompanies the dairying, but on the isolated hill areas around the Forest of Dean and on the Cotswold outliers, livestock rearing and feeding is locally important, while in the sheltered lowlands round Newent and to the northwest there are orchards and a considerable specialization in small fruit production, hop growing and pig and poultry farming.

The existence of this sub-regional specialization reflects the distribution of certain well-defined types of farming practice, the more important of which are analysed in the Farm Management Handbook (1967) of the Universities of Bristol and Exeter. The small dairy farms of the Vale of Severn are represented by 35 holdings with an average size of 113 acres. Milk alone provided 56 per cent of the gross output of these farms and other forms of animal husbandry 33 per cent (cattle 16, poultry 8, pigs 7, sheep 2). This pattern is further illustrated by the farm stock of 29 dairy cows, 25 other cattle, 338 head of poultry, 13 pigs and 38 sheep per hundred acres. Consequently the production of crops accounted for only 11 per cent of the gross output and this in turn reflects the pattern of land use. Permanent and rotation grasses occupied almost 81 per cent of the land, cereals and root crops for stock feeding a further $5\frac{1}{2}$ per cent and crops for sale less than 12 (cereals $10\frac{1}{2}$) per cent. In the Wiltshire vale 25 somewhat larger farms were considered (average size 307 acres) but a broadly similar economy was revealed. Animal husbandry again produced 89 per cent of the total gross output but the concentration on dairying was even more marked since milk accounted for as much as 67 per cent of the output and other elements proportionately less (cattle 13, pigs 4, poultry 4, sheep 1). There was a corresponding difference in the balance of stocking, with

34 dairy cattle and only 18 other cattle, 34 pigs, 112 head of poultry and 7 sheep per hundred acres. Cereals, which gave four-fifths of the gross output from crops, were rather more important than on the Gloucestershire vale farms and were significant in the pattern of land use. Although grasses still accounted for nearly 74 per cent and cereals and roots for animal feeding another 6 per cent, the production of cereals for sale nevertheless occupied nearly 18 per cent of the farm acreage. The 42 Somerset dairy farms (average acreage 192) showed an even more marked concentration on animal husbandry, which yielded 94 per cent of the total gross output (milk 65, cattle 11, pigs 10, poultry 7, sheep 1) with a stock of 36 dairy cows, 19 other cattle, 33 pigs, 11 sheep and 328 head of poultry per hundred acres. Grasses occupied nearly 88 per cent of the farm land while half of the very small output from crops for sale came from cereals, which occupied about 8 per cent of the acreage. That an even greater degree of specialization characterizes some parts of the lowland plain of central Somerset has been shown in a study of 32,000 acres in the Axbridge rural district (G. F. C. Mitchell, 'The Central Somerset Lowlands', *Selected Papers in Agricultural Economics*, Vol. VII, No. 5, 1962, University of Bristol). Here 99 per cent of the crops were for animal feed (94 per cent for milk production) and permanent grass occupied between 89 and 94 per cent of the land on the tiny farms, many of which were of 70 to 80 acres and even so were often fragmented following enclosure and drainage awards. Clearly dairying dominated the economy of all the farms and it was the sole enterprise on 62 per cent of them.

In the sub-regions in south and southwest Somerset, where there is more varied agricultural practice, 27 farms were studied, but within this group a clearer picture emerges if those farms which do engage in dairying are considered separately from those which do not. On the 14 farms (average acreage 365) which produce it, milk was the largest individual item in the gross output (36 per cent) or more than half of the 67 per cent from animal husbandry (cattle 15, pigs 8, sheep 6, poultry 2). Here the farm stock of 17 dairy cows, 20 other cattle, 72 sheep, 28 pigs and 78 head of poultry per hundred acres is much lighter than in the true dairy areas and sheep play a much more important part in the economy. Moreover, only half of the farm land was in permanent or rotation grasses while cereals, three-quarters of which were for sale, occupied just over 40 per cent of the acreage and produced 23 per cent of the gross farm output. On the 13 farms (average acreage 244) which do not produce milk the gross output was shared between animal husbandry (52 per cent; cattle 16, pigs 25, sheep 8, poultry 3) and cropping (48 per cent; cereals 25). There were no dairy cows and only 28 other cattle, but there were 98 sheep, 51 pigs and 106 head of poultry per hundred acres. On these farms, grasses took up about 40 per cent of the land, cereals about 45 per cent and roots about 10 per cent, a proportion suggestive of an approach to true mixed farming.

In south Cotswold (sub-region VII) the 21 farms of the survey had an average size of 230 acres and stock consisting of 23 dairy cows, 20 other cattle, 23 pigs, 20 sheep and 112 head of poultry per hundred acres. They illustrate the fact that dairying is almost as important in this district as in the dairy vales, since milk accounted for 56 per cent of the total gross output and other forms of animal husbandry 27 per cent (pigs 12, cattle 9, poultry 4, sheep 2), leaving only 14 per cent from cereals and 3 per cent from other crops. Rotation and permanent grasses therefore took up 65 per cent of the farm land and feed crops another 10 per cent, but nonetheless nearly 23 per cent was devoted to the production of cereals for sale. The larger size of farms in central Cotswold (sub-region VIII) is shown by the average size of 426 acres for the 22 examples studied. Animal husbandry still produced 55 per cent of the gross farm output, but its mixed character is revealed by the absence of milk, by the share derived from other forms of enterprise (poultry 18, other cattle 14, pigs 13, sheep 10) and by the farm stock which involved no dairy cows, 23 other cattle, 76 sheep, 17 pigs and 650 head of poultry per hundred acres. The very large figures for poultry are indicative of specialist poultry farming in this area and the importance of pig keeping is emphasized by the recent very successful development of the Cotswold hybrid animal. However, the largest individual item in the gross farm output was cereals (37 per cent) which occupied 52 per cent of the farm acreage compared with 42 per cent in rotation and permanent grasses.

The average net farm income for the 102 farms surveyed in the three dairy vales was £15 per acre, in the dairying areas of Cotswold it was £13·1 and on the milk-producing farms in southwest Somerset it was £11·7. This contrasts with a figure of £11·1 on the farms without milk in south Somerset and £7·7 in the districts of Cotswold without dairying. Since the return on capital was also higher on the dairy farms, this suggests that the emphasis on dairying will continue, though increased prices for beef and some reduction in liquid milk consumption at the present time may produce diversification, of which there is some evidence in increased demands for artificial insemination from beef bulls. In arable agriculture the crop figures (Table 21, p. 296) illustrate the trend towards continuous cereal cropping between 1963 and 1967, but changes in 1968, the cessation of seed barley exports and the uncertain world cereal supply situation suggest that this may continue to be modified by the search for profitable break crops and by the reintroduction of oats into the cereal system.

## The Towns and Industries of the Rural Areas

It has already been shown that most of the 35 towns of the Bristol region have a rural setting away from the major industrial and commercial centres of Bristol–Bath, Gloucester–Cheltenham and Swindon. All of them, along with the villages of the region, act to some extent as service centres and many of them could be described as market towns, but these are never their sole functions. These are certainly important functions of the former wool towns of Cirencester, Tetbury and Malmesbury, for example, but it will be seen that even here there has been a significant development of modern manufacturing industry, and though Taunton has been described in the report of the South West Economic Planning Council as a town which is primarily a service and administrative centre, it is not without industrial undertakings. The scale of industrial, commercial and administrative activity ranges widely from towns like Frome, Bridgwater and Trowbridge, with a sizeable complex of industries or important administrative and commercial functions, to relatively small service centres like Wells, Somerton or Malmesbury, with only restricted industrial development.

The nature of the industries involved also shows considerable diversity arising from the variety of manufacturing activity within the larger towns and the specialization of individual concerns in some of the smaller ones. Nevertheless it is possible to suggest five categories of industry which are characteristic of the rural parts of the Bristol region. The first involves the processing of agricultural produce, the second comprises the remains or derivatives of the former West Country woollen industry and the third represents dispersed elements of industries characteristic of the region as a whole, such as engineering and the aerospace industry, the manufacture of footwear and leather goods, and the paper and printing industries and the use of timber. The fourth category does not comprise a single type of industry since it is composed of the highly individual 'one town' industries, whilst the fifth consists entirely of innovations in this area, largely in the fields of electronics, chemicals and plastics, some of which were introduced as a result of wartime relocation, post-war overspill or similar arrangements.

(1a) The high degree of specialization in dairy farming makes the handling and processing of milk by far the most important of the food industries. The recent daily average intake at the creameries of the largest concern in the region, Unigate, exceeded 310,000 gallons, to which should be added over 51,000 gallons handled at the pasteurizing and bottling plants at Bristol, Wootton Bassett and Chippenham. All the company's 11 creameries in the region send some of their intake as liquid milk by road tanker for sale in London and the home counties, and the whole of the intake at Moreton-in-Marsh (16,000 gals.) and Chippenham (11,000 gals.) is disposed of in this way. At the remaining creameries about 52 per cent of the overall intake is processed or manufactured, though the proportion and the nature of processing involved vary greatly from plant to plant. Thus at Watercombe, near Yeovil, the greater part of the intake (22,000 gals.) is manufactured into cheese, whereas at Chard (28,000 gals.) only one-seventh of the milk is used for the production of butter and clotted cream in which the creamery specializes. Chard, however, draws additional supplies of cream for its manufacturing activities from other creameries such as Wellington, where half the intake of 45,000 gals. is made into cream, spray-dried milk powder and cheese. Except at Evercreech (27,000 gals.), where 38 per cent of the milk is used in making butter, cheese and milk powder, the other creameries at Wootton Bassett (31,000 gals.), Melksham (31,000 gals.), Wincanton (41,000 gals.), Bason Bridge, near Highbridge (47,000 gals.) and Sherborne (9,000 gals.) all make cream and butter, but each has other special interests. Thus the relatively small amount of processing at Wootton Bassett and Sherborne also includes the making of yoghurt at the former and cheese at the latter. Of the larger processing plants, Melksham makes and cans evaporated and condensed milks, and Wincanton and Bason Bridge make milk powder and a great range of other products including canned milk puddings, savouries, prepared flavoured drinks and materials for the icecream and other industries, whilst the St Ivel plant of Aplin and Barrett at Yeovil draws milk and milk derivatives from the creamery at Wincanton for the manufacture of lactic cheese and meat and fish spreads, the Somerton plant makes dried milk and there are smaller butter and milk products plants at Wells and Westbury. Among the other large milk-handling and processing companies, Nestlé's creameries include one at Staverton near Trowbridge; Express Dairies has a large creamery at Frome and its plant at Faringdon in the Vale of White Horse is only a little way beyond the eastern boundary of the Bristol region, while Horlicks has establishments at Ilminster, Minehead, Ashcott and Taunton. The main milk-collecting and processing activities of the Cooperative Wholesale Society are concentrated further north at Melksham and Cricklade and, of the Midland companies, Cadburys has a milk plant in Gloucestershire at Frampton-on-Severn and Midland Dairies one at Cricklade. Icecream manufacture is of considerable importance to the latter company which, like others in the industry, draws some part of its processed supplies from the creameries of the Bristol region, and though the large new Walls icecream factory has been sited in the Gloucester–Cheltenham industrial area, its association is in part with the surrounding dairying districts. The Milk Marketing Board, of course, has interests throughout the region and has cheese factories and storage facilities at Cannington near Bridgwater, near Langport and at Wells. There are, too, a great many smaller dairy firms which carry out a certain amount of processing and the farmhouse manufacture of cheese still exists on a limited scale.

(1b) The manufacture of meat products in the rural towns of the Bristol region in former times was largely concerned with bacon curing and the earlier history of the two largest concerns, Harris's of Calne and Bowyers of Trowbridge, has already been traced. In recent years, however, both have been increasingly involved in the production of other foodstuffs, mainly from meat, and the developing national and international market for specially packed and presented prepared foods has resulted in considerable growth and diversification, which is particularly noticeable at Trowbridge where Bowyers' activities now represent a major part of the town's economy as Harris's have long done in Calne. The industry is by no means confined to these two towns, however, and apart from large firms in the industrial areas there are undertakings engaged in bacon curing and pork manufacture in Taunton, Highbridge, Cirencester, Nailsworth and Chippenham, where there is also a plant of the Oxo Company.

(1c) Large-scale operations by the major groups in the industrial areas of Bristol and Gloucester–Cheltenham dominate the whole of the milling industry and comparatively little grain for human food is milled elsewhere in the region, but provender milling associated with the dominant animal husbandry of the area is of local importance in many of the rural towns including Wincanton, Bruton, Chard, Frome, Wells, Radstock, Midsomer Norton, Bridgwater, Melksham, Calne, Seend, Westbury, Chipping Sodbury, Cam and Cirencester.

(1d) In this category of industries involving the processing of agricultural produce, the last general group embraces the production of beverages. Despite the recent closure of undertakings in some of the smaller towns, brewing still continues in Trowbridge and Stroud, but cider and perry making is more characteristic of the rural parts of the region, even though local orchards also supply large manufacturers in other parts of England. Some cider is made on farms and by very small commercial concerns but the bulk of the output comes from four centres: Wickwar in Gloucestershire and Nailsea, Taunton and Shepton Mallet in Somerset. At Shepton Mallet the firm of Showerings has also specialized in the manufacture of bottled perry, one variety of which has been marketed most successfully under the trade name Babycham. Fruit grown in the Bristol region is also used by H. W. Carters in making the blackcurrant syrup 'Ribena' in a factory at Coleford in the Forest of Dean, where apple juice, lemon juice, fruit squashes and other bottled and canned beverages are also produced on a very large scale.

Other individual concerns manufacturing foodstuffs in the rural towns, partly from local agricultural produce, tend to operate on a small scale but there are some noteworthy exceptions, including the Quantock Preserving Company of Bridgwater, who make jams, preserves and canned fruit and vegetables, and Hale-Trent Cakes, who have a factory in Clevedon for the large-scale manufacture of confectionery.

(2) The industrial category which includes remains and derivatives of the once extensive West Country woollen industry is particularly well represented in the Stroud valley, but this is an area to be considered later as a minor industrial sub-region. Elsewhere one or two undertakings survive in each of the districts in which textile working was formerly of great importance. In the valleys of the Cam and Little Avon in Gloucestershire, the Cam mills still produce West of England cloths and Tubbs Lewis manufacture elasticized fabric in a group of mills at Kingswood near Wotton-under-Edge. In the west Wiltshire and north Somerset area the long-established woollen industry of Trowbridge is still carried on by three firms in the town and that of Westbury by a single firm which specializes in the making of West of England cloth. In the nearby Somerset town of Frome, however, direct links with the past were broken when A. H. Tuckers ceased to manufacture wool cloth, though connection with the textile trades was re-established in 1966 when their factory was taken over and enlarged by the Marley group for the manufacture of carpets. In the former worsted and serge area of south Somerset, Fox Brothers still manufactures worsteds, serges and a variety of other cloths in Wellington, with branches in neighbouring towns and in Weston-super-Mare. In Wellington, too, traditional uses of wool for bedding have long been maintained by Price Brothers, who now also use many alternative materials in the manufacture of Relyon beds, bedding and hospital and surgical supplies. Even in Taunton, long ago replaced by Wellington in the woollen industry, textile working survives and in recent times has enjoyed a measure of renewed prosperity following the specialized use of man-made fibres.

(3a) Among the manufacturing activities which exist in dispersed form outside the main industrial areas, the Stroud valley and the Forest of Dean, engineering and the aerospace industry are probably the most characteristic and most important in the Bristol region. It will be recalled that here the early history of the engineering industry was linked with the needs of agriculture and the mechanization of older industries, and in a few cases important traces of this association remain. The large firm of Listers of Dursley became part of the Hawker Siddeley group and concentrates on the manufacture of power plant, marine engines, conveyors, tractors, generating sets, electrical machinery and pumps, but many of these products have important agricultural applications and the firm still makes agricultural machinery, including a moisture extraction unit for drying green baled hay and grain and for ventilating stored vegetables, which was developed at its new plant at Cinderford in the Forest of Dean. Conveyors made by Spencers of Melksham are also still used in agriculture but the firm is now better known for handling gear and conveyors used in industry and transport, particularly in port installations, throughout the world. Elsewhere agricultural engineering as a manufacturing industry is represented in the smaller towns of the Bristol region by only a small number of concerns including a large firm, in Frome, which also specializes in the manufacture of fork-lift trucks and earth-moving equipment, though other firms, including a number in Wellington and Taunton and others in Yeovil, Wells, Warminster and Westbury have products such as bulk storage and conveying plant, ducts and tubing and cooling equipment with far wider present-day applications than their original agricultural ones. Engineering connected with wool working is now only represented in Frome by a firm manufacturing steel carding, which is also used in the tobacco industry, and tools manufactured in Yeovil for glove making also afford a single example of links with other traditional regional industries. General engineering industries have grown up only in the four larger centres of Frome, Bridgwater, Yeovil and Chard, though in Dursley the wide range of activities of Listers, combined with those of a firm of electrical engineers, virtually amount to such a development.

In Frome there are over 12 firms engaged in engineering and foundry work. Most of them employ fewer than 100 workers but among the larger firms are Singers who specialize in hot brass pressing and pressure diecasting for world markets in the engineering industry, Notts Industries who manufacture metal pressings for vehicles, shelving and other industrial uses and who have also specialized in the production of marine life floats and buoyancy gear, and Beswicks who make cartridge fuses and parts for the electrical and electronics industry. The Bridgwater industry is concentrated partly on the manufacture and fabrication of wire by three firms and partly on electrical engineering and the manufacture of batteries in which six firms are engaged, but there is also some more general mechanical engineering and one firm which makes firearms. In Yeovil, apart from the aircraft industry, which is described below, there are over 10 firms engaged in light engineering, one of which is a subsidiary of Westland Aircraft Ltd specializing in the manufacture of metal overhead doors and window frames, and another specializes in tube boring and fabrication and the manufacture of filters. Chard's numerous engineering firms cover a remarkably wide variety of interests, the larger concerns including three engaged in foundry work and casting in brass, bronze and other metals, three in the manufacture of machinery and tools for activities ranging from road making to sheet metal working, two in the installation of aircraft systems and the manufacture of breathing apparatus and one in general mechanical engineering, while the smaller firms are engaged in electrical and light mechanical engineering.

In terms of employment Chippenham might also be regarded as an engineering town because its single major engineering enterprise, the Westinghouse Brake and Signal Company, now has in the region of 4,500 workers. Though originally closely linked with evolution of rail transport, the company is now engaged in the production of braking, control and signalling systems for all forms of transport, as well as equipment for the mining and electrical industries which involves a wide variety of activities in the general engineering and electrical engineering fields.

Elsewhere individual engineering firms, which tend to concentrate on precision machinery or in research and development of electrical and electronic equipment, have their plant in small towns such as Malmesbury and Warminster and in the resorts of Weston-super-Mare, Clevedon and Burnham-on-Sea.

Sub-contracting is such a characteristic feature of the organization of the aerospace industry that a high proportion of engineering firms throughout the Bristol region have some connection with it. Thus at Melksham the New Mendip Engineering Company is part of the Dowty group and undertakes precision engineering for the group's aerospace and other interests. However, outside the main industrial areas the only undertakings wholly and directly involved in aerospace work are located at Weston-super-Mare and Yeovil. The latter town is the home of the Westland Aircraft Company which became involved in activities outside the Bristol region, including the building of hovercraft at Cowes. At Yeovil itself aircraft production is concentrated on the construction of helicopters and another company in the group, Normalair-Garrett Ltd, specializes in pressurization, air conditioning and oxygen breathing apparatus for all British and many overseas aircraft constructors. Westland also have an establishment in Weston-super-Mare and the factories of Rolls-Royce and of another branch of the Bristol aerospace industry, Bristol Aerojets, are nearby in Banwell.

(3b) The manufacture of clothing and footwear is the second of the regional group of industries which is by no means confined to the industrial areas and within this group it is the manufacture of footwear which has the most widely dispersed distribution in the rural towns. The main factories of most of the major companies are located in the Bristol district but the firm of Clarks is exceptional in having its headquarters in the very small country town of Street. Moreover, it is this firm which has most actively pursued a policy of establishing branch factories in most of the other rural towns of Somerset. The function of the branches ranges from the production of completed footwear, sometimes of a specialized type like women's warmlined shoes and slippers made at Minehead, to the manufacture of components. Items for Clarks, for example, form a significant part of the output of the Yeovil leather and new rubber and plastics industries, but in addition footwear components for most of the firms in the industry are made by some of the region's paper, board and plastic concerns like Chamberlains in Stroud. This aspect of the footwear industry is most characteristic of Somerset since, in addition to the three towns already mentioned, there are factories on the outskirts of Bath and in Bridgwater, Weston-super-Mare, Clevedon, Shepton Mallet, Norton–Radstock, Paulton, Castle Cary, Ilminster and Glastonbury, where slippers and boots are made as part of the town's sheepskin industry; the manufacture of components in Gloucestershire is linked mainly with the paper and board industry and in Wiltshire it is represented by a single plant at Warminster.

The glove-making industry, partly because of its long-established system of outworkers, has a similarly dispersed distribution mainly in south Somerset, centred on the gloving town of Yeovil. Fourteen firms in the town itself and a further twenty-four in its neighbourhood are engaged in the manufacture of about 5 million pairs of gloves per year, including about half of all the leather fashion and non-industrial gloves made in Britain. The total labour force is over 7,000 but a high proportion of these are outworkers who do the stitching in their own homes. Elsewhere in south Somerset there are several glove-making firms in Taunton and individual ones in Langport, Somerton and Chard, and in north Somerset at Glastonbury, Wells, Frome, Midsomer Norton and Radstock, while two firms in Warminster and two groups of companies based on Westbury represent the later spread of the industry into west Wiltshire.

The leather industry of Somerset is so intimately linked with the gloving and footwear trades that it is appropriate to consider it next.

Twelve tanneries in and around Yeovil and two at Milborne Port specialize in the treatment of imported fine sheepskins for gloves, hand-bags and garments, though some also produce leathers suitable for shoe uppers, whilst two firms in Glastonbury make leathers for the shoe trade and for sports goods. Both of the Glastonbury firms, Baileys and Clark, Son and Moreland, also dress sheepskins in the fleecy state for making up by themselves and other concerns in the neighbourhood into slippers, boots, garments and rugs. Other sections of the leather industry continue to operate in Bristol; there is one firm in Yatton and another in Westbury which was engaged in the highly specialized manufacture of glacé kid but has more recently added cattle hides, suede kid and brushed suede pigskin.

In the garment section of the clothing industry the towns of south Somerset are again centres of specialization in the manufacture of shirts and collars. This developed early in Taunton where a number of firms have long been established including the large British Van Heusen Company, which now also has factories in Bishop's Lydeard, Crewkerne, Watchet and at Bridgwater, where other firms are also engaged in this trade. Uniforms, formerly for nurses and schools but now for many other users, as well as general clothing, are manufactured on a con-siderable scale by Egerton Burnetts in Wellington, and other firms in Taunton, Wells and Calne make industrial and agricultural overalls, while foundation garments, though mainly produced in the Bristol–Bath area, are also made by Leffmans in Bridgwater and at a branch factory in Somerton.

(3c) The third group of regional industries which is well repre-sented in the rural areas is that which embraces the manufacture of paper, board and paper products, printing and publishing. Since the late nineteenth century, it will be recalled, the actual manufacture of paper and board has become highly concentrated in the Bristol district and to a lesser extent in the Stroud industrial area, so that there are comparatively few remnants of the former widespread distribution in the rural areas. In Gloucestershire the Postlip mills near Winchcombe, which have long specialized in the manufacture of blotting paper, and the Middle mills at Cam, which manufacture fibreboard, are examples of such enterprises on a fairly large scale, as is the Wansborough Paper Company at Watchet in Somerset, which has about 600 employees and uses the local harbour for the import of some of its raw materials. Elsewhere paper making tends to be concerned with manufacture on a relatively modest scale of high quality or very specialized products, like those made at Wookey near Wells. The manufacture of cardboard con-tainers has been introduced at Weston-super-Mare and on a small scale in Taunton, whilst the production of greetings cards at Warminster extends the specialized use of paper and board products into west Wiltshire. It is, however, the printing and publishing activities of Paulton, Midsomer Norton and Frome which form the most important branch of the industry in the smaller towns of the region. Apart from general printing and stationery manufacture, book printing by a number of firms in the Paulton–Midsomer Norton–Radstock district is of sufficient importance to make this one of the principal centres of the trade in Britain. By far the largest of these concerns is Purnells of Paulton, who recently announced a £2 million expansion programme and have also opened a works in Frome where there was already an established book-printing industry. Here the largest firm is that of Butler and Tanner, whose output of 6 million volumes a year includes a high proportion of educational and technical publications. Book, atlas and in particular catalogue printing is a speciality of the firm of D. R. Hillman.

(3d) The last of the manufacturing activities which are well established in the industrial areas but also have an appreciable distribution in other parts of the Bristol region are those involving the use of timber, particularly in the manufacture of furniture. There are, however, no districts in which this type of industry is concentrated and it is usually represented only by individual firms in each locality. In Bridgwater the presence of sawmills and of merchants handling home-grown and imported timber helps explain the group of wood-working firms who specialize in fencing materials, joinery products for the building trade and furniture, but less obvious circumstances underlie the establishment of furniture factories elsewhere. Dursley, where the firm of Bymacks has recently started to make furniture, is not far from the wood-working district in the Stroud–Nailsworth industrial area, but the main reason for the company's move from Dagenham is said to have been the anticipation of a good labour supply being available. It is possible that similar considerations or the availability of sites may account for the opening of a furniture factory at Warminster by a High Wycombe firm, but the initiative of individual companies and the exploitation of laminates and other new materials are probably equally important in the case of these and other organizations like Benchairs at Frome and the Avalon, Yatton and other concerns at Yatton, Clevedon and Weston-super-Mare.

(4) The fourth category of industries which are largely associated with a single rural town in the Bristol region was formerly exemplified by the rubber industry at Melksham, even though the manufacture of rubber components had also continued nearby in Bradford-on-Avon since it was first introduced there in the nineteenth century, and until recently in Frome. The Avon Rubber Company of Melksham is now the parent company of a group which produces most types of rubber goods as well as tyres in other parts of Britain and overseas, as well as at

Melksham and Bradford-on-Avon, and it is still the outstanding representative of this industry in the Bristol region. However, growing production at a newly established factory for the manufacture of rubber components on the trading estate at Calne is expected to continue and the industry has spread even further as a result of the post-war development of major undertakings in the Gloucester–Forest of Dean industrial area, which will be discussed later. On the other hand, the manufacture of transparent wrappings by British Cellophane at Bridgwater still affords a good example of a large undertaking which forms a 'one town' industry in the Bristol region. Nevertheless the firm's original type of cellulose film is now only one of their products and increasing output of polythene, polypropylene and other plastic films involves association with the plastics industry, which has a more general and growing distribution throughout the region.

In the neighbourhood of Westbury in Wiltshire another industry with a large individual plant was introduced to the region in 1962 when the cement works of Associated Cement Manufacturers went into production. Though it draws most of its materials from the chalk areas to the east, the plant's output of about 600,000 tons per year is distributed throughout an area which embraces the whole of the Bristol region and extends some way beyond it to Hereford, Exeter and Southampton. The suitability of Westbury as a distribution centre for much of southern and southwestern Britain presumably also underlies the choice of the West Wiltshire trading estate as the site for a main storage and distribution centre of Tesco stores, and similar circumstances may in part explain the fact that in this small town there are about 800 employees of building firms who operate over much of southern Britain and of the civil engineering firm of A. E. Farr whose work extends throughout the country and overseas.

(5) Wartime relocation of industry, post-war overspill and town development arrangements and planned diversification have been partly responsible for the appearance of a number of new types of manufacturing activity in the Bristol region. This has produced the most marked changes in Swindon, in the Gloucester–Cheltenham industrial area and in the Forest of Dean, but the establishment of individual firms elsewhere has created the final category of industries which can be recognized in the rural towns. Many of them are concerned with advanced technologies or involve the use of new materials but their products are so varied that an impression of their scope can only be given by referring to the actual undertakings in some of the towns. Thus in Cirencester Mycalex and T.I.M. manufacture electrical insulation materials, motors and ticket printing, issuing, recognizing and cancelling machines and the Addo Company makes calculating equip-

**315**

L

ment, whilst in Malmesbury a range of products, mainly connected with the electrical and electronics industry, are made by the special products division of E. K. Cole and by the Linolite Company. Similar interests in specialized mechanical and electrical engineering are characteristic of Wells, where automatic machines and control equipment are made and where E.M.I. Electronics have a factory, and of Corsham, where a number of firms are engaged in precision engineering, electronics and the fabrication of plastics. Work on plastic components and on electrical or electronic components and circuits, often in association with one another, is highly characteristic of many of the smaller units in this group of new industries which have been introduced in Minehead, Wellington, Glastonbury, Calne, Warminster, Trowbridge and Wringhton. Fibreglass is used by two firms in Weston-super-Mare in the manufacture of shipping containers, by two companies in Wellington whose products include vehicle bodies and cabs and machine covers, and by individual firms at Wrington, Marshfield and Corsham. In Frome a plastics industry on a larger scale developed when the long-established rubber-manufacturing firm of Wallington Weston became associated with the Marley group. It now has 750 employees engaged in the production of PVC sheet, laminates and plastic flooring materials.

The chemical industry is little represented in the Bristol region outside the industrial areas, but the move of Cuprinol Ltd from Avonmouth to Frome ten years ago, in association with the local firm of Pinchins, affords an important exception, especially as it is now concerned with the manufacture of a wider range of chemicals in addition to its original wood preservers. In Wellington, too, a long-established firm which formerly specialized only in animal health products now handles a variety of chemical products and has expanded greatly by participation in the recent trend towards presentation in mass-produced aerosols.

In aggregate these five categories of manufacturing activity in the smaller towns produce what amounts to a scatter of minor industrial centres, particularly in the eastern and southern part of the Bristol region in a belt from west Wiltshire to southeast Somerset. In some towns like Cirencester, Malmesbury, Tetbury, Minehead, Clevedon and Wincanton, industry is still on a relatively small scale, and in others like Dursley, Chippenham, Melksham, Calne and Street, single firms still account for a high proportion of the employment in their much larger manufacturing sector. Nevertheless, even in these cases, new industries, sometimes on recently developed trading estates, are tending towards diversification. On the other hand, though there are large undertakings in Bridgwater, Yeovil, Frome and Chard, these towns have already a far wider range of industrial enterprises and further diversification of their activities in recent times is associated with a level of prosperity which adds weight to the suggestion that a number of the smaller towns of the region should be regarded as real or potential industrial growth centres.

## The Industrial Areas

Despite historical circumstances and present-day developments which thus explain the existence of a good deal of widespread manufacturing activity, industrial life is nevertheless dominated by those northern districts which may be described as the industrial areas. Together the Bristol, Bath, Gloucester, Cheltenham and Swindon districts along with parts of the Forest of Dean and the Stroud valley account for at least 75 per cent of the region's manufacturing industry and it is only in the production of leather and leather goods, clothing and footwear and some miscellaneous goods that these areas provide less than half the employment of the whole region. Moreover, despite growth elsewhere and the relatively greater importance of its service functions, the area within twelve miles of Bristol itself remains by far the most important individual centre of manufacturing industry.

### THE LOWER AVON–BRISTOL–SEVERNSIDE INDUSTRIAL AREA

A view of the manufacturing industry of the Bristol district in its regional setting is given by Table 23 which places such occupations in the order of their share of the regional total, though not, of course, in the order of their importance *within* the Bristol district itself. It is significant that many industries in the first four groups were in origin port-oriented and, as some of them remain so today, location close to the waterfront is still common.

TABLE 23

% OF REGIONAL EMPLOYMENT

| | |
|---|---|
| Over 75 | Non-ferrous metal manufacture |
| 50–75 | Chemicals |
| | Food, drink and tobacco |
| | Paper, printing and publishing |
| | Metal goods manufacture |
| 25–50 | Mechanical and electrical engineering |
| | Ferrous metal manufacture |
| | Vehicles |
| | Timber and furniture |
| | Clothing and footwear |

317

The non-ferrous metal industry was formerly represented by a considerable number of firms in the city itself and in the adjacent parts of the Avon valley, but the departure of the Capper Pass Company now leaves only six non-ferrous foundries and two firms of lead merchants and manufacturers. Indeed the replacement of the ancient lead shot tower on Redcliff Hill in 1968 by the new plant of the Sheldon Bush and Patent Shot Company in Cheese Lane symbolizes the latest phase of concentration of the old city industry. However, the Bristol district's present leading position in the non-ferrous metal industry has arisen almost entirely from the activities of the Imperial Smelting Corporation at Avonmouth during this century. Established during the 1914–18 war to help meet the shortage of sulphuric acid and zinc, the plant was located almost alongside the Royal Edward Dock, whence an overhead conveyor now brings imported concentrates of sulphide ores from shipside to the works, where initial sintering releases sulphur dioxide used in the contact process for the manufacture of sulphuric acid. Successively controlled since 1924 by the National Smelting Company, the Imperial Smelting Corporation and the Consolidated Zinc Corporation, later part of the Rio Tinto organization, the undertaking has experienced until very recently continuous growth, the latest rapid phases of which commenced in 1965 with multi-million-pound programmes of expansion and modernization in collaboration with Imperial Chemical Industries and Fisons. From the outset the production of sulphuric acid meant that the corporation was involved in the chemical as well as the metallurgical industries and in more recent times the increasing scale and sophistication of its chemical output has meant that it must be regarded as an important unit in both. Sulphuric acid has always been sold in the London area, the Midlands and South Wales as well as in the Bristol region, but a considerable quantity has also been used in the adjacent Fisons' fertilizer factory for the production of superphosphates from imported rock phosphate brought from the Royal Edward quayside on the conveyor used for ore concentrates. The part of the 1965 programme of development which provided for a new phosphoric acid plant was therefore an extension of earlier interests in the chemical field and since 1946 there has also been considerable development in the manufacture of anhydrous hydrofluoric acid from sulphuric acid and fluorspar. Some part of the output of this acid is sold for use in the petroleum and nuclear energy industries, but it is also the basis of the manufacture of other fluorine compounds at the Avonmouth works, including the Isceons used as refrigerants, as blowing agents in the manufacture of plastic foams and as propellants in the very rapidly expanding aerosols industry. The metallurgical side of the undertaking was primarily concerned with the

318

production of zinc by the horizontal and later the vertical retort processes, but modernization programmes have led to their replacement by the Imperial Smelting process, which was initiated and developed at Avonmouth to allow the concurrent production of zinc and lead in a blast furnace. Metallic cadmium, used in plating, bearings and batteries, is also recovered from the zinc concentrates, and beryllium and beryllium-copper alloy have also been produced for use in the electrical, electronic and nuclear energy industries.

The recent history of the chemical industry itself in the Bristol area is broadly parallel with that of the non-ferrous metal industry. This century has seen the closure of the last of the formerly important soap works, which were the sole survivors of a light chemical industry within the city, and the only remaining chemical plant of any size is the tar distillation works which was established in 1843 on the banks of the Avon at Crew's Hole on the eastern outskirts of the city. Apart from local supplies it long used tar brought from South Wales up the Avon and along the Feeder canal and it was the initial plant on which the activities of the firm of William Butler were based. Though the tar works is still in operation, Butlers, who are now part of the American Tenneco organization, moved to Avonmouth in 1964 largely in order to have centralized production and administration on a site where there was ample room for expansion. In addition to tar acid distillates, Butler Chemicals now also use imported wood and gum rosin, and five trading divisions handle their exceptionally wide range of products which includes rosin sizes, emulsions and printing ink distillates for the paper industry, lubricants, oils, solvents, liquid soap, detergents, antiseptics, disinfectants, pesticides, wood and rope preservatives and special paints. Although Butler Oil Products handle the company's main interests in fuel oils, refining and distillation at its new works are indications that new products may involve it increasingly in the growing petrochemical industry of Avonmouth and Severnside. Availability of ample land was also an important consideration in the nearby location of a factory for Philblack Ltd., who import through Avonmouth a special petroleum fraction for the production of carbon black. Similarly permission granted in 1957 for the industrial use of about 1,000 acres of land a little further north was the essential prerequisite for the establishment of the Imperial Chemical Industries' Severnside plant, which has also been primarily concerned with petrochemical processes and, along with that of the Imperial Smelting Corporation, has been mainly responsible for the special regional importance of the Bristol-Severnside area in their particular industrial groups.

The decision to locate a multi-divisional site on Severnside was taken by Imperial Chemical Industries in the 1950s in the light of market studies for fertilizers produced by the agricultural division, which was to be one of the first occupants of the site. Since the division used the naptha-based pressure steam reforming process prior to the adoption of natural gas as the plant's raw material, nearness to the oil port of Avonmouth, where such petroleum fractions and distillates are handled, was a further important consideration, particularly since other raw materials such as rock phosphate, potash and sulphur were also regular imports. A 70-mile pipeline brings ethylene from the oil refineries near Southampton for the manufacture of ethylene oxide and glycol by the heavy organic division which is sharing the site until production is transferred elsewhere. For a very brief period plasterboard was also manufactured, using the effluent gypsum from the fertilizer plant, but a more important development now being undertaken is the establishment of a third division to manufacture pharmaceutical products.

Industrial association of the kind long practised between the smelting and fertilizer works at Avonmouth has now been established on Severnside, where the South Western Gas Board, whose Sea Bank gas-making plant is also working in part on the I.C.I. pressure steam reforming process, has an arrangement to draw its distillate feedstock through that company's pipeline from Avonmouth and shares other services including industrial water and effluent discharge to the estuary. Some small degree of industrial association even exists with the three groups of nuclear power stations which, like the chemical industries, depend on estuarine sites at Berkeley, Oldbury-on-Severn and Hinkley Point for cooling water. Carbon dioxide used in the power stations as a heat transfer medium is a product of the steam reforming process at the Severnside works and it will be recalled that the nuclear energy industry also accounts for some of the off-site sale of hydrofluoric acid made by the Imperial Smelting Corporation at Avonmouth.

The only other important chemical plant in the Severnside area, Albright and Wilson's phosphorus factory alongside the dock at Portishead, is now ceasing production but the quayside and buildings will continue in use as terminal, storage and distribution facilities for phosphorus brought across the Atlantic in bulk in special vessels from the company's works in Newfoundland, where manufacture is being concentrated because of the availability of low-cost electricity.

The importance of the food, drink and tobacco group of industries in the Bristol district has been more continuous and does not depend as much on twentieth-century developments as does that of the non-ferrous metal and chemical industries, though important changes in location and character have taken place or are about to do so. Thus the long-established manufacture of cocoa and chocolate confectionery was carried on in large factories in the heart of the city and to the northeast in Fishponds and Mangotsfield at the beginning of the present century, but the move by Fry and Son from central Bristol to a largely rural site at Somerdale near Keynsham initiated a period of change which has now completely disrupted the old pattern. Frys' Somerdale factory, now associated with the Cadbury group, is a major concern with several thousand employees and completely dominates the local industry, since in Bristol itself only one other firm of moderate size and a few very small ones remain. Tobacco manufacture, Bristol's other traditional industry in this group, involves about 6,000 workers and is still concentrated in three factories in the Bedminster area of the city which had been established by the early years of the present century. However, it too is now controlled by a single firm in the Imperial Tobacco organization, whose intention to build new factories on a 45-acre site at Hartcliffe in the southern suburbs is likely to result in the disappearance of most branches of the industry from the city area within a few years.

A somewhat similar shift away from the city has occurred in the milling industry, accelerated by the end of direct shipment of overseas grain to the city docks and by war damage. However, immediately above Bristol bridge, waterside sites are occupied by important undertakings, including large flour mills which until recently used grain brought by barge from Avonmouth and the Bristol brewery which has also obtained supplies in this way. The former concentration of milling also led to some degree of association with the bakery and catering trades in this area and the largest of the Bristol yeast factories, operated by the Distillers Company, is located a little further up the harbour near bakery engineers and firms dealing in bakers' and confectioners' sundries. However, the greater part of the Bristol flour-milling industry is now located at Avonmouth, along with the milling and processing of animal feeding stuffs, seed crushing and oil cake manufacture. During the present century large new mills have been built by Spillers and Hosegoods alongside the original Avonmouth dock and other large concerns including the British Oil and Cake Mills Company and the Cooperative Wholesale Society have mills in the adjacent central part of the dock estate.

The general bakery trade is, of course, market-oriented and therefore widely and almost uniformly distributed throughout the Bristol region, but the production of bread and cakes on a near-industrial scale is concentrated in the larger towns and cities and this is most marked in Bristol itself. A dozen large firms, most of them linked with nationwide organizations in the milling and baking industry, have bakeries in the southern and eastern suburbs from Ashton and Bishopsworth round to the Brislington trading estate, Kingswood and Fishponds, with two even further out at Warmley. Besides supplying the Bristol urban area, they all serve districts which on average may extend up to a radius of twenty miles. Other food-manufacturing industries on a considerable scale include the Robertson jam and marmalade concern and three firms who manufacture pork and other meat products of the kind made by the west Wiltshire industry. One still operates in the central area of the city, one in Fishponds and the third, which is part of an international group and is also engaged in the frozen food business, has recently built a large new factory in Kingswood.

The fourth group of industries listed in Table 23 embraces a whole range of activities from the actual manufacture of paper and board to the making and printing of packaging materials and practically every other branch of printing. It was the large-scale manufacture of paper and board which was established at the end of the nineteenth century alongside the city docks and the Avon, where supplies of imported pulp were readily available, and this side of the industry still occupies such sites from Avon Street in the city to St Annes at the head of the docks system and Keynsham further up the river. All still depend heavily on imported materials but a great deal of waste paper and board has also been used and at St Annes Board Mills plant has recently been installed to use home-grown logs. There has long been a tendency for the Bristol industry to specialize in the manufacture of cardboard and the qualities of corrugated and wrapping papers used in the packaging industry. There are six large firms in Bristol and one at Portishead which specialize in making paper bags and sacks and the two largest firms in this group of industries are primarily concerned with packaging. Mardon Son and Hall, whose Bristol factories centre on Temple Street in the city and who also have an establishment at Warmley, have been largely concerned with colour printing and packaging for the tobacco industry but now have group interests covering a very wide field, whilst the firm of E. S. and A. Robinson was the original printing company in what is now an international organization in the packaging industry. Some of its factories are located near the centre of the tobacco industry in Bedminster but it also has others in east Bristol and near Chipping Sodbury, and a considerable part of the manufacture of waxed paper and cartons, in which it specializes, has been concentrated in factories in Fishponds, Warmley and Bitton. A dozen or more other firms in the city and Kingswood area manufacture cardboard boxes, cartons and other containers, and in the new industrial area in Ashton on the southwestern side of the city the large firm of Ashton Containers specializes in the use of fibreboard. Plastics are also used in the packaging industry for boxes and wrappings, and Parnalls in Fishponds,

Colodense in Bedminster and several smaller concerns prepare and print cellulose or plastic wrapping films and containers.

Printing concerns which are not themselves directly engaged in the packaging industry include a few fairly large undertakings, but the vast majority of the sixty or more such firms are small and many of them have long occupied premises in the central and eastern parts of the city, though heavy damage during the last war contributed to a dispersal of small printing works throughout the greater part of the urban area. More recently two of the larger general printing firms have moved, one to the new Ashton industrial area and the other to Wick, some miles to the east of the city, and a book printing company moved to a site on the Bath road near the Brislington trading estate. The nature of the work undertaken is too varied to permit of any kind of general classification but it involves a considerable proportion of high-quality printing including colour and fine art production.

With the exception of those which use timber, none of the remaining industries listed in Table 23 has been linked historically with Bristol's imports and, though some of them do now use such materials, none can properly be described as port-oriented. The first four comprise the groups of metal-using industries which grew up during the nineteenth century and have become collectively by far the most important form of manufacturing activity in the Bristol district. The fact that the production of metal goods is listed first in this group stems from the particular association of Bristol with sheet metal work, which is, in part, related to a former more general connection with galvanizing in the city. Over thirty firms in the district make sheet metal goods or undertake sheet metal fabrications, the majority of them being concerned with air and industrial ducting, chutes, hoppers, cyclones and machine guards and canopies. Many of them have their works near the engineering concerns in the eastern part of the city from St Phillips outwards to Fishponds and Kingswood, but others are located in Bedminster and some of the larger concerns have established plant in the recently developed industrial area of Winterstoke Road in Ashton.

Among the metal-using groups the engineering industries are, of course, of far greater absolute importance, but they present acute problems of description and definition. This is partly because aircraft construction, which is by far the largest individual enterprise in the district, is separately classified in the vehicles group but clearly involves many engineering processes and is, in any case, intimately linked with local engineering because of the prevalence of sub-contracting in the aircraft industry. Moreover, though about half a dozen of the largest engineering firms and perhaps a dozen of the smaller ones have well-defined fields of interest and specialization, there are about 200 concerns engaged in some kind of engineering activity whose functions and products are not only infinitely varied but also change continually. It should be added that the presence of a small ferrous metal industry in Bristol is explained by the output of foundries working to meet the specialized requirements of the local engineering firms.

Among the larger Bristol engineering firms the most common characteristic is a tendency to specialize in the provision and maintenance of equipment for other industries which are well represented in the area, and this is particularly marked in the case of the paper, printing and packaging trades. The large Masson Scott Thrissell Engineering Company, whose factories are in the Easton and St Phillips area of east Bristol, is principally concerned with the manufacture of machinery for printing and making paper, paper bags, boxes and cartons, and one of the divisions of the firm of Strachan and Henshaw has works nearby in Whitehall and Fishponds where it produces printing, slitting and paper-bag-making machinery. By now the output of several engineering firms of this kind is far in excess of local needs and their machines are installed in many countries throughout the world. Moreover, extension into other fields of engineering has taken place and a mechanical handling division of Strachan and Henshaw has works in the old engineering centre of St Phillips and a large factory in the new Ashton industrial area, where it builds hoists and conveyors as well as more specialized handling gear which has led to an interest in developments in the nuclear engineering industry. The important boot and shoe industry in east Bristol is served by three engineering firms who manufacture and maintain shoe machinery and tools in the same district, one of which also has plant near the Clarks footwear factories in Street. A considerable number of firms make equipment for the various branches of the food processing and bakery trades, though often this is combined with engineering for other industries, especially in the case of large concerns like Torrances of Bitton which makes milling machines for paint and ink manufacture as well as for the chocolate industry and which could be described as a chemical engineering firm. In other cases, firms like Holman Brothers at Brislington manufacture compressors and equipment with a more general industrial application and Brecknell Dolman and Rogers specialize in the manufacture of coin-operated and ticket machines and ancillary equipment almost entirely for the service industries and transport. Despite the high level of engineering activity, the manufacture of electrical equipment, except the lightest types and electronic apparatus, is surprisingly uncommon in the Bristol district, the nearest examples being Newmans at Yate and Workman Reed near Yatton, both of whom are concerned with motors, particularly the types suitable for pumping.

The problem of differentiating between the engineering and vehicles industrial groups is well illustrated by the large Douglas engineering firm in Kingswood which formerly manufactured motor cycles, but in that field was later only concerned with Vespa scooters. However, much of the company's present activity stems from its association with the Westinghouse organization since this involves the production of air brakes for commercial vehicles and pneumatic control gear for cranes and excavators, rather than the actual manufacture of vehicles. Indeed the only large firm in Bristol directly concerned with the building of road vehicles is Bristol Commercial Vehicles at Brislington which until recently had to concern itself exclusively with the manufacture of bus and coach chassis for associated transport undertakings.

The vehicles group in the Bristol district, however, is completely dominated by the aerospace industry and this, in turn, is highly concentrated in the group of factories round the airfield at Filton to the north of the city. Aircraft built by the Bristol Aeroplane Company played an important part in the First World War and the company grew so rapidly, particularly in the late inter-war years, that by 1939 it was by far the largest undertaking in the Bristol area, with over 18,000 employees. After vast wartime expansion the company became involved in countrywide adjustments and reorganization of the whole aircraft industry, but the continued importance of the Filton establishments is indicated by the fact that they have provided employment for some 26,000 workers in recent years. During the post-war years the work of the original company was shared by a division concerned with engine production and those engaged in the other aspects of aircraft construction. The former first became associated with the Siddeley organization and then was acquired by Rolls-Royce, so that it operated as the Bristol Engines division of that company. The engine work still continues in Filton but some extension of the company's local interests is suggested by the opening of a Rolls-Royce composite materials establishment at Avonmouth during 1969. The Bristol Aeroplane Company's general work as aircraft constructors and its development of space vehicles now continue as the function of two Filton-based branches of the British Aircraft Corporation. It will be recalled that both Rolls-Royce and the British Aircraft Corporation have factories also near Weston-super-Mare, and both share the general practice of the aircraft industry of sub-contracting and association with specialized engineering concerns in Bristol and elsewhere in the country, notably in the Gloucester–Cheltenham district.

It will have been appreciated that significant changes have taken place during the present century in the location of engineering and the metal-using occupations within the Bristol district, though some large

325

firms and a considerable number of smaller ones still have plant in the original nineteenth-century home of these industries which extended up the Avon valley from the Avon Street area of St Phillips. In the last decade of the nineteenth and the first two decades of the present century the distribution was changed in three ways. The larger concerns led the way in a shift northeastwards from the Avon valley into the Fishponds area of Bristol and beyond the city boundary into Kingswood where most of them remain, along with many firms of moderate size which subsequently joined them. A smaller group of engineering undertakings was set up in the same period to the south of the river in Bedminster, whilst the third shift resulted in the dispersal of a large number of very small firms throughout the whole of the urban area with the exception of the then purely residential districts of Clifton and Redland. In the inter-war period the centre of gravity of employment in these groups of industry was radically changed by the development of the aircraft industry in Filton which was at that time a unique example of a move to the perimeter of the urban area, admittedly because of the specialized requirement of space for the airfield. During the past twenty-five years, however, such outward movements have become a little more general. A number of firms have been established round the trading estate at Brislington, on the Bath Road, and others have moved to the growing industrial area round Winterstoke Road in Ashton near the southwestern limits of the city. Even further afield at Yate the engineering industry was formerly connected with the manufacture of aircraft components by Parnalls, but in the post-war period the company has become part of the Radiation group and is now mainly engaged in the production of domestic equipment. Other firms in Yate, Chipping Sodbury and the Winterbourne, Little Stoke and Patchway areas towards Filton embrace a wide range of light-engineering activity though with some emphasis on tool making and on precision or prototype development work. Structural engineering is not a branch of the industry which in the past was particularly characteristic of the Bristol district, but several large firms now occupy sites on the Brislington estate and in the Ashton area, whose good access facilitates operations throughout the surrounding region. One of the firms, Metal Agencies Engineering, is part of an organization involved in other aspects of Bristol's service function for the building industry in the west of England.

The timber-using industries have no doubt always depended to some extent on supplies from the port, and early works in the centre of the city were within easy reach of the old quays. However, the present-day location of these industries shows little connection with the position of the wharves, yards and saw mills where timber is handled, round the Hotwells part of the city docks or increasingly at Avonmouth. Ten firms are engaged in the general furniture and more specialized chair business, most of them in the traditional furniture district of St Pauls in the centre of the city, though others, including one making a fair proportion of metal chairs, have factories in the Fishponds engineering area. Some manufacturing joinery and prefabricated building firms also have their works near the St Pauls area but far more are located to the east in the Fishponds, Eastville, Easton and St George districts, where there are also six firms who make ladders and six specializing in the manufacture of wooden boxes and packing crates. Indeed the only significant new area involved in the timber industries is in Winterstoke Road alongside the Ashton industrial developments and close to the city docks and the main roads from Avonmouth and Portishead.

By far the largest element in the clothing and footwear industries of the Bristol district is the manufacture of boots and shoes in the Kingswood–Soundwell–Staple Hill area to the east of the city. From the start of the factory industry in the nineteenth century, agricultural and industrial boots of the heavier kind were the speciality of most firms in this neighbourhood and in consequence they suffered badly during periods of recession in the inter-war period and serious unemployment occurred—an otherwise unknown phenomenon in Bristol's recent experience. The inflated wartime demand for footwear for the services helped materially in the district's recovery, but its longer-term prosperity has been maintained largely because of a switch to the manufacture of lighter types of shoe, and in some cases firms concentrated mainly on women's fashion shoes and children's wear for which demand appears to be less variable than is the case with heavier types. One of the larger firms in the district, G. B. Brittons, has not concentrated so much on a single aspect of the market but has been particularly successful in the development of revolutionary techniques of boot and shoe manufacture including the welding of soles and uppers by its associated Moulded Footwear Company. The firm's headquarters are in Kingswood at a factory said to be the largest footwear manufacturing plant in the United Kingdom and it has establishments in the Soundwell–Fishponds area, but its expansion in recent years has also included the creation of important overseas subsidiaries.

In the clothing section of the industry there is a considerable degree of specialization, since four of the larger firms are engaged in the manufacture of foundation garments, and this particular branch of the trade is established in the same area as the footwear industry, with two of the factories in Kingswood, one in Staple Hill and others in east Bristol. Two large firms of general clothing and uniform manufacturers also have their factories in Staple Hill and smaller concerns are grouped in the St Pauls and adjacent districts of the city, so that the large Cooperative Wholesale Society clothing factory at Brislington is the only important exception to the general concentration in the eastern part of the urban area.

Although the pre-eminent position of the Bristol urban area in these groups of regional industries involves most of the district's manufacturing activity, it does not provide an exhaustive list of local industrial occupations. Indeed the presence of an urban market with a population of over half a million ensures that almost every type of industry is represented, though in many cases solely by small individual undertakings. In consequence only those which are of more than local importance and are distinctively associated with Bristol are worthy of note. The leather trade and tanning are among the city's most ancient occupations, but it is natural that most of the leather factors and merchants now operate nearer the boot and shoe industry in the Kingswood area. However, two tanneries remained in the Bedminster district of Bristol, where the manufacture of other kinds of leather goods, including travelling cases and handbags, is long established, though increasing amounts of plastic material are also used. Brush making is another old Bristol craft and this formerly depended on supplies of wood and imported hair and bristle. However, though traditional types of brush are still made in the city, the importance of the Bristol industry in national and overseas markets stems largely from the activities of the Kleen-E-Ze and Pinnacle companies in Kingswood and Hanham, who also developed brushes twisted in wire and use manmade fibres as well as natural hair and bristle. The use of asbestos is a more recent feature of manufacturing industry in Bristol which grew up in the inter-war years. There are several firms which handle a variety of asbestos products but the main development has been in the manufacture of brake and clutch linings by two large firms with factories on the Bath Road close to the Brislington estate. The plastics industry in Bristol is characteristically associated with a number of small firms working in highly specialized fields but, apart from the big packaging concerns which use plastics, there is one large firm in Fishponds using plastic materials and manufacturing plastic-forming machinery.

A long history of industrial diversity and an equally long established pattern of small undertakings, combined with the results of wartime dislocation, ensure that an industrial map of the Bristol district must of necessity be highly generalized. However, Map 15 (back endpaper) demonstrates the fact that manufacturing industry is highly concentrated in the eastern and southeastern parts of the urban area and it is possible to suggest some characteristic features of each of the districts outlined. The first may be defined as the Redcliffe–Bristol Bridge–Queen Square district (1), which is the oldest industrial area in the city since it includes the home of the medieval woollen industry. Today its most important industry is the manufacture and printing of folding cartons, though it also includes the milling, brewing and yeast-making area above Bristol Bridge and the very important commercial and professional areas of Victoria Street and Queen Square. District (2) largely corresponds with the area surrounding the fine squares of St Pauls, which became a centre of the furniture and clothing industries in the late nineteenth century and still has considerable connections with those trades, though in the past twenty-five years it has developed important wholesale functions in the electrical goods and electrical contracting industry in particular. St Phillips, where many Bristol metal-using industries originated, forms the central part of the third district (3), where important engineering concerns still operate amongst a growing number of wholesalers and factors in the metal goods and engineering trades. Further upstream the chemical and plastic plants in Crew's Hole mark the limit of industrial expansion along the Avon valley in district (4), which also includes the very large board mills in St Annes. From St Phillips the metal and engineering industries, in particular, tended to spread northwards and northeastwards during the late nineteenth century into the Easton, St George and Eastville areas of district (5), where there is also some concentration of timber-using industries, especially those concerned with joinery and the manufacture of cases and prefabricated buildings, and a number of clothing and printing works. However, the actual transfer of major works from St Phillips as far north as Fishponds in district (6) led to the latter area becoming in the early part of the present century the main new engineering centre of Bristol, round which sheet metal and timber manufactures also grew up. The large-scale manufacture of waxed cartons and other paper products, the development of a plastics industry and the presence of food-processing concerns have subsequently created a more diverse industrial character in this district, which the creation of the Fishponds industrial estate may help maintain. The large district (7), which includes Staple Hill, Soundwell, Kingswood, Hanham and Warmley, is almost entirely beyond the city boundary and it represents the continuous spread of the urban area as a result of mixed industrial and residential growth during the nineteenth century. It was the home of the factory manufacture of clothing and footwear and it, too, shared in the spread of engineering from the central areas of the city. Later developments included the making of brushes, cartons and other paper products and recent years have seen the establishment of a number of concerns engaged in the large-scale bakery and food-processing industries.

Districts (8), (9) and (10) represent the more restricted southward spread of industry from the Avon valley. In Bedminster (8) this again

329

took the form of mixed development combined with residential growth during the industrial revolution and the area still includes some metallurgical, engineering and leather-working firms along with the dominant tobacco, paper and packaging industries. District (9) is the industrial zone in Ashton which, though geographically an extension of the Bedminster area, contrasts sharply with it since it is largely the outcome of the post-war establishment of large-scale engineering, metal goods and container manufacturing firms. In the main the industries of the Arnos vale–Brislington area (10) belong to the twentieth century. During the inter-war period some development of the clothing and asbestos manufacturing industries took place along the Bath Road, but in recent decades an industrial estate and two industrial/trading estates have been established in the area with the result that there has been an important growth of paper and printing, food-processing and engineering industries.

In district (11) industry is almost entirely confined to the activities of the Filton and Patchway aerospace undertakings and in district (13) to the Portishead dockside plant, with a number of very much smaller concerns in the town itself. Dockside industries at Avonmouth are also included in district (12) as well as the metallurgical, chemical and petrochemical industries of Avonmouth–Severnside, but here additional developments are taking place, some of them associated with new trading estates close to the continuation of the M5 motorway from its interchange with the M4 at Almondsbury to Avonmouth and the new bridge over the Avon giving access to the southwestward extension of the motorway. Most of these developments are in the field of warehousing and distribution, including a recently opened beer bottling plant, but new manufacturing concerns include a composite materials plant for Rolls-Royce and the pharmaceutical division of Imperial Chemical Industries.

The map does not show the small number of manufacturing establishments in the Avon valley between Bristol and Bath or the group of industries in the Yate–Sodbury area. However, though individually some of these concerns are very large and important, their sites are widely spaced and the map serves to re-emphasize the compact nature of the Bristol industrial district and its predominantly rural setting.

It has already been shown that Bristol's role as a regional service and administrative centre gives other sectors of its economy greater absolute importance in terms of employment than manufacturing industry. The growth of its administrative activities in recent decades has tended to accentuate this situation and there are signs that its service function as a distribution centre for southwestern Britain is also growing, possibly as a result of commercial organizations anticipating transport advantages which are arising as the M4 and M5 motorways are completed.

Within the Bristol district the early post-war period saw only slight changes in the location of the service industries, mainly occasioned by bomb damage to large areas in the city centre. A main pre-war central shopping area in Wine Street and Castle Street was totally destroyed and eventually replaced by the Broadmead scheme a few hundred yards away at the junction of districts (1), (2) and (14) on Map 15, though in the meantime shopping centres on main suburban radial roads like Queen's Road, Whiteladies Road, the Gloucester Road, Stapleton Road and East Street and West Street in Bedminster enjoyed increased prosperity. Initially new stores and supermarkets were established only in Broadmead but during the last few years it has been a rapidly growing practice of the supermarket chains to open additional branches on the radial roads and in the new housing estates on the perimeter of the urban area. On the other hand, the creation of true out-of-town shopping centres has not been encouraged and the only development of this type is at Yate, outside the Bristol administrative area. Surrounded by large car parks and in a semi-rural setting, this new centre is at present somewhat reminiscent of North American shopping plazas, but with the growth of the Yate–Sodbury township it may eventually come to resemble more closely the post-war shopping precincts of other British town centres. It remains to be seen whether any changes in the pattern of local government areas will lead to uniform policies on such issues as the desirability of this type of out-of-town retail centre, more of which have been proposed near the M5 motorway to the northwest of the city.

The wholesale trades suffered similar dislocation as a result of war damage, particularly in the Victoria Street area, but until very recently there has been comparatively little planned relocation. In due course repairs and rebuilding re-established Victoria Street and the rest of district (1) on Map 15 as one of the main wholesale centres of the city, which also includes the traditional quayside home of much of the wine trade. Nevertheless, like the retailers, wholesale firms of necessity moved during the war, many of them to St Pauls and St Phillips in the adjacent districts (2) and (3), so that the three areas on the south and east side of the city have become a concentrated central wholesale zone. Others moved further afield into almost every part of the urban area, some to old factories or temporary structures in the industrial areas and others to purely residential districts where a number still occupy disused halls, churches and large houses. More recently, however, there has been a marked tendency for wholesale organizations to seek peripheral or out-of-town sites and this has been particularly true of larger organiza-

331

tions and especially those intending to use Bristol depots as west of England distribution centres for goods delivered by road. To the southeast of the city, Tate and Lyle's plant at Keynsham for the packing and distribution of sugar arriving by bulk road transport is typical of this tendency, as are the large wine bottling and despatch centre at Whitchurch and the grocery, soft drinks and stationery depots on the Brislington trading estate. To the east there are wholesale establishments on the Fishponds trading estate and along the Marshfield road, but the main recent development has been on the former Pucklechurch airfield. Here ample space and good access provide most favourable conditions for six large warehousing, shipping and distributing firms as well as a group of wholesalers, and similar circumstances explain the presence of four firms of hauliers and plant hire specialists. Large wholesale firms in the food trades are also established to the northeast in Yate–Sodbury and here too warehousing is becoming important and there are several haulage and plant hire firms. The most rapid recent growth of the distribution industry, however, has been in the Avonmouth area. This is certainly associated with greatly improved road access and the progress of the motorway programme in the immediate neighbourhood, but it will also be helped by the opening of a rail freightliner depot and by the establishment of an inland clearance depot where unitized and containerized cargoes can be handled. A great deal of new warehouse capacity has been constructed at the north end of the dock area from St Andrew's Road through the Chittening estate towards Severnside and even greater developments seem likely with the establishment of a trading estate and wholesale area close to the M5 approaches to the new Avon bridge.

Although the core of the central business district round Corn Street (14 on Map 15) suffered only slight damage during the war, the very rapid post-war growth of Bristol's office occupations has produced important changes. The most obvious of these has been the expansion of the business district by the construction of office blocks round its margins in Baldwin Street, Marsh Street, Victoria Street, at the foot of Park Street and in Wine Street, Nelson Street and Rupert Street. Before this expansion could be started, however, growing demand for office space, accentuated by the destruction of buildings in other central parts of the city, led many organizations to seek temporary accommodation in residential areas and particularly in the former hotels and large houses of Clifton. Many of these still remain and the perpetuation of a diffuse business district throughout Clifton seems to be envisaged by decisions which have allowed houses in the Pembroke Road area to be replaced by an office block of considerable size and have permitted the residential tower block of Clifton Heights to be used for office purposes.

*Bath.* Though it is separated from Bristol by short stretches of open country, Bath has been included in the Lower Avon–Bristol–Severnside industrial area because it is engaged in manufacturing activities which are characteristic of the district as a whole. The city's fame as a spa, its importance as a shopping and tourist centre and the fact that 77 per cent of its employment is in the service industries all tend to mask the importance of its manufacturing industry. However, the extremely high figure of employment in the service industries stems almost entirely from the presence of a Ministry of Defence staff of some 3,500 in the area and, if this non-commercial element were excepted, Bath would be seen to have an economy in which the manufacturing sector is at least as important as elsewhere in the district.

As in Bristol the engineering industrial groups are collectively by far the most important and account for about half of Bath's manufacturing employment. Since the firm of Stothert and Pitt, which makes lifting, handling and conveying equipment and mobile concrete-mixing machinery, employs two-thirds of the total engineering labour force, the industry is by no means as diverse as that of Bristol, but even so it has a wide range of products including the precision machined goods of the Horstman Gear Company and tools, instruments, spring articles, shoemaking machinery, cranes and foundry goods.

A further third of Bath's manufacturing employment is provided by the clothing and footwear and the paper, printing and publishing industrial groups. The making of foundation garments and the work of two shoe factories dominate the former but, in addition to the Bathford paper mills, there are fifteen firms in the paper and printing industry in the city, including the Pitman printing and publishing firm. Other manufacturing industries are obviously on a small scale except in the furniture and cabinet-making trades, where two of the concerns are large ones.

Although some firms, particularly in the food and printing industries, have plant in the central part of the city, most of Bath's manufacturing industry is highly concentrated alongside the Lower Bristol Road and the Avon, downstream from the railway station to Lower Weston. Upstream there are only one or two industrial sites in the valley, including the paper mill at Bathford, and elsewhere only a large shoe factory in the southwestern suburbs. Since many of the Admiralty employees now work in new establishments built on the hills surrounding the city, the service industries which largely occupy the central area are essentially normal ones involving local administration, professional services and wholesale and retail distribution, though the last has some

**333**

distinctive characteristics associated with the city's history as a spa and a tourist centre.

## THE GLOUCESTER–CHELTENHAM INDUSTRIAL AREA

It will be recalled that the Gloucester–Cheltenham district is one which has experienced considerable economic growth in recent times, particularly in the sector of manufacturing industry. However, this has to be seen against a background of vicissitudes brought about by the vast expansion of the aircraft and aircraft equipment industries after the mid-1930s and the subsequent run-down of aircraft production which was fortunately offset by further development and diversification of the aircraft equipment concerns. The continued prosperity of the Gloucester–Cheltenham area is therefore largely the product of its recent economic history and has been achieved by two types of concern: those which still supply equipment to the home and overseas aircraft industries but have also expanded interests in other fields, and those which have introduced totally new replacement industries into the district.

The former category is best illustrated by the north Gloucestershire establishments of the Dowty group of companies, about two-thirds of whose total labour force of 15,000 is concentrated in the Gloucester–Cheltenham–Tewkesbury district. Dowty Rotol, whose plant is midway between Gloucester and Cheltenham, specializes in the manufacture of landing gear and propellers for the aircraft industries of many countries and also produces equipment for hovercraft. The British aircraft industry is also a principal customer for the gas turbine fuel systems manufactured on the outskirts of Cheltenham by the Dowty Fuel Systems Company. On the other hand, the nearby factory of Dowty Hydraulic Units has less direct connection with the aircraft industry, and home and overseas sales of its products represent considerable diversification of the group's interests. It manufactures hydraulic control gear for earth-moving and mechanical handling machines and the Dowmatic drive employed in vehicles like the Stothert and Pitt mixers. It also makes the Taurodyne hydrostatic transmission which has been used on International Harvester agricultural machinery, and provides the jet propulsion units for amphibious vehicles and boats equipped by Dowty Marine. The other factories in the Gloucester–Cheltenham district supply materials, parts and equipment to group manufacturing plants, though their products are also sold to outside concerns. On the outskirts of Gloucester, Innsworth Metals specializes in precision casting and electroplating, tools are made in Cheltenham by the Gloucester Engineering Company and outside the Gloucester–Cheltenham area factories at Chippenham and Melksham carry out precision machining for the group. Though not directly engaged in commercial manufacture, Dowty Technical Developments at Brockhampton Park near Andoversford is an important industrial unit which centralizes research, development and testing for the factories and is an integral part of the group's north Gloucestershire industrial complex, which also embraces three companies in the Tewkesbury–Ashchurch district, some eight miles away. Although Dowty Electrics in Tewkesbury makes specialist electrical components and equipment for the aircraft industry, it also has products designed for mining and other industries, while the 3 million seals produced each week by Dowty Seals at a factory between Tewkesbury and Ashchurch are used in an even wider range of industries as well as in the group's own plant. Nearby the third company, Dowty Mining Equipment, makes hydraulic props, roof supports and self-advancing support systems which are used in all types of mining throughout the world, and also produces control equipment for automatic coal-face gear designed for the British coal-mining industry. The other large-scale example of expansion and diversification in the aircraft equipment industry is provided by the Aviation Division of Smiths Industries, which has nearly 4,000 employees in the Cheltenham district. In the late 1930s the initial factory for the manufacture of aircraft clocks, watches and instruments was located at Bishop's Cleeve, four miles north of Cheltenham, for strategic reasons, and four further establishments were subsequently added. The original works still produces normal aircraft instruments but it is now also heavily engaged in the construction of aircraft flight control systems, automatic pilots and automatic landing gear, while a post-war unit is concerned with guided weapon autopilots. The activities of the other establishments, which involve engineering laboratories and a plant where all the company's electronic assemblies are made, are also directly concerned with the aerospace industry, but the diverse interests of the group as a whole are reflected in the manufacture of watches at the second factory to be built on the Bishop's Cleeve site.

The British Nylon Spinners' plant at Brockworth, on the Cirencester road about three miles southeast of Gloucester, is one of the more important examples of completely new industries which have been introduced to the district in recent times. It represents a direct replacement of the aircraft industry since it is housed in a factory reconstructed from the old Armstrong Siddeley works, and its opening in June 1960 coincided with the end of production of Javelin aircraft which had threatened serious unemployment in an area where nearly a third of the labour force had at one time been engaged in the aircraft industry. Process operatives among the 2,000 employees are all male, since the plant must be operated on a continuous shift system, and besides local people they include some former miners from the Forest of Dean who were accustomed to continuous shift working. The only bulk material used is nylon polymer chip, which is still brought by road from the north since a scheme to locate additional nylon manufacture on Severn-side, to supplement supplies from Teeside, was abandoned in view of the financial advantages of locating the new plant in a development area in Scotland. Although food processing is by no means new to the area, the scale of operations at the large Walls icecream factory at Barnwood, nearer to Gloucester, is such that its establishment really amounted to a major new industrial development and, since it was also opened when the local aircraft construction industry was declining, it too played an important part in maintaining employment in the Gloucester area. Apart from developments within the Dowty group, few completely new manufacturing industries have been established in Cheltenham since the last war, but office employment has been materially increased by the decision of the Eagle Star Insurance Company to move their head-quarters offices to the district.

Partly because they have physically replaced some elements of the aircraft industry and partly because of planned relocation, most of the large industrial concerns already described occupy sites outside the urban areas of Gloucester and Cheltenham. Innovation, diversification and economic growth are by no means confined to these modern plants, however, and with comparatively few exceptions the pre-war town industries have remained prosperous by adaptation to changing circumstances. Some thirty firms maintain Gloucester's long-standing connection with metal working and engineering, and a number still manufacture modern versions of traditional products such as ferrous and non-ferrous castings, railway equipment, sheet metal work, marine propulsion gear, tools and hydraulic presses, or are engaged in the general engineering field. The most marked characteristic of recent decades, however, has been increased specialization in products which have assumed a new importance in the city. About half a dozen firms are concerned with the manufacture of pumps, valves, compressors and related air and hydraulic control gear, and a similar number concentrate on precision and prototype engineering and the production of tools and electro-mechanical machinery, whilst new interests of individual undertakings include automatic and vending machines, metal extrusion machines and industrial turbine equipment. In Cheltenham the somewhat newer engineering industry shows a slightly greater tendency towards specialization, since there are thirteen undertakings which concentrate on prototype and precision work and many of the twenty-two general engineering concerns also do work in this field. There is, moreover, some emphasis on hydraulics since, in addition to the large Dowty plant, there are two other firms in this branch of the industry as well as factories making not dissimilar equipment, such as valves and steam traps. Electrical and electronic engineering is represented by several firms, tool making is a local speciality and on a small scale there is some sheet metal work and non-ferrous extrusion and casting.

Among the other industries which are generally characteristic of both Gloucester and Cheltenham, those which use wood are the most important. The long-standing timber trade in Gloucester is maintained near the canal by half a dozen firms engaged in importing, saw milling and timber treatment, while a similarly long-established use of wood continues in the adjacent Moreland match factory. Elsewhere in the city there are nine general wood-working and joinery firms and two which specialize in furniture and cabinet making; in Cheltenham there are eight joinery and two cabinet-making works. There are also more than a dozen printing firms in each city and, though many of them carry on very small general printing businesses, more specialized interests are represented by a few larger concerns which now include the Geographia, Burrow and other map and guidebook publishing companies in Cheltenham, for whom printing is done in both cities. A regionally characteristic feature of the clothing industry in Gloucester is the presence of a number of shirt-making firms, but in Cheltenham only one of the four clothing factories specializes in this branch of the trade. In the food industry there is a concentration of large-scale bakery concerns similar to that in Bristol, with some specialization in the manufacture of biscuits and cakes in Cheltenham. However, apart from four firms making plastic products in each city, complete innovations are rare even among the newer urban industries. In Gloucester carpet manufacture has been reintroduced only comparatively recently but in Cheltenham the chemical industry, which includes a large pharmaceutical plant as well as firms of agricultural and general chemists, has now been established for many years.

There is therefore no lack of diversity in the manufacturing activities of the Gloucester–Cheltenham area, but its recovery from the effects of the post-war run-down and reorganization of the aircraft industry and much of its recent economic growth is nevertheless closely linked with the success of large organizations whose interests have made hydraulic engineering and the manufacture of aircraft components vital elements in the economy of north Gloucestershire, notwithstanding the important contributions made by the older urban industries and the new nylon spinning and icecream factories.

337

Though industrial activity is highly concentrated in Stroud itself and the adjacent central parts of the Frome valley round Cairncross and Dudbridge, it also extends up the valleys as far as Nailsworth and Chalford and downstream to the vale at Stonehouse. Following the eventual decline of wool working even in Stroud after the 1880s, manufacturing in the district was maintained partly by the survival of a few specialist textile, paper and wood-working firms, partly by the diversification of its associated engineering industry and partly by the adaptation of disused mills for new industries. In recent years this last aspect of the valley's changing economy has taken on a special importance, since the difficulty of obtaining industrial development certificates in many parts of southern Britain has made the availability of such existing industrial buildings an additional attraction for new industries.

Fine wool is still spun in Stroud and three cloth-making firms continue to manufacture the very high quality and specialized types of cloth which have ensured their survival. These include not only fine woollen cloths for the general clothing trade but also such traditional Stroud products as naval doeskins, venetians, scarlets and other uniform cloths, lawn tennis ball covers, printing filters and billiard cloths. The early growth of a large-scale clothing industry in Stroud, in which steam power was used for the first time, was closely connected with the supply of fine local cloths but, though these are still used, expanding interests now mean that many types of fabric from other sources are also used.

The ancient paper-making industry of Gloucestershire is still represented by a mill at Stonehouse, which also produces paper bags and packaging materials, but elsewhere the manufacture of fibreboard has become more important than paper. One firm which is said to operate the second largest fibreboard mill in Europe includes shoe components among its products and another specializes in the treatment of varnished, embossed and printed fibreboards. The manufacture and printing of paper and board products was also the basis on which the Copeland–Chatterson concern began to make loose-leaf ledgers in Stroud at the end of the last century and business systems forms, stationery, punched cards and index cards still represent a considerable part of the output of its Dudbridge factory, though this now also includes metal and plastic office equipment.

Wood-working industries, originally using mostly Cotswold beech, have survived in the upper valley at Chalford and Brimscombe, where some of the turnery firms also make chairs and build caravans, but the largest of the saw mills is at Stonehouse. This is an old concern

338

specializing in home-grown hardwoods which has expanded greatly by drawing supplies from a large surrounding area and by developing manufacturing as well as milling interests. A highly specialized industry which grew up in Stroud after the decline of the wool industry is the manufacture of pianos involving local metal-working skills as well as the use of home-grown hardwoods and imported woods for cases and later for veneers.

It is, however, the development and adaptation of Stroud's nineteenth-century engineering industry which underlies most of the district's present-day manufacturing activity. The three foundries work in ferrous and non-ferrous metals and are mainly concerned with general castings for the engineering trades, though with particular emphasis on the machine tool industry and on pattern making. In the heavier branches of engineering, the large firm of Daniels makes hydraulic presses, vacuum formers and injection moulding machines for the rubber, plastics and other industries, while Newman–Hender manufactures forged steel valves and fittings, though it is indicative of recent diversification that it also makes egg-grading machines. Similar adaptability in the field of light engineering is illustrated by the firm of Critchley Bros which, during the past ninety years, has successively specialized in the manufacture of pins, wooden and casein and metal knitting needles, metal and plastic electrical components and now plastic and other materials for agricultural engineering. Most of the other engineering firms have developed their present interests or have moved into the area in the last twenty years and diversity is the keynote of a list of their products, which range from heavy mechanical handling gear to scientific instruments. However, a combination of local sheet metal working with electrical engineering has led to specialization by a number of firms in the manufacture of electrical and other control panels and systems, dust extraction plant and ticket issuing machines. There is also some concentration on engineering for air and fluid flow control and for diffusion and filtration plant, whilst very important individual firms with particularly specialized engineering interests include the Sperry Gyroscope Company and the Hoffman Bearing Company at Stonehouse.

The most important group of new manufacturing industries in the Stroud valley is that involving the production and use of plastics. In addition to the large B.P. Plastics firm, which has recently embarked upon a programme to double its output of polystyrene and expanded polystyrene, there are four other companies concerned exclusively with plastics of various types and many others which use locally-made plastic raw materials and intermediates for products like knitting needles, office equipment, hardware, electrical equipment and instruments and for specialized packaging.

## THE FOREST OF DEAN INDUSTRIAL AREA

In common with the Stroud valley, the Forest of Dean suffered the abrupt decline of its traditional occupations after the end of the last century, but their replacement was much longer delayed here, partly because wartime demand led to some recovery in the output of coal and iron until 1918. Thereafter production fell continuously, however, and by the 1930s unemployment reached a level of 46 per cent of the local working population. The fact that in recent years the level of unemployment in the Forest of Dean has only been a little above the very favourable regional average is largely a measure of recovery brought about by the introduction of new industries and the diversification and revival of existing ones, though there has been some migration from the area particularly to the Gloucester–Cheltenham district. Before 1939 attempts to overcome the acute effects of depression in the area depended on local initiative and effort is still maintained by the Forest of Dean Development Association, though an appreciable part of its success must have been due to relocation of industry during the last war and the government's subsequent decision to stimulate further recovery by encouraging industrialists to establish new plant in the area.

Nevertheless, although large-scale coal mining ceased in 1965 and there are now only a few small privately owned coal gales, the extractive industries and agriculture still play an important part in the economy of the Forest. A considerable number of quarries continue in operation in both West and East Dean and to the north of Lydney, producing a great variety of crushed stone, aggregates, chippings, hardcore, roadstone and flux as well as ornamental and building materials which include the well-known Bixhead Blue and Barnhill Grey Sandstones. At an old ironstone and limestone quarry near Cinderford, the Lower Dolomite is now used to manufacture high-quality coloured facing bricks as well as special sulphate-resisting, semi-engineering and common bricks, whilst elsewhere clays, some of them waste from former mining, are used in making bricks, including special hand-moulded types.

The early wood-working industries of the Forest also have very varied modern counterparts, though a great part of the timber grown by the Forestry Commission is of the type used as pit-props or sleepers or for pulp. Saw mills near Lydney, Cinderford, Huntley, Longhope, Newent and Coleford ring the forested area, and in addition to sawn hardwoods and softwoods many of them have individual manufacturing interests. Panel and lap fencing is something of a local speciality, but heavier types of fencing and gates are also produced as well as joinery, prefabricated building extensions, wood mouldings and veneer and melamine-covered mouldings. Even the ancient craft of charcoal burning survives on a single factory basis, though metal smelting is now only one of many industries in which its products are used. However, by far the largest timber-using industry in the area is the manufacture of plywood at Lydney, but at the outset this was in no way connected with the use of local materials. Originally built by the Ministry of Aircraft Production in 1940–1, the factory then used Canadian birch to make plywood for Mosquito aircraft and gliders and became the largest plant of its kind in the country, responsible for about 40 per cent of British plywood production. Under commercial ownership it now uses some local softwoods but mainly employs imported hardwoods for plywoods used in the building, furniture, boat-building and transport industries, as well as foreign and home-grown decorative timbers for veneers, and it also makes highly specialized boards for the nuclear energy industry. The paper industry, which was once more closely linked with local supplies of wood, also survives in the Lydney and Lydbrook districts, where two modern mills produce high-grade and special purpose papers.

Industries engaged in processing agricultural produce have already been described but it should be mentioned that the building of H. W. Carter's Royal Forest Factory at Coleford to make blackcurrant syrup and other beverages was a significant step in the recovery of the West Dean area in the immediate post-war period.

The progress of recovery throughout the Forest, however, has been chiefly associated with the new growth of manufacturing industries, encouraged by government policy and by the establishment of planned industrial sites at Lydney, Cinderford and Coleford. In some cases these are complete innovations but many represent modern developments of the area's nineteenth-century foundry and metal-working industry. Thus one concern, long established in the heart of the Forest, has recently opened a new foundry near Cinderford to make heavy castings used for manhole and similar covers, while at Lydney the manufacture of Watts and Aga domestic boilers by Allied Ironfounders involves the use of castings as well as other aspects of metal work and engineering. The British Piston Company of Coventry also opened a new plant at Lydney in 1962 in order to increase its capacity for sand-cast foundry products and this too may involve increasing engineering activity with the development of machine shops alongside the foundry. In West Dean the long-established manufacture of cables and wire helps explain the presence of an engineering concern producing cable-making machinery as well as a more general heavy engineering industry.

Two of the larger firms which have moved to the Forest of Dean in comparatively recent times, however, were concerns long established in the engineering industry elsewhere which can have had little direct connection with the pre-existing metal-working activities of the area. Listers of Dursley opened their factory at Cinderford as early as 1944 but it was not until 1952 that one of its present main functions, the manufacture of diesel engines, commenced. The factory also makes electrical generating plants and water pumps and some parts of the hay, grain and vegetable drying units already mentioned. The other undertaking, the Albany Engineering Company, moved from London to Lydney after the last war. It is engaged in the manufacture of pumps, particularly for the chemical, oil and motor vehicle industries, for bulk liquid road tankers and for marine use, especially on tankers.

Other new developments related to traditional local activities are exceedingly diverse. Ferrous metal and engineering products include garden tools, wrought-iron work, oil burners and pumps; a modern form of the ancient pin-making craft is still carried on in West Dean by a firm which now also makes general office equipment, while industrial brushes are made at Lydney and Cinderford. Among the newer local trades, commercial vehicle body building grew rapidly after 1950 with the establishment at Lydney of plant for the Duramin Engineering Company of London, which specializes in light alloy vehicle body building, the manufacture of road/rail/sea freight containers and other light alloy fabrications including insulated containers and conveyor troughs.

The rubber industry, which is mainly concentrated on the Lydney industrial estate, is one of the more important forms of manufacturing activity which is completely new to the area. During the last war a long-established Lydney firm developed its tyre-retreading business and in 1948 moved it to a new factory on the estate where it is now also engaged in the manufacture of special purpose tyres. Another firm also supplies the motor industry with rubber goods, but the largest of the group is the J. Allen Rubber Company, now part of the London Rubber Company, which moved from Cheltenham to the Lydney estate in 1951 and also has a factory at Whitecroft in West Dean. The company makes rubber articles for agricultural, industrial and domestic use but specializes in the manufacture of rubber gloves, of which it is the largest producer in Europe. The plastics industry has also been introduced to the Forest of Dean in recent times but, though plastic sheet is used for the manufacture of special garments by the Allen Rubber Company at Lydney, the two principal manufacturers of general plastic goods have their factories at Coleford and Cinderford. Away from these main centres of new and revived manufacturing activity, the largely rural town of Micheldean has seen the recent establishment of the remaining innovations: the manufacture of cameras, cine cameras, projectors and the Rank Xerox electrostatic copying equipment.

## THE SWINDON INDUSTRIAL AREA

Like the Stroud valley and the Forest of Dean, Swindon has suffered the disruption of its former principal industry, but in this case the change has been more recent and abrupt since it was only during the post-war period of railway reorganization that employment in the western region workshops was more than halved from its one-time peak of 12,000 and the town's effective dependence on a single industry brought to an end. However, other industrial organizations which had been relocated or had established branches in Swindon during the war wished to remain and this, reinforced by prompt appreciation of the provisions of the Town Development Act of 1952, largely minimized the blow to the town's economy and indeed led to very considerable diversification of its manufacturing activity. Overspill agreements were reached with authorities in the Greater London area and their effects on the population of Swindon have already been noted. Some of the new industrial undertakings were housed in the town itself and on the railway works estate, but most established themselves on three new industrial estates. By 1957 the Cheney Manor estate, alongside the railway to Gloucester, had been largely taken up and subsequently the Parsonage Farm and Green Bridge estates, to the east of the town on either side of the London line, have been almost fully developed.

Even though it no longer completely dominated the industrial scene and the type of work changed considerably, the British Rail locomotive carriage and wagon works remained an important engineering and vehicle building concern. Moreover, the fact that most of the new large undertakings in Swindon are engaged in metal-working and engineering activities has meant that from an employment point of view the change-over has been a relatively smooth one. During the war the Plessey organization began the manufacture of radio and other components in the town but post-war growth of its Swindon interests has resulted in eleven divisions of the Components group becoming established in the area, five of them on the Cheyney Manor estate and others on railway land. In 1960 Plessey took over the Swindon works of the Garrard Engineering Company, which makes sound reproduction equipment, and in 1965 acquired the capacitor-manufacturing Telegraph Condensor Company. The output of these two concerns is still maintained in addition to the production of machined parts, hydraulic mechanisms and

343

electrical components by other local divisions. Despite the diminished importance of the railway workshops, the industrial group concerned with the manufacture of vehicles is still of the greatest importance in Swindon, since the car body unit plant of the Pressed Steel Fisher Company on the Parsonage Farm estate has now the largest industrial labour force in the district. Nearby the Deloro-Stellite Company, which moved to Swindon from the Birmingham area in 1961, is mainly concerned with the manufacture of stellite, a cobalt-chromium-tungsten metal-cutting alloy, though it too has direct links with the transport industry since this product is also used in gas and steam turbine blades, engine-room steam valves and valve facings for motor engines. A little further to the east of the town at South Marston, the Vickers factory carries out research and prototype development for aeronautical, hydraulic and other work of the engineering group. Elsewhere in the Swindon district the engineering activities of individual firms range from general heavy milling, gear cutting and the building of stationary engines to pattern and tool making and light engineering on the newer estates. In addition to several firms engaged in the manufacture of light electrical components, including one specializing in semi-conductors, two other large firms have introduced to the Swindon industrial estates specialized aspects of electrical engineering involving heavier types of component and equipment. Linton and Hirst make transformer cores and metal parts from electrical steel and ferro-alloys and the Square D Company makes almost all types of electrical control equipment.

Though on a smaller scale than the engineering groups, other forms of manufacturing industry in Swindon have particular importance as sources of employment for women. A number of clothing firms in the town itself include one which has specialized in the manufacture of uniforms, especially for the transport industry, and, in addition to long-established bacon-curing and other food industries, a large food-casing and sausage-skin factory has recently been opened by the Oppenheimer Company on the Green Bridge estate. The manufacture of doors, furniture frames and packing cases is an instance of timber-using activities which have moved to the industrial estates, where the development of packaging is also being carried out by the Metal Box and Sharko-Metal Box companies, who form part of a group of concerns on the Cheyney Manor estate, which make or use plastic goods. Clover Leaf (Products), which manufactures table mats, trays and household goods, is an example of a firm which moved from London to Swindon in 1955.

Although properly described as an industrial town, Swindon's position makes it also an important service centre for much of north Wiltshire and Berkshire and there is some evidence that its commercial functions may grow. The establishment of a depot by the Heinz Company suggests that Swindon might well serve as a distribution centre for much of west and west-central England, especially as it has good links with the M4 motorway, whilst the decision of W. H. Smith and Son to move their offices and depot from London to the Green Bridge estate in Swindon has similar implications.

Although the main reorientation of Swindon's economy belongs to the immediate post-war period, growth has been maintained and the recent announcement that the Union Carbide organization will establish a plant in the area indicates that it may continue. At the present time Swindon is essentially a Wiltshire industrial town whose special economic history in the late nineteenth century and recent involvement in the dispersal of population and industry from London sets it somewhat apart from the rest. Whether or not it will remain appropriate to regard this district as part of the Bristol region must depend largely on long-term planning decisions. If the movement of industrial and commercial undertakings were to continue, possibly on an increasing scale, the links with the metropolis might become the area's most characteristic feature and this would almost certainly be the case if recent proposals for planned urban and industrial development eastwards from Swindon towards the Thames valley were to be adopted.

## The Relationships of Industry in the Bristol Region

Even when the mainly industrial areas have been considered, it remains true to say that there are still everywhere traces of the pattern of small undertakings and diversity of production which characterized the region at the beginning of the present century. However, in recent decades the national trend towards industrial linkage and amalgamations into large industrial groups has been very much in evidence in this part of the country. This has been most marked in the widespread aerospace industry, with its practice of sub-contracting and associated manufacture of components and instruments, but it is also tending to become characteristic of the hydraulics industries of Gloucester–Cheltenham and Swindon, of the electronic and related industries, of the manufacture of packaging materials and paper products and of the food-processing industries. In consequence the patterns of manufacturing throughout the region, though still remarkable for their diversity, are apparently in the process of simplification to a point where it may become reasonable to describe these five types of activity as the region's staple group of industries.

This increasing importance of industrial association and of control by large undertakings or groups makes it more and more difficult to

**345**

postulate for industry simple geographical space relations in terms of input-output analyses, since group or company organization and policy is commonly the determinant particularly of the semi-manufactured input or output of individual plants. Indeed it is only in the case of industries whose input includes a considerable proportion of true raw materials that simple relationships exist, where these materials are available locally or are imported through Avonmouth or the smaller ports.

Local raw materials clearly dominate the input of those food-processing industries concerned with milk products and the same is true to a large extent of the bacon-curing and meat products industry, but milling and cereal manufacturers are much more dependent on foreign grains. Port orientation also characterizes the manufacture of non-ferrous metals, chemicals, paper, board and timber products which use heavy or bulky imported raw or only slightly processed materials, while other industries, including the manufacture of tobacco and chocolate, maintain traditional links with Bristol imports, though their raw materials are neither bulky nor heavy.

For most other industries in the Bristol region, input is mainly of semi-manufactured materials and a survey conducted by Britton (1967) revealed that a little less than half of this was drawn from sources within the region. In some cases this intra-regional linkage is of considerable importance and this is illustrated in the manufacture of paper products and packaging materials, which on the one hand consumes a major part of the region's output of paper, board, cellophane and plastic film, and on the other hand relies to a considerable extent on markets provided by the local tobacco and food industries. The other two main sources of semi-manufactured input are the Midlands and the London area, the former supplying the engineering, electrical engineering and chemical industries and the latter the clothing and footwear, furniture and food industries. In many cases this represents the result of supply arrangements within individual companies or groups and the same is clearly true of the smaller input of textile materials from the north which was largely in the form of nylon polymer chip supplied to the Gloucester spinning factory from the company's chemical plant on Tees-side.

The output relationships of industry in the Bristol region are even less easily defined since many of its products are destined for national and international markets. This is evidently true of the aerospace industry not only for complete aircraft and missiles but also for instruments, engines and other components, whilst it is almost equally true of the fully and semi-manufactured products of other engineering, electrical engineering and electronic industries. Similarly rubber manufactures, whether of gloves, tyres or transport components, have world-wide markets, though a fairly high proportion of the output of tyres and components is shipped initially to the various centres of the British motor vehicle industry or through the London export market. Those industries which are exclusively concerned with the production of semi-manufactured materials have somewhat clearer output relationships. Most of the nylon yarn is sent to the Midlands or the northern textile areas, though this is partly because of the parent company's distribution policy, whilst non-ferrous metals are supplied mainly to users in the Bristol region, in the London area and in the Midlands and north. From the chemical industry, semi-manufactured materials are sent to the Midlands and north because of the manufacturing organization of the principal company involved, but fully manufactured products have a national or international distribution except in the case of fertilizers whose output, like that of animal feeding stuffs, is aimed mainly at supplying consumers in the Bristol region itself, the southwest peninsula and South Wales. Other manufactured consumer goods have a wider distribution: processed human foods are supplied to the London area and to the Midlands as well as to the Bristol region, whilst clothing, footwear and furniture have a nationwide distribution which tends, however, to be dominated by the London market, particularly in the case of furniture.

The closest inter-regional links shown in both industrial input and output are therefore with the London area and with the Midlands, so that rapid economic growth in the Bristol region has even been interpreted as a westward spill of industrial activity from the prosperous London–west Midland–Merseyside axis. Better road connection by the Severn bridge is clearly leading to somewhat closer commercial relationships with South Wales but no evidence is yet available to suggest that industrial linkages have been materially changed. Unless there are important developments in the economy of the southwest peninsula it seems likely that here too there will be little change in its connection with the Bristol region which may continue to depend mainly on the supply of fertilizers and processed imports like animal feeding stuffs.

### The Role of the Port

The foregoing review of industrial relationships has suggested that the main function of the port of Bristol has been the supply of a small group of heavy or bulky commodities and this conclusion is borne out by the trade figures of the port. In 1968, when just over 4 million tons of cargo arrived from foreign ports, individual items accounted for the approximate percentages of the total shown in Table 24.

**347**

TABLE 24

PORT OF BRISTOL 1968

| COMMODITY | APPROXIMATE %S OF TOTAL FOREIGN IMPORTS, BY WEIGHT |
|---|---|
| Grains | 21·0 |
| Petroleum | 19·0 |
| Fertilizer materials | 13·5 |
| Animal feeding stuffs | 13·0 |
| Metal ores | 6·5 |
| Metals | 3·8 |
| Timber | 3·5 |
| Wood pulp | 3·0 |
| Molasses (animal feed) | 3·0 |
| Provisions | 1·5 |
| Chemicals | 1·3 |
| Asbestos | 1·3 |
| Others | 10·0 |

Whereas much smaller items among the other imports, such as tobacco, cocoa and wines, have a value and importance disproportionate to the tonnage involved, it remains true that the shipment of petroleum, grains (mostly maize and wheat), feeding stuffs and fertilizer materials accounted for nearly two-thirds of the port's overseas trade. Ores, metals, timber, pulp and molasses amount to almost a further 20 per cent, making a total of over 85 per cent of foreign imports. Moreover, only a very small part of Avonmouth's petroleum imports arrive direct from foreign ports and in most recent years about $2\frac{1}{4}$ million tons of oil products have been landed from British refineries, thus making up rather more than half of Bristol's 4-million-ton coastwise trade. Clearly such imports represent an exceptional element in this trade and since they are essentially indirect shipments from overseas their addition to the foreign trade would give a clearer picture of Avonmouth's function as an oil port and of its specialization in handling a group of bulky or heavy commodities. When this is done for 1968, the total of foreign imports and coastwise petroleum imports is just over $6\frac{1}{4}$ million tons and the approximate percentages for each commodity are then as shown in Table 25.

On this basis the share of the total taken up by petroleum, grains, animal feeding stuffs and fertilizer materials rises to 78 per cent and with ores, metals, timber, pulp and molasses to over 90 per cent. When it is remembered that foreign exports in 1968 amounted to only a little over 200,000 tons, or 5 per cent of the total overseas trade, it becomes clear that in terms of tonnage the effective function of the port is the handling of this group of imported foodstuffs, fuels and raw materials.

By far the greater part of the trade is made up of cargoes landed at

TABLE 25

PORT OF BRISTOL 1968

| COMMODITY | APPROXIMATE %S OF COMBINED FOREIGN IMPORTS AND COASTWISE PETROLEUM IMPORTS, BY WEIGHT |
|---|---|
| Petroleum | 48·0 |
| Grains | 13·0 |
| Fertilizer materials | 8·5 |
| Animal feeding stuffs | 8·5 |
| Metal ores | 4·0 |
| Metals | 2·5 |
| Timber | 2·0 |
| Wood pulp | 2·0 |
| Molasses | 2·0 |
| Provisions | 1·0 |
| Others | 9·0 |

Avonmouth and the continuation of present trends is likely to accentuate this concentration. Traffic on the Severn waterway is now principally concerned with the coastwise trade in grain, timber, metals and general cargoes. The overseas trade at Sharpness, though prosperous, is still on a very small scale, whilst the ports of the Somerset and Devon coast, with the exception of Watchet where some revival has taken place, are unlikely to increase their trade and within the next ten years the Bristol city docks are scheduled for closure to commercial traffic. The future of the Bristol region's sea-borne trade and communications is therefore likely to depend on the development of facilities in the Avonmouth area. In general terms such developments might be expected to meet and anticipate the consequences of changes in shipping, particularly the growing size of bulk carriers and the increasing importance of container traffic. Since the present Avonmouth docks have commonly been working at full capacity in recent years, and because the surrounding industrial, commercial and transport installations make further extension of dock space problematical, the construction of a completely new deep-water port in the immediate vicinity appeared to be desirable. Accordingly the 1963–4 Portbury plan of the Port of Bristol Authority envisaged the building of such a port to the west of the Avon between the mouth of the river and Portishead but, despite a favourable report from the National Ports Council, several years of deliberation ended without government permission to proceed with the plan. Subsequently, a more modest West Dock scheme was proposed for the same locality but it too failed to obtain the necessary approval of the government. In consequence it has only been possible to undertake modernization and development schemes within the setting provided by the present dock lay-out, though plans have been completed for still another West Dock proposal. With the ending of direct government grants to aid such schemes, however, the whole of the capital will have to be raised by the Port of Bristol Authority and it is therefore uncertain how completely and how soon the need for more deep water berths in the port can be met.

Though the circumstances underlying decisions about the Portbury and the original West Dock proposals were no doubt complex, it seems clear that the present trade imbalance of the port of Bristol was a major consideration. The suggested inadequate profitability of such capital investment appears to have been based on the assumption that the trade of the new port would be on the same lines as that of Avonmouth and that the imbalance would continue. However, the authors of the schemes based a presumption of profitability on the expectation that good deep water berths would attract not only increased imports but also an expanding export trade, once additional shipping lines used the port and more particularly once the exceptionally good motorway connections of the new port were completed. When the Portbury proposals were under consideration, it was by no means clear by what date the motorway system in the west of England would be completed, but this uncertainty has now disappeared, at least as far as the Bristol region is concerned; even the 'spine' road towards the southwest peninsula, advocated by the South West Economic Planning Council, will soon be under construction. This being the case a dock system in the Portbury area would now enjoy the unique advantage of totally unobstructed access to the motorways within a few hundred yards of the quayside and supporters of port development plans are of the opinion that this could attract both export and import cargoes if, as a new port, it were designed with the needs of bulk carriers, unitized and containerized cargoes, and present-day inland transport in mind. Nevertheless the authors of the Severnside Report appear still to base their assessment of port facilities in the area on the assumption that the pattern of trade at Avonmouth, and indeed in the Severn estuary generally, is a permanent one unlikely to be significantly affected by the transport revolution which is accompanying the completion of the country's motorway network. They also seem to discount the direct effects likely to arise from the provision of a really modern deep-water port and offer little encouragement for planning its creation, since they appear to feel that there is little need for further port capacity on the Severn estuary which, though well situated for trade with the rest of the world, would not be conveniently located for trade with the larger ports of northwest Europe.

In the meantime modernization has been undertaken by the re-design of facilities in the oil basin, by the reconstruction of quaysides and sheds round the rest of the Royal Edward Dock, by the provision of special cranes and side-loaders for handling unitized, containerized and other special forms of cargo and by the construction of a large inland clearance depot suitable for the newer systems of commodity stowage as well as for general cargoes. Advantages arising from the completion of the motorway links and the opening of a freightliner terminal at Avonmouth were no doubt foreseen and help explain recent rapid growth of warehousing and distribution facilities on the dock estates and on the new Avonmouth trading estate. Moreover, they will enhance the value of industrial sites on Severnside, for such undertakings as the pharmaceutical plant which is being added to the I.C.I. works, and at Porthishead, where a £250,000 wood pulp terminal has been built for the St Annes Board Mills, possibly in anticipation of the closure of the city docks. Nevertheless any considerable expansion of Bristol's overseas trade must ultimately depend on the provision of new deep-water berths and on the attraction of container traffic and these, in turn, must depend on the future planning of the whole of Severnside's sea-borne trade.

### Planning the Future

The overall impression to be gained from a study of present-day conditions is one of reasonable prosperity throughout the Bristol region, with recent exceptionally rapid economic growth in such localities as Severnside and Gloucester–Cheltenham more than compensating for the absence of marked growth in one or two rural areas like Cotswold and west Somerset. In looking to the future, however, consideration must be given to the possible effects of government policy in seeking a balance between the maintenance of economic momentum in prosperous areas and some redistribution of economic growth on social or other grounds. Moreover, the existence of such a problem is particularly evident in southwestern Britain since the prosperous Bristol region is adjoined by areas in the southwest peninsula and South Wales where some measure of government economic assistance has been thought necessary. Control over the issue of industrial development certificates and financial inducements created by the establishment of development areas are means by which redistribution of economic growth has been attempted and there is evidence of possible effects of such measures on the Bristol region. Thus, in the southwest development area, new factory space, measured in terms of 1965 employment in manufacturing industry, was created at nearly double the rate for the country as a whole, whereas in the Bristol–Severnside district the figure was slightly

351

below the national average. To some extent this may have been due to a pause whilst industry availed itself of productive capacity created by massive capital investment in the Severnside area in the post-war period, but nevertheless even a temporary decline in the rate of investment is significant and some Severnside projects are known to have been abandoned in favour of location in development areas. The effects of competition from such areas are likely to be most marked in cases where very costly projects are planned by large industrial groups whose nationwide organization is capable of incorporating alternative locations for new plant, and it is precisely this kind of development which might have been anticipated in the Severnside district. An obvious exception will arise where technological advantages may accrue from planning innovations or added capacity for an existing integrated heavy industrial plant, and considerations of this kind probably account for the fact that in the recent past the most important investment in the Severnside area has taken place at the works of the Imperial Smelting Corporation and of Imperial Chemical Industries.

Apart from general problems associated with the allocation of nationally planned economic growth, the future of the Bristol region also involves governmental decisions on more specialized issues which include the utilization of the country's estuarine areas, the related development of districts studied under the Maritime Industrial Development Areas (MIDAS) scheme, the evolution of a comprehensive national ports policy and the creation of additional international airports.

It is clearly inevitable that the future of the Bristol region, like that of any other part of the United Kingdom, must depend heavily on government policy, no doubt influenced in local contexts by the advice of the planning councils and planning authorities. However, the report of the South West Economic Planning Council only serves to re-emphasize a fundamental national planning dilemma. Whilst obviously urging the continuation and extension of development area status for parts of the southwest, the report appears to assume that natural economic growth will be allowed to continue in those parts of the planning area which form the Bristol region. Indeed the strategy suggested in the report appears to be based on projected economic and demographic growth rates for the Bristol region and the consequent need to envisage planned control of developments in the Gloucester–Cheltenham district, overall schemes for an enlarged Bristol–Bath area in addition to town developments at Thornbury, Yate and Nailsea, and the encouragement of continued growth in and around Swindon. While these are probably reasonable planning requirements, the report also comments on wider issues that might well invalidate estimates of the region's future on which they are based. It suggests that the country cannot afford to waste opportunities which will be created by the completion of the motorway network and it seems to assume that even greater growth of industry and population should therefore be planned within the region, since it apparently regarded the proper function of the Severnside study to be the selection of localities for such developments rather than an assessment of their desirability.

Like the report of the South West Economic Planning Council, that published as the outcome of the Severnside study appears to start with the reasoned assumption that, during the remainder of the present century, Severnside will see considerable natural economic growth accompanied by an increasing population unless some kind of restriction is imposed upon it. Since the authors of the report see no economic reason to recommend such constraints and since they investigated the possibility of an even more rapid rate of growth if this were positively stimulated by government policy, future planning in the area was largely studied against a background which presupposed a strongly expanding economy and a growing population. However, this was essentially a feasibility study and it is stressed that government decisions to encourage further development of Severnside would be needed in the 1970s if the report's higher estimates of growth by the end of the century were to be realized. It seems equally clear, however, that government policies which actively encouraged investment elsewhere could be just as effective in retarding expansion on Severnside as measures specifically designed for that purpose. That the report refers to possible capital intensive industrial areas to the north of Avonmouth and to the east of Newport (beyond the limits of the Bristol region) is significant because it is precisely this type of development which is most likely to be diverted elsewhere by incentive policies which attract industries to development areas. Thus, though the report expresses the belief that deliberate stimulation of growth on Severnside is a possibility which should be given very careful attention, decisions obviously still rest with the government and must still depend on any general policy for regional economic growth which the government may choose to adopt.

The area covered by the Severnside report includes north Somerset, Gloucestershire, the eastern parts of Monmouthshire and a small area round Ross-on-Wye in Herefordshire. It thus corresponds with the northern part of the Bristol region, though excluding northwest Wiltshire and Swindon and including important areas west of the Wye. The population of Severnside, so defined, was 1,700,000 in 1968 and it was felt that this figure could be doubled during the next thirty years

353

without creating insoluble problems of cost or planning. This would no doubt have involved using many of the 14 sites which were regarded as suitable for major development, in some cases into centres with a population of 250,000, but it is not expected that overall growth will approach such a maximum and so it has not been thought necessary to propose the establishment of large new growth centres. It was estimated that without active government intervention economic growth might lead to an increase in population of 450,000 by 1991 and of 650,000 by 2001. On the other hand much of the planning strategy outlined in the report is based on the calculation that with suitable government stimulation of the Severnside economy the population increase might well be 600,000 by 1991 and about 1,000,000 by 2001.

Some part of this development of Severnside in the next thirty years would be centred in the Monmouthshire–Ross area but within the Bristol region growth might be concentrated near Bristol and Gloucester. The main objective for such a pattern is to create 'three well defined sub-regions (Monmouth–Ross, North Gloucestershire and Bristol–Bath) each with its own major centre of industrial growth and able to reap the benefits of large urban areas.' In the Bristol–Bath sub-region it is suggested that an extra 450,000 people could be accommodated by the end of the century if the Bristol urban area itself were greatly enlarged in the Frampton Cotterell district on the northern side of the city. Provided that local authorities also proceeded with developments such as those already planned at Thornbury, Yate and Nailsea and some further growth occurred at Weston-super-Mare, the population of the sub-region could even increase by as much as 500,000 in this period, whilst the corresponding increase which might be envisaged in the North Gloucestershire sub-region is said to be about 400,000.

The possibility, considered seriously in the Severnside report, that the government might actively encourage exceptionally rapid economic growth rates on Severnside, and not merely allow recent trends to continue, would therefore pose serious problems in planning the accommodation of nearly 1,000,000 extra people in the northern part of the Bristol region during the next thirty years if growth also continued in Swindon and in northwest Wiltshire. In spite of the magnitude of the problems, however, the authors of the Severnside report propose that no additions should be made to the major growth centres of the area, since all their potential development areas are clustered near the existing urban-industrial areas of Bristol–Severnside, Gloucester–Cheltenham and Newport–Pontypool in each of which there has already been considerable recent economic growth. Indeed recommendations in this report, together with proposals elsewhere for development of the Swindon area, suggest that future economic growth and large increases in population in the Bristol region will be very highly concentrated in and around its three existing major industrial areas.

Two main motives for the suggestion that future development on Severnside should be concentrated in this way appear to be largely complementary. On the one hand it is intended to ensure that no individual centre is likely to become excessively large. On the other hand it is thought that growth in the three main centres would be sufficient to render unnecessary a scatter of smaller developments elsewhere which might endanger areas of attractive countryside, use up good quality agricultural land, or prejudice the conservation of beautiful and historic towns and villages. It is therefore suggested that excessive growth should not be encouraged in planning developments at such centres as Thornbury and Nailsea but the report does not rule out some growth of existing medium sized towns. Thus development might be planned near the smaller industrial region of the Stroud valley towns and Stonehouse on the relatively level ground across the river towards Coaley, and some growth of the west Wiltshire towns seems to be implied in the view that growth near Bath could well be diverted in that direction in the fairly near future.

Schemes which involve expansion near the region's largest urban areas could clearly present some challenge to the Green Belt concept of town planning, and many of the proposals which are examined in detail in the Severnside report are of great interest because they seek to make urban growth compatible with conservation. The problem is perhaps most acute in the case of the Bristol–Bath sub-region where strong reasons have been advanced for prohibiting further growth of Bristol in almost every direction. To the southwest and south the attractive countryside round the Avon gorge and in north Somerset is regarded as an asset which should not be sacrificed, whilst to the southeast it was felt that Bath should be protected from excessive growth and that the Green Belt between Bristol and Bath should be retained. To the east of Bristol massive nineteenth century industrial and residential building has left such a legacy of planning and transport problems that to propose further urban growth on any considerable scale in the near future might seem unreasonable. The authors of the report regard much of the land to the northwest of the city as unattractive for residential and urban development, especially as a good deal of industrial development has already taken place to the north of Avonmouth. They therefore urge that no urban growth should be allowed in the area to the west of the M5 motorway and to the south of the M4 motorway, and it is here that

355

some 6,500 acres have been identified as suitable for capital intensive industry.

There remain, therefore, only districts to the north and northeast of the city where it was felt that considerable growth could well be planned. Much of the land is in the valley of the Frome where greatly improved drainage would be needed, but it is suggested that the early stages of development could take place to the east of the valley near the villages of Frampton Cotterell and Winterbourne. About 18,000 acres could apparently be used so that, assuming a population of 18 per acre, nearly 330,000 people could be accommodated. Apart from drainage difficulties the most serious practical problems of such a scheme are likely to be in the field of communications since it might be necessary, for example, to reorientate much of Bristol's public transport system to match a move in the city's effective centre of gravity. However, the new development would give to the whole of the Bristol urban area a much more symmetrical shape athwart the M4 motorway from which actual advantages could accrue, particularly if the suggestion were adopted to construct, at an early stage, through the northern area, urban motorways comparable with the Parkway which links the centre of the present city with the M4. Moreover the Severn tunnel direct railway line crosses the southern part of the proposed area of development close to the M4 motorway and the new out-of-town station at Stoke Gifford would be almost ideally situated near to the geometrical centre of the enlarged city and at a potential focus of urban motorways converging on the M4 some three miles from the M4/M5 interchange at Almondsbury.

Most of the practical problems associated with the Frampton Cotterell development are thus probably capable of highly satisfactory solution and the merits of the scheme seem more likely to be debated on other grounds. The changes which would be necessitated in the Bristol Green Belt have been described as 'a realignment' but critics of the proposals could well regard this as something of an understatement. At present the high ground of Pur Down brings a wedge of almost completely open countryside from the Green Belt to within two miles of the heart of the city. It is true that the word 'realignment' does describe the process whereby the proposed developments would effectively isolate the tip of this wedge and create a more normally shaped Green Belt round the northern perimeter of the enlarged urban area, but it hardly suggests the block of countryside which would be lost in the process. Presumably the new and realigned Green Belt further north would remain inviolate, however, if future planners found the scenery of central Gloucestershire as attractive as the authors of the Severnside report now find the Green Belt in north Somerset.

356

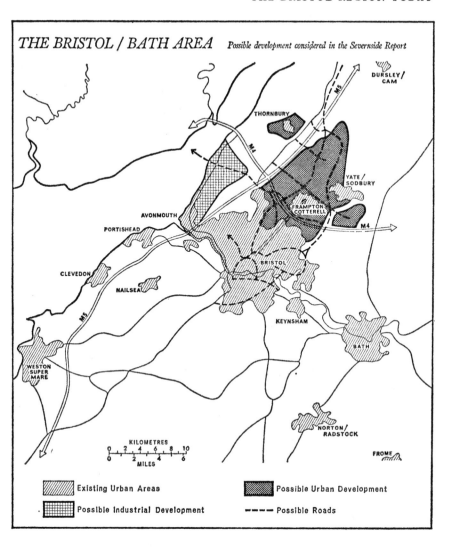

*THE BRISTOL / BATH AREA*   *Possible development considered in the Severnside Report*

DURSLEY / CAM

THORNBURY

M5

M4

YATE / SODBURY

AVONMOUTH

FRAMPTON COTTERELL

M4

PORTISHEAD

CLEVEDON

NAILSEA

BRISTOL

M5

KEYNSHAM

BATH

WESTON SUPER MARE

KILOMETRES
0   2   4   6   8   10
0     2     4     6
MILES

NORTON / RADSTOCK

FROME

Existing Urban Areas

Possible Urban Development

Possible Industrial Development

Possible Roads

357

Criticism could also be levelled at the scheme on the grounds that a fairly rapid increase of 330,000 in the population of Bristol could lead to dangers which the report suggests may accompany excessive size. It is true that Bristol would still not be an exceptionally large city, but in proportion to its present population of 425,000 and in terms of existing facilities the increase would be a vast one and transport is by no means the only urban system which would have to be adapted to meet the new situation. Moreover, though northward extension has the attraction that it would fill a gap and render the eventual shape of the whole urban area more compact, it has the disadvantage that it represents growth even further away from the heart of an already asymmetrical city whose original centre, or rather centres, lie near to its southwestern side. If the potential development area were fully utilized, new urban residential districts would be at distances of 5 to 12 miles from the present downtown shopping area, from the core of the central business district and from the cultural and entertainment centres of the city. While a major shopping development in the Iron Acton–Rangeworthy district could obviate many journeys a good deal of travel would have to be undertaken for purposes other than shopping if newcomers were to participate fully in the life of the Bristol community.

Urban motorways, it is true, could reduce actual travel time across the city to a matter of minutes. It is unfortunately equally true that excellent access to the M4 and M5 motorways would make it possible for many residents in the new parts of Bristol to become, in effect, citizens of whatever community offered them the largest, cheapest and most accessible parking areas around the most comprehensive shopping plazas and entertainment centres; and from the new railway station at Stoke Gifford the attractions of London may soon be little more than an hour away.

In the North Gloucestershire sub-region it is suggested that further growth between Gloucester and Cheltenham should be restricted for reasons comparable with those which led to the recommendation that the Green Belt should be preserved between Bristol and Bath, and the view is taken that Cheltenham, like Bath, should be protected from major growth. Instead it is envisaged that initial development should take place north-northeastward from Gloucester in the direction of Down Hatherley, but that subsequent growth centres should be to the west of the Severn. These would take the form of two new towns, one 7 miles west of Gloucester near Huntley and the other 8 miles north of the city near Staunton. Thus, based on the Gloucester–Cheltenham industrial area, there would be four urban areas kept separate by Green Belts and developed as independent communities. No specific proposals are made for major growth centres directly associated with the smaller industrial region of the Forest of Dean but the towns at Huntley and Staunton and the long-term proposal for town development at Dymock, 12 miles northwest of Gloucester near the M50 Ross spur, would no doubt offer many opportunities for daily travel or for local migration like that which has already taken place from the Forest of Dean to the Gloucester–Cheltenham area; outside the Bristol region similar opportunities would arise from developments in the Monmouthshire–Ross sub-region.

While suggesting that by the end of the century about 9 per cent of the expected population increase throughout the country might therefore be finding accommodation on Severnside, at an important node of the national communications pattern, the authors of the report nevertheless offer little encouragement for the idea that far-reaching revolutionary changes in the use of the Severn estuary and its surroundings will be in sight during the next twenty or thirty years. Thus, though it is foreseen that traffic on the M4–Severn bridge route might necessitate the creation of an additional Severn road crossing, it is clearly not thought feasible that in the period under review this might be provided by the construction of a barrage or barrages which could also be used for water storage, electricity generation and the improvement of navigation. Similarly, though possible plans for an international airport on reclaimed land in the estuary are reviewed and links suggested with MIDAS schemes for a new deep-water port and industrial development which could involve additional population growth in excess of 200,000, it is again felt to be unlikely that such projects will be undertaken in the period covered by the terms of reference for the Severnside study.

No doubt the formulation of a national policy for the development of Britain's estuarine areas does lie far in the future and the possibility of establishing other international airports following the development of Foulness may be even more remote. Moreover decisions on these issues must eventually be taken by the government of the day and the Severnside study group could, at best, only ensure that programmes which they proposed for the next thirty years would not stand in the way of any more imaginative schemes which might one day find favour with the government. Nevertheless it is disappointing that such an important piece of research must lead to the conclusion that safe and relatively uncontroversial development of the region round the Severn estuary is all that can be foreseen in the present century, especially as even these proposals depend on wholly unpredictable government attitudes towards the deliberate stimulation of growth in an already prosperous area.

359

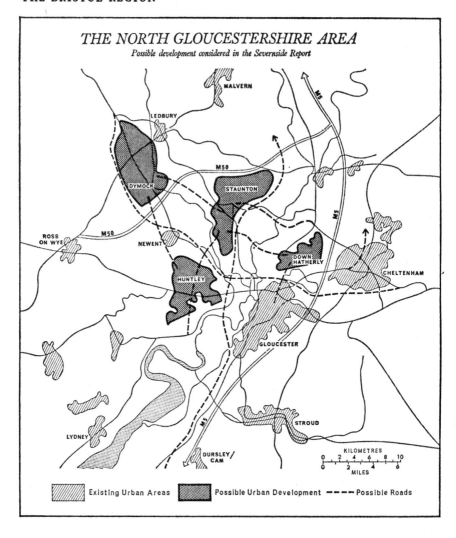

## THE NORTH GLOUCESTERSHIRE AREA
*Possible development considered in the Severnside Report*

Existing Urban Areas    Possible Urban Development    - - - - Possible Roads

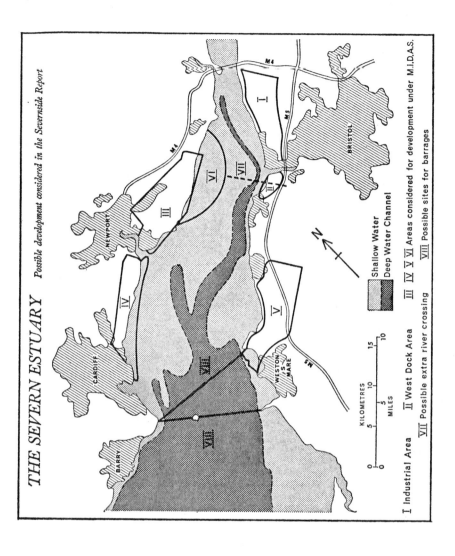

## THE SEVERN ESTUARY
*Possible development considered in the Severnside Report*

BRISTOL

NEWPORT

CARDIFF

BARRY

WESTON S/ MARE

M4

M5

M4

M4

M5

I

II

III

IV

V

VI

VII

VIII

KILOMETRES
MILES

0  5  10  15
0  5  10

N

I Industrial Area

II West Dock Area
VII Possible extra river crossing

Shallow Water
Deep Water Channel

III IV V VI Areas considered for development under M.I.D.A.S.

VIII Possible sites for barrages

Whilst the main outlines of the region's long-term development may thus be largely determined by the policy of the central government, physical planning under present and proposed future legislation remains the responsibility of planning authorities linked with the system of local government areas. It is therefore of considerable interest that the 1969 report of the commission on local government recommended a pattern of areas in the west of England which had great relevance to planning requirements. The suggested South Western Province almost coincided with the existing South West Planning Region and would therefore have combined the Bristol region with totally dissimilar areas on the south coast and in the southwest peninsula. Within the Bristol region, however, quite drastic changes were suggested to create four new operational areas whose geographical character and economy might have made them appropriate units for planning purposes. The Gloucester–Cheltenham industrial district would have formed the core of the new North Gloucestershire unit, which would also have included related areas round Stroud and Dursley and in the Forest of Dean. To the south, a Bristol–Bath operational area would have taken in considerable parts of the surrounding counties to include Thornbury, Yate, Chipping Sodbury, Kingswood, Mangotsfield, and Warmley in Gloucestershire; Chippenham, Melksham, Bradford-on-Avon, and Trowbridge in Wiltshire; and Frome, Weston-super-Mare, and Clevedon in Somerset, thereby incorporating virtually all the urban and industrial areas in the central part of the Bristol region. The two remaining operational areas corresponded with the residual parts of Somerset and Wiltshire, both extended slightly to include in the former the Dorset town of Sherborne and in the latter five Berkshire parishes to the east of the town of Swindon.

The 1969 scheme was replaced in February 1971 by proposals in the White Paper on local government areas which no longer include the establishment of a South Western Province linking the Bristol region with the southwest peninsula and Dorset. Instead, most of the Bristol region would be covered by Areas 25, 26, and 27, which, together, correspond with the counties of Somerset and Gloucestershire, whilst the western part of Area 28 includes the Wiltshire districts which form the remainder of the Bristol region. The proposed Area 26, subsequently given the name Avon, is created by the amalgamation of the city and county of Bristol and the city of Bath with areas of Somerset as far south as Mendip and of Gloucestershire as far north as the rural districts of Thornbury and Sodbury. This Area therefore corresponds with the Bristol–Bath sub-region of the Severnside report and Area 27 corresponds with its sub-region of North Gloucestershire. If the sub-regions suggested in the Severnside report were to be adopted as the basis for future overall planning strategy it would clearly be advantageous if they thus coincided with areas controlled by local government authorities charged with many of the planning responsibilities. Apart from the fact that the transfer of the Sherborne district from Dorset to Somerset is no longer proposed, the residual part of Somerset (Area 25) is identical with the operational area of Somerset in the 1969 scheme. In west Wiltshire, however, there are important changes since it is no longer proposed that the towns of Chippenham, Melksham, Trowbridge, and Bradford-on-Avon should become part of the Bristol–Bath operational area (or Area 26 of the new terminology). Instead they would remain in Wiltshire (Area 28) and, like the Swindon industrial area, would have no closer administrative links than at present with the rest of the Bristol region.

Resilience in the past and an habitual climate of ebullient prosperity may suggest that continued economic success and growth in the Bristol region may be assumed, but the means by which they will be maintained and the degree to which they will develop are less clear. Even the briefest glimpse of future planning problems reveals the extent to which the region's well-being is likely to depend on conclusions reached by a growing number of organizations, whose role appears to be to advise about the decisions which, in the end, will be taken only by the government of the day.

# REFERENCES

The following abbreviated forms are given for the journals listed:

| | |
|---|---|
| *Antiq. J.* | *The Antiquaries Journal* |
| *Arch. J.* | *The Archaeological Journal* |
| *BGAS.* | *The Transactions of the Bristol and Gloucestershire Archaeological Society* |
| *British Assn. Adv. Science.* | *The British Association for the Advancement of Science* |
| *Cotteswold* | *The Proceedings of the Cotteswold Naturalists' Field Club* |
| *EHR.* | *The English Historical Review* |
| *Econ. Geog.* | *Economic Geography* |
| *Econ. Hist. R.* | *The Economic History Review* |
| *Geog. J.* | *The Geographical Journal* |
| *Geol. Mag.* | *The Geological Magazine* |
| *Glast. Ant. Soc.* | *The Glastonbury Antiquarian Society* |
| *Hist. Assn. Bristol.* | *Published by the Bristol branch of the Historical Association* |
| *JRS.* | *Journal of Roman Studies* |
| *J. Roy. Agric. Soc.* | *Journal of the Royal Agricultural Society* |
| *PPS.* | *Proceedings of the Prehistoric Society* |
| *Phil. Trans. Roy. Soc.* | *The Royal Society. Philosophical Transactions* |
| *Proc. Bristol Nat. Soc.* | *Proceedings of the Bristol Naturalists' Society* |
| *Proc. Geol. Ass.* | *Proceedings of the Geologists' Association* |
| *Proc. Speleo. Soc.* | *Proceedings, University of Bristol Spelaeological Society* |
| *Quart. J. Geol. Soc. Lond.* | *Quarterly Journal of the Geological Society of London* |
| *Quart. J. Roy. Met. Soc.* | *Quarterly Journal of the Royal Meteorological Society* |
| *Som. Arch.* | *The Proceedings of the Somerset(shire) Archaeological and Natural History Society* |
| *Trans. IBG.* | *Transactions, The Institute of British Geographers* |
| *Trans. Roy. Hist. Soc.* | *Transactions of the Royal Historical Society* |
| *Wilts. Arch. Mag.* | *The Wiltshire Archaeological and Natural History Magazine* |

THE BRISTOL REGION SELECTED REFERENCES

THE STRUCTURAL BASIS

THE EVOLUTION OF THE LANDSCAPE

ApSimon, A. M., and Donovan, D. T. 'The stratigraphy and archaeology of the late-Glacial and post-Glacial deposits at Brean Down, Somerset'. *Proc. Speleo. Soc.*, **9** (1961), no. 2, 67–136

Arkell, W. J. *The Jurassic system of Great Britain* (Oxford 1933)

Beckinsale, P. R. 'Physical problems of the Cotswold rivers and valleys' *Cotteswold* **35** (1970), 194–105

Beckinsale, P. R. and Smith, K. W. 'Some morphological features of the valleys of the north Cotswolds: The Windrush and its tributaries' *Cotteswold* **31** (1953), 184–95

Bradshaw, R. 'The Avon Gorge' *Proc. Bristol Nat. Soc.* **31** (1966), (2), 203–20

Curtis, M. L. K., Donovan, D. T., Kellaway, G. A. and Welch, F. B. A. *Geology, in Bristol and its adjoining counties*. Ed. MacInnes, C. M. and Whittard, W. F. *British Assn. Adv. Science* (Bristol 1955)

Dewey, H. *British Regional Geology. South-west England*. 2nd Ed. Mem. Geol. Surv. (1948)

Donovan, D. T. 'Geomorphology and hydrology of the central Mendips, Somerset' *Proc. Speleo. Soc.* **12** (1969), no. 1, 63–74

Dury, G. H. 'Meanders of the Coln valley. A new interpretation' *Cotteswold* **31** (1953), 206–19

Gardiner, C. I. 'The making of the valley of the Stroud Frome and an account of its fluviatile deposits' *Cotteswold* **26** (1938), 265–97

Gardiner, C. I., Reynolds, S. H., Smith, S., Trueman, A. E. and Tutcher, J. W. 'The geology of the Gloucester district' *Proc. Geol. Ass.* **45** (1934), 110–44

Godwin, H. 'Studies in the post-Glacial history of British vegetation. VI Correlations in the Somerset levels' *New Phytologist* **40** (1941), 108–32

— 'The botanical and geological history of the Somerset levels' *Advancement of Science* London, **12** (1955), 47

Godwin, H. and Clapham, A. R. 'Studies in the post-Glacial history of British vegetation: VIII Swamping surfaces in Peats in the Somerset levels; IX Prehistoric trackways in the Somerset levels' *Phil. Trans. Roy. Soc.* Series B, **233** (1948), 233–74

Jones, O. T. 'Some episodes in the geological history of the Bristol Channel region' Presidential address, Section C. *British Assn. Adv. Science.* Report, 98th Meeting (Bristol 1930), 57–82

Kellaway, G. A. and Welch, F. B. A. *British Regional Geology. Bristol and Gloucester district.* 2nd Ed. Mem. Geol. Surv. (1948)

Large, N. F. 'Superficial deposits of the Stroud valley' *Cotteswold* **33** (1958), 192–7

Moore, L. R. and Trueman, A. E. 'The Coal Measures of Bristol and Somerset' *Quart. J. Geol. Soc. Lond.* **93** (1937), 195–240

— 'The structure of the Bristol and Somerset coalfield' *Proc. Geol. Ass.* **50** (1939), 46–67

North, F. J. *The evolution of the Bristol Channel with special reference to the coast of South Wales.* National Museum of Wales, Cardiff (1955)

Ollier, C. D. 'The Triassic sandstones of the Bristol region' *Proc. Bristol Nat. Soc.* **29** (1954), 57–70

Palmer, L. S. 'On the Pleistocene succession of the Bristol district' *Proc. Geol. Ass.* **42** (1931) 345–61

— 'Some Pleistocene breccias near the Severn estuary' *Proc. Geol. Ass.* **45** (1934), 145–61

Reynolds, S. H. 'The lithological succession of the Carboniferous Limestone (Avonian) of the Avon section at Clifton' *Quart. J. Geol. Soc. Lond.* **72** (1921), 23–42

Reynolds, S. H. and Greenly, E. 'The geological structure of the Clevedon-Portishead area' *Quart. J. Geol. Soc. Lond.* **80** (1924), 447–67

Sibley, T. F. 'The Carboniferous succession of the Forest of Dean coalfield' *Geol. Mag.* (5) **9** (1912), 417–22

— *Iron Ores. The haematites of the Forest of Dean and South Wales.* Mineral Res. Mem. Geol. Surv. **10** (1919)

Tratman, E. K. 'The hydrology of the Burrington area, Somerset' *Proc. Speleo. Soc.* **10** (1963), no. 1, 22–57

Tomlinson, M. E. 'Pleistocene gravels of the Cotswold sub-edge plain from Mickleton to the Frome valley' *Quart. J. Geol. Soc. Lond.* **96** (1941), 385–421

Trotter, F. M. *Geology of the Forest of Dean coal and iron-ore field.* Mem. Geol. Surv. (1942)

Trueman, A. E. 'Erosion levels in the Bristol district' *Proc. Bristol Nat. Soc.* **8** (1938), 402–28

Tutcher, J. W. and Trueman, A. E. 'The Liassic rocks of the Radstock district, Somerset' *Quart. J. Geol. Soc. Lond.* **81** (1925), 595–666

Welch, F. B. A. 'The geological structure of the central Mendips' *Quart. J. Geol. Soc. Lond.* **85** (1929), 45–76

— 'The geological structure of the eastern Mendips' *Quart. J. Geol. Soc. Lond.* **89** (1933), 14–52

Williams, M. *The drainage of the Somerset levels.* (Cambridge 1970)

Wills, L. J. 'The Pleistocene development of the Severn from Bridgnorth to the sea' *Quart. J. Geol. Soc. Lond.* **94** (1938), 161–242

— *The palaeogeography of the midlands.* 2nd Ed. Univ. of Liverpool (1950)

Wooldridge, S. W. 'The Radstock plateau—a note on the physiography of the Bristol district' *Proc. Bristol Nat. Soc.* **30** (1961), (2), 151–62

Wooldridge, S. W. and Linton, D. L. *Structure, surface and drainage in southeast England* (London 1955)

Yates, R. A. 'Erosion levels of the River Avon drainage basin. A comparative account of the various methods of cartographic analysis' *Thesis. Univ. of Bristol* (1950)

## THE SOILS, VEGETATION AND CLIMATE OF THE BRISTOL REGION SOILS

Avery, B. W. *The soils of the Glastonbury district of Somerset.* Mem. Soil Surv. HMSO (London 1955)

Bristol University. *Gloucestershire, Somerset and Wiltshire land classification.* Univ. of Bristol Reconstruction Research Group (1947), 17–29

Bulleid, A. and Jackson, J. W. 'The Burtle Sand Beds of Somerset' *Som. Arch.* **83** (1937), 171–95

Crampton, C. B. 'Genetic aspects of soils in the Forest of Dean' *Cotteswold* **35** (1970), 206–13

Findlay, D. C. *The soils of the Mendip district of Somerset.* Mem. Soil Surv. (Harpenden 1965)

Land Utilisation Survey of Britain. Reports. *The Land of Britain.* Parts 67 Gloucestershire (1942) 333–4, 86 Somerset (1938) 42–3, 87 Wiltshire (1940) 156–64. Geographical Publications (London 1938–42)

Orwin, C. S. *The reclamation of Exmoor Forest* (London 1929)

Osmond, D. A., Swarbrick, T., Thompson, C. R. and Wallace, T. 'A survey of the soils and fruit in the Vale of Evesham' *Bull. Min. Agr. Fish & Food.* No. 116 (London 1949)

Osmond, D. A. Soils of Gloucestershire, Somerset and Wiltshire, in *Bristol and its adjoining counties.* Ed. MacInnes, C. M. and Whittard, W. F. British Assn. Adv. Science (Bristol 1955)

## VEGETATION

Boley, G. M. 'The vegetation of Berrow, north Somerset. I. The salt marsh community' *Proc. Bristol Nat. Soc.* **9** (1942), 427–33

— 'The vegetation of Berrow, north Somerset. II. The sand dune succession' *Proc. Bristol Nat. Soc.* **9** (1943), 510–20

Heath, G. H., Luckwill, L. C. and Pullen, O. J. 'The heath association of Blackdown, Mendip hills' *Proc. Bristol Nat. Soc.* **3** (1937), 348–64

Hope-Simpson, J. F. and Willis, A. J. Vegetation, in *Bristol and its adjoining counties.* Ed. MacInnes, C. M. and Whittard, W. F. British Assn. Adv. Science. (Bristol 1955)

Hope-Simpson, J. F., Newton, S. E. and Ricketts, M. J. 'Plant communities on Shapwick Heath, Somerset' *Proc. Bristol Nat. Soc.* **30** (1963), 346–61

Jefferies, R. L., Willis, A. J. and Yemm, E. W. 'The late- and post-Glacial history of the Gordano valley, north Somerset' *New Phytologist* **67** (1968), 335–44

Land Utilization Survey, see above under 'Soils'

Moss, C. E. *The geographical distribution of vegetation in Somerset.* Royal Geographical Society (London 1907)

Tiley, G. E. D. 'The calcareous grasslands of the Carboniferous and Oolitic limestones of south-west England: a comparative study with special reference to edaphic conditions' *Thesis. Univ. of Bristol* (1955)

Willis, A. J. and Jefferies, R. L. 'The plant ecology of the Gordano valley' *Proc. Bristol Nat. Soc.* **29** (1959), 469–90

## CLIMATE

Hannell, F. G. Climate, in *Bristol and its adjoining counties.* Ed. MacInnes, C. M. and Whittard, W. F. British Assn. Adv. Science (Bristol 1955)

Land Utilization Survey of Britain. Reports. *The Land of Britain.* Parts 67 Gloucestershire 327–33, 86 Somerset 31–41, 87 Wiltshire 164–8. Geographical Publications (London 1938–42)

Meteorological Office. *Averages of temperature 1931–60* (London 1963)
Meteorological Office. *British Rainfall 1961*. HMSO (London 1967)
Penman, H. L. 'Evaporation over the British Isles' *Quart. J. Roy. Met. Soc.* **76** (1950), 372–83
Potential Transpiration. Technical Bulletin No. 16. Min. Agr. Fish. & Food (London 1967)

### THE PREHISTORIC OCCUPATION

Alcock, L. 'Excavation of South Cadbury Castle 1961' *Antiq. J.* **48** (1968), 6–17
Applebaum, S. 'The agriculture of the British early Iron Age as exemplified at Figheldean Down, Wiltshire' *PPS.* **20** (1954), 103–14
ApSimon, A. M. and Donovan, D. T. 'Marine Pleistocene deposits in the Vale of Gordano, Somerset' *Proc. Speleo. Soc.* **7** (1956), no. 3, 130–6
ApSimon, A. M., Rahtz, P. A. and Harris, L. G. 'The Iron Age. A ditch and pottery at Pagan's Hill, Chew Stoke' *Proc. Speleo. Soc.* **8** (1958), no. 2, 97–105
ApSimon, A. M., Donovan, D. T. and Taylor, H. 'The stratigraphy and archaeology of the late-Glacial and post-Glacial deposits of Brean Down, Somerset' *Proc. Speleo. Soc.* **9** (1961), no. 2, 67–136
Bellows, J. 'On some bronze and other articles found near Birdlip' *BGAS.* **5** (1881), 137–41
Berry, J. 'Belas Knap long barrow, Gloucestershire' *BGAS* **51** (1931), 273–304; **52**, (1932), 123–50
Bonney, N. J. 'Iron Age and Romano-British settlement sites in Wiltshire. Some geographical considerations' *Wilts. Arch. Mag.* **63** (1968), 27–38
Boon, C. 'Gorsey Bigbury. 2nd report' *Proc. Speleo. Soc.* **6** (1950), no. 2, 186–99
Bulleid, A. 'An ancient trackway in Meare Heath, Somerset' *Som. Arch.* **79** (1933), 19–29
— *The lake villages of Somerset*. Glast. Ant. Soc. 3rd Ed. (1938)
— 'Notes on some chambered long barrows of north Somerset' *Som. Arch.* **87** (1941), 56–71
Bulleid, A. and Gray, H. St. George. *The Glastonbury Lake Village*. Glast. Ant. Soc. (1911–17)
Burrow, E. J., Knowles, W. H., Paine, A. C. W. and Gray, J. W. 'Excavations on Leckhampton Hill, Cheltenham, 1925' *BGAS.* **47** (1925), 81–112
Childe, G. *The prehistoric communities of the British Isles* (London 1940)
Clark, J. G. D. 'A microlithic industry from the Cambridge fenland and other industries of sauveterrian affinities from Britain' *PPS.* **21** (1955), 3–20
Clifford, E. M. 'A prehistoric and Roman site at Barnwood near Gloucester' *BGAS.* **52** (1931), 201–54
— 'An early Iron Age site at Barnwood, Gloucestershire' *BGAS.* **56** (1935), 227–30
— 'Notes on the Neolithic period in the Cotswolds' *Cotteswold* **26** (1936), 33–50
— 'Archaeological objects of special interest in Gloucestershire' *Cotteswold* **26** (1937), 159–68
— 'The beaker phase in Cotswold' *Cotteswold* **26** (1938), 256–64
— 'The excavation of the Nympsfield long barrow, Gloucestershire' *PPS.* **4** (1938), 188–213
— 'The Severn as a highway in prehistoric times' *BGAS.* **68** (1949), 5–13
— 'Flint implements from Gloucestershire' *Antiq. J.* **34** (1954), 178–87
— *Bagendon. A Belgic oppidum* (Cambridge 1961)
— 'Two kinds of Beaker pottery from Gloucestershire' *BGAS.* **83** (1964), 34–9
— 'The prehistory of Gloucestershire' *Arch. J.* **122** (1965), 175–7
Coles, J. M. and Hibbert, F. A. 'Prehistoric roads and trackways in Somerset, England. I. Neolithic' *PPS.* **34** (1968), 238–58
Coles, J. M., Clements, C. F. and Hibbert, F. A. 'Prehistoric roads and trackways in Somerset, England. 2 Neolithic' *PPS.* **36** (1970), 125–51
Crawford, O. G. S. *The long barrows of Cotswold* (Gloucester 1925)
— *Archaeology in the field* (London 1953). Includes an appendix on Wansdyke
Crawford, O. G. S. and Keiller, A. *Wessex from the air* (Oxford 1928)
Curwen, E. C. 'The early development of agriculture in Britain' *PPS.* **4** (1938), 27–51

# SELECTED REFERENCES

Daniel, G. E. *The prehistoric chamber tombs of England and Wales* (Cambridge 1950)
— 'The long barrows of the Cotswolds' *BGAS.* **82** (1963) 5–17
Davies, J. A. 'Aveline's Hole, Burrington Combe, an upper Palaeolithic station' *Som. Arch.* **68** (1922), 21–6
Davies, J. A. and Phillips, C. W. 'Report on the excavations at Bury Hill Camp Winterbourne' *Proc. Speleo. Soc.* **3** (1926), no. 1, 8–24
Dobson, D. P. *The archaeology of Somerset* (London 1931)
Donovan, D. T. 'A bibliography of the Palaeolithic and Pleistocene sites of the Mendip, Bath and Bristol area' *Proc. Speleo. Soc.* **7** (1954), no. 1, 23–34
— 'The Pleistocene deposits of Gough's Cave, Cheddar' *Proc. Speleo. Soc.* **7** (1955) no. 2, 76–104
— 'A bibliography of the Palaeolithic and Pleistocene sites of the Mendip, Bath and Bristol area' 1st supplement. *Proc. Speleo. Soc.* **10** (1964), no. 2, 89–97
Dowden, W. A. 'Little Solsbury Hill Camp' *Proc. Speleo. Soc.* **8** (1957), no. 1, 18–29
— 'Little Solsbury Hill Camp' *Proc. Speleo. Soc.* **9** (1962), no. 3, 177–82
Falkoner, J. P. E. and Adams, S. B. 'Recent finds at Solsbury Hill Camp near Bath. A Halstatt-early La Tène site' *Proc. Speleo. Soc.* **4** (1935), no. 3, 183–222
Fell, C. I. 'Shenberrow Hill Camp, Gloucestershire' *BGAS.* **80** (1961), 16–41
Fox, C. 'The distribution of currency bars' *Antiquity* **14** (1940), 427–33
— 'The non-socketed sickles of Britain' *Archaeologia Cambrensis* **96** (1941), 136–62
— 'Somerset from a South Wales viewpoint' *Som. Arch.* **95** (1950), 53–62
Fox, C. and Dickins, B. Ed. *The early cultures of northwest Europe.* (*H. M. Chadwick Memorial Studies*) Cambridge Univ. Includes Daniel, G. E. 'The long barrows in Europe' 1–20 and Clifford, E. M. 'The Cotswold megalithic culture' 21–40 (1950)
Frere, S. S. Ed. *Problems of the Iron Age in southern Britain.* Occasional Paper No. II, The Institute of Archaeology, University of London (1961)
Fry, T. R. 'Further notes on the gravel terraces of the Bristol Avon and their Palaeoliths' *Proc. Speleo. Soc.* **7** (1956), no. 3, 121–9
Garrod, D. A. E. *The upper Palaeolithic age in Britain* (Oxford 1926)
Godwin, H. 'Prehistoric wooden trackways in the Somerset levels, their construction, age and relationship to climatic change' *PPS.* **26** (1960), 1–36
— 'Discoveries in the peat near Shapwick station' *Som. Arch.* **111** (1967), 20–3
Godwin, H. and Clapham, A. R. 'Studies in the post-Glacial history of British vegetation' (1941–55)
— 'Fenland pollen diagrams' *Phil. Trans. Roy. Soc.* Series B, **230** (1941 III), 239–63
— 'Post-Glacial changes of relative land- and sea-level in the English fenland' *Phil. Trans. Roy. Soc.* Series B; **230** (1941 IV), 264–303
— 'Correlations in the Somerset levels' *New Phytologist* **40** (1941 VI), 108–32
— 'Swamping surfaces in the peats of the Somerset levels' *Phil. Trans. Roy. Soc.* Series B, **233** (1948 VIII), 233–48
— 'Prehistoric trackways' *Phil. Trans. Roy. Soc.* Series B, **233** (1948 IX), 249–74
— 'Correlations between climate, forest composition, prehistoric agriculture and peat stratigraphy in the sub-Boreal and sub-Atlantic peats of the Somerset levels' *Phil. Trans. Roy. Soc.* Series B, **233** (1948 X), 275–86
— 'The Meare Pool region of the Somerset levels' *Phil. Trans. Roy. Soc.* Series B, **239** (1955 XIII), 161–90
Godwin, H. and Dewar, H. S. L. 'Archaeological discoveries in the raised bogs of the Somerset levels' *PPS.* **29** (1963), 17–49
Gracie, H. S. 'The Mesolithic age with special reference to Gloucestershire' *Cotteswold* **33** (1959), 107–9
Gray, H. St. George. 'Excavations at the Glastonbury lake village' *Som. Arch.* **48** (1902), 102–21
— 'Report on the excavations at Wick Barrow, Stogursey' *Som. Arch.* **54** (1908), 1–78
— 'The gold torc found at Yeovil 1909' *Som. Arch.* **55** (1909), 66–84
— 'Trial excavation at Cadbury Camp, Tickenham' *Som. Arch.* **68** (1922), 8–20
— 'Excavations at Ham Hill, south Somerset' *Som. Arch.* **70** (1924), 104–16, **71** (1926), 57–76

— 'The disc of Neolithic pottery on Meare Heath, Somerset' *Som. Arch.* **82** (1936), 158–62

Grimes, W. F. Ed. *Aspects of archaeology in Britain and beyond. Essays presented to O. G. S. Crawford.* London. (1951) Includes Grimes, W. F. 'The Jurassic Way across England' 144–71

Grinsell, L. V. *The ancient burial mounds of England* (London 1936)

— 'Some rare types of round barrow on Mendip' *Som. Arch.* **85** (1939), 151–66

— *The archaeology of Wessex* (London 1958)

Grundy, G. B. 'Ancient highways and tracks of Worcestershire and the middle Severn basin' *Arch. J.* **91** (1934), 66–96

— 'The ancient highways of Dorset, Somerset and southwest England' *Arch. J.* **94** (1937), 259–90, **95** (1938) 174–223

Hawkes, C. F. C. 'Hill forts' *Antiquity* **5** (1931), 60–96

— 'The hill forts of northern France' (Review) *Antiquity* **32** (1958), 154–62

— 'The A.B.C. of the British Iron Age' *Antiquity* **33** (1959), 170–82

Hencken, T. C. 'The excavation of the Iron Age camp on Bredon Hill, Gloucestershire' *Arch. J.* **95** (1938), 1–111

Horne, E. 'An early Iron Age site at Camerton, Somerset' *Som. Arch.* **83** (1937), 155–65

Jones, S. J., Grimes, W. F. et al. 'The excavation of Gorsey Bigbury' *Proc. Speleo. Soc.* **5** (1938), no. 1, 3–56

King, D. G. 'Bury Wood Camp. Report on excavations' *Wilts. Arch. Mag.* **58** (1963), 40–7

— 'Bury Wood Camp. Excavations in the area of the southwest opening' *Wilts. Arch. Mag.* **62** (1967), 1–15

Lacaille, A. D. 'Palaeoliths from the lower reaches of the Bristol Avon' *Antiq. J.* **34** (1954), 1–27

McBurney, C. 'Report on the first season's fieldwork on the British upper Palaeolithic cave deposits' *PPS.* **25** (1959), 260–9

Maclean, J. 'A description of the chambered tumuli at Uley and Nympsfield' *BGAS.* **5** (1881), 86–118

O'Neill, H. E. 'Archaeological observations on the Jurassic way in northern Oxfordshire and the Cotswolds' *Cotteswold* **35** (1966), 42–9

O'Neill, H. E. and Grinsell, L. V. 'Gloucestershire barrows' *BGAS.* **79** (1960), (part 1), 5–149

Ordnance Survey. Map of southern Britain in the Iron Age, with text

Parry, R. F. et al. 'Excavations at the caves, Cheddar' *Som. Arch.* **74** (1928), 102–21

Parry, R. F. and Gray, H. St. George. 'Excavations at Cheddar' *Som. Arch.* **76** (1930), 46–62

Phillips, C. W. 'A Romano-British site at Wraxall' *Proc. Speleo. Soc.* **4** (1938), no. 2, 139–45

Piggott, S. 'The early Bronze Age in Wessex' *PPS.* **4** (1938), 52–106

— *The Neolithic cultures of the British Isles.* (Cambridge 1954)

— 'Windmill Hill—east or west?' *PPS.* **21** (1955), 96–101

Radford, C. A. Ralegh. 'The tribes of southern Britain' *PPS.* **20** (1954), 1–26

Radford, C. A. Ralegh and Cox, J. S. 'Cadbury Castle, South Cadbury' *Som. Arch.* **99** (1955), 106–13

Rahtz, P. A. 'Kings Weston Down Camp, Bristol' *Proc. Speleo. Soc.* **8** (1958), no. 2, 30–8

Rahtz, P. A. and M. H. 'Barrow and windmill at Butcombe, Somerset' *Proc. Speleo. Soc.* **8** (1958), no. 2, 89–96

Rahtz, P. A. and Brown, J. C. 'Blaise Castle Hill, Bristol' *Proc. Speleo. Soc.* **8** (1959), no. 3, 147–71

Rahtz, P. A., Barton, R. J. and Tratman, E. K. 'Maes Knoll Camp, Dundry, Somerset' *Proc. Speleo. Soc.* **10** (1963), no. 1, 9–15.

Rankine, W. F. 'Mesolithic finds in Wiltshire' *Wilts. Arch. Mag.* **56** (1956), 149–61

Read, R. F. and Taylor, H. 'The excavation of Mendip barrows' *Proc. Speleo. Soc.* **2** (1922–5), no. 1, 65–74, no. 2, 132–46, no. 3, 211–5

Smith, M. A. 'Some Somerset hoards and their place in the Bronze Age of southern Britain' *PPS.* **25** (1959), 144–87

Sykes, C. M. and Whittle, S. L. 'The Birdcombe Mesolithic site, Wraxall' *Som. Arch.* **104** (1960), 106–23

Taylor, H. 'The Tynings Farm barrow group. 2nd report' *Proc. Speleo. Soc.* **4** (1933), no. 2, 67–127

— 'The Tynings Farm barrow group. 3rd report' *Proc. Speleo. Soc.* **6** (1950), no. 2, 111–73

Tratman, E. K. 'Prehistoric Bristol' *Proc. Speleo. Soc.* **5** (1946), no. 3, 162–82

— 'The prehistoric archaeology of the Bristol region', in *Bristol and its adjoining counties.* MacInnes, C. M. and Whittard, W. F. Ed. British Assn. Adv. Science.(Bristol 1955)

— 'The lost stone circles of north Somerset' *Proc. Speleo. Soc.* **8** (1958), no. 2, 110–8

— 'Gough's old cave, Cheddar, Somerset' *Proc. Speleo. Soc.* **9** (1960), no. 1, 7–21

— 'The Priddy circles, Mendip, Somerset' *Proc. Speleo. Soc.* **11** (1967), no. 2, 97–125

— 'Glastonbury lake village. A reconsideration' *Proc. Speleo. Soc.* **12** (1970), no. 2, 143–67

Tratman, E. K. and Henderson, G. T. D. 'Sun Hole, Cheddar' 1st report. *Proc. Speleo. Soc.* **3** (1927), no. 2, 84–97

Tratman, E. K., Jackson, J. and Donovan, D. T. 'Sun Hole, Cheddar' *Proc. Speleo. Soc.* **7** (1955), no. 2, 61–72

Tratman, E. K. and Taylor, C. 'The Priddy circles' *Proc. Speleo. Soc.* **8** (1957), no. 1, 7–17

Turner, J. 'The Tilia decline, an anthropogenic interpretation' *New Phytologist* **61** (1962), 328–41

*Victoria History of the Counties of England*
Somerset. Ed. Page, W. Vol. I, (London 1906)
*Wiltshire.* Ed. Pugh, R. B. and Crittall, E. Vol. I, (London 1957)

Wainwight, C. J. 'Three microlithic industries from southwest England and their affinities' *PPS.* **26** (1960), 193–201

— 'The excavation of an Iron Age hillfort on Bathampton Down, Somerset' *BGAS.* **86** (1967), 42–59

Wainwright, F. T. 'The Cricklade excavations of 1953' *Wilts. Arch. Mag.* **56** (1956), 162–6

Webster, G. 'The Roman military advance under Ostorius Scapula' *Arch. J.* **115** (1958), 49–98

Wedlake, A. L. and D. J. 'Some Palaeoliths from the Doniford gravels on the coast of west Somerset' *Som. Arch.* **107** (1963), 93–100

Wheeler, R. E. M. and T. V. *Report on the excavation of the prehistoric, Roman and post-Roman site in Lydney Park, Gloucestershire.* Report IX of the research committee of the Society of Antiquaries of London (Oxford 1932)

Wheeler, R. E. M. and Richards, K. M. *The hill forts of northern France.* Report XIX of the research committee of the Society of Antiquaries of London (Oxford 1957)

THE ROMAN OCCUPATION

ApSimon, A. M. 'A Roman field system at Charterhouse-on-Mendip' *Proc. Speleo. Soc.* **6** (1950), no. 2, 201–4

— 'The Roman temple at Brean Down, Somerset' *Proc. Speleo. Soc.* **8** (1958), no. 2, 106–9

— 'The Roman temple at Brean Down, Somerset' *Proc. Speleo. Soc.* **10** (1965), no. 3, 195–258

Baddeley, H. St. C. 'Notes on portions of a late and secondary Roman road system in Gloucestershire' *BGAS.* **52** (1931), 151–85

Barton, K. J. 'The Star Roman villa, Shipham' *Proc. Speleo. Soc.* **9** (1960), no. 1, 30–35

— 'The Star Roman villa, Shipham, Somerset' *Som. Arch.* **108** (1964), 45–93

Blair, P. H. *Roman Britain and early England* (London 1963)

Boon, G. 'The Roman site at Sea Mills' *BGAS.* **66** (1945), 258–95

— 'A Claudian origin for Sea Mills' *BGAS.* **68** (1949), 184–8

— 'Excavations at King's Weston' *BGAS.* **69** (1950), 5–58

Brown, J. C. 'The Roman settlement at Lawrence Weston: the alleged road and the "1850" pavement' *Proc. Speleo. Soc.* **8** (1958), no. 2, 119–23

Brown, P. D. C. and McWhirr, A. D. 'Cirencester 1965' *Antiq. J.* **46** (1966), 240–54

— 'Cirencester 1966' *Antiq. J.* **47** (1967), 185–97

Clifford, E. M. 'The Roman villa, Hucclecote' *BGAS*. **55** (1934), 323–76
— 'Some Roman villas in Gloucestershire' *Cotteswold* **25** (1935), 237–56
— 'The Roman villa, Witcombe' *BGAS*. **73** (1954), 5–69
— 'Stamped titles found in Gloucestershire' *JRS*. **45** (1955), 68–72
— 'Hucclecote Roman villa' *BGAS*. **80** (1961), 42–9
— *Bagendon. A Belgic oppidum* (Cambridge 1961)
Collingwood, R. G. *Roman Britain* (Oxford 1923)
— 'The Fosse' *JRS*. **14** (1924), 252–6
Collingwood, R. G. and Myres, J. N. L. *Roman Britain and the English settlements* (Oxford 1936)
Cox, J. S. 'The Roman town of Ilchester' *Arch. J.* **107** (1950), 94–5
Cra'ster, M. D. 'Roman remains from the Bon Marché' (Gloucester) *BGAS*. **80** (1961), 50–8
Cunliffe, B. 'Excavations at Gatcombe, Somerset in 1965 and 1966' *Proc. Speleo. Soc.* **11** (1967), no. 2, 126–60
Dobson, D. P. and Walker, F. 'Excavations at Sea Mills, near Bristol, 1938' *BGAS*. **61** (1940), 202–23
Donovan, H. E. 'The excavation of a Romano-British building at Bourton-on-the-Water' *BGAS*. **56** (1935), 99–109
— 'Roman finds in Bourton-on-the-Water, Gloucestershire' *BGAS*. **57** (1936), 234–59
Eichholz, D. E. 'The Bristol region in the Roman period,' in *Bristol and its adjoining counties*. MacInnes, C. M. and Whittard, W. F. Ed. British Assn. Adv. Science (Bristol 1955)
Fowler, P. J. 'Excavation of the Romano-British settlement at Row of Ashes farm, Butcombe, north Somerset' *Proc. Speleo. Soc.* **11** (1968), no. 3, 209–36
— 'Fieldwork and excavations in the Butcombe area, north Somerset' *Proc. Speleo. Soc.* **12** (1970), no. 2, 169–94
Frere, S. S. *Britannia. A history of Roman Britain* (London 1967)
Fullbrook-Leggatt, L. E. W. O. 'Glevum' *BGAS*. **55** (1934), 55–104
— 'Glevum' *BGAS*. **86** (1967), 5–16
Gough, J. W. *The mines of Mendip* (Oxford 1930)
Gray, H. St. George. 'The excavation of the amphitheatre at Charterhouse-on-Mendip' *Som. Arch.* **55** (1909), 118–37
— 'A hoard of late Roman coins found on Castle Hill, Wiveliscombe' *Som. Arch.* **92** (1946), 65–75
Green, C. 'Glevum and the second Legion I and II' *JRS*. **32** (1942), 39–52, **33**, (1943), 15–28
Grinsell, L. V. *The archaeology of Wessex* (London 1958)
— 'Somerset archaeology *1931–65*' *Som. Arch.* **109** (1965), 47–77
Haverfield, F. J. *The Romanization of Roman Britain* (Oxford 1923)
Hayward, L. C. 'The Roman villa at Lufton near Yeovil' *Som. Arch.* **97** (1952), 91–112
Hunter, A. G. 'Excavations at the Bon Marché site, Gloucester' *BGAS*. **82** (1963), 25–64
Knowles, W. H. 'Gloucester Roman research committee. Report 1938/9' *BGAS*. **60** (1939), 165–8
Margary, I. D. *Roman roads in Britain*. Vols I and II (London 1955–57)
Musty, W. G. et al. 'The Roman road from Old Sarum to the Mendips' *Wilts. Arch. Mag.* **57** (1960), 30–3
O'Neill, B. H. St. J. and O'Neill, H. E. 'The Roman conquest of the Cotswolds' *Arch. J.* **109** (1952), 23–38
O'Neill, H. E. 'The Roman villa at Whittington Court' *BGAS*. **71** (1952), 13–49
Ordnance Survey. Map of Roman Britain, with text.
Oswald, A. 'Roman material from Dorn, Gloucestershire' *BGAS*. **82** (1963), 18–27
Palmer, L. S. and Ashworth, H. W. 'Four Roman pigs of lead from the Mendips' *Som. Arch.* **101** (1957), 52–88
Pryce, T. D. 'The Roman occupation of Britain, its early phase' *Antiq. J.* **18** (1938), 29–48
Radford, C. A. Ralegh. 'The Roman site at Westland, Yeovil' *Som. Arch.* **74** (1928), 122–43
— 'The Roman villa at Low Ham' *Som. Arch.* **92** (1946), 25–8
— 'The Roman site at Catsgore, Somerset' *Som. Arch.* **96** (1951), 41–77

371

Rahtz, P. A. 'The Roman temple at Pagan's Hill, Chew Stoke, north Somerset' *Som. Arch.* **96** (1951), 112–42

Rahtz, P. A. and Harris, L. G. 'The temple well and other buildings at Pagan's Hill, Chew Stoke, north Somerset' *Som. Arch.* **101** (1957), 15–51

Rahtz, P. A. and Brown, J. C. 'Blaise Castle Hill, Bristol 1957' *Proc. Speleo. Soc.* **8** (1959), no. 3, 147–71

Rennie, D. M. 'A section through the Roman defences in Watermoor Recreation Ground, Cirencester' *Antiq. J.* **37** (1957), 206–15

Richmond, I. A. 'The Roman villa at Chedworth *1958/9*' *BGAS.* **78** (1959), 5–23

— 'Roman Gloucestershire' *Arch. J.* **122** (1965), 177–81

Richmond, I. A. and Toynbee, J. M. C. 'The temple of Sulis Minerva at Bath' *JRS.* **45** (1955), 97–105

Rivet, A. L. F. *Town and country in Roman Britain* (London 1958)

Roman Britain in 1924. 'The Keynsham villas' *JRS.* **14** 233–5

Roman Britain in 1951. 'Pagan's Hill, Littleton villa, Compton Dundon, Lufton villa' *JRS.* **42**, 98–9

Scott-Garrett 'Roman iron mine in Lydney Park' *BGAS.* **78** (1959), 86–91

Seaby, W. A. 'Roman coins from west Somerset' *Som. Arch.* **97** (1952), 189–92

Sykes, C. M. and Brown, G. A. 'The Wraxall Roman villa' *Som. Arch.* **105** (1961), 37–51

Thomas, C. *Rural settlement in Roman Britain* (C.B.A. Research Rpt. 7) includes Cunliffe, B. 'The Somerset levels in the Roman period.' (1966)

Tratman, E. K. 'Some ideas on Roman roads in Bristol and north Somerset' *Proc. Speleo. Soc.* **9** (1962), no. 3, 159–76

*Victoria History of the counties of England*
    *Somerset.* Ed. Page, W. Vol. 1 (London 1906)
    *Wiltshire.* Ed. Pugh, R. B. and Crittall, E. Vol. 1 (London 1957)

Wacher, J. S. 'Cirencester 1960, 61, 62, 63, 64' *Antiq. J.* **41** (1961), 63–71, **42**, (1962), 1–14, **43**, (1963) 15–26, **44**, (1964) 9–18, **45**, (1965) 97–110

Webster, G. 'The Roman military advance under Ostorius Scapula' *Arch. J.* **115** (1958), 49–98

— 'Excavations at Nunnington Park near Wiveliscombe, Somerset' *Som. Arch.* **103** (1958), 81–91

— 'Cirencester, Dyer Court excavations, 1957' *BGAS.* **78** (1959), 44–85

— 'Excavations at the Romano-British villa in Barnsley Park, Cirencester 1961–66', *BGAS.* **86** (1967), 74–83

Wheeler, R. E. M. and Wheeler, T. V. *Report on the excavations of the prehistoric, Roman and Post-Roman site in Lydney Park, Gloucestershire.* Report IX of the research committee of the Society of Antiquaries of London (Oxford 1957)

## THE GROWTH OF SETTLEMENTS AND COMMUNICATIONS UNTIL THE ELEVENTH CENTURY

Attenborough, F. L. *The laws of the earliest English kings* (New York 1963)

Baddeley, H. St. C. ' The battle of Dyrham 577' *BGAS.* **51** (1930), 95–101

Blair, P. A. *An introduction to Anglo-Saxon England* (Cambridge 1960)

Chadwick, H. M. *Studies on Anglo-Saxon institutions* (Cambridge 1905)

Clark, A. 'The nature of Wansdyke' *Antiquity* **32** (1958), 89–96

Copley, G. *The conquest of Wessex in the sixth century* (London 1954)

Darby, H. C. Ed. *An historical geography of England before AD 1800* (Cambridge 1936)

Darby, H. C. and Terrett, I. B. *The Domesday geography of midland England* (Cambridge 1954)

Davidson, J. B. 'On the charters of King Ine' *Som. Arch.* **30** (1884), 1–31

Dobson, D. P. 'Anglo-Saxon buildings and sculpture in Gloucestershire' *BGAS.* **55** (1934), 261–76

Donovan, H. E. and Dunning, G. C. 'Iron Age pottery and Saxon burials at Foxcote Manor, Andoversford, Gloucestershire' *BGAS.* **58** (1937), 157–70

Dunning, G. C. 'Bronze Age settlement and a Saxon hut near Bourton-on-the-Water' *Antiq. J.* **12** (1932), 279–354

English Place-name Society. Vol. 16 *The place-names of Wiltshire*. Glover, J. E. B., Mawer, A. and Stenton, F. M. Cambridge Univ. (1939)

— Vols. 25, 26 *English place-name elements* I and II. Smith, A. H. Cambridge Univ. (1956)

— Vols. 38, 39, 40, 41 *The place-names of Gloucestershire*. Smith, A. H. Cambridge Univ. (1960–64)

Finberg, H. P. R. 'Sherborne, Glastonbury and the expansion of Wessex' *Trans. Roy. His. Soc.* 5th series, **3** (1953), 101–24

— *Gloucestershire studies* (Leicester 1957)

— *The early charters of Wessex* (Leicester 1964)

Fox, A and C. 'Wansdyke reconsidered' *Arch. J.* **115** (1958), 1–48

Fox, C. and Phillips, D. W. 'Offa's Dyke. A field survey' *Archaeologia Cambrensis* **86** (1931), 1–74

Freeman, E. A. 'King Ine' *Som. Arch.* **18** (1872), 1–59

Fullbrook-Leggatt, L. E. W. O. 'Saxon Gloucestershire' *BGAS.* **57** (1936), 110–35

Grundy, G. B. 'Saxon land charters of Wiltshire' *Arch. J.* **76** (1919), 143–301, **77**, (1920), 18–126

— *Saxon land charters of Somerset*. publ. Som. Arch. (Taunton 1927–34)

— *Saxon land charters and field names of Gloucestershire*. publ. BGAS (Gloucester 1935–36)

— 'The ancient woodlands of Gloucestershire' *BGAS.* **58** (1937), 65–155, **59**, (1938), 205–9

— 'The ancient woodland of Wiltshire' *Wilts. Arch. Mag.* **48** (1939), 530–98

Harden, D. B. Ed. *Dark Age Britain. Studies presented to E. T. Leeds* (London 1956) includes Kirk, J. R. 'Anglo-Saxon cremations and inhumations in the upper Thames valley.' 123–31

Hodgkin, R. H. *A history of the Anglo-Saxons*. I & II (Oxford 1935)

Horne, E. 'The Anglo-Saxon cemetery at Camerton' *Som. Arch.* **74** (1928), 61–70

— 'The Anglo-Saxon cemetery at Camerton' *Som. Arch.* **79** (1933), 39–63

Jope, E. M. 'The Saxon building stone industry in southern and midland England' *J. Medieval Archaeology* **8** (1964), 91–118

Kirby, D. P. 'Problems of early West Saxon history' *EHR.* **80** (1965), 10–29

Leeds, E. T. 'The early Saxon penetration of the upper Thames area' *Antiq. J.* **13** (1933), 229–57

Loyne, A. 'The origin and development of Saxon boroughs with particular reference to Cricklade' *Wilts. Arch. Mag.* **58** (1961), 7–15

MacInnes, C. M. and Whittard, W. F. Ed. *Bristol and its adjoining counties*. British Assn. Adv. Science (Bristol 1955)

Mackay, T. F. 'Anglo-Saxon architecture and sculpture in the Cotswold area' *BGAS.* **82** (1963), 66–94

Maitland, F. W. *Domesday book and beyond* (Cambridge 1907)

Meaney, A. L. S. *Gazeteer of early Anglo-Saxon burial sites* (London 1964)

Morgan, F. W. 'Woodland in Wiltshire at the time of the Domesday book' *Wilts. Arch. Mag.* **47** (1935), 25–33

— 'The Domesday woodland of southwest England' *Antiquity* **10** (1936), 306–25

— 'The Domesday geography of Wiltshire' *Wilts. Arch. Mag.* **48** (1937), 68–81

— 'The Domesday geography of Somerset' *Som. Arch.* **84** (1938), 139–55

O'Neill, H. E. 'Saxon burials in the Fosseway at Bourton-on-the-Water' *Cotteswold* **33** (1958), 166–9

Ordnance Survey. Map of Britain in the Dark Ages, with text

Radford, C. A. Ralegh. 'The church in Somerset down to 1100' *Som. Arch.* **106** (1961), 28–45

Radford, C. A. Ralegh and Hallam, A. D. 'The history of Taunton castle in the light of recent excavations' *Som. Arch.* **98** (1953), 55–96

Rahtz, P. A. 'Saxon and medieval palaces at Cheddar, Somerset' *J. Medieval Archaeology* **6** (1962), 53–66

Rahtz, P. A., Harden, D. B., Dunning, G. C. and Radford, C. A. Ralegh. 'Three post-

Roman finds from the temple well, Pagan's Hill, Somerset' *J. Medieval Archaeology* **2** (1958), 104–11

Savage, W. 'Somerset towns' *Som. Arch.* **99** (1954), 49–74

Stenton, F. M. 'The supremacy of the Mercian kings' *EHR.* **33** (1918), 433–52

— *Anglo-Saxon England* (Oxford 1943)

Tait, J. *The medieval English borough* (Manchester 1936)

Taylor, C. S. *An analysis of the Domesday survey of Gloucestershire* publ. BGAS. (Gloucester 1889)

— 'Early christianity in Gloucestershire' *BGAS.* **15** (1892), 120–38

— 'On Gloucestershire in the eighth century' *BGAS.* **16** (1893), 208–30

— 'On the Danes in Gloucestershire' *BGAS.* **17** (1894), 68–95

— 'The Benedictine revival in the Hwiccian monasteries' *BGAS.* **18** (1895), 107–33

— 'On Cotswold in Saxon times' *BGAS.* **20** (1897), 267–306

— 'The origin of the Mercian shires' *BGAS.* **21** (1898), 32–57

— 'Bath, Mercian and West Saxon' *BGAS.* **23** (1900), 129–61

Taylor, H. M. 'The pre-Conquest churches of Wessex' *Wilts. Arch. Mag.* **58** (1962), 156–70

Turner, G. C. 'Some aspects of Celtic survival in Somerset' *Som. Arch.* **97** (1952), 148–55

*Victoria History of the Counties of England*
Somerset. Ed. Page, W. Vol. 1 (London 1906)
Wiltshire. Ed. Pugh, R. B. and Crittall, E. Vol. 2 (London 1955)

### THE CHANGING ECONOMY OF THE BRISTOL REGION FROM THE ELEVENTH TO THE EIGHTEENTH CENTURY

Allen, D. G. C. 'The rising in the west, 1628–31' *Econ. Hist. R.* 2nd Series **5** (1952), no. 1, 76–85

Archer, A. B. 'The history and development of the west of England woollen trade' *Cotteswold* **35** (1967), 28–33

Barton, K. J. 'The excavation of a medieval bastion at St Nicholas's Almshouses, King Street, Bristol' *J. Medieval Archaeology* **8** (1964), 184–212

Beckinsale, P. R. 'Factors in the development of the Cotswold woollen industry' *Geog. J.* **90** (1937), 349–62

Bickley, F. B. *The little red book of Bristol* I & II (London 1900)

Bowden, P. J. 'Wool supply and the woollen industry' *Econ. Hist. R.* 2nd Series **9** (1956), no. 1, 44–58

— *The wool trade of Tudor and Stuart England* (London 1962)

Bristol and Gloucestershire Archaeological Society. *A Gloucestershire and Bristol Atlas.* publ. BGAS. (1961)

Buckatzsch, E. J. 'The geographical distribution of wealth in England 1086–1843' *Econ. Hist. R.* 2nd Series **3** (1950), no. 2, 180–202

Bulley, A. 'To Mendip for coal' I & II. *Som. Arch.* **97** (1952), 46–78, **98** (1953),17–54.

Burt, R. 'Lead production in England and Wales 1700–1770' *Econ. Hist. R.* 2nd Series **22** (1969), no. 2, 249–68

Carus-Wilson, E. M. 'The Merchant Venturers of Bristol in the fifteenth century' *Trans. Roy. Hist. Soc.* 4th Series **11** (1928), 61–82

— *The overseas trade of Bristol in the later middle ages.* Bristol Record Soc. Vol. 7 (Bristol 1936)

— 'An industrial revolution of the thirteenth century' *Econ. Hist. R.* 1st Series **11** (1939), no. 1, 39–60

— 'The English cloth industry in the late twelfth and early thirteenth centuries' *Econ. Hist. R.* 1st Series **14** (1944), 32–50

— 'Trends in the export of English woollens in the fourteenth century' *Econ. Hist. R.* 2nd Series **3** (1950), no. 2, 162–79

— 'Evidence of industrial growth on some fifteenth century manors' *Econ. Hist. R.* 2nd Series **12** (1959), no. 1, 190–205

Collinson, J. *The history and antiquities of the county of Somerset* (Bath 1791)

Cox, J. 'Turnpike houses of the Stroud district' *BGAS.* **86** (1967), 118–50

Cronne, H. A. *Bristol charters 1378–1499*. Bristol Record Soc. Vol. 11 (Bristol 1946)

Darby, H. C. Ed. *An historical geography of England before AD 1800* (Cambridge 1936)

Defoe, D. *A tour through . . . Great Britain*. (London 1769) Intro. Cole, G. D. H. (1928)

Dermott-Harding, N. *Bristol charters 1155–1373*. Bristol Record Soc. Vol. 1 (Bristol 1930)

Farr, G. E. 'Severn navigation and the trow' *Mariners Mirror* 32 (1946), 66–95

— *Somerset harbours including the port of Bristol* (London 1954)

Finberg, H. P. R. *Gloucestershire studies* (Leicester 1957)

Fitzroy-Jones, I. 'Somerset fairs' *Som. Arch.* 91 (1945), 71–81

Fullbrook-Leggatt, L. E. W. O. 'Medieval Gloucester' I & II *BGAS.* 66 (1945), 1–48, 67 (1946), 217–306

Gonner, E. C. K. *Common lands and inclosure* (London 1912)

Gough, J. W. *Mines of Mendip* (Oxford 1930)

Gray, H. L. *English field systems* (Harvard Univ. 1915)

— 'The production and exportation of English woollens in the fourteenth century' *EHR.* 39 (1924), 13–35

Greenhill, B. 'The story of the Severn trow' *Mariners Mirror* 26 (1940), 286–92

Hall, I. V. 'John Knight, Junior . . . Bristol's second sugar house' *BGAS.* 68 (1951), 110–64

Hamilton, A. *The English brass and copper industries to 1800*. Ed. 2 (London 1967)

Hart, C. E. *The free miners* (Gloucester 1953)

Hollis, D. *Calendar of the Bristol apprentices book 1532–1544*. Bristol Record Soc. Vol. 14 (Bristol 1948)

Holmes, G. A. 'Florentine merchants in England 1346–1436' *Econ. Hist. R.* 2nd Series 13 (1960), no. 2, 193–208

Hulbert, N. F. 'A survey of Somerset fairs' *Som. Arch.* 82 (1936), 83–157

Hunt, T. J. 'Some notes on the cloth trade in Taunton in the thirteenth century' *Som. Arch.* 101–2 (1957), 89–107

Jones, S. J. 'The historical geography of Bristol' *Geography* 16 (1931), 180–9

— 'The growth of Bristol' *Trans. IBG.* 11 (1946), 57–83

Kinvig, R. H. 'Historical geography of the west country woollen industry' I & II. *Geographical Teacher* 8 (1916), no. 44, 243–54, no. 45, 290–306

Latham, R. C. *Bristol charters 1509–1899*. Bristol Record Soc. Vol. 12 (Bristol 1946)

Latimer, J. *Annals of Bristol in the eighteenth century* (Bristol 1893)

— *Annals of Bristol in the seventeenth century* (Bristol 1900)

— *History of the society of Merchant Venturers in the city of Bristol* (Bristol 1903)

— *Sixteenth century Bristol* (Bristol 1908)

— *Calendar of the charters of the city of Bristol* (Bristol 1909)

Leland, J. *The itinerary*. Ed. Toulmin-Smith, L. (London 1907–10)

Lennard, R. 'English agriculture under Charles II. The evidence of the Royal Society's "enquiries" ' *Econ. Hist. R.* 1st Series 4 (1933), no. 2, 23–45

— 'English fulling mills. Additional examples' *Econ. Hist. R.* 2nd Series 3 (1950), no. 3, 342–3

— 'The demesnes of Glastonbury Abbey in the eleventh and twelfth centuries' *Econ. Hist. R.* 2nd Series 8 (1956), no. 3, 355–63

McGrath, P. V. 'The Merchant Venturers and Bristol shipping in the early seventeenth century' *Mariners Mirror* 36 (1950), 69–80.

— *Records relating to the society of Merchant Venturers of the city of Bristol in the seventeenth century*. Bristol Record Soc. Vol. 17 (Bristol 1952)

— 'The society of Merchant Venturers and the port of Bristol in the seventeenth century' *BGAS.* 72 (1953), 105–28

— 'Merchant shipping in the seventeenth century. The evidence of the Bristol deposition books' *Mariners Mirror* 40 (1954), 282–93, 41 (1955), 23–37

— *Merchants and merchandice in seventeenth century Bristol*. Bristol Record Soc. Vol.19, (Bristol 1955)

MacInnes, C. M. *A gateway of Empire* (Bristol 1939)

— *Bristol and the slave trade*. Hist. Assn. (Bristol 1968)

MacInnes, C. M. and Whittard, W. F. Eds. *Bristol and its adjoining counties*. British Assn. Adv. Science (Bristol 1955)

Mann, J. de L. 'A Wiltshire family of clothiers. George and Hester Wansey' *Eccon. Hist. R.* 2nd Series **9** (1956), no. 1, 241–53

— *Documents illustrating the Wiltshire textile trades in the eighteenth century.* Publ. Wilts. Arch. Mag. (Devizes 1964)

Mathews, H. E. *The company of soapmakers 1562–1642.* Bristol Record Soc. Vol. 10 (Bristol 1939)

Minchinton, W. E. 'The petitions of the weavers and clothiers of Gloucestershire in 1756' *BGAS.* **73** (1954), 216–27

— 'Bristol. Metropolis of the west in the eighteenth century' *Trans. Roy. Hist. Soc.* 5th Series **4** (1954), 68–89

— *The trade of Bristol in the eighteenth century.* Bristol Record Soc. Vol. 20 (Bristol 1957)

— *Politics and the port of Bristol in the eighteenth century.* Bristol Record Soc. Vol. 23 (Bristol 1965)

Nef, J. U. 'The progress of technology and the growth of large scale industry in Great Britain 1540–1640' *Econ. Hist. R.* 1st Series **5** (1934), no. 1, 3–24

Ogilby, J. *Britannia* (London 1675) Maps of principal roads. Ed. Senex (1719).

Origo, I. *The merchant of Prato. Francesco di Marco Datini* (London 1957)

Parry, R. 'The Gloucestershire woollen industry 1600–1690' *BGAS.* **66** (1945), 49–137

Phelps, W. *The history and antiquities of Somersetshire* (London 1836)

Pontin, K. G. *The history of the west of England cloth industry* (London 1957)

Postan, M. M. 'The fifteenth century' *Econ. Hist. R.* 1st Series **9** (1938), no. 1, 160–67

— 'Glastonbury estates in the twelfth century. A reply' *Econ. Hist. R.* 2nd Series **9** (1956), no. 1, 106–18

Power, E. and Postan, M. M. *Studies in English trade in the fifteenth century* (London 1933). Includes Power, E. 'The wool trade in the fifteenth century.' Carus-Wilson, E. M. 'The Icelandic trade.' Carus-Wilson, E. M. 'The overseas trade of Bristol.'

Ralph, E. and Williams, M. E. *The inhabitants of Bristol in 1696* Bristol Record Soc. Vol. 25, Bristol (1969)

Ramsey, G. D. 'The distribution of the cloth industry in 1561–62' *EHR.* **57** (1942) 361–9

— *The Wiltshire woollen industry in the sixteenth and seventeenth centuries* (London 1943)

Rich, E. E. *The staple court books of Bristol.* Bristol Record Soc. Vol. 5 (Bristol 1934)

Rudder, S. *The history and antiquities of Gloucester* (Cirencester 1781)

Rudge, T. *The history of the county of Gloucester* (Gloucester 1803)

Rutter, J. *Delineation of the north western division of the county of Somerset* (Shaftesbury 1829)

Savage, W. 'Somerset towns' *Som. Arch.* **99** (1945), 49–74

Seyer, S. *Memorials historical and topographical of Bristol and its neighbourhood* (Bristol 1821–25)

Sherborne, J. W. *The port of Bristol in the middle ages.* Hist. Assn. (Bristol 1965)

Shorter, A. H. 'Paper mills in Gloucestershire' *BGAS.* **71** (1953), 145–61

Smyth, J. Maclean, S. S. Ed. *Lives of the Berkeleys* (Gloucester 1883)

Stenton, F. M. 'The road system of medieval England' *Econ. Hist. R.* 1st Series **7** (1936), no. 1, 1–21

Stevens, W. B. 'The cloth exports of the provincial ports' *Econ. Hist. R.* 2nd Series **22** (1969), no. 2, 228–48

Stevenson, W. H. Ed. *Calendar of the records of the corporation of Gloucester* (Gloucester 1893)

Tann, J. 'Some problems of water power. A study of mill siting in Gloucestershire' *BGAS.* **84** (1965), 53–77

— *Gloucestershire woollen mills* (Newton Abbot 1967)

Tate, W. E. 'Gloucestershire enclosure acts and awards' *BGAS.* **64** (1944), 1–70

— 'A handlist of the Wiltshire enclosure acts and awards' *Wilts. Arch. Mag.* **51** (1945), 127–73

— *Somerset enclosure acts and awards* Publ. Som. Arch. (Frome 1948)

Tait, J. *The medieval English borough* (Manchester 1936)

Tawney, A. J. and R. H. 'An occupational census of the seventeenth century' *Econ. Hist. R.* 1st Series **5** (1934), no. 1, 25–64

Tawney, R. H. and Power, E. *Tudor economic documents.* 3 vols (London 1924)

Veale, E. W. W. *The great red book of Bristol I–V.* Bristol Record Soc. Vols. 2, 4, 8, 16, 18 (Bristol 1931–53)

*Victoria History of the Counties of England*
    Gloucestershire. Ed. Page, W. Vol. 2 (London 1907)
    Somerset. Ed. Page, W. Vol. 2 (London 1911)
    Wiltshire. Ed. Pugh, R. B. and Crittall, E. (1956) Vol. 3 (1959) Vol. 4. (1957) Vol. 5 London

Watson, C. E. 'The Minchinhampton custumal and its place in the history of the manor' *BGAS.* **54** (1932), 203–384

Willan, T. S. 'The river navigation and trade of the Severn valley 1600–1750' *Econ. Hist. R.* 1st Series **8** (1937), no. 1, 68–79

Willcox, W. B. *Gloucestershire: a study of local government 1590–1640.* (Yale Univ. 1940)

Williams, A. F. 'Bristol port plans and improvement schemes of the eighteenth century' *BGAS.* **81** (1962), 138–88

THE BRISTOL REGION IN 1800

Billingsley, J. *General view of the agriculture of the county of Somerset* (London 1798)

Collinson, J. *The history and antiquities of the county of Somerset* (Bath 1791)

Cox, C. 'Turnpike houses of the Stroud district' *BGAS.* **86** (1967), 118–50

Darby, H. C. Ed. *An historical geography of England before 1800* (Cambridge 1936)

Davis, T. *General view of the agriculture of the county of Wiltshire* (London 1794)

East, W. G. 'Land utilization in England at the end of the eighteenth century' *Geog. J.* **89** (1937), 156–72

Finberg, H. P. R. *Gloucestershire studies* (Leicester 1957)

Hadfield, E. C. R. 'Canals between the English and Bristol channels' *Econ. Hist. R.* 1st Series **12** (1940), nos. 1 & 2, 59–67

— *British canals* (London 1952)

Hamilton, A. *The English brass and copper industries to 1800.* 2 Ed. (London 1967)

Henderson, H. C. K. 'The 1801 crop returns for Wiltshire' *Wilts. Arch. Mag.* **54** (1951), 85–91

Household, H. *The Thames and Severn canal* (Newton Abbot 1969)

MacInnes, C. M. *Bristol and the slave trade.* Hist. Assn. (Bristol 1968)

MacInnes, C. M. and Whittard, W. F. Ed. *Bristol and its adjoining counties.* British Assn. Adv. Science (Bristol 1955)

Marshall, W. *The rural economy of Gloucestershire* (London 1789)

— *The review and abstract of the county reports to the Board of Agriculture.* (1809–17) Western dept., (1809) Midland dept., (1815) South and western depts. (1815) reprints Newton Abbot

Mathews, W. *The new history and guide to Bristol and directory for the year 1793–94* (Bristol 1794)

Minchinton, W. E. 'Agriculture in Gloucestershire during the Napoleonic Wars' *BGAS.* **68** (1951), 165–83

— 'Bristol. Metropolis of the west in the eighteenth century' *Trans. Roy. Hist. Soc.* 5th Series **4** (1954), 69–89

Morris, J. 'The west of England woollen industry 1758–1840' Thesis summary. *Bull. Inst. Hist. Research* **13** (1936), 106–9

Phelps, W. *The history and antiquities of Somersetshire* (London 1836)

Rudder, S. *The history and antiquities of Gloucester* (Cirencester 1781)

Rudge, T. *History of the county of Gloucester* (Gloucester 1803)

— *General view of the agriculture of the county of Gloucestershire* (London 1807)

Rutter, J. *Delineation of the north western division of the county of Somerset* (Shaftesbury 1829)

Seyer, S. *Memorials historical and topographical of Bristol and its neighbourhood* (Bristol 1821–25)

Tate, W. E. 'Gloucestershire enclosure Acts and awards' *BGAS.* **64** (1944), 1–70
— 'A handlist of the Wiltshire enclosure acts and awards' *Wilts. Arch. Mag.* **51** (1945),
 127–73
— *Somerset enclosure acts and awards* Publ. Som. Arch. (Frome 1948)
Tunnicliffe, W. *A topographical survey of the counties of Somerset, Gloucester, Worcester,*
 *Stafford, Chester and Lancaster* (Bath 1789)
*Victoria History of the Counties of England*
 *Gloucestershire.* Ed. Page W. Vol. 2 (London 1907)
 *Somerset.* Ed. Page, W. Vol. 2 (London 1911)
 *Wiltshire.* Ed. Pugh, R. B. and Crittall, E. Vol. 4 (1959), Vol. 5 (1957) London
Williams, A. F. 'Bristol port plans and improvement schemes of the eighteenth century'
 *BGAS.* **81** (1962), 138–88


NINETEENTH CENTURY CHANGES IN THE BRISTOL REGION


Beckinsale, R. P. *The Trowbridge woollen industry as illustrated by the stock books of John*
 *and Thomas Clark* Publ. Wilts. Arch. Mag. (Devizes 1951)
Bravender, J. 'Farming of Gloucestershire' *J. Roy. Agric. Soc.* **11** (1850), 116–77
Bristol and Gloucestershire Archaeological Society. *A Gloucestershire and Bristol Atlas.*
 Publ. BGAS. (1961)
Bristol Times and Mirror. Reprints. *Work in Bristol* (Bristol 1883)
Buchanan, R. A. *The industrial archaeology of Bristol.* Hist. Assn. (Bristol 1967)
— 'The construction of the floating harbour in Bristol 1804–9' *BGAS.* **88** (1969),
 184–204
Buchanan, R. A. and Cossons, N. *The industrial archaeology of the Bristol region* (Newton
 Abbot 1969)
Buckatzsch, E. J. 'The geographical distribution of wealth in England 1086–1843' *Econ.*
 *Hist. R.* 2nd Series **3** (1950), no. 2, 180–202
Bulley, A. 'To Mendip for coal' I & II. *Som. Arch.* **97** (1952), 46–78, **98**, (1953) 17–54
Cannon, J. *The chartists in Bristol.* Hist. Assn (Bristol 1964)
Census of England and Wales. 'Reports, county reports and tables' HMSO (London
 1831–1961)
Clew, K. R. *The Somersetshire coal canal and railways* (Newton Abbot 1969)
— *The Kennet and Avon canal* (Newton Abbot 1969)
Cooper, N. 'Cheltenham' *Arch. J.* **22** (1965), 181–7
Farr, G. E. 'Severn navigation and the trow' *Mariners Mirror* **32** (1946), 66–95
— *Somerset harbours including the port of Bristol* (London 1954)
Fussel, G. E. 'High farming in southwestern England 1840–80' *Econ. Geog.* **24** (1948),
 53–73
— 'High farming in the west midland counties 1840–80' *Econ. Geog.* **25** (1949), 159–79
Gough, J. W. *The mines of Mendip* (Oxford 1930)
Greenhill, B. 'The story of the Severn trow' *Mariners Mirror* **26** (1940), 286–92
Hadfield, E. C. R. 'Canals between the English and Bristol channels' *Econ. Hist. R.*
 1st Series **12** (1940), nos 1 & 2, 59–67
— *British canals* (London 1952)
Hart, C. E. *The free miners* (Gloucester 1953)
Jenkins, R. 'The copper works at Redbrook and at Bristol' *BGAS.* **63** (1943), 145–67
Johnson, B. L. C. 'New light on the iron industry of the Forest of Dean' *BGAS.* **72**
 (1953), 129–43
Jones, S. J. 'The historical geography of Bristol' *Geography* **16** (1931), 180–9
— 'The growth of Bristol' *Trans. IBG.* **11** (1946), 57–83
— 'The cotton industry in Bristol. *Trans. IBG.* **13** (1947), 61–79
Latimer, J. *Annals of Bristol in the nineteenth century* (Bristol 1902)
Little, B. D. G. *Capper Pass. The first hundred and fifty years* (London 1963)
MacDermot, E. T. revised Clinker, C. R. (1964) *History of the Great Western Railway*
 Vols. I & II. (1833–1921) (London 1927)
MacInnes, C. M. *A gateway of Empire* (Bristol 1939)

Mann, J. de. L. 'A Wiltshire family of clothiers: George and Hester Wansey' *Econ. Hist. R.* 2nd Series **9** (1956), no. 2, 241–53
— 'The later history of the west of England woollen trade' *Cotteswold* **35** (1968), 103–6
Marling, W. H. 'The woollen industry of Gloucestershire. A retrospect' *BGAS.* **36** (1913), 315–33
Minchinton, W. E. 'The beginnings of trade unionism in the Gloucestershire woollen industry' *BGAS.* **70** (1952), 126–41
Morris, J. 'The west of England woollen industry 1758–1840. Thesis summary' *Bull. Inst. Hist. Research* **13** (1936), 106–9
Neale, R. S. 'Industries of the city of Bath in the first half of the nineteenth century' *Som. Arch.* **108** (1964), 132–44
Orwin, C. S. *The reclamation of Exmoor Forest* (London 1929)
Pelham, R. A. 'The application of steam power to the Wiltshire textile industry in the early nineteenth century' *Wilts. Arch. Mag.* **54** (1951), 92–103
Ponting, K. G. *The history of the west of England cloth industry* (London 1957)
Pugh, R. B. 'Chartism in Wiltshire' *Wilts. Arch. Mag.* **54** (1951), 169–84
Rees, H. 'The growth of Bristol' *Econ. Geog.* **21** (1945), 269–75
Shorter, A. H. 'Paper mills in Gloucestershire' *BGAS.* **71** (1953), 145–61
Tann, J. 'Some problems of water power. A study of mill siting in Gloucestershire' *BGAS.* **84** (1965), 53–77
— *Gloucestershire woollen mills* (Newton Abbot 1967)

*Victoria History of the Counties of England*
   Gloucestershire. Ed. Page, W. Vol. 2 (London 1907)
   Somerset. Ed. Page, W. Vol. 2 (London 1911)
   *Wiltshire.* Ed. Pugh, R. B. and Crittall, E. Vol. 4, (1959), Vol. 5 (1957) London
Walrond, L. 'The industrial archaeology of Gloucestershire' *Arch. J.* **22** (1965), 187–8

## THE BRISTOL REGION TODAY

Information collected for government departments or ministries is essential data for a study of the region at the present time. However, this information is usually confidential when in detailed form and is only available for reference in general terms. Local authorities, trade and industrial associations and individual undertakings provide an alternative source of detailed information and a considerable part of the account of present-day conditions in the Bristol region is based on facts provided by them. These were contained in handbooks, brochures and personal communications which are too numerous and sometimes too specialized in interest to be included in the present reference list. The books and articles mentioned below contain more general information and comment about the region in recent times.

Agricultural returns (annual). Ministry of agriculture, fisheries and food. HMSO London
Bird, J. *The major seaports of the United Kingdom* (London 1963)
Bracey, H. E. 'Towns as rural service centres: an index of centrality with special reference to Somerset' *Trans. IBG.* **19** (1953), 95–105
Bristol Engineering Manufacturers Association. Directory
Bristol Incorporated Chamber of Commerce and Shipping. *Gateway to the west.* Bristol as a decentralization area (Bristol 1966)
Britton, J. N. H. *Regional analysis and economic geography. A case study of manufacturing in the Bristol region* (London 1967)
Central Unit for Environmental Planning. *Severnside: a feasibility study.* HMSO (London 1971)
Daysh, G. H. J. et al. *Studies in regional planning* (London 1949). Includes Caesar, A. A. L. 'Gloucestershire, Wiltshire and Somerset' 171–95
Little, B. D. G. *The city and county of Bristol.* 2 Ed. (London 1967)
MacDermot, E. T. revised Clinker, C. R. (1964) *History of the Great Western Railway* (London 1927). See also Nock, O. S. (1967)
Manners, G. 'The Severn bridge and the future' Reprinted address TWW. (1966)

Mitchell, G. F. C. *The central Somerset lowlands*. Selected papers in agricultural economics 7 (1962), no. 5 Bristol Univ.

Neale, W. G. *At the port of Bristol*. Vol. 2, Port of Bristol Authority (1970)

Nock, O. S. *History of the Great Western Railway*. Vol. 3, 1923–47 (London 1967). See also MacDermot, E. T. (1927)

Payne, G. E. *Gloucestershire. A physical, social and economic survey and plan* (Gloucestershire C.C. 1944)

Portbury *Reasons for the Minister's decision not to allow the construction of a new dock at Portbury* (Bristol 1966) HMSO

Shannon, H. A. and Grebenik, B. *The population of Bristol* (Cambridge 1943). National Inst. of Economic and Social Research. Occasional paper 2.

South West Economic Planning Council. *A region with a future*. HMSO (1967)

Tanner, M. F. and Williams, A. F. 'Port development and national planning strategy. Implications of the Portbury decision' *J. Transport Economics and Policy* 1 (1967), no. 3, 1–10.

Universities of Bristol and Exeter *Farm management handbook 1967* (Bristol Univ. 1967)

Unwin, J. T. and Bennett, J. B. *Bristol city centre policy report*. (Bristol Corp. 1966)

Walker, F. 'The port of Bristol' *Econ. Geog.* 15 (1939), 109–24

— 'The industries of Bristol' *Econ. Geog.* 22 (1946), 174–92

— 'The industries of the hinterland of Bristol' *Econ. Geog.* 23 (1947), 261–82

— 'Economic growth on Severnside' *Trans. IBG.* 37 (1965), 1–13

Waterways, British (south western division). *Bristol ports and the Severn ports to the midlands*. 2nd Ed.

# Index

Aalenian, 34, 35
Aarons Hill, 50
Abbas Combe, 46
Abbot's Hill, 44
Abbot's Leigh, 11
Abenhall, 176
Abingdon, 230
*Abona*, 128, 132
Acheulean culture, 105
Acton Turville, 44
Acton Turville Beds, 43
Addo Co., Cirencester, 315
Aerosols, 316, 318
Aerospace industry, 277, 284, 286, 306, 309, 311, 312, 323, 325, 326, 330, 334–37, 344, 345, 346
Aethelflaeda, 155
Agrarian revolution, 195, 196, 205
Agriculture, 160–67, 195–206, 243–51, 263, 280, 289–306, 310, 340
Agricultural engineering, 270, 271, 278, 283, 310, 339, 342
Agricultural land rents, 197, 248
Agricultural sub-regions, 301–306
*Agropyron junceiforme*, 97
*Agrostis*, 94
*Agrostis tenuis*, 95
*Agrostis* with ryegrass, 94, 95
Aircraft equipment, 334, 335, 336, 337, 345, 346
Akeman Street, 128, 137
Albany Engineering Co., Lydney, 342
Albright & Wilson, 320
Alderley, 30, 33, 151, 264
Alderneys, 247
Alder trees, 71, 81, 96
Aldhelm of Malmesbury, 157
Alford, 163
Alham valley, 33, 39
All Cannings Cross, 114, 115
Allen, Ralph, 227, 228
Allen Rubber Co., 342
Allerton series, 86, 87
Allied Iron Founders, 341
Allington, 199
Alluvium, 3, 19, 23, 62, 63, 70, 73, 86, 87, 88, 133, 146, 148, 162

Almondsbury, 10, 21, 23, 27, 61, 129, 152, 179
Alpine orogeny, 53
Alveston, 10, 23, 27, 138
Alvington, 24
American cheese imports, 245, 246
American grain imports, 246, 248, 249, 251, 263
American revolutionary war, 190, 191, 192, 193, 219, 220
*Ammophila arenaria*, 97
Ampney St Peter, 46
Andesites, 7, 85
Andoversford, 33, 54, 116, 143, 335
Anglo-saxon chronicle, 139, 140
Anglo-Swiss Co., 245
Animal feeding stuffs, 246, 248, 284, 291, 292, 295, 308, 321, 347, 348, 349
Animal husbandry, 198, 199, 200, 202, 204, 246, 248, 249, 250, 291, 292, 295, 302, 303, 304, 305, 308
Ansford, 30
Antrim series, 67
Alpin & Barrett, Yeovil, 307
*Aquae Sulis*, 130
Arable land, 68, 69, 70, 71, 72, 86, 161, 162, 163, 165, 172, 196, 197, 199, 200, 202, 203, 205, 244, 246, 247, 248, 250, 290, 292, 295, 296, 297, 302, 303, 304, 305
Arenaceous deposits, 12, 13, 15, 31, 32
*Ariconium*, 135
Arlingham, 126, 129
Armorican, 5, 6, 7, 14, 16, 17, 18, 19, 20, 21, 26, 53
Asbestos manufacture, 328, 330, 348, 349
Ash Tintinhull, 29
Ash woodlands, 78, 91, 92, 94
Ashbrittle, 9
Ashcott Heath, 90, 101, 307
Ashen series, 84, 85, 95
Ashton Containers Ltd., 322
Ashton Court, 117
Ashton seam, 15
Ashton series, 68
Ashton Vale iron works, 253
Ashton Vale Marine Bed, 14

Ashwick, 14

Assessments, 145, 147, 150, 154, 156, 157, 170

Associated Cement Manufacturers, Westbury, 315

Aston Blank, 38, 41

Aston Magna, 31

Athelney, 154

Atlantic period, 109

Atrabates, 121, 130

Aulnage returns, 169

Aurignacian culture, 106

Aust, 119, 146

Aust cliff, 24, 27

Avalon Co., Yatton, 314

Aveline's Hole, 106

Avening, 137

Avon bridge, Avonmouth, 330, 332

Avon fault, 18

Avon gorge, 11, 55, 56, 105, 225, 239, 240, 355

Avon Rubber Co., 277, 285, 314, 315

Avonmouth, 5, 14, 56, 114, 128, 232, 239, 243, 284, 285, 286, 316, 318, 319, 321, 326, 327, 330, 332, 346, 348, 349, 350, 351, 353, 355

Avonmouth basin, 19

Avonmouth dock, 243

Avonmouth Pier & Railway Co., 239, 243

Avonmouth trading estate, 330, 351

Avonmouth West Dock proposals, 349, 350

Awre, 24, 26

Axbridge, 3, 22, 60, 77, 86, 149, 153, 155

Ayrshires, 244

B.P. Plastics, Stroud, 339

Babington, 213

Bacon curing industry, 246, 247, 273, 284, 308, 344, 346

Badbury Hill, 49

Badminton, 138, 161

Badminton Park, 45, 66

Badminton Tunnel, 239

Badsey series, 65, 73, 75

Bagborough, 9

Bagendon, 122, 123, 125, 131, 134

Baileys, Glastonbury, 313

Bajocian denudation, 31, 35

Bakery trade, 321, 322, 324, 329, 337

Ballends castle, 50

Baltonsborough, 68

Banwell, 76, 119, 129, 153, 227, 312

Baptist Mills, 180

Barbados, 189, 194, 220

Barbury Castle, 139, 140

Barley, 165, 166, 197, 200, 201, 203, 246,

248, 249, 295, 296, 297, 305

Barnhill Grey sandstone, 281, 340

Barnstaple, 169, 174, 184, 211, 226, 236

Barnstaple Bay, 9

Barnwood, 59, 61, 105, 106, 107, 110, 336

Barrage schemes, 359

Barren Red group, 15

Barrington, 29, 161

Barrow Gurney, 26, 55

Bason Bridge, 307

Batcombe, 30, 33, 37, 39

Bath, 3, 5, 17, 18, 27, 29, 30, 31, 32, 33, 37, 38, 40, 41, 42, 43, 44, 45, 55, 56, 66, 91, 92, 99, 100, 101, 103, 105, 106, 108, 113, 116, 120, 122, 126, 128, 129, 130, 131, 132, 135, 136, 137, 139, 141, 142, 145, 151, 152, 153, 154, 156, 157, 181, 184, 196, 198, 199, 200, 202, 209, 210, 213, 214, 218, 219, 222, 227, 233, 237, 250, 254, 256, 261, 267, 276, 281, 284, 289, 297, 300, 306, 312, 313, 317, 330, 333, 355, 358, 362

Bath
  Assembly rooms, 227
  The Circus, 227
  The Crescent, 227
  Green Park Station, 234, 237
  Lower Bristol road, 333
  Lower Weston, 333
  Population, 227, 267
  Pump Room, 227
  Spa, 227, 267, 333

Bath Abbey, 142, 156

Bath axis, 5, 6, 7, 8, 14, 16, 17, 20, 27, 28, 31, 32, 34, 35, 37, 39, 53, 54

Bath Hill, 42

Bath stone, 43, 227, 228, 230

Bathampton, 119, 130, 210, 227, 236

Bathampton Down, 117

Bathford, 91

Bathford paper mills, 333

Bâton de Commandement, 106

Bawdrip, 22, 203

Beacon Hill, 6, 7, 8, 16, 50, 60, 79, 84, 85, 103, 111, 128

Beacon Hill (Ilminster), 30

Beakers, 108, 109, 110, 111

Beakers 'A' type, 110, 111
       'B' type, 110, 111

Beans, 205, 295, 297

Bearse, 176

Beau Nash, 227

Beckington, 46, 264

Bedminster, 17, 23, 156, 181, 202, 214, 223, 224, 254, 255, 272, 278, 321, 322, 323, 326, 328, 329, 330

Bedminster Down, 23, 239

Beech woodlands, 66, 91, 92, 94, 109, 276, 338
Beechen Cliff, 33
Beef cattle, 198, 199, 202, 247, 249, 250, 292, 302, 303, 304, 305
Beef herd, 293, 294
Belgae, 121, 122, 123, 125, 130
Belgic cultures, 116, 121, 122, 134
Bell barrows, 112
Benchairs, Frome, 314
Benedictine revival, 158
Berkeley, 5, 24, 27, 82, 156, 247, 264, 320
Berkeley family, 161, 164, 166
Berkeley Hundred, 173
Berkeley Pill, 24
Berkeley Road, 22
Berkshire, 46, 47, 49, 50, 126, 141, 147
Berkshires, 246
Berrow, 97
Beryllium, 319
Beswicks, Frome, 310
Beverstone, 164
Bewdley, 215
Bewley Common, 49
Biddle Combe, 79
Biddlestone, 46
Bideford, 174, 211
Bilberry, 85, 95, 96
Billiard cloths, 259, 338
Birch trees, 96
**Birdcombe site, Wraxall, 106**
Birdlip, 38, 41, 43, 116, 151
Birdlip anticline, 35, 38, 54, 59
Birmingham, 218, 219, 233, 234, 247, 272, 287, 344
Birts Hill, 44
Bishop's Caundle, 46
Bishops Cleeve, 147, 335
Bishopswood, 177, 212
Bishopsworth, 55, 321
Bisley, 41, 43, 54, 170
Bisley Hundred, 173
Bitton, 24, 55, 128, 138, 214, 255, 266, 276, 322, 324
Bixhead Blue sandstone, 281, 340
Black Down Hills, 25, 28, 50, 53, 57, 74, 143, 152
Black Hill, 8
Black Mountain, 108
Black Nore Sandstone, 8
Black Rock Dolomite, 12
Black Rock group, 11, 12
Black Rock Limestone, 11, 12
Blackcurrants, 298, 300, 308, 341
Blackdown, 6, 8, 11, 17, 19, 20, 21, 60, 70, 77, 78, 79, 84, 85, 95, 103, 111, 112
Blackeney Hill, 7

Blackmoor Vale, 46
Blackpool brook, 177
Blackwell Hall, 172, 175, 186, 190, 209, 257
Blagdon, 153
Blagdon reservoir, 22
Blaise Castle, 116, 120, 128, 135
Blakeney, 24, 176, 177
Blandford, 236
Blanket, Thomas, 167
Blankets, 260
Bleadon, 61
Bleadon Hill, 22, 76, 77
Blodley, 212
Blue Lias Limestones, 27, 28
Blunsden, 49
Bodden series, 79
Boot and shoe industry, 224, 273, 274, 275, 277, 285, 306, 312, 324, 327, 329, 333
Boroughs, 154, 155, 156
Boueti Bed, 43
Boulder Clay, 72, 73
Bournemouth, 237
Bourton, 48
Bourton-on-the-Hill, 33
Bourton-on-the-Water, 114, 138, 168
Bourton-on-the-Water villa, 133, 134
Bourton-on-Windrush, 168
Bowden Hill, 47
Bower Ashton, 61
Bower Hinton, 30
Bowyer's, Trowbridge, 246, 308
Box, 33, 43, 266
Box Hill, 42
*Brachypodium pinnatum*, 95
Bracken, 77, 79, 84, 85, 95, 96
Bradford Abbas, 37, 39
Bradford Clay, 42, 43
Bradford-on-Avon, 40, 41, 42, 44, 46, 55, 57, 91, 155, 157, 171, 175, 181, 196, 199, 208, 218, 230, 236, 256, 257, 269, 273, 276, 277, 278, 298, 314, 315, 362, 363
Bradford-on-Avon, battle of, 142
Brandon Hill, 14, 83
Brass manufacture, 179, 180, 212, 222, 272, 311
Bratton Seymour, 39, 41
Breadstone Shales, 6
Break crops, 297
Brean Down, 3, 10, 61, 77, 97, 106, 110, 111, 112, 115, 129, 135
Breccia, 21
Brecknell Dolman & Rogers, Ltd., 324
Bredon Camp, 115, 119, 120, 122
Bredon Hill, 31, 32, 38, 59
Bremhill, 49

Brendon Hills, 9, 70, 71, 74, 92, 111, 135, 145, 152, 252, 302
Brent Knoll, 26, 30, 31, 87, 116
Brent Marsh, 202, 203
Brentry, 13, 27
Brewing, 308, 321, 329
Brick making, 281, 340
Bridgeyate, 55
Bridgnorth, 215
Bridgnorth series, 72
Bridgwater, 3, 10, 20, 21, 24, 101, 149, 169, 174, 203, 211, 214, 218, 226, 231, 233, 236, 250, 267, 269, 270, 272, 281, 282, 285, 287, 289, 302, 306, 308, 309, 310, 312, 313, 314, 315, 316
Bridgwater–Taunton canal, 231
Brimscombe, 338
Brinsea series, 76
**Brislington, 23, 80, 181, 214, 223, 254, 278,** 321, 324, 325, 328, 330
Brislington trading estate, 321, 323, 326, 328, 332
Bristol, 155, 167, 168, 169, 173, 174, 178, 180, 181–94, 211, 213, 214, 219–26, 233, 234, 247, 250, 263, 267, 268, 269, 272, 273, 274, 275, 276, 277, 280, 281, 282, 285, 287, 288, 289, 292, 297, 300, 306, 307, 313, 317, 318–34, 362
Bristol
  Arnos Vale, 23, 330
  Ashton, 321, 323, 324, 326, 327, 330
  **Avon street, 224, 322, 326**
  Baldwin street, 332
  Banks, 193, 224, 268
  Bedminster, East street, 331
  Bedminster, West street, 331
  Berkeley square, 225
  Bordeaux trade, 186, 189, 192
  Brass foundries, 180, 185, 212, 222
  Brittany trade, 189
  Broadmead, 331
  Castle street, 331
  **Central business district, 332, 358**
  Charlotte street, 225
  City docks, 221, 240, 242, 243, 321, 322, 349
  City docks, closure, 349, 351
  Clifton, 23, 224, 225, 278, 326, 332, 333
  Clifton gorge, 11, 55, 56, 105, 225, 239, 240, 355
  Clifton Heights, 333
  Coal supplies, 223
  Coastwise trade, 180, 181–85, 215, 348, 349
  Commercial activity, 181–94, 219, 220, 281, 282, 329, 330, 331, 332, 347-49
  Conham, 224

Corn street, 332
Cornwallis crescent, 225
County status, 181
Crew's Hole, 224, 319, 329
Cumberland basin, 240, 242
Eastville, 23, 327, 329
Engineering industry, 223, 323, 324, 325, 326, 329, 330
Feeder canal, 240, 319
Fishponds, 214, 272, 320, 321, 322, 324, 326, 327, 329
Floating harbour, 221
Food market, 183
Gascony trade, 183, 186, 189, 191, 192
Glass industry, 185, 222, 223
Gloucester road, 331
Growth of, 224, 225
Hartcliffe, 321
Horfield, 278
Hotwells, 180, 222, 223, 225, 239, 326
Icelandic trade, 187
Industrial districts, 255, 278, 328–32 and Map 15
Insurance houses, 193, 194, 224
Irish trade, 182, 183, 185, 188, 189, 192
Iron market, 184, 193, 223
King's square, 225
Kingsdown, 225
Knowle, 55
Levant trade, 188
Manufacturing industry, 167, 168, 169, 174, 179, 180, 184, 185, 188, 212, 221, 222, 223, 224, 268, 269, 278, 284, 285, 286, 289, 317–34
Marsh street, 332
Maryland trade, 189, 190
Mediterranean trade, 182, 183, 187, 188, 192
'Metropolis of the West', 183, 219
Nelson street, 332
Netham, 240
New Cut, 240
Newfoundland trade, 188, 189, 191, 192
Overseas trade, 167, 171, 172, 179, 185–93, 219, 220, 275, 277, 278, 347–50
Park street, 225, 332
Parkway station (Stoke Gifford), 239, 356, 358
Pembroke road, 332
Population, 193, 224, 225, 267, 268, 278, 354, 358
Port dues and charges, 226, 240, 242
Port improvement, 220, 221, 225, 226, 240, 242, 268, 277, 349
Portuguese trade, 185, 186, 187, 188, 189, 191

Potteries, 222
Queen's road, 331
Queen Square, 224, 328, 329
Redcliffe, 318, 328
Redland, 23, 224, 225, 326
Rotterdam trade, 189, 190, 192
Royal York crescent, 225
Rupert street, 332
St Annes, 322, 329
St George, 214, 224, 255, 278, 327, 329
St Jacob-without, 278
St James-without, 278
St Paul, 278, 327, 329, 331
St Philip, 224, 233, 255, 272, 276, 278, 323, 324, 326, 329, 331
St Philip-without, 224
Severn trade, 182, 183, 184
Shipping numbers, 188, 189, 192
Shipyards, 272
Shirehampton, 11
Sneyd Park, 11
Soundwell, 327, 329
South Carolina trade, 191
Spanish trade, 185, 186, 187, 188, 189, 191
Staple Hill, 327, 329
Stapleton, 214, 224, 278
Stapleton road, 331
Sugar houses, 184, 222, 223
Totterdown, 23
Transatlantic trade, 185, 188, 189, 190, 191, 192, 193, 220
Turnpike trust, 213, 218, 219, 220, 240
Tyndalls Park, 225
Victoria street, 329, 331, 332
Virginia trade, 189, 190, 191, 194
West Indies trade, 185, 189, 190, 191, 192, 220, 222
Whitehall, 324
Whiteladies road, 331
Wine street, 331, 332
Winterstoke road area, 323, 326, 327
Wool-cloth shipments, 183, 185, 186, 187, 188, 190, 192, 209
Bristol Areojets, Banwell, 312
Bristol Areoplane Co., 325
Bristol Atlas Works, 272
Bristol Avon gravels, 105
Bristol Avon navigation, 213, 228, 242
Bristol Avonside Mills, 276
Bristol Avonside Works, 272
Bristol Brass Wire Co., 180
Bristol bridge, 321, 328, 329
Bristol Channel, 52, 53, 54, 55, 56, 97, 115, 124, 182, 184, 217, 231, 236, 281

Bristol coalfield, 5, 6, 8, 10, 11, 12, 14, 15, 16, 18, 19, 22, 23, 56, 57, 80, 119, 180, 181, 212, 213, 214, 223, 254, 255, 266
Bristol Commercial Vehicles, Ltd., 325
Bristol Free Port Association, 242
Bristol Staple, 185
Bristol United Colliery Co., 255
British Aircraft Corp., 284
British Cellophane, Bridgwater, 285, 315
British Christianity, 143, 157
British Nylon Spinners, Brockworth, 285, 335, 346
British Oil & Cake Mills, Avonmouth, 321
Bristish Piston Co., 341
British Van Heusen Co., 313
Brittannia Prima, 131
Brittany, 107, 108, 116
Britton, G. B., 327
Broad River, 39
Broad Town, 50
Broadcloths, 168, 169, 170, 172, 173, 174, 175, 183, 200, 207, 208, 209, 210, 256, 257, 259, 260
Broadcloths, coloured, 173, 174, 175, 176, 206
Broadcloths, white, 172, 173, 174, 175, 256
Broadfield Down, 6, 11, 12, 13, 17, 18, 20, 21, 22, 23, 25, 26, 27, 28, 55, 61, 76, 77, 91, 98, 120, 153, 179, 201
Broadmead brook, 40
Broadway, 31, 33
Brockley Coombe, 61, 120, 153
Brockley fault, 18
Brockworth, 285, 335
Broiler chickens, 293, 294, 295
Brokensborough, 46
Brome, 95
Bromham, 65
Bromham series, 65
Bromyard series, 72, 82
Bronze Age, 62, 111–13, 117, 124, 133
Bronze Age wooden trackways, 112
Bronze flat axes, 113
Bronze hoards, 112, 113
Brotherhoods, Chipperham, 271
Broughton Gifford, 46
Broughton Poggs, 46
Brow Down, 152
Brown Earths, 69, 70, 83, 95
Brown & May, Devizes, 270
Brownstone ridges, 7, 8, 14, 82
Brunel, Isambard Kingdom, 234
Brush making, 328
Brussels sprouts, 297

Bruton, 3, 33, 35, 36, 37, 39, 41, 44, 145, 153, 154, 155, 157, 161, 169, 204, 209, 210, 211, 218, 236, 261, 308
Bubb Down Hill, 50
Buckland Denham, 40
Buckskins (cloth), 257, 259
Buckschraft mine, 252
Buckthorne Weston, 48
Building stones, 28, 32, 34, 35, 36, 42, 43, 50, 131, 134, 227, 228, 230, 266, 281
Bulwark, The, 125, 126
Bunter Pebble Beds, 20, 21, 72
Bunter Sandstone, 20, 21, 72
Burford, 43, 151, 164, 199
Burghal Hideage, 154
Burledge Camp, 114
Burlescombe, 231
Burnett, 254
Burnham-on-Sea, 63, 97, 166, 236, 268, 311
Burrell Hill, 31
Burrington, 11, 60, 76, 77, 85, 116, 119, 180
Burrington Oolite, 12
Burrow, 30
Burtle Beds, 62, 86, 203
Burton Downs, 38, 41
Bury Hill, Winterbourne, 115, 116
Butcome, 23, 26
Butcombe Sandstone, 22, 23, 72
Butleigh series, 87
Butler Chemicals, 319
Butler & Tanner, Frome, 314
Butler Oil Products, 319
Butt Moor, 87
Butter, 202, 204, 205, 246, 247, 307
By brook, 42, 45, 91, 107, 138, 170, 227
Bymacks, Dursley, 314

Cadbury Camp, 12, 107, 120
Cadbury Castle, 30, 37, 114, 116, 120, 121, 130
Cadbury Hill, 135
Cadbury's, 307, 321
Cadmium, 319
Caerleon, 126, 128, 131
Cairncross, 338
Calamine, 78, 179, 180, 212, 252, 253, 254
Calamine workings, 179, 180
Calcicolous vegetation, 95
Calcifuge species, 95
Caledonoid, 5
Calleva, 126
Calluna, 79, 84
Calluna vulgaris, 95

Calne, 47, 48, 49, 50, 155, 156, 171, 174, 200, 207, 208, 218, 227, 230, 236, 246, 256, 261, 265, 273, 286, 308, 313, 315, 316
Cam, 30, 206, 276, 308, 309, 313
Cam brook, 25, 33, 37, 40, 41, 42, 54, 88, 138, 229, 237
Cambrian, 3, 6, 7, 19
Camden, 187
Camerton, 18, 112, 115, 122, 126, 128, 132, 138, 213, 229, 237
Camerton colliery, 255
Camulodunum, 128
Canal construction, 184, 193, 215, 217, 229–33
Canal mania, 215, 217, 225, 229
Canals, 184, 193, 213, 215, 217, 229–33, 240, 267, 277
Cannington, 308
Cannington Park, 3, 9, 116, 138
Cannop fault belt, 19
Canynges, William, 187
Capper Pass, Bristol, 272, 318
Caractacus, 126
Carbon 14 dates, 108, 109, 110, 112
Carboniferous, 9, 10, 13, 14, 16, 18, 20, 22, 55, 80
Carboniferous Limestone, 3, 7, 9, 10, 11, 13, 16, 17, 18, 20, 21, 22, 23, 26, 27, 36, 37, 55, 56, 70, 75, 76, 77, 78, 91, 92, 108, 111, 120, 132, 159, 179, 201, 240, 281, 298
Cardiff, 6, 193
Carding engines, 209, 210
Carex arenaria, 97
Carr, Isaac & Co., 258
Carters, H. W., Coleford, 300, 309, 341
Cassimeres,, 208, 256
Castle Cary, 3, 30, 33, 37, 67, 73, 101, 153, 169, 204, 209, 210, 218, 237, 262, 266, 312
Castle Combe, 45, 91, 168, 170, 171, 172, 176, 199, 227, 264
Castle Hill, 49
Castle of Comfort, 103, 212
Catcombe, 83
Catcott Burtle, 62
Catcott complex, 86
Catcott Heath, 89
Catcott series, 86
Catsgore villa, 133, 134
Cattle, 166, 198, 199, 202, 203, 204, 205, 244, 248, 249, 250, 292, 293, 294, 302, 303, 304, 305
Cattle Hill, 39
Cattle plague, 245
Catuvellauni, 122

Causeway camps, 107
Ceawlin, 141
Celestine, 24, 281
Ceol, 141
Ceratodus Bone Bed, 25
Cereals, 165, 166, 197, 200, 201, 203, 246, 248, 249, 295, 296, 297, 302, 303, 304, 305, 306
Cerney, 168, 215, 281
Chalford, 338
Chalk, 3, 47, 50, 54, 65, 74, 103, 108, 141, 142, 151, 161, 184, 199, 200, 251, 291, 297, 300
Chalk Hill, 38, 41
Chamberlain, Stroud, 312
Champion's works, 180, 212, 222
Chapmanslade, 47, 50
Charcoal burning, 341
Chard, 29, 50, 169, 201, 204, 210, 211, 235, 236, 259, 262, 266, 307, 308, 310, 311, 312, 316
Charfield, 8, 10, 22, 26, 263
Charlcott Hill, 49
Charlton, 46
Charleton Horethorne, 37, 39, 41, 44
Charlton Bank series, 68, 69, 70
Charlton Mackrell, 22
Charmy Down, 40, 42
Charnian, 5
Charterhouse, 8, 79, 111, 128, 129, 132, 133, 134, 135, 178, 201, 254
Charterhouse, manor of, 179
Cheddar, 14, 60, 77, 78, 79, 90, 98, 106, 116, 155, 156, 163, 168, 227, 298, 300, 302
Cheddar cheese, 245, 250
Cheddar gorge, 60, 135
Cheddarian culture, 106
Chedworth, 42
Chedworth villa, 133, 134
Chedzoy, 22, 62, 153, 203
Chedzoy series, 86
Cheese and butter country, 199, 244
Cheese Hill, 44
Cheese longhorn cattle, 203, 205, 244
Cheese production, 166, 199, 202, 203, 244, 245, 246, 247, 249, 250, 307, 308
Chelborough Hill, 50
Chelm Combe, 106, 108
Cheltenham, 29, 30, 32, 35, 73, 99, 100, 114, 143, 151, 167, 217, 228, 233, 235, 245, 248, 267, 279, 282, 284, 286, 289, 297, 300, 303, 306, 317, 334, 335, 336, 337, 342, 358
Cheltenham, population, 228, 267, 268
Cheltenham Sands, 73
Cheltenham series, 73

Cheltenham Spa, 228, 267
Chelwood, 81
Chelwood series, 72
Chemical industries, 286, 306, 316, 317, 318, 319, 320, 324, 329, 330, 337, 346, 347
Cheney Manor industrial estate, Swindon, 343, 344
Chepstow, 10, 21, 235
Cherhill, 50
Cherrington, 138
Chew Magna, 101, 213
Chew Stoke, 72, 135
Chew valley lake, 22, 60, 71
Chewton, manor of, 179
Chewton Mendip, 8, 25, 69, 153, 254, 264
Chickerell series, 66
Chilthorne Domer, 29
Chilton Foliat, 168
China Eugene mine, 252
Chinnock brook, 39
Chippenham, 42, 43, 46, 47, 48, 108, 151, 154, 156, 168, 171, 200, 208, 218, 230, 231, 233, 235, 236, 245, 246, 256, 258, 261, 265, 271, 273, 282, 284, 287, 289, 307, 308, 311, 316, 335, 362, 363
Chippenham Forest, 144, 145, 146, 149
Chipping Camden, 30, 31, 32, 34, 35, 38, 59
Chipping Norton Limestone, 38, 41
Chipping Sodbury, 5, 10, 13, 14, 22, 26, 35, 143, 151, 167, 248, 281, 289, 308, 322, 326, 330, 331, 332, 362
Chisleborough Hill, 32
Chittening estate, 332
Chittoe, 48
Chocolate, 223, 274, 277, 284, 320, 321
Christian Malford, 161, 200
Church lands, 156, 157, 158, 205
Churchdown, 31
Churchill, 14, 60, 61, 71, 119, 153, 298
Cider, 298, 308
Cider apple orchards, 67, 166, 298
Cider orchards, commercial, 298
Cinderford, 10, 13, 16, 252, 281, 310, 340, 341, 342
Cirencester, 35, 42, 43, 44, 45, 46, 49, 99, 100, 116, 122, 125, 126, 128, 129, 130, 131, 132, 136, 137, 152, 156, 164, 167, 170, 172, 174, 178, 199, 207, 209, 211, 217, 218, 233, 247, 265, 286, 306, 308, 315, 316
Cirencester, battle of, 141, 142
Cirencester Park, 45
Civil War, 175, 177, 187
Clan Down, 37
Clandown colliery, 254

Clandown fault, 19
Clanna anticline, 13
Claphanger Common, 29
Clapton, 14
Clapton coalfield, 20
Clapton-in-Gordano, 8
Clark, Son & Moreland, Glastonbury, 275, 313
Clark, C&J, Street, 274, 312, 324
Clarks of Trowbridge, 257
Cleeve Cloud, 30
Cleeve fault, 18
Cleeve Hill, 31, 32, 33, 35, 38, 41, 54, 114
Cleeve Hill syncline, 35, 54
Clevedon, 6, 8, 11, 14, 17, 18, 25, 76, 77, 91, 95, 108, 120, 153, 179, 202, 219, 236, 268, 281, 286, 300, 309, 311, 312, 314, 316, 361
Clevedon fault, 19, 20
Clevedon–Failand ridge, 21, 56, 61, 99, 201
Clevedon–Portishead ridge, 17, 21, 61, 201
Cliff Hill, 39
Clifton Down group, 12, 13
Clifton Down Limestone, 12, 13, 19
Clifton Down Mudstones, 12
Climate, 62, 64, 69, 72, 83, 84, 97–104
Clothiers, 171, 173, 207, 208
Clothing manufacture, 267, 285, 312, 313, 327, 328, 329, 330, 337, 338, 344
Cloverleaf (Products), Swindon, 344
Clutton, 18, 80, 81, 213
Clutton fault, 19
Clyffe Pypard, 50
Clypeus Grit, 36
Coaches, 219
Coal, 131, 132, 176, 180, 181, 182, 212, 213, 214, 230, 251, 253, 254, 255, 260, 261, 263, 266, 277, 280, 335, 340
Coal Commission, 176, 253
Coal Measures, 10, 14, 15, 17, 18, 20, 23, 37, 55, 72, 80, 81, 92, 197
Coaley, 355
Coalfields, 5, 14–16, 18, 19, 180, 181. See also entries under Bristol coalfield, Somerset coalfield and Forest of Dean
Coalpit Heath, 81, 233, 255
Coalpit Heath basin, 19
Coalpit Heath series, 81
Coalpit Heath tramways, 233, 234, 255
Cockayne's experiment, 175
Cocoa and chocolate industry, 274, 277, 284, 320, 321, 346, 348
Codrington, 11
Cogmill, 56
Coker Hill, 44
Colchester, 128
Cold Ashton, 42, 138

Cole, E. K., Malmesbury, 316
Coleford, 13, 15, 181, 213, 300, 309, 340, 341, 342
Coleford High Delf seam, 15
Colerne, 42, 227
Coleshill, 47, 49
Colluvium, 59, 60, 63, 66, 79, 88
Colne St Aldwyn, 45
Colodense Ltd., 322
Combe Down, 42, 43, 227, 237
Combe Hay, 41, 229
Combwich, 116
Common bent, 95
Communications, 150–53, 158, 184, 213, 214–19, 229–43, 263
Compton Bassett, 50
Compton Dando, 22, 81
Compton Dundon, 88, 153, 204
Compton Greenfield, 61
Compton Martin, 112
Compton Pauncefoot, 33
Compton series, 87, 88, 89
Condensed milk, 307
Condicote, 38
Congresbury, 22, 120, 153, 157
Conham, 180
Coniferous woodlands, 81, 92, 94, 96
Consolidated Zinc Corp., 318
Containerized cargoes, 332, 349, 350
Coombe Hill, 38
Cooperative Wholesale Society, 307, 321, 328
Coopers Hill, 38
Copeland-Chatterson Ltd., Stroud, 338
Copper smelting, 180, 194, 222
Coral Rag, 48, 49, 65
Corallian, 47, 48, 49, 50, 64, 65, 94, 200, 246, 302
Corinium, 125, 126, 131
Cornbrash, 44, 45, 46, 47, 65, 66, 199, 249
Cornish miners, 254
Corsham, 43, 44, 46, 108, 114, 122, 161, 196, 199, 266, 273, 316
Corsley, 50
Corston, 45, 110
Corton Denham, 29, 30, 32
Corton Hill, 32, 33, 37
Cossington, 26
Cotham Beds, 25
Cotswold, 3, 5, 29, 30, 31, 33, 34, 35, 36, 38, 40, 41, 42, 44, 45, 46, 54, 57, 59, 61, 65, 66, 67, 68, 73, 75, 91, 92, 95, 97, 98, 99, 100, 103, 104, 106, 107, 108, 109, 110, 111, 114, 115, 116, 117, 119, 120, 121, 122, 123, 125, 126, 129, 131, 134, 136, 137, 138, 139, 140, 141, 142, 143, 144, 145, 147, 148, 150, 151, 152,

153, 158, 159, 160, 161, 163, 164, 165,
168, 169, 170, 171, 172, 174, 176, 184,
186, 195, 196, 197, 198, 199, 200, 203,
205, 206, 207, 217, 218, 239, 240, 244,
247, 248, 249, 251, 263, 264, 266, 276,
279, 291, 292, 298, 300, 302, 303, 305,
351
Cotswold rotation, 197, 199, 248, 249
Cotswold sheep, 172, 198
Cotswold/Southdown cross, 198
Cotswold sub–Edge zone, 59, 60, 105
Cotswold wool, 172
Cotteswold Sands, 31, 32, 33, 66, 170
Cotton grass, 96
Cotton manufacture, 222, 263
Count of Mortain, 156
Coutances, Bishop of, 156
Cow down, 163, 196
Cowage brook, 49
Cowbridge, 25
Craig Llwyd axes, 110
Cranham, 38, 41
Cranmore, 46
Crannogs, 117
Cream, 307
Crease Limestone, 12
Creech Hill, 33, 37, 120
Creech St Michael, 276
Cremation burials, 137, 138
Cresswellian culture, 106
Cretaceous, 48, 49, 50, 52, 53, 57, 74, 101
Crewkerne, 3, 31, 32, 35, 37, 39, 50, 67,
101, 158, 169, 204, 209, 210, 211, 218,
261, 262, 266, 313
Cricklade, 49, 148, 154, 155, 200, 218, 230,
307
Cripple Hill, 30, 32
Critchley Bros., Stroud, 339
Cromhall, 10, 12, 13, 14, 21, 23, 214
Crop returns (1801), 197
Croscombe, 169
Cross-leaved heath, 96
Croyden Hill, 9, 83, 92
Crudwell, 46
Crumpmeadows fault, 19
Cucklington, 48
Culm Measures, 8, 9
Cuprinol Ltd., Frome, 316
Currency bars, 116, 123
Curry Mallet, 161
Curry Rivel, 163

Dairy Shorthorns, 203, 205, 244, 247
Dairy vales, 70, 198, 199, 200, 244, 245,
246, 247, 248, 284, 295, 302, 303, 305
Dairying, 70, 163, 165, 166, 195, 196, 198,
199, 200, 201, 202, 203, 204, 205, 244,

245, 246, 247, 248, 249, 250, 284, 291,
292, 294, 295, 302, 303, 304, 305, 306,
307, 308
Damp oak forest, 68, 91, 92, 94
Danby Lodge, 10
Dancing Hill, 39
Dancombe brook, 40
Danes, 154
Daniels, Stroud, 339
Dark Ages, 92, 176
Dauntsey, 200, 239
Debenhams, Taunton, 282
Deciduous woodland, 91, 92, 94, 96
Defoe, Daniel, 163, 166, 193, 217
Deloro-Stellite Co., Swindon, 344
Denchworth series, 64
Denudation, 52, 54, 55, 56, 62, 63
Deorham, battle of, 131, 137, 140, 141,
142, 145
Derbyshire, 212
Deschampsia flexuosa, 95
Devizes, 108, 174, 207, 230, 236, 245, 261,
270
Devonian, 7, 8, 9, 74, 82, 83, 84, 92, 94,
96
Didcot, 231, 235
Dilton Marsh, 47, 48, 50
Diocletian, 131
Disc barrows, 112
Distillers Co., 321
Ditcheat, 163
Dobunni, 121, 122, 123, 125, 130, 131,
134, 135
'Dockization' schemes, 221, 240, 242, 243
Doeskins (cloth), 259, 338
Dolebury, 79, 116, 212
Dolomites, 10, 11, 12, 281
Dolomitic Conglomerate, 20, 21, 22, 23,
24, 37, 77, 201
Domesday fisheries, 148
Domesday mills, 148, 149, 151, 170
Domesday plough teams, 147, 150
Domesday population, 147, 148
Domesday survey, the, 143, 144, 145, 146,
147, 148, 149, 150, 152, 153, 155, 156,
170
Domesday vills, 147, 148, 149, 151, 152,
153
Doniford stream, 205
Dorchester, 129, 130
Dorchester-on-Thames, 137, 157
Dorn Hill, 31
Dorset, 46, 48, 54, 57, 217, 218
Dorset Downs, 50
Double-looped palstaves, 113
Douglas Engineeering Co. 325
Doulting, 36, 37

Doulting stone, 36
Dowlas, 169, 210, 261
Down Hatherley, 358
Downside stone, 28
Dowty Electrics, Tewkesbury, 335
Dowty Fuel Systems, Cheltenham, 334
Dowty group, 284, 311, 333, 334, 335, 336, 337
Dowty Hydraulic Units, Cheltenham, 334
Dowty Marine, Cheltenham, 334
Dowty Mining Equipment, Ashchurch, 335
Dowty Rotol, Cheltenham, 334
Dowty Seals, Tewkesbury, 335
Dowty Technical Development, Andoversford, 335
Dozens (cloth), 169
Drainage, 51, 54, 56, 57, 60, 70, 81, 166, 356
Drainage (Somerset levels), 89, 145
Draycott, 60
Draycott Moor, 90
Drybrook, 10
Drybrook Limestone, 12
Drybrook Sandstone, 12, 13
Duck stamped pottery, 115, 120, 121, 124
Dudbridge, 338
Dulverton, 168, 169
Dumbleton, 31
Dumnonii, 121, 123
Dundas aqueduct, 229
Dundon, 22, 70
Dundry, 22, 23, 26, 27, 28, 34, 35, 36, 37, 53, 55, 56, 115, 120, 139
Dundry Freestone, 36
Dunes, 63, 97
Dunkerton, 37, 213, 229, 237
Dunkery Beacon, 9, 83, 96, 103, 152
Dunkhorn Hill, 40
Dunster, 9, 83, 103, 168, 169
Duramin Engineering Co., Lydney, 342
Durdham Down, 11
Durotriges, 121, 123, 125, 130
Dursley, 27, 28, 30, 33, 173, 206, 218, 227, 259, 265, 269, 270, 271, 278, 289, 310, 314, 316, 342, 362
Durston junction, 236
Dymock, 82, 359
Dyrham Park, 33, 144, 147

Eagle Star Insurance Co., Cheltenham, 282, 336
Eaker Hill, 8, 84, 85
East Bicknor, 176
East Brent, 203
East Coker, 44, 45, 261
East Flower Hill fault, 19

East Harptree, 77, 78, 112, 180
East Hill, 39
East India Co., 206, 211, 260
Eastcourt House, 45
Eastington, 115
Easton colliery, 255
Ebbw Vale Co., 253
Ebor gorge, 60, 106
Ebrington Hill, 31, 38
Ecclesiastical history, 156–58
Edford colliery, 255
Eddington Burtle, 62
Eddington-on-Polden, 112
Edgerton Burnetts, Wellington, 313
Eighteenth century, 70, 165, 166, 173, 175, 176, 177, 178, 179, 180, 181, 183, 184, 185, 190, 191, 192, 193, 194, 195–228, 255, 256, 268
Elasticized fabric, 263, 309
Elberton, 11, 12, 138
Electrical contracting, 329
Electrical engineering, 283, 286, 310, 311, 315, 316, 317, 324, 337, 339, 343, 344, 346
Electrical wholesaling, 329
Elevation and exposure, 97, 98, 100, 101, 102, 103, 248
Ellandun, battle of, 142
Ellick series, 85, 95
Elm, 68, 94
Elmbridge, 177
Emborough, 78
E.M.I. electronics, Wells, 316
Emmerson's works, 180, 212
Employers' associations, 207
Employment, 167, 171, 173, 174, 181, 207, 213, 255, 256, 258, 259, 261, 262, 263, 269, 271, 274, 275, 276, 277, 280, 281, 282, 283, 286, 287, 289, 312, 313, 317, 321, 325, 326, 333, 335, 336, 340, 343, 344
Employment structure, 280, 281
Enclosure, 92, 161, 162, 163, 164, 166, 177, 196, 197, 199, 200, 201, 202, 204, 248, 250
Enclosure Acts, 162, 163, 196
Engineering industries, 226, 227, 251, 265, 266, 267, 269, 270, 271, 272, 273, 274, 277, 284, 286, 306, 309, 310, 311, 315, 316, 323, 324, 325, 326, 333–37, 338, 339, 341, 342, 343, 344, 346
English Channel, 217
English elm, 94
English Stones, 24
Englishcombe, 33, 37, 139
Epi-Palaeolithic cultures, 106
Erica cinerea, 95

*Erica tetralix*, 96
*Eriophorum augustifolium*, 96
*Eriophorum vaginatum*, 96
Ermine Street, 38
Ermine Way, 126, 128, 129, 132
Erosion surfaces, 54–57
Ethylene, 320
Ethylene glycol, 320
Ethylene oxide, 320
Evaporated milk, 307
Evaporites, 24
Evenlode valley, 147
Evercreech junction, 237, 261, 307
Every year land, 165, 197
Evesham, 151, 156, 161, 273
Evesham series, 68, 69, 70, 75
Ewen, 46
Exeter, 187, 218, 219, 233, 236
Exford, 9, 83, 165
Exmoor, 3, 6, 7, 9, 25, 83, 92, 96, 103, 145, 152, 250, 302
Exmoor Forest, 9
Exmoor National Park, 96
Exmoor Society, The, 96
*Exon Domesday*, 149, 150, 164
Express Dairies, 307
Extractive industries, 163, 176–81, 212–14, 231, 251–55, 266, 280, 281, 283, 340

Failand, 11, 17, 18, 23, 25, 108, 117, 120, 153
Fairford, 45, 46, 137, 139, 147, 148, 239
Falfield, 27
Fallow, 161, 165, 197, 202, 204, 205, 296
Farleigh Hungerford, 40, 43, 44, 46, 169
Farm sizes, 244, 246, 299, 300, 302, 304
Farmborough compression belt, 18, 27
Farmhouse cheese making, 245, 250, 308
Farr, A. E., Westbury, 315
Farrington colliery, 255
Farrington group, 15
Farrington Gurney, 26, 69, 213
Fastolf, Sir John, 171
Faulting, 5, 6, 18, 19, 20, 24, 26, 37, 39
Fen peat, 62, 63, 96
Fen vegetation, 96, 109, 145
Fencing, 341
Fertilizer materials, 318, 320, 348, 340
Fertilizers, 318, 320, 347
*Festuca ovina*, 95
*Festuca rubra*, 95, 97
FethanLeag, battle of, 140
Fibreglass, 316
Field drainage, 244
Field systems, 146, 160, 161, 162
Filton, 27, 55, 239, 325, 326, 330
Findall mine, 252

Fishing, 117
Fishponds industrial estate, 329, 332
Fisons, Avonmouth, 318
Fladbury series, 87, 88, 89
Flax, 169, 204, 210
Flax Bourton, 56, 61, 153
Flaxley, 177, 212, 227, 266
Flooding, 81, 86, 87, 89, 90, 104, 112, 117, 145, 146, 198, 202, 218
Florentine wool buyers, 164, 172, 186
Flour milling, 308, 321, 329, 346
Fly boats, 230
Fluorspar, 318
Fodder crops, 291, 292, 295, 296, 304
Fog, 99, 104
Folding, 5, 6, 9, 13, 14, 16, 17, 18, 19, 20, 26, 27, 31, 35, 52, 53, 54
Foley family, 177, 178
Food processing industry, 245, 246, 247, 251, 265, 273, 274, 278, 284, 285, 306, 307, 308, 317, 320, 321, 322, 329, 333, 337, 341, 344, 345, 346
Food processing machinery, 273, 274, 324
Footwear components, 285, 312, 338
Ford, 91
Foreland Grits, 9
Forest Clay, 64
Forest Marble, 38, 39, 40, 41, 42, 43, 44, 45, 46, 47, 66, 153
Forest of Braydon, 48, 94, 144, 145, 146, 148, 164
Forest of Dean, 5, 6, 7, 8, 10, 11, 12, 13, 14, 15, 16, 18, 19, 24, 71, 80, 81, 82, 90, 92, 94, 103, 111, 115, 117, 119, 122, 131, 134, 135, 144, 145, 146, 147, 155, 158, 160, 164, 165, 174, 176, 177, 178, 179, 180, 181, 182, 194, 196, 197, 212, 223, 226, 230, 247, 252, 253, 266, 279, 280, 281, 283, 286, 287, 288, 300, 303, 309, 310, 315, 317, 336, 340–43, 359, 362
Forest of Dean Development Association, 340
Forest of Dean Iron Co., 252
Forest of Dean (Mines) Act 1838, 253
Forest of Dean (Mines) Act 1904/6, 253
Forest of Selwood, 47, 94, 142, 144, 145, 146, 149, 154, 157, 204
Forestry Commission, 92, 176, 340
Forges, 177, 178, 212
Fosseway, 126, 128, 129, 132, 135, 139, 141, 152, 153
Foundation garments, 313, 327, 333
Fox Bros., Wellington, 309
Frampton Cotterell, 23, 56, 72, 80, 81, 131, 161, 197, 266, 354, 356
Frampton-on-Severn, 307
Free Miners, 176, 177, 179, 253

Freestones, 41, 42
Freezing Hill, 30, 37
French wars, 220
Frenchay, 56
Freshford, 33, 114, 122, 169, 175, 210, 264
Friesians, 244
Frocester, 161, 247
Frome, 3, 5, 8, 17, 37, 39, 40, 41, 43, 44, 45, 46, 92, 107, 110, 112, 129, 155, 156, 157, 169, 174, 175, 181, 209, 210, 215, 218, 227, 235, 236, 237, 250, 254, 255, 256, 257, 259, 261, 264, 265, 276, 281, 283, 285, 286, 287, 306, 307, 308, 309, 310, 312, 314, 316, 362
Frome gap, 110, 112, 114, 122, 128, 152, 204
Frost heaving, 60
Frost hollows, 99
Frosts, 99
Fruit production, 72, 166, 204, 292, 296, 297, 303
Fry's, Somerdale, 321
Fuddle brook, 40
Fullers Earth, 38, 40, 41, 42, 65, 66, 170
Fullers Earth Clay, 34, 38, 39, 40, 41, 42, 43, 44, 66
Fullers Earth Rock, 39, 40, 41
Fulling mills, 167, 168, 169, 170, 173, 174, 211, 256
Furniture manufacture, 275, 314, 327, 329, 333, 337, 346, 347

Gales (mining), 176, 177, 253, 255, 340
Galvanizing, 272, 273, 323
Garden Cliff, 26
Gare Hill, 50
Garrard Engineering Co., Swindon, 343
Garrison theory, 154
Gatcombe, 129
Gatcombe Hill, 45
Gauge war, 234, 235
Gault Clay, 47, 50, 65, 200
Geology, 3–51
Geomorphology, 51, 52–63
Germany, 173
Gewissae, 139, 140
Gibbet Hill, 44
Gig-mills, 171, 173, 174, 207, 257
Glacial conditions, 57–63, 72, 73
Glass, 185, 222, 223
Glasshouse cultivation, 73, 296, 303
Glastonbury, 25, 26, 30, 31, 75, 89, 96, 112, 134, 145, 167, 204, 211, 236, 275, 312, 313, 316
Glastonbury Abbey, 143, 146, 156, 157, 158, 162, 164, 179
Glastonbury culture, 116, 121, 123, 124

Glastonbury lake village, 116, 117, 123
Glastonbury syncline, 53
Glevum, 125, 126, 131, 132
Gleying, 67, 68, 70, 71, 86
Gloucester, 21, 31, 54, 57, 59, 62, 75, 101, 105, 115, 125, 126, 128, 129, 131, 132, 148, 152, 154, 155, 156, 157, 167, 174, 178, 181, 182, 183, 184, 196, 197, 198, 212, 215, 217, 219, 226, 232, 233, 234, 235, 245, 247, 248, 267, 271, 272, 273, 275, 276, 279, 281, 285, 286, 289, 297, 300, 303, 306, 308, 315, 317, 334, 335, 336, 337, 346, 358, 359
Gloucester and Berkeley canal, 217, 232, 233
Gloucester Carriage & Wagon Co., 271, 276
Gloucester–Cheltenham industrial area, 279, 280, 282, 284, 286, 288, 292, 308, 315, 325, 334–37, 340, 351, 352, 354, 358, 359, 362
Gloucester and Cheltenham tramway, 233
Gloucester dairy cattle, 198, 205
Gloucester Engineering Co., Cheltenham, 334
Gloucester population, 267
Gloucester, port of, 183, 226
Gloucester cattle, 244
Gloucester ship canal, 217, 226, 232, 233
Gloucestershire agricultural tables, 244, 251, 290, 291, 292, 293, 296, 299
Glove making, 211, 266, 271, 274, 275, 312
Goat Hill, 44
Goblin Combe, 61, 120
Goblin Combe Oolite, 12
Godney Moor, 90
Godney series, 90
Golden Valley, 170
Golden Valley Mills, 276
Goldhill series, 65
Gordano valley, 61, 76, 96, 101, 153, 202, 297
Gorse, 77, 84, 85, 95, 96
Gorsey Bigbury, 110
Gough's cave, Cheddar, 106
Grabbist Hill, 9
Grain imports, 278, 321, 348, 349
Grand Western canal, 231
Grass farming, 68, 70, 78, 79, 86, 161, 195, 196, 198, 199, 201, 202, 204, 278, 290, 291, 292, 295
Grass leys, 69, 70, 71, 198
Grassland, 66, 67, 82, 86, 94, 95, 96, 97, 161, 244
Gravels, 22, 59, 60, 65, 73, 74, 75, 76, 107, 200, 281
Gravette implements, 106

*Great Britain*, S.S., 242
Great Burrington, 167
Great Hinton, 48
Great Oolite, 38 45, 57, 65
Great Ridge, 53
Great seam, 15
*Great Western*, S.S., 242
Great Witcombe, 33, 54, 59
Great Welsh glacials, 57
Green belts, 355, 356, 358
Green Bridge industrial estate, Swindon, 343, 344, 345
Greensand, 47, 49, 50, 65, 74, 94, 108, 200
Greinton series, 70, 71
Grey Marls, 24, 25, 70, 71
Grimboldsash Hundred, 173
Grittleton, 162
Grittleton House, 45
Gulley Oolite, 12
Gunn's Mill, 177
Gypsum, 24, 320

Haddon Hill, 83, 94
Haden Co., Trowbridge, 270
Hair cloth, 262
Hale Combe, 8
Hale-Trent Cakes, Clevedon, 309
Hallatrow, 229, 237
Hallen Marsh junction, 19
Hallstatt culture, 114
Ham complex, 70
Ham Green, 105
Ham Hill, 116, 120, 121, 130
Ham Hill stone, 32
Hambridge series, 74, 75
Hambrook, 23
Hamdon Hill, 32
Hampen Marley Beds, 42
Hampshire Basin, 53
Hand axes, 105
Hanging Hill, 37
Hanham, 55, 180, 222, 274, 277, 285, 302, 328, 329
Hangman Grits, 9, 83
Hanover Hill, 39
Hanseatic League, 182, 183, 186
Haresfield Beacon, 30
Harptree, 72, 77, 78, 112, 180, 254
Harptree Hill, 60, 153
Harptree, manor of, 179
Harris's of Calne, 246, 273, 308
Hartcliffe fault, 18
Hartpury, 26
Hawker Siddeley, 310, 325
Hawkesbury, 30, 33, 37, 40, 41, 151, 161, 167, 168, 170
Hawkesbury Upton, 41, 42

Hawling, 41
Hazel, 94, 109
Head deposits, 22, 23, 59, 60, 61, 70, 73, 75, 76, 79, 85
Heath grass, 95
Heather, 95, 96
Heddington, 50
Hedgerows, 92, 94, 244
Heinz Co., Swindon, 344
Hembury (Devon), 107
Henbury, 21, 146
Hengistbury Head, 123
Henton, 22
Herefords, 198
Herne Hill, 29, 30
Heywood, 48, 200
High Ham, 22, 70, 88, 145
High Littleton, 81, 213
High Vein seam, 15
Highbridge, 62, 203, 236, 281, 307, 308
Highworth, 47, 49, 200, 218
Hill, 27
Hill fog, 104
Hill forts, 114, 115, 116, 117, 119, 120, 121, 130
Hill forts (lists), 119, 120
Hillman, D. R., Frome, 314
Hillsley, 30, 33, 37, 38, 151
Hilmarton, 49
Hilperton, 47
Hinkley Point, 320
Hinton Blewett, 26
Hinton Charterhouse, 38, 39, 40, 42, 43, 44
Hinton Hill, 42, 138
Hinton Sands, 43
*Hippophae Rhamnoides*, 97
Hod Hill, 125
Hoffman Bearing Co., Stonehouse, 339
Hog's Back, 53
Holcombe, 213
Hollybush seam, 15
Holman, Bros., 324
Holt, 236
Holt Hill, 44
Holton, 46
Holway Hill, 32, 37
Holwell cave, 9
Honeybourne series, 65, 73, 75
Hope Hill, 61
Hope Mansell anticline, 13
Hops, 203, 303
Horlicks, 307
Hornbeam, 94
Hornsbury, 29
Horsechestnut, 94
Horsington, 46
Horsley, 206, 264

Horstman Gear Co., Bath 333
Horticulture, 166, 292, 302, 303
Horton, 30, 33, 37, 138, 161
Hosegoods Ltd., 321
Hotwells group, 13
Hotwells Limestone, 13
Hucclecote, 115
Hucclecote villa, 133, 134, 136
Hullavington, 46
Humidity, 98
Hundreds, 153, 154, 173
Hungerford, 139, 140, 236
Hunstrete, 213
Hunstrete fault, 19
Hunting pink, 256, 258, 259
Huntley, 21, 24, 340, 358, 359
Huntspill, 62, 166, 203
Huntspill river, 63, 89
Huntworth series, 74
Hurcot series, 69, 70
Hydraulic engineering, 283, 286, 325, 334, 335, 336, 337, 339, 344, 345
Hydrofluoric acid, 318, 320
Hwiccii, 142, 146, 156, 157, 159
Hyena Den, Wookey, 106

Iberian peninsula, 115, 120, 183, 186, 187, 188, 189, 192
Ice cream, 307, 308, 336
Icknield Way, 137
Iford, 169
Ilchester, 125, 126, 128, 129, 132, 133, 134, 136, 145, 152, 154, 181
Ilfracombe Beds, 9
Ilminster, 29, 30, 67, 74, 145, 155, 204, 210, 211, 218, 236, 259, 261, 262, 302, 307, 312
Imperial Chemical Industries, 285, 318, 319, 330, 352
Imperial Smelting Corp., 285, 286, 318, 319, 320, 352
Imperial Tobacco organization, 321
Industrial association, 320, 345
Industrial development certificates, 338, 351
Industrial groups, 283
Industrial groups,
    Clothing and footwear, 283, 285, 312, 313, 317, 327, 328, 329, 333, 346, 347
    Engineering and electrical goods, 283, 284, 287, 333
    Food, drink and tobacco, 283, 284, 317, 320, 321, 322
    Leather and leather goods, 283, 306, 317, 328
    Other manufactures, 283

Paper, printing and publishing, 283, 285, 313, 314, 317, 322, 323, 333
Timber and furniture, 283, 314, 317, 327
Vehicles, 283, 284, 317, 325, 344
Industrial location, 283, 287, 320, 325
Industrial revolution, 193, 208, 213, 234, 251, 260, 288, 330
Industrial structure, 280, 281
Inferior Oolite, 5, 31, 33, 34, 35, 36, 37, 38, 41, 45, 65, 66
Ingsdons Hill, 33
Innox Hill, 44
Innsworth Metals, Gloucester, 334
Input–output analysis, 346
Iron Acton, 16, 55, 56, 72, 81, 138, 197, 205, 214, 297, 358
Iron Acton fault, 19
Iron Age, 62, 107, 113, 114–24, 131, 133, 134
Iron Age coins, 121, 122, 123
Iron Age hill forts (lists), 119, 120
Iron Age tribes, 121, 122, 123, 125, 130, 131
Iron First 'A' culture, 114, 115
Iron First 'B' culture, 115
Iron furnaces, 177, 178, 212, 252
Iron manufacture, 155, 177, 178, 194, 266, 317
Iron mining, 115, 117, 123, 131, 132, 135, 176–78, 194, 212, 252, 253, 266, 340
Iron pans, 79, 83, 84
Iron Second 'B' cultures, 115
Iron Third 'C' cultures, 122
'Isceons', 318
Isle Abbotts series, 74
Isle Brewers series, 74, 75
Itchington, 23

Junction bed, 29, 30, 67
Jurassic, 3, 10, 22, 30, 32-47, 49, 52, 53, 54, 57, 65, 66, 67, 90, 101, 116, 149, 203, 240
Jurassic scarp, 30, 32, 34, 35, 36, 37, 149, 151
Jurassic Way, 116, 129, 151

Kale, 295
Keinton Mandeville, 163
Kellaways Beds, 46
Kemble, 46, 137, 144, 199, 239
Kemble Beds, 42
Kenn, 62
Kennard Moor, 87
Kennet and Avon canal, 217, 228, 229, 230, 231, 233
Kennet valley, 106, 139
Kerseys, 169, 259

Keuper Marl, 20, 21, 22, 23, 24, 25, 60, 61, 70, 71, 72, 74, 76, 88, 89, 201
Keuper Sandstone, 21, 24, 71, 72
Keynsham, 23, 26, 56, 156, 210, 222, 289, 320, 322, 332
Keynsham villa, 133
Kidney Hill fault, 19
Kilcott valley, 38
Kilmersden, 18, 213
Kimmeridge Clay, 48, 49, 64, 65, 72, 200
King Alfred, 154
King Arthur's cave, Ross, 106
King Cynegils, 157
King Ine, 143, 146, 157
Kingroad anchorage, 242
King's Sedge Moor, 89, 145, 203, 204, 218
Kings Weston, 19, 129
Kings Weston Down, 114, 120, 133
Kings Weston Hill, 11
Kings Weston villa, 133
King's Wood Warren, 50, 94
Kingsbury, 162
Kingsbury camp, 49
Kingsbury Episcopi, 29, 30
Kingsclere monocline, 53
Kingscote, 42
Kingsdown, 42, 122
Kingsettle Hill, 50
Kingsholm, 125, 126, 131
Kingston St Michael, 46
Kingstone, 30
Kingswood, 22, 55, 223, 263, 274, 277, 285, 309, 321, 322, 323, 326, 327, 328, 329, 362
Kingswood anticline, 6, 15, 17, 19, 25, 26, 53, 61, 68, 72, 80, 180, 181, 214, 223, 224, 225
Kingswood colliery, 255
Kingswood Great seam, 15
Kingswood & Parkfield Colliery Co. 255
Kington Magna, 48
Kleen-e-ze Co., 328
Knapp series, 85, 86
Knighton Hill, 44
Knowle Hill, 50
Knowle Moor, 89, 90
Kyneton, 8

La Tène culture, 114, 116
Lace, 210, 262
Lacock, 46, 47, 108, 114, 122, 199
Ladden brook, 55, 56
Lake villages, 115, 116
Lamyat, 30, 33
Land tenure, 162
Langard Budville, 21
Langford, 76

Langford series, 75, 76, 84
Langley Hill, 38
Langport, 25, 26, 28, 53, 87, 89, 132, 145, 154, 155, 169, 204, 236, 237, 308, 312
Lansdown Hill, 30, 33, 37, 40, 130
Lassington, 26
Latcham series, 87
Latteridge, 23
Lavas, 7
Lawrence Weston, 21
Le Catillon hoard, 121
Leaching, 104
Lead mining, 78, 117, 123, 125, 128, 129, 133, 134, 135, 152, 178, 179, 212, 252, 253, 254
Lead shot, 179, 188, 222, 318
Leather working, 274, 275, 312, 313, 328
Lechlade, 46, 101, 147, 148, 218, 247, 281
Leckhampton, 114, 119, 137, 151
Leckhampton Hill, 30, 33
Leffmans, Bridgwater, 313
Leicester/Cotswold crossbreds, 172, 198
Leigh Delamere, 46
Leigh Woods, 55
Leighterton, 138
Leland, 163, 165, 166
Levallois technique, 105
Lias, 3, 16, 22, 23, 24, 25, 26, 27, 28, 29, 31, 34, 40, 52, 53, 55, 57, 60, 67, 69, 72, 73, 74, 78, 79, 87, 88, 89, 112, 145, 147, 149, 150, 152, 163, 196, 203, 251
Lightmoor collieries, 253
Lillington Hill, 44
Lime trees, 92
Limestone quarrying, 240, 281
Limpley Stoke, 210, 237, 273, 277
Lincoln, 126, 128
Linden decline, 110
*Lindinis*, 125, 130
Linen manufacture, 169, 204, 210, 261, 262, 288, 289
Ling, 95, 96
Linolite Co., Malmesbury, 316
Linton (Forest of Dean), 177
Linton & Hirst, Swindon, 344
Listers, Dursley, 270, 271, 310, 342
Little Sodbury, 30, 32, 33, 37
Little Solsbury (Bath), 114, 115, 116, 117, 119, 130
Littleton, 23, 138
Littleton villa, 133, 134
Litton, 26
Liverpool, 184, 193, 218, 220, 221, 226, 242
Livery cloths, 256
Livestock numbers, 293, 303–305
Llandovery, 7

Local government areas, 362, 363
Lodge Hill, 37, 47
London, 49, 173, 175, 183, 184, 186, 187, 188, 193, 198, 206, 209, 210, 211, 215, 217, 219, 228, 233, 245, 261, 287, 307, 318, 343, 344, 346, 347, 358
London basin, 53
London cloth market, 172, 175, 186, 190, 209, 257
London liquid milk supply, 245, 247, 250, 307
London Royal Africa Co., 190
London, trade to, 172, 346, 347
Long Ashton, 13, 23, 61, 97, 98, 101, 129, 202
Long barrows, 107, 108, 109, 124
Long Burton, 45
Long Lode series, 67
Long mounds, 107
Longhope, 177, 340
Longleat Park, 47, 48, 50, 94
Longridge Hill, 38
Longtree Hundred, 173
Low Ham villa, 133, 134, 136
Lower Asholt, 9
Lower Avon-Bristol-Severnside industrial area, 282, 286, 288, 317–34, 351, 352, 354
Lower Calcareous Grit, 48, 49, 64
Lower Coal Measures Series, 14, 17
Lower Coal Series, 15, 18, 19, 20, 80, 181
Lower Cromhall Sandstone, 12
Lower Devonian, 9
Lower Dolomite, 12, 340
Lower Drybrook Sandstone, 12, 13
Lower Failand, 8
Lower Freestone, 34, 35
Lower Lias Clay, 27, 28, 29, 37, 67, 68, 73, 75, 94, 198, 202, 203
Lower Limestone (Inferior Oolite), 34
Lower Limestone Shales, 11, 20, 79, 85
Lower Severn axis, 5, 6, 7, 12, 14, 16, 17, 18, 19, 20, 27
Lower Stone, 8
Lower Tremadoc, 6
Lower Trigonia Grit, 35
Lower Westbury Beds, 25
Luckington fault, 19
Lucott Hill, 9
Ludlow Sandstones, 6
Lufton villa, 133
Lulsgate fault, 18
Lulsgate series, 76, 77, 78, 80, 95
Lusty Hill, 39
Luxborough, 135
Lydbrook, 177, 252
Lydford series, 88

Lydney, 10, 13, 18, 115, 119, 177, 235, 252, 266, 340, 341, 342
Lydney Park, 135, 136
Lyneham, 47, 49, 200
Lynmouth, 9
Lynton Beds, 9
Lysaght Co., Bristol, 272, 273

McAdam, 240
Madder, 183, 203
Maes Down, 37
Maes Knoll, 37, 115, 139, 140, 141
Maesbury, 8
Maesbury series, 84, 95
Magdalenean culture, 106
Maglemose culture, 106
Maiden Bradley, 128
Maiden Castle, 121, 125, 130
Maiden Hill, 38
Malago valley, 23, 56
Malmesbury, 45, 46, 47, 48, 154, 155, 157, 168, 171, 199, 218, 239, 261, 262, 286, 302, 306, 311, 316
Malmesbury Abbey, 142, 156, 157, 161
Malvern Hills, 5, 57
Malvernoid, 5, 13, 16, 17, 18, 31
Mangotsfield, 214, 224, 234, 278, 321, 362
Mangotsfield junction, 234
Manufacturing industry, 268, 269–77, 279, 280, 282–89, 306–30, 333–47
Maperton, 39
Marden brook, 47
Mardon, Son & Hall, 322
Mardon's mill, 276
Marine influences, 98
Mark, 87, 166, 203
Market gardening, 65, 71, 72, 73, 75, 76, 81, 201, 204, 246, 248, 292, 303
Markets, 155, 156
Marksbury, 18, 37, 213
Marksbury fault, 19
Marley Group, Frome, 309, 316
Marlstone ledge, 67, 151, 153, 248
Marnhull, 47
Marnhull series, 66
Marram, 97
Marshes Hill, 30
Marshfield, 40, 41, 42, 171, 174, 316
Marston Bigot, 44
Martock, 29, 32, 67, 161, 262, 269, 275
Martock series, 67
Masson Scott Thrissell Engineering Co., 324
Masterton Down, 50
Match manufacture, 276, 337
Max series, 88, 89
May Hill, 5, 6, 13, 16, 19, 21, 24, 82, 103

Meadowland, 146, 147, 148, 149, 162, 166, 198, 201, 204, 205, 247, 248
Meare, 26
Meare lake village, 116, 117, 123
Meat processing industry, 308, 322, 346
Mechanical engineering, 270–74, 283, 310, 311, 315, 316, 317, 324, 341, 342, 343, 344
Mediterranean produce, 183, 187, 189, 192
'Medley cloths', 175, 176, 208, 210
Meldun, 157
Melksham, 47, 48, 199, 200, 235, 245, 269, 270, 277, 278, 289, 307, 310, 311, 314, 315, 316, 335, 362, 363
Melksham Forest, 144, 145, 146, 148
Mells, 14, 18, 37, 39, 44, 116, 122, 156, 213, 264
Mells colliery, 255
Mells Down, 44
Meltons, 256, 258, 259
Mendip, 3, 5, 6, 7, 8, 10, 11, 12, 13, 14, 16, 17, 18, 19, 20, 21, 22, 25, 26, 27, 28, 29, 30, 31, 33, 34, 36, 37, 38, 39, 44, 53, 55, 56, 60, 61, 68, 69, 70, 71, 72, 75, 76, 77, 78, 79, 82, 84, 85, 88, 92, 95, 97, 98, 99, 100, 103, 104, 106, 107, 108, 109, 110, 111, 112, 113, 114, 115, 117, 120, 121, 122, 124, 128, 129, 132, 133, 134, 135, 142, 145, 149, 150, 152, 153, 156, 176, 178, 179, 180, 201, 202, 203, 211, 212, 218, 237, 240, 250, 253, 254, 281, 297, 298, 302, 362
Mendip archipelago, 25
Mendip caves, 106, 111, 114
Mendip complex, 78, 79, 80, 95
Mendip coombes and gorges, 59, 60, 106
Mendip Liberties, 178, 179
Mendip mining laws, 179
Mendip Royal Forest, 178
Mendip sheep, 198
Meon Hill, 115, 119
Mercia, 140, 141, 142, 153, 154, 155, 157, 158, 159
Merino wool, 173, 200, 207
Merridge, 9
Mesolithic cultures, 106, 107, 108, 109, 111
Mesozoic, 3, 5, 6, 25, 52, 54, 56, 57, 59, 63, 78
Metal Agencies, Engineering, 326
Metal Box Co., Swindon, 344
Metal ores, 78, 115, 117, 123, 125, 128, 129, 131–35, 152, 176–78, 179, 180, 251, 252, 348, 349
Metals, 155, 177, 178, 179, 180, 222, 223, 252, 254, 255, 273, 286, 318, 348, 349
Metal using industries, 222, 223, 226, 265,

269, 270, 271, 272, 273, 274, 276, 317, 323, 326, 329, 330, 336, 339, 341, 342, 343
Micheldean, 7, 10, 18, 82, 343
Michelsberg culture, 107
Mickleton, 59
Micklewood Beds, 6
M.I.D.A.S., 352, 359
Middle Ages, 94, 153, 159, 160, 164, 165, 169, 172, 178, 179, 180, 181, 182, 185, 225, 226
Middle Cromhall Sandstone, 13
Middle Lias, 28, 29, 30, 31, 33, 34
Middle Lias Marlstone, 29, 30, 32, 59, 66, 67, 151, 153, 248
Middle Mills, Cam, 313
Middlezoy, 22, 62, 106, 156, 163, 203
Midelney series, 89
Midford, 41, 229, 237
Midford Sands, 31, 32, 33
Midland Dairies, 307
Midsomer Norton, 22, 213, 266, 276, 283, 289, 308, 312, 314
Milborne Port, 5, 36, 37, 39, 44, 153, 154, 158, 163, 211, 275, 313
Milbury Heath, 8
Milk, 202, 205, 292, 303, 304, 306, 307, 308
Milk condenseries, 245, 273, 307
Milk and dairy herd, 293, 294
Milk, liquid, 202, 205, 244, 245, 247, 249, 250, 278, 305, 307
Milk Marketing Board, 308
Milk processing industries, 245, 246, 247, 273, 284, 306, 307, 308, 346
Mill buildings, 206, 207, 208, 209, 211, 256, 257, 338
Millgrit seam, 15
Milling machinery, 273
Millstone Grit Series, 13, 14, 80
Millwrights, 269, 270
Milton Clevedon, 30
Milverton, 155, 211, 236, 259, 261, 264
Minchinhampton, 43, 126, 138, 143, 161, 168, 170
Minchinhampton Freestones, 42
Mindel-Riss interglacial, 105
Mine law courts, 177
Minehead, 53, 236, 268, 286, 307, 312, 316
Mineries (Mendip), 179, 254
Mines Royal Act, 180
Mining and quarrying, 176–81, 212–14, 230, 240, 251–55, 264, 266, 280, 281, 283, 340
Ministry of Agriculture, Fisheries & Food, 289–99

Ministry of Aircraft Production, 341
Ministry of Defence, 281, 333
Minsterworth, 26
Miocene earth movements, 52, 53, 54, 56
Miserden, 38, 41, 42, 43, 54, 264
Mixed farming, 201, 202, 204, 249, 292, 302, 303
Molasses, 348, 349
*Molinia*, 85
*Molinia caerulea*, 96
Molybdenum in soils, 68
Monkton Farleigh, 42, 44
*Mons Badonicus*, 141
Montacute, 275
Montacute House, 32
Moons Hill Complex, 85
Moons Hill series, 85
Moorewood, 15
Moorgreen fault, 19
Moorland, 83, 96, 201
Morelands, Glastonbury, 275, 313
Morelands, Gloucester, 337
Moreton-in-Marsh, 148, 247, 307
Morgan's Hill, 139, 140
Morte Slates, 9
Mosquito netting, 262
Motor transport, 240, 325
Motorways, 330, 331, 332, 345, 350, 351, 353, 355, 356, 359
Moulded Footwear Co., 327
Mountain Limestone, 11
Mousterian culture, 106
Mozing mills, 174
Multivallate hill forts, 119, 120
Municipal Corporation Commission, 226
Mushroom production, 298
Muster rolls, 167, 171
Mycalex, Cirencester, 315

Nails, manufacture of, 155, 178, 188
Nailsea, 14, 19, 202, 308, 352, 354, 355
Nailsea coalfield, 19, 20, 23, 223, 254
Nailsea glass, 223
Nailsworth, 143, 206, 227, 259, 269, 270, 276, 308, 314, 338
Naish House fault, 18
Naphtha, 320
Nash Hill, 47
National Forest Park, 176
National Ports Council, 349
Naunton, 38, 41, 43
Neolithic, 107–10, 111
Neolithic cultures, 107–10, 123, 124
Neolithic pottery, 107–110
Neolithic wooden trackways, 109, 112
Nestlés, 245, 307
Netham, 240, 273

Nethercombe, 171
Netting, 169, 210
Nettlebridge, 18, 81
Nettlebridge colliery, 255
Nettleton Shrub, 135
New Cross, 30
New Dock Co., 240
New Draperies, 172
New Mendip Engineering Co., Melksham, 311
New Passage, 235
New Rock, 15
New Rock colliery, 255
New Wear, 212
Newbury, 15, 215, 217
Newbury colliery, 255
Newbury Hill, 40
Newent, 71, 72, 303, 340
Newman-Hender, Woodchester, 270, 272, 339
Newmans Ltd., Yate, 324
Newnham, 24
Newport, 193, 215, 273, 353
Newton Park, 139
Nibley, 80, 81
Nibley Knoll, 38
Nibley series, 80, 81
Nineteenth century, 173, 178, 180, 181, 184, 193, 194, 195–228, 229–78, 279
Nineteenth century population changes, 263–68, 278
*Nodens*, 135
Non-ferrous metal industry, 155, 177–80, 193, 212, 222, 223, 253, 254, 272, 311, 317, 318, 319, 330, 336, 337, 339, 342, 344, 346, 347
Non-ferrous ores (imported), 278, 318, 348, 349
Nordrach series, 78, 79, 80, 84, 95
Normalair-Garret, Yeovil, 284, 311
North Bradley, 44, 46
North Cadbury, 67
North Cheriton, 46
North Curry, 158
North Drain, 89
North Hill, 8, 17, 18, 60, 79, 80, 84
North Hill fault, 18
North Hill (Minehead), 9, 83
North Nibley, 30, 264
North Newton series, 71, 72
North Wiltshire canal, 230
North Wootton, 45
Northleach, 34, 38, 41, 151, 164, 167, 196, 217
Norton, 46
Norton-Radstock, 283, 312
Norton St Philip, 40, 210

Notgrove, 41
Nottingham Hill, 30, 33, 54, 73
Notts Industries, Frome, 310
Nuclear power stations, 320
Nunney, 37, 39
Nunney brook, 39
Nylon polymer, 336, 346
Nympsfield, 41, 43, 129, 264

Oak woodlands, 68, 78, 81, 91, 92, 94, 96
Oaksey, 46
Oakwood mine, 252
Oare, 9
Oats, 165, 166, 197, 200, 201, 203, 246, 248, 249, 295, 296, 297, 306
Odd Down, 41, 42, 139
Offa, 140
Office employment, 281, 282, 332, 333
Oilcake manufacture, 273, 321
Oilseed imports, 273, 278, 321
Old Red Sandstone, 6, 7, 8, 9, 10, 11, 14, 18, 20, 24, 37, 52, 72, 79, 82, 84, 85, 95, 134
Old Sarum, 128, 139, 140, 152
Old Sling mine, 252
Old Sodbury, 30, 33, 37, 40, 42, 116, 217
Oldbury, 24
Oldbury-on-Severn, 320
Oldland, 15
Oldland Colliery Co., 255
Oldmixon Crescent estate, Weston-super-Mare, 288
Oligocene earth movements, 52
Olive oil, 186, 188, 191
Olveston, 10, 12, 23, 138, 146
Oolites, 10, 12, 42, 43, 59, 65, 73, 91, 92, 95, 145, 147, 150, 159, 199, 203
Oolitic Marl, 34
Open fields, 146, 160, 161, 162, 163, 196, 200, 201, 204
Oppenheimer Co., Swindon, 344
Orchards, 67, 76, 78, 166, 201, 203, 204, 248, 296, 297, 298, 303, 308
Ordovician, 6
Organic soils, 70, 85, 89, 90
Ostorius Scapula, 125
Othery, 22, 70, 71, 203
Otterhampton, 26
Out-of-town shopping centres, 331, 358
Out-of-town station (Stoke Gifford, Bristol Parkway), 239, 356, 358
Outports, 220, 239, 242, 243, 268
Over, 10
Over Compton, 32
Over Stowey, 9
Overalls and uniforms, 313, 327, 344
Overbury, 186

Overspill arrangements, 279, 306, 343, 344
Overtown, 38, 41
Owlpen, 173, 264
Oxenton, 31, 38, 54, 114, 119, 138
Oxford Clay, 44, 45, 46, 47, 48, 49, 50, 57, 64, 67, 72, 94, 101, 149, 150, 199, 204
Oxfordshire, 43, 46, 47, 122, 138, 217
Oxo Co., Chippenham, 308
Ozleworth valley, 38

Packaging industry, 274, 283, 285, 322, 323, 324, 328, 330, 338, 340, 344, 345, 346
Packaging machinery, 274, 283
Pagan burials, 137, 138, 139, 142, 143
Pagan's Hill, 114, 135, 136
Painswick, 34, 35, 38, 54, 170, 206, 259, 265
Painswick Hill, 54
Painswick syncline, 35, 54
Palaeolithic, 21, 105, 106
Palaeozoic, 3, 5, 7, 21, 22, 24, 25, 54, 56, 57, 63, 67, 72, 76
Panborough, 87
Paper bags and sacks, 274, 322, 338
Paper making industry, 227, 273, 274, 276, 277, 278, 285, 306, 312, 313, 314, 322, 323, 324, 329, 330, 338, 341, 346
Paper making machinery, 274, 324
Paper-pulp imports, 276, 278, 322, 348, 349
Parent materials, 64–90
Park End, 212, 252
Park End colliery, 253
Parkfield colliery, 255
Parkfield seam, 15
Parnalls, Yate, 326
Parnells, Fishponds, 322
Parrot seam, 15
Parsonage Farm industrial estate, Swindon, 343, 344
Patchway, 55, 56, 330
Patney, 237
Paulton, 18, 37, 72, 213, 237, 254, 266, 285, 312, 314
Paulton fault, 18
Paven Hill, 49
Pawlett, 26, 95, 203
Pea Grit, 34
Peasdowne, 40
Peat, 3, 62, 63, 89, 90, 96, 117, 146
Pecketts, 272
Pen Hill, 8, 12, 17, 19, 33, 37, 79, 84, 85, 103
Penistones (cloth), 259
Pennant Sandstones, 14, 15, 81, 134
Pennant Series, 15, 19, 20, 80, 81

Pennard, 25, 26, 29, 30, 67, 68
Pennard Sands, 29, 30
Pennard series, 67
Pennine trends, 54
Pennsylvania, 40
Penpole Point, 179
Penselwood, 47, 94, 142
Pensford, 15, 18, 81, 169, 181, 213, 237, 254
Periclines, 5, 6, 7, 8, 11, 12, 13, 16, 17, 18, 19, 20, 21, 25, 27, 60, 79, 82, 84, 85
Periglacial conditions, 57–63, 85, 91
Permanent grass, 244, 290, 295, 296, 297, 303, 304, 305
Permanent pasture, 244, 246, 247, 249, 251, 290, 295, 296, 297, 303, 304, 305
Permian, 9, 20, 70, 74
Perry making, 298, 308, 309
Perseverence mine, 252
Pershore series, 73
Peterborough culture, 109, 111
Petrochemical industries, 286, 319, 320, 330
Petroleum imports, 232, 233, 278, 348, 349
Petters, Yeovil, 271
Pharmaceutical chemicals, 320, 330, 337, 351
Philblack Ltd., Avonmouth, 319
Phosphoric acid, 318
Phosphorus, 320
Piano fabrics, 259
Piano manufacture, 259, 276, 339
Pickwell Down Grits, 9
Pig rearing, 166, 204, 246, 248, 284, 292, 303, 304, 305
Pigmeat industry, 246, 247, 284, 308, 322
Pigs, 246, 247, 293, 294, 295, 303, 304, 305
Pill, 55, 61, 219
Pillowell fault, 19
Pilton, 22
Pilton Beds, 9
Pin making industry, 226, 339, 342
Pines Express, 237
Pinkney House, 45
Pinnacle Co., 328
Pitmans, Bath, 333
Pitminster, 25
Place-names, 138, 142, 143, 144, 145, 146, 147
Plastic films, 315, 322, 346
Plastics industries, 286, 306, 315, 316, 318, 322, 328, 329, 337, 339, 340
Pleistocene breccias, 61
Pleistocene glaciations, 57, 59
Pleistocene transgression, 55
Plessey organization, Swindon, 343
Pliocene transgression, 55

Plywood manufacture, 341
Podimore series, 73
Podzolisation, 79, 83, 84
Polden Hills, 22, 25, 26, 28, 61, 62, 69, 70, 71, 87, 88, 109, 112, 129, 132, 136, 145, 146, 149, 152, 153, 163, 202, 203, 204, 298
Pollen analysis, 109, 112, 116, 117
Polsham series, 75
Poole, 210, 215, 236, 237
Poole Keynes, 46
Population distribution, 256, 263–68, 279, 289, 353, 354, 356, 358, 359
Porlock, 9, 53, 157
Porlock valley, 83, 99
Port of Bristol Authority, 243, 349, 350
Port of Bristol, trade, 181–93, 226, 276, 277, 278, 347–51
Port Improvement, Bristol, 220, 221, 225, 226, 240, 242, 268, 277, 349
Portbury, 8, 61, 139, 140, 243, 349, 350
Portbury plan, 349, 350
Portishead, 6, 8, 11, 14, 25, 56, 108, 139, 163, 239, 243, 268, 297, 320, 327, 330, 349
Portishead Beds, 8
Portishead dock, 243
Portishead Down, 8
Portishead Pier & Railway Co., 239, 243
Portishead wood-pulp terminal, 351
Portland Beds, 49, 50
Port oriented industries, 317–23
Portskewett ferry, 235
Postlip, 227, 276, 313
Potatoes, 81, 200, 201, 203, 204, 205, 246, 248, 296, 297
Potential transpiration, 103, 104
*Potentilla erecta*, 95
Poulton, 44, 46
Poultry, 292, 293, 294, 303, 304, 305
Precipitation, 101, 102, 103, 104
Prehistoric agriculture, 109, 112, 113, 117, 122, 123
Prehistoric period, 105–24
Prehistoric trackways in Somerset levels, 109, 112
Pressed Steel Fisher, Swindon, 344
Pressure steam reforming process, 320
Preston, 46
Price Bros., Wellington, 309
Priddy, 8, 60, 78, 79, 85, 111, 112, 135, 254
Priddy Circles, 79
Priddy series, 79
Printing and publishing, 227, 276, 277, 278, 285, 306, 313, 314, 322, 323, 329, 330, 337

Printing machinery, 324
Priston, 33, 40
Providence Hill, 13
Provisions, 278
*Pteridium aquilinum*, 95
Ptolemy, 121
Publow group, 15
*Puccinellia maritima*, 97
Puckington, 30
Pucklechurch, 16, 26, 144, 214, 266, 332
Pucklechurch airfield, 332
Pump manufacture, 324, 336, 342
Purbeck Beds, 49, 50
Puriton, 26, 129, 153
Purnells, Paulton, 314
Purple moor grass, 96
Purse Caundle, 39, 41
Purton, 47, 49, 142, 200

Quantock Preserving Co., Bridgwater, 309
Quantocks, 3, 6, 7, 8, 9, 16, 21, 25, 27, 53, 55, 60, 70, 71, 83, 84, 92, 96, 103, 111, 120, 145, 147, 149, 152, 201, 205, 302
Quantoxhead, 26
Quartz Conglomerate, 7, 8, 82
Quartzitic Sandstone Group, 14, 19, 20, 80
Quaternary, 51, 56–63
Quaternary deposits, 3
Quaternary earth movements, 25
Queen Charlton, 55, 254
Queen's Sedge Moor, 89
Quennington, 227

Radiation group, 326
Radstock, 18, 37, 40, 44, 115, 181, 213, 229, 235, 237, 254, 255, 266, 283, 308, 312, 314
Radstock basin, 5, 14, 15, 16, 18, 19, 181, 254, 280
Radstock Group, 15
Radstock shelf, 27, 28, 34
Rael Hill, 38
Rag Ruff seam, 15
Ragstones, 35
Railway gauges, 234, 235, 237, 239
Railways, 184, 213, 214, 230, 231, 233–40, 243, 245, 246, 249, 252, 254, 255, 263, 266, 267, 268, 271, 272, 277, 311, 332, 343
Railways,
    Avonmouth Pier & Railway Co., 239, 243
    Berkshire & Hampshire Extension, 236, 237
    Birmingham & Gloucester, 233, 234, 247
    Bristol & Exeter, 231, 233, 235, 236, 239, 243

Bristol–Gloucester, 214, 233, 234, 235, 247
Bristol–New Passage, 235
Bristol & North Somerset, 237, 254
Central Dorset, 236
Central Somerset, 236
Cheddar Valley, 236
Clifton Down Extension, 239, 243
East Gloucestershire, 239
East Somerset, 236
Great Western, 231, 233, 234, 235, 236, 237, 239, 243, 245, 268, 271
Great Western Union, 233
London–Bristol, 233, 235, 239
London Midland Region (B.R.), 237
London Midland and Scottish, 237
Midland, 234, 235, 237, 239, 243
Portishead Pier & Railway Co., 239, 243
Somerset & Dorset, 235, 236, 237
South Wales railways, 234, 235, 237, 239
South Western, 235, 236, 237
Wiltshire Somerset & Dorset, 235
Wiltshire Somerset & Weymouth, 235, 236
Rainfall, 83, 84, 101, 102, 103, 104
Raised bogs, 62, 63, 90, 96, 117
Ram Hill fault, 19
Ramsbury, 157
Rangeworthy, 55, 80, 358
Rank Xerox, Micheldean, 343
Reafforestation Acts (Forest of Dean), 177
Red Devon cattle, 202, 250
Red Down, 49
Red fescue, 95, 97
Red Marls, 24, 70, 71, 205
Red Measures, 15, 16, 80
Red Somerset cattle, 202
Redbrook, 177, 180, 212
Redcliffe Hill lead shot tower, 318
Reform Act (1832), 155, 226
Religious houses, 156–58
Religious houses (lists), 158
Rendcombe, 42
Retail services, 331, 333, 334, 358
Rhaetic, 22, 23, 24, 25, 26, 27, 28, 68, 70, 78
Rice grass, 96
Ridgeway, 10
Ridgeway, The, 151
Ridgeways, 110, 151
Rinyo-Clacton culture, 109
Rio Tinto organizations, 318
Riss glacial, 105
River development, 54, 56, 57, 61, 62
River traffic, 150, 151, 181, 184, 212, 214, 240
Rivers, 150, 151, 184

Rivers,
Avon (Bristol), 8, 10, 11, 12, 17, 21, 23,
26, 27, 31, 33, 37, 40, 41, 42, 43, 46,
47, 48, 53, 54, 55, 56, 57, 62, 71, 72,
82, 101, 105, 107, 108, 110, 111, 113,
114, 116, 117, 119, 120, 122, 128, 132,
138, 139, 140, 141, 142, 146, 149, 152,
153, 156, 157, 158, 159, 161, 169, 170,
171, 174, 181, 184, 200, 201, 202, 204,
206, 210, 214, 217, 221, 230, 233, 242,
243, 248, 250, 255, 278, 297, 298, 300,
349
Avon (Little), 57, 82, 173, 206, 309
Avon (Warwickshire), 57, 59, 132, 138,
148, 165
Axe, 22, 29, 57, 60, 62, 86, 87, 89, 90,
105, 121, 149, 153, 202, 203
Biss, 47, 138
Brue, 22, 28, 30, 33, 39, 46, 47, 57, 62,
68, 87, 89, 145, 147, 149, 169, 202,
203, 204
Cam, 30, 33, 38, 39, 57, 173, 206, 309
Cale, 46, 47
Cary, 87
Cherwell, 122
Chew, 22, 88, 109, 114, 115, 129, 138,
153, 169, 206
Coln, 33, 61, 139, 143, 148, 151
Firehead, 74
Frome, 23, 39, 40, 42, 44, 46, 47, 55,
56, 81, 138, 169, 221, 356
Frome (Stroud), 30, 33, 38, 43, 54, 57,
148, 170, 215, 338, 339
Isbourne, 54
Isle, 29, 74, 302
Kenn, 62, 202
Lox Yeo, 22, 76
Mells, 39, 40
Otter, 105
Parrett, 21, 32, 39, 57, 61, 68, 74, 86,
87, 89, 121, 136, 142, 143, 149, 150,
152, 169, 184, 203, 214, 231, 302
Ray, 49
Severn, 6, 7, 10, 12, 14, 17, 21, 22, 24,
26, 52, 54, 56, 57, 59, 62, 67, 82, 86,
95, 96, 101, 105, 108, 115, 116, 119,
122, 126, 129, 131, 132, 144, 146, 148,
165, 178, 182, 185, 195, 196, 198, 214,
215, 229, 232, 247, 349, 358
Stour, 46, 47
Thames, 48, 49, 54, 57, 107, 109, 110,
114, 119, 137, 138, 139, 140, 141, 143,
144, 147, 148, 151, 159, 165, 200, 215,
217, 229, 230, 281
Tone, 169, 184, 203, 214, 226, 231, 302
Trym, 21
Usk, 215

Windrush, 34, 61, 139, 148, 151, 165
Wye, 7, 10, 11, 24, 103, 113, 119, 135,
177, 182, 185, 215
Yeo, 22, 23, 29, 32, 36, 37, 39, 57, 62,
120, 129, 130, 133, 149, 152, 153, 169,
202, 203
Road metal, 240, 281
Road patterns, 150-53, 239, 240
Roads, condition of, 181, 184, 200, 213,
214, 217, 218, 219, 239, 240
Robin's Wood Hill, 31
Robinson, E.S&A Ltd., 322
Robertsons, Bristol, 322
Rockhampton, 27
Rodborough, 170, 265
Rodborough Common, 38
Roddenbury Hill, 47
Rode, 169, 264
Rodmarton, 116
Rodmore, 227
Rolls Royce, Bristol Engines Division,
284, 312, 325
Roman agriculture, 130, 131, 132, 133, 134
Roman baths, 130, 131
Roman coal mining, 131, 132
Roman coins, 133, 136
Roman field systems, 134
Roman iron mining, 131, 132, 135
Roman lead mining, 125, 128, 129, 133,
134, 135, 152
Roman occupation, 63, 121, 125-36, 145,
149, 151, 155, 158, 178
Roman pottery, 132
Roman quarrying, 131, 132
Roman roads, 126, 128, 129, 130, 131, 132,
133, 152
Roman temples, 135, 136
Roman villas, 129, 130, 132, 133, 134, 136
Romanization, 130, 131, 133, 136, 137
Romano-British Clay, 63, 86, 89, 90
Romans, 43
Rookham, 79
Rope manufacture, 169, 210
Ross-on-Wye, 3, 5, 215, 353
Ross series, 72, 82
Rotation grass and lucerne, 290, 295, 296,
303, 304, 305
Rough grazing, 290, 291, 296
Round barrows, 109, 111, 112, 113
Roundway, 50
Rowberrow, 78, 180
Rowley, 227
Rownham ferry dock, 221
Royal Edward dock, 243, 318, 350
Royal Forests, 160, 176, 178. See also
Forests of Braydon, Dean and Selwood
and Chippenham, Exmoor, Mendip and

Melksham Forests
Royal Fort, 14
Royal lands, 156–58, 161, 176
Rubber glove making, 342, 346
Rubber industry, 273, 276, 277, 278, 312, 314, 315, 316, 339, 342, 346, 347
Run-rig, 162
Rye grass, 94, 95

Sacking, 261, 262
Sailcloth, 169, 210, 261, **272**
St Annals mine, 252
St Annes Board Mills, 322, 351
St Briavels, 21
St Briavels Hundred, 176
St Catherine, 33
St Congar, 157
St Cuthbert works, Priddy, 254
St Decuman, 157
St Dunstan, 158
St Dyfrig, 157
St George's Land, 12
St Leonards, 177
St Mary, Redcliffe, 36
St Patrick, 157
St Petroc, 157
*Salix atrocinera*, 96
Sallow carr, 96
Sallow trees, 96
Salmonsbury, 114, 115
Salt marsh grass, 97
Saltway, The, 38, 129, 132
Salters Path, 151
Saltford, 57
Saltways, 151, 153
Sand and gravel, 281
Sand Hall series, 70
Sand sedge, 97
Sandford, 60
Sandford Orcas, 30, 32, 153
Sandy Lane, 108, 128, 132, 302
Sandyridge, 200
Sapperton, 57, 138
Saucer barrows, 112
Sauveterrian cultures, 106
Savernake Forest, 139
Saw-milling, 275, 314, 326, 337, 338, **339**, 340, 341
Saxon agriculture, 67, 143, 145, **146**, **147**, 148, 150, 152
Saxon brooches, 137, 138
Saxon cemeteries, 137, 138, 139
Saxon hide, 146, 147, 154
Saxon land charters, 142, 143, **144**, **145**, 146, 147, 151
Saxon land use, 143, 146, 147, **148**, **149**, 150, 152

Saxon palace (Cheddar), 155
Saxons, 137–59
Scarplands, 3, 65
Scottsquar ridge, 38
Scribbling machines, 209
Sea Buckthorne, 97
Sea Crouch, 97
Sea grass, 96
Sea-level changes, 59, 62, 63
Sea Mills, 128, 129, 132, 135, 220, 239
Seasons of the year, 98, 99, 100, 101
Seat Hill, 44
Seavington St Michael, 30
Secondary Neolithic cultures, 107, 108, 109, 110, 111
Sedgemoor series, 89
Seed grasses, 198, 201, 204, 205, 249, 290, 297
Seend Cleeve, 48, 49, 50, 200, 252, 308
Seend Hill, 48
*Seiglingia decumbens*, 95
Selsey Common, 38
Semington, 46, 47, 230
Semington brook, 47, 138
Serge manufacture, 169, 174, 176, 198, 207, 211, 221, 259, 260, 261, 309
Service industries, 224, 266, 268, 280, 281, 282, 289, 306, 315, 317, 324, 330, 331, 333, 344, 345
Settlement patterns, 137–59
Seventeenth century, 70, 146, 160, 162, 164, 165, 166, 167, 172, 173, 174, 175, 177, 178, 179, 180, 181, 185, 188, 190, 196, 206, 208, 213, 221, 225, 256
Severn bridge, 347, 359
Severn bridge (railway), 235
Severn-Cotswold culture, 108, 124
Severn estuary, 63, 108, 114, 124, 193, 226, 350, 359
Severn navigation, 214, 215, 232
Severn Navigation Co., 232
Severn trows, 215
Severn tunnel, 19, 62, 235, 239
Severnside, 286
Severnside study, 350, 353, 354, 355–61
Sevington, 46
Shakemantle mine, 252
Shapwick Heath, 90, 106, 109, 112, 116
Sharko-Metal Box Co., Swindon, 344
Sharpness, 7, 8, 62, 232, 235, 349
Sharpness docks, 232, 349
Sheep, 172, 198, 293, 294, 295, 303, 304, 305
Sheep rearing, 117, 123, 150, 159, 163, 164, 197, 198, 200, 201, 204, 205, 247, 249, 292, 302, 303, 304, 305
Sheep's fescue, 95

Sheepskin goods, 275, 312, 313
Sheep walk, 163, 196, 198
Sheldon Bush & Patent Shot Co., 318
Shepton Mallet, 3, 7, 33, 36, 37, 60, 68, 79, 169, 181, 204, 209, 211, 218, 237, 261, 262, 266, 308, 312
Shepton Montague, 33, 39
Sherborne, 32, 36, 37, 39, 41, 44, 45, 157, 218, 307, 362
Sherborne Abbey, 32
Sherborne series, 65, 66
Shipham, 21, 77, 78, 84, 133, 135, 180
Shirehampton, 11, 105, 219
Shires (Mercia), 154
Shires (Wessex), 153, 154
Shirt making, 313, 337
Shore Hill, 50
Shorthorns, 244, 247
Shortwood fault, 19
Siddeley organization, 325, 335
Siddington, 46
Silchester, 126, 128
Silk manufacture, 211, 261, 275
Silures, 125, 126, 129
Silurian, 3, 6, 7, 8, 19, 82, 84, 85
Simonsbath, 9, 83, 96, 165
Singers, Frome, 310
Sissons, Gloucester, 272
Siston, 22, 26, 266, 302
Slaughterford, 42, 91, 227, 276
Slave Hill, 48
Slave trade, 190, 191, 220, 221
Slimbridge, 73, 75, 164
Small Down, 37, 120
Smith, W. H. & Sons, Swindon, 345
Smitham Hill, 79, 103
Smiths Industries, Cheltenham, 284, 335
Sneyd Park, 11
Snowfalls, 99, 100
Snowshill, 151
Soap industry, 319
Society of Merchant Venturers, 221, 226, 240
Society of Mineral and Battery Works, 179
Soil drainage, 64–90
Soil moisture deficit, 103, 104
Soil quality, 65, 71, 73, 74, 75, 80, 81, 82, 83, 86, 88, 90
Soil series, 64–90
Soils, 45, 60, 61, 64–90, 196, 197, 198, 199, 200, 201, 204, 205, 248, 249, 297, 302
Soldier's Hole, Cheddar, 106
Solent, The, 54
Solifluxion, 59, 61, 85, 105, 106
Solutrean culture, 106
Somerford, 200
Somerset agricultural tables, 244, 290, 291,

292, 293, 296, 299
Somerset coal canal, 229, 230, 231, 237, 254, 257
Somerset coalfield, 5, 6, 14, 15, 16, 18, 19, 22, 80, 180, 181, 212, 213, 214, 229, 237, 239, 254, 255, 266, 280, 283
Somerset levels, 3, 21, 22, 62, 63, 67, 68, 70, 86, 87, 90, 95, 96, 109, 110, 112, 117, 145, 146, 149, 150, 153, 154, 158, 202, 203, 250, 251
Somerset levels, drainage, 63, 202, 203
Somerset sheep, 198
Somersetshire, 163
Somerton, 25, 26, 53, 69, 70, 87, 116, 132, 133, 155, 163, 204, 306, 307, 312
Somerton series, 69
South Brewham, 46
South Cheviton, 46
South Petherton, 67, 158, 161, 204
South Petherton series, 67
South Wales, 25, 49, 56, 108, 110, 111, 113, 173, 178, 182, 183, 184, 193, 194, 212, 214, 222, 226, 230, 232, 248, 252, 253, 255, 272, 273, 318, 319, 347, 351
South Wraxall, 46
Southampton, trade through, 164, 183, 186, 187, 209, 210, 217, 218
Southern Overthrust, 18
Southwest Economic Planning Council, 279, 282, 291, 292, 306, 350, 352, 353
Southwest peninsula, 8, 97, 114, 121, 162, 347, 351, 362
Southwestern Gas Board, 320
Southwestern Second 'B' cultures, 115
Southwestern Third 'B' cultures, 115, 116, 121, 124
Southwold, 196, 199
Spain, 173, 175, 185, 186, 187, 188, 189, 191, 192, 207, 209, 210, 211
'Spanish' cloths, 175, 176, 189, 208, 210, 256, 257
Sparkford, 26, 67, 73, 74
Spartina Townsendii, 96
Spelter (Zinc), 212, 273
Spencers, Melksham, 270, 310
Sperry Gyroscope Co., Stonehouse, 339
Spetchley series, 71
Sphagnum, 96
Spillers Ltd., 321
Spirthill, 49
Sprays Hill, 50
Spye Park, 49, 50
Square 'D' Ltd., Swindon, 344
Stalbridge, 46, 47
Stalbridge Weston, 46
Stanley, 168
Stanton Drew, 156, 213

Stanton St Quintin, 46
Stanton Wick, 80, 81, 114
Stanway, 151, 168
Staple Hill, 50, 55, 152, 285, 327
Stapleton colliery, 255
Star villa, 129, 133
Staunton, 176, 358, 359
Starveall, 147
Staverton, 47, 307
Steam ploughing, 244
Steam power, 209, 213, 230, 257, 269, 270
Steeple Ashton, 48
Stert, 165
Stille, 5
Stinchcombe, 32, 33, 38, 173
Stock Hill, 60, 84
Stocking manufacture, 211
Stockland Bristol, 87
Stocklinch, 29
Stogursey, 111, 112
Stoke Bishop, 8, 11
Stoke Gifford, 23, 61, 239, 356, 358
Stoke Gifford fault, 19
Stoke Moor, 89
Stoke St Mary, 25
Stoke-sub-Hamdon, 30, 32, 161, 275
Stoke Trister, 47, 48
Stompe of Malmesbury, 171
Ston Easton series, 68, 69
Stone, 19
Stonehenge, 113
Stonehouse, 28
Stonehouse, near Stroud, 30, 33, 265, 338, 339, 355
Stonesfield Slate Beds, 40, 41, 42
Stoney Down, 50
Storms, 104
Storridge Hill, 50
Stothert & Pitt, Bath, 333, 334
Stour Hill, 48
Stour Provost, 48
Stourport, 215, 232, 233
Stourton Caundle, 46
Stowell, 41
Stowford, 169
Stow-on-the-Wold, 138, 147, 148, 151, 196, 217
Strachan & Henshaw Ltd., 324
Straits (cloth), 169, 174
Strawberry growing, 76, 77, 98, 202, 298, 300, 302
Street, 26, 129, 274, 276, 289, 312, 316, 324
Stretcholt, 62
Strontium, 24, 281
Stroud, 29, 30, 33, 35, 36, 38, 41, 54, 59, 66, 91, 92, 103, 122, 144, 148, 151, 184, 196, 206, 207, 209, 215, 218, 227, 233,

257, 258, 259, 260, 261, 264, 265, 269, 270, 276, 282, 286, 287, 289, 302, 308, 309, 312, 313, 314, 338, 339, 340, 343–45, 355, 362
Stroud canal, 184, 215
Stroudwater industrial area, 151, 164, 166, 170, 171, 173, 206, 209, 288, 313, 317, 338, 339, 340, 355
Stroudwater scarlets, 170, 173, 174, 206, 259, 338
Stroudwater woollen district, 148, 170, 171, 173, 174, 206, 209, 288, 313, 338
Structure, 3–51
Sturminster Newton, 48, 50, 236
Sub-Atlantic period, 112
Sub-Boreal period, 109
Suetonius, 125
Sugar beet, 72, 82
Sugar trade, 184, 185, 189, 190, 191, 220
*Sulis Minerva*, 130, 131, 135
Sulphuric acid, 318
Summer Hill, 38, 41
Sun Hole, 108
Sunshine records, 100, 101
Superficial deposits, 59, 64, 65, 67, 70, 71, 72, 74, 75, 76
Superphosphates, 318
Swainswick, 33
Swansea, 181, 193, 194
Swell, 41
Swindon, 47, 49, 94, 103, 108, 139, 142, 156, 218, 230, 233, 235, 245, 267, 271, 279, 280, 281, 282, 284, 288, 289, 306, 315, 317, 352, 353, 355, 362, 363
Swindon industrial area, 280, 287, 288, 315, 343–45, 352, 363
Swindon population, 267, 268, 343
Swindon railway works, 268, 271, 343
Sycamore, 92
Symonds Yat, 119

Tael fans, 59
Tanning, 274, 313, 328
Tar distillation, 319
Tate & Lyle, Keynsham, 332
Taunton, 53, 101, 105, 112, 143, 145, 147, 154, 167, 168, 169, 174, 201, 203, 204, 206, 207, 209, 210, 211, 214, 215, 218, 227, 231, 236, 237, 239, 250, 259, 261, 262, 266, 267, 269, 276, 281, 282, 298, 306, 307, 308, 310, 312, 313
Taunton direct line, 236, 237
Taunton, manor of, 149, 156
Taunton series, 74
Taynton Freestones, 42
Tea Green Marls, 24, 25, 69
'Teart' pastures, 68

Teazles, 173, 174
Tedbury camp, 37
Tellisford, 169
Temperature, 98, 99, 100
Temperature ranges, 99, 100
Temple Cloud, 80
Temple Cloud fault, 18
Temple Combe, 46, 236, 250
Temple Guiting, 165, 168
Tenneco organization, 319
Terry Hill, 40, 44
Tertiary earth movements, 25, 52–6
Tertiary physical history, 25, 51, 52–6
Tesco Stores, Westbury, 315
Tetbury, 42, 44, 45, 163, 164, 172, 174, 196, 207, 209, 217, 239, 306, 316
Tewkesbury, 24, 25, 26, 28, 72, 101, 103, 144, 148, 151, 156, 167, 182, 183, 196, 232, 334, 335
Textile machinery, 171, 173, 174, 207, 208, 209, 210, 257, 258, 259, 269, 270, 271
Thames navigation, 229, 230
Thames–Severn canal, 215, 229, 230, 231, 232
Thornbury, 8, 18, 21, 27, 82, 144, 151, 156, 247, 248, 281, 352, 354, 355, 362
Thonbury anticline, 5, 10, 18, 23
Thornford, 39
Three-field cultivation, 160, 161
Througham, 42
Thrupe series, 85, 96
Tickenham, 11, 12, 120, 153
Tickenham fault, 18
Tickenham series, 76
Ticking (cloth), 169, 210, 261
Tidenham, 144
Tiddenham Chase, 10, 11, 13
T.I.M., Cirencester, 315
Timber imports, 190, 192, 226, 233, 271, 275, 278, 348, 349
Timber trade, 190, 192, 226, 233, 348, 349
Timberscombe, 157
Timber using industries, 226, 233, 271, 272, 275, 276, 306, 314, 317, 326, 327, 329, 337, 338, 340, 341, 344, 346
Timsbury, 37
Timsbury colliery, 255
Tinkers Hill, 48
Tintern, 10, 11, 177, 215
Tintern Beds, 8
Tites Point, 6, 19, 22, 24, 26, 82
Tiverton, 231
Tiverton branch canal, 231
Tobacco growing, 166, 167
Tobacco trade and manufacture, 184, 185, 189, 190, 191, 222, 223, 274, 277, 278, 284, 285, 321, 322, 330, 346, 348

Tockenham, 49
Tockington, 129
Tog Hill, 37
Tolland, 9
Toomer Hill, 44
Topsham, 231
Tor grass, 95
Tormarton, 41, 42, 138, 151
Tormentil, 95
Torrances, Bitton, 324
Tortworth, 5, 8, 10, 19, 82
Tortworth inlier, 5, 6, 7, 18, 19, 22, 24, 27, 82
Tourist industry, 281
Town Development Act (1952), 287, 343
Towns, origin of, 154, 155, 156, 159
Trackways, 110, 113, 141, 150–53
Tranchet implements, 106
Transport, 150–53, 184, 212, 214–19, 263 271, 272
Treborough, 135
Trenchard Group, 15
Trent, 29
Trias, 3, 9, 10, 16, 19, 20, 21, 22, 23, 24, 25, 52, 55, 57, 59, 60, 68, 69, 70, 71, 72, 78, 88, 197, 202, 203
Trip series, 66
Trowbridge, 46, 47, 94, 149, 171, 181, 199, 208, 209, 218, 230, 235, 236, 245, 246, 256, 257, 258, 260, 261, 264, 265, 269, 270, 281, 289, 306, 307, 308, 316, 362, 363
Trym valley, 11, 21
Tubbs Lewis, Kingswood, 309
Tuffs, 7
Tulle, 262
Tunley Hill, 37
Turbary Moor complex, 90
Turnips, 197, 198, 200, 201, 203, 205, 249
Turnpike trust (Bristol), 213, 218, 219, 220, 240
Turnpike trusts, 184, 213, 218, 240
Tweeds, 257
Twerton, 210, 254, 255
Two-field cultivation, 160, 161
Tyley Bottom, 38
Tynings farm, 110, 111, 112
Tytherington, 12, 24, 138

*Ulex gallii*, 95
Uley, 33, 38, 206, 207, 264
Uley blues (cloth), 173
Umbrellas, 276
Undy, 21
Unigate Dairies, 307
Union Carbide, 345
Unitized cargoes, 332, 350

Univallate hill forts, 119, 120
University of Bristol, 292, 303, 304
University of Bristol Reconstruction Research Group, 90
University of Exeter, 292, 303
Uphill, 12, 106, 128, 153
Upper Calcareous Grit, 48, 49, 64
Upper Coal Measures, 16
Upper Coal Series, 15, 18, 19, 80, 81, 181
Upper Cromhall Sandstone, 13
Upper Devonian, 9
Upper Drybrook Sandstone, 13, 14
Upper Freestone, 34, 35
Upper Lias, 30, 31, 32, 33, 34, 35, 66, 67, 153, 202
Upper Lias Clay, 29, 32, 33, 34, 41, 57, 66
Upper Lias Sands, 29, 32, 33, 34
Upper Llandovery Sandstones, 6
Upper Slaughter, 33
Upper Soudley, 10
Upper Tremadoc, 6
Upper Trigonia Grit, 35, 36
Upton Cheyney, 22, 23, 30
Upton Noble, 44, 46
Upton St Leonards, 31, 33
Uxella, 121

Vaccinium myrtillus, 95
Vale of Berkeley, 129, 152, 247
Vale of Evesham, 27, 28, 148, 166, 196, 197, 198, 247, 248, 292, 303
Vale of Gloucester, 27, 28, 68, 73, 247
Vale of Ilchester, 204
Vale of Moreton, 30, 31, 32, 57, 72, 303
Vale of Moreton anticline, 32, 34, 35, 54
Vale of Pewsey, 17, 44, 47, 48, 49, 50, 53, 65, 112, 114
Vale of Severn, 57, 125, 133, 139, 291, 303
Vale of Taunton Dene, 71, 74, 75, 204, 205, 250, 302
Vale of Wardour, 6, 16, 26, 47, 48, 49, 50, 53
Vale of Warminster, 53
Vale of Wellington, 74
Vale of White Horse, 48, 49, 230, 307
Vale of Wrington, 98, 133, 145, 202
Vales, 195, 196, 197, 198, 199, 200, 204, 219, 245, 300
Valley mist, 99, 104
Valley-side soil complex, 83
Vallis Limestone, 12
Vegetables, 72, 73, 75, 77, 203, 204, 205, 292, 296, 297, 298
Vegetation, 65, 68, 79, 80, 84, 90, 91–97
Velvet Bottom, 135
Venetians (cloth), 338
Verlucio, 128, 132

Verulamium, 128
Vespasian, 125
Vesulian transgression, 35, 46
Vickers Engineers, South Marston, 344
Vicunas (cloth), 259
Viney Hill, 7
Vobster, 5, 213, 237
Vobster colliery, 15, 255

Wagon transport, 181, 217, 218
Walking sticks, 276
Walls ice cream factory, Gloucester, 308, 336
Walmore, 26
Walton-in-Gordano, 101
Wansborough Paper Co., 313
Wansdyke, 139, 140, 141
Wanstrow, 41, 44
Warehousing, 330, 332, 351
Warminster, 156, 175, 181, 208, 218, 235, 261, 275, 310, 311, 312, 313, 314, 316
Warmley, 15, 180, 222, 322, 329, 362
Warren Hill, 50
Watchet, 26, 154, 157, 227, 236, 253, 276, 313, 349
Water power, 168, 170, 173, 208, 209, 211, 256
Watercombe, 307
Waterley Bottom, 38
Wattonensis Bed, 39
Wavering Down, 76
Wavy hair grass, 95
Wedmore, 22, 24, 26, 61, 68, 70, 87, 89, 110, 112, 153, 203
Wedmore series, 70
Wellington, 207, 209, 210, 211, 218, 259, 260, 261, 265, 269, 279, 307, 309, 310, 313, 316
Wellow, 37
Wellow brook, 25, 33, 37, 40, 42, 44, 54, 139, 237
Wells, 3, 8, 60, 77, 106, 153, 157, 158, 168, 169, 211, 236, 276, 286, 306, 307, 308, 310, 313, 316
Wells Cathedral, 36, 156
Wells, episcopal manor of, 179
Welsh Christianity, 157
Wenlock, 6, 7, 8
Wenlock Mudstones, 7
Wenlock Shales, 6
Wentlloog series, 86, 87
Wessex, 107, 108, 112, 117, 120, 137, 139, 140, 141, 142, 143, 146, 150, 153, 154, 155, 157, 158, 159
Wessex culture, 111, 112, 124
Wessex, origins of, 137, 139
West Ashton, 48

West Buckland, 112
West Chinnock, 39
West Chinnock Hill, 32
West Cranmore, 39, 44
West Harptree, 72
West Harrington, 69
West Midlands, 97, 178, 193, 198, 206, 252, 303
West Saxons, 137, 139, 140, 141, 142, 143
West Sedge Moor, 89
West Town, 101
West Wiltshire trading estate, 315
Westbury Brook mine, 252
Westbury Moor, 89
Westbury-on-Severn, 26
Westbury-on-Trym, 6, 8, 11, 27, 158, 278
Westbury-on-Trym anticline, 8, 11, 17, 18, 19, 21, 23, 25, 27
Westbury (Wiltshire), 47, 48, 49, 117, 135, 171, 235, 237, 245, 252, 259, 275, 279, 307, 309, 310, 312, 313, 315
Westcombe, 33
Westerleigh, 55, 214
Western Second 'B' culture, 119, 120, 122
Western Third 'B' cultures, 115, 121, 122
Western Third 'C' cultures, 116
Westhay Moor, 90
Westhay series, 90
Westinghouse Brake & Signal Co., 271, 311, 325
Westland Aircraft Co., Yeovil, 284, 311
Westland villa, 133
Weston Down, 8
Westonbirt, 45
Weston-super-Mare, 3, 5, 61, 77, 99, 100, 101, 106, 117, 122, 129, 135, 163, 179, 202, 239, 268, 284, 287, 288. 309, 311, 312, 313, 314, 316, 354, 362
Weston-under-Penyard, 135
Weston Zoyland, 62, 163, 203
Whatley, 8, 39
Wheat, 165, 166, 197, 200, 201, 203, 246, 248, 249, 295, 296, 297
Wheat Act, 249
Wheatenhurst, 168
Whitbian, 31
Whitchurch, 55, 177, 333
Whitcliff Park, 27
White Lias, 27, 28
White Way, 129
Whitecroft fault, 19
Whitminster, 59
Whitnell Corner, 79
Whitney, 151, 239
Whittington, 157
Whittington Villa, 133, 134
Wholesale trades, 329, 330, 331, 332, 333

Wick, 6, 11, 13, 17, 22, 55, 323
Wick Hill, 49
Wickridge, 38
Wickwar, 7, 8, 10, 11, 12, 22, 23, 55, 56, 94
Wigpool, 13
William of Moion, 156
Williamstrip Park, 45
Williton, 109
Willow herb, 96
Wiltshire agricultural tables, 244, 251, 290, 291, 292, 293, 296, 299
Wiltshire Bacon Co., 246
Wiltshire & Berkshire canal, 49, 230, 231, 232
Wiltshire sheep, 198
Wiltshire United Dairies, 245, 246, 250
Wincanton, 46, 47, 169, 204, 209, 210, 218, 236, 265, 307, 308, 316
Winchcombe, 30, 31, 38, 43, 59, 143, 155, 156, 167, 168, 170, 196, 227, 276, 313
Winchcombe Abbey, 155, 156, 158, 161, 162, 164, 165
Winchcombe anticline, 54
Winchester, 130, 157
Winchester Cathedral, 156, 168
Wind direction, 97, 98, 99
Wind-borne deposits, 61, 63, 69, 76, 77, 78, 79, 84
Windmill Hill culture, 107, 108, 124
Windmill Hill (Somerset), 44
Wine trade, 183, 186, 188, 191, 222, 223, 278, 331, 332, 348
Winford, 13
Winscombe, 76, 79, 156, 180
Winsham, 29
Winterbourne, 23, 56, 197, 266, 302, 326, 356
Witcombe, 11, 30, 31, 133, 134
Witham Friary, 46, 178, 179, 236
Witham Park, 50, 94
Withypool, 83
Wiveliscombe, 9, 168, 169, 211, 236, 259
Woden's Burh, 141
Wood pulp, 276, 278, 322, 348, 349
Woodchester, 33, 110, 143, 270, 272
Woodchester villa, 133, 134
Woodland, 45, 47, 48, 62, 64, 66, 68, 69, 70, 71, 77, 78, 81, 82, 90, 91, 92, 94, 96, 107, 108, 138, 140, 142, 143, 144, 145, 148, 149, 150, 201, 204
Woodland clearance, 109, 143, 144, 145
Woodmancote, 173
Wookey Hole, 60, 77, 106, 116, 276, 313
Wool cloth exports, 167, 171, 172, 175, 184, 185, 186, 188, 190, 192
Wool markets, 164, 172, 174, 186, 207, 209
Wool production, 117, 134, 156, 162, 163,

164, 200, 205, 206, 207, 209
Wool quality, 172, 173, 174, 198, 206, 207
Woolaston, 227
Woolavington, 156, 203
Wool-combing, 174, 207, 211
Wool-combing machines, 260
Woolhope, 5
Woolhope Limestone, 6
Woollen industry, 41, 117, 155, 156, 162, 163, 164, 165, 167–76, 185, 196, 199, 206–12, 218, 221, 222, 230, 251, 255–63, 264, 265, 278, 288, 289, 306, 309, 329, 338, 339
Woolverton, 46
Worcester, 156, 182, 218, 232, 233
Worcester, diocese of, 156, 158
Worcester series, 70, 71, 75
Worcester syncline, 19
Workman Reed Ltd., Yatton, 324
Worle, 179
Worlebury Hill, 61, 77, 116, 117, 119, 122
Worsted manufacture, 169, 172, 174, 207, 211, 258, 259, 260, 309
Wootton Bassett, 49, 239, 307
Wotton Hill, 38
Wotton-under-Edge, 5, 29, 30, 33, 38, 43, 45, 138, 143, 144, 151, 206, 207, 218, 227, 259, 264, 309
Wraxall, 98, 117
Wraxall villa, 133
Wrington, 77, 149, 153, 156, 298, 316
Wrington fault, 18

Wrington series, 77, 78
Wroughton, 50
Würm glaciation, 106
Wych elms, 92

Yarlington, 33
Yate, 13, 23, 24, 55, 161, 214, 247, 281, 324, 326, 330, 331, 332, 352, 354
Yate Rocks, 12, 13
Yate shopping centre, 331
Yate-Sodbury township, 331, 354
Yatton, 101, 135, 236, 298, 313, 314, 324
Yatton Keynell, 44
Yeast manufacture, 321, 329
Yenston, 46
Yeovil, 5, 29, 30, 31, 32, 35, 36, 37, 44, 45, 66, 67, 132, 133, 134, 169, 204, 209, 210, 211, 218, 235, 236, 237, 250, 261, 266, 267, 271, 274, 275, 276, 282, 284, 286, 287, 289, 307, 310, 311, 312, 313, 316
Yeovil Sands, 31, 32
Yeovilian, 31
Yetminster, 45
Yoghurt making, 307
Yorkshire, 206, 218, 230, 256, 260, 261

Zeals, 48, 50
*Zerna erecta*, 95
Zinc, 179, 180, 252, 253, 318, 319
Zinc production, 179, 180, 212

UNIVERSITY LIBRARY
NOTTINGHAM

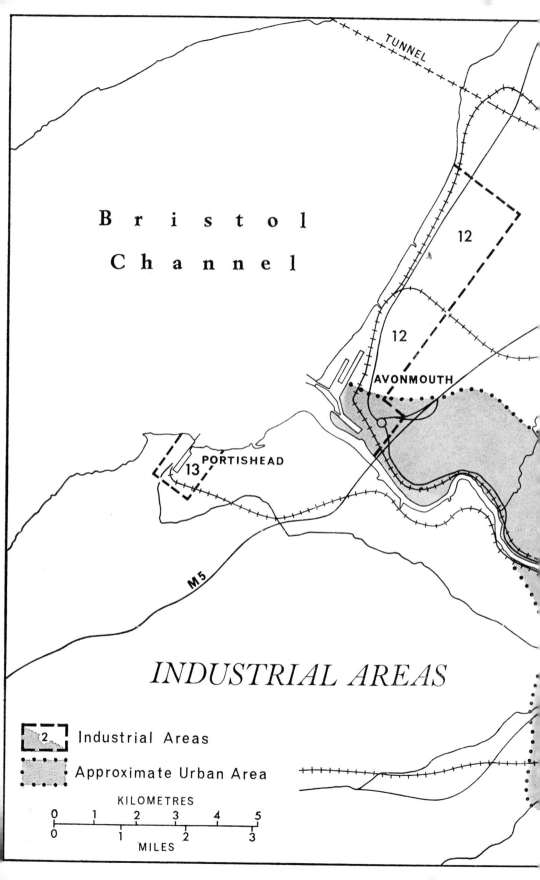

**B r i s t o l**
**C h a n n e l**

TUNNEL

12

12

AVONMOUTH

PORTISHEAD

13

M 5

*INDUSTRIAL AREAS*

Industrial Areas

Approximate Urban Area

KILOMETRES

0    1    2    3    4    5

0         1         2         3

MILES